# The Challenges of Globalization

# The Challenges of Globalization

*Economy and Politics in Germany, 1860–1914*

Cornelius Torp

Translated by Alex Skinner

berghahn
NEW YORK • OXFORD
www.berghahnbooks.com

Published by
Berghahn Books
www.berghahnbooks.com

English-language edition


German-language edition

Die Herausforderung der Globalisierung



The translation of this work was funded by Geisteswissenschaften International – Translation Funding for Humanities and Social Sciences from Germany, a joint initiative of the Fritz Thyssen Foundation, the German Federal Foreign Office, the collecting society VG WORT and the Börsenverein des Deutschen Buchhandels (German Publishers & Booksellers Association).

**Library of Congress Cataloging-in-Publication Data**

Torp, Cornelius.
[Herausforderung der Globalisierung. English]
The challenges of globalization : economy and politics in Germany, 1860–1914 / Cornelius Torp ; translated by Alex Skinner.
pages cm
Translation of: Die Herausforderung der Globalisierung.
Includes bibliographical references.
ISBN 978-1-78238-502-8 (hardback : alk. paper) — ISBN 978-1-78238-503-5 (ebook)
1. Germany—Economic conditions—19th century. 2. Germany—Economic conditions—20th century. 3. Germany—Politics and government—19th century. 4. Germany—Politics and government—20th century. I. Title.
HC285.T6713 2014
330.943'084--dc23

2014009649

**British Library Cataloguing in Publication Data**

A catalogue record for this book is available from the British Library

Printed on acid-free paper

ISBN: 978-1-78238-502-8 hardback
ISBN: 978-1-78238-503-5 ebook

# Contents

# Figures and Tables

## Figures



## Tables

# Acknowledgements

When the original German edition of this book was published in 2005, research on the history of globalization was still in its early stages. In the intervening period the topic has received a lot of attention. The fact that my book is now available in English and can contribute to the ongoing debate on this topic is down to the generous support of Geisteswissenschaften International (Translation Funding for Humanities and Social Sciences from Germany), a joint initiative of the Fritz Thyssen Foundation, the German Federal Foreign Office, the collecting society VG WORT and the Börsenverein des Deutschen Buchhandels (German Publishers & Booksellers Association).

A number of friends have helped me greatly during this entire period. My thanks go above all to Hans-Ulrich Wehler, whose recent death has left behind an unfillable gap. I will sorely miss his support and willingness to engage in critical dialogue. I continue to benefit from Manfred Hettling's stimulating insights and friendship. And I would be a much poorer individual without the advice of Claudius Torp, in his dual role as brother and fellow historian.

Alex Skinner did a fantastic job of translating the text. My thanks to Caitlin Mahon for her exceptionally judicious and meticulous copyediting. Thomas Weisser compiled the index with admirable attention to detail. The translation project was fully supported from the outset by my German publisher, Vandenhoeck & Ruprecht, particularly in the shape of Martina Kayser and Margarita Wolf. And I owe a special debt of gratitude to Marion Berghahn for her readiness to include my book in her programme of publications. It was a pleasure to work with her and the other consummate professionals at Berghahn Books.

# Abbreviations

| | |
|---|---|
| AA | Auswärtiges Amt (Foreign Ministry) |
| BA | Bundesarchiv (Federal Archive) |
| BdI | Bund der Industriellen (Industrialists' League) |
| BdL | Bund der Landwirte (Agrarian League) |
| BR | Bundesrat |
| CVDI | Centralverband Deutscher Industrieller (Central Association of German Industrialists) |
| CVH | Centralstelle für Vorbereitung von Handelsverträgen (Central Department for Trade Treaties) |
| DHT | Deutscher Handelstag (German Trade Federation) |
| DKP | Deutsch-Konservative Partei (German Conservative Party) |
| DLR | Deutscher Landwirtschaftsrat (German Agricultural Council) |
| Fs. | Festschrift |
| GDP | Gross domestic product |
| GNP | Gross national product |
| GStAPK | Geheimes Staatsarchiv Preußischer Kulturbesitz |
| *GW* | *Die gesammelten Werke* (Bismarck) |
| HK | Handelskammer (chamber of commerce) |
| HVV | Handelsvertragsverein (Trade Treaty Association) |
| Langnamverein | Verein zur Wahrung der gemeinsamen wirtschaftlichen Interessen in Rheinland und Westfalen (Association for |

| | |
|---|---|
| | the Protection of Common Economic Interests in the Rhineland and Westphalia) |
| MdR | Mitglied des Reichstags (member of the Reichstag) |
| MF | Finanzministerium (Preußen) (Finance Ministry, Prussia) |
| MHG | Ministerium für Handel und Gewerbe (Preußen) (Ministry of Trade and Commerce, Prussia) |
| ML | Ministerium für Landwirtschaft, Domänen und Forsten (Preußen) (Ministry of Agriculture, Estates and Forestry, Prussia) |
| NDP | Net domestic product |
| NNP | Net national product |
| PA AA | Politisches Archiv des Auswärtigen Amtes (Foreign Ministry Political Archive) |
| RI | Reichsamt des Innern (Imperial Ministry of the Interior) |
| RSA | Reichsschatzamt (Imperial Treasury) |
| RT | Reichstag |
| SPD | Sozialdemokratische Partei Deutschlands (Social Democratic Party) |
| *StDR* | *Statistik des Deutschen Reichs* (Statistics of the German Empire) |
| *StenBerAH* | *Stenographische Berichte über die Verhandlungen des Preußischen Hauses der Abgeordneten* (Stenographic reports on the proceedings of the Prussian House of Representatives) |
| *StenBerRT* | *Stenographische Berichte über die Verhandlungen des Deutschen Reichstags* (Stenographic reports on the proceedings of the German Reichstag) |
| *StenBerZollparl.* | *Stenographische Berichte über die Verhandlungen des Deutschen Zollparlaments* (Stenographic reports on the proceedings of the German Customs Parliament) |
| *StHbDR* | *Statistisches Handbuch für das Deutsche Reich* |

| | |
|---|---|
| *StJbDR* | *Statistisches Jahrbuch für das Deutsche Reich* |
| VDEStI | Verein Deutscher Eisen- und Stahlindustrieller (Association of German Iron and Steel Industrialists) |
| VSW | Vereinigung der Steuer- und Wirtschaftsreformer (Association of Tax and Economic Reformers) |
| WA | Wirtschaftlicher Ausschuß (Economic Committee) |

# Introduction

Today, globalization is commonly regarded as 'the leitmotif of our age'.[1] Both its emphatic supporters and vehement critics tend to underline its novelty. They see globalization as the symbol of the present era, an 'invention' of the late twentieth century. But globalization has a history. Admittedly, when this history began is subject to dispute. Some historians believe they can trace the beginnings of global contacts and networks far back into the pre-Christian era.[2] A significantly larger group, influenced by Immanuel Wallerstein and Fernand Braudel, date the beginning of globalization to the early sixteenth century. From this perspective, the discovery of the Americas, the expansion of the Spanish and Portuguese colonial empires and the rise of an essentially global trading network mark the beginning of a new era.[3]

If we take the degree of global integration reached today as our benchmark, however, then from an economic history perspective there are good reasons to begin the history of globalization in the nineteenth century. It was only in the decades after 1800 that a world that was certainly networked but still primarily determined by regional dynamics began to turn into a global lattice of interactions. It was only then that a process of global economic integration began (and it is in this limited sense that I understand globalization in the present work) that sets apart the period since the mid-nineteenth century from all other eras according to every economic criterion, and in both qualitative and quantitative terms. But even during this era globalization was an anything but linear process. In fact, we can discern two clearly distinct waves of globalization. The first, the central concern of the present book, gained increasing traction from around 1850, culminating in the golden era of the world economy between roughly 1890 and 1914. This was followed by a phase of 'deglobalization' in which the two world wars, the world economic crisis beginning in 1929 and burgeoning protectionism undid much of the global economic integration that had been achieved.[4] It was only after the Second World War that a second thrust of globalization gradually took hold, one that intensified further towards the end of the twentieth century and persists to this day.

On the eve of the First World War, the revolution in transport brought about by the steamship and railway, the radical transformation of communication through telegraphy and telephony, and the enforcement of the international gold standard and concomitant establishment of what was virtually a common currency propelled global economic integration to a level that still seems impressive today.[5] From the mid-nineteenth century, world trade grew at such a rapid and steady rate that shortly before the globalization backlash against the global economy during the world wars and the interwar period, global trade had already reached a level of intensity comparable with that of the 1970s. This explosion in the volume of world trade was flanked by a large-scale convergence in international commodity prices, which points to the emergence of a highly integrated global market.[6] At the same time, in the second half of the 'long' nineteenth century, the new worldwide potential for investment allowed international capital mobility to rise to a level that in some respects even surpasses current conditions.[7] Finally, in the years between 1850 and the First World War, mass migration reached a level unsurpassed to this day. If we consider European emigration overseas, transnational migration within Europe, which also ran into the millions, and internal migration within specific countries, which was greater than ever before, it seems entirely reasonable to think in terms of a world labour market and global wage structure in the late nineteenth century.[8]

It stands to reason that such a fundamental change in global parameters was bound to affect the various nation-states, their societies and their politics. This applies, for example, to mass migration and the resulting upheaval in traditional ways of life and values, along with its repercussions for nationality laws and the discourse of nationalism.[9] But it applies perhaps even more to the field of foreign trade policy, since here the global economy and national politics rubbed up against one another more directly than anywhere else. Contemporaries were already aware of this: virtually no other political topic was such a constant focus of public interest, and no other problem was the subject of such bitter controversy as tariff and trade policy.

Globalization and the rapidity with which it advanced came as a shock to the national economies of the nineteenth century, one that profoundly disrupted familiar realities. Absolute and relative prices changed at a breathtaking pace, new social and political fronts emerged and those affected negatively by global market integration got organized and mobilized support. Most countries responded to the new situation by erecting protectionist barriers. Among the larger countries, only the U.K. remained faithful to free trade – though even here there was a protectionist movement of considerable vigour. Despite differences in the details, meanwhile, almost the whole of continental Europe turned to protectionism from the late 1870s onwards, and this intensified up until the First World War. Much the same applied to the Latin American states and those British colonies that had become independent; during the same period, they introduced protective tariffs for their industries that generally exceeded their European equivalents. From the beginning of the nineteenth century the U.S. was a stronghold of protectionism, but here too tariffs on industrial products increased again strongly from the 1860s on. My argument in this book is that we can only adequately interpret German tariff and trade policy before the First World War as part of an *international* response to a wave of global economic integration that was increasing at a furious pace.

This book focuses on the effects of the first wave of globalization on the economy, society and politics of the German Empire and on how its foreign trade policy responded to the challenges of this novel integration of the global economy. My intention here is neither to endorse an understanding of globalization as an anonymous force coming from outside nor to imply that the German Empire was its 'victim'. The German economy was an important part of the global economy before the First World War. German firms played a significant role in shaping and driving forward the first wave of globalization; a fair number of them were among the leading multinational companies and can be considered early 'global players'. At the same time, it would be wrong to view globalization as the autonomous result of purely economic forces. In many respects, it was the product of political action and parameters created by policies – from the development of the transport infrastructure, through the gold standard, to import restrictions and export subsidies.[10] German tariff and trade policy, like other fields of state action and like the foreign trade policies of other states that interacted with it, influenced and moulded the specific historical form of globalization before 1914. So if I pay particular attention to how globalization changed economic relations and the conditions of political action in the German Empire, I do so with an awareness that this involves privileging a specific perspective on the complex interplay between globalization on the one hand and national economy and politics on the other. This does not mean, however, that I aim to systematically disregard other aspects.

The present study of the German Empire's integration into the global economy and its foreign trade policy before the First World War is conceived as a historical analysis of the relationship between economy and politics under the conditions of global economic integration. At the same time, the book's subject matter places it at the heart of political economy. This term, which has a long tradition but has enjoyed a new phase of increasing popularity since the late 1960s, tends to cover a highly heterogeneous range of approaches. What they have in common is that all reject the neoliberal mainstream's attempt to disregard the political and social context of economic processes and analyze them as if they were governed by natural laws.[11] Distancing themselves from an understanding of economic theory reduced to mere economics, the various schools of political economy have focused on analyzing the interdependence of politics and economy. The study of international economic relations, foreign trade policy and protectionism has always played a prominent role here. The various currents within political economy have led to the establishment of competing, at times complementary and sometimes fundamentally contradictory approaches, and these have provided the cornerstones of a broad and intensive debate.[12] In the present work, I seek to contribute to this ongoing debate from a historian's perspective.

The state with which I am centrally concerned here, the German Empire, was the second-largest trading nation in the world before the First World War and played a key role in the global economy. Closely followed by the U.S., it was soon snapping at the heels of the long-dominant trading power of the U.K. In 1913, Germany accounted for around 13 per cent of global trade, just 4 per cent behind the U.K. – in 1880, the U.K.'s share had been more than twice that of Germany.[13] Conversely, it is hard to overstate the significance of foreign trade to the German economy. On the eve of the First World War, foreign trade as a share of gross domestic product was a substantial 35.1 per cent.[14]

I trace the course of German foreign trade policy until the outbreak of the First World War, which tore apart the web of international economic relations and subjugated foreign trade policy to its own imperatives. There are two aspects, meanwhile, to the book's historical starting point. First, as far as its scope and the empirical research is concerned, it focuses on the quarter century before the First World War. This period was characterized by the highest degree of global economic integration before 1914 and is therefore most likely to provide us with relevant information on our topic; it is also the period that has been researched the least. Second, there are good reasons to extend the present study back to the early 1860s, at least in broad outline. This is essential because only this longer period allows us to make statements about historical tendencies in the relationship between economics and politics. Further, there are a number of reasons to consider the early 1860s a turning point. First, it provides us with an overview of almost the entire span of the first wave of economic globalization. Second, with the conclusion of the Cobden Treaty between the U.K. and France, the year 1860 marks the beginning of a new, free trade–oriented era of trading relations in Europe. And third, the Franco-Prussian trade treaty of 1862 was of great significance to what would later become the German Empire, as it forced the entire German Customs Union (Deutscher Zollverein) into the European trade treaty system. This not only signalled the temporary victory of economic liberalism, but also anticipated the Lesser German solution in economic policy terms.

Methodologically, the present study seeks to overcome the dead end of a diplomatic history of foreign economic relations by fusing the analysis of economic and political history. The parts of the book focused on economic history make use of the classical analytical toolkit of foreign economic theory, while also benefiting from recent debates in this theoretical field. This applies especially to the assessment of protectionist measures. Into the late 1970s, this field was almost completely dominated by the dogma of free trade, which decried all state intervention in foreign trade. In theoretical terms, this view, and the whole of foreign trade theory along with it, is based on the theorem of comparative costs, whose classical formulation is found in David Ricardo's *Principles of Political Economy* of 1817.[15] With reference to his famous example of two goods and two countries (the U.K. with its cloth and Portugal with its wine), Ricardo managed to show that for the productively superior country, which can produce every good more cheaply than other countries, trade can still be an advantage. In other words, it is not the absolute but relative cost advantage that is crucial to the emergence of foreign trade. Regardless of whether differences in production technology, as in Ricardo's work, or differing factor endowments, as in the Heckscher-Ohlin-Samuelson model, are considered responsible for comparative cost advantage, implicitly or explicitly the entire conceptual framework rooted in Ricardo's idea works with two crucial assumptions: constant returns to scale and perfect competition. On these premises, the free exchange of goods without state intervention always appears to represent a Pareto optimum – if not necessarily with respect to specific sectors, then certainly in terms of the economy as a whole. Classical foreign trade theory concedes just one exception to this rule: the optimum tariff or terms of trade argument, though this is marginalized as practically irrelevant.

The advocates of new trade theory, whose most prominent representative is Nobel Prize winner Paul Krugman, reject this idea. In contrast to orthodox foreign trade theory, they assume that certain markets are characterized by imperfect competition and increasing returns to scale. This step not only allows economies of scale to join comparative cost advantage as an autonomous source of foreign trade relations. It also has far-reaching economic policy implications. On these changed premises – as supporters of the new theory have concluded – there is no fundamental reason to disdain trade policy interventions. If they target specific, so-called strategic sectors or those featuring high positive external effects, protectionist measures may in fact have beneficial effects on the economy as a whole.

Given this recent theoretical development, which questions the free trade thesis in its traditional form, it is very difficult to justify the formerly common tendency of economists and economic historians to condemn every kind of protectionism from the outset. It seems more reasonable to examine the effects of trade-restricting measures on a case-by-case basis and then come to a conclusion. There is nothing surprising about the fact that after weighing things up in this way we may still wish to argue for free trade policies – but now on pragmatic grounds.[16]

In terms of political history, the present study centres on the foreign trade policy decision-making process and the actors involved in it within the ministerial bureaucracy, diplomatic service, political parties and economic interest groups. The main focus here is on the decision-making processes on the German side. Other states' foreign trade policy actions, meanwhile, to which German actions were geared and with which they interacted, are comprehended solely as impulses coming from outside. I chose to leave the social and political processes underlying other countries' actions largely out of my account partly because I lacked the time and resources to include them. But this decision also allowed me to get to grips with German foreign trade policy towards not just one other state but several other states. This provided me with the basis for a detailed comparative analysis of German trade policy strategy towards the United States and Russia during the peak period of globalization. In this case, historical comparison, whose general methodological benefits require no repetition here, can even operate under the ceteris paribus conditions so favourable to every comparative study. In focusing first on Russia and then on the U.S., the only changing variable is the trade partner under consideration, while the basic constellation of actors remains much the same on the German side.

The present study operates on an intermediate level of abstraction. Essentially, this means that it concentrates on the interactions of collective actors of relevance to foreign trade policy in ministries and imperial offices, political parties or their parliamentary groupings in the Reichstag, and agrarian and industrial interest groups. Individual actors generally appear merely as representatives of these collective entities or in cases where they themselves enjoyed significant room for manoeuvre. Analytically, then, the present study operates far below the highest level of abstraction – often chosen in historical studies on foreign policy themes – that declares states as a whole acting subjects and conceives of them as interacting with one another. Rather than treating the state as a black box in this way, one that 'entails a highly potent form of reductionism',[17] I dissolve it into a plethora of collective actors and their interactions. But I must also highlight what my analysis does not consider. With a few exceptions, it disregards everything below its analytical level, such as conflicts and decision-making processes within ministries or – in the economic sphere – the role of individual firms.

This study ascribes particular importance to the triad of interests, institutions and ideas. It analyzes in detail the interests of the various groups of producers and consumers, without simply deriving them from their socioeconomic situation. Instead, it allows for the fact that interests are never straightforwardly 'given' through the socioeconomic situation, but always undergo a – sometimes complex – process of interpretation. It also gets to grips with the organization of economic interests and the institutional conditions that foster or hamper their political enforcement. Further, I examine the importance and relative autonomy of discursive constructions and pay particular attention to the worldviews and interpretive schemes of contemporaries, which became manifest in the trade policy debate carried on by experts and within a broad political public sphere. Against the background of these structural conditions of action, I then focus on analyzing specific political decision-making processes and the economic and political actors involved in them. I place particular emphasis on the subjective character or *agency* of the individual and collective actors who shaped German trade policy while acting under a specific range of conditions.

The present study draws on a wide range of sources, but is based primarily on analysis of unpublished archival material. Most significant here are the files of the Foreign Ministry's Trade Policy Department in the Federal Archive (Bundesarchiv) in Berlin, which survive in almost complete form and have never been comprehensively analyzed. Almost as important are the collections of the Imperial Treasury (Reichsschatzamt), the Imperial Ministry of the Interior (Reichsamt des Innern) and the Imperial Chancellery (Reichskanzlei), which have also been preserved by the Federal Archive, as well as the files of the Prussian ministries in the Prussian Privy State Archives (Geheimes Staatsarchiv Preußischer Kulturbesitz) in Berlin-Dahlem. I evaluated the personal files of the staff working in the Trade Policy Department in the Foreign Ministry's Political Archive for the period of relevance to this study. I also drew on a wealth of published sources. These include the statistics published by the Imperial Statistical Office (Kaiserliches Statistisches Amt), stenographic transcripts of Reichstag proceedings, minutes of party conferences and association meetings, and an extensive range of heated and polemical texts by contemporary economists on foreign trade policy. Other key materials are leading newspapers and magazines, through a selection of which I sought to convey the spectrum of political opinion.

Few fields of historical research have developed with the kind of dynamism displayed by the history of globalization and global history over the last few years. Just a decade or so ago no more than a handful of economic historians and historically interested economists had highlighted the stupendous growth in global economic integration in the nineteenth century, particularly its second half.[18] Subsequently, these have helped stimulate an ever-broadening stream of studies in economic history – a significant number of them on global commodity flows – with the same kind of thrust.[19] Further, in view of transnational political linkages, imperialism and cross-border cultural transfers, the notion of the nineteenth century as the peak period of globalization has become established within the discipline of history as a whole and has found its way into a number of global historical syntheses, now with the status of verified fact.[20] Without denying the differences between contemporary globalization and that of the nineteenth century, historical research on globalization has, first, asserted that there is no qualitative difference between the two processes and brought out the many parallels between global integration today and that of a century ago.[21] Second, it has shown that there is more to globalization than the homogenization of the world and the blurring of boundaries. In fact, increasing global integration and interpenetration have themselves consistently helped accentuate new boundaries and processes of fragmentation – from protective barriers through nationalisms to ethnic differences – or generate them in the first place.[22]

On the international level, the surge in historical research on globalization has gone hand in hand with a new interest in tariff and trade policy during the era of accelerated world market integration in the 'long' nineteenth century, so that we now have a number of new and detailed and sometimes excellent studies on the U.K. and U.S. in particular, along with certain other countries.[23] This does not apply to German foreign trade policy in the same way. It is in fact fair to say that there is a pronounced lack of empirical studies on the topic – and this applies especially to the period from the 1880s onwards. This is surprising not least because historians studying the German Empire long ago recognized the centrality of tariff and trade policy as a field of political conflict, quite often ascribing to it a key role in their competing interpretations of the empire.

There is far-reaching agreement among these otherwise diverging perspectives regarding the key stages of German foreign policy and its superficial evaluation. It is accepted that the German customs tariff of 1879, whose protective duties were extended over the course of the 1880s, marks a clear turning point after a quarter century of advancing trade liberalization. Following the interlude of the trade-friendly Caprivi treaties, which were associated with the lowering of agricultural tariffs, historians agree that the Bülow tariff of 1902 returned German tariff and trade policy to the protectionist approach begun under Otto von Bismarck. At the same time, in light of the rupture with the principles of Caprivi's trade policy and the further raising of tariffs over the levels of the Bismarck era, they see the German Empire transitioning to high protectionism.

There are marked differences between the different narratives on the empire, meanwhile, when it comes to explaining German protectionism and its evaluation in detail. One highly influential perspective can be traced back to Berlin historian Eckart Kehr, who died at a young age in 1933. This was later developed and expounded to great effect by Alexander Gerschenkron, Hans Rosenberg and Hans-Ulrich Wehler, and sees the long-standing political alliance between heavy industry and big agrarians as the driving force of German tariff and trade policy.[24] In this view, from the late 1870s on, this alliance between 'rye and iron' set in motion a class-based and anticonsumerist form of protectionism in the field of tariff policy. But it did much more than this. As a conservative 'cartel of the state-preserving and productive classes' with a firmly antisocialist thrust, it determined the fate of German politics. Briefly interrupted by the Caprivi years, 'Junkers and smokestack barons' succeeded in ruthlessly advancing their protectionist interests, implementing a protectionist policy blatantly intended to benefit them at the expense of consumers and exports. At the same time, as it struggled to defend its own power, the ill-starred alliance between big industry and big landowners did much to lead the empire into the disaster of the First World War and placed a heavy burden on German history as a whole. Against this background, the protectionist turn of 1879, as the birth of this unholy alliance, has at times been viewed as 'one of the great mistakes of nineteenth-century German and thus European history', with consequences up to and including National Socialism.[25]

This far-reaching interpretation has not gone uncontested. It was soon pointed out that it was not so much the Prussian Junkers who took up the cudgels for agricultural tariffs in the run-up to 1879 as the agrarian associations and agricultural councils in the farming regions, particularly of western Germany.[26] The findings of James C. Hunt fit neatly with this picture. As he has elaborated, it was not just the big agrarians that benefited from the cereal tariffs but also the small and medium-sized farms supposedly manipulated by them; these also gained effective protection from international competition through a number of de facto protectionist animal disease controls and veterinary measures. In light of this, there can be no question of an agricultural protectionism that one-sidedly favoured the cereal producers east of the Elbe.[27] And in a general sense too, the influence that Wehler and the other 'Kehrites' had ascribed to the elites of the empire came under increasing fire from the late 1970s onwards. The key to understanding the history of the German Empire, as a group of British historians in particular have underlined, lies not in 'manipulation from above' but rather in self-mobilization 'from below'.[28] Finally, some historians questioned the durability and resilience of the agrarian-industrial alliance. Particularly during the era of the 'politics of rallying together' (*Sammlungspolitik*), as the new version of the protectionist alliance of 1878/79 initiated by the government around the turn of the century has been called, critics have suggested that the structural fragility and disunity of the coalition of agriculture and heavy industry was plainly apparent.[29]

The explanation of German protectionism that highlights the dominant influence of the agrarian-heavy industrial power cartel and its critique, which eschews any comprehensive alternative interpretation of this kind, differ on many key points. Despite this, they – and thus also research on German tariff and trade policy – have certain things in common. Not only have they been crying out for in-depth empirical examination for decades, but both entail a narrowing of perspective in at least two respects. First, these competing interpretations focus entirely on the political and social power relations within the German Empire; they seek to explain the empire's foreign trade policy as the product of specifically German domestic political constellations. The flip side of this focus is the systematic failure to cast light on the international context. They pay insufficient attention to the influence of other states' foreign trade policy measures on German policies and fail to get to grips with the significance of trade policy interactions for the system of international relations as a whole. They also fail to evaluate the level of German protectionism in international comparison.

Second, the vast majority of historical research has been limited to analysis of the political decision-making process and has paid virtually no attention to the economic structures and processes that were, after all, the object of the political interventions. With a few exceptions,[30] this applies to the economic consequences of tariffs and other foreign trade policy measures. But it applies above all to the global and domestic economic preconditions for political action. The relevant historians thus almost entirely disregarded the embedding of the German national economy in a highly integrated world economy and its effects on the foreign trade policy decision-making process.

In contrast to this perspective, which is fixated exclusively on the German Empire, the present work situates German foreign trade policy consistently in the context of the first wave of globalization before 1914. The book begins with an attempt to reconstruct the embedding of the German national economy in a global economy undergoing a dramatic process of integration (chapter 1). I first consider the statistical data underpinning the present study and the associated methodological problems. I then seek to establish the role of the German Empire within global trade, before reversing perspective to examine the significance of foreign trade to the German national economy as a whole, along with the relationship between economic shifts and fluctuations in imports and exports. I then go on to calculate the balance of trade and balance of payments and analyze their development; in condensed form, they tell us about the German Empire's economic relations with the rest of the world. Consideration of these factors is at least as important as the examination of the terms of trade that follows, that is, changes in the price relationship between imported and exported goods. I then focus on the structure of foreign trade from two different perspectives. Analysis of the country- and sector-specific structure of imports and exports and their transformation should tell us about the economically based dependencies and room for manoeuvre that characterized German foreign trade policy. Finally, I attempt to assess the significance of the globalization process for key sectors of the German economy. Based on examination of their competitive situation in the world market, I seek to bring out the trade policy interests of agriculture, machine building and the electrical industry, the chemical industry, the textile industry and heavy industry.

Building on this foundation of economic history, I then trace the history of German foreign trade policy from the early 1860s until the mid-1890s. I look first at the period of free trade (chapter 2), which, according to a common myth, symbolized the entire nineteenth century. In fact, outside of the U.K., it was no more than an interlude that lasted for just under twenty years. Chapter 3 attempts to get to grips with the reintroduction of what were initially moderate protective tariffs in 1879 and the autonomous tariff policy under Bismarck that followed it, which expanded the system of agricultural protection. Finally, the Caprivi trade treaties, along with their domestic and foreign policy implications, stand centre stage (chapter 4). The question that runs through the entire book, including chapters 5 and 6, is to what extent the room for manoeuvre, decision-making processes and outcomes of German foreign trade policy were transformed by the first wave of economic globalization.

Chapter 5 is devoted to detailed study of the interaction between foreign trade policy, global economic integration and domestic politics around the turn of the century and provides a new interpretation of the genesis of the Bülow tariff of 1902 beyond the fronts that have emerged within the debate on the 'politics of rallying together'. I begin by examining in-depth the economic interest groups within German society, which were affected by globalization in different ways, and their political representation. I pay special attention to the question of which of the latent economic interests identified in the first part found political articulation, but also the problematic endeavour of organizing the interests of both producers and consumers. In the next step, I examine the central role of the Prussian-German ministerial bureaucracy, which, far from forming a monolithic bloc, was deeply split over the customs tariff issue. Finally, I examine the stance of the political parties and the legislative process in the Reichstag that resulted in the Bülow tariff.

In chapter 6 I shift perspective and, for the period between the turn of the century and the First World War, investigate the German Empire's trade policy relations with its trading partners. Country-specific peculiarities make it impossible to cover the empire's multifarious trade policy relations in any complete way, so I focus on German trade policy towards Russia and the U.S. On the eve of the First World War, these two countries were not just Germany's most important trading partners; they also represented the two major variants of treaty-based trade policy relationships with the German Empire. Above all, though, the ultraprotectionism practiced by both was the most important challenge facing German trade policy before the First World War.

CHAPTER 1

# The German Empire in the World Economy before 1914

On the eve of the First World War liberal economist Paul Arndt summed up the effects of Germany's integration into the world economy:

> *The impact of global trade and commerce extends to the smallest German cottage.* Products from almost every country in the world are to be found in the most modest of households. If we take a cursory glance at our everyday surroundings, at every turn we see objects whose origins lie entirely or partly in other countries. Even in the homes of the less well-off we find bread from Russian, Romanian, North American, Argentinian or Indian wheat, eggs from Italy or Russia, fish from the coast of Norway or Scotland ... rice from East India, coffee from Central or South America or from Dutch India ... textiles of American, Egyptian or Indian cotton, of South African or Australian wool, of Russian flax, which may have been spun and woven in England or France ... glassware from Austria or Belgium ... and so on and so forth. But even goods produced by German labour from German raw materials are now subject to foreign influences. Their production, price and saleability often depend on conditions abroad. We would be hard put to find a single product in Germany whose production is completely unrelated to foreign market conditions.[1]

Arndt's assessment is not only striking testimony to the attentive pre-1914 observer's awareness of economic globalization. It also points up how the German Empire's integration into the world economy impacted on people's lives and highlights, across social classes, the ubiquitous presence of the world market in everyday life.

## Statistical Foundations and Methodological Problems

It is in fact hard to overstate just how integrated into the global economy the German economy was towards the end of the 'long' nineteenth century. This integration was based primarily on Germany's position within global trade, and in what follows – partly determined by my emphasis on trade policy – this will be a key focus. If we want to reconstruct the German Empire's integration into the world market before 1914, it is essential to examine two issues. First, we must investigate the role of the German economy within the global economy: Germany's share of world trade and the structure of its international trade relations. Second, we must scrutinize the importance of world trade to the German Empire: the consequences of global economic integration for specific sectors of the economy and for the German economy as a whole. In both cases, any attempt to portray Germany's integration into the world economy is confronted by grave methodological problems. These relate above all to the statistical data available on foreign trade and involve three key aspects.

One fundamental problem relates to the reliability and completeness of German foreign trade statistics. For the periods prior to the founding of the German Empire there is no sound data at all. For the territory of the German Customs Union from the 1830s and 1840s onwards we might draw on the 'commercial certificates' produced by its member states; but these merely provide customs statistics whose main deficiency is that they related solely to goods subject to customs duties. Important outbound or inbound duty-free commodities were not included in the statistics at all, and for goods that were included, only quantities and not values were recorded. Significant changes were made only with the foundation of the German Empire, when German foreign trade statistics were completely reorganized and calculated on a uniform basis.

For the period from 1872, the present study uses the figures on 'special trade' (*Spezialhandel*) provided by the publications of the newly established Imperial Statistical Office (Kaiserliches Statistisches Amt). Up to and including 1879, however, these too must be cited with great caution. Since there was as yet no legal obligation to register every commodity that crossed the customs frontier, we must work on the assumption that the foreign trade figures are marred by a number of uncorrectable errors. These errors related primarily to export statistics, and the Imperial Statistical Office saw them as so serious in some cases that from 1875 on it initially refrained from calculating export values because of the 'tremendously unreliable character of the documentation on exports'.[2] In 1881, the Imperial Statistical Office took the view that 'with respect to all exported items it is impossible to get anywhere near the truth by comparing results before and after 1 January 1880'.[3] Later, however, it changed its view, made a belated calculation of the value of exports and concluded that 'in general terms'[4] for the period from 1872 to 1879 the foreign trade figures were in fact compatible with those for the following years, an assessment shared, with all due caution, by the present study.

Then, from the beginning of 1880, the 'law concerning statistics on trade in goods between the German customs area and other countries' came into effect. Only now were German foreign trade statistics placed on a reasonably satisfactory basis. Three key innovations were responsible for this. First, from 1880 it was made compulsory to declare all goods imported, exported or transported across the boundaries of the customs area. Second, all entries on imports and exports now systematically recorded values as well as quantities. The assessment of values continued to involve considerable uncertainties. Recorded values were long based exclusively on the annual estimation of average prices for specific types of goods by a commission of 170 experts appointed specifically for this purpose. Only from 1906 was the obligation to declare gradually extended to the values of exported goods; from 1911 on the value of all exports was recorded.[5] Until 1928, in contrast, import values are estimates.

Third and finally, from 1880 onwards the countries of origin and destination of imported and exported goods were also recorded. Only from this point forward, then, can we say anything about the regional structure of German foreign trade and its transformation. Furthermore, it was only now that contemporaries could access data on the significance of specific trading partners and the composition of trade with them – information whose importance can scarcely be overstated in the context of trade treaty negotiations. The statistical data on the origin and destination of German foreign trade, however, must also be used with caution. The definition of country of origin and country of destination, for example, changed in the period under investigation. Until 1906, what mattered was from which country's domestic trade a product had come or which country's domestic trade it was entering into, in short, which were the countries of purchase and sale, but this information was subsequently replaced by identification of the countries of production and consumption. That these two categories by no means always coincide is plainly apparent. Australian wool that arrived in the German Empire via a British middleman is from the U.K. in one system and Australia in the other. We may assume, however, that the distinction between the two methods of assessment was of greater relevance in theory than in practice. First, on the whole the change in the statistics left behind no notable irregularities. Second, from 1880 on, 'the countries through which goods are transported directly or in which goods are merely reloaded or repackaged … [were to be] left out of account when indicating the origin and destination of the goods'.[6] This eliminated the greatest potential for distortion. In compliance with this regulation, countries of purchase and origin as well as countries of sale and consumption did in fact coincide in the vast majority of cases. When this was not the case, it was often quite impossible to discover the information demanded by the new system. This applied above all to exports, when, for example, the exporter delivered products to a British or Belgian trader and had no idea in which country they were resold or ultimately consumed.[7] Before and after 1906, unintentional and intentional false declarations must have represented a significantly larger source of statistical errors than the change in the declaration system. The Imperial Statistical Office could uncover these in specific instances. In 1883, for example, the statistics showed imports into the German customs area of more than 270,000 tonnes of iron ore from the Netherlands' domestic trade. Reexamination ultimately revealed that the ore in fact came from Spain and had merely been imported via a Dutch port.[8] At times, erroneous declarations could lead to significant misrepresentation of trade with specific countries. For example, between 1880 and 1884 imports from Belgium supposedly increased by 54.7 per cent and imports from the Netherlands by 73 per cent – increases that can only be explained as a result of the 'increase in the procurement of overseas goods as they transit via Belgian or Dutch ports to Germany' and the false declaration of these purely transiting goods.[9] From a present-day perspective, unfortunately, we have little option but to highlight such obvious deficiencies in the statistics. As a rule, it is not possible to systematically correct them: in most cases neither the German statistics nor those of Germany's trading partners provide us with any means of doing so.[10]

The second serious difficulty in analyzing German foreign trade statistics before 1914 lies in the classification of goods. This was based on the structure of the Statistical Index of Goods (Statistisches Warenverzeichniss), which was introduced in its original form in 1872 but subsequently underwent a number of changes. Over the course of time additional products, but above all the expert assessment of import and export values, whose accuracy depended in large part on the distinctions made by the Statistical Index, required a marked increase in the individual items listed. The index valid from 1872 showed 457 article numbers for imports and 403 for exports; by 1906, this had grown to 2,030 import items and 1,879 export items. There were also several changes in the number and designation of product groups, which encompassed a range of individual numbers, and in the principles governing the assignment of individual items to these categories.[11]

The evolution of the Statistical Index places limits on the potential to compare over long periods of time the import and export figures shown in the statistics. First, entirely new types and groups of products were included, and second, the content of specific groups of products changed, with quite different items being allocated to the same or a similar category over the course of time. Following the introduction of the new Statistical

Index of 1906, which included a 'classification of goods quite different from the earlier version and a highly detailed listing of individual goods', the Imperial Statistical Office came to the conclusion that 'comparison of the results of foreign trade from 1 March 1906 with those of earlier years' was possible only 'for annual totals and with respect to goods listed in the same way in the new Statistical Index and in the older version'.[12] In line with this, in subsequent years statistical surveys always showed foreign trade in two separate categories: on one side, 'goods comparable' with the data provided prior to the reorganization of the index, and on the other the – larger – category of 'non-comparable goods'.[13]

When it comes to the classification of goods, however, it is possible to eliminate the most serious shortcomings of the statistics. This requires us to break free from the differing classifications found in the different versions of the Statistical Index and reorganize the individual items in accordance with a system valid for the entire period under investigation. In principle, we can define superordinate categories for grouping individual items in line with quite different criteria; often, however, it makes sense for practical reasons to base our categories on a broadly accepted contemporary schema such as the international classification produced by the Brussels Convention of 1913, which most industrial states, including the German Empire, agreed to adopt in order to standardize international trade statistics.[14]

The third and probably the greatest potential for falsification and distortion of German foreign trade statistics prior to the First World War lies in the fact that until 1906 they related to the German customs area rather than the German Empire. But the decisive rupture in the statistics on German foreign trade had occurred earlier, in 1888/89, after the Hanseatic cities of Hamburg and Bremen joined the Customs Union on 15 October 1888. After this the German customs area was largely identical with that of the German economic area, and the latter, with a few exceptions that we can disregard in light of their negligible trade turnover, was identical with the territory of the German Empire.[15] Prior to joining the Customs Union, in statistical terms Hamburg and Bremen were considered trading partners, and they accounted for a substantial portion of German trade. In the year they joined, 1888, the 'customs enclaves on the Elbe and Weser' accounted for 555 million marks or 17 per cent of German imports and 808 million marks or 25.2 per cent of exports.[16]

It is hard to assess the consequences of the Hanseatic cities' accession to the German customs area for import and export value series. The Imperial Statistical Office assumed a drop in exports because 'those quantities of goods formerly listed as moving from the free trade of the German customs area to the customs enclaves on the Elbe and Weser for consumption in these locations and thus included in the export records … are no longer shown since these cities joined the customs area'. This fall in German exports of consumer goods, which was substantial because of the large population of Hamburg and Bremen, which, it was noted, was 'capable of high levels of consumption', contrasted with an increase caused by the export of goods produced in the Hanseatic cities, but the latter was markedly smaller than the former. In the case of imports, on the other hand, the expansion of the Customs Union brought about an increase 'and not just because of the accession of a population with such outstanding purchasing power but also because since the two cities joined the customs area the statistical records extend to commodities of foreign origin which, as the staple items of these cities, are imported in large quantities'.[17] The Imperial Statistical Office's diagnosis is confirmed by the countervailing movements of total imports and exports for the years 1888/89. While exports decreased by 3 per cent, imports saw an increase of 19 per cent, which can only be explained by the change in the basis of calculation.[18]

Evening out this statistical rupture by correcting the foreign trade figures prior to 1889 in accordance with the calculation basis that applied from that date onwards is no easy task. The cleanest solution in methodological terms would be to reduce the value of exports for the German customs area by the proportion entering the Hanseatic cities, while adding exports from Hamburg and Bremen not entering the Customs Union, and to proceed in the same way with respect to imports. Unfortunately, this approach is infeasible because the statistics, especially for Hamburg, fail to distinguish sufficiently between the origins of exports and destinations of imports.[19] In order, despite this, to ensure the comparability of foreign trade statistics across the rupture of 1888/89, economist Fritz Soltau suggested raising the import figures for the period from 1880 to 1888 by one-fifteenth and reducing the export figures by one twenty-fifth.[20] This procedure is problematic, however, as it is based on the statistical interpolation of the increases of 1886/87, 1887/88 and 1889/90, which are themselves heterogeneous and the result, moreover, is subjected to what seems to be a quite arbitrary correction. For want of superior alternatives, then, for total German imports to 1888 the present work is based on the uncorrected figures found in the customs area statistics. At the same time, I have tried to factor in the rupture in the statistics when interpreting them. For aggregate German exports, I was able to draw on recent estimates by Arthur Lewis, who corrected the figures in the German statistics with the help of the statistics of Germany's trade partners – a procedure that admittedly throws up new problems.[21]

The Hanseatic cities' accession to the Customs Union had an even graver impact on the figures for trade with specific trade partners than on total exports and imports. This is because a substantial proportion of customs area exports to the Hanseatic cities was not consumed there but exported onwards, and because the regional structure of the trade carried on by Hamburg and Bremen differed significantly from that of the Customs Union. As a result, the customs area statistics up to 1888 – measured against the German economic area – systematically underestimated exports to the Hanseatic cities' main countries of export, while overstating exports to the countries of western Europe, most of which were reached by land. The fluctuations in the statistics after the cities joined the customs area are testimony to the scale of the distortion before 1889. While in 1889 German exports to the Netherlands, Belgium and France together supposedly lay at around 10 per cent below the value of 1888, at the same time exports to the U.K. increased by 35 per cent. The value shown in the statistics for exports to the U.S. increased by 159 million marks or 67 per cent from 1888 to 1889, while the 'increase' in exports to South America was no less than 173 per cent.[22] Similar examples could be mentioned with regard to imports. There is no incontestable method of correcting the foreign trade figures up to and including 1888. The Hanseatic cities' statistics do not provide the necessary information[23] and their trade partners' figures are also unsuited to this purpose; in a number of ways they are incompatible with one another and with the German statistics. The only solution is therefore to begin analyzing the regional structure of German foreign trade only from 1889 on and to disregard the data up to 1888, which is available only from 1880 (see above); in light of the other distortions we have to accept, this is a relatively minor disadvantage.

The overall picture that emerges from the preceding remarks is as follows. German foreign trade statistics before the First World War exhibit a number of grave shortcomings that confront any historical study with serious methodological problems. From 1889 onwards, however, there exists a statistical foundation that allows us to make reasonably certain statements about the volume of German foreign trade and its commodity and regional structure. For earlier years, meanwhile, we must operate on a far less reliable basis. It is possible to reconstruct the data series for aggregate exports and imports and for specific commodities until 1880, and with reservations until 1872, but not for the regional structure of German foreign trade. On the other hand, a glance at the trade statistics of other countries shows that we can still regard the statistical material available for German foreign trade as relatively reliable and satisfactory. This applies not only in comparison with Dutch and Russian foreign trade statistics, which are considered notoriously unreliable, but in some ways even with respect to the U.K., where instead of country of origin and destination, until 1904 it was ports of dispatch and arrival that were recorded, which tells us little about the regional structure of trade.[24]

## German Exports and World Trade

If we begin, against this background, to reconstruct the development of German foreign trade and the world market integration of the German Empire before the First World War, our first step should be to adopt a bird's-eye view. From this vantage point the tremendous growth in German exports is plainly apparent. In current prices, exports increased from an annual average of 2,308 million marks for the five-year period 1872–76 through 2,785 million marks for 1884–88 and 4,128 million marks for 1897–1901 to an annual average of 8,246 million marks for 1909–13. German exports reached their provisional peak the year before the First World War began, attaining the landmark figure of 10,097 million marks – the first time exports had exceeded a figure of ten billion. Alongside the many short-lived fluctuations, which will be discussed later on, the export figures clearly show two distinct phases of long-lasting growth. The first extends from 1872/73 to 1894 and is characterized by a comparatively small average annual increase in exports of just 1.2 per cent. In the second period, meanwhile, which extends from 1895 to the outbreak of the First World War, exports increased rapidly at an average annual rate of 6.8 per cent.[25] German exports as a whole thus grew even more rapidly than world trade. Figure 1.1 brings out this state of affairs by contrasting the indices of world exports and German exports for the period from 1872 to 1913. From 1880, the German export index always exceeded its world

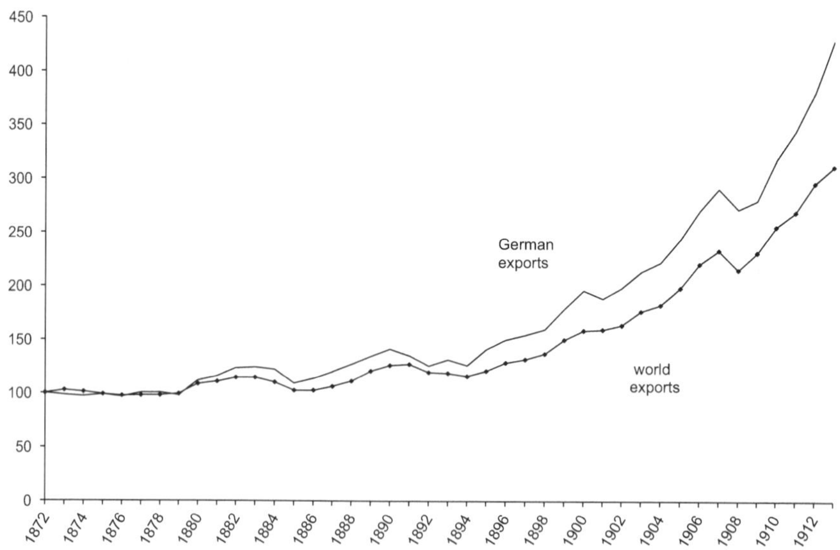


**Figure 1.1.** German exports and world exports, 1872–1913 (1872 = 100)
*Source:* Appendix, table 1.

benchmark; only in the phase of its accelerated growth from 1895, however, did German exports begin to differ markedly from the development of world exports.

The growth of German exports, which was above the international average, enabled the German Empire to climb – seemingly inexorably – through the ranks of exporting countries. Of the major exporting nations identified in table 1.1, which accounted for just over half of global exports in the four decades before the First World War, only the German Empire managed to increase its share continuously. Only U.S. exports grew more during certain periods, but from the turn of the century on they lost ground again. The U.K. and France, meanwhile, suffered a drastic decline in their share of world exports in the period with which we are concerned. Shortly before the war, France was virtually eliminated from the leading group of exporters; the U.K., the U.S. and Germany were now at about the same level. This comes out even more clearly than in the table if we base ourselves not on the export figures for the five-year period 1909–13 but solely on the figures for the year before the war. In U.S. dollars, the U.K. was in the lead at 2,553 million, closely followed by the German Empire at 2,454 million and the U.S. at 2,448 million.[26] The situation with regard to imports was rather different. With imports of 3.2 billion dollars – financed in large part by service exports (transportation, insurance and so on) and the reflux of earnings from foreign capital investments – the U.K. was still out in front, followed by Germany with 2.6 billion dollars and the U.S., which imported goods amounting to 1.8 billion dollars.[27]

**Table 1.1.** Share of global exports, 1874–1913 (in %)

| | *1874–78* | *1879–83* | *1884–88* | *1889–93* | *1894–98* | *1899–1903* | *1903–8* | *1909–13* |
|---|---|---|---|---|---|---|---|---|
| *German Empire* | 9.5 | 10.0 | 10.6 | 10.4 | 11.0 | 11.5 | 11.8 | 12.2 |
| *France* | 11.7 | 10.2 | 9.8 | 9.4 | 8.7 | 8.4 | 7.8 | 7.5 |
| *U.K.* | 17.3 | 16.7 | 17.0 | 15.9 | 14.7 | 14.2 | 13.9 | 13.5 |
| *U.S.* | 10.0 | 12.1 | 10.9 | 12.0 | 12.8 | 14.3 | 13.4 | 12.7 |

*Sources:* My own calculations based on Lewis, 'Rate of Growth', 38–59, table 3; appendix, table 1.

## Foreign Trade and the German Economy

German exports not only grew faster than world trade but also than the economy of the German Empire as a whole. In constant 1913 prices, from 1872 to 1913 the German net national product at factor costs more than doubled, while exports saw a fivefold increase over the same period.[28] Comparison of annual real-term growth rates of exports and net domestic product (NDP) at factor costs (figure 1.2) shows that both growth processes were subject to heavy fluctuations, and these were even more pronounced in the case of exports. If we begin by summarizing annual growth rates by business cycle[29] and forming their arithmetical mean, the following picture emerges: in the first half of the 'Great Deflation' (1874–83), the NDP grew by an average annual rate of just 1.22 per cent, while exports grew by 3.57 per cent. In the second half (1883–90), NDP growth increased by an annual average of 3.02 per cent, but was still exceeded by export growth at 4.18 per cent. In the following decade (1890–1900), because of the economic boom beginning in 1895, the average annual growth rate of the NDP reached 3.46 per cent, its highest level during the empire, before falling back slightly in the 1900–7 period to 2.71 per cent and then climbing again to 3.26 per cent for 1907–13. The real-term growth in exports, meanwhile, rose continually from annual averages for 1890–1900 of 4.30 per cent through 5.86 per cent during the 1900–7 period to 6.47 per cent for 1907–13.[30]

Average growth rate of exports rose constantly from one economic cycle to the next, seemingly independent of growth trends in the national economy. This suggests that we ought to be sceptical about the thesis that during the 'Great Deflation' periods of depression had given a special boost to exports because during these periods the excess supply caused by the drop in domestic demand was shunted onto the world market at dumping prices.[31] This claim of a causal connection between economic

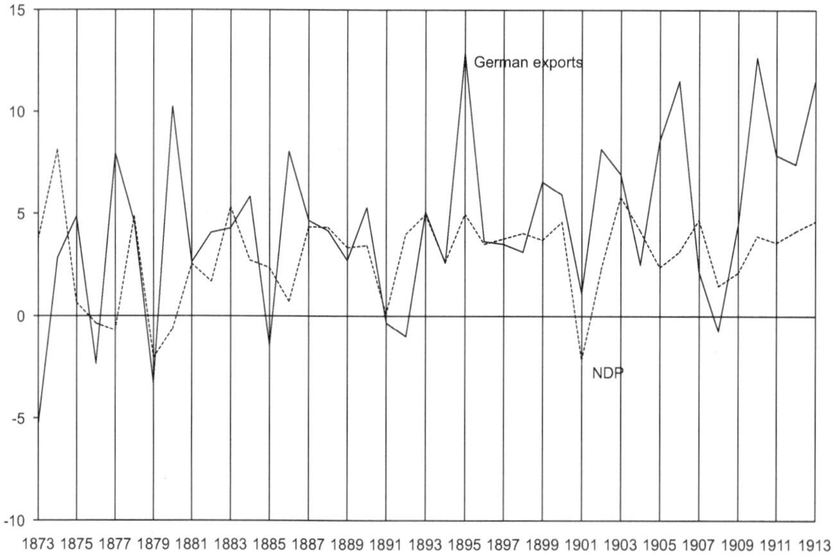


**Figure 1.2.** German exports and net domestic product, 1873–1913 (in constant prices). Change over the preceding year as a %

*Sources:* My own calculations based on Holtfrerich, 'Growth', 130, table 2 (NDP at factor costs); Lewis, 'Rate of Growth', 30, table 2 (exports 1872–1889); Hoffmann, *Wachstum*, 531, table 129 (exports 1890–1913).

contraction and increased exports undoubtedly applies to specific sectors such as the iron and steel industry. But with respect to total exports the only confirmation comes from export figures provided by Walther G. Hoffmann up to and including 1888, which are excessively high. According to the export figures convincingly corrected by Arthur Lewis, meanwhile, during economic boom years average growth in exports is above that of the years of recession, even in the period up to 1895.[32] Comparison of annual growth rates of exports and NDP (figure 1.2) also point to a generally positive rather than negative correlation between the two quantities. Rather than hinting at export endogeneity, however, this correlation leads to the opposite conclusion: that exports, which ultimately represent nothing other than foreign demand for German products, were a demand element of great relevance to the economy as a whole and their fluctuations must therefore have been reflected in the long-term development of the NDP. This connection is particularly evident in the marked decline in exports of 1876, 1879, 1885, 1891, 1901 and 1907/8, all of which are likely to have helped cause the weakening of the domestic economy that went hand in hand with them.

If we then contrast the development of real German imports with that of real NDP (figure 1.3), it emerges that both imports and exports were subject to greater fluctuation than economic activity as a whole but also grew

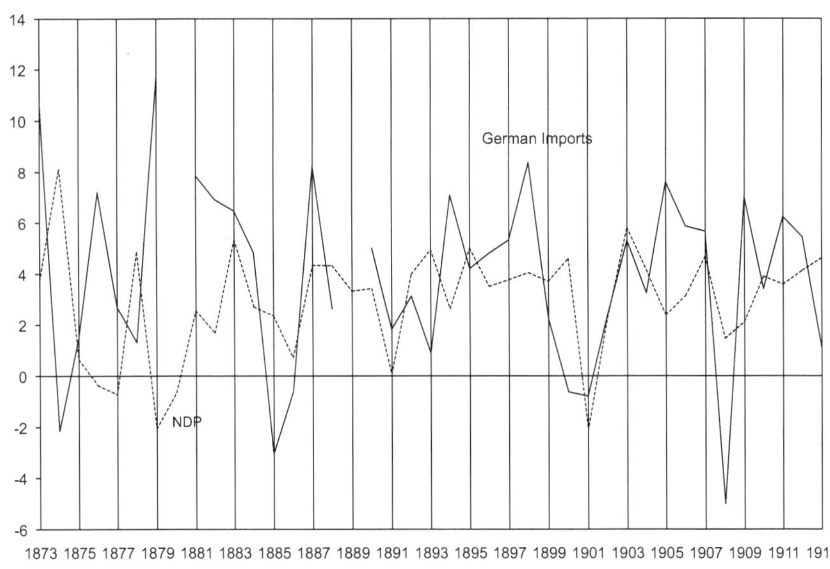


**Figure 1.3.** German imports and net domestic product, 1873–1913 (in constant prices). Change over the preceding year as a %

*Sources:* My own calculations based on Holtfrerich, 'Growth', 130, table 2 (NDP at factor costs); Hoffmann, *Wachstum*, 537–38, table 131 (imports).

faster on average than NDP. Unlike exports, however, average import growth rates aggregated according to economic cycles show no tendency to increase or any other trend throughout the period under investigation: German imports grew at an average annual rate of 4.82 per cent in the 1874–83 period and by 3.35 per cent for 1883–90; for 1890–1900 the annual growth rate climbed again to 3.84 per cent, but then declined slightly to 3.58 per cent in the 1900–7 period and 3.41 per cent for 1907–13.[33]

Foreign trade theory generally assumes that imports are a function of national income, such that its magnitude is endogenously linked to domestic economic trends.[34] Analysis of annual fluctuations in the growth of NDP and imports lends credence to this assumption with respect to the German Empire prior to 1914. Only in a small number of cases, however, does a significant aligned swing of NDP and imports in the same year point to the causal relationship between them: the downswing of 1890/91, the economic upturn of 1901/2 and the brief crisis of 1907/8. In other cases, meanwhile, the movements of NDP and imports were characterized by a slight phase shift. Interestingly, in most cases imports did not follow trends in the overall economy but foreshadowed them. The import declines of 1873/74, from 1882 on, of 1899/1900 and of 1913, like the increases of 1879, 1886/87 and 1894, indicate that both economic crises and upturns often make their presence felt earlier in the seismographic swings in import growth than in the rather more sluggish production trends in the overall economy.

The fact that both the exports and imports of the German Empire grew even faster than its domestic or national product meant that an ever-greater proportion of German commodity production was exported abroad, while the German national economy became increasingly dependent on imports from other countries. The best, most straightforward indication of the growing importance of foreign trade to the German economy as a whole is the development of export and import rates, in other words, the relationship between exports or imports and gross national product (GNP) or gross domestic product (GDP).[35] As apparent from table 1.2, the German import rate, which was already more than 15 per cent in the 1870s or, given the excessively low estimates of imports until 1888, even higher, had increased again by a solid quarter by the First World War. For the five-

**Table 1.2.** German export and import rates, 1874–1913 (exports and imports as % of GNP, in constant 1913 prices, five-year averages)

| | *1874–78* | *1879–83* | *1884–88* | *1889–93* | *1894–98* | *1899–1903* | *1904–8* | *1909–13* |
|---|---|---|---|---|---|---|---|---|
| *Export rate* | 8.5 | 9.7 | 10.5 | 10.6 | 11.0 | 12.0 | 13.7 | 15.8 |
| *Import rate* | 15.2 | 14.9 | 14.6 | 17.1 | 17.8 | 17.9 | 18.6 | 19.2 |

*Sources:* My own calculations based on *StJbDR*; Hoffmann, *Wachstum*; Lewis, 'Rate of Growth', 30, table 2; Ritschl and Spoerer, 'Bruttosozialprodukt', 51, table A.1.

year period 1909–13, the German economy thus depended on imports to an extent that amounted on average to almost one-fifth of its GNP.

The growth in the export ratio was even more impressive. Because of the permanently increasing growth rate, in the forty years before the First World War it almost doubled its initial value. In the last year of the period under investigation, 1913, no less than 17.8 per cent of the commodities produced in the empire were sold abroad. It is testimony to the high degree of global economic integration prior to the First World War that this value placed the empire only in the middle range of industrialized countries. While the German export rate was well above that of France (13.9) and ever further above the U.S. (6.1), it still lagged a bit behind the U.K. (20.9); but in 1913 the highest export rates by far were to be found in Belgium (50.9) and the Netherlands (38.2), whose highly developed industries depended far more on selling their products on the world market than applied in countries with a large domestic market. We may perhaps better assess the degree to which the German economy was globally integrated prior to the First World War if we not only compare it with the economies of other contemporary industrialized countries but also undertake an intertemporal comparison. This shows that the export rate of the empire on the eve of the First World War was surpassed by West Germany – even after the 'economic miracle', which was based in significant part on the stunning success of German exports – only slightly in the 1970s (19.7 per cent in 1973) and not until 1987 to any great extent (26.4). Even by the late 1980s, the U.S. export rate amounted to less (5.7) than one-third of the German value for 1913; during the same period Japan, long considered the modern exporting country par excellence, achieved just half (9.7) of this amount.[36]

## Trade Balance and Balance of Payments

Before the First World War, the value of German imports continuously exceeded that of exports. Figure 1.4 brings this out for the period for which we have reasonably reliable import and export data by showing not just trends in aggregate imports and exports but also the balance between them (exports – imports). What we must bear in mind here, however, is that the available import and export figures – as is still common today – are based on different recording methods. Exports are registered through the so-called f.o.b. (free on board) method to the amount of the pure value of commodities as they cross borders; imports, on the other hand, are estimated in line with the so-called c.i.f. (costs, insurance, freight) method, in other words, inclusive of these particular costs. As a result, even a trade balance that is in a state of perfect equilibrium in terms of the value of

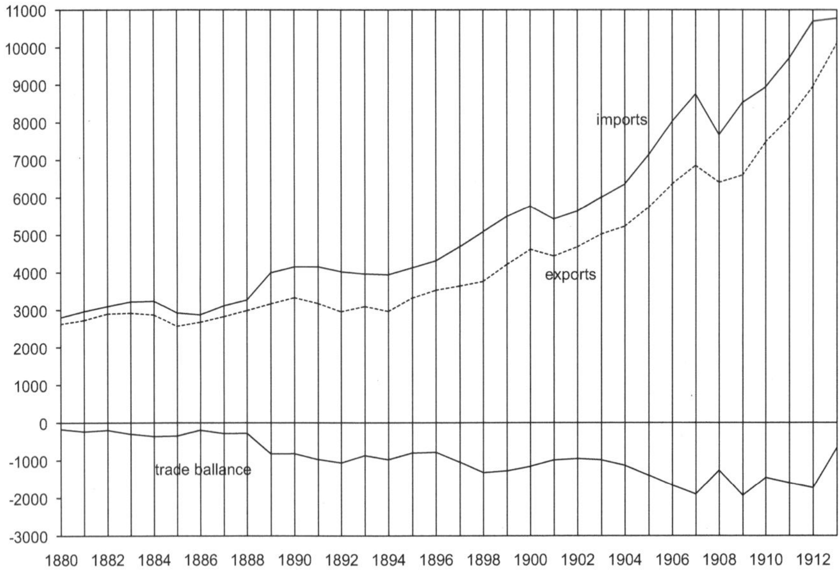


**Figure 1.4.** German trade balance, 1880–1913 (millions of marks, in constant prices)
*Sources:* imports: *StHbDR,* section 2; *StJbDR* (special trade excluding precious metals); exports: 1880–1888: Lewis, 'Rate of Growth', 30, table 2; 1889–1913: *StHbDR,* section 2; *StJbDR* (special trade excluding precious metals); trade balance = exports – imports.

goods looks like a deficit in the statistics; the different ways of recording imports and exports artificially increase negative trade balances while conversely 'massaging' the balance of invisible trade because the foreign services already added to the import value are 'missing' in the recording of actual imports of services.[37] In the case of the German trade balance before the First World War, a large part of its consistently negative status is surely due to the differing methods of recording imports and exports, and thus determined solely by accounting procedures. One of the key pieces of evidence here is the fact that while the German Empire's trade deficit grew in absolute terms over the course of time, it fell in relation to German imports because of the falling costs of transportation, from 22.5 per cent of imports in 1889–93 through 18.9 per cent during the period 1899–1903 to 15.2 per cent for 1909–13.[38]

The overall picture of the balance of payments provides a more comprehensive view of the empire's integration into the world economy than the visible balance alone. Attempts to work out the balance of payments with all its subaccounts for the German Empire before 1914 are beset by a number of problems and uncertainties. Reliable figures exist only for the import and export of goods and thus for the balance of trade, and for the import and export of precious metals included in the foreign exchange account. For the other subaccounts we are dependent on more or less persuasive estimates. Walther G. Hoffmann has made the only attempt so far to work out the values of relevance to the balance of payments. His estimates, however, are based on a number of dubious assumptions and overall seem quite incapable of conveying a realistic picture of the German balance of payments prior to the First World War. This is especially evident in his marked overestimation of the surplus in the German invisible trade balance, which amounts to 47 per cent (1898) of net exports, according to Hoffmann.[39] I have therefore corrected Hoffmann's calculations on a number of occasions in the present work.

Let us look first at the balance of capital transactions. As in Hoffmann's work, I too draw on the figures published in the *Der deutsche Ökonomist* from 1883 on for foreign securities issued in Germany as the best available ballpark figures for annual German net capital exports.[40] Again like Hoffmann and following a number of contemporary authors, I estimate the level of German capital investment in foreign securities for 1913 at about twenty billion marks. The fundamentally justified objection that in both cases we are actually dealing with gross rather than net figures may be countered with the fact that in comparison with German foreign investment, foreign capital investment in Germany played a merely subordinate role; according to the calculations of Herbert Feis, at the end of 1913, by far the most important capital exporter in the world, the U.K., held German securities amounting to a total of just 131 million marks, in contrast to German capital investments in British securities of well over ten times this figure.[41] Further, I have attempted to deal with the problem of using gross rather than net figures by making defensive, low estimates. This applies both to annual capital outflows, which exclude such things as securities acquired on foreign stock exchanges, and to the total value of German assets abroad, which lies at the lower end of contemporary estimates.[42]

In contrast to Hoffmann, however, I view the values indicated for annual capital exports and total assets as what they originally were: data that refer only to German foreign investment in the shape of portfolio investments – and that therefore capture just one dimension of the long-term capital account. For the second element of long-term capital transactions, direct investment, which Hoffmann implicitly views as marginal, we have just a few contemporary estimates, though these are of a magnitude that suggests an urgent need to factor them in. Building on a study by the Imperial Naval Office (Reichsmarineamt), Sartorius von Waltershausen estimates German direct investment overseas for 1904 at 8,030 to 9,225 million marks, which will have contrasted with a negligible amount of foreign direct investment in Germany. He puts net investment in Europe at 1.5 billion marks.[43] If we again make defensive calculations, we arrive at a figure for German foreign investment in the form of direct investment of around 9.5 billion marks for 1904. If we continue to draw on Sartorius von Walterhausen's figures for 1898 and work on the assumption that the total volume of German direct investment abroad and the total volume of portfolio investments grew in line with a linear regression curve,[44] then we arrive at a figure for German net capital exports in the form of direct investment of just under 200 million marks a year on average, which must be added to the capital account. If we follow this approach to making estimates, we arrive at a net figure for German direct investment abroad for 1913 of around 11 billion marks, and thus of about 31 billion marks for German capital investment as a whole (portfolio and direct investment).[45] This figure fits neatly with the estimates made by Paul Arndt, which also find support among other economists, who put the gross value of German portfolio and direct investments abroad at 'at least 35 billion marks' for 1913.[46]

Finally, available estimates for the total volume of German foreign investment allow us to calculate capital returns flowing back into the German Empire,[47] which in balance of payments terms form part of the invisible trade balance. Hoffmann assumes that the return on German capital invested abroad was equal to the long-term interest rate in Germany and was 3 per cent for 1913.[48] But this assumption seems quite unrealistic, as we can expect that the yield of foreign investments will have included a risk premium that must be added to the German capital market interest. Schaefer's findings do in fact suggest a much higher yield on German portfolio investments abroad, whose arithmetical mean for the 1883–1913 period amounts to 5.4 per cent.[49] This value is taken as the basis for the present work as well. As we now have time series on the balance of trade, foreign exchange and capital account and on the balance of capital returns as a component of the invisible trade balance, we may calculate the balance of the remaining services as a residuum of the other subaccounts. Here we make use of the trivial insight that due to the principle of double entry bookkeeping, the balance of payments as a whole must always be balanced.

On the basis of the assumptions outlined above, we arrive at annual estimates for the specific subaccounts of the balance of payments that are at times quite different from Hoffmann's time series.[50] Table 1.3 summarizes the findings in the form of five-year averages. Across the 1883–1913 period we find a clear balance of payments structure: the expanding trade deficit contrasted with a structural surplus in the balance of invisible trade and capital account movements. I have already talked about the persistent deficit in the German Empire's visible trade balance, which expanded over time. But this deficit was more than offset by the active invisible balance,

Table 1.3. German balance of payments, 1883–1913 (millions of marks, current prices)

| | 1883–88 | 1889–93 | 1894–98 | 1899–1903 | 1904–8 | 1909–13 |
|---|---|---|---|---|---|---|
| *Exports* | 2,807 | 3,143 | 3,439 | 4,588 | 6,112 | 8,246 |
| *Imports* | 3,104 | 4,053 | 4,426 | 5,661 | 7,583 | 9,726 |
| *Trade balance* | –297 | –910 | –987 | –1072 | –1472 | –1480 |
| *Return on capital (balance)* | 786 | 980 | 1,139 | 1,304 | 1,464 | 1,618 |
| *Other services (balance)* | 184 | 513 | 655 | 400 | 840 | 699 |
| *Invisible trade balance* | 970 | 1,494 | 1,794 | 1,704 | 2,304 | 2,318 |
| *Current account* | 673 | 584 | 808 | 631 | 833 | 838 |
| *Capital account proper* | 681 | 549 | 721 | 486 | 585 | 643 |
| *Reserve account* | –7 | 34 | 87 | 145 | 248 | 195 |
| *Capital account* | 673 | 584 | 808 | 631 | 833 | 838 |

*Source:* Calculation of five-year averages based on appendix, table 2.

so that the current account as a whole (trade balance + invisible balance) was highly positive over the long term. What is striking here is that the lion's share of the surplus generated within the context of the invisible balance can be put down to the enormous capital returns that flowed back to the empire from German foreign investment. In comparison with them, the other services, above all transportation, played a still important but subordinate role. In the period under consideration as a whole, the surplus in the invisible trade balance reached a level that made it possible not only to offset the trade deficit but also to finance significant net capital exports and a positive foreign exchange account. The balance of long-term capital movements exhibited fairly pronounced fluctuations from year to year but maintained an essentially unchanging basic level, while over time average annual German precious metal imports climbed markedly above exports, generating a surplus.

Short-term capital transactions represent the major remaining uncertainty in the German balance of payments prior to 1914. Unfortunately, we lack sufficient evidence to make even a rough estimate of the magnitude of such transactions. The general assumption is that the German Empire was a net debtor in the field of short-term capital transactions.[51] In this case, both the capital account surplus and the invisible balance surplus would be reduced. It is also possible that factoring in international short-term capital transactions would offset the annual fluctuations in the invisible and capital balance to some degree. But this would do nothing to change the fundamental balance of payments structure of the German Empire as outlined above. The role of the empire was that of a classical creditor nation that was in the process of expanding its position through further net capital exports – though at a stable rather than increasing rate. This leads on to two further points.

First, the enduring imbalance between the individual subaccounts demonstrates that the impact attributed to 'gold automatism' in theory, namely, a balance of payments adjustment in the real economy, fails in practice if autonomous capital movements disrupt the assumed price-specific flow mechanism. As German net capital exports largely offset the current account surpluses, they tended to counteract the adjustment mechanism ascribed to the gold standard – the current account remained enduringly uneven, with its active balance developing into a structural constant.

Second, this enduring current account surplus points to a latent potential for trade policy conflicts. As the debtor countries could service their debts over the long term only if they themselves generated current account surpluses, which given their passive invisible balance could arise only from higher trade balance surpluses, we may assume they would exhaust every restrictive trade policy option in order to achieve the required export surplus. On the other hand, the persistent German current account surplus indicates that there was little willingness in the creditor country to accept the current account deficit necessary to the intertemporal stability of the foreign trade equilibrium, as this would have entailed a risk for the German economy of structural adjustment crises. Here again, then, we would expect the deployment of trade policy instruments – this time with the aim of securing the status quo.

## The Development of Import and Export Prices

Price movements in foreign trade featured a number of clear basic trends. If we trace the price indices for German imports and exports weighted for import and export values from 1880 to 1913, and it is only for this period that we have sufficient data to do so, then overall (figure 1.5) the import price index shows a U-shaped curve. The prices of German imported goods declined by more than one-quarter until the mid-1890s, but then increased again and were at about their initial level by 1913. Export prices also exhibited a marked decline during the 'Great Deflation', which was in fact rather more pronounced than in the case of import prices. In contrast to these, however, they then increased only negligibly, so that in 1913 the export price index was far below its initial level. The consequence of the contrasting development of import and export prices was a significant worsening of the German terms of trade (t.o.t.), of the real exchange rela-

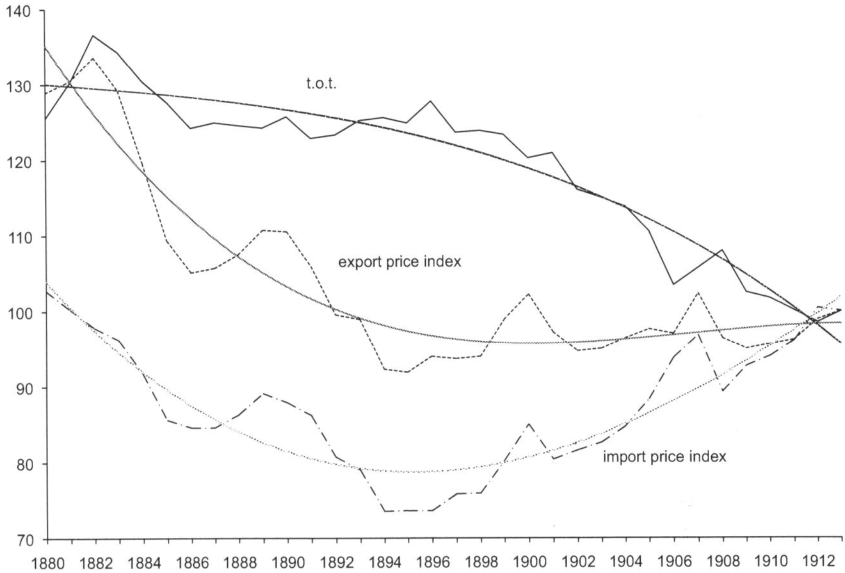


**Figure 1.5.** Terms of trade, 1880–1913 (1913 = 100)
*Source:* Hoffmann, *Wachstum*, 548, 607, 613.

tionship, which is a quotient of the export and import price index. In other words, in quantitative terms the German economy had to increase the volume of its exports disproportionately in order to finance imports. As figure 1.5 shows, this was a long-lasting trend, though one that increasingly gained ground when import prices rose significantly faster than export prices from the mid-1890s.[52]

There are many possible reasons for this development. Foreign trade theory identifies a number of factors that may influence terms of trade. Processes of economic growth, changes in preference structures, trade policies, changes in exchange rates and capital movements may in theory have an impact on the real terms of trade.[53] But which of these factors exercises the crucial influence in specific cases, the importance of each within a combination of mechanisms, is very difficult to assess empirically.[54] This is due not just to the wide range of variables but also to the fact that economic research lacks any equivalent of the experiments found in the natural sciences that allow us to create in practice the ceteris paribus conditions found in theory and thus to isolate the influence of individual factors. Often, then, it is as good as impossible to separate out analytically the effects of the various influences, which overlap in reality. This applies all the more when, as in this case, phenomena are investigated across long time periods, such that short-term and long-term effects may overlap.

Rather than attempting, with scant prospect of success, to determine the significance of the various factors that might explain the worsening of the German terms of trade, then, I merely wish to highlight two aspects here.

First, the German Empire clearly did not succeed in improving its own terms of trade through the introduction or raising of customs duties. Foreign trade theory as applied to the real economy identifies such an effect to the benefit of the tariff-imposing country as a predictable result of an equilibrium model featuring two countries and two products, the assumption – likely a realistic one in the case of Germany – being that the tariff-imposing country is big enough to influence international prices, in other words, international supply is not infinitely elastic. In contrast to this assumption about the connection between tariffs and the real exchange relationship, there is no indication at all of a positive reaction of the terms of trade to protectionist measures by Germany. Instead, the terms of trade seem to have developed to the country's long-term disadvantage more or less independently of the various trade policies pursued. We might counter the possible objection that from a German perspective the real exchange relationship would have gotten even worse in the absence of tariffs by pointing to the example of the U.K., with its free trade focus, whose terms of trade developed far less negatively during the period under investigation than those of Germany.[55]

Second, the significance of the negative development of the German terms of trade should not be overstated. On the one hand, the real relationship of exchange derived from import and export prices, which, to be more precise, we should describe as commodity terms of trade, seems to have changed clearly to the disadvantage of the German Empire. Trade developed to the detriment of the German economy in the sense that Germany received ever fewer imported goods per unit of exported goods. On the other hand, it is possible and likely that this development went hand in hand with such a substantial increase in productivity that the factoral terms of trade in fact increased at the same time. This is because of the efficiency of production factor input in the German export sectors, which was enhanced by increased productivity. If these overcompensated for similar phenomena in other countries and the worsening of the real exchange relationship, then despite falling commodity terms of trade the German economy received more imported goods per unit of production factors deployed for export. But the increase in the factoral terms of trade brought about in this way is just one aspect of the increase in national wealth. The other is the growth in productivity itself, which was based substantially on realizing economies of scale. These would have been impossible without exports, which facilitated the expansion in production that underpinned the economies of scale.

## The Regional Structure of German Foreign Trade

The geographical structure of German foreign trade played a crucial role in trade relations with specific countries. If we begin by adopting a bird's-eye view and focusing on exports and their distribution across different parts of the world, we will notice a remarkable persistence of spatial structure. As table 1.4 shows, in the quarter century before the First World War (as discussed earlier, it is only for this period that we have reliable figures for a regional analysis of German trade),[56] no less than three-quarters of German exports always went to other European countries. This clear and enduring dominance of intra-European exports, however, was not peculiar to Germany, but reflects general European trends. It is true that annual intra-European exports made up just 67.9 per cent of total European exports on average for 1909–11; but this figure is due in significant part to the strong extra-European orientation of the large British export trade. If we limit ourselves to the countries of continental Europe, meanwhile, intra-European exports for 1909–11 amounted to 78 per cent, a figure even higher than that for Germany.[57] It would be wrong to interpret the large European share of German exports as an indication that the integration of the German Empire into the world economy was at a low level. One good way of bringing this out is to make a comparison with the present. Even present-day Germany's export economy, which has enjoyed great success in the global market, exported 73.3 per cent of its products to other European countries in 2000 – just slightly less than a century before.[58]

At first sight, the share of German exports going to the Americas seems not to have changed much. But this conceals a fundamental shift in the importance of North and South America as markets for German goods. While North America declined markedly as a target region for German exports, from 12.7 per cent of total German exports in 1890 through 9.1 per cent in 1901 to 7.7 per cent in 1913, exports to South America increased in the same period from 5.1 per cent (1890) to 7.6 per cent (1913).[59] The

**Table 1.4.** Regional structure of German exports, 1889–1913 (as a % of total exports)

| | *Europe* | *The Americas* | *Asia* | *Africa* | *Australia and Oceania* |
|---|---|---|---|---|---|
| *1889–93* | 78.0 | 17.4 | 3.0 | 0.8 | 0.7 |
| *1894–98* | 78.5 | 15.5 | 3.7 | 1.5 | 0.8 |
| *1899–1903* | 78.3 | 14.4 | 4.5 | 1.7 | 1.0 |
| *1904–8* | 75.1 | 16.6 | 5.1 | 2.0 | 1.0 |
| *1909–13* | 75.4 | 16.4 | 4.7 | 2.2 | 1.0 |

*Source:* Five-year averages based on table 3 in the appendix.

development of exports to Asia and Africa can also be described from two different perspectives. On the one hand, the share of German exports going to Asia more than doubled between 1889 and 1913, while undergoing a 6.5-fold increase in absolute terms. German exports to Africa underwent a threefold increase in the quarter century before the First World War.[60] On the other hand, even these rates of increase change nothing about the fact that shortly before the First World War Africa and Asia together accounted for no greater a share of German exports than the Netherlands. The German colonies too were conspicuous by their insignificance to the export economy: in 1913 they absorbed no more than 0.5 per cent of aggregate German exports.[61]

The impression that German exports were marked by great continuity of geographical structure is further qualified when we depart from the level of continents to that of importing countries. Table 1.5 lists the eight most important trading partners of the German export economy in order of the total volume of German goods that they absorbed between 1889 and 1913. The table not only shows once again the dominance of Europe, but also the fact that German exports underwent regional diversification over the course of time. In 1890 the main importing countries accounted for no less than 73 per cent of German exports, but just 66 per cent on the eve of the First World War. The growing remainder was distributed mainly among smaller export partners in northern Europe, South America and Asia. Regardless of a clear absolute increase in exports to all destination countries, the distribution of German exports to specific trade partners also changed markedly. The U.K. remained the leading importer of German goods throughout the period under examination; but its importance diminished significantly, above all from the turn of the century. The share of German exports going to the U.S. also declined over the quarter century before the First World War. In contrast to the U.K., it was the interplay of highly protectionist American tariff policies and rapid industrial development that was responsible for this, increasingly putting the U.S. economy in a position to satisfy domestic demand. In contrast to the U.K. and the U.S., after the low point in trade relations between Germany and Russia arising from the Russo-German tariff war in the early 1890s it proved possible to increase exports to Russia, which accounted for a growing share of German exports; by 1913 it had become the third most important importing country.

No such dramatic trend applied to the five other most important destination countries for German exports (all of them neighbours of the German Empire), whose share remained more or less unchanged between 1889 and 1913. What all of them have in common is that the goods bought from Germany made up a greater share of their import structure than of

**Table 1.5.** German exports: Main trading partners, 1889–1913 (exports in millions of marks and as a share of total exports)

| | I. U.K. | | II. Austria-Hungary | | III. U.S. | | IV. Netherlands | | V. Russia[a] | | VI. France | | VII. Belgium | | VIII. Switzerland | | % share I–VIII of total German exports |
|---|---|---|---|---|---|---|---|---|---|---|---|---|---|---|---|---|---|
| | m. of marks | % | m. of marks | % | m. of marks | % | m. of marks | % | m. of marks | % | m. of marks | % | m. of marks | % | m. of marks | % | |
| *1889* | 647 | 20.4 | 319 | 10.1 | 395 | 12.5 | 249 | 7.9 | 174 | 5.5 | 209 | 6.6 | 137 | 4.3 | 170 | 5.4 | 72.7 |
| *1890* | 690 | 20.7 | 332 | 10.0 | 417 | 12.5 | 258 | 7.8 | 184 | 5.5 | 231 | 6.9 | 151 | 4.5 | 176 | 5.3 | 73.3 |
| *1891* | 679 | 21.4 | 331 | 10.4 | 357 | 11.2 | 268 | 8.4 | 145 | 4.6 | 237 | 7.5 | 153 | 4.8 | 181 | 5.7 | 74.0 |
| *1892* | 629 | 21.3 | 321 | 10.9 | 346 | 11.7 | 234 | 7.9 | 130 | 4.4 | 201 | 6.8 | 141 | 4.8 | 169 | 5.7 | 73.5 |
| *1893* | 670 | 21.7 | 339 | 11.0 | 354 | 11.4 | 240 | 7.8 | 136 | 4.4 | 201 | 6.5 | 148 | 4.8 | 183 | 5.9 | 73.4 |
| *1894* | 632 | 21.3 | 353 | 11.9 | 271 | 9.2 | 243 | 8.2 | 171 | 5.8 | 188 | 6.3 | 150 | 5.1 | 185 | 6.2 | 74.1 |
| *1895* | 676 | 20.4 | 374 | 11.3 | 368 | 11.1 | 245 | 7.4 | 208 | 6.3 | 202 | 6.1 | 159 | 4.8 | 216 | 6.5 | 73.8 |
| *1896* | 713 | 20.2 | 400 | 11.3 | 383 | 10.9 | 262 | 7.4 | 232 | 6.6 | 201 | 5.7 | 168 | 4.8 | 239 | 6.8 | 73.7 |
| *1897* | 699 | 19.2 | 406 | 11.2 | 397 | 10.9 | 263 | 7.2 | 241 | 6.6 | 210 | 5.8 | 189 | 5.2 | 249 | 6.9 | 73.0 |
| *1898* | 741 | 19.7 | 426 | 11.3 | 333 | 8.9 | 278 | 7.4 | 273 | 7.3 | 205 | 5.5 | 187 | 5.0 | 253 | 6.7 | 71.8 |
| *1899* | 801 | 19.0 | 450 | 10.7 | 377 | 9.0 | 321 | 7.6 | 325 | 7.7 | 216 | 5.1 | 207 | 4.9 | 281 | 6.7 | 70.8 |
| *1900* | 862 | 18.7 | 486 | 10.5 | 440 | 9.5 | 364 | 7.9 | 313 | 6.8 | 277 | 6.0 | 253 | 5.5 | 284 | 6.2 | 71.1 |
| *1901* | 907 | 20.5 | 464 | 10.5 | 385 | 8.7 | 372 | 8.4 | 302 | 6.8 | 249 | 5.6 | 236 | 5.3 | 257 | 5.8 | 71.6 |
| *1902* | 958 | 20.5 | 480 | 10.3 | 449 | 9.6 | 392 | 8.4 | 300 | 6.4 | 253 | 5.4 | 261 | 5.6 | 278 | 5.9 | 72.1 |
| *1903* | 982 | 19.6 | 500 | 10.0 | 469 | 9.4 | 417 | 8.3 | 323 | 6.4 | 272 | 5.4 | 268 | 5.3 | 297 | 5.9 | 70.3 |
| *1904* | 985 | 18.9 | 555 | 10.6 | 495 | 9.5 | 410 | 7.8 | 300 | 5.7 | 274 | 5.2 | 277 | 5.3 | 320 | 6.1 | 69.2 |
| *1905* | 1042 | 18.2 | 580 | 10.1 | 542 | 9.5 | 433 | 7.6 | 346 | 6.0 | 293 | 5.1 | 313 | 5.5 | 359 | 6.3 | 68.2 |
| *1906* | 1067 | 16.8 | 649 | 10.2 | 637 | 10.0 | 444 | 7.0 | 406 | 6.4 | 383 | 6.0 | 356 | 5.6 | 374 | 5.9 | 67.9 |
| *1907* | 1060 | 15.5 | 717 | 10.5 | 653 | 9.5 | 452 | 6.6 | 438 | 6.4 | 449 | 6.6 | 343 | 5.0 | 446 | 6.5 | 66.6 |
| *1908* | 997 | 15.6 | 737 | 11.5 | 508 | 7.9 | 454 | 7.1 | 450 | 7.0 | 438 | 6.8 | 323 | 5.0 | 401 | 6.3 | 67.3 |
| *1909* | 1015 | 15.4 | 767 | 11.6 | 606 | 9.2 | 454 | 6.9 | 445 | 6.7 | 455 | 6.9 | 349 | 5.3 | 413 | 6.3 | 68.3 |
| *1910* | 1102 | 14.7 | 822 | 11.0 | 633 | 8.5 | 499 | 6.7 | 547 | 7.3 | 543 | 7.3 | 391 | 5.2 | 453 | 6.1 | 66.8 |
| *1911* | 1140 | 14.1 | 918 | 11.3 | 640 | 7.9 | 532 | 6.6 | 625 | 7.7 | 599 | 7.4 | 413 | 5.1 | 482 | 5.9 | 66.0 |
| *1912* | 1161 | 13.0 | 1035 | 11.6 | 698 | 7.8 | 609 | 6.8 | 680 | 7.6 | 689 | 7.7 | 493 | 5.5 | 521 | 5.8 | 65.7 |
| *1913* | 1438 | 14.2 | 1105 | 10.9 | 713 | 7.1 | 694 | 6.9 | 880 | 8.7 | 790 | 7.8 | 551 | 5.5 | 536 | 5.3 | 66.4 |

*Sources: StDR* (1889–1905); *StJbDR* (1906–13). All figures excluding precious metal exports.

[a] Including Finland until 1896.

the German export structure; in other words, in purely percentage terms the German Empire was more important to their imports than they were to the German export economy. In fact, prior to the First World War German exports dominated most European markets. More than a few countries were dependent on German goods for anything from one-third to almost one-half of their total imports, as in the case of Switzerland (31.6 per cent), Russia (34.6 per cent) and Austria-Hungary (45.8 per cent) in the year 1900.[62]

Finally, we can also learn about the regional structure of German exports by looking at the export difference factor (EDF), which indicates the standardized deviation of a country's actual share of German exports from the share we would expect on the basis of its share of world imports.[63] An EDF of 0 means that actual trade precisely matches the share of world trade; the lowest value of EDF = –1 means that no trade is occurring at all; the more positive the EDF, the more it points to trade of above-average intensity. Given that transport routes influence the EDF and thus the average EDF for neighbouring countries is +1.0, while that for transatlantic trade is –0.3, three figures stand out among the export difference factors calculated for 1900: the figures for Austria-Hungary (+2.1) and Switzerland (+1.8) indicate that Germany's export intensity was significantly higher than we might expect for these countries. The comparatively small French EDF, particularly for a neighbouring country, of –0.4, meanwhile, indicates that France was far less important to German exports than we might have expected in light of its position within world trade and its geographical position.

The geographical structure of German imports also reveals the dominance of intra-European trade. In contrast to exports, however, Europe clearly began to lose its predominant position with respect to imports during the quarter century before the First World War. Even more clearly than in the five-year averages listed in table 1.6, this is evident if we look at the first and final year of the period under examination: while 79.3 per cent of German imports still came from other European countries in 1889, this had fallen to 54.7 per cent by 1913.[64] Due to the sharply increasing demand for raw materials and foodstuffs from overseas, meanwhile, the extra-European regions became significantly more important as sources of German imports. By far the largest share of German imports from outside Europe was provided by the Americas; from the turn of the century, they were consistently the source of more than one-quarter of total German imports. Throughout the period under examination the U.S. was much more important than the other countries of South and North America. Between 1889 and 1913, the U.S. share of total German imports from the two American continents was between 50 and 70 per cent.

**Table 1.6.** Regional structure of German imports, 1889–1913 (as a % of total imports)

| | *Europe* | *The Americas* | *Asia* | *Africa* | *Australia and Oceania* |
|---|---|---|---|---|---|
| *1889–93* | 72.8 | 19.9 | 4.4 | 1.3 | 1.5 |
| *1894–98* | 66.8 | 22.7 | 6.5 | 1.8 | 2.2 |
| *1899–1903* | 62.8 | 25.9 | 6.6 | 2.6 | 2.1 |
| *1904–8* | 60.1 | 26.5 | 7.7 | 3.2 | 2.4 |
| *1909–13* | 57.2 | 26.3 | 9.0 | 4.5 | 3.0 |

*Source:* Five-year averages based on table 3 in the appendix.

The growing importance of the non-European world to German imports, which accounted for a 45.3 per cent share in 1913, notably higher than the equivalent figure of 31 per cent one hundred years later, is also confirmed if we turn our attention to the leading supplier countries for the German Empire (table 1.7).[65] It is the development of the U.S. as the main supplier for the German economy that is most impressive here. In addition, two other non-European territories managed to advance into the ranks of the eight most important German trading partners before the First World War, namely, British India and Argentina.[66] Their shares of German imports more than doubled between 1889 and 1913, placing them on almost the same level as France on the eve of the war. Most of the German Empire's important European importing partners (Austria-Hungary, Belgium and above all the U.K.), meanwhile, suffered a drastic decline in their share of German imports and in some cases, such as Belgium, even an absolute long-term decline in trade. In 1889, the U.K. was still the undisputed leader among countries importing to the German Empire. By 1913 it had fallen to third place, accounting for just half the volume of imports from the U.S. This was due in significant part to the fact that the U.K. began to lose its function as a middleman for the German economy, as the required goods were increasingly obtained directly from overseas areas. Of the leading European trading partners, only Russia – apart from a brief decline in 1892/93 as a result of the Russo-German trade conflict – managed to stabilize its share of German imports at a high level.

If we leave the level of individual trade partners, table 1.7 also reveals another tendency: just as with exports, there was a diversification of import relations in the quarter century before the First World War. The trading partners listed in table 1.7 accounted for just under 71 per cent and the eight largest supplier countries (listed in footnote 67) for no less than 77.7 per cent of German imports in 1889,[67] but this had sunk to 63 per cent by 1913.[68] If we go on to link analysis of the regional structure of imports with findings on exports, two things stand out.

**Table 1.7.** German imports: Main trading partners, 1889–1913 (imports in millions of marks and as a share of total imports)

| | I. U.S. | | II. Russia[a] | | III. Austria-Hungary | | IV. U.K. | | V. France | | VI. British India | | VII. Belgium | | VIII. Argentina | | Share I–VIII of total German imports |
|---|---|---|---|---|---|---|---|---|---|---|---|---|---|---|---|---|---|
| | m. of marks | % | m. of marks | % | m. of marks | % | m. of marks | % | m. of marks | % | m. of marks | % | m. of marks | % | m. of marks | % | |
| *1889* | 317 | 7.9 | 519 | 13.0 | 530 | 13.3 | 665 | 16.7 | 271 | 6.8 | 95 | 2.4 | 336 | 8.4 | 85 | 2.1 | 70.6 |
| *1890* | 397 | 9.6 | 523 | 12.6 | 583 | 14.1 | 601 | 14.5 | 258 | 6.2 | 129 | 3.1 | 314 | 7.6 | 74 | 1.8 | 69.4 |
| *1891* | 403 | 9.7 | 579 | 14.0 | 569 | 13.7 | 565 | 13.6 | 251 | 6.0 | 157 | 3.8 | 247 | 6.0 | 109 | 2.6 | 69.4 |
| *1892* | 535 | 13.3 | 382 | 9.5 | 563 | 14.0 | 548 | 13.6 | 254 | 6.3 | 150 | 3.7 | 204 | 5.1 | 87 | 2.2 | 67.8 |
| *1893* | 427 | 10.8 | 352 | 8.9 | 571 | 14.4 | 565 | 14.3 | 236 | 6.0 | 179 | 4.5 | 188 | 4.7 | 93 | 2.3 | 65.9 |
| *1894* | 450 | 11.4 | 439 | 11.1 | 572 | 14.5 | 512 | 13.0 | 211 | 5.4 | 164 | 4.2 | 170 | 4.3 | 104 | 2.6 | 66.6 |
| *1895* | 483 | 11.7 | 568 | 13.8 | 513 | 12.4 | 536 | 13.0 | 223 | 5.4 | 162 | 3.9 | 177 | 4.3 | 118 | 2.9 | 67.5 |
| *1896* | 528 | 12.3 | 628 | 14.6 | 547 | 12.7 | 551 | 12.8 | 230 | 5.3 | 171 | 4.0 | 173 | 4.0 | 108 | 2.5 | 68.2 |
| *1897* | 652 | 13.9 | 698 | 14.9 | 583 | 12.5 | 568 | 12.1 | 243 | 5.2 | 205 | 4.4 | 182 | 3.9 | 109 | 2.3 | 69.2 |
| *1898* | 876 | 17.2 | 725 | 14.3 | 627 | 12.3 | 566 | 11.1 | 261 | 5.1 | 221 | 4.3 | 197 | 3.9 | 143 | 2.8 | 71.2 |
| *1899* | 894 | 16.3 | 621 | 11.3 | 716 | 13.1 | 673 | 12.3 | 298 | 5.4 | 230 | 4.2 | 243 | 4.4 | 194 | 3.5 | 70.6 |
| *1900* | 1004 | 17.4 | 671 | 11.6 | 704 | 12.2 | 714 | 12.4 | 303 | 5.3 | 205 | 3.6 | 216 | 3.7 | 233 | 4.0 | 70.2 |
| *1901* | 986 | 18.2 | 669 | 12.3 | 680 | 12.5 | 553 | 10.2 | 272 | 5.0 | 197 | 3.6 | 183 | 3.4 | 201 | 3.7 | 69.0 |
| *1902* | 893 | 15.9 | 759 | 13.5 | 696 | 12.4 | 557 | 9.9 | 303 | 5.4 | 214 | 3.8 | 195 | 3.5 | 202 | 3.6 | 67.8 |
| *1903* | 934 | 15.6 | 822 | 13.7 | 724 | 12.1 | 594 | 9.9 | 330 | 5.5 | 253 | 4.2 | 205 | 3.4 | 271 | 4.5 | 68.8 |
| *1904* | 943 | 14.8 | 805 | 12.7 | 703 | 11.1 | 615 | 9.7 | 366 | 5.8 | 295 | 4.6 | 231 | 3.6 | 337 | 5.3 | 67.6 |
| *1905* | 991 | 13.9 | 973 | 13.6 | 752 | 10.5 | 718 | 10.1 | 402 | 5.6 | 278 | 3.9 | 274 | 3.8 | 369 | 5.2 | 66.7 |
| *1906* | 1236 | 15.4 | 1068 | 13.3 | 810 | 10.1 | 824 | 10.3 | 434 | 5.4 | 322 | 4.0 | 291 | 3.6 | 372 | 4.6 | 66.8 |
| *1907* | 1320 | 15.1 | 1107 | 12.7 | 813 | 9.3 | 977 | 11.2 | 454 | 5.2 | 407 | 4.7 | 297 | 3.4 | 443 | 5.1 | 66.5 |
| *1908* | 1284 | 16.8 | 945 | 12.3 | 751 | 9.8 | 698 | 9.1 | 420 | 5.5 | 307 | 4.0 | 262 | 3.4 | 446 | 5.8 | 66.7 |
| *1909* | 1263 | 14.8 | 1364 | 16.0 | 755 | 8.9 | 724 | 8.5 | 485 | 5.7 | 317 | 3.7 | 290 | 3.4 | 438 | 5.1 | 66.1 |
| *1910* | 1188 | 13.3 | 1387 | 15.5 | 759 | 8.5 | 767 | 8.6 | 509 | 5.7 | 404 | 4.5 | 326 | 3.6 | 357 | 4.0 | 63.8 |
| *1911* | 1343 | 13.8 | 1634 | 16.8 | 739 | 7.6 | 809 | 8.3 | 524 | 5.4 | 440 | 4.5 | 340 | 3.5 | 370 | 3.8 | 63.9 |
| *1912* | 1586 | 14.8 | 1528 | 14.3 | 830 | 7.8 | 843 | 7.9 | 552 | 5.2 | 533 | 5.0 | 387 | 3.6 | 445 | 4.2 | 62.7 |
| *1913* | 1711 | 15.9 | 1425 | 13.2 | 827 | 7.7 | 876 | 8.1 | 584 | 5.4 | 542 | 5.0 | 344 | 3.2 | 495 | 4.6 | 63.2 |

*Sources: StDR* (1889–1905); *StJbDR* (1906–13). All figures excluding precious metals.

[a] Including Finland until 1896.

First, the German Empire's trade balance with its various key trading partners, in other words, the balance of exports and imports, developed in contradictory ways. On the one hand, the empire managed to continuously improve its visible trade balance with all the leading industrialized countries of western and central Europe. Vis-à-vis the U.K., the Netherlands and Switzerland, the empire succeeded in greatly increasing a trade surplus that had already existed in the early 1890s; with respect to Belgium, Austria-Hungary and France, what had formerly been a trade deficit was converted into a growing surplus around or just after the turn of the century. On the other hand, the trade deficit with the U.S. and Russia, as suppliers of raw materials and foodstuffs, increased rapidly and enduringly.

Second, despite these processes of change, four of the German Empire's trading partners set themselves apart from all others over the period under consideration in terms of their economic importance. With a total annual average trade volume (imports + exports) of between around 1,200 million marks (Russia) and around 1,550 million marks (U.K.), the U.K., U.S., Austria-Hungary and Russia played an outstanding role in German foreign trade between 1889 and 1913; the German Empire's next most important trading partner, France, accounted for an average annual trade volume of less than 700 million marks. At the same time, there was a fundamental shift within the quartet of the empire's main trading partners. While the U.K. was substantially more important to German foreign trade in the five-year period of 1889–93, with aggregate annual average imports and exports of 1,252 million marks, than Austria-Hungary (892 million marks), the U.S. (790 million marks) and Russia (625 million marks), by the eve of the First World War this hierarchy had been turned virtually upside down. The empire's main trading partners were now Russia and the U.S., with an average total trade volume of 2,103 and 2,076 million marks, respectively, for the 1909–13 period; the U.K. (1,975 million marks) was now in third place and Austria-Hungary (1,711 million marks) in fourth.

## The Commodity and Sectoral Structure of Imports and Exports

Investigation of the regional structure of German foreign trade and how it changed over time requires complementary analysis of its composition with respect to commodities and sectors. Again, it makes sense to begin at a high level of abstraction and first divide traded goods into just five categories: foodstuffs, luxury consumables (coffee, cigarettes and so on), raw materials, semifinished goods and finished goods.[69] If we apply this scheme to German imports since 1880, we find that over the entire period leading up to the First World War foodstuffs as a share of German imports – which grew at a breathtaking pace – increased slightly but basically remained at the same level. In 1880, foodstuffs made up 25.2 per cent of German imports, and the figures were 25.4 per cent in 1890, 26.3 per cent in 1900 and 26.6 per cent in 1910. Luxury consumables, meanwhile, which constituted 7.9 per cent of imports in 1880 and 9.1 per cent in 1890, subsequently failed to keep up with the growth of imports as a whole and as a share of imports fell to 6.6 per cent in 1900 and just 4.8 per cent in 1910. The picture looks quite different with regard to raw materials. As a share of German imports, they grew continuously from 1880 (35.8 per cent) through 1890 (37.6 per cent) and 1900 (39.7 per cent) to 1910 (45.1 per cent). While imports grew faster than GNP, the growth in raw materials imports outstripped that of imports as a whole. Raw materials imports thus grew much faster than GNP. Only when we factor this in do we get a clear sense of the extent to which the German economy's demand for foreign raw materials increased: on the eve of the First World War, the value of raw materials imported was almost five times the figure for 1880. Imports of semifinished and finished goods, meanwhile, grew impressively in absolute terms, but not in relation to other groups of imported goods. Semifinished products as a share of the German Empire's imports declined from 1880 (18.9 per cent) through 1890 (17.4 per cent) and 1900 (16.5 per cent) to 1910 (14.5 per cent), while the figures for finished goods are 12.2 per cent for 1880, 10.6 per cent for 1890, 11.1 per cent for 1900 and 9.0 per cent for 1910.[70]

The five-year import averages for the most important goods, shown in table 1.8, allow us to gain a more detailed picture of the commodity structure of German imports. First, the figures reflect the division of German imports into different types of commodities as outlined above. Of the main imported goods listed, seven (oil-bearing fruits and seeds, wood and wood pulp, coal, ores, cotton, wool, skins and pelts) are in the category of raw materials, while three (wheat, barley, eggs) are foodstuffs; this contrasts with just two semifinished products (textiles and copper) and one luxury consumable (coffee). Second, we find that foreign trade in the various goods within a product category could develop in quite different ways. In the case of cereals, for example, wheat imports grew four times over between 1880–84 and 1909–13, while barley imports saw an almost eightfold increase. The picture was quite different with respect to trade in rye. After 1906, the empire developed from a net importer to a net exporter country, whose export surplus grew to 90.7 million marks in 1913[71] – a consequence of the interplay of tariffs and the import certificate system, which I discuss in more depth later (chapter 6) in the context of Russo-German trade relations. In the case of industrial input factors,

**Table 1.8.** Imports of specific goods and groups of goods, 1880–1913 (millions of marks, in current prices)

| | *1880–84* | *1885–89* | *1890–94* | *1895–99* | *1900–4* | *1905–9* | *1909–13* |
|---|---|---|---|---|---|---|---|
| 1. *Wheat* | 98 | 70 | 135 | 186 | 252 | 360 | 409 |
| 2. *Barley* | 50 | 61 | 95 | 116 | 128 | 254 | 382 |
| 3. *Eggs* | 16 | 31 | 62 | 80 | 109 | 143 | 178 |
| 4. *Coffee* | 132 | 158 | 211 | 163 | 151 | 171 | 218 |
| 5. *Oil-bearing fruits and seeds* | 53 | 60 | 98 | 114 | 173 | 247 | 424 |
| 6. *Wood and wood pulp* | 80 | 104 | 146 | 239 | 220 | 313 | 354 |
| 7. *Coal* | 24 | 37 | 64 | 69 | 103 | 168 | 180 |
| 8. *Ores of all types* | 36 | 71 | 75 | 106 | 158 | 275 | 359 |
| 9. *Cotton* | 188 | 209 | 220 | 229 | 360 | 481 | 577 |
| 10. *Wool* | 216 | 231 | 239 | 255 | 269 | 391 | 456 |
| 11. *Skins and pelts* | 145 | 133 | 137 | 178 | 275 | 418 | 527 |
| 12. *Textiles (yarn and raw silk)* | 295 | 327 | 283 | 320 | 319 | 440 | 473 |
| 13. *Copper* | 15 | 15 | 35 | 69 | 107 | 201 | 257 |

*Sources:* My own calculations (five-year averages) based on *StJbDR* (nos 1–4, 7, 9–10, 13); Hoffmann, *Wachstum*, 526–27, table 128 (nos 5–6, 8, 12); Jasper, 'Strukturwandlungen', 347 (no. 11).

meanwhile, import trends naturally depended mostly on the growth dynamics of a given branch of industry. All the production factors needed for the textiles industry, for example, regardless of processing stage, exhibit substantially slower import growth than semifinished copper, which was processed further by the dramatically expanding German electrical and machine-building industries. Third and finally, table 1.8 documents the wide spread of imports, which took in virtually every sector of the economy, and their impressive absolute growth, which intensified further during the economic boom beginning in 1895. What we need to bear in mind here, however, is that the import figures listed above are in current prices and the real increase in imports across the period under consideration probably occurred more evenly, as import prices – as discussed above – initially showed a downwards trend before moving up again in the mid-1890s.[72]

As a result of the increase in imports, which left all domestic economic growth figures in the shade, the world market became ever more important in supplying the German economy. Again, the best place to find quantitative evidence of this is on the level of specific imported goods. In the case of goods produced both abroad and domestically, the first way in which we might verify the notion that imports became increasingly important to the domestic market is to trace the relationship between import volume and domestic production over time. If we turn first to wheat, the most important agricultural import to the German Empire, what we find is the development presented in figure 1.6. Wheat imports, which accounted for less than 10 per cent of German production in 1880, increased significantly relative to domestic production in the next two decades in the context of at times substantial harvest-related fluctuations before reaching an exceptional figure of 85 per cent of German wheat production in 1901 as a consequence of a bad harvest in the empire. Subsequently, even after the increase in customs duties brought about by the Bülow tariff, which came into force in 1906, wheat was imported in large quantities until the First World War, amounting to between 50 and 70 per cent of domestic production, depending on German crop yields. In the case of the other important imported cereal, barley, the import rate increased even more dramatically: while barley imports amounted to just 10.3 per cent of German crop yields in 1880, the corresponding figure was 38.5 per cent for 1895 and a massive 88.2 per cent for 1913.[73]

These figures do not, however, sufficiently clarify the extent to which German consumers actually depended on foreign supplies for their cereal consumption. It would be conceivable, for example, for German wheat imports to have been countered by correspondingly high wheat exports, whose rerouting to the home market might have largely compensated for any loss of foreign supplies. To determine the degree of import de-

**Figure 1.6.** Relationship between wheat imports and production in the German Empire, 1880–1913 (in %)

*Source:* Appendix, table 5.

pendency, beyond the comparison of production and import volumes, we must therefore contrast net imports, in other words, the difference between imports and exports, with domestic consumption, which may be calculated as the sum of domestic production and imports minus exports (production + imports – exports).[74] In this way we obtain the share of German wheat consumption that it was necessary to import from abroad in order to satisfy existing demand. Of course, this figure too merely represents a descriptive measurement of import dependency that can respond sensitively to political interventions in foreign trade; it cannot help us to predict the economic costs caused by a fall in imports or the resulting substitution effects among producers and consumers. If we apply this concept to wheat supplies to the German Empire before the First World War, it emerges that dependence on supplies from abroad increased substantially over the long term. While an average of just 14.8 per cent of the wheat consumed in Germany had to be bought from abroad in the 1880s, on average net imports already met 26.5 per cent of domestic demand in the 1890s. Finally, in the first decade of the new century, indigenous production satisfied just one-third – 34.3 per cent – of German wheat consumption.[75] Only in the last few years before the war did the share of domestic demand met by net imports decline again slightly. Interestingly, the reason for this lay not in falling import figures but in sharply increasing German wheat exports, which witnessed an anachronistic renaissance caused by the interplay of customs tariffs and the import certificate system.

Again, barley outstripped wheat. In 1880, indigenous production covered 97 per cent of German demand for barley, with just 3 per cent coming from abroad. By 1895, however, net imports as a share of German barley consumption had already risen to 27 per cent. By 1913, the figure was 47 per cent – almost half of German demand for barley was met by foreign imports.[76] Almost all these imports consisted of feed barley, on which German livestock farming was profoundly dependent, particularly in the case of pig feed. Overall – to cite the cool-headed calculations produced by Bernhard Harms, founder of the Kiel Institute for the World Economy (Kieler Institut für Weltwirtschaft) in 1916, in the middle of the war – per head of population German imports of foodstuffs, luxury consumables and of cattle had grown from 21.1 marks in 1872 to almost twice that amount, 39.1 marks, by 1913.[77]

Far more even than in the case of foodstuffs, however, the German economy was dependent on imports for a large number of industrial input factors. This applied not just to raw materials such as cotton, which had to be imported for climatic reasons, or to materials not naturally present in the German Empire or available in insufficient quantities, as in the case of oil (in 1901–5, a notably increased annual production of 64,998 tonnes contrasted with imports of 1,002,411 tonnes).[78] German industry also became significantly more dependent on the world market in the case of those raw materials being concurrently produced on a substantial scale within the German Empire. This applied even to a raw material such as iron ore, though in terms of output the empire was its second-largest producer in 1912, after the U.S.[79] If we look solely at quantitative data on production, imports and exports, then in comparative terms import dependency with respect to iron ore does not appear to have been particularly pronounced: foreign imports covered 24.6 per cent of German needs in 1913; in fact, it was not until 1898 that imports exceeded exports.[80] A very different picture emerges, however, if we look not at quantitative data but at values, as these reveal that on the world market German ores sold for less than one-fifth (in 1910)[81] of the price that the German iron and steel industry had to pay for foreign iron ores, whose chemical composition (phosphorus content) made them vital to the production process. Factoring in data on values clearly brings out the increase in import dependency. In the mid-1880s, net imports as a share of the German iron and steel industry's iron ore consumption came to just 5.1 per cent, but ten years later this had climbed to 32.6 per cent and in the first decade of the twentieth century had increased substantially to an annual average of 49.9 per cent. Finally, again in terms of net value, 62 per cent of the ores converted into iron in German furnaces came from mines outside of the German economic area in 1913.[82]

That the German economy's dependence on supplies from the world market extended beyond the sphere of foodstuffs, luxury consumables and raw materials is evident when we turn to the semifinished product of copper. Until the late 1880s, demand for this commodity stagnated at a low level within the German Empire. As a result of the massive growth of the electrotechnical industry, German domestic demand for copper then doubled in a year (1888/89) and saw further huge increases in subsequent years. Indigenous copper production, which was 20 to 30 per cent below German consumption even in previous years, was now utterly incapable of satisfying the increased demand. As early as 1889, copper imports exceeded total German production by more than one-third. Since copper production in the German Empire grew continually but too slowly to keep pace with the lightning increase in demand, domestic production increasingly fell behind imports, so that shortly before the First World War imports amounted to around five times the German annual production of copper.[83] For net imports as a share of German copper consumption, this resulted in the trend shown in figure 1.7: following the rupture of 1888/89, which catapulted German dependency on the world market to 50 per cent, the proportion of domestic copper demand met by foreign imports rose in

**Figure 1.7.** Share of German copper demand met by net imports, 1880–1912 (in %)
*Source:* Appendix, table 6.

near-linear fashion until the copper processing industry in Germany was dependent on foreign supplies of copper to meet more than 80 per cent of its needs in the last few years before the war.

From the founding of the German Empire until the First World War, the development of the commodity and sectoral structure of German exports was diametrically opposed to that of imports. In this period, Germany advanced to the status of industrial exporting country par excellence. Foodstuffs and luxury consumables as a share of German exports declined by more than half in the quarter century before the war: from 22.4 per cent in 1880, through 15.2 per cent in 1890 and 11.8 per cent in 1900, to 10.7 per cent in 1910.[84] From the mid-1870s on, sugar was the single most important agricultural export. The complex interleaving of cost reductions in sugar beet cultivation and in the production of beet sugar on the one hand and initially concealed but then open export premiums on the other hand turned the German Empire into the largest beet sugar producer and exporter in the world in the last few decades of the nineteenth century.[85] In the early 1890s, sugar exports as a share of total German exports reached their maximum level at more than 7 per cent, but in the following years and until the war they fell back again to around 2 per cent, since the value of sugar exports – as table 1.9 shows – generally stagnated, while German exports as a whole expanded rapidly. At times more than 60 per cent of German sugar production went abroad, until the abolition of all export premiums, agreed to in the Brussels International Sugar Convention of 1902; this prompted the German sugar industry to focus more on the domestic market, and the export rate to fall to 30–40 per cent (1910–12).[86]

**Table 1.9.** Exports of specific goods and groups of goods, 1880–1913 (millions of marks, in current prices)

| | *1880–84* | *1885–89* | *1890–94* | *1895–99* | *1900–4* | *1905–9* | *1909–13* |
|---|---|---|---|---|---|---|---|
| 1. *Sugar* | 161 | 160 | 211 | 215 | 189 | 203 | 202 |
| 2. *Coal* | 72 | 86 | 108 | 141 | 216 | 273 | 391 |
| 3. *Leather and leather goods* | 152 | 184 | 146 | 153 | 160 | 233 | 298 |
| 4. *Ironware* | 212 | 210 | 242 | 339 | 541 | 693 | 956 |
| 5. *Textiles (fabrics and clothing)* | 681 | 738 | 656 | 669 | 834 | 989 | 1,031 |
| 6. *Machines, motor vehicles and electrotechnical products* | 56 | 57 | 79 | 175 | 298 | 585 | 864 |
| 7. *Chemical and pharmaceutical products* | 252 | 230 | 281 | 363 | 433 | 603 | 818 |

*Sources:* My own calculations (five-year averages) based on *StJbDR* (nos 1–2); Hoffmann, *Wachstum*, 522, table 126 (nos 5–7); Jasper, 'Strukturwandlungen', 359, 364 (nos 3–4).

In general, during the period under consideration raw materials as a share of the German Empire's exports consistently accounted for about 15 per cent, based on current prices; in constant 1913 prices, meanwhile, in other words, in real terms, raw materials as a share of exports declined by about one-quarter between the 1870s and the First World War.[87] Furthermore, there were shifts within the export of raw materials. The leading raw materials export was coal, which doubled to more than 5 per cent as a share of exports between 1880 and 1913; this means that coal alone made up a good one-third of total raw materials exports shortly before the war.

In contrast to primary products (foodstuffs, luxury consumables and raw materials), industrial products as a share of German exports increased substantially. As early as 1880 (in current prices), they made up 63.1 per cent of exports. By 1913, this had increased to 74.4 per cent. Semifinished products showed the highest rates of growth; as a share of exports, they accounted for 21.3 per cent during the year before the war. This meant that since 1880, as a share of exports they had increased by one-third in nominal terms and almost twice over in real terms, while the real volume of semifinished exports saw an almost eightfold increase during this period. This was an expression of the intensifying international division of labour and the associated increase in interindustrial trade. Even the highly dynamic growth in semifinished exports, however, changed nothing about the fact that the finished goods that were the final result of the production process clearly dominated German exports and, since 1883, consistently accounted for more than half of them.[88]

In parallel to the triumphant march of German industrial exports across the world, there was a fundamental change in their structural composition. From a sectoral perspective, it is the relative decline in textile exports that stands out most. In 1880, textile exports (semifinished and finished products) still made up more than one-quarter of total German exports and more than 40 per cent of industrial exports; by 1913 both shares had more than halved. The new leading economic sectors of the chemical engineering industry, the electrotechnical industry and the machine-building industry, as well as the iron and steel industry, meanwhile, increased markedly as a share of exports. In 1880, the export of all the products of these industrial branches together made up no more than 17 per cent of total exports and 27 per cent of industrial exports. In the year before the First World War, meanwhile, these sectors were responsible for one-third of total German exports and almost half (45 per cent) of industrial exports. This shift in the structure of German exports, away from the textiles industry and other 'old' export sectors with their generally consumption-oriented products towards 'new' export sectors with their focus on producer goods, however, was anything but linear.[89] Into the late 1880s, there was no fundamental change in export relations. Only from around 1890 did the dominant position of textile exports begin to erode. At the same time, the new leading export sectors began their meteoric rise. While the absolute value of textiles exports (in current prices) grew by just 59 per cent between 1890 and 1913, the export value of the iron and steel industry grew by 433 per cent, that of the chemical industry by 293 per cent and that of the machine-building, electrotechnical and motor industries by no less than 1,249 per cent. With this breathtakingly rapid shift within the structure of exports, Germany was at the cutting edge of a secular trend in the international trade of industrial goods, one that characterized much of the twentieth century. How 'modern' the German export structure was prior to the First World War is evident if we compare it with the British competition. While yarns, fabrics and clothing had sunk to well under 20 per cent of industrial exports in Germany in 1913, in the U.K., its early industrialization its undoing in this regard, almost half of exports came from the textiles sector.[90]

## Economic Sectors and Globalization: International Competitive Position and Economic Interests

Finally, based on the import and export structure outlined above and a sector-specific analysis of competition in the world market, I attempt to produce an economic interest profile for the German economy with respect to the advancing globalization of economic relations. Within the framework of a cost-benefit analysis informed by the available economic data, the question here is which sectors profited most from increasing world market integration and which found themselves in trouble because of it. To put it differently, from the perspective of trade policies: which economic sectors would have been the winners from protectionist interventions in international trade relations? Conversely, which sectors would we expect to have had an interest in the free play of global economic forces and the dismantling of restrictions on trade?

Methodologically, it is important to note that in bringing out the interests of various sectors, I am not aiming to portray the ideas advocated by the various economic associations. Instead, the aim is to present ideal-typical constructions in Max Weber's sense, conceptual constructs that clarify what the various producer groups' attitudes towards trade policy would have been had they geared themselves towards the sector-specific advantages and disadvantages of world market integration, in other words, if they had been driven by a purely instrumental economic rationality. The heuristic benefit of such an approach is obvious. Only by comparing those interests that were in fact articulated and that made a social impact with the kind of interest profile envisaged above, only by establishing the distance between the two, can we discover the extent to which the formation of interests matched the condensed, ideal-typical model and to what extent it was partly shaped by other motives and intervening factors.[91] In no way is this to make the case for any kind of economic determinism in which we simplistically derive trade policy outcomes from specific webs of economic interest. Neither is this a modern critique of ideology that sets out to contrast the 'false' consciousness of various social groups with their 'true', supposedly objectively definable interests. Instead, the aim is the analytical isolation of one explanatory factor: the interests of specific sectors arising from their incorporation into the international economy – rather than those resulting from other economic realities. The aim is to assess on this basis the importance of this factor as a causal explanation of the views on trade policy that were in fact espoused and to what extent other factors played a role.

Every attempt to delineate the basic structure of producers' differing trade policy interests is necessarily more or less simplistic. Fully reliable statements can be made only on the level of the individual firm. Even within the same economic sector, such as the textiles industry, individual firms' tariff and trade policy interests may differ significantly quite regardless of whether we are talking about spinning or weaving mills, dyeworks, embroidering plants, or small or large firms, whether they are located within the linen, wool, cotton, silk or jute industry, how high the level of mechanization is, where their major markets are or where they get most of their raw materials. Regardless of these differences, which certainly exist, we can distinguish between different groups of producers with similar interests if we look between the lowest level of abstraction, that of the individual firm, and the highest, that of the German economy as a whole, at the intermediate level of economic sectors. We shall leave to one side those sectors that depend directly and exclusively on foreign trade – as applied to much of the shipping industry, for example – and that therefore inevitably had an interest in the expansion of international trade relations, along with those branches that were comparatively unaffected by economic globalization. Instead, our focus will be on those spheres of the primary and secondary sector – agriculture, the electrical industry, machine building, the chemical industry, iron and steel production and the textiles industry – that were both highly relevant to the national economy and especially influenced by increasing integration into the world market. The interest profiles that emerge are as follows.

## *Agriculture*

More clearly than in any other economic sector, it was among cereal growers that economic considerations prompted demands for protectionist interventions. The cereal producers of western and central Europe were the big losers in the first wave of globalization. As a result of the revolution in the international transport system, a functioning world market in agriculture took shape during the last third of the nineteenth century. Europe saw nothing less than an invasion of overseas cereals due to dramatically falling transportation costs in combination with the opening up of vast areas of virgin soils to agriculture – in the U.S. alone, after the end of the Civil War the wheat-growing acreage increased within ten years (1869–79) from 7.7 to 14.9 million hectares, four times the total German wheat-growing land.[92] In contrast to earlier times, from the mid-1870s on German and other European cereal growers were increasingly confronted by overseas and Russian competitors whose economies of scale generally allowed them to undercut European prices.

German export markets collapsed, and competitive pressures then intensified in the home market as well. Within just ten years, net imports of wheat shot up from almost nothing in the first half of the 1870s to an annual average of 612,605 tonnes for the period 1883–85 – which equated to no less than one-quarter of German crop yields.[93] Because cereal production on the world market expanded so dramatically while demand grew relatively slowly (if continuously), prices plummeted. The world market price for wheat, for example, sank, if we work with an index based on

British prices (1913 = 100), by almost two-thirds from 1873 (173.8) to a low point in 1894 (64.6); it then increased again until the war, but never came anywhere near the level of the early 1870s.[94] Much the same applied to the other types of cereal crops.[95]

It is a much-discussed question whether German farmers did everything necessary to adapt to the changed competitive realities through rationalization, intensification and introduction of new production methods. Two arguments may be put forward against the criticism that they failed to adjust sufficiently, though no doubt a fair number clung to antiquated production structures and techniques. First, critics of German agriculture have claimed that farmers should have reduced their arable farming to a small number of optimal areas while going all-out to focus on animal production. But in fact, this is both problematic and unrealistic. The proposed switch of much of German cereal growing to livestock farming would probably have led to similarly ruinous competitive conditions in the field of livestock and meat production as already existed in the market for cereals; furthermore, because of the soil and weather conditions in many regions, such a transition was not even possible. Second, it should be recognized that between 1870 and 1914 no other European country experienced the kind of leap in productivity that occurred in German agriculture. Though German agriculture was still in the middle of the European range in terms of productivity in 1870 according to the calculations of J. L. van Zanden (regardless of whether we base our calculations on agricultural production per hectare or per unit of labour), after a tremendous effort it had almost reached the peak of agricultural efficiency achieved in Belgium, Denmark and the Netherlands by 1910.[96] This massive increase in productivity was achieved above all by the use of land-saving technologies, in other words, artificial fertilizer – by 1910, only Belgium and the Netherlands used more – and imported feedstuffs. Increasing mechanization, the advance of so-called labour-saving technologies, also played a significant, though ultimately less important, role.[97]

In light of this, Germany's cereal producers, and especially the large farms east of the Elbe, which were particularly dependent on the market, faced a simpler and harsher reality. In a global market in agriculture, most German cereal producers were no longer competitive. Due to their comparatively high production costs (the key factors here being the use of artificial fertilizers and the high cost of land, the latter affecting purchases, leases and *Erbabfindungen,* or compensation paid to coheirs), many agricultural enterprises in Germany were unable to match the low prices offered by foreign competitors. These could produce at far lower costs either because, as in the U.S., they had a surplus of both cheap and fertile land at their disposal or, as in Ukraine, Russia and India, workers earned a pittance.[98] Coolly calculating contemporaries were already aware of this. This is evident in the assessment reached by Max Weber following his in-depth examination of the position of large estates in East Prussia in the context of the survey of agricultural workers carried out by the Association for Social Policy (Verein für Socialpolitik) in the early 1890s: 'From a commercial and industrial perspective', Weber concluded, 'the agriculture in the East [is] a declining, increasingly uncompetitive business' as the 'international competitive conditions [have made] land in the east of Germany worthless from the point of view of production for the world market'.[99] Against this background of a structural crisis of agriculture, many German estate owners and peasants faced a choice between accepting a massive loss of income, which could ultimately force them to leave the market, in other words, give up their enterprises, and placing their hopes in protective tariffs or other state subsidies.

Farmers focused mainly on livestock rearing faced a rather different situation. First, for them the development of a world market in agricultural products meant not just a battle with new competitors, but also a cost-lowering factor, as they could buy cheap feedstuffs from overseas and Russian producers. And they did so on a massive scale. By the First World War, German imports of feedstuffs, barley, maize, fish meal, oil cake and so forth had increased to an annual figure of around one billion marks, which amounted to no less than one-third of the feed necessary to maintain German livestock. This made the German Empire the largest importer of feedstuffs in the world. Without the development of a global market in feedstuffs, the formidable growth of animal production in the German Empire prior to 1914 would have been out of the question: only the internationalization of feedstuff supplies made it possible to lastingly break through the closed agricultural loop of fertilization, feed production, feeding and husbandry within the same farm and to compensate for the lack of usable land available for livestock rearing.

Second, in the case of livestock and meat the competitive pressures brought to bear by the world market proved less of a threat than with respect to cereals – and this would have been true even if the German Empire had not placed massive restrictions on the import of animal products through a series of veterinary and disease-control measures. Again going by a British price index, world market prices for livestock, meat and dairy products certainly fell following a relative boom in the 1870s, from 100 in 1867–77 by no less than one-quarter to 73 in 1896; but this was a substantially more moderate decline than in the case of cereals, and was fully offset by 1914 as a result of another price increase.[100] This had less to do with trends in the global supply of livestock products, which like cereals expanded rapidly, than with the fact that the increase in demand for livestock and meat kept pace with the growth in supply because of growing real incomes and shifts in consumption in the industrialized countries.

Third and finally, small and medium-sized farms, which accounted for the vast majority of German livestock, were far more flexible than the large farms that specialized in cereal cultivation in terms of their capacity to adapt to shifting market conditions.[101] This was because they were based on a 'mixed' approach to production, with livestock farming being complemented by the cultivation of cereals and root crops. The diversification of their production allowed farmers to respond adequately to changes in the relative prices of various agricultural products: if the price of rye was low, it was used as animal feed. If on the other hand the price of cereals rose and livestock prices fell, then rye could be sold on the market. In this way, cereal cultivation functioned as a kind of economic insurance over the course of the 'pork cycle'.

Nevertheless, even those farmers focused mainly on livestock rearing had far more reason to welcome than to fear protectionist agricultural policies. It was in fact somewhat later, from the late 1880s, when an increasing number of refrigerated ships were available, that the pressure of international competition began to make itself felt in the market for livestock and meat (though to a lesser extent than in the case of cereals). In view of rapidly growing domestic demand, state protection against the harsh competitive conditions in the world market promised to ensure a respectable producer's surplus for German stockbreeders. The introduction of generally effective import restrictions on livestock, meat and meat products at the same time as unhindered access to the world market in feedstuffs must have been economically optimal for them. With respect to the types of cereals usually used as animal feed, above all barley and oats, this entailed a potential conflict of interest with cereal producers, who once again could only profit from protectionist measures.[102]

## *Machine Building and the Electrical Industry*

Very different in nature were the economic interests of machine building and the electrical industry; I deal with them together since in many ways, in terms of globalization, their interests were comparable and also because the two industries were closely linked with respect to production, sometimes inextricably. From a purely commercial perspective, at least in the last two decades prior to the First World War, both industries were inevitably keen on the freest possible access to the world market and the dismantling of all trade restrictions on the part of the German Empire. There were several reasons for this. First, most firms in the German machine-building industry and particularly in the electrical industry were a match for their international competitors. In fact, they were often far superior to them. As a result, they had no need for tariff protection or other forms of state subsidy. Second, determined by their prime position in the world market, both sectors attained most of their profits through exports. Every impediment to free cross-border goods traffic by other states and every trade policy implemented by the German government that would have provoked such impediments would have been viewed as a threat to this exporting success. Third, for both the machine-building and electrical industries, a global market unburdened by state barriers to trade offered the most cost-effective and often the only possibility of obtaining the raw materials they needed – above all metals.

From the mid-1890s until the First World War, German machine building went through an unprecedented boom, which went hand in hand with an enormous growth in exports. Within just two decades, from 1893 to 1913, German machine exports grew by a factor of ten in absolute terms, while they increased from 2.2 to 6.7 per cent as a share of total exports. At the turn of the century, German machine exports amounted to just half of British exports; by 1913, with a world market share of about 30 per cent, Germany had almost caught up with the U.K. and easily beat the U.S. into third place.[103] But the German machine-building industry's phenomenal track record should not lead us to conclude that German machine producers were in pole position in every market segment – the market in machines was too diverse for that. In the case of office equipment, typewriters, cash registers and a number of machine tools, German mechanical engineers proved unable to match their U.S. counterparts – their most dangerous rivals in other fields as well – with respect to price and quality. By and large, however, the German machine industry's triumphant progress across the globe prior to the First World War confirmed the assessment of F. C. Huber, professor at the technical university and secretary of the chamber of commerce in Stuttgart, who stated proudly in 1901, 'Dependent on other countries just a few decades ago, today the German machine-building industry is among the front-runners, and when it comes to efficiency, first-rate work, fine materials and outstanding construction, is probably second to none.'[104]

For many machine-building firms in the German Empire, exports compensated for a domestic demand that was meagre in comparison with the U.K. and U.S.; in this way they created the precondition for a production volume that facilitated the degree of specialization and standardization essential if these firms wished to keep up with their British and American rivals. By the turn of the century, export dependency – the share of total production sold abroad – had thus reached a high level in many firms in the machine-building sector and continued to increase up until the war.

In the early 1890s, the Hannoversche Maschinenbau A.G., the Hanomag, for example, still built its locomotives mainly for the domestic market and sold just 7 per cent (1890–94) of its production outside of Germany; by 1910–13, exports as a share of total locomotive production had grown to 40 per cent.[105] In certain cases, in highly specialized firms whose products occupied a leading position globally, sales within the German Empire actually became less important than those on the world market. From 1906, year after year, Bosch, the Stuttgart-based firm known worldwide for its magnetos, exported more than 80 per cent of its products to other countries.[106] In the still young automobile industry, exports also played an increasingly important role. The findings of the production surveys carried out in 1909 and 1910 in the motor vehicle industry show impressively that the home market for German automobiles during this period grew significantly more slowly than foreign demand. While domestic sales in cars and trucks increased from 6,227 to 6,885 units from 1909 to 1910, exports more than doubled, from 1,000 to 2,226 units – in other words, two-thirds of the increased sales of the German motor industry were due to an increase in exports.[107]

In terms of global competition, the German electrical industry was even better placed than the machine-building industry. More than in any other economic sector, the electrotechnical industry was dominated by large companies. The process of concentration that began in 1901/2 gave rise to two sector-leading companies: the Siemens-Schuckert-Werke and the Allgemeine Elektricitäts-Gesellschaft (AEG), founded by Emil Rathenau in 1883 (which traded under the name Deutsche Edison-Gesellschaft until 1887). On the eve of the First World War, going by their near-identical balance sheet totals, these were the two largest German industrial firms after the Fried. Krupp AG, accounting together for around three-quarters of German electrotechnical production. Both electrical giants maintained numerous subsidiaries in other countries and behaved in many respects like present-day multinational companies. With 81,795 employees, of whom no less than 18,348 worked beyond the borders of Germany, Siemens was the largest electrical company in the world in this respect. Exports, also dominated by these two large companies, but in which the many small specialist firms that coexisted with them also played a significant role, were of crucial importance to the German electrical industry. More than one-quarter of German electrical production was sold abroad in 1913; in the case of Siemens, the figure was no less than 36.2 per cent. After the turn of the century, the German Empire's electrotechnical industry attained a seemingly unassailable position in the international market. The year before the war, it accounted for a world market share of more than 46 per cent. It exported well over twice as much as the British and more than three times as much as the American electrical industry, which was the only one even close to the size of its German counterpart.[108]

## Chemical Industry

Alongside the electrical industry, the other showpiece of German exports was the chemical industry. This applied above all to organic chemistry and in particular to the dyes industry. Like all other export industries, it too was dependent on the world market in a dual sense. First, it obtained much of the chemical raw materials it processed from abroad. Second, it was inevitably keen to sell its products unimpeded in other countries. In terms of the degree of its export dependency and its place in the world market, however, the situation of the German dyes industry was unique. By the late 1870s, the German chemical industry – whose international lead was due primarily to the achievements of chemical research in Germany and its incorporation into the production process – already met around half of global demand for synthetic dyes; on the eve of the First World War, this had increased to almost 90 per cent. Outside of Germany, Switzerland was the only country with a dyes industry worth mentioning. The absolute dominance of German firms in the world market went hand in hand with their dependence on it. As early as the 1880s and 1890s, for instance, the Badische Anilin- und Sodafabrik, the BASF, sold around three-quarters of its dyes production abroad. After the turn of the century, the importance of the world market to German dyes producers increased even further: the Kleine I.G., also known as the Dreibund or triple alliance, which included Bayer and Agfa as well as BASF, sold almost 82 per cent of its dyes outside the borders of the German Empire in 1913. At the same time, there were major regional shifts within the export sector. The 'old' markets in Europe and North America increasingly lost ground to new, rapidly expanding markets, chiefly in Asia – in 1913, China, British India and Japan together absorbed almost 22 per cent of the Kleine I.G.'s exports. In cases where exports were impeded or threatened by tariffs or patenting problems over long periods of time, major German chemicals companies responded by creating foreign subsidiaries. Mainly in France and Russia, but also in the U.K. and U.S., German dyes producers made copious direct investments from the late 1870s onwards in order to circumvent actual or anticipated interventions in world trade. By 1914, all major dyes companies had developed into multinational concerns.[109]

But it was not just with respect to the biggest-selling dyes that the German chemical industry was the undisputed world leader. It also led in all other spheres of organic chemistry, because laboratory experiments on the synthesis of dyes had tremendous 'spin-off' effects on other, entirely new fields of production. The new product classes developed from by-products and intermediate products of dye synthesis included pharmaceutical compounds such as salvarsan, Pyramidon and aspirin, photographic materials, synthetic fibres and explosive materials. In the pharmaceutical sector especially, the leading role played by the German chemical industry in the global market rested not just on the shoulders of the major dyes producers such as Bayer and Hoechst, which unlike BASF had expanded their research and production to the promising sphere of pharmaceuticals; significant too were a number of highly efficient firms specializing in pharmaceuticals such as Schering, Knoll and Co., Merck and C. F. Böhringer, whose products also enjoyed a global reputation. Just how dependent the other industrialized countries were on the products of the German chemical industry became apparent only after the outbreak of the First World War, when supplies from Germany stopped and there was no available alternative. In a speech to the annual conference of the Chemical Society in March 1915, William Henry Perkin (named after his father, the discoverer of mauveine, the first synthetic aniline dye, and former assistant to Adolf von Baeyer in Munich), reeling from the precarious situation that had arisen in the U.K. due to the cessation of German imports, complained that

> it has long been our habit to import almost all our organic fine chemicals from Germany. It may indeed be said that Germany has no competitor worth considering in the whole domain of organic chemical industry. That we should have allowed trades of such magnitude to pass almost completely into the hands of a foreign nation seems incredible, and, as the inevitable result, we are face to face with the serious position that, the foreign supply having stopped, stocks are rapidly vanishing and prices are rising to such an impossible level that the progress of several of our industries is greatly hampered.[110]

Though not as dominant as in the field of organic chemistry, in the field of inorganic chemistry the German chemical industry was still highly competitive internationally. This applies, for example, to acids produced in large quantities such as sulphuric, hydrochloric, nitric and phosphoric acid, which were urgently required as basic components in fertilizer production, the dyes industry, the metals industry and many other branches of production. From the 1880s, however, contrary to all the assertions made by the manufacturers, which have sometimes been given the status of fact in recent historical research,[111] this also applied to soda production. As late as the 1870s German soda producers, whose production was based on the then predominant Leblanc process, proved incapable of competing with their British rivals because of the far higher cost of raw materials in Germany. In the recession beginning in 1873, just under one-third of

German soda plants fell victim to the cheaper British Leblanc soda and were forced to close down; by 1877, imports accounted for 49 per cent of German soda consumption. But this situation changed fundamentally as a result of a technological innovation: the ammonia-soda process developed by the Belgian Ernest Solvay. This was doubly advantageous: production costs were low and it resulted in a purer form of soda.

From 1880 on, the soda industry in Germany quickly went over to using the superior ammonia-soda process – like the U.S. and the other industrialized countries of continental Europe – while the established British soda producers, whose capital was locked into their Leblanc soda plants, invested only tentatively in the new production method. As a result, competitive conditions in the international soda market changed substantially within a few years. Recent historical studies show clearly that German soda producers working with the Solvay process were entirely capable of competing on the world market, even without tariff protection, from the early 1880s.[112] As early as 1884, Germany made the transition from net importer to net exporter of soda; just ten years later, the German soda industry had become the world's second largest exporter of soda and produced more soda ash via the ammonia-soda process than any of its international competitors. The Trade Treaty Association (Handelsvertragsverein, or HVV) was thus quite right to state in its submission to the imperial chancellor in 1903 that there was 'no … need for tariff protection for soda', and that such tariffs merely enabled the soda syndicate that controlled the German market to raise the domestic price above the world market price and thus make extra profits: the Solvay-Gesellschaft, by far the largest German soda producer and the dominant member of the cartel, managed to achieve a dividend of 45 per cent.[113]

## *Textile Industry*

In contrast to the electrotechnical and chemical industries, the textile industry was a 'mature' industry at the end of the nineteenth century. All the key technological innovations – self-actor, ring-spinning frame, combing machine and power loom – had already appeared on the scene in the middle of the century and begun their triumphal progress across the globe, with varying rapidity in different locations. The major advances were in the past. What mattered now was to disseminate and optimize a largely mature and proven technology. The industrial 'stragglers' – above all the U.S. and Germany – managed to reduce their developmental gap with the British textile industry; but they were unable to catch up with the pioneer of the industrial revolution in this sector, let alone overtake it through technological advances. Until the First World War and beyond, British textile production maintained a clear edge over its competitors, both in terms of productivity and volume of output. Its dominance was particularly pronounced in the cotton industry. As late as 1913, British cotton factories contained almost 40 per cent of spindles worldwide.[114] Heavily concentrated in and around Manchester and Glasgow, the British cotton industry had by far the most modern equipment, the best-educated and most efficient workers and the largest production facilities. The U.K. also maintained its preeminence in the second most important field of textile production in economic terms, the wool industry, beyond the end of the nineteenth century, though its lead here was not as dramatic as in cotton processing. This was reflected in the dominant position of the British textile industry in the world market. Despite its international competitors' notable efforts to catch up with it, in 1913 the U.K. still accounted for 42.9 per cent of world textile exports. The two largest textile exporters after the U.K., France and Germany, meanwhile, took a world market share of just under 15 per cent each.[115]

The German textile industry was heavily dependent on world trade at an early stage. It imported a substantial quantity of yarn, but above all the vast majority of the raw materials it processed. First came cotton, which from the outset had to be imported in its entirety, and wool, an ever-increasing share of which came from abroad because the growing demands of the textile industry coincided with the decline of sheep farming in Germany. Conversely, the German textile industry had always exported a large proportion of its products. As early as the 1840s, exports of cotton and woollen goods from the German Customs Union outstripped imports many times over; shortly before the First World War, in his pertinent study of the German textile industry, Alwin Oppel calculated that it sold almost half its production of more than 2 billion marks outside the empire.[116] In view of its complexity, it is impossible to identify a homogenous set of trade policy interests for the German textile industry. The competitive conditions in the world market for cotton products differed from those in the international trade in wool products, which in turn faced circumstances different from those of products such as linen and silk. Particularly during the economic boom from 1895 on, a rapidly expanding sector such as the cotton industry (which actually managed to increase its previously shrinking share of German net value added after the turn of the century) had economic interests quite different from those in a declining sector such as the linen industry. Finally, the competitive position of the producers of unfinished materials differed from those of the manufacturers of fine cloths, just as the interests of a large firm operating with the latest machines diverged from those of a small only partly mechanized one. But the biggest gap in interests within the German textile industry, and this applies throughout the period under consideration, lay between its two most economically important branches, spinning and weaving, and cut across the materials processed by them.[117]

The superior British import competition with which German spinners found themselves confronted prompted them to call for tariffs or other protective measures. This applied less to the producers of coarse yarn types, which were highly competitive internationally and even generated a German export surplus in their category. It very much applied to that part of German spinning that produced finer yarns. For all yarn types with a degree of fineness higher than 45 in the British system of yarn classification, imports covered two-thirds or more of German consumption. Overall, with respect to all types of yarn taken together, yarn imports exceeded exports continuously and substantially from the first statistics produced by the German Customs Union to the First World War. For the years 1905–9, for example, net imports of cotton and wool yarn amounted to an average of 103.8 million marks, of which the former accounted for 54.9 million and the latter 48.9 million. The origin of yarn imports demonstrates how inferior not just German spinners but also those in other countries were to their British counterparts. In 1907–9, an impressive annual average of two-thirds (188 million marks) of total German imports of wool and cotton yarn came from the British Isles; in 1910, the figure for cotton yarn alone was 91 per cent of imports.[118]

The trade policy interests of the German weaving industry, which employed more than 486,000 workers – according to the occupational census of 1907 – and thus more than 2.3 times as many as spinning (in 1882 the ratio was 3:1), conflicted radically with those of spinning.[119] For the latter, every tariff on the yarns it processed raised its production costs, thus threatening its competitiveness on the world market. The special economic significance of this problem was due first to the substantial export volume of German weaving, which in the case of wool and cotton alone amounted to an average of 553 million marks for the 1901–5 period; this corresponded to an export share of almost 11 per cent, leaving other exported goods in the shade. Second, the extremely high competitive pressures in the world market for textiles meant that even small cost increases could result in loss of market share.[120] Conversely, the majority of German weavers – and the same goes for other export-oriented sectors of the German textile industry such as the dyes, bleach and printing industries – had no heightened interest in tariff protection for their own products because, unlike the soda industry, for example, they lacked a cartel; in view of the marked export surplus characteristic of most woven goods, this would have been necessary to make prices on the domestic market reflect any additional tariffs that might have been imposed. Much of the weaving industry, then, along with other branches of the German textile industry that exported their products, would have been among the beneficiaries of policies supportive of free trade.

## *Heavy Industry*

A conflict of interest very similar to that found in the textile industry was also latently present in heavy industry; here, however, it was overlaid by a different kind of constellation, which was due to the interplay of cartel formation and vertical integration and thus of two structural features of the German mining, iron and steel industry that became increasingly manifest from the foundation of the empire until the First World War. Fundamentally, in other words, without taking account of the particular organizational character of heavy industry in Germany, the interests of the various stages of production, that is, of mines, smelting works, steel mills and rolling mills, were very different. What was output for firms at the upstream stage of production that had to be sold at the highest possible price entered the next stage as a raw material and thus as a cost factor that must be minimized by buying as cheaply as possible. How different economic interests on the various rungs of the processing ladder could be is apparent if we look at the British iron and steel industry. Here the producers of semi-finished goods struggled under the pressure of international competition, while the processing industry had the same phenomenon – the opportunity to obtain cheap steel from abroad – to thank for a substantial reduction in costs and enhanced competitiveness. In principle, with respect to trade policy, all that the different segments of heavy industry – like other branches of the secondary sector – had in common was an interest in low agricultural tariffs; such tariffs fostered wage increases by increasing workers' living costs and threatened to trigger retaliatory measures by trading partners calculated to impede the export of industrial goods.

In fact, the economic interests of German heavy industry were rather different. The winners and losers from protectionist measures were not the ones we might have expected in light of these considerations, in contrast to the situation in other countries. This was due, first, to the development of cartels, which was especially pronounced in German heavy industry both in comparison with other countries and with other sectors of industry, and which had major consequences for prices and foreign trade. The first wave of cartelization in Germany occurred during the period of economic crisis in the 1870s and 1880s. Whether we should therefore consider cartels, to cite Friedrich Kleinwächter's famous 1883 dictum, the 'children of hardship'[121] seems doubtful because many cartels proved unstable and fell apart during periods of economic crisis, precisely when they should have proved their value. Furthermore, with hindsight it is evident that as far as the number and efficacy of cartels is concerned, cartel formation really took off only from around the turn of the century and thus reached its peak during a period characterized not by economic crisis but by a sustained economic boom. There has been a wide-ranging and contentious debate among historians on the market power and success of cartels. A number of historians have rightly underlined the chronic instability of most cartels and highlighted the risks of overstating their overall economic relevance and influence. In this context, however, heavy industry is a special case. First, it generated the three most respected and important cartels in German industry in the shape of the Rhineland-Westphalia Coal Syndicate (Rheinisch-Westfälisches Kohlensyndikat), formed in 1893, the Pig Iron Association (Roheisenverband), founded in 1897 and transformed into a tightly administered syndicate in 1904, and the Steelworks' Association (Stahlwerksverband), created in 1904. Second, and this is the crucial point for us, the cartels mentioned above and their predecessors succeeded in maintaining a price level in the German domestic market above the world market price for many of their products, though not all, over long periods of time. In the rails market, for example, this policy of price differentiation was maintained continuously from 1879 until the First World War; the domestic price was always between 10 and 40 per cent higher than the world market price.[122] Through their ability to separate the German market from the world market, the cartels created the preconditions for an export-oriented industry such as heavy industry to benefit from protective tariffs on their products in the first place and thus to develop an economically based interest in them. Without the pricing power of the cartels in the domestic market, meanwhile, and here practical experience and economic theory are in accord, the import duties on most heavy industrial products would soon have fallen victim to domestic producers' price competition and would therefore have been economically meaningless: there would have been nothing stopping domestic producers from selling a portion of their otherwise export-bound production on the German market.[123]

The second factor that had a significant impact on the trade policy interests of German heavy industry was the tendency for vertical integration that typified it in the decades before the First World War.[124] The first good reason for the progressive combination of several production stages in the same firm – for the comprehensive integration of mines, blast furnaces, steel and rolling mills and sometimes even machine-building factories – was the cost advantage arising from rationalization of operating procedures and the deployment of technological innovations. The introduction of the 'direct process', the unmediated transfer of molten pig iron from blast furnace to converter, which rendered further fuel-intensive smelting in the cupola furnace redundant; the minimization of transportation; the use of the furnace gases released during the blast furnace process to drive gas engines; the rolling out of steel 'in one heat' – all of this generated considerable savings in energy and other costs, endowing the major 'mixed works' with a clear competitive advantage.[125] The second key force driving the emergence of combined firms was the increasing formation of cartels. By investing in upstream production stages, for example, through the linkage of a foundry and steel plant or colliery and smelting works, companies could avoid both high cartel prices and the need for supplies from the cartels, which were often inadequate, especially in boom periods.[126] Here, the fact that the consumption of the 'mixed works' was not usually counted as part of their share of cartel sales played as important a role as it did in the integration of downstream production stages, which allowed the combined firms to avoid cartel discipline: rather than selling it via the cartel, they processed a large part of their production within the firm. In this sense, the development of German heavy industry confirmed the insight of New Institutional Economics that high transaction costs, which transaction cost theory considers an expression of significant market imperfections (in this case, regulation by cartels), prompt firms to replace market exchange as far as possible with transaction cost–reducing organizational solutions – the most prominent of which is the internalization of transactions by means of vertical integration.[127]

The advance of 'mixed works' had a lasting impact on trade policy interests within heavy industry. The potential for conflict that would have existed in the event of operational separation of different stages of production was eliminated within the large, vertically integrated heavy industrial firms. Because they had comprehensively shifted the procurement of raw materials and intermediate products from market to company, because they obtained almost everything from their own plants, the 'mixed works' had few reasons to be interested in unhindered, duty-free access to the world market as supply source.

In short, the advance of cartelization and vertical integration had a significant impact on the economic interest structure of German heavy industry with respect to tariff and trade policy. Rather than a conflict of interests between the various production stages, what emerged in Germany was an opposition between the highly cartelized 'mixed works' on the one hand, which benefited from protectionist measures at all stages of the value-creation process, and 'pure works' on the other, for whom tariffs made intermediate products more expensive. Ultimately, this was a conflict between unequal opponents. It was one that the 'pure works', mostly rolling mills, could not win. They were hemmed in on one side by cartels, which dictated material prices and allocation quantities, and on the other side by large competitors in the finished goods market able to produce at low costs. 'Pure works' increasingly disappeared from the scene, leaving the way clear for the heavy industrial giants.[128]

Before the First World War, tariffs, cartels and vertical integration formed a complex of mutually reinforcing factors within German heavy industry. Just as cartelization and the advance of the 'mixed works' led to a tendency to embrace protectionist measures among major firms in the iron and steel industry, as outlined above, existing tariffs fostered the formation of cartels and vertical integration. The combined impact of these three factors (and here the description of German heavy industry's place in the world market merges seamlessly into the history of the impact of protectionist intervention) played a significant role in the sharp rise in production and exports in the German iron and steel industry in the decades before 1914.

Particularly when compared with the U.K., the growth of German iron and steel production following the foundation of the empire seems impressive. In the early 1870s, British heavy industry still produced about four times as much pig iron and more than twice as much steel as its German counterpart. By 1893, however, Germany overtook the U.K. in steel production for the first time; the same applied to pig iron production by 1903. In the last few years before the First World War, Germany left the U.K. far behind in terms of production. In the case of pig iron, the U.K. was responsible for 14 per cent of world production in 1911–13, and just 10 per cent when it came to steel; German producers, meanwhile, accounted for almost one-quarter of global output in both cases. Only the American iron and steel industry, backed by its huge domestic market, outdid its German counterpart on the eve of the First World War in terms of production volume, accounting for no less than 40 per cent of world production of both pig iron and steel in 1911–13. In the field of exports, meanwhile, the German iron and steel industry rose to the status of undisputed world market leader during the period under consideration. Throughout the nineteenth century, British heavy industry had clearly dominated the global market. In 1880, for example, British exports of iron and ironware were four and a half times that of Germany, and even in 1899 they amounted to two and a half times the German figure. After the turn of the century, however, German iron and steel producers increasingly wrested market share from their British competitors, outstripping them at a breathtaking pace in terms of export volume. In 1913, Germany exported 6.5 million tonnes of iron and ironware, beating the U.K. into second place by a large margin with its exports of 5.1 million tonnes.[129]

The triumph of the German iron and steel industry on the world market has often been put down to particularly progressive production methods and the use of technology superior to that of its competitors. Conversely, British businessmen have been faulted for failing to recognize the signs of the times and, in large part because of a blinkered conservatism, failing to introduce technological innovations and modernize the production process as a whole to the degree necessary.[130] In the context of such arguments, the interplay of tariffs and cartels in Germany played at most the indirect role of fostering the growth of German production and exports by creating conditions that reduced the risks associated with investment in new capital-intensive technologies.[131] I do not privilege such arguments here, however, as there are two problems with them. First, every international comparison of the technological efficiency of iron and steel production in the nineteenth century is beset by a number of methodological difficulties with respect to data and implicit criteria. All such studies must therefore be approached with great caution, as evident in the ultimately very different estimates that have been made of the productivity of the British steel industry in comparison with its American and German counterparts.[132]

Second, comparison of technological efficiency and thus the claim that the German iron and steel industry was more efficient would make sense only if steel – as the product with respect to which the different production processes were being compared – was a homogenous product. But this is not the case. In the 1880s, the vast majority of the German steel industry began to use the Thomas rather than the Bessemer process, which allowed the use of phosphorus-rich ores such as Lorraine Minette and was particularly well suited to the production of cheap, ordinary steel with no special strength requirements. In the U.K., meanwhile, the Thomas process, the basic version of the Bessemer process, never played a significant role. Building on a Bessemer industry that continued to exist and in parallel with the advance of Thomas plants in Germany, in the U.K. there was a transition to the Siemens-Martin process, which required significantly more time than the Bessemer or Thomas process, but resulted in higher-quality types of steel. In contrast to the U.K., Germany's Siemens-Martin capacity, which had also been rapidly developed from the mid-1890s, was used mostly for scrap processing; by the time of the First World War it still had nowhere near the importance to German steel production as in the case of the U.K.[133] In the three decades before the First World War, then, the product mix of the German and British steel industries developed in different ways: the rise of a Thomas process–based industry producing inexpensive ordinary steel featuring Siemens-Martin works for scrap processing in the former, and a dominant Siemens-Martin industry based on pig iron and serving a higher quality and price segment with a residual Bessemer capacity in the latter. International comparisons of efficiency that smooth out these differences run the risk of precipitately and illegitimately attributing technological superiority to German heavy industry. This would at least be quite wrong in the market segment in which British and German producers competed with one another directly, namely, the production of Siemens-Martin steel, much of which was used for shipbuilding. It was not until after the turn of the century that Germany managed to produce steel that equalled the British variety typically used in the shipyards. Even then, however, British Siemens-Martin steel enjoyed a better reputation in international shipbuilding than its German counterpart, one it proved impossible to match. In some cases even German shipyards had to be forced to use domestically produced materials by government guidelines.[134]

In view of this, the direct stimulus to the exports and production of the German iron and steel industry provided by the combined system of tariffs, cartels and vertical integration was far more important than its indirect effects. That contemporaries already saw a connection between tariffs and export capacity is evident in the words of Karl Richter, chairman of the Association of German Iron and Steel Industrialists (Verein Deutscher Eisen- und Stahlindustrieller, or VDEStI) and head of the Royal Iron and Steel Works (Königshütte) of Upper Silesia, who declared in 1878, 'In my opinion we would export even more if tariffs were reintroduced because we could sell even more cheaply in foreign markets if our prices were higher at home.'[135] But the impression raised by this argument, that export was an end in itself, indicates that the historical actors lacked a complete grasp of these economic interrelationships. For a better understanding of the export-promoting effect of import restrictions – which standard neoclassical theory also fails to explain – we need the economic model developed more than one hundred years later by Paul Krugman, leading light of new trade theory.[136]

Krugman's approach breaks with two basic assumptions of neoclassical theory, perfect competition and constant economies of scale, working on the assumption of both oligopolistically distorted and segmented markets on the one hand and the presence of economies of scale on the other – conditions, in other words, which apply to the iron and steel industry prior to the First World War. The basic idea here is that under these conditions the total or partial exclusion of foreign competition from the domestic market through tariffs or other protectionist measures has far-reaching consequences. In a first step, it leads to an increase in sales and production for domestic industry, which takes over the market share of excluded foreign competitors. The growth in output based on protection of the domestic market then allows indigenous producers to realize economies of scale, as expressed in declining marginal costs as production increases.[137] This is reflected in falling average costs and increases the competitiveness of the industry subject to protectionist measures on the world market – at the expense of foreign competition, which faces the opposite trend of falling production and rising marginal costs. The growth in the exports of domestic producers fostered in this way – German heavy industry in this case – in turn stimulates an increase in production, which sets in motion once again the cycle of increased output, falling marginal costs and export growth. Ultimately, then, import restrictions induce an increase both in production volume and in the exports of the protected industry – with the seemingly paradoxical result that under certain circumstances a trade-restricting measure may even result in an expansion in trade volume.

The explanatory model put forward here for the exporting success and enormous growth in production of the German iron and steel industry also casts new light on the export dumping that it sometimes practiced. Contemporaries and historians have of course placed special emphasis on the close connection between economic crises and the heavy industrial price dumping sometimes fostered by the cartels' export premium policy.[138] This highlights the situational causes of dumping, drawing attention to the function of exports during a domestic recession as an outlet for unsellable surplus production, which could be sold abroad at rock-bottom prices. Meanwhile, the factors identified here to explain the advance of German iron and steel producers on the world market (increasing economies of scale and the existence of differently priced markets brought about by the interplay of tariffs and cartels) indicate the structural and persistent causes of heavy industrial dumping. It is not just that successful dumping on foreign markets can be practiced only on the basis of cartels or cartel-like agreements and through the imposition of tariffs, because otherwise goods sold at low prices abroad might flow back over the border and swamp the domestic market. A cost-based analysis of the problem also shows that under the conditions identified above, a dumping policy, in other words, selling abroad at prices lower than total production costs,[139] may in fact represent a profitable strategy over the long term. This applies if, through the spreading of fixed costs across a larger output and the exploitation of economies of scale, the expansion of production that goes hand in hand with the dumping of exports leads to a reduction in average costs – which overcompensates for the decline in average returns caused by dumping prices or makes production profitable in the first place.

From the perspective of present-day business economics, whether an export order is accepted by a firm at a price above or below total production costs is largely irrelevant – what matters is not production costs but marginal costs, in other words, the variable costs of the additional production necessary to meet the order. Only when the target price of an export transaction is less than the marginal costs has an economic loss been suffered. As economic historian Ulrich Wengenroth's calculations also show, those export transactions described by the historical actors involved as 'losses', which were carried out at below-average costs, were almost certainly still well above marginal costs and were therefore in fact 'profits'.[140] Even when we factor in that the concept of marginal costs was as unknown to contemporaries as the optimization calculations built upon it, which are now part and parcel of business economics (in Germany, the relevant cost accounting tools were developed only in the 1920s), we may still assume that in practice, through experience and tentative experimentation, many businesses came up with a strategy that approximated the cost accounting postulate. In any case, the resolution adopted at a meeting of the governing board of the Bochumer Verein coal and steel company in 1878 that 'it is vital that export transactions be carried out even at low prices because insufficient activity in the domestic economy *alone* is not profitable' at least indicates that key actors were fully aware of the fundamental problem at an early stage.[141] The extent of German heavy industry's dependence on exports, which were urgently needed to reduce unit costs even in economically favourable periods, is evident in the fact that exports as a share of the semifinished and finished products shipped by the Gewerkschaft Deutscher Kaiser, a major steel producer, during the decade 1903–12 oscillated steadily around the 30 per cent mark. In the case of the Fried. Krupp AG, where the export quota climbed to a peak of three-quarters during the depression beginning in 1873, exports accounted for one-third of total sales on average during the economic boom years from 1895 to 1913, though they reached around 50 per cent in certain years.[142]

CHAPTER 2

# Foreign Trade Policy in the Free Trade Era

## The Cobden Treaty and the European Free Trade System

The trade treaty between the U.K. and France named after British free trader Richard Cobden ushered in the age of free trade in Europe. After the signing of this treaty in 1860, almost all European countries concluded treaties with one another within just a few years, transforming Europe into a zone of relative free trade within a breathtakingly short period. One hundred years before the Treaties of Rome, there emerged something like a common European market. What had happened? On the initiative of Cobden and his French counterpart Michel Chevalier, a French economist and member of the Conseil d'Etat, intensive British-French negotiations began in mid-1859. These led to the signing of the momentous trade treaty by the beginning of the following year. The motives for signing the treaty entailed a number of complex elements on both sides of the English Channel. Overall, though, it was political interests that dominated in both the U.K. and France.[1]

In foreign policy terms, the key British actors hoped to reduce the tensions between the two countries, which had rapidly worsened. War seemed within the realm of the possible. Cobden even believed that implementing the principle of free trade across the board and the concomitant intensification of international economic relations would render the instruments of traditional diplomacy superfluous and secure lasting world peace. 'Free Trade is God's diplomacy, and there is no other certain way of uniting people in bonds of peace', he assured the French emperor at the secret negotiations.[2] In domestic policy terms, for Cobden and his supporters from the aspiring middle classes support for free trade was associated not just with a radical critique of what they saw as vastly excessive British arms expenditure, but also with an attack on the dominance of the aristocratic elite, which continued to determine foreign policy and the country's fate in other ways as well.

For the French too, political considerations played a central role. Following his victories over Austria at Magenta and Solferino, Napoleon III was eager to improve political relations with the U.K. in order to gain support for his next moves in continental Europe. Particularly in view of France's impending, though not yet official, annexation of Nice and Savoy, the planned trade treaty seemed a great opportunity. In addition, the French emperor and his advisers were fundamentally convinced of the principle of free trade and expected the new British competition to stimulate the modernization and growth of French industry. Napoleon III had, however, never managed to achieve a majority in the French parliament for any unilateral reduction of tariff levels because protectionist deputies were in the overwhelming majority. But he alone had the authority to conclude a trade treaty – and this was one of the key factors that made it possible.

The Cobden Treaty meant a radical break with traditional French trade policy, which was not only protectionist but often prohibitive. France pledged to abolish all import bans. From 1 October 1861, French import tariffs would amount to a maximum of 30 per cent of the value of goods; this regulation came into force earlier with respect to coal, iron, steel, tools and machines. By 1 October 1864, tariffs were to be reduced again to a maximum of 25 per cent ad valorem. In return, the U.K. significantly reduced import duties on wine, spirits and silk products – goods, in other words, of great importance to the French export trade. Export duties on British coal were eliminated completely. At the same time, the number of imported goods subject to tariffs was reduced from 419 to 48. This brought the process of liberalization of British foreign trade to a provisional peak, a process initiated by Sir Robert Peel in 1842, when British customs tariffs applied to more than four thousand items.[3]

But the most important and momentous element in the Cobden Treaty was the most-favoured-nation clause in Article 19. This was not a completely new treaty innovation, but it was the first time that such a clause had been incorporated into a significant trade treaty after an interval of thirty or forty years during which reciprocal agreements had dominated.[4] In the 'unconditional' version set out in the British-French agreement of 1860, the most-favoured-nation clause stated that all tariff reductions or other concessions granted to third parties by one of the contracting parties in future must automatically be extended to the other contracting party as well. The far-reaching importance of this regulation is evident in the fact that the Cobden Treaty was followed within a few years by a series of further trades treaties based upon it. The treaties signed by the U.K. and France with many other European countries were followed by bilateral agreements among these countries, giving rise to a comprehensive network of trade treaties. Since all of them included the most-favoured-nation clause, every new tariff reduction that was agreed immediately benefited every other trading partner with which a given country had signed agreements. In this way, beginning with France, continental European protective tariffs fell like dominoes. '[W]e secured the alliance and co-operation of France', stated Louis Mallet, close ally of Cobden and member of the Board of Trade, from a British perspective in 1866, 'in breaking down the whole of the prohibitory laws of Europe'.[5] Within just half a decade, the whole of western and central Europe had merged into a zone of largely free trade. Tariffs and other trade restrictions had not vanished entirely, but in comparison to the past they had been dramatically reduced.

That things would develop in this way could not have been predicted in 1860. It quickly became clear, however, that the Cobden Treaty had breathed new life into European trade policy. Just a few months after the treaty had been concluded, the French government began to sound out the potential for further trade treaties with other European countries – it approached Prussia in June 1860. Again, it was not just economic policy concerns that motivated this proposal. The foreign policy aims that Napoleon III associated with a trade treaty between France and Prussia were at least as important. The French emperor aimed not just to intensify Franco-Prussian relations, but also hoped to pull the rug from under any coalition between Prussia and Austria intended to curb French hegemonic aspirations in Europe – by using the treaty to incite conflicts within the German lands.

## Genesis and Consequences of the Franco-Prussian Trade Treaty of 1862

The French treaty proposals received a sympathetic response from the Prussian government. After consulting with the other members of the Customs Union, on whose behalf Prussia acted in such cases, negotiations began in Berlin on 11 January 1861. Historians have examined in-depth the course of the negotiations as well as the various stages of the conflict that flared up within the Customs Union over the assumptions embedded in the Franco-Prussian trade treaty once it had been concluded, so there is no need to describe them in detail again here.[6] What matters for our purposes is to scrutinize the key reasons why the Prussian government was so keen to reformulate trade policy on a free trade basis by pushing the Franco-Prussian trade treaty forward even in the face of resistance from other members of the Customs Union.

In the first instance, an ideological factor played a crucial role. The Prussian ministerial bureaucracy was overwhelmingly convinced of the correctness of the principle of free trade. This was especially true of the officials entrusted with the trade treaty negotiations. The central figure here was not Johann Friedrich von Pommer Esche, who formally led the Prussian delegation, but Rudolph von Delbrück, a delegate from the Prussian Ministry of Trade and Commerce (Ministerium für Handel und Gewerbe). Delbrück and his colleagues were acting against the background of a largely consistent and fairly strong tradition of free trade ideas within the Prussian bureaucracy. This tradition extended back to the Stein-Hardenberg reforms and was first manifested within the Prussian customs system of 1818, which was extremely liberal in international comparison and was adopted by the Customs Union when it was founded in 1834.[7] Later, between 1854 and 1859, the Prussian government repeatedly attempted to implement a reduction in tariff rates within the Customs Union. In the 1840s, at the insistence of the southern German states, these had been raised, and without the help of the legislature, they had taken on a protectionist character. This was because the prices of many goods, particularly industrial ones, had fallen markedly over the course of time, while the weight-based tariffs imposed by the Customs Union had remained unchanged, so that they had de facto increased significantly as a share of the value of goods. Prussia's efforts with regard to tariff policies, however, had generally met with resistance from other members of the Customs Union at the General Conferences of the 1850s and had come to nothing because these members threatened to use the veto that the Customs Union treaty granted each state. In view of this unsatisfactory tariff policy stagnation, the Franco-Prussian trade treaty offered the Prussian administration a good opportunity to overcome the middle powers' blockade policy and achieve its desired reform of the Customs Union tariffs: the tariff changes sought by Prussia were built into the trade treaty, and Prussia declared their adoption a prerequisite for the Customs Union treaties, which were up for renewal in 1865.

The fundamentally pro–free trade tendency within the Prussian ministerial bureaucracy received a powerful boost from the astonishing progress made by the free trade doctrine in the political sphere from the late 1850s. 'More or less everyone', stated Gustav Schmoller in retrospect, 'was caught up in the great surge of free trade theory'.[8] This applied not just to the Prussia of the 'new era', but also – to varying degrees – to the other German states and virtually all of Europe.[9] Bolstered by the economic upturn that began following the first world economic crisis of 1857–59, increasing numbers of contemporaries embraced a pronounced free trade optimism, with which European liberals increasingly identified. The future appeared to belong to the free exchange of goods across borders, which held out the promise of international prosperity and peace. Within public debates the pioneering figures of the free trade doctrine increasingly managed to associate their views with progress, while stigmatizing support for protective tariffs as reactionary. When two of the 'strongholds of the isolationist system', France and Belgium, embraced a trade policy inspired by notions of free trade in 1860 and 1861 respectively, many observers in Prussia and the other German states felt that the Customs Union risked missing an opportunity to play its part in a new age of economic policy. 'We had stood still or gone backwards', as Delbrück put it, 'while the rest of the world was moving forward. Could we afford to sit apart from this movement? We could not.'[10]

The Congress of German Economists (Kongreß deutscher Volkswirte), founded in Gotha in 1858, soon became the main engine of the German free trade movement. While calls for domestic freedom of commerce had stood centre stage during its first meetings, from 1860 on trade policy issues increasingly dominated. Subsequently, the Congress rapidly began to present itself as the spearhead of the German free trade movement and as a committed pioneer of reforms to the Customs Union constitution. The Congress's great political influence did not rest on its clout as an organization. It met just once a year and always in a different location; it was not a 'members' organization', but an open conference in which anyone who paid the entry price could take part in discussions and vote on resolutions; it lacked the continuity and cadre of public relations functionaries so typical of later associations. Nor was there any homogenous free trade doctrine that might have been preached from the 'pulpit' of the Congress. The Congress of German Economists was instead a forum used by the very different groups within the German free trade movement to promote their ideas.[11]

The significant political impact of the trade policy demands made by the Congress can be explained only in light of its members and their function as disseminators. Officials, lawyers and secretaries of chambers of commerce, who were overrepresented at Congress meetings, had all kinds of opportunities to disseminate free trade ideas in their professional lives as well as to implement them. But even more significant to the public impact of the Congress was the fact that virtually from the beginning its opinion-forming core consisted of journalists and other writers. They included radical apostles of free trade John Prince-Smith and Julius Faucher, who published chiefly in the most important economic journal of the free trade movement, the *Vierteljahrsschrift für Volkswirtschaft und Kulturgeschichte*, and expounded their convictions at numerous meetings and conferences. But the core group of the Congress also included representatives of the daily and weekly press such as Otto Wolff, chief of the *Ostseezeitung*, Viktor Böhmert of the *Bremer Handelsblatt* and Otto Michaelis, responsible for the economic section of the influential Berliner *National-Zeitung* since 1856. Furthermore, the Congress of German Economists was closely integrated in terms of personnel with the National Association (Nationalverein), founded in 1859, through figures such as Rudolf von Bennigsen, Gustav Freytag, Karl Braun, Hermann Schulze-Delitzsch and many others; in this way it exercised a lasting influence on the economic policy views of the Lesser German liberals involved in it.[12]

In contrast to these ideological relations and to what occurred later on, in the early 1860s organized economic interests played no major role in advancing the new direction in Prussian-German trade policy. There were no doubt broad economic circles that thought they would benefit if foreign trade policies were reorganized on a free trade basis, above all the export-oriented agricultural producers east of the Elbe, the wholesale trade in the North Sea and Baltic Sea cities, and a plethora of branches producing consumer goods. But they generated no interest-based organizations that advanced the liberalization of trade policy remotely as effectively as the Congress of German Economists.[13] At the meetings of the Congress, meanwhile, representatives of industry, trade and agriculture were in the minority; the educated middle class clearly dominated. Furthermore, it would be wrong to imagine that the different sectors of the rapidly developing commercial production within the Customs Union had any uniform interest in free trade. There were undoubtedly economic sectors of a staunchly protectionist persuasion. Around 1860, the two most important were the heavy industry of Rhineland and Westphalia and the southern German cotton spinners, whose main fear was the adverse effects they were likely to suffer from their superior British competitors. Even they, however, exercised no lasting influence on the trade policy decision-making process during this period.

On the other hand, this does not mean that economic interests were of no significance to the trade policy approach taken by Prussia and the Customs Union. The opposite is true. Yet such interests generally entered into political decision making not as a result of any large-scale campaign 'from below', in other words, as the expression of well-organized economic interest groups, but primarily as perceived and interpreted by ministerial bureaucrats, parliamentarians and journalists. They tended to believe that German industry – and this also applied to those branches that continued to call for protective tariffs – had developed so far in the preceding decades that they could now withstand the pressures of international competition. Prussian trade minister August von der Heydt, for example, was convinced that 'market expansion was more important to industry than the level of the customs tariff'.[14] Against this background, the key actors expected that concluding a trade treaty with France, which would have meant a massive reduction in French import duties, would give the German Customs Union access to a new and lucrative market. Indeed, in the absence of a treaty there was a risk that German industry would be lastingly disadvantaged in the French market compared to its British competitors once the Cobden Treaty came into effect, and that the same would apply to other European competitors following the conclusion of further bilateral agreements. As Delbrück stated in retrospect,

> Neither politically nor economically, given our geographical position and highly developed commerce, could we have endured a situation in which we were shut out of a market right in front of our noses, that of the continent's richest country, if this market, as was bound to occur and did in fact occur, was going to be opened up to every other part of Europe.[15]

The conception of the economic interests of German producers underpinning such remarks was quite out of sync with the demands they actually made. This conception was actually based far more on Delbrück's perception and interpretation. Furthermore, the ministerial bureaucracy enjoyed tremendous latitude and room for manoeuvre at this point. All of this is evident in the fact that before concluding the trade treaty with France, though the Prussian government consulted a number of select experts, it consciously avoided any systematic survey of chambers of commerce or any more broad-based enquiry: the leading figures felt that they had sufficient information and were afraid of protectionist opposition.[16]

Conditions within the Prussian camp, as outlined above, may well have been favourable to the advance of free trade, but the real impulse came from the field of 'classical' power politics. Since the revolution of 1848/49, the problem of tariff policies had increasingly been caught in the slipstream of conflicts between Austria and Prussia. Soon after successfully putting down internal opposition in 1849/50, the new Austrian prime minister Felix Fürst zu Schwarzenberg and his trade minister Karl Ludwig von Bruck, who was also freshly appointed, had put forward plans to gradually create a large-scale central European customs union. The vision of a large economic area taking in all the German states, its boundaries marked by protective tariffs, with the 'heft of a seventy million-strong confederation',[17] which was itself intended to be merely a preliminary step towards political union, represented a highly ambitious alternative to the German Customs Union, which was up for renewal in 1852–54. At the same time, the Austrian initiative was also an undisguised threat to Prussian leadership in the field of trade policy. Through clever political tactics the Prussian government had managed to thwart the plan for an immediate customs union with Austria in the early 1850s, extend the Customs Union in its conventional form and thus secure for the time being Prussia's preeminence within Germany in terms of economic policy. At the same time, however, the trade treaty of February 1853, agreed as a compromise between Austria and Prussia, had created a makeshift solution that hung like a sword of Damocles over Prussia's dominance within the Customs Union: from this point forward, Austria and the Customs Union formed one customs area, but one that remained divided by a tariff wall; both sides agreed to a large number of preferential tariffs not granted to any other trading partner; and Article 25 provided for negotiations on the establishment of the full customs union envisaged by Austria to begin by 1860 at the latest.[18]

Under these conditions, the pursuit of a firm free trade line in tariff policy developed into Prussia's most important instrument in the struggle for hegemony in central Europe. The greatest possible reduction in the Customs Union's tariff rates – this was the rationale of Prussian strategy as pursued seamlessly from Manteuffel to Bismarck – would make accession so unattractive to Austria, with its great need for protective tariffs, that it was bound to reject the idea. In line with this, in a cabinet order of 19 May 1856, Friedrich Wilhelm IV had already decreed, for political reasons, that the best course of action was to 'implement without delay a reduction in the Customs Union tariff on a scale that Austria cannot emulate any time soon'.[19] This was easier to decree than implement, however: as we have seen, the liberal revision of the Customs Union tariffs sought by Prussia came to grief repeatedly in the late 1850s due to the partly politically and partly economically motivated blockade tactics pursued by a number of members and the paralyzing effect of the *liberum veto* regulation that applied within the Customs Union. Only with the Cobden Treaty and France's offer shortly thereafter to enter into negotiations on a similar Franco-Prussian agreement did unanticipated events provide the Prussian government with a way out of its structural dilemma. In terms of international trade policy, concluding a treaty with France that included comprehensive tariff reductions was intended to evade the tariff blockade in the Customs Union while at the same time pulling the rug from under Austria's plans for a customs union. In the early 1850s, Austria seemed even less able to pursue a comprehensive liberalization of tariff policy than it had been in the years before. First, the economic crisis of 1857–59 had hit Austria harder than Prussia, prompting Austrian industrialists suffering from the economic slump to articulate their protectionist interests with ever-greater vehemence. Second, the unfortunate course of the war in upper Italy had not only profoundly shaken the foreign policy prestige of the Danube Monarchy, but also plunged it into a deep financial crisis that eliminated all room for manoeuvre with respect to tariff reductions due to fears over loss of revenue.[20]

Right from the start of the trade treaty negotiations with France, the political calculations of Prussia's statesmen were centrally informed by their determination to nip in the bud Austria's plans for central Europe. Subsequent remarks by Delbrück, the pivotal figure in the negotiations on the Prussian side, leave no room for ambiguity:

> We were well aware that a treaty with France would push any German-Austrian customs union into the unforeseeable future, place major obstacles in the way of so-called parification [equalization] of tariffs and generally impede further development of the February Treaty, but we had no wish for any German-Austrian customs union or parification of tariffs; what we wanted, as least as far as I was concerned, was merely a limited expansion of the February Treaty.[21]

The Prussian government lost no time in pressing on with the negotiations on a trade treaty with France. After three rounds of negotiations, a treaty was signed on 29 March 1862 that provided for substantial tariff reductions on both sides, to be implemented by 1 January 1866. France essentially granted the Customs Union the tariff concessions that the U.K. had already received through the Cobden Treaty and Belgium through the treaty of 1 May 1861. In return, Prussia, acting on behalf of the Customs Union, pledged to radically reorganize the entire tariff system on a free trade basis, the key concessions to France being the halving of duties on silk and wine. In addition, the trade treaty, as well as France's treaties with the U.K. and Belgium, included a pledge to grant each other most-favoured-nation status. This made it clear that as soon as it lapsed in 1865, the preferential tariff system agreed between the Customs Union and Austria in the treaty of February 1853 would inevitably come to an end, as it was incompatible with the most-favoured-nation principle.[22]

Before the conclusion of the Franco-Prussian negotiations, opposition to the planned trade treaty began to mount within the Customs Union. Keenly supported by the Austrian government, the southern German members of the Customs Union in particular raised objections to a treaty whose ultimate effect would be to squeeze Austria out of the Customs Union completely and strengthen the influence of Prussia. But it was only after the agreement had been signed that the conflict over adoption of the trade treaty negotiated between Prussia and France by the other Customs Union states reached its peak of intensity. Austrian foreign minister Johann Bernhard von Rechberg did his utmost to stir up anti-Prussian opposition within the Customs Union. In an official memorandum of 7 May 1862, he contested Prussia's right 'to unilaterally change the entire system of tariffs, and do so by means of a treaty with a third power' in light of the provisions in the treaty of February 1853. 'In quite plain terms' he expressed the view that the treaty with France had no other purpose than 'to turn Austria's separation from the rest of Germany with respect to trade into a permanent state of affairs'.[23] In an attempt to achieve a last-minute change of course, in July the Vienna government even put forward an alternative to Prussian trade policy that made major concessions to the Customs Union; this drew heavily on the old Bruckian plans for a customs union and – should the treaty with France be renegotiated – proposed the rapid liberalization of trade in goods within the German lands and Austrian accession to the Customs Union in the near future.[24]

The Prussian government wasted no time in brusquely rejecting the Austrian offer and was unwavering in pursuit of its chosen course. In order to 'demonstrate to the world that the country is behind the government's trade policy', in a historically unique act the government put the contentious trade treaty to a vote in the Prussian House of Representatives before its definitive signing.[25] After the House of Representatives and the Prussian Upper House had voted in favour of the treaty, with just twelve votes against in the former case and unanimously in the latter, the Berlin government finally signed it on 2 August 1862 despite the fact that at this point only Saxony, Oldenburg and the Thuringian states had officially approved it. When Bavaria, Württemberg and Hanover subsequently refused to approve the trade treaty with France, the Prussian ministerial bureaucracy brought things to a head: the Prussian deputies were presented with a resolution that 'characterized rejection of the treaties as a rejection of continuation of the Customs Union with Prussia and recommended moving swiftly to open negotiations on the further existence of the Customs Union with those governments party to the treaties'. This too was passed by an overwhelming majority.[26]

Bismarck's appointment as prime minister in September 1862 left the basic thrust of Prussia's trade policy unchanged. Even more than his predecessors, however, he used this policy as an instrument of power politics; with even greater determination he strove to give Prussia the whip hand over economic policy within the German Confederation. Within Prussian domestic politics he found a way of standing shoulder to shoulder with the liberal opposition with respect to economic policy by consistently maintaining a free trade approach. But his hopes that this would help him find a way out of the cul-de-sac of the constitutional conflict – over the reform of the Prussian army and the balance of power between parliament and king – were disappointed. The liberal parliamentary majority unanimously supported Bismarck's approach to the Customs Union, and the German National Association (Nationalverein), Congress of German Economists and ultimately even the German Trade Association (Deutscher

Handelstag, or DHT), still firmly committed to a Greater Germany when it was founded in May 1861, supported the Customs Union's accession to the western European free trade zone. But the opposing camps with respect to the military and the constitutional issue remained irreconcilable. For Bismarck, however, the crucial factor was the confederal dimension of tariff and trade policy. Even more clearly than Albrecht von Bernstorff before him, he saw this policy as the lever that could squeeze Austria out of the German Confederation and settle the German question in Prussia's favour. As Bismarck explained in his great Christmas memorandum of 1862, it was not the German Confederation, which was wholly disadvantageous to Prussia, but the Customs Union that constituted the 'most appropriate basis for dealing jointly with the material and ultimately political interests of the German states'. Whether the 'German Confederation continued to exist or not', the 'potential inherent in the Prussian state' could 'come to fruition only *alongside* or *outside* of it'. The Prussian prime minister thus strongly advocated 'liberation from the web of confederal treaties' and a fundamental reorganization of the Customs Union in the interests of Prussia. With respect to speedy ratification of the French treaty by the other Customs Union states, Bismarck was pessimistic: in view of the strong anti-Prussian opposition, there was 'no prospect of the trade treaty being accepted in the *current* phase of the Customs Union'. Only linkage of the trade treaty and institutional reform of the Customs Union through the treaties up for renewal in 1865/66 held out the hope of untying this Gordian knot. There was, however, no doubt in his mind that the Prussian strategy he had outlined would succeed over the long term, because 'the trade system created by France's treaties with England, Belgium, Prussia and Switzerland is of such importance as to make it almost impossible over the long term for the majority of Customs Union states to remain outside of it'. If sticking resolutely to the trade treaty with France 'created a situation by virtue of which the Customs Union with Prussia offered the only route into the system as a whole for the German states … then we would be in a very good position to compel those states to accept our conditions for the renewal of the Customs Union'.[27]

Bismarck allowed himself to be persuaded – by Delbrück's energetic opposition – to postpone for the time being the planned Customs Union reform, which aimed to abolish individual states' vetoes and establish a customs parliament,[28] and he also failed to receive from France the desired assurance that it would refrain from entering into direct negotiations with the other Customs Union states on entry into the 'entire system of French trade treaties'.[29] Yet the political scenario of the next few years otherwise developed largely along the lines that he had laid down. After months of fruitless negotiations with the other members of the Customs Union, in mid-December 1863 the Prussian government – in a repeat performance of its approach to the first Customs Union crisis of 1851/52 – gave notice that the Customs Union treaties would cease to apply from the end of 1865 and made their renewal ultimately dependent on acceptance of the Franco-Prussian trade treaty. The survival of the Customs Union and approval of Prussian free trade policies were now officially linked through an undisguised threat.

As a result, the anti-Prussian front gradually began to crumble. Ultimately, the small and medium-sized Customs Union states could in no way afford to risk the Lesser German economic unity that had already been achieved. The cross-border economic links facilitated by three decades of the Customs Union were far too intensive; the smaller partners in particular were far too economically dependent on the range of options to buy and sell commodities provided by the integrated internal market of the Customs Union area.[30] In fiscal terms as well, small and medium-sized states were highly dependent on the revenues of the Customs Union. The alternative of a separate confederation with Austria as aired by the anti-treaty members of the Customs Union in the case of its dissolution could in no way provide sufficient compensation. And in early 1864, as Austria joined Prussia to fight for Schleswig-Holstein, Vienna's support for the opposing middle-sized states declined markedly. As a result, one member of the Customs Union after another agreed to the conditions for the renewal of the union dictated by Prussia. Saxony was the first on 11 May 1864; it was not long before it was joined by the Thuringian states, Baden, Braunschweig, Frankfurt and the Electorate of Hesse, after the elector had been paid a substantial bribe by Karl Mayer von Rothschild[31] on Berlin's behalf.[32] In July the Hanover government gave in to the pressure to conform, which came in significant part from its own liberal parliament, and acceded to the Prussian trade system along with Oldenburg. Bavaria, Württemberg, Hessen-Darmstadt and Nassau made up the last line of resistance. Given the lack of Austrian support and ever more vigorous public demands to continue the tried-and-tested Customs Union with Prussia, however, even they were ultimately forced to capitulate. The Bavarian king Ludwig II summed the situation up in August, stating that fundamentally his government had 'no other choice' than to submit to Prussia as it would 'sooner or later be forced to join the rest of Germany again in any case … given the powerful interests [involved]'.[33] On 12 October 1864 the four southern German states accepted the Prussian conditions. On 16 May of the following year, all members signed the new Customs Union treaty; this extended the alliance for a further twelve years on the basis of acceptance of the Franco-Prussian trade treaty and a new tariff informed by free trade principles.[34]

The trade treaty concluded between the Customs Union and Austria on 11 April 1865 completed Prussia's economic policy victory. The preferential tariff system that had existed between the Customs Union and Austria since 1853 was abolished and replaced by a simple most-favoured-nation relationship, which placed Austria on the same level as France and all the other trade treaty partners. A further blow to the Austrian camp emanated from Article 25 of the treaty of February 1853, which entailed a binding commitment to negotiations on Austria's accession to the Customs Union over the course of the treaty period; this was not incorporated into the new treaty and was instead replaced by a vague plan to 'begin negotiations in the near future on the issue of a general German customs agreement' – a promise that was further qualified by an explicit statement that 'these [negotiations] are in no way intended to restrict the autonomy of any of the parties to the treaty to formulate laws on tariffs and trade'.[35] Bismarck had originally been prepared to go quite far to accommodate Austrian demands for renewal of Article 25 in consideration of the foreign policy relations between Prussia and Austria. In 'a pactum de contrahendo' he saw a form of politically unthreatening lip service, as he considered a tariff union between the Customs Union and Austria 'an impracticable utopia due to the differences in their economic and administrative conditions'.[36] In taking this view, however, Bismarck was met with the implacable opposition of Prussian finance minister Karl von Bodelschwingh, Prussian trade minister Heinrich zu Itzenplitz and above all their 'free trade spiritus rector', Delbrück.[37] In an extensive memorandum, Delbrück, who underlined the strength of his feelings by threatening to resign, explained that Article 25 in its traditional form was nothing other than the 'seed of future strife', an 'ever-ready means of paralyzing Prussia's capacity for trade policy action'. Convinced that 'no trade policy idea is now more antipathetic to every political or trade policy party in Prussia' than 'that of a customs union with Austria', and that therefore 'approval of a new Article 25' would face 'serious difficulties' in the Prussian House of Representatives, he ultimately got his way in the ministry and won over the king. Bismarck suffered a serious political defeat and had to make the empty formula mentioned above palatable to the new Austrian foreign minister, Alexander von Mensdorff.[38]

In the spring of 1865, with the renewal of the Customs Union treaties and the signing of the treaty with Austria, the die had been cast with respect to the German question, at least as far as trade policy was concerned. The Lesser German solution had prevailed in economic policy terms; Prussia's hegemonic position within the Customs Union had been confirmed far more impressively than during the first Customs Union crisis. None of this meant that any automatic or inevitable process had been set in motion with respect to later political unification, but an important preliminary step had been taken. The door to a customs area shared with the other German states, an option that Austria had so far left slightly open, had now slammed shut; the notion of a central European economic area of seventy million people centred on Vienna, as envisaged by Schwarzenberg and Bruck and further developed by Rechberg, had proved a chimera. With the conclusion of the bitterly contested trade treaty with France, the German Customs Union had taken a decisive step towards integration into the rapidly developing European free trade zone. The subsequent trade treaties that the Customs Union concluded with Belgium, the U.K. and Italy, the same year it was itself renewed, signalled consistent progress along the chosen path. All these treaties were bilateral agreements on the model of the Cobden Treaty and contained the most-favoured-nation clause. They bound the Customs Union, as long as it existed, firmly into the western and central European network of free trade agreements, just as these went a long way to creating this network.[39]

## The Apex of German Free Trade Policy from 1866 On

The Austro-Prussian War and its political consequences were the prelude to the second phase of the Customs Union's free trade-era policies. The events of 1866 created the preconditions for a fundamental institutional reorganization of the Customs Union. The Prussian annexations and the founding of the North German Confederation made the political and economic importance of Prussia even more obvious than it already was. In view of the existing power relations and economic dependencies, the four southern German states that remained outside of the North German Confederation were essentially left with no other choice than to more or less willingly accept the Prussian proposals on the reorganization of the Customs Union. There were few options open to them given Bismarck's blatant threat to otherwise abandon the customs union with southern Germany. On 8 July 1867, by signing the revised Customs Union treaties, Baden, Hessen-Darmstadt and – after some to-ing and fro-ing – even Württemberg and Bavaria consented to the reform of the Customs Union constitution that the Prussian ministerial bureaucracy and Bismarck had wanted for so long.

Out of what was originally a fairly loose customs league of independent states with a veto for every member there now developed a customs federation with a full-fledged bicameral system and majority decisions, a federation that in many ways foreshadowed the constitution of the later German Empire and that its Prussian initiators certainly saw as a preliminary step on the path to closer political unity. The cumbersome General Conference was replaced by the Federal Customs Council, in which the North German Confederation had forty-two out of a total of fifty-eight votes. While Prussia had just seventeen seats, it was entitled to hold the presidency and it was the only state that had a veto over all decisions. The second chamber, the Customs Parliament, consisted of members of the North German Reichstag and deputies from the southern German states, all of them elected by universal direct and secret male suffrage. This ensured the dominance of the densely populated north under Prussian supremacy in the Customs Parliament. Right from the start, in the sphere of trade and tariff policy the reformed Customs Union was a fully functional organization – despite all the restrictions that the new structure of the Customs Union placed on its powers (the National Liberal Ludwig Bamberger, whose more far-reaching hopes were disappointed, regarded the Customs Parliament as a 'living reminder of the imperfect and unbalanced character of our … constitution', but also as an 'objectively indispensable tool'),[40] and despite all the resistance in the southern German states to closer ties with Prussia and the institutional restructuring of the Lesser German economic union.[41]

The institutional reorganization of the Customs Union opened up the possibility of implementing an accelerated free trade policy, which represented the continuation of previous policies but also entailed a qualitatively new dimension. Key decisions on personnel within the Prussian-German executive after 1866 show clearly that there was a determined expansion of the free trade system. The key post of president of the newly established chancellery, the top authority of the North German Confederation, was filled by architect of Prussian trade policy Rudolph von Delbrück. In close cooperation with the majority in the North German Reichstag, he immediately set about realizing a massive programme of liberal reforms that went far beyond the sphere of trade policy or even economic policy. One of Delbrück's first acts on taking office was to appoint Otto Michaelis senior counselor in the chancellery. Michaelis was a prominent pioneer of free trade ideas as editor of the trade policy section of the *National-Zeitung*. He initially sat for the Progress Party in the Prussian House of Representatives and, after it split, for the National Liberals in the North German Reichstag. Probably more than any other personnel decision, Michaelis' appointment symbolizes the efforts made to balance out Bismarck's influence by bringing in some of his liberal opponents from the period of the constitutional conflict as well as the Customs Union executive's commitment to liberal economic reforms domestically and the full implementation of free trade with other countries.[42] In the years after 1866, the same signals went out when it came to the key positions within the Prussian ministerial bureaucracy – above all other new appointments, this applies to the appointment of the staunchly pro-free trade Otto Camphausen as Prussian finance minister in 1869, which also occurred on Delbrück's initiative.[43]

In terms of content, the second phase of the free trade era, which lasted beyond the founding of the German Empire until the mid-1870s, was characterized by two key features that distinguished it from the preceding period. First, tariffs were again reduced significantly both in terms of their number and level; with a few exceptions, all protective tariffs were removed in favour of a pure revenue tariff system. Second, the Customs Union and later the German Empire gave up reciprocal free trade and began to practice unilateral free trade. In analogy to the principles of British free trade policy, Germany now lowered tariffs through stand-alone legislation to levels below those agreed in trade treaties, without demanding anything in return from its trading partners.

The transition from a moderate to a pronounced free trade policy occurred in two stages. The first step was the autonomous customs tariff reform of 1870, which entailed the passing of two parliamentary bills. This was the result of a two-year legislative process that began with the conclusion of the trade treaty of 1868 between the Customs Union and Austria. This treaty, which replaced the agreement of 1865, contained a wide range of new and substantive tariff reductions – the pig iron tariff, for example, which had already been lowered through the trade treaty with France from 2 marks to 1.50 marks per 100 kilograms, was now reduced even further to 1 mark. The trade treaty with Austria met with vigorous resistance from some southern German protectionists in the Customs Parliament. 'If Germany were to be overrun by the Huns and Vandals, its cities aflame', railed Moritz Mohl, a deputy from Württemberg, against the planned treaty and the entire thrust of German trade policy, 'they would cause the same kind of destruction wrought by free trade as it ruins our businesses'.[44] But this bitter opposition was shared by just a few parliamentarians; in the end, the Austrian trade agreement achieved an overwhelming majority of 246 votes to 17.[45]

The situation was initially quite different with regard to the bill to amend the Customs Union tariff submitted to the Customs Parliament at the same time. Building on the treaty with Austria, it aimed to achieve a comprehensive simplification of the customs tariff and was intended to pave the way, on the model of the U.K., for the transition from a protective to a pure revenue tariff system, in which tariffs are applied exclusively to goods not produced domestically, so that their impact is limited to that of an indirect excise duty. If the tariff bill, which provided for exemption from duty for forty-five groups of goods previously subject to it and for twelve further significant tariff reductions, initially met with the resistance of the majority of deputies in the Customs Parliament, this was not because it was too pro–free trade. The dispute was over the plan contained in the government's bill to counterfinance the loss of revenue caused by the tariff reductions, a plan based on a higher tax on tobacco and the introduction of a petroleum tariff. The planned mineral oil tariff in particular was firmly rejected by the liberal parliamentary majority. Crucial here was not just free traders' basic opposition to any new tariff and fears over the burden this would place on consumers. Liberals also feared that a tariff on a product like petroleum – growing so rapidly in terms of consumption and imports – would mean allowing the government to impose 'a tax on an entirely incalculable and unknown scale', whose yield threatened to undermine the Customs Parliament's already limited budgetary significance.[46] The tariff reductions provided for in the government's draft bill, meanwhile, did not go far enough for many radical free traders – particularly the deputies from the Progress Party and the agrarians from east of the Elbe; they called for the speeding up of free trade reforms.

Only in 1870, after tariff amendments had failed to win approval in the Customs Parliament in the two previous years, was a compromise reached that was supported both by the majority of deputies as well as the "Bundesrat", the assembly of representatives from the member states of the North German Confederation (from 1867), which was absorbed into the German Empire in 1871. In terms of content, this compromise rested on two pillars. First, the government abandoned the petroleum tariff, for which there was no support in the Customs Parliament, but gained approval for a financially less profitable increase in the coffee tariff. Second, beyond the many generally uncontroversial tariff reductions, the pig iron tariff was again reduced by a further 50 per cent, which was not originally envisaged in the government's draft bill. This compromise went some way to satisfying the wishes of the radical free traders, who had joined forces in the Customs Parliament to establish the Free Trade Commission (Freihändlerische Commission), which had supported total abolition of the pig iron tariff since 1869.[47] At the same time, however, the more far-reaching and as yet unfulfilled demands for free trade, which were gaining increasing traction in published opinion, in the Customs Parliament and within the Prussian-German ministerial bureaucracy indicated that the customs tariff reform of 1870 did not mean that the government had reached the end of its chosen course.[48]

The free trade era reached its peak and at the same time its conclusion with the further reform of the customs tariff in 1873, which represented the second step on the path of unilateral free trade and at the centre of which stood the removal of iron tariffs. This had been preceded by a lively campaign against the retention of the remaining fragments of protective tariffs, a campaign that began shortly after the foundation of the German Empire in 1871. This was supported, first, by the free trade dogmatists from the ranks and circles of the Economic Congress (Volkswirtschaftlicher Kongress), who could get their work published in the *Vierteljahrsschrift für Volkswirtschaft, Politik und Kulturgeschichte,* the *Hamburger Nachrichten,* the *Hamburgische Börsen-Halle,* the *Ostseezeitung* and other newspapers closely associated with trade.[49] Second, the estate owners of northern and northeast Germany and their newly created organizations, the Congress of German Farmers (Kongreß Deutscher Landwirte) and the German Agricultural Council (Deutscher Landwirtschaftsrat, or DLR), were increasingly vociferous and vehement in their insistence that iron tariffs be abolished, which they expected would reduce the costs of agricultural equipment and machines.[50]

In fact, the economic preconditions for a further reduction in tariffs could hardly have been more favourable than they were in the early 1870s. The German economy had benefited from several years of a booming economy, culminating in a surge in investment and demand following the end of the Franco-German War in 1871; most businesses could look back on 'golden years' of growth and prosperity. This applied especially to the iron industry, which was more productive and internationally competitive than ever before; because of the tax and tariff revenue that had grown during the economic upturn and French reparations, the German Empire and the individual states found themselves in a fiscally saturated position, which made it possible to reduce tariffs without having to provide financial compensation.

The initiative for the abolition of the iron tariffs initially came from the Reichstag in 1873. In May, the conservatives Friedrich von Behr and Nicolaus von Below tabled a corresponding motion, which was supported not only by a large number of Prussian agrarians such as the Counts of Dohna-Finckenstein and Eulenburg, Wilhelm von Minnigerode and Friedrich von Wedell-Malchow as well as most of the National Liberals, but also by the leading Centre Party deputies Ludwig Windthorst and Bishop von Ketteler.[51] The seemingly inexorable, triumphant march of free trade had convinced them of its superiority. 'On all tariff matters, I act firmly in support of free trade', declared Windthorst. The '*liberal* tendency in the trade system', which he increasingly 'trusted', was 'always advancing, and every attempt to permanently reverse it will fail miserably'.[52] But the Reichstag deputies' bill never went to a vote. The imperial government announced a tariff amendment, which had been prepared by the chancellery with the full approval of the Prussian Ministry of Trade and the Prussian Finance Ministry (Finanzministerium) at virtually the same time as the parliamentary initiative and was put before the Reichstag a few weeks later.[53] The government's proposed bill took up most of the radical free traders' as yet unfulfilled demands. Its core aim was to remove tariffs on pig iron and semifinished products of iron, locomotives, steam kettles, machines and rail vehicles. 'The tremendous economic upturn in all fields of commercial activity requires us, and the financial position of the empire allows us, to take a step further along the path of customs tariff reform that we have already set out on', to quote the bill's short and pithy introduction.[54]

The tariff amendment was passed unchanged by the Bundesrat but met with the resistance of deputies in the Reichstag, who were close to German heavy industry. Influenced by the nascent economic crisis, the large number of petitions and submissions emanating from them was testimony to their increasingly vociferous support for retaining the remaining protective tariffs. In the Reichstag, heavy industrialist Karl Ferdinand Stumm pointed out that the economic situation had gotten notably worse during the first half of 1873 and that 'the iron business is now stagnant in a way we have not seen for twenty or thirty years'.[55] Like the Free Conservative Wilhelm von Kardorff, who was closely linked with Silesian industry through his own holdings, Stumm asserted that the iron and steel industry in Germany already enjoyed less state protection than in almost any other industrial state; specifically, the misapplication of the French export rebate, the *titres d'aquit-à-caution,* functioned as a kind of export premium, disadvantaging German heavy industry vis-à-vis its international competitors, and was likely to do serious damage if tariffs were removed.[56] While these arguments had some effect on parliamentarians, the protectionist opposition merely managed to achieve a partial postponement: the proposed compromise drawn up by Johannes Miquel, Friedrich Hammacher and Friedrich von Varnbüler and ultimately accepted by the overwhelming majority of the Reichstag ensured that full exemption from duty would come into force immediately, on 1 October 1873, only for pig iron and a small number of other important articles. Other iron and steel goods, machines and a number of other goods, meanwhile, initially saw substantial tariff reductions and would become duty-free only on 1 January 1877.[57] While this certainly granted heavy industry a period of adjustment, it also advanced and largely completed the project of reorganizing the customs tariff on a free trade basis.

Nothing demonstrates the sweeping ideological dominance of free trade dogma as the driving force of Prussian-German liberal foreign trade policy better than the fact that the Customs Union and later the German Empire not only continued to pursue this policy after 1866, but in fact stepped up the pace of reform, gradually and autonomously approaching a fully formed free trade system. When all 'power politics' reasons for the pursuit of free trade had ceased to apply because of the decision to take a belligerent approach to the Prussian-Austrian conflict, and when integration into the European network of trade treaties was secure and further liberalization of its own customs tariff no longer held out the promise of reciprocal measures by trading partners, Prussia-Germany went over to unilateral free trade and made further drastic reductions in its tariffs. The key reason for this is to be found within the intellectual horizons and motivations of the historical actors involved in the trade policy decision-making process. The great majority of them were now convinced of the incontrovertible correctness and beneficent economic effects of free trade. In contemporary thinking, free trade was inseparably associated both with a long period of economic boom that had only briefly been interrupted and featured unprecedented economic growth and with the success story of German unification. The doctrine of free trade was also celebrating its triumph in the rest of Europe. The words with which Reichstag deputy Behr 'justified' his motion to abolish iron tariffs while ascribing to the free trade doctrine axiomatic validity, eliciting no protest, were symptomatic of the hegemonic position occupied by the idea of free trade within the political culture around 1870 vis-à-vis other trade policy options. 'Nothing', stated Behr, could be further from his mind than 'wishing to prove the necessity for eliminating iron tariffs. Axioms, gentlemen, require no proof.'[58] Perhaps even more striking evidence of the discursive preeminence of free trade is the fact that even supporters of iron tariffs such as Stumm felt compelled to explicitly profess their faith in the principle of free trade, merely daring to state that it was not yet the right time to remove tariffs.[59]

The preeminence of the free trade idea within contemporary trade policy discourse and thought thus represented the structurally most important and also most enduring driving force of an increasingly radical Lesser German free trade policy. In the early 1860s, the impulses emanating from the Cobden Treaty and the intensifying Prussian-Austrian conflict provided the crucial historical spark that set in motion the reorganization of German tariff and trade policy on a consistent free trade basis. In comparison to these factors, the importance of economic interests – as hinted earlier – was fairly negligible. The role of the large farm owners east of the Elbe, who had an interest in free trade, should not be overstated in this context either. First, the conservative agrarians developed only relatively late, namely, from the late 1860s, into leading proponents of free trade reform. The Prussian ministerial bureaucracy and the free trade liberals, meanwhile, had been advancing the agenda much earlier. Second, the Prussian large estate owners' interest in free trade was not simply a direct expression of their economic situation, but at least as much the product of their perceptual filter, which was informed by the socially dominant free trade ideology. And in fact, agriculture benefited comparatively little from the removal of the iron tariffs – the main goal of their free trade agitation – as it consumed only around 5 to 7 per cent of German iron production and was burdened by existing tariffs only to a vanishingly small degree.[60]

'Political conditions imposed free trade, while economic ones permitted it', as Walther Lotz put it in 1892 with regard to the causes of Prussian-German free trade policy.[61] He understood that the importance of the constellation of economic interests that applied in the 1860s and early 1870s lay less in the fact that they had hugely advanced the project of free trade reform than in the fact that they had placed no great barriers in its way. Because of the favourable economic situation, despite a marked increase in international trade, domestic producers suffered very little or not at all at the hands of foreign competition and thus felt no increased inclination to defend or pursue superfluous protective tariffs. Furthermore, economic globalization had not yet reached certain fields of commercial and above all agricultural production, or had done so only in limited fashion. All of this was to change fundamentally over the next few decades.

## CHAPTER 3

# The Shift towards Protectionism

By the mid-1870s the winds of trade policy had already begun to blow in a new direction. In 1879, just two years after the abolition of iron tariffs, the Reichstag approved a comprehensive package of industrial and agricultural tariffs, though this was merely the prelude to the increasingly protectionist legislation of the 1880s. The protectionist turn of 1879 has attracted a lot of attention. In political economy, like Peel's repeal of the Corn Laws in 1846, it forms part of the standard repertoire of prominent historical examples repeatedly used to illustrate and empirically verify explanatory theories.[1] For many historians it is a turning point of crucial importance to German history, a key element in the conservative 'refoundation' of the German Empire.[2] Hans Rosenberg went so far as to describe 'the historical turn of 1879 as one of the great errors in nineteenth-century German and thus European history' and to ascribe to it profound consequences, up to and including National Socialism.[3] This is surely overstating things. Just like the thesis of the 'second foundation of the empire', it overestimates the extent to which the decisions of 1879 shaped or enduringly determined the empire's development. Furthermore, with respect to tariff and trade policy we need to keep in mind both that there was a concurrent global protectionist turn, as well as the fact that the German customs tariff of 1879 merely implemented a moderate system of protection. This applies to what were initially very moderate cereal tariffs, but also to protective industrial tariffs; here, the tariff reductions implemented autonomously since the mid-1860s were essentially rescinded. Nonetheless, after a quarter century of intensifying trade liberalization, the tariffs of 1879 symbolize an important turning point.

## Economic and Political Parameters

If we turn to the structural conditions that facilitated and advanced the trade policy turn, the first key factor is the economic depression that began in 1873, which brought to an end the booming economy of the 'founding years'. The consequences of this severe economic crisis, which was triggered by a buildup of overcapacity and lasted until 1879, have often been described: stock market crash and credit crisis, financial losses and declining incomes, diminishing demand and sales slump, company collapse and unemployment, weak growth and falling prices. As in 1857–59, only this time far more painfully, the crisis that began in 1873 also showed just how much economic globalization had linked together the different national economies. The downturn was soon affecting all the main industrial countries, and it culminated in the first great global economic crisis. The global scale of the depression worsened the crisis of the German economy, as it did mutatis mutandis in every other country. First, foreign demand for German exports collapsed at almost the same time as domestic demand. Second, international competition made itself painfully felt in both foreign markets and the German domestic market as competitors everywhere attempted to sell off their surplus production at low prices.[4]

In view of this international competitive pressure, which was real enough but sometimes grotesquely overstated by those affected, it was not long before key actors began to mobilize, organize and articulate their economic interests as they sought to gain state protection from the forces of the world market. Unsurprisingly, those branches of the economy traditionally geared towards protectionism were out in front, above all western German heavy industry and the southern German textile industry. Their sectoral associations, which had emerged shortly after the foundation of the German Empire, the Association for the Protection of Common Economic Interests in the Rhineland and Westphalia (Verein zur Wahrung der gemeinsamen wirtschaftlichen Interessen in Rheinland und Westfalen), also known as the Long Name Association (Langnamverein), and the Association of Southern German Cotton Industrialists (Verein Süddeutscher Baumwollindustrieller), soon functioned as the nucleus of protectionist interests. For tactical reasons, the Association of German Iron and Steel Industrialists, the VDEStI, founded in October 1874, the first heavy industrial interest organization to serve the whole of Germany, initially restricted itself to demanding the retention of those tariffs earmarked for abolition on 1 January 1877.[5] Wilhelm Löwe, the voice of the VDEStI in the Reichstag, left his brother-in-law Louis Baare of the Bochumer Verein coal and steel company in no doubt that given the still strong position of free traders in the parliament the only way this demand would be met was if 'the issue is viewed as lying outside the combat zone of free trade and protective tariffs. … If we make it an issue of protective tariffs, we'll lose.'[6] Only once it had become clear, towards the end of 1875, that neither the Reichstag nor the government were prepared to agree to retention of the iron tariffs did those forces within the VDEStI who propagated an openly protectionist approach and advocated reintroduction of the pig iron tariff increasingly gain the upper hand. At the same time, Ruhr industrialist August Servaes declared that the best way to achieve these objectives was to bypass the ministerial bureaucracy and parliament and 'as far as possible ... go directly to the imperial chancellor'.[7]

The organization of protectionist interests reached a new level with the foundation of the Central Association of German Industrialists (Centralverband Deutscher Industrieller, or CVDI) in February 1876. In this first umbrella organization of German industry, representatives of the various protectionist sectors came together to jointly pursue their economic policy goals. Representatives of the glass and soda industry, the paper and leather industry, and the wool and linen industry were present at the birth of the CVDI. Yet it was clearly the interests of the cotton spinners and especially those of the heavy industrialists, who initially put on a show of polite reserve, that dominated. Right from the start, the CVDI 'reeked of iron'.[8] A. Lohren's draft articles of association already expressed the thrust of the association's politics with striking clarity: 'Combating the doctrine of free trade, which is plunging national labour into ruin to the benefit of foreign labour.'[9] In the early days, the CVDI's near-exclusive objective was the 'protection of national labour' through a system of protective tariffs. In order to ready public, parliament and government for such a shift in trade policy, the CVDI engaged in a major press and petitioning campaign. Right from the start and with great success the CVDI claimed to be the only organization speaking for the whole of German industry. This was only possible because the CVDI succeeded in mediating between the different and sometimes sharply diverging interests of the industrial sectors present within it and putting forward a transsectoral catalogue of protectionist demands.[10] Getting others to accept this claim was also facilitated by the fact that the only possible rival, the German Trade Association, the DHT, was completely paralyzed with respect to trade policy as a result of the 'divergent interests present within it'.[11] Having disappointed the hopes placed in it as an organizational platform by the free traders, from 1876 the DHT increasingly departed from its formerly strict free trade line and, particularly after the trading cities on the Baltic renounced their membership in protest, increasingly came under the sway of the CVDI.[12]

The second important economic force fostering the trade policy shift was the globalization of the agricultural market, whose impact I described in detail earlier (see the section on agriculture in chapter 1). From the mid-1870s, the German cereal economy increasingly found itself exposed to competition from low-cost overseas and eastern European producers, both in its export markets and in Germany itself. From the outset, the

German Empire was afflicted by import surpluses in rye and barley; from 1876 it also became a net importer of wheat.[13] A far bigger blow to the individual farmer was the long-term downward trend in cereal prices as a result of the rapid expansion of international supply beginning in the late 1870s. But it was only in the mid-1880s that the extent of the price decline became truly apparent. Overall, in the second half of the 1870s the average market price of wheat in Prussia, at 210 marks per tonne in 1876, 230 in 1877, 202 in 1878 and 196 in 1879, was below the average price of 1866–1875 (228). But it still remained within the range familiar from the previous decade. Only in 1883 did the price fall sharply to 185 marks per tonne, before sinking further to 157 marks by 1886.[14] Price trends were very similar for other cereal types. The overall index of cereal prices in Germany declined from 117 points in 1873 to 90 points in 1878; it then underwent a short-term recovery before beginning a downwards slide in 1882 that reached its temporary low of 77 index points in 1887.[15]

The changed economic situation, though still highly opaque in the early 1870s, was reflected in German agriculturalists' attitude towards trade policy. What had been a solid free trade front began to crumble. Before 1879, however, German farmers did not join the protectionist camp as 'suddenly'[16] and unanimously as Lujo Brentano and August Bebel later claimed; it is by no means true that they became 'just as committed to protectionism … from one day to the next … as they had previously been to free trade'.[17] The agrarian organization that ultimately proved the staunchest proponent of protective agricultural tariffs was the Association of Tax and Economic Reformers (Vereinigung der Steuer- und Wirtschaftsreformer, or VSW), founded in February 1876, an organization close to the German Conservative Party. Manorial lords from east of the Elbe clearly dominated among its almost seven hundred members. But even the Tax and Economic Reformers did not commit to a protectionist trade policy right from the start. Instead, their original articles of association were ambiguous with respect to foreign trade policy: 'Committed to the principle of free trade, we oppose protective tariffs but see customs duty and consumption taxes as an open question.' This was a compromise formula that fused a fundamental commitment to free trade with a pragmatic, open attitude to protectionist alternatives. It was not until 1879 that it was superseded by an unambiguously protectionist credo.[18] The VSW's catalogue of demands initially foregrounded issues unrelated to trade policy: tax relief for estates, removal of the railways' differential tariffs, revision of trade regulations and stock corporation law, increased scope to take action against farm workers in breach of contract – all of this was inseparably bound up with a radically antiliberal, right-wing conservative programme. Only very gradually and in the face of significant resistance within its own ranks did a protectionist position take hold within the VSW, based on demands for an even-handed protectionist approach to agriculture and industry. With respect to their propaganda activities in favour of a shift in trade policy, the Tax and Economic Reformers lagged far behind the CVDI before 1879.[19]

Even more divided and generally more reserved in its attitude towards protectionist tendencies was the German Agricultural Council, the DLR, the official representative organ of German agriculture, founded in 1871. Even at its conference held just a few months before the adoption of the customs tariff reform in January 1879, the DLR proved unable to pass an unambiguously protectionist resolution. A call for the 'introduction of moderate customs duties that take equal account of the interests of agriculture and industry' failed to attain majority support. The Agricultural Council was just as unable to agree on a clear free trade line. The formula that was finally agreed to stated that if 'in the event that the currently applicable customs tariff is revised, as is being considered, and for fiscal policy reasons tariffs on formerly duty-free inbound items [are] unavoidable and … low revenue tariffs (import duties) [must] be introduced for them', then the DLR expected 'the interests of agriculture to be taken into account in the same way as those of industry'.[20]

Interestingly, it was not the landowners of northeastern Germany who expounded a staunchly protectionist line within the DLR. In fact, the delegates from West and East Prussia, along with the representatives of Schleswig-Holstein, Oldenburg, Mecklenburg, Alsace-Lorraine, Baden and Hesse were among the most energetic opponents of any kind of tariff protection. Only the representatives of three provinces in West Prussia voted unambiguously for cereal tariffs: Hanover, Hesse-Nassau and Rhineland, along with the delegate representing Upper Silesian agriculture.[21] Other hotbeds of agricultural protectionism – as evident from analysis of the activities of regional agrarian associations and agricultural councils – were to be found in the Kingdom of Saxony and in Westphalia.[22] Initially, then, it appears that the demand for agricultural tariffs did not come from the Prussian Junkers – in this respect, the VSW was probably a quite unrepresentative cutting edge – but from those German agricultural regions dominated by peasant farmers that found themselves within or near major industrial zones; they were therefore more oriented towards a stronger domestic market and open-minded about the protectionist preferences of industry.

This dual pressure exerted by the world economic crisis from 1873 on and the structural crisis of agriculture that hit Germany along with the rest of western and central Europe soon afterwards brought about a dual shift in the political framework, which also fostered the swing towards protectionism. First, the economic crisis fundamentally discredited economic liberalism, and political liberalism soon after. In view of the economic misery, the idea of a natural harmony of economic interests and the self-regulating capacity of the market quickly lost much of its appeal. Unbridled progressive optimism was increasingly replaced by pessimistic prognoses. Everywhere, people began to look for someone to blame – and ever-greater numbers of political actors identified the liberal legislation and economic policies of the previous years as the culprit. Wilhelm Wehrenpfennig, the political correspondent and coeditor of the *Preußische Jahrbücher,* had diagnosed this attributional mechanism as early as 1876:

> Those who have invested their wealth in depreciating shares criticize the stock corporation law rather than their own carelessness. Those who have seen their robust securities decline in value blame our wrongheaded economic policies rather than acknowledging the propensity for change of all earthly things, which has given us times of plenty followed by lean years since the time of the pharaohs. The industrialist complains about the customs tariff, the peasant about freedom of movement, and both about the railways' freight rates, whose shareholders in turn explain the decline in the value of their holdings as a result of our public administration imposing the wrong rules. Institutions that have existed for centuries in other cultures, such as the principles of our trade regulations, are attacked as dangerous innovations. Even such urgent and successfully implemented reforms as that of our coinage and banking system attract the most fanciful blend of accusations and complaints.[23]

Economically liberal ideas – or 'Manchesterian' ones, to use the disparaging term that was often used – suffered a profound and comprehensive loss of prestige. It was not only the idea of free trade that this applied to, but that was certainly included. Rather than a belief in the universal validity of the free trade principle, the view expressed by Gustav Schmoller in 1879 to the Association for Social Policy (Verein für Socialpolitik) increasingly took hold: 'Protective tariffs and free trade … are not fundamental issues but subordinate tools of political or economic therapy'; Schmoller also asserted that 'times of boom, of increasing exports, of the opening up of overseas markets … [are] the natural eras of free trade, just as, conversely, times of international market stagnation, depression, and crisis naturally trigger demands for protective tariffs'.[24] Calls for state intervention to tackle the crisis became generally louder. The longer the economic downturn dragged on, and the greater the number of economic sectors that found themselves facing existential crisis, the less convincing the liberal faith in the self-healing power of the market became. Hans Rosenberg was right to count the ideological shift in climate that this entailed – the enduring delegitimization of liberal economic thought and the profound loss of faith in political liberalism that went hand in hand with it – among the 'most striking characteristics of the era with the most historically momentous intellectual and practical impact among the trends apparent between 1873 and 1896'.[25]

The second change in the political framework occurred in the field of international trade policy. Protectionism had been on the advance again worldwide since the mid-1870s. Many states responded to the pressure of international economic competition, which had increased greatly concomitant with the advance of economic globalization, by establishing protective tariffs and other barriers to trade. During the world economic crisis this pressure initially bedeviled those branches of industry affected by import competition, but it hit European agriculture with full force not long afterwards. Austria-Hungary, for example, abrogated its trade treaties as early as 1876, ensuring its capacity to pursue an autonomous tariff policy. In 1878 a protective tariff was implemented that still seemed relatively moderate compared to its successors of 1882 and 1887. But it entailed a marked tariff increase for some goods, particularly yarns and textiles, and also required payment of import duties in gold; this de facto amounted to a further general tariff increase. At around the same time, through its customs tariff of 30 May 1878, Italy also took the first step towards a protectionist system. Russia went over to the collection of customs duties in gold in early 1877 – and because of the substantial discrepancy between the exchange rates of paper and gold roubles, this increased the tariff burden on incoming goods by 33 per cent.[26] In Canada, the customs tariff of 1879 marks the turn towards protectionism. From now on, agricultural goods were burdened with an average import duty of 20 to 50 per cent of their value, while the equivalent figure for industrial goods was 20 to 30 per cent.[27] Over the course of the 1870s, Argentina and Brazil also introduced protective tariffs for their still young industries. Finally, following a period of moderate tariffs, the U.S., a bastion of protectionism since the start of the century, had begun to pursue a highly protectionist course as early as 1861 in the form of the Morrill tariff, a course it then consistently pursued.

These signs of a shifting international trade policy climate were keenly noted in the German Empire – just as observers in other countries took note of the protectionist tendencies in Germany. For proponents of protective tariffs, the successes of the protectionist movement in other states exercised a kind of demonstration effect. They gave them the feeling that their demands were in line with the zeitgeist, that they constituted an appropriate and justified response to the economic situation. Pointing to the advance of protectionism across the world was also an excellent means of justifying tariffs in one's own country as a necessary countermeasure. As Ludwig Windthorst described this situation in the Reichstag, no one should believe that 'if all the nations round about us are going down the protectionist path, we alone can open our gates and let in the flood of goods that our own industry ought to be producing'.[28] In an address to the Association for Social Policy, Schmoller even anticipated a 'general tariff war' for which the German Empire must 'arm' itself. Only a 'reformed tariff', one that 'puts us more or less back in the same position as other continental European countries', would give German trade policy the necessary bargaining chips and allow it to achieve favourable trade treaties.[29]

## Bismarck

Despite the historical significance of the complex of economic-political change outlined above, which can only be fully grasped in retrospect, there was no inevitability about the turn of 1879 in the German Empire. The foreign competition in a global market characterized by falling transportation costs, competition that made itself painfully felt in the economic downswing and in the structural crisis of agriculture, the crisis of economic liberalism, and the shift towards protectionism emerging across the world – these things were perhaps necessary but certainly not sufficient conditions for the transformation of trade policy. The influence of the interest organizations was too meagre, the agrarians were still too irresolute and the free trade idea was still too deeply entrenched in too many heads. But what the changes described above generated was the condition of possibility for a protectionist shift, a set of circumstances that was initially still very unfixed and that opened up new room for political manoeuvre. Bismarck was quick to recognize this and consistently exploited it. On the level of political events he was the key driver of the shift in trade policy; we cannot explain how the customs tariff of 1879 came about without Bismarck. We may briefly sum up his motives from three perspectives.

First, fiscal policy was of key importance. Over the course of the debate on reform of customs tariffs, Bismarck ostentatiously sought to highlight fiscal policy – as in his letter to the Bundesrat of 15 December 1878 setting out his intentions. He explained that with respect to the tariff issue, for him 'the imperative of financial reform … [was] of prime importance'.[30] This emphasis was also apparent when he presented the customs tariff bill to the Reichstag in person.[31] From the mid-1870s on, the empire's financial problems were in fact increasingly palpable. As its own source of revenue, the empire merely had a few remaining tariffs, a number of consumption and transaction taxes, and a range of operating and administrative revenues of which only that from the postal and telegraph system was significant. Other than that, it was dependent on the so-called *Matrikularbeiträge,* in other words, financial contributions from the states, imperial assets based on French reparations and borrowing. When revenues from tariffs and the indirect taxes accruing to the empire fell rather than grew as a result of the economic downswing, when the French war reparations had been spent but imperial expenditure, particularly on the armed forces, continued to rise, the empire increasingly had to fall back on financial contributions from the states, such that they increased annually from 51 million marks in 1874 to 70 million in 1878/79.[32] In the late 1870s, national debt increased even more dramatically. In 1877, it stood at only 16 million marks, but it soared to 72 million in 1878 and 139 million in 1879.[33] The financial crisis also afflicted the individual states. Increasingly, they faced pressure from two sides: from increasing financial contributions and, thanks to the economic crisis, from falling revenues generated by the direct taxes accruing to them. Further, the entire tax system was extremely antiquated and seemed to be reaching the limits of its capacity – there was thus an irrefutable need for comprehensive reform. Bismarck saw the fundamental reorganization of the tax and fiscal system as a central and pressing political task. Towards the end of 1875, in a speech to the Reichstag, he made his first public reference to the 'Herculean task' of 'total tax reform', a vital step that must include 'tariff reform'.[34] After a number of failed attempts to find new sources of revenue for the empire, given the rising tide of protectionism in the country a comprehensive system of import tariffs increasingly began to seem like the solution. Overall, he thought, salvation no longer lay in a small number of select fiscal tariffs but in a return to the 'principle that every item that crosses our borders should be liable to duty', though with the exclusion of a number of indispensable industrial raw materials.[35] The additional revenue expected as a result of the revision of the customs tariff (Bismarck reckoned on a figure of at least 80 million marks), should – this was the reform's first goal – ensure 'the empire's financial autonomy', making it more independent of the states.[36] Rather than an 'irksome boarder', the empire must now take on the role of 'the individual states' generous provider'.[37] In other words, the new customs revenue should put the empire in a position to reverse the flow of financial contributions.

The states' finances thus having been much improved, and this was the second goal of Bismarck's plans, they would be in a position to restructure their own tax systems. Prussia, for example, would have been able to abolish the class tax as well as the income tax for all incomes up to 6,000 marks while also relieving the tax burden on agriculture and local government authorities.[38] Third, a step would have been taken towards Bismarck's goal of 'leaving the troubled waters of direct taxes for the plain sailing of indirect ones'.[39] Bismarck believed that indirect taxes and duties were perceived as less burdensome by taxpayers and should therefore be given preference, while in much of Germany direct taxes 'had reached a level that is oppressive and does not seem justified economically'.[40] Finally, the entire issue also had an antiparliamentary aspect. The adoption of a customs tariff that would apply over a lengthy period of time would have undermined the Reichstag's revenue appropriation rights, which it de facto possessed as a result of its annual assessment of the states' financial contributions.[41]

Second, Bismarck's motivations also included a changing attitude towards trade policy under the influence of the economic crisis from 1873 on. The mounting flood of petitions and memoranda, the protectionist press campaigns and agitation pursued by the economic interest organizations, the gloomy economic prognoses of Bismarck's banker Gerson von Bleichröder and his criticisms of the government's free trade course – these things could not fail to register with a politician as convinced as Bismarck was of the decisive role played by material interests.[42] In any case, Wilhelm I was soon to vote for a '"system of moderate protective tariffs"' and insisted that he '"had always had reservations about the lowering of tariffs and fought the elimination of iron tariffs in the last sitting of the state council"'.[43] Delbrück's resignation in April 1876 seems symbolic of the imperial chancellor's changed view of trade policy. Delbrück had always been the figurehead of economic liberalism in the government. Though Bismarck later gave varying versions of Delbrück's departure and the reasons for it, there is no doubt that Bismarck's turn away from the 'principle of free trade', the fact that he was no longer willing to back Delbrück 'if he continued to base his economic policy on Manchesterian principles', played a significant role – and this was also the impression that was made.[44]

As with many of his contemporaries, Bismarck's shift away from free trade towards protectionism occurred in two stages. First, he turned his back on the idea of unilateral free trade. Very much in line with a reciprocal trade policy, he felt that the government must see to it that 'with respect to the export of the most important products of German industry to other states, the conditions that apply are at least as favourable as those under which the import of industrial goods from those states to Germany takes place'.[45] In order to achieve this, Bismarck called for retaliatory trade policy measures to be taken against those countries that discriminated against German producers through import duties or export subsidies. In Bismarck's opinion, the 'unjust chicanery' to which German heavy industry was 'exposed as a result of France's *aquits-à-caution*' could only be 'brought to an end by means of genuine retaliatory measures'.[46]

Over the course of 1877, while deeply engaged in trade policy issues following Delbrück's departure and surrounded by protectionist advisors such as Wilhelm von Kardorff and Christoph Tiedemann, Bismarck then entered the second stage of his support for protectionism, his focus shifting from retaliatory to protective tariffs. The German economy must now be protected not just from other countries' trade policies but also from international economic competition. As Bismarck saw it, protective tariffs must apply not just to industry but to agriculture as well. At a time when many agrarians were still vacillating over their trade policy stance, Bismarck saw 'Germany's agricultural population', which was increasingly exposed to international price competition, as 'close to ruin' and viewed state intervention to help it as a 'question of survival'. But Bismarck felt that German agriculture could only be effectively helped 'if we protect it against competition from Russia, Austria and America'.[47] The solidarist protectionist system now taking shape ever more clearly in Bismarck's thinking and statements, one that encompassed virtually every branch of the economy, was not only of great benefit to fiscal policy. It also had the enormous advantage of being easier to implement politically. With a cool gaze, Bismarck concluded that political resistance to protection for specific economic sectors was directed mostly 'against the advantages' that 'this provides certain branches of production, supposedly at others' expense'. Bismarck thus saw a tariff system that avoided such 'privileges' as far more viable. This system 'would be applied equally to *all* items that cross our borders from abroad by imposing on them without exception an ad valorem duty, thus ensuring, on the basis of a justified national egotism, that German production as a whole and without exception is placed on a rather more favourable footing than that of other countries'.[48]

Finally, Bismarck was also motivated by domestic political considerations, which went far beyond the field of economic and fiscal policy. Since this field is one of the most discussed and best researched in the political history of the German Empire, a brief discussion will suffice here. In short, Bismarck sought to rework the parliamentary and thus ultimately social basis of power on which his policies relied. For a number of different reasons – including Bismarck's enduring conflicts with the left wing of the National Liberals around Eduard Lasker, his implacable resistance to all demands for further parliamentarization and liberal system change, his fear that the heir to the throne might pursue reformist policies and his increasingly polarizing claim to power itself, which 'could tolerate *no* [additional] autonomous power of any kind'[49] – towards the end of the 1870s the chancellor increasingly sought to squeeze the National Liberals out of their key parliamentary position.

Such aspirations, which had long been aired, suddenly seemed much closer to reality. Once again under the heavy influence of Bismarck, party political alternatives to the 'governing coalition' of Free Conservatives and

National Liberals began to appear. First, following their refoundation as the German Conservative Party in 1876, the German Conservatives now sought to join the government. Second, from 1878 on it began to look as though the Kulturkampf might soon be over, which meant that working with the Centre Party on specific issues in the Reichstag now entered into the realm of the possible. Against this background, Bismarck could now hope to achieve a viable parliamentary basis that would tie him less to a specific party and was further to the right within the party political spectrum – if possible including the National Liberals, but excluding their left wing.

Over the course of time it became ever clearer that the issue of protective tariffs, like the Anti-Socialist Law, was an excellent means of achieving the desired rightward shift within the governing Reichstag majority, inflicting severe losses on the National Liberals in the Reichstag elections of 1877 and 1878 and driving a wedge between the party's centre and left. In addition, the debate over tariffs promised to increase the importance of material interests within German politics. Bismarck welcomed this increasing economization of politics and both promoted and exploited it through his cooperation with the interest organizations. 'The scholars without business, without property, without trade, without industry, who live from wages, fees and coupons', he declared to the Prussian finance minister Arthur Hobrecht in 1878, 'will have to subordinate themselves to the producing population during the years of economic challenge or give up their seats in parliament'.[50] This reflected his profound aversion to a liberalism whose conception of politics was informed by the values of the educated bourgeoisie and whose parliamentary representatives 'feel no heat from our sun and remain dry when it rains … who are engaged neither in industry nor agriculture nor carry out a trade, unless they feel fully employed in representing the people according to various schools of thought'.[51] It is also indicative of his support for a party system geared more towards material interests. In Bismarck's eyes, this not only had the advantage of being more realistic and predictable, but also seemed to give the government a more pronounced role as intermediary – which would allow it to play the various interest groups off one another.

It would no doubt be wrong to conceive of the motivations described above as a 'master plan' that had existed all along, a polished political strategy doggedly pursued across the years. That would be to retrospectively implant into the course of history an intentionality that it did not possess, to misconstrue the historical process that led to the turn of 1879 as the work of a strategically planning and fully autonomous actor. Instead, the emphasis must be on the diverse range of interactions between supraindividual forces and tendencies, the actions taken by a variety of actors and their individual motives, and the openness of historical situations. Right in the middle of this period of intense change, for example, at the end of 1877, Bismarck negotiated for months with National Liberal parliamentary leader Rudolf von Bennigsen about his possible entry into the Prussian and imperial governments. Had this been agreed, it might have shifted the trajectory of events in a different direction, though this is not inevitable. And yet – though the 'domestic situation' often changed 'with kaleidoscopic rapidity',[52] though Bismarck's decisions were often a response to alternatives arising from a given set of circumstances – certain goals do emerge as central to his actions over the long term: the disciplining of the National Liberals, the rightward shift of the parliamentary base and the expansion of his own room for manoeuvre through mobilization of economic interests. They might retreat into the background for a time, and they did not fit together neatly to form an elaborate or internally consistent plan. But they were fundamental constants of Bismarck's policies.[53]

## The Turn of 1879

The genesis of the customs tariff of 1879 demonstrates the thrust of the economic and political trends described at the beginning of this chapter, but above all it sheds light on Bismarck's crucial role and the extent to which he cooperated with the various economic interest groups in order to achieve his goals. This applied in two respects even in the buildup to the actual legislative process. First, in 1878, Bismarck managed to establish an enquiry into the situation of the iron, cotton and linen industries, thus addressing one of the key demands of the Central Association of German Industrialists, or CVDI. The very limitation to those branches of industry in which protectionist interests were most strongly represented left no room for doubt about the expected and intended results of the enquiry. The same applied to the appointment of members of the investigative committees, which was carefully supervised by the chancellor, ensuring that in all cases protectionists would have an a priori majority. Finally, the way in which the enquiry went about its work resembled farce rather than unbiased investigation. This applied in particular to the iron enquiry, which was carried out in close contact with the interest organizations. The set of questions that underpinned the committee's information gathering was based on CVDI guidelines. The participating experts, the vast majority of whom had also been proposed by the CVDI and the Association of German Iron and Steel Industrialists, or VDEStI, were then heard in private by the investigative committee, but not before the CVDI general secretary Henry Axel Bueck, residing in the Kaiserhof Hotel, had provided them with a detailed briefing in advance of their appearance; subsequently, he corrected the stenographic reports of their testimony to create the impression of unanimity. In view of this well-rehearsed performance from the textbook of interest-based politics, it comes as no surprise that the iron enquiry ultimately delivered the result desired by Bismarck and the associations. The report was one long lament for the economic plight of the German iron industry and called unanimously for state protection from foreign competition.[54]

Second, in the face of heavy resistance from the Prussian State Ministry (Staatsministerium), after the second assassination attempt on the emperor Bismarck dissolved the Reichstag. Through the new elections, in which he exercised a considerable influence, he created the parliamentary prerequisites for a shift in trade policy. As never before, in 1878 Bismarck managed to stamp his favourite topics onto the election campaign: the struggle against social democracy, the need for a new, anti-Manchesterian economic and trade policy, the precedence of economic over constitutional issues and a general shift away from a politics based on ideas to one informed by interests. Implicitly and explicitly, the government's entire election campaign targeted the National Liberals, and once again particularly their left wing; the goal was the domestic isolation of the National Liberal Party, their transformation into another straightforwardly pro-Bismarck party in addition to the Free Conservatives. In order to achieve this, Bismarck used every tool of election propaganda at his disposal in an attempt to turn the elections into a plebiscite on himself. At the same time, the interest organizations, which the chancellor did all he could to encourage and carefully deployed against the 'antigovernment' parties, now entered into the Reichstag elections with their novel campaigning methods. On the whole, the outcome of the election was a success for Bismarck. While there was no electoral earthquake, there was a clear shift to the right. First, the National Liberals lost 29 of their 128 seats, with the worst losses suffered by the left wing; the Progress Party also fell back from 35 to 26 seats. Second, both conservative parties enjoyed a surge in support: the German Conservatives went up from 40 to 59 seats and the Free Conservatives from 38 to 57.[55]

In the newly elected Reichstag, on 19 October 1878, one day after the Anti-Socialist Law had finally been approved, there emerged a protectionist majority for the first time. Under the aegis of Baron von Varnbüler, 204 of the 397 Reichstag deputies came together to form the Free Economic Union (Freie Wirtschaftliche Vereinigung) and issued a moderately protectionist declaration.[56] 'In view of the trade policies being pursued in most of the countries around Germany, in recognition of the deficiencies of the German customs tariff, which is damaging the prosperity of the people, and in light of the ongoing crisis afflicting German commerce and agriculture', the parliamentarians came out – though initially in a rather vague way – in favour of a fundamental turn towards protectionism.[57] Better than the final vote on the customs tariff, in which party discipline and superordinate political perspectives played a major role, the party political profile of the advocates of protective tariffs can be seen in the distribution of signatures beneath the 'declaration of the 204'. It was signed by 81 deputies from the Centre Party, 39 Free Conservatives, 36 German Conservatives and 27 National Liberals. This corresponded to 87 per cent of the Centre grouping, 69 per cent of the Free Conservatives, 60 per cent of the German Conservatives and 28 per cent of the National Liberals. So at this stage only the Centre Party was pursuing a genuinely uniform and staunchly protectionist course. Both conservative parties, meanwhile, continued to include a strong free trade minority. Particularly in the case of the German Conservatives, with their clear links to agrarian interests, this points again to the ambiguous stance on trade policy in German agriculture, particularly east of the Elbe, in the early 1870s. This impression is reinforced if we look solely at German Conservative deputies from agrarian eastern Germany: only 52 per cent of them signed the protectionist resolution.[58]

His hand strengthened by the 'declaration of the 204', Bismarck abandoned all reserve and went on the offensive. On 28 October 1878 he informed the governments of the other member states of his plan to reform the customs tariff, and on 12 November in the Bundesrat he proposed setting up a tariff commission to prepare the new legislation. In a letter to the Bundesrat of 15 December that was eventually made public, the so-called Christmas letter, he officially unveiled his views on the scale of the reform project and set out the principles and goals of his new customs and trade policy.[59] On 3 January 1879 the tariff commission, led by former Württemberg minister Varnbüler, wasted no time in beginning its work; by 26 March it had already produced a draft customs tariff. This immediately went to the Bundesrat, which approved it just a few days later on 3 April without it even having been presented to the committees for scrutiny in the normal way. In the Reichstag the debate on the customs tariff bill, introduced by Bismarck himself with a lengthy speech, began on 2 May; finally, on 12 July 1879 the new customs tariff was approved by parliament at a third reading by 217 votes to 117.[60]

In light of the rapidity of the legislative process and emphatic result of the parliamentary vote, it is easy to forget the substantial difficulties that Bismarck's programme of protective tariffs came up against in the associations and parties, the states and even the Prussian State Ministry. But the shift away from free trade itself, it turned out, was not the main obstacle, since after years of economic crisis fundamentalist free traders were now in the minority almost everywhere. In fact, the core problem was the form of the planned protectionist system. Particularly problematic was the interlinkage of agrarian and industrial protective tariffs. On the one hand, even those agrarians who had campaigned intensively for their sector to be protected from international competition felt quite disinclined to support the introduction of tariffs on industrial goods. This was because these tariffs seemed likely to increase the cost of agricultural equipment and machines. They had fought fanatically for their abolition just a few years before. On the other hand, industry – and this applies both to export industry as well as those branches facing import competition – had absolutely no interest in tariffs on agricultural products because these would inevitably increase the prices of foodstuffs. This in turn would ultimately increase wages and thus costs. Despite the 'steadfast alliance' of agriculture and industry invoked so often and so ostentatiously at the interest organizations' meetings, as, for example, at the tenth Congress of German Farmers (Kongreß Deutscher Landwirte) in February 1879, despite appeals from the organizations' functionaries to 'speak with one voice',[61] this fundamental discrepancy of interests reared its head again and again. The structure of the agrarian-industrial protectionist alliance was thus highly fragile. In early 1879, for example, both the CVDI and the VDEStI still refused to actively support demands for agricultural tariffs. At the same time there were calls among agrarians to abandon the alliance with industrial protectionists. In the Bundesrat too there was no lack of resistance to agricultural tariffs. The tariff commission that he had appointed failed to back the level of cereal tariff that Bismarck wanted – not just the representatives of other states, but also Prussian delegates either voted for tariff-free status or a much lower rate. Finally, in the Reichstag, the rye tariff, which was higher than that proposed in the Bundesrat bill, was also rejected at the first attempt.[62]

Only against this background can we fully grasp Bismarck's crucial importance to bringing about the tariff policy volte-face of 1879. He was not only the main force driving the customs tariff rapidly through the legislative bodies; he also managed, right to the end, to maintain the linkage between industrial and agrarian tariffs and hold together the constantly diverging protariff parliamentary groups. He used every tactical instrument at his disposal to achieve this. He threatened some while making promises to others; he applied public pressure and mobilized the interest organizations against the political parties. He left the Prussian ministers and the representatives of the other states in no doubt as to the indivisibility of his protectionist programme. When the tariff committee began its deliberations, he even went so far as to task Tiedemann with 'telling Varnbüler explicitly that he would go along with the protectionist flow only as long as agriculture was also given protection. If this failed to happen, he would try again with the free traders.'[63]

Through a plethora of responses to petitions and letters sent to him that were released for publication, the so-called peasants' letters, Bismarck sought to convince the public that the state should pay agriculture 'the same attention as industry'.[64] At the same time he set out to gain good publicity from the agricultural organizations, as his 'efforts only had a chance of success if the majority of the relevant agricultural population throw their weight behind them'.[65] In the buildup to the Reichstag debate on the new customs tariff, in correspondence with Karl Ernst von Thüngen-Roßbach, condemned by Lasker as the 'unconditional assumption of the agrarian programme … in the agitational sense', the chancellor openly encouraged the Bavarian 'tax reformer' to support his agricultural demands more emphatically and vociferously than before.[66] The 'decent tariff'[67] on cereals demanded by Thüngen-Roßbach could be achieved only if 'above all, the representatives of agriculture in the Reichstag take action, get together and table motions'. He, Bismarck, had done everything within his power to 'keep agriculture on equal terms with industry', but he required 'greater and more practical support on the official and journalistic level' if he was to have any prospect of success.[68]

It bears repeating: Bismarck did not create the protectionist movement. It was the product of superordinate economic and political processes that began to gain traction in the 1870s. The international triumph of protectionism in the final quarter of the nineteenth century leads us to suspect that protectionist efforts would have borne fruit sooner or later within German tariff and trade policy. But when and how the change of direction in trade policy actually occurred, under what political conditions and in what form – for this Bismarck bore much of the responsibility. In the context of the policy shift of 1879, he was the 'man of action', the architect. His crucial role also points to the fairly large room for manoeuvre that the executive still enjoyed under the circumstances of the time, and that enabled the chancellor to pursue largely autonomous goals that transcended the field of trade policy.

Conversely, this does not mean either that Bismarck acted in line with a long-term strategic plan or that he was entirely successful in achieving his goals. Even in the closing stages of the negotiations on the tariff reform, he had to accept significant curtailments of his fiscal policy objectives. It emerged that the customs tariff reform only stood a chance of being accepted in the Reichstag if Bismarck either accommodated the National Liberals or the Centre Party on the issue of 'constitutional guarantees'. In order to counter the risk to the Reichstag's revenue appropriation rights arising from the increased revenues likely to result from the new tariffs,

Rudolf von Bennigsen of the National Liberals proposed granting the parliament the right to set the coffee tariff as well as the tariff and consumption tax on salt on an annual basis. Initially, the Centre Party also called for annual approval of the salt tax, but gave this demand up over the course of the negotiations. It was, however, uncompromising in its insistence on the adoption of the so-called Franckenstein clause, according to which the revenues from tariffs and the tobacco tax in excess of the sum of 130 million marks per year should be divided between the individual states in line with their population. Since the empire's financial needs were well above 130 million marks, this would leave it dependent on the states' financial contributions, though in contrast to the past these would be partly financed in advance through transfers from the empire. This meant that the Reichstag would retain its right to set the budget, as it would continue to be responsible for the annual setting of the states' financial contributions, while the federal element would be strengthened, as the empire was still dependent on the contributions from the individual states, which were enjoying a marked increase in revenue.

For a number of reasons, Bismarck decided to join forces with the Centre Party and adopt the Franckenstein clause. Ultimately, conceding to the Centre Party's federalist demands seemed to him less dangerous than extending the authority of the Reichstag as associated with Bennigsen's motion. Second, cooperation with the Centre Party was a good way of laying the foundation for an end to a messy Kulturkampf. Third, Bismarck's relationship with the National Liberals had by now deteriorated so much that giving into their constitutional conditions, even to the smallest extent, was anathema to him. Fourth and finally, in contrast to Windthorst, Bennigsen could not guarantee that his parliamentary grouping would vote as one for the package of tariffs and taxes; only with the Centre Party, then, could a secure majority be obtained in the Reichstag. By opting for the 'pittance paragraphs of the so-called Franckenstein clause',[69] the chancellor sacrificed his main fiscal policy goal of making the empire financially independent of the states. In return, he received a stable Reichstag majority for the customs tariff reform and a substantial increase in state revenue. Ultimately, this was fiscally beneficial both to the individual states and the empire, and he avoided paying the price of additional constitutional guarantees.[70]

## The 'Autonomous' Tariff Policy of the 1880s

For the German Empire the introduction of the customs tariff of 1879 was merely the first step in a tariff policy that increasingly tightened the protectionist screw over the following decade. Subsequent to a number of minor revisions in 1881, 1882 and 1884, it was above all the tariff reforms of 1885 and 1887 that strengthened the German system of protective tariffs. It was overwhelmingly agricultural interests that benefited from the expansion of the protectionist system. While the customs tariff of 1879 had primarily implemented a system of protective industrial tariffs – addressing the concerns of heavy industry and the textile industry in particular – and had introduced only meagre duties on cereals, agricultural tariffs were clearly to the fore in the tariff amendment of 1885, though they were linked with a number of tariff increases for the products of cotton spinning, the lace and embroidery industry, the brick and asbestos industry and a few other smaller industrial sectors. Finally, the tariff reform of 1887 was a purely agrarian affair and was limited almost exclusively to a further major increase in cereal tariffs.[71] As a result, as we can see in table 3.1, if we take as our starting point the complete absence of tariffs in the 1870s, the tariff burden grew in three stages, to 50 marks per tonne in the case of wheat and rye, 40 marks for oats and 22.5 marks for barley. In relation to German wholesale prices, for wheat and rye, the two most important types of cereal, this meant an increase in the tax burden of up to 30 and 40 per cent, respectively. In view of this development, the warning given by Eduard Lasker in 1879 in the Reichstag debate on customs tariff reform took on a virtually prophetic quality. For the time being, Lasker predicted, 'the industrialists have triumphed over the farmers with respect to grain tariffs', since the latter had 'been compensated with something that is not equivalent'. Soon, however, 'the farmers [would] ... force their way into the limelight with the powerful backing of the chancellor', to encash the 'bill' they had drawn and ask, 'Where is the rest of our money?'[72]

The tariff policy of the 1880s found its necessary supplement in the trade treaty policy pursued by the German government. With respect to its own customs tariff, between 1877 and 1892 the German Empire almost exclusively concluded pure most-favoured-nation treaties. In other words, it merely assured a given treaty partner that it would not be treated worse than any other state with which trade treaties had been signed. The alternative treaty variant, an agreement in which both sides lowered or at least fixed (i.e., ruled out increases in) tariffs for particular goods for the duration of the treaty, was used only in a small number of exceptional cases. The German government concluded such trade treaties only with Spain (1883, 1885), Italy (1883), Switzerland (1881, 1888) and Greece (1885) – and even in these cases, the German customs tariff was fixed or reduced only in a small number of cases, chiefly with respect to items categorized as raw materials and consumer goods. The far more important trade treaties with Belgium (1865) and Austria-Hungary (1868), meanwhile, which en-

**Table 3.1.** Cereal tariffs and prices, 1880–89

| | *Wheat* | | | *Rye* | | | *Oats* | | | *Barley* | | |
|---|---|---|---|---|---|---|---|---|---|---|---|---|
| | I Tariff in m. per t | II Price in m. per t | III Tariff as per cent of price | I Tariff in m. per t | II Price in m. per t | III Tariff as per cent of price | I Tariff in m. per t | II Price in m. per t | III Tariff as per cent of price | I Tariff in m. per t | II Price in m. per t | III Tariff as per cent of price |
| *1880* | 10 | 218 | 4.6 | 10 | 188 | 5.3 | 10 | 148 | 6.8 | 5 | 158 | 3.2 |
| *1881* | (1 January 1880) | 220 | 4.5 | (1 January 1880) | 195 | 5.1 | (1 January 1880) | 151 | 6.6 | (1 January 1880) | 152 | 3.3 |
| *1882* | | 204 | 4.9 | | 152 | 6.6 | | 132 | 7.6 | | 132 | 3.8 |
| *1883* | | 186 | 5.4 | | 145 | 6.9 | | 128 | 7.8 | | 132 | 3.8 |
| *1884* | | 162 | 6.2 | | 143 | 7.0 | | 131 | 7.6 | | 139 | 3.6 |
| *1885* | 30 | 161 | 18.6 | 30 | 141 | 21.3 | 15 | 134 | 11.2 | 15 | 132 | 11.4 |
| *1886* | (1 July 1885) | 151 | 19.8 | (1 July 1885) | 131 | 23.0 | (1 July 1885) | 120 | 12.5 | (1 July 1885) | 122 | 12.3 |
| *1887* | 50 | 164 | 30.4 | 50 | 121 | 41.4 | 40 | 98 | 40.8 | 22,5 | 109 | 20.7 |
| *1888* | (26 November 1887) | 172 | 29.0 | (26 November 1887) | 135 | 37.2 | (26 November 1887) | 123 | 32.5 | (26 November 1887) | 115 | 19.6 |
| *1889* | | 188 | 26.6 | | 156 | 32.2 | | 150 | 26.7 | | 131 | 17.1 |

*Sources:* I: Kaiserliches Statistisches Amt (ed.), *Deutsche Landwirtschaft*, 151–52, 154–55; II: 1880: *Monatshefte zur Statistik des Deutschen Reichs* 43, 1880, XII 52*; 1881–89: *StHbDR*, section 1, 474 (wheat, rye, oats: Berlin wholesale prices; barley: Danzig prices of domestic brewing barley); III: my own calculations (III = I ÷ II × 100).

tailed comprehensive tariff commitments, were not renewed but replaced by pure most-favoured-nation treaties.

At one time, in the early 1860s, the most-favoured-nation clause had gone a long way to turning Europe into a zone of relative free trade with astonishing rapidity, as it ensured that every new tariff reduction agreed through trade treaties was immediately generalized (see chapter 2). Now, in the 1880s, it became apparent that it did not have this impact without accompanying trade treaties entailing comprehensive tariff concessions. For the German government, the conclusion of pure most-favoured-nation treaties in this period had a dual advantage. First, as a most-favoured nation giving nothing in return, Germany benefited from the tariff reductions that the other states had granted one another within the framework of the European network of trade treaties, which was still largely intact. It is true that there was no trade treaty with France, the linchpin of this treaty system, but in line with Article 11 of the Treaty of Frankfurt, signed in 1871 after the Franco-German War, there was a mutual commitment to the most-favoured-nation principle with respect to all the tariff policy concessions granted to the U.K., Belgium, Austria-Hungary, Russia, Switzerland and the Netherlands. Second, and this is the key point in this context, the general limitation to pure most-favoured-nation agreements was the necessary condition for the German Empire's autonomous tariff policy beginning in 1879. Only foregoing the trade treaty commitment to specific tariff items put German tariff policy in a position to increase its tariff rates at any time – an option that, as we have seen, was used extensively.[73]

Which factors propelled and fostered German protectionism in the 1880s? It was to a great extent trends and forces already nascent in the buildup to the shift of 1879 that now made their full impact.

This applies, first of all, to by far the most important cause of the rapid development of German agricultural protectionism in the final decade of the Bismarck era: the globalization of the market in agricultural goods, particularly cereals, which was entering its peak period. Following price developments that exhibited no clear trend in the second half of the 1870s, the development of a functioning world market in cereals was reflected irrefutably, and in a way that was evident to everyone, in a dramatic price drop beginning in the early 1880s. As evident in table 3.1, which shows average annual prices in Berlin (as far as available), which were about average for the whole of Germany, the price of the four main types of cereals declined by between 28 and 38 per cent of their initial value between 1881 and 1886/87. Contemporaries were fully aware of the causal nexus of globalization and declining prices. There was 'no doubt', to quote the government's justification for the tariff amendment of 1885 in the Reichstag, 'as to the cause of the phenomena and that our cereal prices are undergoing a steady decline, regardless of the strong growth of the population and meagre increase in the area under cultivation'. While earlier, 'because of the costliness and slowness of transportation', each country was dependent on a relatively limited area for its cereal supplies and 'the price level of cereals was almost entirely dependent on the crop yields from this area', now,

> as a result of the perfection of the means of communication, which has opened up the interior of continents through railways, replaced sailing ships with steamers and made the movement of goods quicker and cheaper, cereals have ... become the object of a powerfully organized world trade, which pulls boundless new territories into a cycle of production that brings together in the same market the products of the most remote areas and diverse climates.

In this way, German agriculture was 'exposed to competition from countries whose rich soils are often available for almost cost-free occupation' and that can be cultivated by machine,

> while in other territories, because of the people's modest needs, the costs of manual labour remain far below the levels reached in this country and finally, in most of our competitor countries, the burden on the land for state and municipal purposes is negligible. ... Under these circumstances, we are unlikely to see positive changes in our agriculture in the near future. In all probability, the pressure of overproduction will make itself felt on cereal prices for many years and may even increase.[74]

In view of this, with unprecedented intensity and unanimity the agrarian interest organizations went on the offensive vis-à-vis state institutions and the public in order to achieve emergency aid for agriculture, which was under pricing pressure. Calls for higher cereal tariffs played a prominent role here. The Bundesrat, Reichstag, chancellery and the ministries of the individual states found themselves bombarded by mass petitions, some of them signed by tens of thousands of people. The greater the fall in prices, despite tariffs, the more the agrarians stepped up their protectionist demands. Two years after the Reichstag had accepted the 1885 tariff reform by an overwhelming majority, a reform that went significantly beyond the government bill at various points in its tariff increases – the tariffs for wheat and rye were trebled over the figure for 1879 – the German Agricultural Council, for example, again called for a doubling of the most important cereal tariffs.[75]

But the fact that this call for protective tariffs by the DLR made it into the government's tariff amendment practically unchanged is not just connected to the high level of political pressure applied by the agricultural producers. It is also related to the fact that the government – and this mainly means Bismarck, who added the office of Prussian trade minister to his remit in 1880 – was only too pleased to accommodate agricultural desires. This is the second force that helped to foster German protectionism in the 1880s. After 1879, the chancellor intimated repeatedly that he 'placed great importance' on raising the existing tariffs;[76] again and again, he threw his political weight behind strengthening tariff protection, particularly for agriculture.[77] At the same time, the focus of his arguments shifted. He had justified the tariff reform of 1879 to the outside world overwhelmingly on fiscal policy grounds, but it was now the notion of protection that came increasingly to the fore. The government bill aimed to achieve nothing less than the 'protection of national labour', as Bismarck explained in 1885 in the Reichstag debate on amending the customs tariff.[78] But no other branch of industry so urgently required state protection as German agriculture, which 'is in a worse condition than all others' and whose 'disastrous' state the chancellor never tired of describing at length.[79] As Bismarck saw it, another reason to help out the agrarians with protective tariffs was that in case of war only a strong agricultural base could ensure that the country could largely provide for its own cereal needs, while too much dependency on cereal imports would make the German Empire vulnerable. This argument invoking an autarkic war economy played a major role, particularly in the public defence of cereal tariffs. 'What position would we be in at times of war … if we really got to the point of being unable to grow the cereals that we must necessarily consume', Bismarck asked in a 1882 Reichstag speech, 'if we have no Russian cereal imports and are perhaps blocked at the same time from maritime routes, in other words if we have no grain at all?'[80]

Regardless of his ongoing willingness to grant state protection to agriculture, it is evident that with respect to calls for agricultural tariffs, Bismarck was increasingly driven rather than the driver. In 1878/79, he had left no stone unturned to encourage agrarian tariff campaigns and the engagement of those advocating agricultural interests. By 1887, like Prussian agriculture minister Robert Lucius, he increasingly perceived the pressure from conservative landowners in the Prussian House of Representatives as troublesome 'agrarian greed'.[81] His efforts to achieve new protective measures for agriculture no longer went far enough for the agricultural interest organizations. The conservative *Kreuzzeitung* saw agriculture standing 'like Cinderella … before the gates of the castle and before the gates of ministries', waiting 'for help'. It even went so far as to openly reproach Bismarck: 'Those government officials who, under present-day conditions', take it upon themselves 'to deny agriculture its most urgent needs … do not fully grasp the importance of the historical moment' and 'are betraying the history of the state at an important moment'.[82]

A third force, the momentum of the system of protective tariffs established in 1879, also helped expand protectionism. I do not just mean the general problem of economic policy that existed in the German Empire and in many other comparable cases, namely, that the introduction of tariffs for certain economic sectors aroused protectionist desires in other branches that did not in fact require protection, thus generating new calls for protective tariffs. In a more specific sense, this also applies to the internal logic inherent in every protectionist system, according to which certain tariffs, unless they are completely ineffective, necessarily trigger the introduction of other tariffs. A well-known example of this is the complementary relationship between flour tariffs and those for cereals. If there is no tariff on flour or if it is not set at a high enough level, in accordance with the extraction rate, then the relevant actors will simply import flour rather than cereals, thus avoiding the cereal tariffs. Another example is the impact of the tariff on wine introduced in 1879. In 1880 it led to a substantial increase in the import of wine grapes from Austria-Hungary and Italy, as they still entered the country duty-free. In order to make this avoidance of the wine tariff impossible and ensure that German winegrowers got the full benefit of the planned tariff, in 1881 the German Empire added a grape tariff to the wine tariff. However, this applied not just to the wine grapes relevant to wine production, but also to table grapes. Although these were a completely different type of grape, the payment of duty on them was accepted, nolens volens, as it was impossible to reliably distinguish between the different types of grapes at the border.[83]

Finally, the development of the German system of protective tariffs was also propelled by the international wave of protectionism, the beginnings of which could already be seen at the end of the 1870s, but which made its full impact only during the following decade. In terms of its economic cause, as in Germany the worldwide protectionist trend was a response to the new competitive relations and redistribution of income that the first wave of globalization had brought in its wake. Further, however, the system of international trade policy relations itself generated a dynamic that fostered protectionism. Tariff increases in one state frequently provoked matching responses by trading partners. Sometimes, costly protectionist measures were based on no more than the anticipation of similar steps by the other side. In this way, over the course of the 1880s there developed a vicious circle or, better, an upward spiral of tariff increases and other trade-inhibiting measures.

The result was an out-and-out trade policy arms race in which, apart from the German Empire, all other major continental European states – Russia and Austria-Hungary, France and Italy – were involved. Having already raised the real customs burden by one-third in 1878 by demanding tariff payments in gold, from 1880 on the Russian government ramped up customs duties every year – partly by making major increases in tariffs on individual product groups, and partly, as in 1885 and 1890, by imposing additional tariffs on almost all incoming goods. The new Russian customs tariff of 1891, which amalgamated all the new tariffs of the preceding years as well as imposing another rise, marked the provisional peak of a development that made Russia the home of across-the-board, high protectionism, ahead even of the U.S. For Austria-Hungary, the German customs tariff of 1879 and the failure of the German-Austrian negotiations on a comprehensive tariff treaty triggered the tariff revision of 1882. On the German model, this introduced agricultural tariffs and entailed numerous tariff increases, and even went beyond German rates for industrial tariffs. In 1887, a wide range of tariffs saw additional increases – here again we see the attempt to do everything possible to avoid falling behind concurrent tariff increases in neighbouring countries. In France the obstacles to an increase in agricultural tariffs were removed through the tariff law of 1881, which exempted most agricultural goods from the impending trade treaty negotiations. In lockstep with Germany, the tariffs on cereals and livestock were increased substantially in 1885 and 1887. Finally, the Méline tariff, introduced in early 1892 after three years in the pipeline, marked the final victory of protectionism in France. In Italy too, a fundamental tariff revision in the direction of protectionism had been underway since the early 1880s. The result was the general customs tariff of 1887, which placed tariffs for agricultural and industrial goods on a level similar to those in Germany, France and Austria-Hungary.[84]

In brief, far more clearly than in the run-up to 1879, let alone the free trade era from 1860 on, in the 1880s it was the impulses emanating from a rapidly advancing economic globalization that determined the course of German foreign trade policy. This is not to endorse an economic determinism, but rather to identify a factor that exercised an increasing influence on the direction of tariff and trade policy via the articulation and organization of the relevant interest groups. Once established, the protectionist system also exhibited a substantial self-perpetuating power. The significance of other influences, meanwhile, declined along with the government's capacity to instrumentalize foreign trade policies in pursuit of other political goals.

CHAPTER 4

# The Caprivi Trade Treaties

## Caprivi's 'New Course' for Trade Policy

Following Bismarck's departure the approach to trade policy changed once again. New imperial chancellor Leo von Caprivi broke with the autonomous tariff policy and concluded a series of trade treaties that laid down the German Empire's approach to tariffs over the long term, namely, a twelve-year period. Agreements were reached with Austria-Hungary, Italy, Switzerland and Belgium in 1891 and with Serbia, Romania and Russia in 1893/94.[1] Every treaty followed the same principle: the German Empire reduced agricultural tariffs, with tariffs on breadstuffs (wheat and rye), for example, falling from 50 to 35 marks per tonne. In return the treaty partners declared their willingness to lower tariffs on German industrial exports. The system of agricultural protection, which had developed rapidly under Bismarck, was thus cut back moderately in order to clear the way for the export of German industrial goods. Perhaps even more important to the producers than the tariff reductions granted by trade partners was the predictability achieved by the fixing of customs tariffs through the treaties and the lengthy period they covered. Caprivi rightly highlighted this point when he presented the first series of trade treaties to the Reichstag. 'Scientific works' and 'reports by chambers of commerce' agreed, according to the imperial chancellor, that 'the first requirement for every industry is being able to count on longer periods of time, knowing what it must adapt itself to; if it is granted such longer time periods, it will find a way to rise to the challenges it faces'.[2]

The main reason for the new shift in trade policy strategy was the risk entailed in the international trade policy situation of the early 1890s for a German economy that was by now largely geared towards the world market. On the one hand, the German economy's dependence on foreign trade had increased continuously in the wake of advancing globalization. In 1889–93 the German import rate was already 17.1 per cent of GNP, and the economy could only afford these imports because 10.6 per cent of

German GNP was sold abroad.[3] On the other hand, as the final decade of the nineteenth century began, protectionism, which had been mounting worldwide since the late 1870s, reached a level that threatened to do severe damage to German exports and thus to the economic development of the German Empire as a whole. Two key export markets increasingly closed their borders to German industrial goods. In the U.S., the McKinley tariff of 1890 marked a new peak in the country's high protectionism. Immediately after it came into force, German exports to the U.S. declined dramatically; from 1890 to 1894, they fell from 417 to 271 million marks.[4] Russia too increasingly shut itself off from foreign industrial imports over the course of the 1880s. Repeated Russian tariff increases, which were partly the result of a strategy of forced industrialization, but partly a direct response to increased German agricultural tariffs, almost halved German exports to Russia from 1880 to 1887.[5] The *Lombardverbot,* a ban on Russian securities decreed by Bismarck in 1887, failed to dissuade the Russian government from pursuing its protectionist course and instead helped intensify the economic conflict between the two countries. German exports were hit particularly hard by Russian differential tariffs on coal and pig iron, which put Upper Silesian imports entering the country through the land border at a clear disadvantage to British imports arriving at seaports.

Against the background of this partial loss of key export markets, those responsible for German foreign trade policies came under pressure to take action when the existing European trade treaty system threatened to collapse at the same time. Hitherto, despite Germany's withdrawal under Bismarck, the network of long-term tariff treaties centred on France that had been established by Cobden and Chevalier in 1860 had remained largely intact and had held protectionist moves in the participating states in check. Through its most-favoured-nation treaties and Article 11 of the Treaty of Frankfurt, the German Empire had benefited from the comparatively low tariff level of the French treaty system without having to make tariff concessions of its own. As foreign secretary Adolf Marschall von Bieberstein put it, the empire had eaten 'fruits from a tree' that 'did not belong to us, that we had not planted and to whose costs we had contributed nothing'. When this tree 'was felled … overnight', because political forces in France that did not want to renew the trade treaties and wished to adopt an autonomous tariff policy succeeded, 'that was the end of the fruit' that had fallen into the lap of the German Empire without it giving anything in return.[6] 1892 threatened to become an annus miserabilis for German trade policy and German exports. By far the majority of European trade treaties, no less than fifteen in number, expired at the beginning of this so-called meteoric year.[7] Should France fail to renew its trade treaties, and in late 1890 this was viewed as certain, then in many European states the autonomous customs tariffs that had already been drawn up would have replaced the conventional tariffs in 1892, dramatically increasing the level of protectionism. A trade policy 'war of all against all' began to seem a real possibility.[8]

The likely radical increase in barriers to the European market, which was so central to German exports, barriers that threatened to have not just a protectionist but also prohibitive effect, would have been a heavy blow to the German national economy. It was not just the government that took this view but also the Reichstag, which adopted the first series of the Caprivi trade treaties by an overwhelming majority. Indeed, had such an important segment of demand within the German economy as that represented by exports fallen away towards the end of the nineteenth century, it would have dangerously slowed down the engine of German economic growth – with all the negative consequences for the labour market and wage levels that were bound to ensue. Germany was going through its third, largest and final wave of emigration. The demographic-economic pressure had already driven just under 1.5 million people overseas between 1880 and 1890,[9] while the economic downturn that began in 1890/91 also made a major impact in this respect. It was precisely this danger of an export-induced economic collapse that Caprivi had in mind when he declared to the Reichstag deputies towards the end of 1891 that 'we must export: either we export goods or we export people. We cannot go on like this, with an increasing population but without the industrial growth to match.'[10]

From the mid-1870s, economic globalization was initially reflected in German foreign trade policies in a one-sided way, namely, in mounting protectionist pressures. It now faced restrictions from an opposing source. In the changed international trade policy situation of the early 1890s, the high degree of German dependence on foreign trade made continuing the policy of increasing protectionism pursued under Bismarck an alternative that could only be realized at great expense to the German economy. This was also how the responsible actors within the Prussian-German government saw things. Without illusion, Caprivi presented his diagnosis of German import dependence before the Prussian State Ministry, highlighting the danger that the 'brutal [trade policy] approach being pursued by North America and Russia as well' might cause Germany 'greater suffering than a European war. We can do nothing about it because we cannot do without imports of such things as cotton and petroleum.'[11] Germany, he underlined before the Reichstag, was 'not in a position … to meet its own needs over the long term. We are utterly reliant on the exchange of products and goods with other states because of the laws of nature, the size of our territory, our climate and our soil.' The dependence of the

German economy on imports and exports – merely two sides of the same coin – 'undoubtedly' made it appear that 'continuing along the same path' of erecting trade barriers 'would be the ruin not just of our industry, and of our workers, but perhaps of our state as well'. Against this background there was just one possibility:

> to attempt to conclude tariff treaties with other states, and in this way expand our markets, gain new markets and those things which our industry can no longer find inside the country, things it has lost abroad as other countries, such as those I have already mentioned, seem determined to close themselves off from us on a long-term basis – to replace these things by coming to agreements with other nearby nations.[12]

Despite Caprivi's assertions, the conclusion of the trade treaties he mentioned was not primarily intended to open up new, previously untapped markets to German exports and dismantle existing trade barriers. Instead, given the protectionist wave spreading across the world, the goal was to create a more or less equivalent replacement for the imploding French treaty system. Only in exceptional cases did the treaty negotiators succeed in reducing the other side's import tariffs to a level much below previous rates. But what was achieved was a general safeguarding of the status quo with respect to Germany's trade treaty partners – the prevention of the new tariff increases looming on all sides. The question discussed so often by historical researchers as to whether the Caprivi trade treaties gave a boost to German exports and resulted in increased growth for the economy as a whole – both of which would presuppose a significant change from the previous situation – is in fact flawed to begin with.[13]

For contemporaries, the dramatic change in the statistical construction of international economic reality towards the end of the 1880s lent credence to the idea that it was imperative to support German exports. The accession of Hamburg and Bremen to the Customs Union in October 1888 and the concomitant change in the basis for calculating imports and exports led to the rupture discussed earlier in German foreign trade statistics (see chapter 1). From 1889 on, German exports seemed lower and imports markedly higher than would have been the case according to the previous system of calculation. As a result, practically overnight a gaping chasm opened up in the trade balance that went way beyond anything that had been seen before. In 1888, imports had exceeded exports by just 57 million marks, which meant that the trade balance was as good as equalized. The statistics for 1889, meanwhile, suddenly showed a trade deficit of 825 million marks,[14] which had come about almost exclusively as a result of changes in the underlying statistical principles. While informed contemporaries were well aware of this fact, the statistical manifestation of the trade deficit still shaped their perception of reality. Only now could it become a discomfiting problem, as it appeared to indicate that 'we … [are] not in a position to pay for what we need to live and to keep our industry motoring along over the long term'.[15] In other words, it was only the rupture in the statistical construction of reality that gave rise to the contemporary perception of a 'calamity'[16] that must be addressed by fostering exports.

Towards the end of 1889, the relevant imperial authorities had already begun to consider trade policy strategies to be implemented following the collapse of the European trade treaty system expected to occur in 1892. Initially, the emphasis was on plans for a central European customs union that built on the old project promoted by Bruck and Schwarzenberg, plans that were also subject to intensive discussion among leading economists at the time.[17] In his memorandum of 25 March 1890, Max von Berchem, director of the Trade Policy Department of the Imperial Foreign Ministry (Auswärtiges Amt) until 1886 and subsequently undersecretary of state,[18] worked under the assumption that it was urgently necessary 'to maintain exports, which have shown no progress for two years'.[19] The fact that, from a present-day perspective, this was a misdiagnosis based on the statistical distortion that arose in 1888/89 – the data series for German exports adjusted for the effects of the Hanseatic cities' accession to the Customs Union shows an increase of 12.1 per cent between 1887 and 1889[20] – changes nothing about the perceptual framework that guided the actions of Berchem and others and highlights once again the reality-creating force of statistical constructs. In order to secure the future of German exports, Berchem proposed the creation of a central European customs union that, in addition to Germany and Austria-Hungary, would include France and Italy as well. The goal was 'to enlarge the internal market by equalizing tariffs while retaining the protective tariff system vis-à-vis countries outside of the Customs Union and strengthening the tariff system vis-à-vis nontreaty states'.[21] A significant influence on Berchem was exercised by his school friend Lujo Brentano,[22] who had called several times over the years for a 'tariff policy agreement with Austria-Hungary and the Christian Balkan states and the securing of this customs area through high protective tariffs on agricultural and industrial products',[23] but Berchem shifted his conception of a central European customs union westwards. The proposals put forward by Gustav von Lindenfels, senior adviser in the Trade Policy Department of the Foreign Ministry (and an expert on trade with western Europe),[24] pointed in a similar direction; he too advocated the most comprehensive possible tariff policy rapprochement between Germany and its neighbours and the introduction of an aggressive general tariff to be applied to all nontreaty states, which was aimed at the U.S. and, even more, at Russia.[25]

It was not long, however, before the view took hold within the ministerial bureaucracy that the project of a central European customs union was not a realistic alternative, either politically or economically. Max von Schraut, for example, undersecretary of state with responsibility for Alsace-Lorraine within the Imperial Ministry of the Interior, had great doubts about France's willingness to enter a customs union dominated by Germany. Above all, though, he highlighted Germany's dependence on the world market and the risk that the founding of a central European customs union featuring high protective tariffs vis-à-vis other countries might '*hamper German exports to these other countries*'. In view of their global orientation, German export interests were 'geared not towards isolation along with a few other countries but towards freedom of action with respect to the general world market'.[26] The trade policy strategy that Caprivi finally declared the official line on 14 July 1890[27] had been set out a week before in a memorandum by Otto Huber, senior adviser in the Imperial Ministry of the Interior.[28]

Like Schraut, Huber did not consider the plan to establish a central European customs union viable. Instead, he proposed that Germany conclude a series of bilateral trade treaties that would entail comprehensive tariff reductions and fixed tariffs on both sides. Treaty negotiations were to be entered into first with Austria-Hungary. On the basis of the conventional tariff agreed on with the Danube Monarchy, the German government would then enter into trade treaty negotiations with other countries. In contrast to a customs union, which would have implied a distinction from nonunion states, the proposed tariff treaties would facilitate the coexistence of straightforward most-favoured-nation agreements with other trade partners important to the German economy. In his memorandum, Huber had already explicitly pointed out that trade treaties favourable to the German export industry could be achieved only if the empire lowered its agricultural tariffs markedly in return.[29] Despite the open opposition of Prussian agriculture minister Lucius von Ballhausen, Huber's proposed 30 per cent reduction in the wheat and rye tariff was ultimately included unaltered in the trade treaties concluded under Caprivi.[30]

It is hard to assess the importance of so-called high politics to the concluding of the Caprivi trade treaties. Overall, issues in international politics certainly appear to have played a role in the thinking of the decision makers in Berlin, without having been decisive. What is certain is that Caprivi was not an exponent of the unrealistic postulate repeatedly propagated by Bismarck in his public announcements – including in his opposition to the trade treaties concluded by his successor – of a clear separation between economics and politics in international relations, explicitly referring to it as a 'mistake'.[31] It was also clear that the treaties with

Austria-Hungary and Italy were bound up with the politics of alliance. Towards the end of the 1880s the German Empire found itself in a 'quiet' tariff war with the other members of the Triple Alliance. The imperial chancellor thus defended the trade treaties before the Reichstag by arguing that 'if we enter into an alliance with other states ... it then becomes impossible to remain in a state of permanent economic war with them'.[32]

Influenced by the theory of world empires, which assumed that a small number of powerful global empires – most often mentioned were the U.S., the British Empire, Russia and sometimes China – would eventually supersede the prevailing system of international power relations,[33] Caprivi went a step further and spoke in favour of a continental European policy of détente through economic means:

> The stage of world history has been enlarged: the proportions have changed and a state that has played a role in history as a major European power may, as far as its material powers are concerned, be among the small states in the foreseeable future. If the European states wish to maintain their global position, then in my view they will not be able to avoid ... banding closely together. It is not impossible that a time will come when they will grasp that they have better things to do than suck the blood out of one another. They will have to deploy every means at their disposal in the battle for economic survival.[34]

In the Prussian State Ministry as well, Caprivi cited the foreign policy dimension of the trade agreement with Austria-Hungary to justify it. It is 'impossible over the long term' to 'maintain a political alliance when one is at war in trade policy terms. The value that the political alliance would have for us is so great that in order to maintain it we should not shy away from making sacrifices even in the field of trade policy.'[35]

But both in the State Ministry and before the Reichstag, arguments in favour of the trade treaties based on the politics of alliance also had an important tactical function. They were designed to provide additional legitimation for the lowering of German agricultural tariffs, and to take the sting out of the expected protests from agrarian conservatives. This is evident not just in the fact that the economic motives outlined above were very much to the fore during the entire decision-making process. It is also apparent in the fact that before the crucial discussion in the State Ministry on the treaty with Austria-Hungary, Caprivi explicitly tasked the Foreign Ministry with helping him prepare by providing him with foreign policy arguments in favour of the trade treaty, thus arming him against any agrarian objections.[36] Overall, then, there is much to suggest that for Caprivi and the Prussian-German ministerial bureaucracy, improving foreign relations was no more than a subsidiary objective in concluding the trade treaties, an objective that was also very well-suited to justifying the treaties in domestic political terms, but one which, on the whole, was clearly subordinate to the central economic aim of enhancing the conditions for German exports.[37]

Among the most interesting aspects of the decision-making process on the German side in the run-up to the first series of trade treaties is the fact that the stimulus for changing the course of trade policy clearly came from the ranks of the executive, while very few initiatives intended to foster exports came from organized industrial interest groups.[38] In 1887 and 1890 the German Trade Association, or DHT, produced three memorandums on Germany's trade relations with Austria-Hungary and Italy that argued against an autonomous tariff policy and in favour of concluding tariff treaties; the top bureaucrats in Berlin drew on these in preparation for the treaty negotiations.[39] But they were basically informative in character and seem to have left no particular impression on the trade experts at the Foreign Ministry or the other imperial offices and ministries. The decision to pursue industry-friendly trade treaties on the basis of a reduction in agricultural tariffs was thus not due to the influence of economic interest groups; it was an autochthonous product of the administrative apparatus. To be more precise, since even this apparatus was internally divided, the new trade policy course was due to the fact that a particular group within the executive, which was absolutely convinced of the need to foster exports, got its way. Adolf Wermuth, who worked in the Imperial Ministry of the Interior, identified its axis as the 'Huber-Goering-Caprivi leadership'.[40]

Indeed, there was only one thing the government could expect from organized economic interests: opposition. Once information about the impending trade treaty negotiations with Austria-Hungary had filtered through to the public, it was the agricultural interest organizations that mobilized first. In a series of petitions, the various regional agricultural associations expressed their opposition to the planned agricultural tariff concessions.[41] The national agricultural associations, the German Peasants' League (Deutscher Bauernbund), the Congress of German Farmers (Kongress Deutscher Landwirte), the Association of Tax and Economic Reformers (Vereinigung der Steuer- und Wirtschaftsreformer) and the German Agricultural Council (Deutscher Landwirtschaftsrat), also expressed their opposition.[42] But industrial interest groups also responded critically to the government's trade policy initiative. In a position statement initiated by Carl Ferdinand von Stumm that appeared in the *Berliner Politische Nachrichten* on 6 February 1891, the executive board of the Central Association of German Industrialists, or CVDI, explicitly declared 'that German industry seeks no advantages that can only be obtained at the expense of agriculture'.[43] It is difficult to gauge the key reasons why the CVDI adopted this stance. The first major motivating factor was undoubtedly a desire to reassure agriculturalists as to the ongoing stability of the agrarian-industrial alliance. Second, and closely bound up with this, some of the leading figures in the CVDI were afraid that the ultimate effect of lowering agricultural tariffs would be to endanger the survival of protective industrial tariffs.[44] Third, the CVDI felt that it had not been involved enough in preparing the trade treaty negotiations to promote the interests it represented. Fourth and finally, the CVDI critique of trade policy may also have been an expression of the dissatisfaction felt by many industrialists with the general political line inherent in the 'new course', which aimed to integrate the needs of the workers and Social Democrats.[45] The least likely explanation is that put forward by the general secretary of the CVDI, Henry Axel Bueck, who claimed that through its declaration the CVDI wished to strengthen the hand of the German negotiators at the trade treaty negotiations taking place in Vienna.[46] In any case, the CVDI's intervention made precisely the opposite impression on the government. It published an article in the *Reichsanzeiger* sharply critical of the CVDI's declaration and questioning its right to speak for German industry.[47]

It was only under the influence of this conflict and very gradually that the government's trade treaty policy gained public support from those branches of industry with a particular interest in exports. On 23 March 1891, the Association for the Protection of the Interests of the German Chemical Industry (Verein zur Wahrung der Interessen der Chemischen Industrie Deutschlands, or Chemieverein) stated that for German industry 'there is absolutely no reason to support the unconditional retention of agricultural tariffs at their current levels', should it prove necessary to lower them in order to achieve favourable trade treaties.[48] The DHT too expressed its support for the trade treaty policy being pursued by Caprivi.[49] But even this changed little about the impression of organizational weakness left by the export-oriented industrial branches. As a result of the worsening economic recession, meanwhile, the heavy industrial-agrarian solidarity declared by the CVDI soon began to crumble. By late April 1891, the CVDI was rushing to assure the government that in principle it took a very positive view of the trade treaties. Ultimately, when it came to the vote in the Reichstag towards the end of 1891, those deputies close to the CVDI voted in favour of the trade treaties and thus the lowering of cereal tariffs.[50]

Trends in cereal and foodstuff prices in the early 1890s made it much easier to enforce the first series of trade treaties and the reduced agricultural tariffs they entailed. By the late 1880s, the price of cereals had recovered markedly from the lows of 1886/87. The Berlin wholesale price for wheat increased from 151 marks per tonne in 1886 to 195 marks in

1890, while the price of rye increased steadily from 121 marks per tonne in 1887 to 170 marks in 1890.[51] This was partly the result of a succession of rather modest harvests; above all, though, it was due to the protective tariffs raised again in 1887. In 1891, the coincidence of a poor German harvest with crop failures in a number of countries from which Germany imported cereals then led to an explosion in the price of cereals and foodstuffs. In Berlin, the average annual price of wheat shot up to 224 marks per tonne and peaked in May at 241 marks; in Mannheim, the average annual price was no less than 241 marks, peaking at 253 marks in November. The price of rye, which had formerly been significantly lower than that of wheat, temporarily exceeded the latter towards the end of 1891 and at 211 marks per tonne (Berlin price) reached an average annual level not seen since the 1850s.[52] As the imperial statistics immediately showed, this also meant that the price of wheat and rye in Germany was higher than the world market price to the full amount of the tariff of 50 marks, and in the west and south of the empire the figure was at times even higher.[53] The situation seemed to worsen dramatically when Russia, Germany's most important supplier of rye by far, issued a ban on the export of rye in response to an extremely poor harvest in late July 1891; by the end of the year, this had been extended to all types of cereals and cereal products.[54]

The substantial price increase, which lasted for several years and applied not just to cereals but in much the same way to other foodstuffs such as potatoes and meat and was reflected in a major increase in the cost of living, bolstered the social and political protest movement against the agricultural tariffs in general and cereal tariffs in particular. The issue of cereal tariffs had already been an important one in the Reichstag elections of 1890 and had helped ensure that the left liberals, and above all the Social Democrats, had seen a major increase in support. In January 1891, the bills put forward by Eugen Richter of the Free-Minded Union and Social Democrat Ignaz Auer were considered in the Reichstag, both of which aimed to reduce or eliminate cereal tariffs, but after a long and contentious debate neither managed to obtain majority support.[55] Over the course of the year, the reduction or temporary abolition of cereal tariffs was also discussed several times in the Prussian State Ministry.[56] In contrast to the French government, however, which implemented a temporary cereal tariff reduction in May 1891, the German government upheld the existing tariffs. The main reason was the fluctuating trade treaty negotiations with Austria-Hungary, in which Caprivi desperately needed the high German cereal tariffs as a 'bargaining chip' to wring reduced industrial tariffs from Germany's negotiating partner.[57] Despite the precarious supply of foodstuffs and the rapid increase in their cost, the imperial chancellor took the view that the 'conclusion of the trade treaties', which were intended to ensure 'a twelve-year framework favourable to industry and also of benefit to workers', was incompatible with a precipitate lowering of cereal tariffs.[58] Caprivi also spoke in support of their retention in this vein before the Prussian House of Representatives.[59] Looking back on the vote there in spring 1891 a few months later, he claimed that there was 'such a strong current of support for a temporary reduction in the agricultural tariffs' that 'if the Prussian government had lifted a finger to achieve it ... then the House of Representatives would have come to a fairly unanimous decision to temporarily lower the tariffs'.[60]

As the year wore on, the protest movement against the agricultural tariffs and the rising cost of foodstuffs continued to grow. There were protests against price increases across the empire; the agitation against agricultural tariffs in both the Social Democratic and left-liberal press was in full flow. When the trade treaties with Austria-Hungary, Italy and Belgium were presented to the Reichstag in December 1891 and cereal prices, far from having fallen, remained at their highest levels, many members of the parliament viewed the tariff reductions associated with the treaties as overdue, and they met with resistance from just a relatively small minority. Centre Party deputy Peter Reichensperger was representative of the views of many others. He was fundamentally convinced of the necessity 'of granting appropriate protection to domestic agriculture', but took the view that it was 'absolutely impossible to maintain the tariff of 5 marks [per 100 kilograms of wheat and rye] on a long-term basis'.[61] Even agrarian conservatives such as Hermann von Arnim conceded 'that lowering the rye tariff at some point was absolutely necessary'.[62] At the final vote, it was not just the Social Democrats who voted in favour of a government bill for the first time in their history, along with the left liberals. The entire Centre Party and almost all Free Conservatives and National Liberals voted in favour of the trade treaty with Austria-Hungary. The only substantial opposition came from the German Conservatives, two-thirds of whom voted against the treaty.[63] The development of cereal prices around 1890 ran counter to the downward trend in the price of foodstuffs, which had lasted since the 1870s, and was reflected in massive consumer protests. This created extraordinarily favourable political parameters for enforcing the reduction in agricultural tariffs contained in the trade treaties, opening up what political scientists often call a window of opportunity.[64]

## The Agrarian-Protectionist Countermovement

This window closed faster than it had opened. Directly after the Reichstag had approved the trade treaties with Austria-Hungary, Italy, Belgium and

Switzerland in December 1891 and January 1892, the price of wheat and rye, the two most politically sensitive cereal types, began to plummet. In January 1892, a tonne of wheat in Berlin still fetched 214 marks, already making it 10 marks cheaper than the annual average for 1891. By the end of the year the price went into free fall, dropping to 149 marks. In the two following years, the downward trend persisted, though at a slower rate. The annual average price of wheat in Berlin fell from 224 marks per tonne in 1891 through 176 marks in 1892 and 152 marks in 1893 to 136 marks in 1894. Price trends followed a very similar pattern in the case of rye. Again, the Berlin price declined from 211 marks per tonne in 1891 through 176 marks in 1892 and 134 marks in 1893 to 118 marks in 1894, not much more than half its initial value.[65] In the case of both cereal types, the year 1894 marked a low point in price trends not reached again in the entire period up to the First World War; by 1895 the price of wheat had begun to climb slightly, and then more markedly from 1896, while in the case of rye the recovery began only in 1897. Essentially, the price drop, which, after 1891, affected wheat and rye far more than other cereal types, simply continued the downward trend that had begun in the 1870s. This price drop was a manifestation of the oversupply on the world agricultural market triggered by globalization over the two previous decades as new cereal producers continued to enter the market, and this oversupply was only slowly soaked up by a corresponding increase in demand in the second half of the 1890s. In this sense the price drop was not an exception but rather a return to the development that had begun with the globalization of the agricultural market, one briefly interrupted in the preceding years by the conjunction of exceptionally bad harvests and the raising of German cereal tariffs. The significance of the tariff reduction implemented by Caprivi to the drop in price was comparatively minor. This becomes immediately apparent if we compare the reduction of the tariff by 15 marks per tonne with the difference in price between 1891 and 1894, which amounted to 88 marks per tonne in the case of wheat and 93 in the case of rye.

Nonetheless, the conjunction of the reduction in agricultural tariffs stipulated in the Caprivi treaties and the fall in the price of wheat and rye in the early 1890s was the crucial trigger for an unprecedented wave of mobilization and organization of agricultural interests. This found its most spectacular and also its most consequential expression in the establishment of the Agrarian League (Bund der Landwirte, or BdL) in February 1893. This event should not, however, obscure the fact that there were also a number of long-term factors that helped advance the formation of a mass agrarian movement. Most significant here was the structural crisis in agriculture since the late 1870s, a direct consequence of economic globalization. While the prices of agricultural goods, above all cereals, continued to fall because of stiff competition on the world market, production costs in German agriculture fell only a little or not at all during the 'Great Deflation'. Expenditure on machines, buildings and fertiliser certainly fell in the 1880s, but wages remained on the same level or even increased, while existing debts were increasingly perceived as an oppressive burden because of falling property and agricultural prices – this applied especially to the large landowners, who often had a great deal of mortgage debt. Everywhere the differing trends in product prices and production costs led to a fall in agricultural profits, frequently to greater debt and to economic ruin for a significant number of farmers.[66]

The perception of crisis was intensified by the overall economic significance of the agricultural sector. This had diminished in the wake of ongoing industrialization, as Germany was rapidly transformed from an agricultural into a modern industrial state, a development that increasingly entered the consciousness of historical actors in the last few decades of the nineteenth century. A diffuse sense of dissatisfaction and uncertainty increasingly spread through rural areas over the course of the 1880s. David Blackbourn puts this collective mental disposition down to the invasion of rural society by the 'other', which he identifies as the expansion of the school system, the military service and the railways.[67] This was reflected in the growing alienation of many farmers from state authority and the traditional system of agricultural associations, fostered the spread of exclusionary ideologies such as anti-Semitism and antiurbanism and led to a crisis of the old dignitaries' parties, which an increasing portion of the rural population felt poorly represented by.

By the early 1890s this complex of agrarian crises had fused into an explosive mix. The conjunction of falling cereal prices and the conclusion of the Caprivi trade treaties, which were perceived as antiagriculture, was the spark that ignited this tinderbox. The call for radical organization by Ruprecht, a tenant farmer from Ransern, in December 1892, which preceded the establishment of the BdL, has become famous in this connection. Ruprecht suggested

> nothing more and nothing less than that we throw in our lot with the Social Democrats and create a solid front against the government, show them that we are no longer willing to be treated as we have been. … We have to stop complaining and start shouting! … We must shout so loudly that the whole country hears us … we must shout so loudly that we are heard all the way to the steps of the throne! … [W]e have to engage in politics, the politics of interest no less; … for it is only by ruthlessly pursuing straightforward interest-based politics that we might perhaps ensure the survival of today's farmers. … So we must cease to be liberal, ultramontane or conservative and to vote on this basis. Instead we must come together to form a single great agrarian party and thereby seek to exercise greater influence on the parliaments and on legislation.[68]

The history of the foundation of the BdL, and its astonishingly rapid rise to one of the most influential interest organizations with one of the largest memberships in the empire, has been researched in-depth, so there is no need to go over it again here.[69] It is important to see the success of the BdL, which was dominant above all in the Protestant areas of northern and central Germany, not in isolation but in the context of the foundation of other organizations such as the Bavarian Peasants' League (Bayerischer Bauernbund) in 1893 and the concurrent transformation in the programs and political style of the existing Catholic peasants' associations. Through a complex interplay between rural self-mobilization and the activities of the organizations' leaders, a broad agrarian protest movement developed throughout the empire during the Caprivi era. Far more radically and with far greater organizational force than previous agricultural organizations, these defined, articulated and sought to enforce politically the interests of 'agriculture'. Despite all the differences in their programmes, organizational structure and ideological tendencies, which could be substantial, what held the various agrarian interest organizations together was agricultural protectionism, the demand that German agriculture be protected from international competition.[70]

The first effects of the agrarian protest movement were already felt at the Reichstag elections of 1893. Though the BdL – still in embryonic form just a few months after its establishment – was unable to intervene in the election campaign, as it did later, with the full weight of its well-oiled propaganda machine, it managed to get more than one hundred of the newly elected Reichstag deputies to commit to its programme. These parliamentarians pledged their support for a catalogue of demands agreed by the league's constitutive assembly, in which agricultural protectionism played a prominent role. At the top of the BdL's list of demands was 'sufficient tariff protection for the products of agriculture and ancillary trades'. The second point in the BdL programme specified what this meant, namely, 'absolutely no reduction in existing tariffs and no trade treaties with Russia and other countries that will result in the lowering of German agricultural tariffs'.[71] That the agricultural protectionist front in the new Reichstag extended far beyond the circle of those deputies committed to the league, the majority of whom came from the two conservative parties, is evident in the fact that the Economic Alliance (Wirtschaftliche Vereinigung) propagated by the BdL and initiated in July 1893 under the aegis of Wilhelm von Kardorff, Berthold von Ploetz and Diederich Hahn managed to attract the support of 140 parliamentarians, more than one-third of the parliament.[72]

The cross-party character of this parliamentary grouping already shows that agricultural protectionism was not just the concern of the German Conservatives and Free Conservatives. The agrarian element in these two parties was large, so there was little conflict with the agricultural interest organizations over economic policy goals. The National Liberals and Centre Party, meanwhile, came under massive political pressure due to the interplay of the agricultural crisis, the growing politicization of the peasantry and the increasing organization of agrarian interests. At the elections of 1893 the National Liberals found themselves confronted with the impending loss of their rural constituencies in a number of regions. In rural Hesse, for example, Otto Böckel's anti-Semitic Central German Peasants' Association (Mitteldeutscher Bauernverein) enjoyed great success, breaking into what was formerly a National Liberal domain. The only thing that prevented these elections from being a complete disaster for the National Liberals was the fact that they had entered into an alliance with the BdL, which provided them with the organizational backup for the election campaign that they themselves lacked. Seven of the nine National Liberal candidates in Hesse were supported by the BdL, while the other two were sympathetic towards it. It is true that this put an end to the anti-Semites' meteoric rise; but the price paid by the National Liberals in Hesse was an overall dependence on the BdL and the concomitant 'agrarianization' of their economic policy platform.[73]

Political Catholicism too faced the threat of voter desertion and major internal conflicts as a result of the agrarian protest movement, which formed partly within the Catholic peasants' associations while also distancing itself from them. In Westphalia, the mood in the countryside was far less explosive than in other regions. This part of the country also had a successful tradition of representation of agrarian interests stretching back to 1862 in the shape of the Westphalian Peasants' Union (Westfälischer Bauernverein), which had close links with the Centre Party. Yet even here there were tensions. In the elections of 1893, Catholic landowner Burghard von Schorlemer-Alst, who was the founder and leader of the Westphalian Peasants' Union, ensured that agrarian candidates stood in three constituencies, having tried in vain to persuade the Centre Party's official election committees to place more emphasis on agrarian candidates.[74] In May 1893 the Centre Party grouping in the Reichstag launched its election campaign with an official statement that is striking testimony to the difficult situation in which the party now found itself with respect to tariff and trade policy. Initially the parliamentary party believed it must defend its solid backing for the first of Caprivi's trade treaties in the preceding legislative period. It had supported the treaties because they

> entailed the fixing of the protective tariffs at least at the level stipulated in these treaties for twelve years, because they gave the political-military Triple Alliance an economic basis and thus greater stability and security over time; and because without them … a chaotic customs war, particularly among our

allies, would have damaged both German industry and agriculture and the Alliance, so necessary to Germany security and to maintaining world peace.

This justification was one-sided in its emphasis on the foreign policy aspects of the trade treaties and the successful defence of the protective tariff principle and made no mention at all of the most important aspect, namely, the promotion of German exports. With respect to future trade policy decisions, what the Centre Party leaders were trying to do here was undermine the agricultural protectionists' increasingly scathing criticisms by underlining that in 'future trade treaty bills ... the interests of German agriculture and of German businesses large and small [must] be our primary concern and doubly assured of our strictest scrutiny and most careful consideration'.[75]

## The German-Russian Trade Treaty

While the domestic political resistance to Caprivi's export-friendly trade policy, which involved a moderate reduction in agricultural protection, thus grew markedly, the advancing globalization of economic relations made it seem vital to continue and expand it. More than anywhere else this dilemma was apparent in Germany's trade relations with Russia. Over the course of the 1880s, a full-blown tariff arms race had developed between the two countries. The increases in Germany's agricultural tariffs in 1887 and the ban on Russian securities decreed by Bismarck in the same year had not compelled the St. Petersburg government to relent. Seemingly unimpressed by German threats, in August 1890 it again raised its tariffs and in June the following year it implemented the so-called Mendeleev tariff, a level of protection that exceeded even the American McKinley tariff of 1890 and had a virtually prohibitive effect on a number of important German exports to Russia. Caprivi initially continued his predecessor's confrontational trade policy course. The trade treaties concluded under his aegis in 1891, which came into force on 1 February 1892, had a clear anti-Russian edge. The reduced agricultural tariffs contained in them not only benefited trade treaty partners, but every state with which the German Empire had a formal or informal most-favoured-nation relationship. In 1892, this made Russia, to which neither of these things applied, the single largest agrarian exporting state to whose products the higher tariffs of the previous general tariff applied rather than the lower tariff rates in the new German treaties.

Negotiations on a trade policy compromise failed to deliver because the German side regarded the reciprocal measures offered by Russia as insufficient. On 1 August 1893 the Russian government reacted to Germany's still differential tariffs, which were hitting Russian agricultural exports hard, by subjecting German goods to a maximum customs tariff specially created for this purpose. This increased most of the tariff rates in the Mendeleev tariff by a further 20 to 30 per cent. What had been a 'cold' customs war between Germany and Russia had thus entered its hot phase. Reciprocal retaliatory trade policy measures escalated: the German Empire responded to the punitive Russian tariffs by adding another 50 per cent to the German general tariff on all goods from Russia. From late summer of 1893, a tariff of 35 marks per tonne applied to breadstuffs from the U.S., Hungary, Romania, and Argentina, while the figure was 75 marks per tonne for breadstuffs from Russia. The Russian government retaliated by imposing an additional 50 per cent increase on existing tariff rates. At the same time, it increased the charges on German ships (*Kronslastengelder*) by a factor of ten, from 10 kopeks to 1 rouble per 2 tonnes.[76]

The German-Russian tariff war was a severe blow to the trade of both countries. Overall, imports from Russia, which had still amounted to 579 million marks in 1891, collapsed to just 352 million by 1893; German exports fell from 184 million marks in 1893 to 136 million in 1894.[77] In Russia, it was above all its export-oriented agriculture that was hit by German retaliatory measures. German imports of Russian wheat fell from 91.2 million marks in 1891 to 2.6 million in 1893, and those of rye from 99 million marks to 9.8 million. As a result of this economic conflict, Russian farmers lost a large part of their most important market within just two years. In 1891, Russia accounted for a share of more than 54 per cent of German cereal imports, but this had plummeted to just 14 per cent by 1893.[78] In no time at all, global competition had largely driven Russian cereals, disadvantaged by the differential tariff, from the German market. The U.S. increased its share of German wheat imports from 15.8 to 44.8 per cent between 1891 and 1893 at the expense of Russia; Romania saw an increase from 4.7 to 20.4 per cent and Argentina from 1.4 to 21.5 per cent. Russia's share of rye imports also fell from 73.5 to 43.6 per cent between 1891 and 1893; in this case the main beneficiaries were Romania and Bulgaria, and briefly, in 1892, the U.S. as well.[79] In view of this massive loss of market share and the reduced income associated with it, Russian agrarians mobilized to attack their government's conflictual approach. The agricultural protests intensified further when a good harvest in 1893 dramatically increased Russian cereal supplies, while the German market, which used to be the main source of demand, remained largely closed.

On the German side the tariff war impacted trade, shipping and all those branches of industry exporting to Russia. As a result of the punitive tariffs and the large increase in Russian shipping costs, the German Baltic shipping companies, which had already had to accept losses before the customs war broke out because the differential tariff on Russian cereals deprived them of return freight, found themselves facing an existential threat from the summer of 1893; they managed to maintain a weak, loss-making trade in order to avoid being completely crushed by international competitors.[80] As early as the 1880s, German industrial exports were already stagnating because of increasingly radical Russian high protectionism, and had even declined significantly for a time. Now, as a result of the discriminatory approach to German goods concomitant with the customs war, German producers were in danger of losing their market share, particularly to their British competitors. 'Orders that otherwise went to Germany, and indeed with respect to important products of German industry', as the government's memorandum on the German-Russian trade treaty summed up this state of affairs, had 'now been placed with other states, from which the Russian buyers could obtain the goods at low tariff rates'.[81] In view of the acute risk of being excluded from the Russian market, which was regarded as having great potential for the future, it is no surprise that 'German trade and industry made it abundantly clear that it was of the utmost importance that they be freed from the shackles that the … customs war had placed on them as soon as conceivably possible'.[82] Within trade and industry there was soon a broad consensus regarding the necessity of bringing the economic war rapidly to an end and concluding a trade treaty with Russia. This included heavy industry, which also showed clear interest in the Russian market. The tendency, which united trade and industry, to push for a trade policy compromise with Russia was further strengthened by the economic downturn that had persisted since 1890 and now prompted producers to step up their search for foreign markets.

In view of the economic losses caused by the customs war and under pressure from those economic circles interested in flourishing trade relations – agriculture in Russia and trade, shipping and industry in Germany – the two governments soon entered into talks intended to end the economic hostilities. On 10 February 1894 – six months after the outbreak of the 'hot' customs war – a trade and shipping treaty was concluded between Germany and Russia with a life span of ten years. The German Empire guaranteed the reduced agricultural tariffs stipulated in the series of treaties recently concluded with Austria-Hungary, Italy, Switzerland and Belgium and fixed a number of other tariffs for the duration of the treaty. A large proportion of Russian tariffs were either reduced or at least fixed in return. They also came to an agreement on most-favoured-nation status, so Germany benefited from the fifteen tariff reductions contained in the trade treaty that Russia had previously concluded with France, which were not included in the German-Russian agreement. In addition, the two parties agreed a series of further measures designed to facilitate bilateral economic relations.[83] While none of this made any difference to the highly protectionist character of the Russian customs tariff, most tariffs were reduced to a level at which they no longer had a prohibitive effect and, most importantly, eliminated the disadvantaging of German exporters vis-à-vis their international competitors.

Historians have repeatedly claimed that the conclusion of the German-Russian trade treaty clashed with the plan for a central European customs union originally pursued by Caprivi.[84] This is incorrect. First, as we have seen, because of the German economy's world market orientation, the conception of a central European customs union, initially aired in the Foreign Ministry, was soon rejected as unrealistic. Second, because of the most-favoured-nation clause, the tariff reductions agreed to in the trade treaties with Austria-Hungary, Italy, Belgium and Switzerland applied from the outset to almost all of Germany's other trading partners as well, so a central European system of preferential tariffs had never existed. Third and finally, already in the early stages of the new trade policy approach, key actors in Berlin were considering expanding the trade treaty system to Russia. Given the importance of reciprocal trade relations and the problems that applying a separate tariff policy to Russia would bring in its wake, by late 1890, before the start of the negotiations with Austria-Hungary, the trade experts at the Foreign Ministry were aware of the potential of concluding a German-Russian trade treaty.[85] From the perspective of the German government, the reason why it took until 1894 to reach such an agreement was, first, because Russia had previously failed to offer anything adequate in return and, second, because of the strong domestic political opposition from the agrarians. In this sense the customs war also helped make it clear to the protectionist hard-liners on both the Russian and German sides that the present situation could not go on, in other words, that there was no alternative to concluding a trade treaty.

We might sum all this up by saying that in 1893/94, for the first time in history, German foreign trade policy was subject to simultaneous pressure on two fronts, both of which emanated from advancing globalization and, through a kind of pincer movement, increasingly limited the political room for manoeuvre. On one side there emerged a powerful agricultural protectionist movement, a response to the economic problems of German agriculture associated with world market integration. This movement called explicitly for a strengthening of the system of agricultural protection while bitterly resisting any attempt to reduce existing tariffs. From the other side, the integration of the German economy into the world market was already well advanced, imposing major restrictions on trade policy. Germany's great dependence on imports and exports made it seem inevitable that a policy of isolation from the world market and a trade policy confrontation would entail massive economic losses and was thus unviable. Furthermore, there was resistance to such a policy from those economic interest groups that profited from the globalization of markets and aimed to achieve the intensification and political safeguarding of international trade relations. In the context of discussions on the German-Russian trade treaty and, even earlier, during the debate on the treaties with Romania and Serbia, the domestic political effects of the dual pressure exerted by economic globalization came clearly to the fore. Three phenomena were particularly important.

First, the conflicts generated by world market integration intensified the emphasis on socioeconomic divisions within the political landscape of the empire, in other words, an increasing orientation towards material interests. The dispute over Caprivi's trades treaties did much to politically activate the crucial conflict, also emphasized by Seymour Martin Lipset and Stein Rokkan in their concept of cleavage, between the agrarian and industrial sector, while also overlaying this conflict with the clash between urban consumers and rural producers.[86] Over the course of the trade policy debates of the early 1890s, the political landscape became increasingly polarized along this fault line. On one side stood the advocates of agricultural protectionism and their parliamentary auxiliaries, above all the German Conservatives. Count Mirbach's claim before the Reichstag that Caprivi's trade treaty system 'would culminate in the systematic impairment of indigenous agriculture and systematic privileging of foreign agriculture' was fairly moderate.[87] Count Kanitz's assessment of the consequences of the trade treaty with Russia and its ten-year period of validity was far more dramatic: 'the ten years that lie ahead of us' will cost German agriculture 'more than an ill-starred war'.[88] Finally, for the chief editor of the *Kreuzzeitung,* Wilhelm von Hammerstein, the German-Russian trade treaty was not, as claimed by the Foreign Ministry secretary Marschall, a 'milestone', but rather a 'gravestone' bearing the inscription, 'The last resting place of German agriculture'.[89]

On the other side there developed a phalanx that extended from the Social Democrats, who emphasized the consumer's standpoint, to the representatives of industrial export interests. All the organizations of trade and industry were unanimous in their support for the trade treaty with Russia. The CVDI was 'delighted to see the conclusion of the German-Russian trade treaty' and declared that it 'regarded its rejection by the Reichstag as highly detrimental to commercial activity and trade, the Fatherland's general economic situation and especially the interests of the workers'.[90] While the representatives of heavy industry such as Bueck and Stumm went to great lengths to emphasize the 'common interests of industry and agriculture', and repeatedly made speeches to agrarians stressing their loyalty,[91] this was patently the end of the trade policy alliance between heavy industry and agriculture, which had existed since 1879, and this was recognized on all sides. The BdL had already refused to support Stumm's candidacy at the Reichstag elections of 1893 because of his unwillingness to commit to rejecting the trade treaty with Russia. It made no difference to the league, as BdL functionary Heinrich Suchsland coolly informed him, 'whether the votes in favour of the trade treaty are cast by an extreme free trader or a moderate one'.[92] When it emerged that those Reichstag deputies closest to industry would support the Russian treaty during the crucial vote, the alienation between the former partners in the protectionist front reached its peak. As Hammerstein saw it, industry had violated the terms of its 'pact' with agriculture.[93] In light of their advocacy of the trade treaty, Mirbach accused the industrialists of displaying the 'greatest ruthlessness' and declared that 'the solidarity of interest between agriculture and industry … was thus scarcely worth the paper it was written on', and 'in practical terms' was 'long since forgotten'.[94] Social Democratic deputy Bruno Schoenlank commented with delight on the outbreak of conflict between his political opponents: 'we are already seeing the expression of the natural opposition between major industry and agrarians', which would 'intensify ever further' in future.[95]

Finally, the trade treaty with Romania was adopted by the Reichstag by just 189 to 165 votes. The only reason that the vote was rather less tight in the case of the Russian treaty, 200 to 146, was that a number of deputies had overarching political reasons to vote for it. The results of both votes showed not just how much the camp opposed to Caprivi's trade treaty policies had now grown – in late 1891, the Austro-Hungarian treaty had gained the support of 243 deputies in the Reichstag with just 48 votes against.[96] They also revealed that while the Social Democrats and left liberals were as unanimous in their support for the treaties as the German Conservatives were in their opposition, the trade treaty issue deeply divided the Free Conservatives and National Liberals, and above all the Centre Party. Of Centre Party deputies, 44 voted for and 49 against the treaty with Romania; the agreement with Russia received 45 votes in favour and 39 against, after a number of the opponents of the treaty chose not to attend rather than contribute to the conflict within the parliamentary party. The disputes over the trade treaties were so intense that Centre Party leader Ernst Lieber feared for the party's survival. Should there be an election campaign centred on economic policy, following the putative rejection of the Russian trade treaty and subsequent dissolution of the Reichstag, 'no one would take up arms against one another to defend their cause as ferociously' as members of the Centre Party: 'north against south, east against west, city against country, commerce against agriculture'.[97]

Second, the conflict between agricultural protectionist and world market–oriented interests had a tendency to extend into the Prussian-German ministerial bureaucracy. Support for Caprivi's trade treaty policy came chiefly from the various imperial offices and particularly from the representatives of the Foreign Ministry and the Imperial Ministry of the Interior.[98] Among the Prussian ministers, on the other hand, only the trade minister Hans von Berlepsch came out unreservedly in support of the new trade policy course. The arguments put forward by those officials who supported the trade treaty policy and the lowering of agricultural tariffs concomitant with it were centred, first, on economic policy, highlighting the need to secure German export markets and encourage industrial growth. Second, they underlined the social policy significance of the trade treaties. They were intended, so the argument went, to improve the material lot of industrial workers and thus exercise a socially pacifying effect, creating more employment opportunities in the industrial export sectors while at the same time lowering the cost of foodstuffs. Third, representatives of the Foreign Ministry in particular cited foreign policy reasons for the trade treaties. This applied above all to the treaty with Austria-Hungary, which was intended to stabilize the Triple Alliance, and that with Russia, which would improve the dramatically worsening German-Russian relations and help prevent any further French-Russian rapprochement.

The opponents of the Caprivi trade treaties within the executive were to be found predominantly in the Prussian ministries. We can identify two hotbeds of resistance: the Prussian Ministry of Agriculture, Estates and Forestry (Ministerium für Landwirtschaft, Domänen und Forsten) and the Prussian Finance Ministry. The agriculture minister – whether Lucius or, from late 1890, Heyden – and his high-ranking subordinates, such as Hugo Thiel and Richard Wentzel, saw themselves first and foremost as the custodians of agricultural interests, especially those of the landowners east of the Elbe. Like them, Prussian finance minister Miquel also tried on several occasions either to prevent a reduction in the agricultural tariffs or to undermine the conclusion of the treaties as a whole. He was so energetic in his opposition that Wilhelm II, who was convinced of the need for the trade treaties, felt obliged to persuade him otherwise by posing the at once flattering and threatening question as to whether 'the greatest finance minister of the century wants to put at risk his emperor's very own work over a minor tariff issue'.[99] When Miquel then gave his view of the trade treaty with Russia in the Reichstag on 1 March 1894, he began with an in-depth appraisal of the 'desperate situation' of agriculture and signalled the Prussian government's willingness 'to take effective action to ensure [that agriculture received] as much relief as possible'; he went on to express support for the German-Russian trade treaty not offensively by pointing to its economic and political importance but with the defensive and rather tortuous argument that it would 'not bring about ... a significant worsening of the situation of agriculture', since German agricultural tariffs had already been lowered by the preceding trade treaties.[100]

The rejectionist attitude towards Caprivi's trade policy so widespread in the Prussian ministerial bureaucracy found perhaps its clearest expression in the behaviour of two high-ranking Prussian officials, Karl Gamp and Andreas von Bernstorff, both of whom were also members of the Reichstag and voted against the trade treaty with Russia.[101] Earlier, shortly after the Reichstag debate on the German-Romanian trade treaty, at a meeting of the Prussian State Ministry, Caprivi complained about the public opposition to the trade treaties expressed by Gamp and other officials, describing it as incompatible with their status as officials and calling for them to be banned from participating in 'the campaigns of the Agrarian League'. Due to the opposition chiefly of Miquel and Prussian prime minister Count zu Eulenburg, however, he failed to achieve either this or his goal of regulating the parliamentary activities of these recalcitrant public servants; he merely managed to ensure that they received a mild reminder of the decree on officials (*Beamtenerlaß*) of 1882.[102]

Third and finally, as the disputes over the Caprivi trade treaties raged, it became ever more apparent that trade policy and especially tariff policy decisions, in addition to their material dimension, also had an important symbolic dimension, and that this was becoming increasingly important and hampering attempts to reach a compromise between the conflicting interests. A paradigmatic case was the political struggle over the last of the Caprivi treaties, the trade treaty with Russia. There was in fact no rationally comprehensible economic motive for the mass agrarian opposition to this treaty. The argument put forward again and again by opponents of the trade treaty was that the influx of Russian cereals to Germany – which could be expected once the German conventional tariff had been approved with respect to Russia – would exercise additional price pressure on the German market and thus worsen the crisis of agriculture. This was a chimera. The foreign secretary, Marschall, was quite right to point out to the Reichstag that this assertion was based on the false premise that 'price formation in the case of cereals' as in the '"good old days"' was a 'national matter' and that 'the impact of the cereal tariff would be country-specific'. In the 'age of steamships, telegraphs and railways' this notion seemed 'untenable' even to contemporaries, since a functioning 'world market' in agricultural goods had taken shape and 'as a consequence of this, price formation for cereals [was] *international* in accordance with the production surplus of the entire world on the one hand and the needs of the various countries, which consume more than they produce, on the other'.[103] So whether Russian cereals flowed directly into the German market or exercised price pressure indirectly via the world market, the consequences for German agriculture would be more or less the same. The German Empire had granted the reduced agricultural tariffs in the trade treaty not just to Austria-Hungary but also to all major cereal-exporting states apart from Russia because of the most-favoured-nation principle. Cereals, the price of which depended on the world market, thus simply entered Germany from the other regions with a cereal surplus at the lower tariff rates.

Because of this, the differential tariff on Russian cereals had no protective effect for German agriculture, but merely led to a situation in which 'the most-favoured nations send us their rye and replace it with Russian rye'.[104] The German punitive tariff of 75 marks on a tonne of Russian breadstuffs had no effect on prices and thus damaged Russian exporters, who had to turn to other markets, but failed to protect the German market. This was also evident in the fact, conceded by the agrarians, that the price difference between Russian and German cereals at no point exceeded the German treaty tariff of 35 marks per tonne.[105] Furthermore, the differential treatment of Russian products through certificates of origin might be effectively maintained on a temporary basis but hardly over the long term, as it was possible for traders to avoid them. For example, according to Marschall, no one could prevent 'Russian wheat, Russian rye and Russian cereals from being taken to most-favoured nations, turned into flour there' and then imported to Germany at the reduced tariff rates.[106]

The meaninglessness of rejecting the German-Russian trade treaty on economic grounds, however, changed nothing about the agrarians' implacable opposition, and neither did the sometimes substantial concessions that the government made to them in other areas. The removal of the differential tariffs for the transportation of flour and cereals on the Prussian railway was clearly addressed to the agriculturalists of southern and western Germany. They had first been introduced only in 1891 because of the then poor supply situation in order to facilitate the transportation of cereals from the areas of surplus in the north and east to the other parts of Germany. It is true that they failed to make any great impact, but right from the outset they were met with the implacable opposition of southern and western German peasants and millers, who regarded them as an important competition-intensifying factor. In the Reichstag, it was primarily the Centre Party, which was closely linked with the Catholic peasants' associations, that embraced these demands. Perhaps even more crucially, the Bavarian government, which found itself confronted with massive 'pressure from the ultramontanists and supporters of the Peasants' League' in the Bavarian parliament, linked its support for the German-Russian trade treaty in the Bundesrat with the abolition of the differential tariffs.[107]

On the other hand, by eliminating the 'certificate of identity' (*Identitätsnachweis*), the government gave the agrarians east of the Elbe something they had long wanted. The law of 14 April 1894 introduced a bill of entry system. The cereal exporter would now receive an 'import certificate' when exporting that could be used to pay duties when importing cereals and certain other goods. Since the certificate of identity for imported and exported cereals had been abolished and the individual exporter was not necessarily identical with the importer, just as the place of import was not necessarily identical with the place of export, the import certificates were straightforwardly tradable. The bill of entry system in combination with the abolition of the certificate of identity de facto functioned as an indirect export subsidy. As a consequence, immediately after the new rule had come into force, eastern German cereal exports to Scandinavia and the U.K., which had almost ground to a halt, saw a major revival. At the same time, the abolition of the certificate of identity and the newly created export outlet this had created reduced the price pressure on eastern German areas of cereal surpluses. This reduced the price difference between western and eastern Germany and, in contrast to the past, the cereal producers of the northeastern provinces could now benefit more fully from tariff protection. Economically speaking, this was a highly valuable form of compensation. It not only more than compensated eastern German agriculture for the effects, of little relevance in any case, of the German-Russian trade treaty, but also for the reduced agricultural tariffs entailed in the agreement with Austria-Hungary.[108]

If the agrarians – and not just those in the east of Germany – were nonetheless up in arms about the German-Russian trade treaty, the first reason was their specific perceptual filter. Influenced by the economic crisis in which they found themselves and contrary to what any sober *ex ante* reflection would have suggested, they overestimated the extent of what they feared would be additional competitive pressures; at the same time, they underestimated the value of the compensation they had been granted. Second, the trade treaty with Russia had now taken on a symbolic importance that went far beyond its purely economic significance. From the perspective of the agrarians, it stood for the whole proindustry and antiagriculture trade policy propagated by the chancellor they despised, for the betrayal they had suffered at the hands of their former heavy industrial allies and for the fact that German agriculture had been left in the lurch by the government and all its allies in its 'life and death … struggle for survival'.[109] This added further ideological depth to the already gaping chasm between the opposing economic policy fronts. Every concession made by the opposing side seemed inadequate, every form of compensation third-rate and all compromise out of the question.

CHAPTER 5

# The Conflict over the Bülow Tariff

## *The Genesis of the Customs Tariff Reform of 1902*

At the turn of the twentieth century, the political conflict over the question of which tariff and trade policy the German Empire should pursue in response to advancing globalization reached a new peak. No sooner had the Caprivi treaties come into force than the agricultural protectionist groups began to push furiously for their revision, engaging in an unprecedented campaign of agitation to this end. In response, by early 1895, the emperor had already tasked Chlodwig von Hohenlohe-Schillingsfürst, who had just taken office after the fall of Caprivi, with 'putting together a programme acceptable to the agrarians'.[1] Though the Caprivi treaties would cease to apply only at the end of 1903, by 1897 the responsible imperial ministries and the Economic Committee on the Preparation and Assessment of Trade Policy Measures (Wirtschaftlicher Ausschuß zur Vorbereitung und Begutachtung handelspolitischer Maßnahmen), an economic policy advisory board made up of representatives of agriculture, industry and trade, had already begun to prepare the new customs tariff to replace the general tariff in place since 1879. The tariff rates in the new tariff – and this is what made it politically significant – would form the foundation for all future trade treaty negotiations. At the same time, its structure and subdivisions were intended to reflect the increasing differentiation and specialization of the production of goods. When the tariff reform was finally passed by the Reichstag five years later in December 1902, contemporaries would look back over a political conflict that is among the most bitter, enduring and most consequential disputes in the entire history of the German Empire.

The political struggle over the form of the Bülow tariff also found expression in a closely associated debate. Initially led by a number of prominent economists but subsequently encompassing ever-broader circles of the German public, this revolved around whether Germany's development into a highly developed industrial state should be welcomed and encouraged or slowed down in order to retain the country's basic character as an agrarian state.[2] This controversy, which seems oddly anachronistic given how far the country's industrial transformation had already advanced, was triggered by the dispute over the Caprivi treaties and essentially continued until the First World War, but clearly reached its peak between 1897 and 1902.

The members of the diametrically opposed camps within the 'agrarian state' versus 'industrial state' debate stylized the decision on the Bülow tariff as one that would set the course for the German Empire's economic, social and political future. Indeed, this conflict was only superficially concerned with the correct approach to foreign trade policy. It was also about more than purely economic structural change. In essence, it revolved around the conflict between two fundamentally different models of society. On one side stood those who, like Lujo Brentano, Max Weber and Heinrich Dietzel, considered Germany's further development into an industrial state inevitable and were in favour of this development and the social changes concomitant with it. Since they fundamentally supported Germany's further integration into the world economy, they either advocated a largely free trade-based trade policy or a system of moderate protective tariffs that would not hamper the conclusion of new trade treaties. Supporters of the 'agrarian state', on the other hand, such as Adolph Wagner, Karl Oldenberg and Max Sering, saw the global economic division of labour that had emerged merely as a transitional stage[3] and were convinced of the 'impossibility of a lasting export industry'.[4] They therefore fought against Germany's transformation into an industrial state dependent on exports, in which agriculture would become increasingly unimportant. But though this led them to call for increased tariff protection for agriculture, intended to counteract further structural economic change and preserve existing agrarian structures, the participants in the academic debate did not wish to be seen as lackeys of the agrarian interest groups. As Wagner underlined, their call for a policy of agrarian protectionism was based chiefly on the fundamental sociopolitical conviction, permeated by the cultural critique of the fin de siècle, that '*preserving a substantial indigenous rural landowning and agriculturalist population in both absolute and relative terms* ... is a *crucial precondition* for the well-being and enduring socioeconomic, physical, ethical, cultural and political health and security of the *entire nation*'.[5]

There are two key reasons why I have opted not to provide a detailed account and analysis of the dispute over Germany's future as an agrarian or industrial state. First, this dispute is one of the best-researched aspects of the trade policy conflicts that marked the run-up to the customs tariff reform of 1902.[6] In the main the relevant sources are easily accessible, and we have full and detailed accounts of the opposing views. Second, there would appear to be good reasons to doubt the notion, repeatedly aired by historians in one form or another, that the 'socially conservative, romantic-agrarian mind-set [expressed in the debate on an agrarian versus industrial state] characteristic of a large number of often very influential university professors … did much' to 'lay the groundwork for comprehensive agricultural protectionism'.[7]

The first reason to doubt the implicit or explicit assertion that the dispute had a formative influence on the outcome of the trade policy decision-making process is that, as it unfolded, neither camp managed to achieve discursive supremacy. Ludwig Pohle, one of the prominent exponents of the agrarian state concept, was quite correct in his view that 'German economics … [is divided] into two camps with respect to trade policy issues', of which 'neither surpasses the other in terms of the number and significance of its supporters'.[8] Against this background, the most we can say in light of the debate on an agrarian versus industrial state is rather more modest: in contrast to the U.K., there was no dominant free trade discourse in Germany before the First World War that might have represented a significant barrier to protectionist aspirations.

Second, arguments highlighting the importance of agrarian-conservative ideas in the German debate are unable to explain why the establishment of a system of protective agricultural tariffs was not a specifically German phenomenon but an international one in the late nineteenth century. We would have to ask why agricultural protectionism also played a role in France, Austria, Italy and a number of other continental European states, despite discursive structures and traditions of thought quite different from those of Germany.

In any case, and this is the third point, it seems methodologically impermissible to make a direct causal linkage between supposedly prevalent patterns of thought and discourse and the results of the political decision-making process. Ultimately, if there is any methodologically legitimate way to trace their influence, this can only be on the level of individual actors and their motivations. Only a detailed analysis of the political decision-making process is capable of showing the role ultimately played by such influences and how we should assess their significance in comparison with other intervening factors.

## Economic Interests and Their Organization

That economic interests play an important role in foreign trade policy decisions is uncontested – and this applies nowadays just as much as it did in days of the German Empire. Beyond this commonplace, however, a sphere of more challenging theoretical problems opens up. This includes the question of which units of economic interest we should be working with in the first place and how to separate them from each other. Even more difficult is the question of how to grasp theoretically the relationship between the initial constellation of economic interests, the political decision-making process and its trade policy results.

One of the fundamental problems with those explanations, so common in economic history, that highlight economic interests is the need to avoid a circular argument that ultimately derives the *explanans* from the *explanandum*. These are based on the idea that because certain interests benefited particularly from a particular foreign trade policy, this policy obviously reflects their economic dominance and political efficacy. In order to avoid this risk, interest-oriented approaches usually define the key material interests and the groups of actors embodying them a priori on the basis of specific theoretical assumptions. We can identify two main types of approach based on their underlying premises.

The first, represented, for example, by Ronald Rogowski's study *Commerce and Coalitions,* is based on the application of the so-called Stolper-Samuelson theorem.[9] This works on the assumption of production factors fully mobile between sectors (the Heckscher-Ohlin model) and states that restrictions on trade through tariffs generally benefit the owners of a factor that is relatively scarce within the national economy, while the free international exchange of goods is advantageous in the case of abundantly available factors.[10] Working with just three production factors, namely, labour, capital and land, Rogowski comes to the conclusion that we can go a long way in explaining the different trade policy approaches of the U.K. and much of the European continent from the late 1870s on with the help of the Stolper-Samuelson theorem. According to this view, in the U.K., with its plentiful capital and labour, there was a successful coalition between these two factors to the benefit of free trade, against the wishes of protariff agrarians, while in most continental European countries the scarcity of capital and land generated a protectionist alliance between owners of capital and land – which took the form of the alliance between 'rye and iron' in Germany – that succeeded in enforcing its will against the 'surplus factor' of labour.[11]

The second, alternative analytical framework for explaining trade policy decisions through economic interests is provided by the Ricardo-Viner model, which works on the assumption that production factors are not fully mobile but instead sector-specific to some extent, in other words, tied to a specific branch of production. The application of a variant of this approach to a historical case can be seen in Douglas Irwin's study of the

British general election of 1906.[12] Irwin works with a sector-specific model in which the production factor of labour is incompletely mobile between the various economic sectors.[13] Under these conditions, we can expect that trade policy interests are not – as predicted by the Stolper-Samuelson theorem – geared towards production factors, but towards economic sectors; in line with these interests, alliances form in specific branches. These crosscut class since the owners of all those factors involved in a particular sector see their fate as linked primarily with the economic situation of this branch. According to Irwin, we can largely explain the Liberals' victory in the elections of 1906 and along with it the continuation of British free trade policies with the help of the sector-specific model that underpins his work. For Irwin, most voters decided how to vote in accordance with the international competitive position of the economic sector in which they were employed: export-oriented sectors privileged concepts of free trade, while those engaged in import competition were protectionist in character. Ultimately, then, according to Irwin's analysis, the fact that the U.K. stuck with free trade before the First World War was due to the clear predominance of export-dependent sectors in the British economy.[14]

Such approaches generally have the advantage of clearly formulated premises and formal elegance, and at times they show a high degree of explanatory power in cases where we wish to understand how global economic changes impact on the development of domestic political forces. But they are generally of little use if our aim is to explain the historically specific form taken by a particular trade policy. Because they tend to distinguish only very crudely between free trade and protectionism they are unable to do justice to the different varieties of protectionist policies found in reality, which are of great relevance in terms of their economic effects, or the endless gradations that lie between the extremes of radical free trade policies and ultraprotectionist ones. They generally share two other basic weaknesses.

First, with respect to the interests of the individual and social actors they have defined, these approaches generate a myth of clarity. They only take account of the producer interests arising from affiliation to a particular factor or sector, while leaving consumer interests out of account. In view of the significance of the consumption of imported foodstuffs and other goods to the individual household, this is particularly problematic for employees, who are also considered only as producers but not as consumers – no consideration is given to the conflict of interests that may ensue for the individual or group as a result of these differing social roles.[15] Further, even interests within specific groups of producers – whether organized on a sectoral or factoral basis – are by no means always as clear-cut as they are generally imagined to be. How opposed the economic interests within an economic branch may be is evident, for example, in the conflicts of interest between weavers and spinners in the textiles industry or between the producers of semifinished products and the processing industry within the iron and steel sector.

Second, the approaches described above exhibit economic determinism. This is based on the idea that through their impact on the constellation of domestic economic interests, global economic changes find more or less direct expression in national trade policy strategies. These approaches fail to take adequate account of the fact that interests are not simply predetermined by the socioeconomic situation but are subject to a complex process of interpretation, whose outcome is influenced by socially dominant perceptual filters and worldviews. They also fail to pay enough attention to the organization of interests and their political enforceability.

Therefore, in the present study I take a different tack. In a first step (chapter 2), I attempted to identify an ideal-typical economic interest profile for the German economy in view of the increasing globalization of economic relations. My efforts here were informed by the question, which is consonant with the sector-specific orientation of the more realistic (at least over the short term) Ricardo-Viner model, as to which economic branches or subsections of these branches were among the winners and losers of globalization. By implication this revealed which branches or subbranches benefited from particular protectionist interventions and which did not. In a second step, I shall now compare ideal-typical interests with the views that were in fact articulated by the various economic interest organizations in the German Empire on the cusp of the twentieth century. At the same time, I extend the spectrum of interests considered through the addition of consumer interests. Here, with respect to both the interests of producers and consumers, I pay particular attention to the question of which factors foster the articulation, organization and political enforcement of particular interests while impeding or thwarting others. This casts some initial light on what the interest-oriented approaches outlined above tend to treat as the black box of the trade policy decision-making process. Furthermore, I examine the role of the other actors and institutions involved in this process – parties, ministerial bureaucracy and Reichstag. With regard to the formation and organization of economic interests, my analysis is guided by two theoretically grounded hypotheses.

First, building on the findings of endogenous tariff theory, I work on the assumption that those producers interested in protectionist measures generally possess a structural organizational advantage over those circles benefiting from the free exchange of goods.[16] This is because the effect of a protectionist restriction is usually palpable and immediate, while the harm caused by it tends to be indirect and diffuse. For import-competitive producers keen on protection, the incentive to get organized is comparatively high, since the utility arising for them from the enforcement of trade restrictions is clearly recognizable and individually significant. This does not apply in the same way to those affected negatively by protective measures. This includes those export branches that do not themselves benefit from protective tariffs but are afraid of retaliatory measures by foreign countries that might curtail their opportunities for export. In contrast to the protective impact of an import restriction, however, the losses they can anticipate only occur in the future, are difficult to quantify in terms of scale and tend to take the form of opportunity costs, which are generally viewed as less significant. Much the same applies to consumers, the second important group to which the costs of protection are passed on. In addition to the problem, which applies in this case, of measuring the loss of welfare suffered, the price-increasing effect brought about by the trade restriction is widespread, so the individual consumer may be damaged in a way that is scarcely perceptible on the individual level.

The second hypothesis that guides my analysis is based on the theory of collective action. Often, historical, political-scientific and economic researchers take it for granted that groups whose members have a shared economic interest and act rationally will get organized and take collective action in order to achieve the group's goals. In accordance with the empirically backed findings of the theory of collective action in the wake of Mancur Olson, meanwhile, the present work assumes in the first instance that joint group action is unlikely – at least if we are talking about numerically large or, to use Olson's terms, latent groups.[17] Even if it was to the advantage of all members of a large group to work together to promote their collective interests, in normal circumstances they will not do so of their own accord – even if there is complete agreement within the group on a common objective and on how to realize it, and especially if the group members are actors rationally pursuing their self-interest. This is because, for those in favour of them, regardless of whether they are producers in specific economic branches or consumers, a liberal foreign trade regime, protection in the form of tariffs or other economic policy goals take on the character of 'public goods'. In other words, every firm in an import-competitive branch of the economy benefits from protection from foreign competition – quite regardless of how much the individual member of an economic sector has campaigned for its adoption as policy. Conversely, the cheapening of import goods through the liberalization of foreign trade policies also benefits those consumers that have not actively sought to have tariffs dismantled. Since no one can be excluded from using the collective good – whether a given group benefits from a tariff increase or tariff reduction – for rationally acting actors there is no incentive to invest time, money or energy in its political implementation or to join a relevant interest organization. Even if the utility of a protective tariff for a particular group of producers was to greatly exceed the costs entailed in its enforcement, why should the individual actor pursuing his self-interest make even the slightest sacrifice in order to achieve this common goal, when those who have contributed nothing will ultimately share in the benefit obtained in the same way?

Every social group with a shared economic interest in a collective good is confronted with this so-called free rider problem. The only real exceptions to this are numerically small groups in which either a single member gains a large enough advantage from the provision of public goods to prompt him to bear the entire costs alone, or in which face-to-face communication allows the coordination of a collective approach and the punishment of deviant behaviour.[18] But the larger the number of individuals or businesses that benefit from a collective good, the smaller, ceteris paribus, is the incentive for the individual group member to make an effort to achieve the common goal. If larger groups fail to get to grips with the free rider problem in one way or another, either no organization will emerge to pursue the common interest in the first place or it will be unstable and weak. According to Olson, the fundamental factor in overcoming the problems involved in collective action is always the existence or creation of so-called selective incentives that exclude the free riders who contribute nothing to achieving the group objective – only on this basis can a stable and effective interest organization develop. Selective incentives may be negative or positive in character. In the former case, pressure is exerted on those who refuse to do their bit to help organize and enforce the common interest. Positive selective incentives, meanwhile, are additional benefits provided by an interest organization that accrue exclusively to its members but not nonmembers – in contrast to a collective good. Furthermore, consciously departing from the framework of orthodox neoclassical assumptions, Douglass C. North has pointed out that ideologies too may function to overcome the free rider problem by prompting the individual to take action to achieve a superordinate goal – contrary to any simple, hedonistic cost-benefit calculation.[19]

## *The Agrarian Interest Organizations*

As in most other continental European countries, within German agriculture the constellation of economic interests provided fairly favourable preconditions for the development of a well-organized and strongly protectionist agricultural lobby. Despite their very different production profiles, virtually all farmers who produced for the market in some way found themselves exposed to the pressure of global agricultural competition and benefited from protective measures aimed at agricultural goods – albeit to varying degrees (see chapter 2). Historians have long disputed that such a shared interest in agricultural protectionism truly existed. In the wake of the contemporary liberal critique and especially under the influence of Eckart Kehr and Alexander Gerschenkron, for three decades after the Second World War West German historiography was dominated by an interpretation that assumed that German agriculture was split into two blocks with diametrically opposing interests.[20] On this view it was a case of big landowners from east of the Elbe, who had specialized in growing cereals, versus peasant farmers from west of the Elbe, the majority of whom were engaged in livestock farming. While the former generally had a great interest in cereal tariffs, the latter, along with consumers, had to bear the resulting economic costs in the form of more expensive feed cereals. Against this background, so the argument goes, we can explain the support for higher corn tariffs among peasants west of the Elbe only in light of their manipulation by the Junkers and the agrarian interest associations dominated by them. However, James C. Hunt has rightly argued that most peasants were engaged in mixed farming and had reached a high degree of self-sufficiency with respect to bread- and feedstuffs, and in good years were even in a position to put their cereal surpluses on the market.[21] For exponents of this view, peasant farmers' efforts to achieve higher cereal tariffs were very much in their own interests rather than the result of successful brainwashing by the big agrarians. Hunt also highlights the fact, generally overlooked in the research, that German livestock farmers had received effective protection from international competition through a number of de facto protectionist legal regulations intended to prevent animal diseases and veterinary measures, so it is simply not true that agrarian protectionism only benefited cereal producers.[22]

In terms of economic interests, but also, closely linked with them, farm size and type of farming, it is probably better to assume an – admittedly simplistic – tripartite division of German agriculture, as opposed to the bifurcation that is all-pervasive within the historical research and that even Hunt fails to fundamentally question.[23] The first bloc was made up of Prussia east of the Elbe, which was dominated by large estates and extensive cereal growing, with an emphasis on rye. Second, we can identify an area dominated by large-scale peasant farms in northern Germany, taking in the provinces of Hanover and western Schleswig-Holstein and the grand duchy of Oldenburg; here market-oriented livestock rearing clearly predominated. The East Prussian *Köllmer* and Westphalian *Meierhöfe* came under the same category. Third, and resistant to easy classification, is the region of central, western and southern Germany characterized by small and medium-sized peasant farms and dominated by mixed farming and intensive land use; here, alongside cereals and livestock, vegetables, fruit and wine also played an important role.[24]

What held the three segments of agrarian interests together was the threat posed by the globalization of the agricultural market and the concomitant price pressure, though this made itself felt earlier and more intensely in the case of cereals than with respect to other agricultural products. As submissions from chambers of agriculture from every part of the empire, contemporary surveys and more recent studies in regional history all show, this was reflected in a general attitude in favour of comprehensive agricultural protectionism that bound together the different categories of farmers both horizontally and vertically.[25] The crucial elements in this protectionism, trade restrictions on cereals and livestock, always benefited not just one but several major agrarian groups. So on the one hand it is true that individual large estates in the east of Germany profited particularly from the cereal tariffs because of their size. On the other hand, in the empire as a whole, of the land used to grow rye – the classical cereal of Prussia east of the Elbe – just 21 per cent was located on large farms, while 75 per cent was owned by medium-sized farms (featuring more than two hectares of cropland), which also sold a fair portion of their yield and thus benefited from the tariffs.[26] It is in fact wrong to assume that the growing of breadstuffs was generally of more importance to large estates than peasant farms: measured by their share of farmland, the large estates of more than one hundred hectares were actually below the average figure achieved by small and medium-sized peasant farms with an area of more than half a hectare.[27] A similar picture emerges with respect to the impact of frontier barriers and livestock tariffs implemented to prevent the spread of animal diseases. Again, the benefits accrued not just to the large peasant farms of northern Germany that specialized in livestock rearing and called for significant tariff increases[28] but also, on a smaller scale, to the countless small and medium-sized farms of southern and western Germany that sold their surplus meat on the market.

Given this broadly shared interest in agricultural protectionism, potential conflicts among agrarians – emphasized by left-liberal contemporaries and the historians who adhered to their interpretation – tended to recede into the background. Such conflict was essentially limited to the issue of protection for feedstuffs, which the large livestock farmers in particular wished to obtain on the world market at the lowest possible tariff rates in order to keep costs down, while farmers growing feed crops sought tariff increases. In addition, the large agrarian interest organizations managed to effectively dampen the remaining potential for conflict. With respect to those agricultural products used exclusively or primarily as livestock feed, such as oil-bearing fruits, seeds, fodder beets or maize, they pushed for no or negligible tariff increases.

Further, from the Agrarian League (Bund der Landwirte or BdL) through the Association of Tax and Economic Reformers (Vereinigung der Steuer- und Wirtschaftsreformer or VSW) to the German Agricultural Council (Deutscher Landwirtschaftsrat or DLR), the agrarian interest organizations never tired of emphasizing the commonality of agricultural interests and seeking to strike a balance between different agrarian interests. They always put together comprehensive catalogues of protective demands that avoided favouring particular groups of farmers and that, they claimed, granted 'the necessary protection to all the products of German agriculture on the basis of *total equality*'.[29] BdL president Baron Conrad von Wangenheim put it in paradigmatic terms: 'The new customs tariff ... should benefit no particular branch over any other', while '*all* important branches of agriculture' ought to 'receive the *most equal possible degree of protection*'. The league, he explained further in a speech in late 1900, was 'far less concerned to ensure that an article is given special treatment, that it is subject to a particularly high tariff; what matters far more to us is that the *mass* of agricultural products *as a whole* enjoy a certain degree of protection on the basis of the greatest possible equality, so that agriculture in all its branches is also guaranteed equal development'. But the 'basic precondition for proceeding on this basis' is 'that we are united *among ourselves*. If we ourselves begin to fight about such things as the size of specific tariff items then we might as well forget about fighting this battle in the first place.'[30] The VSW was also keen to establish a unified agrarian front by formulating a programme of agricultural protectionism that provided incentives – for every farmer, if possible. It demanded that 'in fixing the level of agricultural tariffs ... it is not just cereal and livestock tariffs that must take the form of protective tariffs but also those tariffs' that 'are of particular benefit to *small farms,* such as tariffs on eggs, on live and dead poultry, on bed feathers'.[31]

There are good reasons here to follow Hans-Jürgen Puhle and suspect that such statements were ideologically motivated, that they functioned first and foremost as instruments of manipulation through which the leaders of the agrarian organizations hoped to secure the support of those running small and medium-sized farms.[32] But this is only half-true. First, the slogans of the agrarian interest organizations generally reflected what the agrarian protest movement, which was based mostly on self-mobilization 'from below' rather than taking its instructions 'from above', had articulated since the early 1890s.[33] Second, such slogans were more than mere rhetoric: they reflected comprehensive catalogues of demands, championed by the agricultural interest groups using every political means at their disposal. The protectionist wish lists propagated by the leading agrarian interest organizations covered just about every agricultural product and – unless they had become embroiled in the close political combat of the Reichstag – diverged from one another only in detail.

The agrarians wanted to see a dramatic increase in the livestock tariff in the new customs tariff. The DLR called for an eightfold increase in the tariff rates for cattle, while the BdL demanded a fourfold increase for pigs.[34] Separate from this, since its foundation in 1893 the latter had called for the borders to be closed as much as possible to foreign cattle under the pretext that they were likely to spread disease.[35] In the case of eggs, the board of the DLR and the *Deutsche Tageszeitung,* an organ of the BdL, spoke almost with one voice in calling for the treaty tariff to be raised by 2 marks to 37.50 and 40 marks, respectively. Overall, what the agrarians had in mind amounted to a virtually seamless system of protection for agricultural products; in many cases, this would have not just a protectionist but prohibitive effect.[36] Most politically charged was undoubtedly the envisaged increase in cereal tariffs. In place of the Caprivi rates of 3.5 marks per 100 kilograms of wheat and rye, and 2 and 2.8 marks respectively for barley and oats, the DLR demanded a tariff rate of 7.5 marks for all cereal types, which must remain above 6 marks even within the framework of the trade treaties.[37] This was not enough for the BdL, which agitated for a minimum rate of 7.5 marks for rye, wheat, barley and oats.[38] Following joint consultations with the BdL and the Union of German Peasant Farmers' Association (Vereinigung der deutschen Bauernvereine), the Bavarian Peasants' League (Bayerischer Bauernbund) too propagated a tariff increase of at least 7 marks for the four main types of cereal.[39]

But the demands with which the agrarian interest organizations bombarded the imperial government and the governments of the states through a plethora of submissions and that they addressed to the public via the numerous newspapers close to or controlled by them were not limited to specific tariff rates. What the agrarians sought was a fundamental reorganization of the entire system of customs tariffs. The current general tariff, whose rates the government itself believed it could have reduced in trade treaty negotiations, in order to maintain corresponding reciprocal measures of benefit to the empire's own export goods, should be replaced – and here all the agrarian organizations agreed – by a dual tariff of the kind introduced a few years earlier by France in the shape of the Méline tariff.[40] The advantage of the dual tariff system that the agrarians wished to implement for all goods or 'at least for agriculture'[41], was, they believed, that it fixed both the maximum and minimum tariff for every product. Even in trade treaty negotiations – and this was the key point – the negotiators could not go below this fixed minimum tariff. The agrarians would thus retain a legally guaranteed tariff protection; this would make renewal of the Caprivi treaties, which they perceived as a debacle and required Germany to keep agricultural tariffs low, practically impossible.[42] Essentially, the agrarian proposals aimed to prevent entirely the conclusion of new long-term trade treaties and to return to Bismarck's autonomous tariff policy. Should this ultimate aim prove impossible to achieve, the agrarians wanted to see safeguards built into the new customs tariff, right from the outset, that would prevent subsequent lowering of agricultural tariffs through trade treaty agreements.

The call for the '*general* elimination of the privileges currently granted to most states through the *most-favoured-nation clause* ... by terminating their most-favoured-nation status' was along the same lines.[43] Renunciation of the most-favoured-nation concept, inherent in every trade agreement made by the German Empire, would not only have meant breaking with a principle consistently upheld since 1860, but would have completely undermined the existing trade treaty system and dramatically curtailed the applicability of German tariff concessions. In addition, the call for a radical change of trade policy course was regularly flanked by a series of demands for nontariff trade restrictions to be included in the customs tariff law. The most prominent of these demands was the elimination of mixed entrepôts for cereals and the abolition of customs credits, both of which would have greatly hindered cereal imports.[44]

With the odd deviation or difference in emphasis here and there, this catalogue of demands for agricultural protection was advocated unanimously by all agrarian organizations active across the empire and regionally. By far the most powerful organization among them, with the greatest public appeal, was the Agrarian League, the BdL. Historians have already analyzed and discussed the reasons for this in-depth, namely, its success in claiming to speak for agriculture as a whole, its organizational strength, its specific ideology and its position within the political system of the German Empire, so there is no need for us to recapitulate their work here.[45] But it is still interesting to ask why, within the entire spectrum of organized interest groups around the turn of the century, not one single economic policy association was able to match the BdL's success and influence. To preempt the issue a little: why, despite its much greater economic momentum, did industry and trade fail to produce a similarly powerful and effective interest organization?

Our preliminary theoretical reflections suggest that we should highlight two aspects. First, the BdL was able to build on the constellation of interests outlined above within German agriculture, which offered fairly favourable preconditions for a trade policy campaign. Almost every farmer was negatively affected by the globalization of the agricultural market, so agrarian producers' interest in protectionism was intense and widespread. Trade policy interests within the secondary and tertiary sector, in contrast, were markedly more heterogeneous, and the consequences of protectionist intervention for historical actors were significantly more difficult to predict. Both factors meant far less favourable conditions for the development of a strong organization taking a unified foreign trade policy line.

Second, like no other economic interest organization, the BdL succeeded in getting the problems of collective action under control. The league showed considerable skill in wooing members and gaining their support through a whole package of positive selective incentives. Through the affiliated commercial organizations, it not only offered them discounts on the purchase of seeds, artificial fertilizers, feedstuffs and agricultural machinery, but also provided them with technical and legal advice and helped them obtain inexpensive insurance.[46] In contrast to the collective good of 'tariff protection', from which no farmer could be excluded, these benefits accrued exclusively to members of the league. The league's ideology, which combined evocation of the unity of 'country people' and the primacy of agriculture with conservative-cooperative elements, social Darwinist ideas and a radical anti-Semitism, may also have helped deal with the free rider problem and gain the BdL a large number of supporters. The approximately 250,000 individuals[47] who were members of the league at the turn of the new century made it not only the largest economic interest association outside of the trade unions, but also enabled it, through members' financial contributions, to maintain its elaborate organization and highly effective propaganda machine.

In terms of the political enforcement of agrarian desires, in the run-up to the customs tariff decision of 1902 there was a kind of division of labour between the agrarian organizations, which was certainly not their initial intention and which went far from smoothly. On the one hand, the German Agricultural Council, the DLR, in which the more moderate agrarians had the upper hand, sought to exert its influence on the executive. Its mainly aristocratic representatives were able to build on the traditionally privileged position of the social strata they represented within the Prussian-German hegemonic cartel and make use of their excellent connections in the ministerial bureaucracy. Provided with information by the government on a preferential basis and consulted on important matters, in 1897 the DLR was asked (as a matter of course) to identify five delegates to represent the interests of agriculture on the newly formed tariff policy advisory board, the thirty-member Economic Committee on the Preparation and Assessment of Trade Policy Measures, together with five agrarians appointed by the government.[48] In the Economic Committee's Commission on Agriculture, Foodstuffs and Luxury Consumables

(Landwirtschaft sowie Nahrungs- und Genußmittel) the agrarians, very much among their own kind (just three of the thirteen commission members came from outside agriculture),[49] could articulate their protectionist aspirations virtually unchallenged and influence the organization of the new customs tariff.

The Agrarian League, on the other hand, whose manner and demands were far more radical and uncompromising than those of the DLR, took a sharply oppositional stance towards the government from its foundation onwards and maintained a 'chronically bad relationship with the central ministerial bureaucracy'.[50] It took on the task of disseminating protectionist propaganda and influencing the Reichstag, in which the customs tariff bill might still be changed and which would ultimately have to pass it. On the whole the BdL was highly successful in its activities.[51] Here it benefited greatly from the crisis of the traditional dignitaries' parties, which lacked the organizational substructure so vital in the emerging age of the 'political mass market' (H. Rosenberg). The BdL filled this lacuna by aiding the election campaigns of those politicians it chose to support through its highly effective propaganda machine and mobilizing people to vote for them. In return, the candidates had to pledge in writing and in advance their support for the BdL's electoral platform – the league was subsequently meticulous in monitoring their adherence to this commitment during parliamentary votes, and would never fail to punish anyone who broke with it by withdrawing its support and ostracizing them. At the Reichstag elections of 1898, which produced the Reichstag that ultimately decided on the customs tariff in 1902, and in whose success the tariff issue played an important role, the BdL managed to obtain a prior commitment to its programme from no less than 118 of the 397 deputies elected – most of them members of the two conservative parties.

But even in those cases where BdL candidates did not prevail, the league's electoral agitation was not without effect. In many agrarian constituencies, because of the league's aggressive presence the candidates it did not support could win their seat only because they largely embraced its agricultural protectionist demands. For the National Liberal and Centre Party deputies in particular, the price paid for winning their seats in the Reichstag was the thoroughgoing 'agrarianization' of their trade policy views. When the air had cleared after the election campaign, the Reichstag that assembled was one in which a clear majority favoured strengthening tariff protection for agriculture. Those who supported continuing von Caprivi's trade treaty policy also had to come to terms with this fact. As the *Kölnische Zeitung*, which leaned towards the National Liberals and was in favour of trade treaties, commented before the Reichstag negotiations on the new customs tariff had even begun, there could be 'no possible doubt' that 'it will be impossible to achieve a Reichstag majority for the trade treaties without moderately increasing the cereal tariffs'.[52] But what a 'moderate increase' meant was still subject to much dispute.

## *The Associations of Trade and Industry*

In contrast to agriculture, which was generally battered by the new competitive conditions in the world market, though to varying degrees, economic globalization had a highly variable impact on the secondary and tertiary sectors of the German economy. Branches troubled by the international competitive pressures contrasted with those which, because of their outstanding competitive position in the world market, made most of their profits through export while at the same time benefiting from the opportunity to obtain primary products cheaply from foreign countries; other parts of the German economy, meanwhile, were comparatively little affected by globalization, since internationally tradable goods played only a negligible role for them. Even within a single economic branch, foreign economic interests could diverge significantly. An example of this was the textile industry, where the opposition between the spinners, who found themselves exposed to superior British import competition, and the weavers, whose interest lay in obtaining cheap and high-quality yarn from the U.K. as smoothly as possible, was only the most intense branch-internal conflict of interest (see chapter 1).

This fragmentation of economic interests found expression in a broad spectrum of trade policy positions, extending from manifestly protectionist to fundamentally free trade perspectives. These were far from the best conditions for the development of a powerful organization with clearly formulated tariff and trade policy objectives. This applied less to the level of trade and regional associations, of which there was no lack in the German Empire, and whose membership structure generally reflected homogenous interests – from the Union of Saxon Spinning Mill Owners (Vereinigung Sächsischer Spinnereibesitzer) through the Association of German Cotton Yarn Consumers (Verband deutscher Baumwollgarnkonsumenten) to the Association of Breweries of Berlin and Environs (Verein der Brauereien von Berlin und Umgegend). But it certainly applied to the cross-sectoral central and umbrella organizations of trade and industry, which were faced with the virtually impossible task of formulating a trade policy strategy capable of achieving consensus, but which were the only bodies with the organizational capacity and legitimacy to influence not just specific tariffs but also the basic character of tariff and trade policy.

Again, it is testimony to how much easier it was to organize and promote protectionist interests, as opposed to the free exchange of goods, that in advance of the Bülow tariff, of the industrial interest organizations it was the one with the most protectionist views, namely, the Central Association of German Industrialists (Centralverband Deutscher Industrieller or CVDI), that had the greatest opportunity to exercise an influence, and it was the most protectionist forces that initially held sway within it. In the CVDI, the notion of protective tariffs had the full weight of organizational tradition behind it. When it was founded in 1876 in response to the global economic crisis that had persisted since 1873, the key driving force was the desire to 'protect national labour'; the struggle against free trade had welded its members together.

By the turn of the century, the CVDI had developed from a body solely concerned with tariff-related agitation into a central industrial organization engaged in a wide range of activities. The CVDI had excellent connections within the Prussian-German ministerial bureaucracy and had made itself 'indispensable' by functioning as an 'intermediary between businesses and the central state administration'.[53] It was consulted as a source of expertise on every important economic policy issue and was involved in the preparation of draft laws; its representatives sat on the relevant advisory boards, panels and committees. By the turn of the century the CVDI had succeeded in gaining member associations from every significant branch of industry, so it could claim with some justification to represent German industry as a whole. Nonetheless, in the shape of the textile industry and particularly heavy industry, the CVDI's approach continued to be determined primarily by the two economic branches that had set the tone when it was founded. In other words, its approach to trade policy and other issues as well was dominated by the spinners' associations and the cartelized coal and steel industry, which had a proclivity for protectionist strategies in terms of both their interests and traditions.

This protectionist bias and the CVDI's excellent connections with the government were clearly evident in the establishment of the Economic Committee. The initiative to establish this tariff policy advisory board, which formally came under the ambit of the Imperial Ministry of the Interior and whose members were leading representatives of economic interest groups, came from the executive director of the CVDI, Henry Axel Bueck. '[I]n its whole approach, in its composition and purpose, and in the impact it is eventually likely to make', Bueck emphasized, the Economic Committee corresponded 'on the whole' to the 'proposals made [in the] memorandum [he himself had] submitted' in June 1897;[54] the course was set for the establishment of the new body in a conversation between Miquel, Bueck and Emil Russel, who was a member of the board of both the CVDI and the German Trade Association.[55] In the shape of Max Frey, Carl Krafft, Eduard Lang, Gustav Koenig and Richard von Vopelius, the

CVDI sent five 'avowed protectionists'[56] to sit on the Economic Committee. Interestingly, three of them, Frey, Krafft and Lang, had a background in the textile industry. Koenig, president of the German Sugar Industry Association (Verein Deutscher Zuckerindustrieller), and Vopelius, president of the German Association of Glass Industrialists (Verband der Glasindustriellen Deutschlands), were representatives of two branches of industry close to agriculture. Heavy industry, meanwhile, remained politely in the background – only Vopelius was considered close to it.[57] The Imperial Ministry of the Interior for its part was so kind as to nominate another five industrialists close to the CVDI or members of it, who were also known for their protectionist views.[58] In light of its composition, there could be no doubt about the Economic Committee's trade policy orientation: in the shape of these industrialists and the ten representatives of agrarian interests, the remaining ten members of the Economic Committee, who were supposed to represent the interests of trade and the export industry,[59] found themselves confronted by a 'phalanx of protectionists'[60] who could outvote them on all important issues. The Economic Committee, then, seemed to have laid the institutional foundation for the protectionist reorientation of German foreign trade policy.

The longer the political disputes over the customs tariff dragged on, however, the more clearly the differences in trade policy interests within industry came to light, even in the CVDI. A first taste of things to come was provided in 1897/98, when conflict broke out between cotton spinners and weavers over the level of yarn tariffs.[61] For a time, the CVDI leadership managed to wrest a unifying formula from both parties in tough negotiations. Two years later, this had become unthinkable. In circulars of 9 February and 5 May 1900, the CVDI called on its members to give their views on the customs tariff scheme and on the level of the individual tariff rates.[62] The original goal had been to achieve an intraindustrial compromise on the basis of the responses received and to present the government – as in 1879 – with a coherent and comprehensive catalogue of demands supported by all CVDI members in a spirit of solidarity. But the leadership of the CVDI had 'not yet' succeeded in 'inducing such unanimity', despite its 'many earnest efforts'. In contrast to 1879, 'on this occasion [it proved impossible] to persuade large sections of German industry … to subordinate their special interests to the interests of the whole'.[63]

The demands of the different branches diverged greatly, while the German economy's integration into the international trade system was now far advanced. The tariff question thus seemed too important for anyone to have been willing to agree to a common line. This was abundantly clear once again at the CVDI board meeting on 19 and 20 June 1900, in which the agenda was dominated by the results of the members' survey and how best to proceed: 'When the responses on the specific tariff rates were examined in great depth', the CVDI's executive director stated, 'conflicting views based on diverging interests were frequently in evidence'.[64] The dispute between the associations of spinning and weaving broke out again with striking vigour; but in the iron and steel industry too, and in a number of other branches, conflicts of interests between the producers and processors of semifinished products proved unbridgeable. The board of the CVDI managed to achieve a unanimous vote only with respect to two of the just under one thousand tariff rates included in the customs tariff bill, those for pig iron and cement.[65] In all other cases, driven by the fear that the CVDI would fall apart, the decision was made not to resolve the conflicts of interest that had emerged by means of a majority decision. Instead, the CVDI would simply collate all the responses submitted to it, some of which were quite contradictory, and pass them on to the government.[66]

There were also profound disagreements within the CVDI on the question of whether the new customs tariff should take the form of a uniform or dual tariff. Once again, consensus could not be reached either in the CVDI commission or executive board: 'views were divided'. Once again, both bodies chose not to settle 'this extraordinarily important issue by majority decision', and thus entirely avoided establishing what the CVDI's official position was. In a vain attempt to shift attention away from its own inability to make a decision, the CVDI leadership sought salvation by declaring that it 'is the task of the imperial executive, in accordance with the far more comprehensive knowledge and experience at its disposal in dealing with foreign affairs',[67] to make a choice between a uniform and dual tariff. There could be no clearer indication of the internal disunity of this leading industrial association – never otherwise noted for its restrained approach to the provision of political advice – than this peculiar 'vote of confidence'.

Even these tortuous manoeuvres, however, could do nothing to change the fact that those trade associations and firms that felt that their foreign trade interests were not being adequately reflected in the CVDI now turned their back on the association. The major dye works left the CVDI around 1900 because of tariff issues. Their trade association, the Association for the Protection of the Interests of the German Chemical Industry (Verein zur Wahrung der Interessen der Chemischen Industrie Deutschlands or Chemieverein for short), had already left the CVDI in 1889/90, since the chemical industry 'not only received no support [from it], but was in fact often harmed [by it]'.[68] The paper processing industry also broke with the CVDI in 1902 by leaving the Association of German Paper Manufacturers (Verein deutscher Papierfabrikanten), which was a member of the industrial umbrella organization.[69] So profound were the conflicts of interest that emerged within the CVDI over the tariff issue that the exasperated Anton von Rieppel, a member of the executive board, proposed in 1902 that tariff and trade policy issues be left entirely to the individual trade associations in future, with the CVDI limiting itself to the sphere of social policy.[70]

How did the escalating dispute over the new customs tariff – and the fact that export interests were also gaining ground within the CVDI – impact on the 'politics of rallying together' being pursued by agriculture and industry in an attempt to promote the 'protection of national labour', an alliance discussed with equal avidity by contemporaries and historians[71] and one that Prussian finance minister Miquel did his utmost to nurture? The founding of the Economic Committee was very much in line with this project. It aimed to revive the protectionist coalition of 1879, and its composition – the generally moderate agrarians of the DLR on one side, convinced protectionists from the ranks of the CVDI on the other – seemed to lay the groundwork for an agrarian-industrial alliance on a protectionist foundation. The CVDI too left no one in any doubt that it was prepared to back the raising of agricultural tariffs. From the perspective of the industrialists, however, there was a point beyond which tariff increases should not go. This point was reached if the strengthening of German agricultural protection began to pose a serious risk to the conclusion of new trade treaties, in other words, the continuation of Caprivi's trade treaty policy.

There could be no clearer expression of this ambivalent stance towards agrarian demands than the resolution passed by the meeting of CVDI delegates in early February 1901 – with just one vote against. On the one hand, the assembly acknowledged 'that the current difficulties of German agriculture require an adequate increase in cereal tariffs'. On the other hand, it 'expected' that 'this increase should be of a level compatible with the common good and in particular a level that does not rule out the possibility of concluding long-term trade treaties'.[72] From the perspective of the CVDI, then, the key compromise reached by the assembly cannot be summed up in Eckart Kehr's classical formula: 'for industry the fleet, imperialism and expansion; for the Agrarians the tariffs and maintenance of the social superiority of the Conservatives'.[73] As Geoff Eley has brought out convincingly, this notion had already come to grief because the fleet was quite unable to fulfil the unifying function ascribed to it and was generally regarded as a disruptive factor by everyone concerned.[74] The compromise on tariff and trade policy was instead to be achieved in accordance with the following principle: to the agrarians an increase in protective agricultural tariffs, to industry the continuation of the policy of long-term trade treaties. This compromise was explicitly accepted by the moderate agrarians,[75] but – and this is what made it so fragile – it was permanently threatened by the BdL's extensive tariff demands and agitation against the trade treaties.

But the crisis between the interest organizations of agriculture and industry only broke out openly after the government had published its customs tariff bill in the summer of 1901. The dual tariff contained in the government bill for wheat, rye, barley and oats prompted the CVDI executive board to abandon its former restraint on the question of a uniform or dual tariff and raise 'the most serious reservations about the provision set out in the draft law', according 'to which only the tariff rates for cereals must under no circumstances be reduced by treaty-based agreements. This stipulation', the board went on, was apt 'to put at risk or even render impossible the conclusion of any trade treaties at all. This is not a risk that industry can run, and it was never the intention of the Central Association to allow higher cereal tariffs without the concurrent conclusion of new trade treaties.'[76] This stance initially led to polarization within the CVDI, which came clearly to light at the assembly of delegates on 1 October 1901.[77] On one side stood the 'agrarian industrialists'[78] – represented by Koenig and Vopelius, who were also on the Economic Committee – who wished to maintain the alliance with agriculture at any cost, up to and including the extremists of the BdL; they defended the principle of the dual tariff and saw the solution as the imposition of a minimum tariff on all industrial articles. On the other side stood the other members of the CVDI, who rallied around their chief executive, Bueck. Though essentially very open-minded about agrarian demands, he made a speech critical of Koenig's views,[79] came out firmly against the dual tariff and eventually came out on top – despite a resolution worded in such a way as to conceal dissent.[80] That Bueck, with his pro–trade treaty views, represented not just the concerns of those businesses within the finishing industry that were members of the CVDI, but at least as much the interests of western German heavy industry, which feared for its export opportunities, is already apparent in the fact that just three days after the CVDI's resolution was published, the Association of German Iron and Steel Industrialists, the VDEStI, expressed its vigorous opposition to the 'fixing of minimal tariff rates for cereals, and the laying down of minimum tariff rates in general'.[81]

What a fundamental challenge this represented to the agrarian-industrial front is evident in the reaction of the agrarian press. Immediately after the CVDI executive board had stated its position on the government bill in early August 1901, the *Deutsche Tageszeitung*, a BdL organ, declared that if the 'Central Association' stuck to its 'view' then 'the so-called *politics of rallying together is finished*', since 'as is well-known … [the agrarians had] declared their willingness' to 'support long-term trade treaties' only 'on the condition that legally enshrined minimum tariffs are introduced'.[82] On this occasion, the *Kreuzzeitung*, which usually took a less radical line than the BdL press, threatened open confrontation: 'in the parliament, however, Mr. Bueck will soon come to understand that the friends of agriculture will vote against any increase in any industrial tariff and thus against the entire tariff bill if they are not granted the minimum tariff on cereals. … Mr. Bueck will be laughing on the other side of his face when the decision is made.'[83] The 'flood of invective'[84] that the agrarian press heaped on the CVDI after its vote against the dual tariff for cereals, and the open conflict that this 'dirty trick' unleashed between it and 'its former allies, the agrarians',[85] did not mark, as the *Freisinnige Zeitung* crowed, the detachment of the CVDI 'from Miquelian talk of the politics of rallying together'[86] or the final abandonment of attempts at agrarian-industrial cooperation. But they did show very clearly the extent to which globalization had intensified domestic economic conflicts of interest and, as a result, how unstable and brittle every conception of collective action that pinned its hopes on finding a balance between trade policy interests must inevitably be. The potential for conflict was far greater than it had been in 1879, and all parties involved felt that there was much more at stake.

The second of Germany's central industrial associations, the Industrialists' League (Bund der Industriellen, or BdI), was also initially keen on the 'politics of rallying together'. This is astonishing given that the BdI chiefly represented the export-oriented finishing industry and had emerged in 1895 by highlighting its differences from the CVDI and heavy industry.[87] From late 1896, the BdI ameliorated its initially confrontational stance towards agrarians and heavy industry and increasingly sought to collaborate with the CVDI. There were two main reasons for this. First, there seemed to be scant prospects that the aspirations of the finishing industry would be taken into account in the reworking of the customs tariff: in the absence of cooperation with more influential interest groups, the BdI was fairly insignificant. Within the BdI, therefore, the more strongly protectionist wing around general secretary Wilhelm Wendlandt temporarily held sway. With respect to tariff policy, it was in favour of cooperating with the CVDI and balancing the interests of industry and agriculture, including the finishing industry. Second, the further increase in American tariffs brought about by the Dingley tariff of 1897 and the bogeyman of the 'American peril' in general helped bring about an alliance within the BdI in favour of protectionist measures. The motives underlying the actions of the groups involved in it varied greatly. While a number of BdI members suffered from the increasing American competition and expected higher tariffs to better protect them from their unwelcome competitors, the other group of tariff supporters saw their own export opportunities as threatened by American high protectionism and merely wished to use German tariff increases as a temporary means of wresting trade policy concessions from the U.S.[88]

Over the long term, however, neither the 'American peril' nor the association's principle of making no fundamental decision on free trade versus protectionism and instead 'supporting the increase or lowering of import tariffs ... on a case-by-case basis'[89] proved capable of papering over the conflicts of interest within the association. The longer the dispute over the Bülow tariff went on, and the more concrete the form it took, the more clearly the faction in the BdI opposed to its leadership's collaborative course articulated their views and advocated resistance to the tariff bill. Before the passing of the Bülow tariff in the Reichstag, this group managed to gain the upper hand, prompting the BdI board to declare themselves against the 'serious damage being done to the nation's interests as a whole, but particularly those of industry'[90] as a result of the planned agricultural tariff increases – and officially taking the league into the camp opposed to the protectionist front. This change, of course, was also facilitated by the increasingly obvious fact that the BdI had largely failed to achieve the tariff policy demands of the industrial branches it represented.

There are three key reasons for the negligible influence exercised by the Industrialists' League. First, in contrast to the established CVDI, the still young BdI enjoyed no privileged access to the government or ministerial bureaucracy. This difficult starting point was compounded by the fact that the BdI leadership focused their lobbying efforts exclusively on the Imperial Ministry of the Interior, though it was well-known that the Imperial Treasury was also playing a significant role in the tariff preparations.[91] Second, the heterogeneity of the interests represented in the BdI impeded the formulation and determined pursuit of a clear trade policy line. In the BdI, as in the CVDI, despite its members' heavy dependence on exports, it was initially those producers keen on protectionist measures who held sway, their demands having the advantage of being easy to specify and enforce through specific tariff rates. Only after some delay, when the customs tariff bill presented a specific outcome to which critics could address themselves, did an antiprotectionist faction increasingly take shape within the BdI, though it was unable to make any fundamental difference to the association's general paralysis with respect to tariff policy. Third, the BdI proved incapable of overcoming the difficulties involved in collective action. Neither the association's ideology, which was in a state of flux around the turn of the century and was yet to incorporate its later focus on medium-sized businesses and its associated emphasis on the contrast between producers of raw materials and the finished goods industry, nor the privileges with which the league provided its members were sufficiently appealing to mobilize its own clientele. The BdI's membership numbers and growth, at least in the early days, were very modest. The league's income from membership fees was thus negligible, resulting in a chronic lack of funds. Significantly, this prevented the development of an effective bureaucratic apparatus of the kind that characterized the BdL and the CVDI.[92]

The fragmentation of economic interests, which was a major headache for umbrella organizations like the CVDI and the BdI that covered such a broad spectrum of interests, was a less daunting problem for the trade policy associations. Because they were founded to pursue specific objectives, they only attracted members who at least more or less agreed with them. At the same time, their membership basis extended beyond the secondary sector, taking in industrialists and representatives of trade and the banks. While producers keen on protectionist intervention clearly felt represented by the existing associations, in the context of impending customs tariff reform around the turn of the century exponents of a liberal tariff and trade policy believed they could assert their interests only by founding new organizations. The Central Department for Trade Treaties (Centralstelle für Vorbereitung von Handelsverträgen) emerged in 1897 under the aegis of the Chemieverein with the participation of a number of associations specifically focused on industrial exports and the BdI.[93] The year before, representatives of the major Berlin banks, trade, shipping and the export industry had jointly founded the Protection Association against Agrarian Encroachments (Schutzverband gegen agrarische Übergriffe), whose declared goal was the 'the defence of all economic interests threatened by agrarian encroachments'.[94] Finally, on 11 November 1900, following preparatory discussions chiefly involving representatives of wholesale trade and shipping from Hamburg and Bremen, the Trade Treaty Association (Handelsvertragsverein or HVV) was launched.[95] Under the presidency of Georg von Siemens (of the Deutsche Bank), the HVV rapidly developed into the most important fighting organization opposed to the protectionist front; its membership grew rapidly, peaking at 16,700 in May 1902, and it launched vigorous campaigns immediately after its establishment.

All these associations of economically liberal provenance shared a fundamentally defensive character. They did not fight under the banner of free trade or call for further reductions in existing tariffs. Their objective was merely to secure the trade policy status quo. The HVV's articles of association, for example, explicitly identified the 'Association's purpose' as 'maintenance of German tariff and trade policy as established through the existing trade treaties and opposition to attempts to dismantle it'.[96] Like the Protection Association against Agrarian Encroachments and the Central Department for Trade Treaties before it, the Trade Treaty Association emerged as a defensive reaction among export-oriented economic circles to agrarian efforts to revise Caprivi's trade policies, which had been gaining traction since the mid-1890s. Even in their choice of names, the newly founded organizations consciously kept their distance from anything that might have looked like a dogmatic free trade stance. In view of the powerful current of protectionism and in order to facilitate the conclusion of new trade treaties, their aim was to prevent excessive tariff increases and ensure that the customs tariff did not take the form of a dual tariff.[97] But given the existing balance of political forces, the representatives of the export industry and trade were under no illusion that they could prevent some increase in the level of protection. For the liberal trade associations, the least likely source of support for their foreign trade interests was the democratically elected parliament, whose composition made it seem to them like a hotbed of protectionism. They placed 'greater trust',[98] meanwhile, in the government, at least parts of which seemed willing to listen to their demands.

It is hard to gauge the impact made by the activities of the Trade Treaty Association and other similar special-purpose associations. There is very little evidence that they exercised a direct influence on the tariff policy decision-making process; with respect to membership and organizational clout they seem to have been the poor relation of the Agrarian League. All of this indicates that, on the whole, the organizations of those opposed to the protectionist front enjoyed little success. Two factors go a long way to explaining this. First, the founding of the HVV, as the most important antiprotectionist economic association, occurred too late to exercise much influence. Most of the preliminary work on the tariff had already been done by the ministerial bureaucracy and the Economic Committee, and by late 1900 the fundamental decisions had already been made with respect to a large number of issues.

Second, the HVV's capacity to take effective action was impaired by a split over tactics as the debate on the customs tariff wore on.[99] While the more pro–free trade portion of the HVV's members advocated delaying adoption of the customs tariff in the Reichstag through targeted obstruction until the elections of 1903, the opposing camp eventually called for the organization to support the government bill and thus accept a marked increase in the level of protection. Interestingly, in addition to Hamburg shipowner Albert Ballin, who Chancellor Bernhard von Bülow sought to sway by sending Heinrich von Tschirschky as his special representative and who was even persuaded to try to influence the Hanseatic city's press and chamber of commerce,[100] the latter group included representatives of the major chemical and electrotechnical firms. While most other branches expressed trade policy views that can be straightforwardly traced back to their economic interests, the willingness of these two flagships of German exports to countenance protectionist compromises seems to contradict the expectations expressed earlier (chapter 2), namely, that – given their high degree of dependency on the world market and dominant competitive position – they should really have been among the most energetic protagonists of the greatest possible degree of trade liberalization. This was because the major corporations of the chemical and electrical industry could take a far more relaxed view of likely export problems than small and medium-sized firms. Much like modern multinational companies, they were the only firms in a position to engage in capital exports and circumvent other states' restrictive foreign trade policies by constructing branch factories abroad. This gave companies such as Siemens or AEG competitive advantages on the international market over their smaller German competitors, and as they attempted to calculate their complex web of interests these advantages seem to have more than made up for the disadvantages that they too would suffer from any intensification of German tariff protection.[101]

In contrast to industry, trade had no central association of its own – again, this supports the thesis that those economic circles eager to see the free cross-border exchange of goods had poorer organizational potential than those in favour of protectionism. The German Trade Association (Deutscher Handelstag or DHT) was of course not solely concerned with representing the interests of trade. The DHT, which acted as a free association, certainly formed the umbrella organization for all chambers of commerce and other commercial bodies in the German Empire. But the chambers of commerce did not represent only the tertiary but also the secondary sector in a given district. A survey carried out shortly after the turn of the century showed that in 1902, of 3,070 members of chambers of commerce, far more than half, 1,716, were engaged in industry rather than trade.[102] Within the DHT, the chambers of the coastal cities, entirely dominated by wholesale trade and shipping, thus stood alongside those completely dominated by industrialists; in others a mixed picture prevailed. The lattice of interests within the DHT was further complicated by the fact that, apart from the corporations of trade and industry that businesses were legally obliged to join, there were a number of free industrial associations among its members. These included the Dortmund Mines Association (Verein für die bergbaulichen Interessen im Oberbergamtsbezirk Dortmund) and the Northwestern Group of the VDEStI (Nordwestliche Gruppe des VDEStI) as well as the Chemieverein and the Association for the Protection of Common Economic Interests in the Rhineland and Westphalia (the Langnamverein).[103]

Unsurprisingly, then, like no other economic organization the German Trade Association encompassed the full spectrum of diverging foreign trade policy interests that came to the fore within trade and industry due to the pressures exerted by the first wave of globalization. The DHT's internal disunity was laid bare at the plenary assembly of 8 January 1901. The motion put forward by the Kassel Chamber of Commerce that the DHT should declare itself 'firmly against any increase in the tariffs on foodstuffs'[104] was passed by a wafer-thin majority; with 147 votes to 144, the assembly was split into two almost equally large blocs. At the next plenary assembly of 30 September 1901, the DHT board sought to prevent any repeat demonstration of its own disunity by putting a draft resolution to the assembly that did not reject all increases in agricultural tariffs per se, but merely

> explicitly [emphasized its] reservations about the *extraordinary* increase in tariffs on foodstuffs in the tariff bill (the risk posed to trade treaties, increased cost of living, weakening of purchasing power with respect to industrial products, and impairing of the ability of German commerce to compete with foreign companies).[105]

'It seemed more desirable', explained the DHT General Secretary Soetbeer in his address, 'to put forward a more flexible version if a large majority could be persuaded to support it, rather than suggest something more radical that would have resulted in the kind of division we saw in January'.[106] But the efforts by the DHT leadership to avoid the open expression of internal tensions proved largely in vain. On one side, Wilhelm Beumer, who represented heavy industry in the Rhineland and Westphalia, made a point of expressing his commitment on behalf of the Langnamverein and Northwestern Group of the VDEStI to the 'community of interest between agriculture and industry' and declared that he was 'unable to support the declaration [proposed by the board] against the raising of tariffs on foodstuffs'.[107] On the other side, the free trade–oriented chambers of commerce criticized the board's draft resolution as too 'mild' and called on the DHT to be far more vigorous in its opposition to the 'pretensions of the agrarian movement'.[108]

And yet, in contrast to 1879 and 1885, when, 'because of the starkly opposing interests'[109] and the fear that it might otherwise fall to pieces, the DHT chose to express no view at all on agricultural tariffs, this time a crucial vote took place. The motion put forward by a number of chambers of commerce dominated by heavy industry, which described 'a moderate increase in *tariff rates* on *cereals* and *other agricultural products* … as necessary from the perspective of agriculture and permissible from the standpoint of consumers', was overwhelmingly rejected. The board's motion, which expressed its 'strong support' for a 'significant reduction in tariffs on foodstuffs in the tariff bill', was passed by a similarly large majority.[110] There was by now too much at stake for most members of the DHT – as evident in the submissions and petitions from individual chambers of commerce, which ran to the thousands[111] – because of the German economy's high degree of dependency on foreign trade, and they perceived the intensification of German agricultural protectionism as too great a threat to their own export interests to continue to forgo an emphatic vote against the projected increases in agricultural tariffs in order to avoid conflict.[112]

Furthermore, the debates and resolutions of the DHT left no one in any doubt that certain key tariff and trade policy demands were unanimously supported by all branches of industry and trade. At the top of the list was the demand for the continuation of the policy of long-term trade treaties begun under Caprivi. For German exports, far more important than the level of specific tariff rates was the predictability, the '*stability* of conditions',[113] that long-term trade treaties guaranteed with respect to the foreign trade policies of other states. Second, all members of the DHT were unanimous in believing it imperative that the trade treaties continue to adhere to the most-favoured-nation principle.[114] Third and finally, the DHT came out more or less unanimously against the dual tariff and thus against legally enshrined minimum tariff rates because it feared these would hinder the conclusion of new trade treaties or render them impossible.[115]

## The Social Democrats and the Interests of Consumers

Endogenous tariff theory generally considers consumers, with their preference for the lowest possible tariffs on consumer goods, chronically difficult to organize.[116] So despite the fact that in quantitative terms they constitute the most significant of the groups negatively affected by trade restrictions, the assumption is that they are inadequately represented within the political process. In a rational choice model, the utility likely to accrue to the individual from active participation in an interest organization seems too small relative to the costs for such participation to be likely to occur. The incentive to become politically engaged is reduced even further by the nonapplicability of the exclusion principle, in other words, by the fact that the desired free access to the world market, as a public good, benefits all consumers regardless of their political efforts. Most consumers do more than just consume; as employers or employees they are also the producers of certain goods or services and in this role they sometimes have conflicting and more central protectionist interests, which is another reason why consumer interests find it difficult to develop a strong lobby.

At first glance, this seems to be contradicted by the fact that consumers in the German Empire had a very well-organized and politically successful representative of their interests in the shape of the Social Democratic Party (Sozialdemokratische Partei Deutschlands, SPD). But this paradox is more apparent than real, and highlights the fact that consumer interests played a fundamentally different role for the SPD than did producer interests for the associations of agriculture, industry and trade. In contrast to the relationship between producer interests and economic associations, for the Social Democrats consumer interests were not the point of departure for or the foundation of their organization. The SPD began life as a workers' party rather than a consumers' party and only later discovered that articulating consumer interests could have great public appeal. Thus, in its foundational phase the SPD did not face the specific problems of collective action that it would have as a genuine representative of consumer interests. Its later electoral successes may have been due to the great emphasis it placed on consumer interests, but its organizational strength had other roots.

Christoph Nonn has provided an in-depth analysis of the development of the SPD into a consumers' party in his thorough study of consumer protest and the party system in Wilhelmine Germany. Nonn links the transformation of the SPD into a consumers' party causally with the increase in meat prices after the turn of the century. The Social Democrats, it is claimed, increasingly made themselves the 'mouthpiece' of protests over price increases triggered by the cost of meat, which – in contrast to the price of bread – rose markedly in the last few years before the First World War. In terms of its public profile and clientele, in the decade before 1914 the SPD thus increasingly represented consumer interests.[117]

Here, in contrast, I suggest that the process rightly identified as such by Nonn entered its crucial phase earlier, namely, before the turn of the century, and had other causes. When public protests broke out in 1905 as a consequence of the first wave of price increases, the course had already long been set for the development of the SPD into a party of urban consumers. The rise in the price of meat and other animal products was not the cause of the transformation of the Social Democratic Party, though it undoubtedly gave it another major boost. Of crucial importance to the reorientation of the SPD was the dispute, which began with the debate on the Caprivi treaties, on the German Empire's tariff and trade policy, which had been put on the agenda by globalization and culminated in the political battle over the Bülow tariff. Over the course of the final decade of the nineteenth century, foreign trade policy came to occupy an ever more central place in the sphere of public interest. Initially, the initiative for this undoubtedly came from the agricultural producers, among whom the long-standing fall in the price of agricultural products, in combination with the cereal tariff reductions contained in the Caprivi treaties, led to unprecedented and enduring mobilization in the early 1890s. The protectionist demands of the agrarian interest organizations had provoked a counterreaction on the political left even before the turn of the century. Since it looked ever more likely that agrarian demands for protectionism would be met, the SPD increasingly presented itself as a bulwark of consumer interests. In the long-standing conflict over the customs tariff reform of 1902, it sharpened its profile as the advocate of urban consumers. This process can be observed both on the level of internal party debate and with respect to the Reichstag elections and the election campaigns that preceded them.

On the level of internal party debate, we can see that the consumer perspective and free trade principles did not originally form part of the German Social Democrats' core ideology. The Gotha Conference of 1876 declared 'that the battle between protectionism and free trade that has broken out within the propertied classes is quite alien to the socialists of Germany'. In the 'question of whether or not there should be protective tariffs', the Social Democrats at the time saw no question of principle but 'merely a practical question' that must 'be decided upon on a case-by-case basis'.[118] But the pragmatism of the Gotha resolution was fundamentally revised at the SPD conference of 1898 in response to the efforts to establish a protectionist front and the preparations being made for the reorganization of the customs tariff. Of course, there was no lack of opposition to committing the Social Democrats to a fundamentally free trade perspective. Max Schippel, who made the speech on tariff and trade policy, declared that under certain circumstances protective tariffs were also in the interests of the workers, that 'the issue of protective tariffs and of free trade [could] never become a class issue for workers', and thus suggested that the party make no firm commitment in this respect but instead 'keep its options open'. For him, the workers were 'not pure consumers' but rather 'participants in the present-day organism of production'.[119] Ignaz Auer, secretary of the party executive, also came out against the fundamental SPD commitment to opposing all protective tariffs – agricultural or industrial – contained in Karl Kautsky's draft resolution. He underlined that 'in terms of practical agitation, party members' had had 'very bad experiences' when taking such a firm approach.[120] Ultimately, however, the party leadership around Bebel managed to overcome internal party resistance to an unambiguous SPD position. After the situation had been mildly diffused with respect to industrial tariffs (there was in any case consensus within the party regarding the rejection of agricultural tariffs), Kautsky's resolution was passed 'by a very large majority'.[121]

At the party conference in September 1900, the free trade course that had been raised to the status of party doctrine two years before was confirmed and extended. According to the resolution passed by the party conference, the new customs tariff that was gradually taking shape would leave 'the consumer, chiefly the working class, powerless and helplessly at the mercy of the prices dictated by a united business world'. Against this background the SPD declared its 'rejection of all tariffs and all tariff increases, particularly on foodstuffs' and support 'for a trade treaty policy whose objective is to progressively dismantle mutual restrictions on trade and foster global free trade'.[122] In terms of party strategy, it was by this point at the latest, as they tried to get to grips with key tariff policy issues, that the German Social Democrats committed themselves unambiguously to the defence of consumer interests and the principle of freedom of trade.

When the customs tariff bill then appeared in 1901 with its massive tariff increases for cereals and meat,[123] the SPD immediately resolved to undertake a major campaign of agitation 'against this planned robbery of the people'.[124] The following year, the party executive could report to the conference that in 'thousands of gatherings in every part of the empire … there have been protests against the hunger tariffs, while sharply worded resolutions have expressed our opposition to the attempt', under 'the guise of "protecting national labour", to exploit consumers, and above all the working population, to benefit a few thousand big landowners and the industrial magnates [*Schlotjunker*] in the most flagrant way by artificially raising the prices of the most essential everyday comestibles'.[125] The SPD's antiprotectionist propaganda campaign, which emphasized the consumer standpoint rather than the class perspective and included not just word-of-mouth agitation but also an extensive leafleting campaign, culminated in a mass petition, a clever mise-en-scène by the party, against the 'profiteering and hunger tariff'. This was signed by almost 3.5 million individuals. As the party leadership explicitly stated, not all of them were workers, but in fact represented '*every* section of the population'.[126]

We can also trace the SPD's transformation into a consumers' party by looking at Reichstag elections. This applies first of all to the thematic emphases of election campaigns. As early as the elections of 1890, in view of the temporary boom in the price of foodstuffs, the SPD made its agitation against agricultural tariffs, which had been raised once again in 1887, part of its election campaign, helping it achieve a magnificent result. In 1898, the defence of consumer interests and opposition to demands for protective agrarian tariffs in particular were once again among the key themes of the SPD's election campaign. Finally, at the elections of 1903, which took place just a few months after the Bülow tariff had been approved by the Reichstag, resistance to the customs tariff and the struggle against 'bread profiteers' stood centre stage in the SPD campaign. The SPD increasingly emphasized the consumer standpoint and antiprotectionism, which went hand in hand with a reining in of public expressions of revolutionary Marxist rhetoric. In this sense the party was both pacesetter and part of a process whose origins lay in the early 1890s, one that fundamentally changed the empire's political culture. Over the course of this process, propelled on the other side of the political spectrum by the agrarian interest organizations, above all the BdL, both the content and style of political debate were transformed. In the elections held between 1890 and 1903, the government proved increasingly incapable of determining the key themes of the election campaigns. Increasingly this was done by the propaganda machines on the right and left of politics, which focused on appealing to the masses. In the shape of tariff and trade policy – the demand for agricultural protectionism on the one hand and opposition to the 'hunger tariffs' on the other – they placed at the centre of the political battle a topic that underlined the socioeconomic conflicts within German society and, above all, one that starkly highlighted one of the key latent sources of tension, namely, the conflict between rural producers and urban consumers.[127]

The recent electoral studies by Jonathan Sperber and Brett Fairbairn, who base their arguments on elaborate statistical analyses, confirm that these developments saw the SPD increasingly establish itself as a consumers' party. In terms of its membership structure, the SPD remained a working-class Protestant party limited by confessional boundaries for the entire duration of the empire. From 1890 on, however, it increasingly managed to tap into a new pool of voters beyond its original social milieu. In the 1890s, the SPD began to make inroads among working-class Catholics, a trend that intensified after the turn of the century, though the religious factor continued to impede the party's political advance. Above all, though, by underlining the shared interests of consumers, the SPD managed to attract the votes of an increasing portion of the urban bourgeoisie and especially the rapidly growing 'new middle class' of white-collar workers and civil servants. According to Sperber's calculations, 42 per cent of voters from the Protestant middle class – though this umbrella term captures only very imperfectly the conditions in Germany at the time – voted for the SPD at the Reichstag elections of 1903; this was only a slightly smaller proportion than it managed to attract among working-class Protestants.[128] The flip side of the Social Democrats' spectacular gains among urban consumers across classes was its persistent failure in the agrarian regions. In the early 1890s, under the slogan coined at the party conference in Halle, 'Into the countryside!', the SPD was still trying to gain a foothold among rural labourers and peasant farmers through a comprehensive campaign of rural agitation; this helped it achieve its first rural successes – particularly through the efforts of Otto Braun in East Prussia. In subsequent years, its increasingly radical and uncompromising opposition to all protectionist measures intended to support agricultural prices, a dominant aspect of the party's public profile, did much to prevent any further gains in these areas.[129]

## The Splintering of the Executive

Depending on one's methodological standpoint, the debate on the reorganization of the customs tariff either highlighted the profound conflicts of interest between agriculture and industry, within trade and industry, and between agrarian producers and urban consumers, or constructed these conflicts discursively in the first place. In any case, the Prussian-German executive was directly affected. The fundamental antagonism between the representatives of a protective tariff policy designed to close Germany off as much as possible from the world market and the representatives of a proglobalization, export- and consumer-oriented trade policy extended into the offices of the ministerial bureaucracy and became entangled with the at times significant competition between the different departments.

### *The Dispute over the Tariff Scheme*

The conflict that arose between the Imperial Treasury and the Imperial Ministry of the Interior over the arrangement of the individual items in the new customs tariff provided a taste of the disputes to come. The officials at the Imperial Treasury had begun preparing for the revision of the customs tariff under the leadership of Arthur von Posadowsky-Wehner. Under his successor, Max von Thielmann, who had previously been ambassador in Washington, D.C., and played a significant role in the conclusion of the German-Russian trade treaty in 1894 as leader of the German delegation, this work was seamlessly continued. For his part, when he moved to the Imperial Ministry of the Interior in 1897, Posadowsky tried to bring responsibility for preparing the new customs tariff under its ambit and immediately began to draw up a tariff bill in competition with that of the Imperial Treasury. No one, however, disputed the need to reform the customs tariff, which essentially harked back to the Prussian tariff of 1818.[130] What organizing principle should underpin the new customs tariff, however, was a matter of great controversy.

At the beginning of October 1898, the Imperial Treasury went on the offensive and submitted its draft customs tariff, completed in August, which initially contained the new tariff scheme only but no tariff rates, to the federal governments and other imperial departments.[131] The structure of the draft tariff was geared towards the stages of the manufacturing process. First came raw materials, then semifinished products and finally finished products. Posadowsky expressed vehement opposition to this structure. He asserted that the new customs tariff was intended 'to establish not merely a financial tariff system, but rather a system of tariffs adapted to national labour in its entirety, one consisting chiefly of protective tariffs'. In his view, the Imperial Treasury's draft tariff, which was 'constructed on the opposition between material and product', did not provide a suitable basis for this. Only the 'economic tariff system' favoured by the Imperial Ministry of the Interior, in which the tariff items were arranged in accordance with the different branches of industry, would do justice to the overarching political imperatives and represent 'genuine progress vis-à-vis the current domestic and foreign tariff schemes'.[132] At the same time, Posadowsky presented the completed section of the alternative drawn up by the Imperial Ministry of the Interior, which aggregated the products of 'agriculture and of the food and luxury consumables industry' and which was to be prominently placed right at the start of the customs tariff.[133]

The secretary of the interior received strong support from Prussian agriculture minister Ernst von Hammerstein in particular. With great openness, the latter expressed the true nature of the dispute over the tariff scheme, namely, the fact that 'the arrangement of the groups of individual dutiable goods in many cases also entails a preliminary decision on the gradations of the tariff rates' and that 'as a consequence the inclusion of types of goods in one group or another [will] often determine in advance the level of the tariff on a given product'.[134] In the tariff scheme developed by the Imperial Ministry of the Interior, 'which divides up goods according to branches of industry … and thus [aims] to dedicate special sections to the products of agriculture and forestry and the foodstuff industry', Hammerstein felt that the interests of agriculture, which he saw himself as representing, would be far 'better safeguarded and asserted' than in the 'systems drawn up [by the] Imperial Treasury based on a natural scientific perspective and the opposition between material and finished product', because in the latter agricultural products, as 'primary products', would be 'unreasonably placed on the backburner' in comparison with other categories of goods; this 'would be a heavy blow to those affected'.[135] The Prussian agriculture minister thus found himself in perfect harmony with the German Agricultural Council, which – and this is unlikely to be a coincidence – had called immediately before, in December 1898, for agrarian products to be brought together in one category in the new customs tariff in order to underline from the outset agriculture's special need for protection.[136]

The conflict over the arrangement of customs tariff items was indivisibly bound up with the dispute over the extent to which economic interest groups should be involved in preparatory work on the tariff. While the Imperial Treasury, with its generally positive attitude towards the expansion of trade, sought to keep all economic interest organizations – not just protectionist ones – out of the trade policy decision-making process as far as possible, and explicitly informed the other departments 'that the bill [should] be treated as confidential' and 'in particular to refrain for now from imparting it to chambers of commerce and similar bodies',[137] the opposite applied to the protectionist ministries. In line with the maxim propagated by Prussian finance minister Miquel, '[N]ot to make any rules within the political sphere without being certain that they enjoy the consent of the propertied classes',[138] Posadowsky, also called 'the imperial answer to Miquel'[139] by the left-liberal press, sought to give the protectionist interest groups precedence within the preliminary work on the customs tariff reform.

Very much in this vein was the establishment of the Economic Committee, which was brought to life as a tariff policy advisory board reporting to the Imperial Ministry of the Interior and was, from the outset, conceived in such a way that it was dominated by protectionists (see above). Establishing the Economic Committee was only secondarily a matter of drawing on economic expertise to inform the impending customs tariff reform. More important still was its political function: it was to signal to the interest organizations that the imperial leadership was listening to their tariff policy demands, while also providing them with a forum within which they could reach agreement in the spirit of collective action. The first task of the Economic Committee was to carry out a comprehensive production survey. This was intended to serve as the basis for the draft tariff bill developed by the Imperial Ministry of the Interior and within the framework of which producers were explicitly urged 'to express [their] wishes … particularly with respect to foreign competition both at home and abroad'.[140] Regarding the findings of the production survey, Posadowsky repeatedly pointed out that he thought it 'especially important that account be taken of this preparatory work, to which the most outstanding representatives of the branches of industry affected have contributed … because those involved in industry would not understand if the activities of their representatives were left out of account'.[141]

With regard to the structure of the customs tariff, a 'characteristic compromise' proposed by Prussian finance minister Miquel was finally agreed to after about a year of conflict[142] between supporters of the drafts drawn up by the Imperial Treasury and the Imperial Ministry of the Interior.[143] With respect to the basic conception of the tariff, the approach that held sway was the Imperial Treasury's systematic one, which could also point to the support of the federal governments outside Prussia.[144] In the case of agriculture, however, the organizing principle of the Imperial Treasury's template was violated. Agricultural products were aggregated within a dedicated section as a coherent block that preceded the other categories within the tariff bill.[145] The second change made to the draft provided by the Imperial Treasury was the revision of the section dealing with the iron industry to ensure that it reflected the views of the interested parties within heavy industry. In the early stages of the ministerial bureaucracy's preliminary work on the customs tariff reform, then, it was the two branches of the economy with the greatest organizational power and most strongly protectionist tendencies that succeeded in asserting their interests.

## *The Conflict over the Tariff System*

The conflict over the customs tariff scheme had not yet been resolved when Posadowsky launched a general attack on the principles of the existing trade policy system. In a comprehensive memorandum, he outlined the trade policy situation of the German Empire and explained that the 'unification of the tariff treaty and most-favoured-nation system' brought about by the conclusion of Caprivi's trade treaties was 'untenable over the long term', because the pure most-favoured-nation approach allowed a number of mainly non-European states to enjoy the tariff reductions guaranteed by Germany in the tariff treaties without making any concessions of their own, so that 'major benefits [fell] into their laps without them giving anything in return'.[146] With respect to the future, the secretary of the interior thus advocated breaking with the trade policy system that had pertained hitherto, which fused together the long-term bilateral trade agreements featuring extensive reciprocal tariff concessions with the universal validity of the most-favoured-nation principle, which generalized the tariff reductions stipulated in the treaties. As Posadowsky saw it, there were two basic alternatives for German trade policy. It could either move towards a reciprocity-based system making only limited use of the most-favoured-nation principle or 'generally forego reducing and fixing the … most important tariffs' and return to the system of autonomous tariff policy and straightforward most-favoured-nation approach that applied during the Bismarck era. Because the second approach entailed the risk that Germany would face the U.S. with no trade policy 'weapons' at its disposal and with nothing to 'defend itself against Great Britain's efforts to band together with its colonies', Posadowsky gave priority to the first option, in other words, the conclusion of bilateral trade treaties and restricted use of the most-favoured-nation approach.[147]

In the view of the Imperial Ministry of the Interior, in order to be better equipped to deal with future trade treaty negotiations the new German customs tariff should be 'arranged in such a way that every foreign state, in line with the level of its imports to Germany, has an interest in achieving favourable tariff rates here, while no state can obtain preferential tariff rates without granting us privileges of equal value'.[148] As Posadowsky saw it, a dual tariff of the kind introduced by France in 1892 in the form of the Méline tariff would be the best way of meeting this requirement.[149] In contrast to the existing customs tariff, for every tariff item it should specify not one but two tariff rates, a minimum and maximum. The maximum tariff would apply to those states unwilling to grant Germany trade policy concessions within the framework of reciprocal treaties. The minimum tariff, meanwhile, would represent the legally enshrined 'minimum protection' and mark the lowest possible level that German negotiators working on trade treaties could propose. On the one hand, the idea here was that the maximum tariffs would provide the German Empire with 'sufficient bargaining counters'[150] to wrest from other states – it was the U.S. that the key actors generally had in mind here – tariff reductions in treaty negotiations. On the other hand, the minimum tariff was the insurance, unanimously demanded by all agricultural organizations, against any move to go below the fixed limits in later trade treaties. Even during periods of high agricultural prices, this would have made a repeat of the agricultural tariff reductions implemented by Caprivi in the early 1890s by the treaty route impossible or at least much more difficult.

That this aspect clearly predominated for the supporters of the dual tariff is evident in the preferences of the Prussian Finance Ministry and the Prussian Ministry of Agriculture, both of which expressed their avid support for the Imperial Ministry of the Interior. 'To achieve the objective we aim to achieve in drawing up a new German customs tariff, namely, of granting national labour the necessary protection and in particular ensuring an improvement in the position of agriculture', to quote Prussian finance minister Miquel, who left no one in any doubt about his priorities, it was 'particularly important that the circles involved, and again, agriculture in particular, are provided with guarantees that we will not go below the level of protection regarded as necessary in formulating our treaty-based tariff and trade relations with other states'.[151] Prussian agriculture minister Hammerstein also saw the 'main task' of the customs tariff reform as '*helping German agriculture and doing everything possible to eliminate the heavy pressure it has been under for some time now*'.[152] This could best be done, as both he and the radical agrarians believed, by returning to Bismarck's autonomous tariff policy. Since even he could not avoid 'acknowledging the interest of trade and industry in trade treaties that run for a reasonable and specific length of time',[153] and therefore considered it unlikely that the government would turn its back on the trade treaty policy begun by Caprivi, in the interests of agriculture he must at least insist on the introduction of a minimum tariff. Only the dual tariff could guarantee agriculture the minimum level of protection necessary over the long term. Ultimately, the introduction of a dual tariff would have meant nothing less than the self-disempowerment of the executive and a corresponding shift of authority to the legislative branch. By enshrining a minimum tariff in law, rather than leaving the government complete room for manoeuvre, as it had done previously, to reach agreements on lower rates in treaties and decide ex post facto whether to accept the resulting trade agreement, the Reichstag would have determined in advance the extent of possible tariff reductions within the framework of trade treaties.

Vigorous opposition to the change of course intended by the Imperial Ministry of the Interior, in collaboration with the Prussian Finance Ministry and the Prussian Ministry of Agriculture, soon sprang into life within the Prussian-German ministerial bureaucracy. The Foreign Ministry, Imperial Treasury and Prussian Ministry of Trade and Commerce (Ministerium für Handel und Gewerbe) joined forces to advocate the retention of the existing trade policy system, based on a unified tariff, long-term trade treaties and general application of the most-favoured-nation principle. Contra the Méline tariff, constantly held up as a shining example by supporters of a dual tariff,[154] the Imperial Treasury asserted that since French foreign trade had lagged far behind its German counterpart since its introduction, it 'seems justified to conclude' that 'the customs tariff of 1892 has not fulfilled the hopes placed in it. Industry has begun to fall behind to some extent, while there has been no improvement in the situation of agriculture.'[155] According to the Imperial Treasury, one crucial reason not to adopt a dual tariff was that the tariff rates in the maximum tariff were set too high in relation to the German economy's actual need for protection, and would have to apply to raw materials and semifinished products as well if they were to effectively fulfil their intended function – as bargaining chips to prompt other states to make concessions. This utterly excessive maximum tariff, which was motivated by purely tactical concerns, would ultimately come into force vis-à-vis every country with which Germany had not concluded a trade treaty, and would therefore result in a 'per se unjustifiable increase in the price of the goods affected as well as harming domestic consumers'.[156]

Apart from the manufacturing industry, which would no longer be able to obtain certain primary products customs-free, German exports would suffer as well as other countries took retaliatory measures. Above all, 'given the sense of irritation with Germany there, the application of any maximum tariff, of even the most modest kind, to imports from the United States of America … [would] likely [trigger] an immediate customs war' with unforeseeable consequences.[157] The Foreign Ministry backed the idea – in contrast to the claims of the opposing camp – that, even as a starting position, the dual tariff would be worse than a uniform tariff in trade treaty negotiations rather than an advantage. The enshrining in law of minimum tariffs would inform the governments of other states which concessions the German Empire was fundamentally prepared to make. They would then regard the maximum tariff 'as merely a sham tariff and view the reductions at issue as a matter of course, for which it is unnecessary to concede anything significant in return'.[158] Trade treaties favourable to German exports could not therefore be achieved on the basis of a dual tariff.

Above all, though, the Foreign Ministry took up the cudgels for unlimited application of the most-favoured-nation principle. 'More than that of some other states', German exporting industry was

> keen to avoid differential treatment in foreign countries. We export a large number of different products, but we enjoy a solid monopoly only with respect to a very small number of articles, and in virtually every field we are subject to competition from highly developed foreign industries. What this means is that without too much trouble we can be driven from the relevant foreign markets through differential tariff treatment.[159]

But it was precisely such disadvantages vis-à-vis their international competitors that would threaten German exporters if the German Empire broke with the most-favoured-nation principle. In addition, when it came to 'preserving or renouncing the most-favoured principle', even more than with respect to setting the general tariff level, it was crucial to take 'account of the potential political repercussions'. Since the Cobden Treaty of 1860, the most-favoured-nation clause had been a taken-for-granted component of every trade treaty. Though by now free trade theory was in retreat and the idea of protective tariffs had gained ground, at least within European trade policy, the view was firmly anchored that tariff policy differentiation, in other words, a failure to grant most-favoured-nation status, was a 'violation of the principles of international economic intercourse', an 'infringement of the other party's legitimate interests'.[160] By withholding most-favoured-nation status, the German Empire thus ran the risk 'of inflaming public opinion in other countries, prompting their governments to take retaliatory economic measures against us and consequently causing serious repercussions in the genuinely political field'.[161] So at least with respect to the major European powers, which were also Germany's leading trading partners, because it was so important to avoid such political disgruntlement it was advisable to uphold the most-favoured-nation principle without qualification.

In contrast to the customs tariff scheme, with respect to the dual tariff the warring departments could no longer bridge the gulf between their differing views; they were unable, of their own accord, to agree to a solution acceptable to both sides.[162] A meeting of the six ministers and imperial secretaries involved, held on 6 October 1900 under the chairmanship of Hohenlohe, who was still in office, ended inconclusively.[163] So it was one of the first tasks facing Bernhard von Bülow, who was appointed imperial chancellor shortly afterwards, to resolve the issue of a dual versus uniform tariff and end the logjam within the Prussian-German executive. At a meeting on 27 October that both he and all the relevant departmental chiefs again attended, he managed to find a compromise that seemed acceptable to everyone. The customs tariff would be structured as a dual tariff for the most important agricultural products and a small number of industrial goods and as a uniform tariff for all other items.[164] On the one hand, this was a partial victory for the agrarians pushing for minimum agricultural tariffs, while on the other hand, it was a formula that deferred any detailed decision on the nature and quantity of goods to which a dual tariff should apply.

Since Bülow had unambiguously espoused the uniform tariff as foreign secretary, all sides expected a clear decision to reject the dual tariff.[165] We can identify two key factors that would have prompted him to accommodate the advocates of the dual tariff and seek a fundamentally dilatory solution. First, by indicating his willingness to reach an accommodation with respect to the tariff issue, he hoped to break the opposition to his canal bill among the agrarians in the Prussian House of Representatives. Bülow's opening speech in the Prussian Landtag of 9 January 1901 was along the same lines. Here he also linked the Mittelland canal project with approval for increased agricultural tariff protection.[166] Second, in late October 1900, the agricultural interest organizations enjoyed a clear advantage over those of industry and trade with respect to the development and public articulation of their view on the dual tariff issue. While all agricultural associations had expressed their unanimous and unambiguous support for a customs tariff featuring minimum and maximum rates, the CVDI had just declared itself incapable of coming to a clear position as a result of internal differences, while the DHT had yet to express its view.[167] The compromise suggested by Bülow reflected the agrarians' temporary discursive hegemony, while also being intended to give the protest movement against the dual tariff time to develop; it was gradually getting off the ground in industrial and trade circles and the supporters of the existing tariff system within the ministerial bureaucracy urgently required its support.

Meanwhile, the conflict between the departments on the issue of the customs tariff system shifted to specifying the tariff items for which a dual tariff should be introduced. In what was by now its third draft tariff, which underpinned the commissarial deliberations among the relevant ministries and imperial offices in March 1901, the Imperial Treasury provided for dual rates for thirty-one tariff numbers – all of them agricultural products. While the Prussian Ministry of Trade expressed broad agreement with this, the Foreign Ministry took the view that 'even the number of dual rates provided for in the draft goes beyond what is necessary and is questionable in trade policy terms', and proposed limiting the dual tariff to breadstuffs and livestock along with directly derivative products.[168] The Imperial Ministry of the Interior, Prussian Finance Ministry and Prussian Ministry of Agriculture, meanwhile, expressed their vehement opposition to any further reduction in the dual rates. The representatives of the Imperial Ministry of the Interior alleged that the restriction of the dual tariff supported by the Foreign Ministry would 'not seem adequate to the agricultural circles and the parties close to them in the Reichstag'.[169] The assessment of the Prussian Ministry of Agriculture was graver still. Through Caprivi's customs and trade policy, which had 'profoundly damaged the interests of German agriculture', the government had 'lost the trust of broad swathes of the very parts of the population which, intimately entwined with the interests of the state due to their property ownership, formerly provided the most solid support for its policies'. If this undesirable development was to be corrected, agriculture must be granted a comprehensive, minimal level of protection, which would ideally go beyond the dual rates proposed in the Imperial Treasury's draft. If the Foreign Ministry were to get its proposal accepted, on the other hand, 'the great expectations [harboured by] agriculture' would 'give way to a general sense of disappointment' and 'a storm would be unleashed that would [inevitably] lead to an acrimonious struggle between the government and the parliament, with consequences that cannot be ignored'.[170]

The same animosity was also in evidence with respect to whether the dual tariff should be restricted to agricultural products or extended to certain industrial goods. While the Foreign Ministry, Imperial Treasury and Prussian Ministry of Trade, in order to avoid making it even more difficult to conclude trade treaties and because they feared that were this to happen there would be a protectionist arms race within industry, came out against the introduction of minimum tariffs for specific industrial products, the Imperial Ministry of the Interior, Prussian Finance Ministry and Prussian Ministry of Agriculture came out in favour.[171] Still espousing the 'politics of rallying together' propagated mainly by him and Miquel, Posadowsky pointed out that 'it would lead to serious internal difficulties if the fundamentally different treatment of industry drove a wedge between it and agriculture at a time when both groups are dependent on one another's support in the impending parliamentary negotiations on customs tariff reform'.[172] The secretary of the interior therefore proposed introducing dual rates for pig iron, a number of semifinished products of the iron industry, leather, paper and various yarns and thus for the products of the most protectionist industrial interest groups, 'whose support the government cannot do without as it replaces the customs tariff'.[173] Since the Foreign Ministry, Imperial Treasury and Prussian Ministry of Trade categorically refused to support such an extension of the dual tariff, in the spring of 1901 the camps within the ministerial bureaucracy were once again as irreconcilably opposed as they had been half a year earlier.

## *The Dispute over Tariff Rates and the Completion of the Tariff Bill*

The more time that passed by, the more the dispute over the tariff system was overlaid by a third conflict revolving around the level of the tariff rates. The dynamics of the interdepartmental conflict was the same as with the dispute over the dual tariff: the Imperial Ministry of the Interior, Prussian Finance Ministry, and Prussian Ministry of Agriculture sought to raise the tariff level significantly across the board – this applied chiefly to the products of agriculture, but to a lesser extent to the products of import-competing branches of industry as well. The Foreign Ministry, Imperial Treasury and Prussian Ministry of Trade, meanwhile, sought to keep the tariff increase within strict limits. At the commissarial conference, which brought together the leading expert officials of the three Prussian and three imperial departments in March 1901 and which had in fact been arranged by Bülow at the suggestion of Miquel in order to resolve the remaining differences of opinion, these divergent views came into collision with one another.[174] After nine days, there were still seventy tariff rates on which it had proved impossible to reach agreement.[175]

More than three-quarters of these problem cases related to agricultural products and foodstuffs. The quixotic ideas of the Ministry of Agriculture often made it particularly difficult to reach a consensus. In the case of livestock tariffs, for example, it requested an increase higher than that envisaged in the Imperial Treasury's template, yet because of the move from quantity-based to weight-based tariffs, this already provided for an increase of between two and six times the existing tariff burden. It is true, the ministry conceded, that there were 'negligible imports of livestock … at present because of the impact of the veterinary prohibition on certain imports and the meat inspection law'. But the sensible course of action was 'to use this favourable set of circumstances and introduce the highest possible livestock tariffs so that if the ban on certain imports, etc. is eliminated at some point, the high tariff would mean that German livestock farming would have nothing to fear from foreign countries'. So in this case it was not the acute threat emanating from international competition that was cited to justify a prohibitive protective tariff, but the potential risks posed by the advancing globalization of the agricultural market. In view of the likely increase in global supplies of animal foodstuffs, it was crucial, 'in the interests of German agriculture, to act quickly to prevent the kind of competition and plunging prices suffered by the previous generation with respect to grain growing'.[176]

Unsurprisingly, the tariffs for the four main cereal types proved particularly controversial. Table 5.1 shows the various proposals for the minimum tariff still being espoused by the imperial and Prussian ministries during the second round of consultation. The Ministry of Agriculture was by far the most ambitious, proposing either a minimum tariff of 70 marks per tonne for wheat and rye and 50 marks per tonne for oats and barley or, alternatively, 60 marks per tonne for all cereal types. It could point to the views of the Economic Committee, in which a plenary majority had also expressed support for a minimum tariff of at least 60 marks for rye, wheat and oats.[177] The Foreign Ministry was most moderate in its tariff proposals, favouring the introduction of a minimum tariff for wheat and rye only. For oats and barley, meanwhile, it called for a uniform rate that could be lowered in treaty negotiations at the negotiators' discretion. The Foreign Ministry also emphasized that the minimum tariff for rye should be set somewhat lower than that for wheat. The idea was that this would facilitate the conclusion of a trade treaty with Russia, which was by far

**Table 5.1.** Departments' requests for minimum tariffs on cereals, March 1901 (marks per tonne)

| | *Wheat* | *Rye* | *Oats* | *Barley* |
|---|---|---|---|---|
| *Tariff enshrined in treaty* | 35 | 35 | 28 | 20 |
| *Proposal from Ministry of Agriculture* | 70 or 60 | 70 or 60 | 50 or 60 | 50 or 60 |
| *Proposal from Prussian Ministry of Finance* | 60 | 55 | 50 | 40 |
| *Proposal from Imperial Ministry of the Interior* | 60 | 60 | 50 | 35 |
| *Proposal from Prussian Ministry of Trade* | 55 | 50 | 50 | 50 uniform rate |
| *Proposal from Imperial Treasury* | 55 | 50 | 50 | 50 uniform rate |
| *Proposal from Foreign Ministry* | 55 | 50 | 60 uniform rate | 50 uniform rate |

*Source:* Findings of the commissarial consultation among the relevant imperial and royal Prussian departments on the draft customs tariff law, 29 March 1901, BA, R 1501, 118904, fols 11–12)

Germany's most important supplier of rye and thus had a particular interest in the rye tariff.[178]

If we compare the minimum tariffs proposed by the various ministries with one another and with the existing conventional tariff, two main aspects stand out. First, even the lowest proposed tariffs amounted to a dramatic increase in protectionism. The long-standing pressure exerted by the agrarian interest organizations and the majoritarian arithmetic in the Reichstag, as the Foreign Ministry resignedly acknowledged, made it seem 'inadvisable ... in light of domestic politics' to countenance a tariff rate of less than 50 marks for the different types of breadstuffs.[179] Second, the differences between the various proposals, which seemed negligible in comparison to the projected increase, still contained enough explosive material to make it very difficult for the different parts of the Prussian-German ministerial bureaucracy to reach consensus. Mediation talks between the ministries were thus broken off with no resolution of the cereal tariff issue.

Two tactical moves by Bülow were necessary to overcome the standoff between the imperial and Prussian ministries and end the dispute within the government on the customs tariff bill – at least for a time. The first was the comprehensive ministerial shake-up of early May 1901.[180] Bülow used the government's retreat on the canal issue, into which it had been forced by the conservatives in the Prussian House of Representatives, to rid himself of his keenest competitor in the Prussian State Ministry, namely, Prussian finance minister Miquel. He was replaced by former minister of the interior Georg von Rheinbaben. Hammerstein, who was unwavering in his insistence on a minimum tariff of 60 marks for cereals and whose tariff demands had greatly impeded efforts to find a compromise in other ways as well, had to leave the Prussian Ministry of Agriculture and was replaced by Victor von Podbielski; this former chief of the Imperial Post (Reichspostamt), though once a member of the BdL, was considered a fairly moderate agrarian conservative. Ludwig Brefeld, last of the three Prussian ministers involved in preparing the customs tariff, also left his post. The new Prussian trade minister was Theodor Möller, formerly a member of the Reichstag as a deputy for the National Liberals. Möller had been a member of the Economic Committee and overall favoured a moderately protectionist course. Before they took up their posts, all the new cabinet members had to pledge their support for a political programme comprising three key points: 'the drawing up of new trade treaties and, in line with this, a moderate approach both to those cereal tariffs earmarked for increase and to the preferred form of the minimum tariff, such that the tariff does not hinder the conclusion of treaties, and continued support for the canal project'.[181] In terms of the customs tariff issue, which played a key role here, this was consonant with Bülow's policy of the 'middle way', as he had outlined it at the October conference. 'It is particularly important', Bülow underlined there, 'to arrange the minimal rates in such a way that they do not go beyond the minimum level of unavoidably necessary protection and in no way create obstacles to the conclusion of trade treaties'.[182] The cabinet reshuffle was intended to clear the way for the compromise that was clearly being impeded by the old ministerial team.

Bülow's second coup was the convening of a tariff policy conference in early June of 1901, to which he invited not just the leaders of the imperial and Prussian ministries involved in the preliminary work on the tariff bill, but also the finance ministers of the larger states, namely, Bavaria, Saxony, Württemberg, Baden and Hesse.[183] Bülow pursued twin objectives through this conference. First, involving the other states from the outset was intended to ensure the customs tariff bill smooth passage through the Bundesrat. Second, the presence of the governments of the federal states, known for their moderate tariff policy approach, was intended to demonstrate to the more protectionist ministries that a high protectionist tariff bill would not find majority support in the Bundesrat and compel them to back down. Bülow was generally successful in both respects. Before the conference had even begun, as they sat together 'in one of the window bays in the main hall of the Bundesrat', he had come to an agreement with Bavarian finance minister Emil Riedel[184] on the parameters of a common strategy: above all, the customs tariff should be designed in such a way that it presented no insurmountable obstacles to the conclusion of new trade treaties. The number of dual rates should thus be kept to a minimum. Finally, cereal and livestock tariffs should certainly be increased substantially, but not on the scale demanded by the agrarians, as this would have increased the price of foodstuffs to the point of endangering the social peace.[185]

The outcome of the tariff policy conference was very much in line with this. Of the thirty-one dual rates included in the Imperial Treasury's proposal, just four survived the first day: the customs tariff law was to stipulate a minimum tariff only for rye, wheat, oats and barley, and the trade treaty negotiators must not go below this level. Rheinbaben's attempt to argue, much like his predecessor, that it was necessary 'to set minimum rates for important industrial articles and avoid disrupting the solidarity between agriculture and industry',[186] like Posadowsky's efforts to salvage the dual tariff for livestock, got nowhere due to the unanimous opposition of the Foreign Ministry, Imperial Treasury, Ministry of Trade and the federal states.[187] The decisions on tariff rates reflected the views of the ministries advocating a lower level of protection. The minimum rate for wheat was set at 55 marks per tonne; for rye the figure was 50 marks (reflecting the difference from the wheat tariff requested by the Foreign Ministry); for oats too a tariff rate of at least 50 marks would apply; finally, a minimum tariff of 30 marks was stipulated for barley.[188] This still meant a major increase in tariffs, but was at the lower end of the proposals that had been aired.

Two other developments facilitated this turning point in the standoff on tariff rates. First, from early May 1901, the customs tariff bill was no longer linked with the Mittelland canal project: the government had withdrawn the canal bill because the Landtag committee seemed set to reject it. Thus, with respect to the tariff issue, Bülow no longer had to factor in the agrarian conservatives in the Prussian House of Representatives in the same way as he had before. Second, an antiprotectionist front gradually began to gain traction within trade and industry. This provided a counterweight, at least to a certain extent, to the agrarian protectionist propaganda that had completely dominated the public political sphere. The Trade Treaty Association had been launched as the main platform of the 'antiprotectionist front', and the German Trade Association too had come out almost unanimously against the dual tariff and for a continuation of Caprivi's trade treaty policy at its plenary assembly of 8 January 1901.[189]

Overall, the events described above paint an ambivalent picture of the capacity to steer political events enjoyed by the new imperial chancellor and Prussian prime minister.[190] On the one hand, he undoubtedly succeeded in getting the decision he wanted with considerable tactical skill. He thus put his stamp on the customs tariff bill as the politically responsible leader of imperial policy. On the other hand, the 'middle way' policy that Bülow championed was not based on any substantive trade policy concept; there was no long-term strategy informed by specific principles. It was instead based chiefly on pragmatic and tactical concerns, was geared entirely towards the views of the opposing camps and raised the steering of a skilful course between them to the status of political programme. This does not indicate that the imperial chancellor was in control of the situation. Nor does the fact that, despite the preceding reshuffle, he needed the federal states to make the departments advocating a more protectionist approach see reason. The political situation was Bülow's master far more than the other way round. Economic globalization had made tariff policy one of the main fields of conflict and fostered the development of diametrically opposing fronts that extended all the way into the Prussian-German ministerial bureaucracy; these factors systematically limited the imperial leadership's room for political manoeuvre. Given the growing pressure from all sides, Bülow and the empire's other key political actors were concerned only to find a compromise on the customs tariff issue that would do at least reasonable justice to the different interests.

This shrank to a bare minimum their capacity to pursue autonomous objectives beyond the sphere of tariff policy: right from the start, fiscal policy aspects, for example, played an utterly subordinate role in the consultations on the customs tariff bill.[191]

In the summer of 1901, as he sought a compromise on the customs tariff issue, Bülow was to discover just how fine and fragile a line he was walking. After first disseminating reports on the new tariffs in the press through deliberate indiscretion, he finally had the tariff bill published in the *Reichsanzeiger* on 26 July 1901.[192] The press reaction was horrendous. Shortly after publication of the bill, the *Berliner Börsen-Zeitung* summed up the situation by stating that the new customs tariff had 'met with anything but a favourable response in the press'. 'Free traders, protectionists and agrarians' were 'unanimous in their condemnation of the government bill, each for completely opposing reasons'.[193] The social democratic and left-liberal papers tried to outdo one another in expressing their rejection of the tariff bill. *Vorwärts* called for an 'uncompromising battle' against the 'new bread and meat profiteers' tariff'.[194] The *Frankfurter Zeitung* condemned the 'massive increase in the cost of living in Germany' that would result from the new customs tariff and that could 'not be condemned strongly enough from an economic, political or social perspective'.[195] Finally, the headline 'To arms!' appeared in the *Freisinnige Zeitung*, which urged its readers to '[r]esist this flawed tariff and trade policy! *Down with the customs tariff!*'[196]

On the other side of the political spectrum, the conservative agrarians complained just as strongly about the supposedly too low agricultural tariff rates, which were well below what they wanted. But the tariff bill received a far from euphoric reception in the publications of the other political camps as well.[197] Responses were almost entirely critical, and only occasionally did the government receive cautious support. The unfavourable press response eventually prompted Bülow, who was extremely sensitive in this regard, to push Posadowsky to do 'everything he could to ensure' that 'the more important conservative and agrarian organs such as the *Kreuz-Zeitung*, *Neueste Nachrichten*, *Post*, *Schlesische Zeitung* and *Deutsche Tageszeitung*, along with agricultural corporations, openly and firmly support the … tariff rates that have become widely known'. Otherwise, the imperial chancellor warned, 'I fear that His Majesty will be attracted to the view that the agrarian party is insatiable, and that it should be regarded as a mistake to have stipulated such high agricultural tariff rates in the bill without gaining the approval and support even of the conservatives'. Should the 'conservative and agrarian press now make a number of demands', this could 'have the gravest of consequences for the conservative parties' whole attitude towards the government'.[198]

Bülow's evocation of looming dangers made little impact. After Posadowsky's intervention, the *Post* and *Kreuzzeitung* did express lukewarm support for the government's customs tariff.[199] The *Deutsche Tageszeitung*, organ of the BdL, however, stuck to its verdict on the 'completely inadequate customs tariff', which could not 'satisfy' even 'the humblest of farmers'.[200] The storm of protest that the tariff bill unleashed within Germany was matched by the unanimously negative reaction it provoked abroad. The international press – above all the Austro-Hungarian and Russian press – spoke largely with one voice in condemning the German customs tariff and discussed the possibility of a customs war.[201] So the logjam within the executive had only just been overcome when it became clear that even the policies of the 'middle way' could not bypass the political minefield associated with the customs tariff issue. Before the tariff bill had even made its way from the Bundesrat to the Reichstag, it was clear that there were major conflicts still to come.

## The Bülow Tariff and the Parties in the Reichstag

After the tariff bill had been passed by the Bundesrat with only insignificant modifications, it came before the Reichstag on 19 November 1901. 'There a battle flared up' that was 'unprecedented in the history of the Reichstag. … In the toughness and duration of the struggle over the decision, the customs tariff war is unsurpassed', as Adolf Wermuth, then director in the Imperial Ministry of the Interior and as such a leading figure in the preparation of the tariff bill, stated as he looked back over the events that followed. He went on:

> It comprised a full year of consultation and obstruction. The supporters of the customs tariff had a significant majority at their disposal; but in the problematic nature of the material and the number of customs tariff items to be decided on, its opponents enjoyed the most favourable defensive position imaginable. This is why the very first reading attracted 48 speakers in 9 sessions. Then came the committee stage, taking up three-quarters of the year and no less than 116 sessions. And finally the closing battle, from 16 October to 14 December 1902, in 48 plenary sessions, fought with skill, cunning and passion. Victory required changes to parliamentary procedures on two occasions. The uproar in the year of the customs tariff thus had an effect on how the Reichstag conducts its business that can still be felt today.[202]

Committed to paper two decades later, this bellicose depiction still conveys the dramatic nature of the events and the crucial importance that historical actors ascribed to the tariff issue in economic, political and social terms. The disputes over the Bülow tariff in the Reichstag were in fact the most bitterly fought and longest-lasting parliamentary conflict in the history of the German Empire.

## The Basic Parliamentary Constellation

The tariff bill that the government presented to the Reichstag consisted of two parts: the customs tariff law, which, in addition to a number of technical provisions, included minimum rates for the four main types of cereals, and the customs tariff, which laid down the autonomous rates for 946 items.[203] After Bülow had introduced the government bill, on the first day of the Reichstag negotiations, 2 December 1901, with only a short, carefully balanced, low-content speech,[204] the task of justifying the bill in detail the following day fell to Count Posadowsky-Wehner, by far the best economic policy expert on the government benches. In dramatic terms he set out the ultimate reasons for the projected increase in German tariff protection: the revolution in the transportation system had 'compressed the globe like a rubber ball'[205] – it would be hard to think of a more vivid description of the 'death of distance', something often invoked in the contemporary globalization debate as well. The development of 'modern transport conditions' had 'placed countries thousands of miles away from us in a geographical market situation such that they could just as well be right in front of our customs offices'. German agriculture in particular, 'by far the largest' economic sector in Germany, employing eighteen million people and providing for their dependents,[206] had been exposed to overwhelming international competitive pressure as a result. This the state must counteract through tariff increases, unless one was willing to accept a further worsening in the already precarious economic situation of agriculture, along with the ensuing social and political consequences.

In the Reichstag there was in fact a broad majority, extending from the conservative parties through the Centre Party to the National Liberals, in favour of the customs tariff reform being pursued by the government, and especially the raising of agricultural tariffs. But at the first reading of the tariff bill, and especially in the subsequent sessions of the Reichstag Committee, to which the plenary assembly referred the bill after nine session days, it became clear that the protectionist majority itself was completely disunited. Once again, the main bone of contention was the degree to which the tariffs for agricultural products should be raised by the new customs tariff. The protectionist Reichstag majority split into three parts regarding what should be seen as 'sufficient' tariff protection for agriculture.[207]

1. It was in fact only the National Liberals who were firmly in favour of the government bill.[208] Bülow's policy of the 'middle way', which aimed to increase tariff protection for agriculture but keep it within certain lim-

its so as not to render impossible the conclusion of new long-term trade treaties, not only dovetailed with the wishes of western German heavy industry, with whom the National Liberal leaders were closely linked.[209] It also offered a route out of the dilemma faced by the National Liberal Party because it included an extremely broad spectrum of trade policy views, ranging from the agricultural protectionism of Count Oriola to the fundamentally free trade stance of the *National-Zeitung*, the official party organ under the leadership of Artur Dix.[210] The government bill was intended to function as a compromise solution reasonably acceptable to both sides and to avoid a split vote among the National Liberal Reichstag grouping of the kind that had occurred, with far-reaching political consequences, in 1879, as well as in connection with the tariff increases of 1885 and 1887.

2. On the extreme right, meanwhile, by far the largest portion of the German Conservatives declared the protection for agriculture provided for in the government's tariff bill to be completely inadequate. This was very much in line with the views of the Agrarian League, with which the German Conservative Party had entered into a close alliance, every one of its deputies pledging their support for its programme in the elections of 1898.[211] But the Anti-Semites, the deputies of the Bavarian Peasants' League and a number of chiefly Bavarian members of the Centre Party also took the same line – albeit in sometimes varying ways. In its official statements, the BdL characterized the government bill as 'the worst thing that could have happened to German agriculture through the revision of the customs tariff system'[212] and called for minimum rates for the main types of cereal of at least 75 marks per tonne, along with a significant extension of the dual tariff system. In both the Reichstag and the Reichstag Committee, Baron von Wangenheim, president of the BdL and German Conservative Reichstag deputy, threatened to vote against the customs tariff if the level of the agricultural tariff was not raised substantially.[213]

3. Between these two camps stood the quantitatively larger group of those in favour of protective tariffs, made up of deputies from the Imperial Party (Reichspartei), the vast majority of Centre Party members and a small number of German Conservatives. In contrast to the extreme agrarians, the Reichstag deputies of this middle segment of the majority parties were among the 'friends in principle'[214] of the tariff bill in that they did not condemn it wholesale and viewed it as a viable basis for negotiation. They too, however, regarded the agricultural tariff increases proposed by the government as inadequate and sought to reinforce the already conspicuous tendency towards agricultural protectionism in the tariff bill. Perhaps even more clearly than the radical demands of the agrarian conservatives in thrall to the BdL, this broad support for a significant increase in agricultural tariff protection reflects the high degree of political pressure exerted

by the barrage of demands made by the agrarian associations over so many years. Since the goals of the Christian peasants' associations differed from those of the Agrarian League only marginally, beyond confessional differences this pressure affected every party with a substantial number of agrarian voters. As well as the direct influence of the agricultural interest organizations to which the deputies and their parties found themselves exposed, there was also the – hard to measure – indirect impact made by the agrarian protectionist groupings on contemporaries' thinking – a result of their success in shaping the trade policy debate through their early and strong presence, as well as the homogeneity of their demands.

In the Reichstag, this divided protectionist majority was confronted on the political left by staunch opponents of the tariff bill who firmly rejected any increase in tariff protection and especially an increase in agricultural tariffs. The left-liberal parties and the Social Democrats were as one in their opposition to the customs tariff bill, but differed with respect to their methods of opposition and to some extent also their motives.

The SPD, which placed the consumer perspective centre stage (as discussed earlier in this chapter) along with the Free-Minded Union (Freisinnige Vereinigung) under the leadership of Theodor Barth, pursued a strategy of parliamentary obstruction. They intended to delay the Reichstag negotiations on the new customs tariff in every conceivable way and if possible prevent its adoption in the current legislative period; this would allow them to use it as a compelling campaign topic in the Reichstag elections due in the summer of 1903. In early November 1901, before the Reichstag negotiations had even begun, August Bebel gave a speech in which he publicly announced that his party would use every means at its disposal in order to delay the parliamentary processing of the tariff bill. To the amusement of his listeners he declared, for example, that the SPD intended to move for a time-consuming roll call vote for at least 700 of the 946 items in the customs tariff: 'It is a point of principle for us that everything should be done as thoroughly as possible. *Every roll call vote takes half an hour, so we will need 350 hours to vote.*'[215] On this basis, voting in the Reichstag alone would have taken about fifty session days – and this was just the tip of the obstructionist iceberg.

No less radically than the SPD, Eugen Richter's Free-Minded People's Party (Freisinnige Volkspartei) and the small group of deputies from the German People's Party (Deutsche Volkspartei) rejected the 'system of *universal protectionism*'[216] that it believed the new customs tariff would establish. Just like the Social Democrats, the left liberals too couched their arguments in terms of consumer interests. In contrast to the SPD, however, most of them were not free traders on pragmatic grounds; they were convinced of the beneficent effects of the free international exchange of goods as a matter of principle. Beyond this, however, their free trade views were also based on material interests, as they were closely linked with trading and shipping circles. But the main difference from the SPD, and also the key line of division within left liberalism – between the Free-Minded Union on the one hand and the two 'people's parties' on the other – revolved around which tactics to deploy to fight the tariff bill. Eugen Richter too wanted the bill subjected to in-depth deliberation in the Reichstag, but in the name of his party he firmly rejected the parliamentary delaying tactics practiced by the SPD and the Free-Minded Union. The main reason he cited for his strong condemnation of the approach taken by the other opposition parties was a principled one: systematic obstruction was contrary to the spirit of parliamentarism.[217] But two tactical motives also played a role: first, Richter believed that the differences within the majority parties and the scope of the subject matter were enough to prevent adoption of the customs tariff before the end of the parliamentary term, and he feared that obstruction might even help weld together the internally divided majority, prompting it to take united action. Second, participation in parliamentary obstruction would have brought the Free-Minded People's Party into irreconcilable opposition to the Centre Party, which took a basically positive view of the customs tariff reform and on whose support Richter's party would be largely dependent in the impending second-round elections of 1903.[218]

## *The Resolutions of the Reichstag Committee*

When it began its work on 9 January 1902, the 16th Committee, to which the Reichstag had referred the tariff bill, attracted an entirely exceptional degree of public interest. The Committee was composed of twenty-eight members of the various Reichstag groupings; its sittings were also attended by a number of government representatives. When it concluded its negotiations on the customs tariff law and customs tariff at the third reading on 6 October, it had completed a true marathon of well over one hundred session days. So that it could continue to deliberate during the parliament's summer recess, the government was even willing to compensate Committee members financially – despite the inherent risk of reopening the issue of parliamentary expenses, which had caused it so much trouble.[219] The proceedings of the Committee advanced at a sluggish pace. Right from the outset, the Social Democrats sought to spin out its deliberations through amendments and filibusters. Before long, it began to appear 'doubtful' that the customs tariff would ever emerge from the depths of the Committee deliberations to 'see the light of day'. 'The Social Democrats', as the *Zukunft* stated, not without some admiration, 'use every trick in the book to obstruct proceedings; and in the shape of their deputy Stadthagen they have a record-breaking world champion in this regard. The Committee convenes almost daily. Mr. Stadthagen then rises to speak; and once he has risen, he is loath to sit back down.'[220] In this way, debates lasting for hours, on even the most insignificant of the just under one thousand tariff items, became the norm.

But at least as much as the left's delaying tactics, the Committee's work was hampered by constant conflicts within the protectionist majority and by the government's stubborn refusal to accept changes to its bill. Free Conservative Kardorff, elected as chair of the Committee, resigned after just one month. When the Centre Party and the conservatives, despite having already agreed on a compromise in arduous confidential discussions, were initially unable to agree on a collective approach to cereal tariffs within the Committee,[221] he prompted a row over a procedural issue and resigned as chair 'amid scenes of general agitation and much clamour and shouting from the Social Democrats'.[222] 'I do not believe', he wrote to his wife a week later, 'that the tariff will get off the ground. The government is weak, the Centre Party and National Liberals unreliable and it is very hard to unite the majority parties.'[223]

Those agrarians who shared the views of the BdL were a constant source of new problems. When they realized that they were not going to achieve their extreme demands for agricultural tariffs, they had no qualms about working with the left liberals and Social Democrats in their attempts to remove a number of industrial tariff rates. The *Deutsche Tageszeitung,* the publication of the Agrarian League, had already announced such an approach in advance: the 'increases in agricultural tariff rates' agreed in the Customs Tariff Committee so far were 'so negligible that no one [could] expect them to result in any really *significant* future increase in the prices of agricultural products' and 'agriculture has been *definitively denied* the kind of effective tariff protection necessary if it is to be able to compete with industry on an equal basis'. There was now just one way to 'establish the *complete parity of agricultural and industrial tariff protection*' supposedly sought by the agrarians: a '*major reduction in industrial protective tariffs*'. Certainly, this violated 'the principle of effective protection for all national labour', but was the result of the '*predicament*' into which the agrarians had been forced by the lack of solidarity shown by 'leading champions of industry in particular'.[224]

In the Reichstag Committee, the representatives of the Agrarian League immediately set about making good on this threat. He 'voted for exemption from duty with a heavy heart', declared the director of the BdL, Diederich Hahn, on one of the occasions when he supported the abolition of an industrial tariff, 'but if the National Liberals support an increase in agricultural tariffs at the second reading' he hoped to 'be in a position to vote for the industrial tariffs'.[225] Given the views of the majority of Committee members, one of the main reasons why the extreme right, in collaboration with the left, managed to lower many industrial tariffs at the first reading was that the parties positioned between these two wings often failed to put up a united front. This was a direct consequence of intraindustrial conflicts of interests, chiefly between the different stages of production within an industrial branch, conflicts that extended all the way into the Customs Tariff Committee. As evident in the paradigmatic deliberations on textile tariffs, in such contentious cases the voting behaviour of Centre Party, National Liberal and Imperial Party deputies[226] was often geared towards the industrial interests that predominated in their constituencies, and as a result they were utterly disunited. Under these circumstances it was easy for the left-wing parties and agrarians to realize their objective – a shared one, despite their very different motivations – of dismantling the government bill.

When the Customs Tariff Committee completed its first reading of the tariff bill in the summer of 1902, the government's original proposal had been stripped of much of its content. In light of the problems thrown up by the first reading, there seemed very little chance that the Committee would have ended its second and third readings of the customs tariff bill before the end of the parliamentary recess in October. Throughout the Committee's deliberations, imperial chancellor Bülow had remained very much in the shadows, so that, as Eugen von Jagemann, a delegate from Baden, put it, 'the failure of its work cannot seem attributable to him';[227] in the summer, he gave serious consideration to the idea of dropping the entire customs tariff project.[228]

It was only because of the pressure exerted by the impending failure of the entire tariff reform, and the associated possibility of putting at risk the increase in agricultural protective tariffs already in prospect, that a number of agrarians relented and the protectionist majority parties managed to agree a common approach. Following confidential preliminary talks among the different groupings of the protectionist majority, the second reading of the tariff bill by the Reichstag Committee was accomplished in just eight sessions, far more rapidly and with far less conflict than expected. Helpful too was the fact that the political left had decided to desist from its obstructive approach for the time being before resuming it – with far greater public impact – on the floor of the Reichstag. Though the Committee undid a large number of the changes it had made to the government bill at the second reading – particularly with respect to industrial tariffs – its amendments were still extensive. There were three key aspects to the modifications made to the original tariff bill as a result of the Committee's resolutions.

First, the Customs Tariff Committee increased the minimum rates included in the government bill for the four main types of cereals. Wheat was now to be subject to a tariff of at least 6 instead of 5.5 marks per quintal, while the figure for rye and oats was 5.5 rather than 5 marks. The barley tariff was even increased from 3 to 5.5 marks.[229] This was the result of a compromise supported chiefly by the Centre Party, the German Conservatives and the Imperial Party.[230] As expected, the Social Democrats and left liberals voted against the increase in the minimum rates, but so did most National Liberals, who advocated the adoption of the tariffs proposed by the government. The tariff increase did not go far enough, meanwhile, for either Wangenheim, the German Conservative president of the BdL, or Georg Heim, leader of the Bavarian Christian Peasants' Union (Bayerischer Christlicher Bauernverein) and Reichstag deputy for the Centre Party. Both abstained. Wangenheim stated before the Committee that the cereals tariff should 'help compensate' for 'the lower production and carrying costs [enjoyed by] other countries vis-à-vis Germany as a consequence of better climatic soil conditions, a less developed culture associated with lower wages or more favourable transportation conditions'. 'Neither the tariff rates in the government bill nor those in the Schwerin-Herold-Kardorff amendment' took sufficient account of this, unlike the minimal rate of 7.5 marks for all main cereal types demanded by the BdL.[231] Ultimately, the Committee's decision was a major blow to the government. Through its leading representatives both within and outside the Committee, it had already declared on a number of occasions that it would 'at no point be willing to countenance the compromise amendment' and that there was no prospect of it relenting.[232]

Second, through the votes of its protectionist majority, the Customs Tariff Committee increased the tariff rates in the autonomous tariff for livestock and meat well above the level in the tariff bill and supplemented them with minimum rates not to be reduced further in trade treaties.[233] This would mean extending the legally enshrined minimum protection, which applied only to the four main cereal types, to livestock and meat. This idea was very much in line with the aspiration, held by all the agrarian interest organizations, with their comprehensive catalogue of demands, to balance the different interests within agriculture, namely, those dividing cereal growers from livestock rearers, as discussed above. It was not just the left-wing parties that protested against this increase in agricultural tariff protection; government representatives did so almost as vigorously. The minister of the interior, Posadowsky, who had himself advocated extending the dual tariff to livestock just a year earlier, now defended the compromise reached within the executive and declared the minimum tariffs put forward by the Customs Tariff Committee 'unacceptable' in terms of both their substance and level.[234] Oswald von Richthofen, foreign secretary, emphasized that 'setting minimum tariff rates would make it very difficult if not impossible to conclude trade treaties, particularly with Austria-Hungary'.[235] But it was all in vain – the committee could not be persuaded to reverse its decision. Both the government and the protectionist majority parties became ever less willing to compromise. Both sides struck an increasingly harsh tone. The minutes of the Committee show Centre Party deputy Heim going so far as to brusquely inform the government representatives that their intransigence was making it

> completely impossible for the customs tariff to get off the ground. [Heim and his colleagues] do not sit on the Committee to have their eardrums burst. Blundering on in the same old way will achieve nothing. His party is determined to uphold the fixing of the most important livestock tariffs. No customs tariff without fixed rates![236]

Third and finally, at the second reading, the Centre Party – this time with the support of the SPD and against the votes of the conservatives, National Liberals and left liberals – managed to ensure that a paragraph was inserted into the draft customs tariff law that reserved the expected additional yield from the agricultural tariffs for a system of widows' and orphans' insurance. This was to be introduced by the imperial government by 1910 at the latest and was called the Heim amendment.[237] Through this measure, the Centre Party leadership sought to reconcile the party's left wing, more geared towards the interests of workers and consumers, to the increased tariffs on foodstuffs and sharpen the party's social policy profile for the elections due in 1903. Though the additional income expected from the customs tariff reform was in fact urgently needed in order to consolidate the imperial finances, which were in a terrible state, this resolution by the Customs Tariff Committee did not meet with the government's resistance in the same way as its other initiatives. In the Bundesrat, the non-Prussian states initially came out against using tariff revenue to fund a system of insurance for widows and orphans 'in light of their financial position'. Ultimately, however, both in the Prussian State Ministry and on the imperial level the view that prevailed was the one championed by Posadowsky and Bülow: it was necessary 'to accept Heim's amendment' if 'we want to convince the Centre Party to support the customs tariff and get it through the Reichstag in the face of the strong opposition'. But as the government saw it, the other reason to link the customs tariff with the system of insurance for widows and orphans was that it believed this would 'take a lot of the steam out of the Social Democratic agitation against the agricultural tariffs and [gain us] a powerful slogan for the next election campaign'.[238]

## *The Kardorff Compromise and the Adoption of the Customs Tariff*

As the plenary assembly of the Reichstag began the second reading of the tariff bill, the gulf between the government and the majority parties was clearly in evidence. Bülow made it very plain that the government would continue to reject the strengthening of agricultural protectionism inherent in the Committee's resolutions and that it could 'no more agree to ... an increase in the minimum rates for the cereal tariffs' than 'to any extension of these rates to articles in the tariff other than the four main types of cereals'.[239] Were the Reichstag majority to insist on the demands made by the Customs Tariff Committee and reject the bill, the imperial chancellor threatened, agriculture would ultimately lose even the tariff increases on offer from the government, since 'allied governments would be left with no other choice' than 'either, where possible, to tacitly allow the existing trade treaties to remain in effect or to enter into trade treaty negotiations on the basis of the old tariff'.[240]

The government's determination to resist the demand, supported by the majority of the parliament, for a further strengthening of agricultural tariff protection was due – in contrast to what Bülow later claimed[241] and to the impression made in most historical accounts[242] – less to the strength of its convictions about tariff policy or superior tactics than to the lack of alternatives perceived by the imperial leadership. Given the extremely difficult process of achieving compromise that had already taken place within the executive, which resulted in the government bill, Bülow believed he had already gone to the outer limits of acceptability in terms of agricultural protection. For various reasons it seemed to him impossible to take a single step further in this direction and towards the Reichstag majority. First, it would have been extremely difficult if not impossible for the Bundesrat to agree to a further increase in agricultural tariffs.[243] Second, the emperor had made it clear to Bülow that he categorically 'ruled out' any 'extension of the minimum tariff' and 'any kind of increase' in the minimum rates 'for rye and wheat'.[244] Third, any further increase in tariffs for foodstuffs was bound to drive even larger numbers of voters into the arms of the SPD in the impending elections, and the SPD was already expected to do very well. Fourth and finally, the government took the view that the increase in the level of agricultural tariff protection demanded by the Reichstag majority would have added to the difficulties of concluding new trade treaties, and even invoked the danger of customs wars with such important German trading partners as Austria-Hungary, Russia and the U.S., all of which exported large quantities of agricultural goods to Germany.

The representatives of the Centre Party and the two conservative parties, who had worked together to ensure that the Customs Tariff Committee enhanced the agricultural protections in the tariff bill, made it abundantly clear in the Reichstag that they were no more willing to change their position than the government was. Count Schwerin-Löwitz emphasized that the Committee's resolutions 'only became possible' because 'a number of Committee members had proved willing to make huge sacrifices in terms of their own convictions regarding the necessary level of the cereal tariffs'. In plain language, what this meant was that the agrarian conservatives on the Committee had already compromised as much as they could and already caused themselves problems with the BdL. Now it was the government's turn to show 'at least a little of the same willingness to compromise'.[245]

For contemporaries, parliamentary procedures had become a matter of course, while the Reichstag had achieved a considerable degree of self-confidence over the decades (though neither development should be confused with parliamentarization in the sense of a step-by-step transition to a parliamentary system of government). This is evident in the striking fact[246] that Imperial Party member Wilhelm von Kardorff, hardly the greatest advocate of parliamentarism, explained his party's insistence on the Committee's resolutions by arguing that the government's failure to compromise with the Reichstag majority and its 'like it or lump it' approach to the customs tariff issue were reducing 'general levels of respect for parliament'.[247] 'The parliament', the Reichstag deputy explained, was 'a legislative element with equal status, and the proposals made by the parliament have the same right to serious consideration by the allied governments as the proposals made to the parliament by those governments'.[248]

In light of the irreconcilable views held by the protectionist Reichstag majority and the government, but also because of the ongoing disunity of the majority parties – the National Liberals did not agree with the Committee resolutions, and there were alternative proposals on the right for far higher minimum tariffs (see table 5.2) – in autumn 1902 the prospect of the customs tariff reform being successfully concluded seemed slimmer than ever. This was also the prevailing view in published opinion. Shortly after the beginning of the second reading, with great satisfaction, left liberal Reichstag deputy Theodor Barth stated in the *Nation*: '[I]n the absence of a miracle – and miracles are a rare event in parliamentary life – it is ... very unlikely that the government's customs tariff bill will be passed into law before the elections of the coming year.'[249] Those organs of the press close to the conservatives or the Centre Party differed in tone but not substance. They too were as one in believing that the customs tariff reform was close to failure.[250] The chances of the tariff bill passing rapidly through the Reichstag were worsened by the fact that the SPD and the Free-Minded Union now took the opportunity to resume their delaying tactics with renewed vigour. On the very first day of the second reading, left liberal Georg Gothein spoke against the minimum tariffs on breadstuffs for two-and-a-half hours.[251] Social Democrat Otto Antrick managed a three-and-a-half hour speech the following day.[252] As well as almost endless obstructive speeches, there were extremely time-consuming roll call votes, which the left demanded on even the most insignificant details. Finally, the SPD grouping was highly successful with its tactic of leaving the hall en bloc before votes they themselves had triggered in order to make the parliament, which was often half-empty due to the exhausting debates, incapable of passing a resolution.[253]

The fact that a compromise was ultimately achieved and the tariff reform was passed by the Reichstag before the end of the year was due to the fact that the political costs of its failure would have been far too high for the protectionist majority parties. Had the government withdrawn its bill, the marked increase in agricultural tariff protection it provided for would have been lost for the foreseeable future. Upon rational reflection, the protectionist parties and associations could not afford to put at risk what was achievable under the circumstances that pertained. This would be particularly dangerous because the SPD's campaign of agitation against the 'hunger tariffs' was already in full swing, and it was extremely unlikely that the elections due in 1903 would result in a Reichstag as open to protectionism as the existing one. Against this background, when confronted with the fact, repeated by Bülow in the Reichstag on 21 October, that 'the Committee's proposal with respect to the minimum tariffs [is] unacceptable to the allied governments at every stage of the deliberations',[254] the deputies from those parties defending the Committee's resolutions – as sardonically noted by left liberal Ernst Müller-Meiningen in the parliament – had no real option left than to 'roll over [as] nicely' as possible.[255]

So while the verbal jousting continued in the plenary Reichstag, behind-the-scenes negotiations were going on among the majority parties and talks were held between their representatives and the government to sound out the potential for an agreement. During the entire process of negotiation, it was the Centre Party leadership that was clearly in control of events. It is thus hardly surprising that the compromise finally agreed to in late November, after weeks of intense struggle, bore its stamp to a considerable degree. Among the German Conservatives, meanwhile, right to the end there was strong opposition to any concessions to the government. At the key meeting of the parliamentary party, only a wafer-thin majority of twenty-one to twenty deputies voted for the compromise negotiated with the government. They only did so because Bülow had threatened to otherwise let the entire tariff, with its agricultural tariff increases, come to grief, and because many German Conservatives were plagued by the anxiety that they might otherwise lose all of their influence on the imperial leadership to the Centre Party.[256]

Through the agreement finally reached between the government and the majority parties and which – named after the first person to sign this crucial proposal – entered the history books as the 'Kardorff compromise', the imperial leadership got what it wanted with regard to the key areas of dispute. The cornerstones of the compromise were as follows. First, the majority parties forewent the extension, as agreed in the Customs Tariff Committee, of the minimum tariff beyond the four main types of cereals: the minimum tariffs for livestock were eliminated. Second, through gritted teeth, the Centre Party, Imperial Party and a majority of the German Conservatives also accepted the minimum rates in the government bill for wheat, rye and oats (see table 5.2). Third, with respect to the barley tariff, the imperial leadership sought to accommodate the agrarian wing of the Centre Party, which in return abandoned its demands, which went beyond those resolved in the Committee. The barley tariff was split in two: the minimum rate for malting or brewing barley was increased from 30 marks per tonne, as provided for in the government's tariff bill, to 40 marks (see table 5.2). Feed barley, meanwhile, was eliminated from the minimum tariff entirely; its tariff level within the general tariff could be reduced in the context of trade treaties in the absence of any predetermined lower limit.[257] The compromise thus took account of the interests of livestock farmers, who imported large quantities of barley from abroad to feed their animals.[258] Fourth – and this too was a concession to the Centre Party – the government declared its willingness to use the additional income from the foodstuff tariffs to establish a system of insurance for widows and orphans (Heim amendment in the Committee, Trimborn amendment in the Reichstag). Fifth, the lowering of certain generally unimportant tariffs for agricultural equipment was the 'golden bridge'[259] that allowed the majority of Conservatives to accept the compromise. Sixth and finally, the majority parties agreed to accept the entire customs tariff en bloc, in other words, without a debate and a vote on every single item, in order to rapidly complete the second reading and circumvent attempts at obstruction. This was a profound intervention in the Reichstag's rules of procedure,

**Table 5.2.** Minimum tariffs on cereals in the Reichstag, 1902 (marks per tonne)

| | *Wheat* | *Rye* | *Oats* | *Barley* |
|---|---|---|---|---|
| *Current treaty tariff* | 35 | 35 | 28 | 20 |
| *Government bill* | 55 | 50 | 50 | 30 |
| *Resolutions by the Customs Tariff Committee* | 60 | 55 | 55 | 55 |
| *Wangenheim amendment (BdL)* | 75 | 75 | 75 | 75 |
| *Heim amendment (Bavarian Centre Party)* | 60 | 60 | 60 | 60 |
| *Kardorff compromise* | 55 | 50 | 50 | 40 (malting barley only) |

*Sources: StenBerRT,* 1900–3, Attachments, no. 704, 711, 715, 790

whose permissibility was highly contested, and made up the true substance of the so-called Kardorff amendment[260] – the changing of the minimal tariffs in line with the previously achieved compromise, meanwhile, was considered only at the third reading on formal grounds.[261] Though the initiators of the Kardorff amendment were to be found in the upper echelons of the Centre Party, it was agreed that the leader of the Free Conservatives would be the first to sign it and thus provide it with a name. This was because it was hoped that Kardorff's standing as a conservative parliamentarian, cofounder of the Agrarian League and opponent of the Caprivi trade treaties would smooth the way for a favourable reception of the compromise on the agrarian right.

On 27 November 1902 everything hung in the balance once again. The second reading of the customs tariff law had been completed; deliberations on the customs tariff itself were now to begin. Reichstag president Franz von Ballestrem had no sooner stated that there were no objections to the *modus procedendi* he had proposed than Kardorff raised a procedural motion. He announced that 'in a few minutes the House will be presented with a subsidiary motion that seeks … to express the en bloc adoption of the law'.[262] Only at this moment did Centre Party deputy Peter Spahn arrive with the motion, which had only just been composed, and which was immediately handed to the president in handwritten form.[263] Had this intervention occurred just a moment later – after deliberations on the tariff had begun – then in line with the Reichstag's rules of procedure nothing could have been done to prevent full deliberation on all 946 items in the customs tariff. Given the SPD's delaying tactics, this would likely, in fact almost certainly, have prevented the tariff reform from being adopted during the current legislative period and would perhaps have scuppered it entirely.

The motion proposed by Kardorff triggered a five-day procedural debate on its permissibility. Passions peaked over the course of this debate. SPD deputy Paul Singer accused the majority parties of 'brutally violating the minority and the rules of procedure'.[264] Carl Ulrich, also a Social Democrat and long-standing minister-president of Hesse during the Weimar Republic, became so furious that he marched through the hall shouting loudly for several minutes while completely ignoring Ballestrem's calls for order.[265] There was massive conflict within the opposition. While Eugen Richter declared Kardorff's motion contrary to the rules of procedure, he roundly condemned the parliamentary obstruction practiced by the other left-wing parties and asserted that 'the Social Democrats and Free-Minded Union' themselves bore 'a large part of the responsibility' for the collective approach taken by the internally fragmented protectionist Reichstag majority. According to him, 'the different views on the size of the tariff had receded' in the face of 'growing indignation' over the 'forms taken by opposition to the customs tariff'.[266]

Once the majority parties had finally succeeded in settling the issue of procedural permissibility through a vote, the real debate on the Kardorff motion began. Once again, the SPD and the Free-Minded Union pulled out all the stops to obstruct things. Despite this – after the rules of procedure had been changed again by the Gröber motion – the third reading of the tariff bill took place on 13 December. During it, Social Democrat deputy Antrick set an unusual record in German parliamentary history: only after eight hours of uninterrupted filibustering did he leave the rostrum. At half past five in the morning on 14 December, the crucial final vote was finally held. The customs tariff law, together with the customs tariff, was adopted by 202 votes to 100 with 1 abstention. Apart from the Social Democrats and the left liberals, a group of no less than thirty deputies on the agrarian right drawn from the ranks of the German Conservatives, the BdL, the Bavarian Peasants' League and the Anti-Semites voted against the customs tariff.[267]

I shall conclude by summing up the analysis of the parliamentary decision-making process presented above and locating it within the overall context of the development of the Bülow tariff. Three points stand out.

First, the majority of the legislative branch – the German Reichstag elected according to universal, secret and equal male suffrage – proved substantially more protectionist than the executive or, to be more precise, the part of it that finally triumphed. Had things gone wholly according to the will of the parliamentary majority, then the customs tariff, particularly its agricultural part, would have been far more protectionist in character than it actually was. In this sense the government looked after the interests of the exporting industry, trade and consumers more effectively than their representatives in the Reichstag. The reason for this is obvious: the executive was not exposed to pressure from protectionist interest associations in the same direct way as the legislative branch. In the run-up to the Bülow tariff, it was the agrarian interest organizations – above all the BdL – with their vociferous demands for protection from global competition that managed to get the majority of deputies (by helping their election campaigns) into a relationship of direct dependency and to influence them indirectly via massive, long-term campaigns within the public political sphere. The greater willingness of parliamentary institutions to give in to the protectionist desires of interest groups compared with the executive is not a feature specific to the late German Empire; this foreign trade policy phenomenon is found in other cases as well. The best-known example is undoubtedly the genesis of the Smoot-Hawley tariff of 1930, which raised the U.S. tariff level to unique heights, never seen before or since, and helped worsen the world economic crisis.[268] As a result of the disastrous impact of the Smoot-Hawley tariff, a few years later the U.S.

Congress agreed to surrender its trade policy authority to the executive: it was less directly exposed to the influence of protectionist interests than members of Congress in their constituencies and was therefore generally more protrade in character.

Second, the fact that the Reichstag grappled with the Bülow tariff for more than a year is striking testimony to the tremendous potential for discord inherent in the tariff issue, which made it the main field of parliamentary conflict around the turn of the century. There was massive political antagonism, and not just between the political left and the protectionist majority; the relationships between the majority parties themselves and between them and the government were also characterized by intense conflicts. What had happened was the exact opposite of what Miquel had predicted when he made the case for his preferred 'politics of rallying together' before the Prussian State Ministry in November 1897. He had suggested that 'a national economic policy, particularly collaboration between the major economic groups ... [is] apt to bring the parties closer together' and push existing 'political antagonisms ... into the background'.[269] But rapidly advancing economic globalization affected the living conditions and income prospects of different social groups in many different ways, ultimately engendering fundamental conflicts of interest and political tensions. As a result, in the final stages of the customs tariff reform the imperial leadership was solely concerned to somehow rid itself of this conflict-ridden subject without allowing the whole project to collapse within the highly treacherous political waters.

It would thus be quite wrong to view the Bülow tariff as the successful result of a long-term strategy consistently pursued by the agrarian-industrial front. If such a strategy ever existed in elaborated form (and the beginnings of such a strategy can certainly be seen in the establishment of the Economic Committee), as the decision-making process advanced it rapidly degenerated into a politics of muddling through. How unsuccessful the customs tariff reform was with respect to agrarian-industrial collaboration is evident, apart from anything else, in the vehement rejection of the Kardorff compromise by the Agrarian League, the leading association representing the key agrarian beneficiaries. The BdL not only condemned the agricultural protection in the new tariff as totally inadequate and accused every Reichstag deputy who had pledged to support its programme but had voted for the Kardorff compromise of betraying their common cause.[270] In 1902/3, it even allowed the tariff issue to cause the only serious rift with the German Conservative Party before the First World War after the majority of its deputies dared to vote for the tariff despite the BdL's warnings.

Third and finally, historical researchers influenced by the work of Eckart Kehr have repeatedly asserted that there was a close relationship between the customs tariff bill and the second naval law of 1900 in that both were parts of a *do ut des* pact mediated by the government between industry and agriculture.[271] Neither the negotiations on the customs tariff in the Reichstag nor the decision-making process in the Prussian-German ministerial bureaucracy provide any evidence to support this theory.[272] Certainly, in the run-up to the naval law – and in the context of the canal bill – government representatives gave vague assurances that they would take due account of agricultural interests over the course of the impending customs tariff reform.[273] But there can be no question of any long-term strategic linkage of the customs tariff bill with the fleet.[274] In the decision-making process that culminated in the Bülow tariff, there is no evidence, either on the level of government or parliament, of any master plan stretching back over years that would have made construction of the fleet and tariff increases elements in a comprehensive agrarian-industrial barter. The customs tariff reform was a political phenomenon sui generis. Compromises between the various political and economic groups were generally sought not in other political fields but with respect to the customs tariff itself.

There was a single but telling exception: the so-called Trimborn Act, which stipulated that additional income from the foodstuff tariffs should be used to establish a system of insurance for widows and orphans. The Centre Party ensured its inclusion in order to gain the support of its own working-class clientele for the tariff, but in contrast to the supposed connection between the customs tariff and the fleet, it thus had a purely instrumental function. At the same time, it dashed all hopes of financing through the new tariffs the costly fleet-building programme that had just been launched.[275] Ultimately, the linkage of the customs tariff and the system of provision for dependents highlights once again how difficult it was to achieve a politically and socially sustainable solution to the tariff issue. The key actors believed that the only way to ensure that the customs tariff revision would be sufficiently accepted by society as a whole was to flank it with compensatory measures to assuage the losers. Though in embryonic form and with little success, this was an attempt to put together a package of tariff and social policy measures of the kind that we see again and again in the history of international trade policy, whenever the key imperative has been to enforce a change of trade policy regime – whether in the direction of liberalization or protectionism – in the face of opposition from those negatively affected by it. Examples range from the agricultural assistance that Robert Peel linked with the elimination of corn tariffs, through the social policy programme inherent in the tariff reform propagated by Joseph Chamberlain, to the far-reaching compensatory strategies that accompanied the shift in U.S. foreign economic policy in 1934/35.[276]

CHAPTER 6

# German Trade Policy after the Turn of the Century

## *A Two-Country Study*

The Bülow tariff of 1902, which came into being amid intense political struggles, merely provided the legal foundation for German trade policy up until the First World War. Only the practice of bilateral trade policy relations could show whether its critics were right to claim that the increased agricultural duties it contained were obstacles to the conclusion of new, long-term, comprehensive tariff treaties and thus to the continuation of Caprivi's trade treaty policy. The Caprivi treaties, concluded in the early 1890s, expired at the end of 1903. Immediately after the adoption of the new customs tariff, therefore, trade treaty negotiations were in the offing with all treaty partners. In many cases, after the turn of the century the German Empire also reworked its trade relations with the numerous states with which it had not concluded major customs tariff agreements and instead had a most-favoured-nation or similar relationship.

Since it is impossible to give an account of German trade policy as a whole before the First World War as manifest in the diverse range of bilateral relations with its various trading partners, I shall examine it here by looking at the development of Germany's trade policy relationship with two specific states. This is the only way to gain a true sense of the German government's room for manoeuvre and the exigencies of trade policy – given its close entanglement with international economic processes, foreign policy parameters and domestic political developments. German trade policy towards Russia and the U.S. is central to my account here. This is because, first, these two states were Germany's most important trading partners before the First World War. The total annual average volume of German trade with Russia was 2,103 million marks for the period 1909–13, while the figure for the U.S. was 2,076 million marks, higher figures than for any other country (see tables 1.5 and 1.7).

Second, in terms of the contractual nature of their trade policy relationship with the German Empire, the U.S. and Russia represented the two basic models. While Germany had concluded a comprehensive twelve-year customs tariff treaty with the Russian Empire, it had a less stable most-favoured-nation relationship with the U.S. Third, in several respects the Russian and American cases provided similar starting conditions for German trade policy, making them particularly well suited to a comparative analysis. Both countries were large territorial states enjoying a very positive trade balance with Germany, from which they almost exclusively imported industrial goods, and both had a strong interest in the export of agricultural products. Above all, though, both challenged German trade policy in much the same way through the extreme form of high protectionism they practiced. The fact that German trade policy towards Russia took a very different form from that towards the U.S. before the First World War – and this is the fourth point – is thus particularly interesting and in need of explanation.

## Russia

### *Expansion of Trade and Intensification of the Trade Policy Conflict*

German-Russian trade had boomed since the conclusion of the trade treaty of 1894. It rapidly recovered from the slump triggered by the customs war that had preceded the agreement.[1] Having sunk from 579 million marks in 1891 to 352 million marks in 1893, as early as 1895 the value of German imports from Russia reached 568 million marks, close to its initial level, before surging to 822 million marks by 1903.[2] The value of German exports to the Russian Empire, which had sunk to 136 million marks in 1893 as a result of Russian high protectionism, grew rapidly to reach a figure of 325 million marks by 1899 before stagnating at this level for a number of years.[3] According to German foreign trade statistics, under the conditions of the trade treaty policy inaugurated by Caprivi two features dominated the development of German-Russian trade: high, almost equal growth rates for imports and exports and a persistent German trade deficit, which was still climbing in absolute terms.

A quite different picture of the development of trade between Germany and Russia emerged, however, if one looked at the Russian trade statistics. According to them, after the tariff treaty had come into force Russian imports from Germany grew far more rapidly than Russian exports to Germany. As a result, Russia's trade balance with Germany, which even the Russian statistics had formerly shown to be very positive, showed a negative balance from 1896, one that had increased rapidly by 1899 and persisted in subsequent years. The main reason for the huge divergence in the Russian and German trade statistics lay in different methods of determining countries of origin and destination. While the German statistics recorded exports' ultimate destination and country of origin whenever possible, while disregarding straightforward transit countries, the Russian trade statistics often recorded as imports from Germany goods that came from other countries and had merely transited through the German customs area. Further, they classified the substantial portion of Russian exports that reached the German Empire not by land across the border between the two countries but by sea via other countries – this applied in particular to cereal imports that entered Germany from the southern Russian ports on the Danube, Black Sea and Sea of Azov via the Netherlands or Belgium – not as exports to the German Empire but as trade with the transit countries.[4] The discrepancy between German and Russian foreign trade statistics was further aggravated by a number of other differences between the calculation and assessment methods used by each side.

Judged by the principles of modern-day foreign trade statistics, despite certain shortcomings (see chapter 1) the German figures undoubtedly provided a far more realistic picture of trade between Russia and Germany than the Russian figures. Informed contemporaries both in Germany and Russia were essentially aware of the reasons for these substantial statistical differences and of the Russian figures' limited validity.[5] This did not prevent repeated trade policy conflicts between Berlin and St. Petersburg over how trade between Germany and Russia had *really* developed since the trade treaty of 1894 had come into force.[6] The dispute over the correct statistical construction of reality had a predeterminative function. If one side succeeded in establishing its calculation method as generally binding, and it was generally the German trade experts that had the greatest success here because of the methodological superiority of the imperial statistics, this amounted to a quite significant preliminary decision with respect to the definition of the two sides' economic interests, how to evaluate the consequences of the existing trade agreement and the demands that could legitimately be made in future trade treaty negotiations.

In contrast to the absolute quantity of imports and exports, there was little disagreement with respect to the basic commodity structure of trade between Germany and Russia. The vast majority of German imports from Russia consisted of the products of agriculture and forestry. Of the 822 million marks worth of imports from Russia identified by the German statistics for 1903, 101 million marks were accounted for by wheat, 73 million by rye, 106 million by barley and 38 million by oats – together, the four main types of cereals accounted for 39 per cent of total imports reaching the German Empire from Russia that year.[7] At the same time, the huge quantities of Russian cereals, the vast majority of which entered Germany in the west via the Elbe and Rhine, made Russia by far the largest supplier of cereals to Germany. In the case of rye and oats, Russian agriculture had already occupied this position throughout the 1880s, while in the case of barley it finally beat Austria-Hungary in 1894. In the case of wheat – and again this points to the existence of a functional and highly flexible world market – the share of the German import market provided by the main supplier countries of Romania, Russia, Argentina and the U.S. shifted dramatically year to year; here too, however, Russia led the pack for a time from 1903 on. On an average annual basis, between 1901 and 1904 the Russian share of German rye imports was 88.6 per cent; the figure for oats was 81.3 per cent, for barley 66.8 per cent and for wheat a not insubstantial 34.6 per cent.[8]

Unsurprisingly given the gap in industrial development between the two countries, meanwhile, it was primarily industrial products that Germany exported to Russia. But the different branches of German industrial exports to the Russian Empire exhibited very different growth dynamics: the growth in exports was comparatively small in the case of heavy industrial products requiring simple processing. Russian heavy industry was vigorously stimulated under the aegis of finance minister Sergei Yulyevich Witte, who held office from 1892 to 1903, and was sealed off from global competition by high protective tariffs. It was increasingly able to cover the rapidly growing domestic demand, with the production of Russian pig iron, steel and cast iron growing by more than 200 per cent between 1890 and 1900.[9] Goods higher up in the hierarchy of production, which Russian industry either did not produce at all or whose quality or quantity was deficient, meanwhile, showed very high rates of export growth. For example, while German exports of 'raw metal goods', which competed with the products of Russian heavy industry, grew by a mere 16 per cent between 1895–97 and 1903–5, exports of 'finished metal goods' grew by around 261 per cent over the same period.[10] Around the turn of the century the most technologically advanced sectors of the German metals processing industry, namely, the machine-building and electrotechnical industries, were particularly successful in exporting to Russia. In just seven years, the compound export category of 'tools, machines and vehicles' climbed from 11.3 million marks in 1892 to a value of 67.2 million marks by 1899 – equating to more than one-fifth of German exports to Russia.[11]

As a consequence of the dramatic growth in exports, within just a few years the Russian Empire had become the most important export market for a number of technologically advanced products of German industry – and, given its potential for industrial development, also the most promising future market. By 1900, with the Russian state continuing to put massive resources into railway building (the rail network had almost doubled in size in the preceding decade alone),[12] Russia had become the main importer of German locomotives, accounting for 5 million marks of a trade worth 15.7 million in total. In the same year, Russia was also the most important destination for German steam engine exports (5 million marks out of total German exports of 19.4 million), agricultural machinery (6.2 out of 13 million marks), electrical machines (5.5 out of 23.3 million marks), machine tools (2 out of 7.9 million marks) and other 'machines for industrial purposes' (10.6 out of 80.6 million marks).[13] For the German chemical industry too the Russian Empire represented a rapidly growing market of great significance. Exports of chemical products to Russia, however, showed only moderate growth around the turn of the century because the Russian policy of high protectionism had already prompted German dyes producers to change their approach. In order to avoid the rising tariffs, since the late 1870s German businesses had increasingly shifted their production for the Russian market to Russia – initially for final production only but subsequently for the production of intermediate products as well.[14] In the main, through extensive direct investment in the Russian Empire – exceeding all other investment worldwide – the big German chemicals companies thus managed to substitute for the exports impeded by Russian tariffs and attain a dominant position on the Russian market through subsidiary companies.

In both Russia and Germany, then, there were significant economic actors keen on a bilateral trade relationship featuring an absolute minimum of protectionist intervention. The situation only became difficult in trade policy terms because there were also import-competitive sectors in both countries that were unable to cope with the pressure of world market competition and therefore sought protectionist measures. Given the intensity of reciprocal trade relations, these were bound to have a particularly deleterious effect on the other country's exports. On the German side this applied above all to agriculture. Its organizations were already up in arms in 1893/94 over the conclusion of the German-Russian trade treaty (see chapter 4). In the years that followed their relentless propaganda, which again took aim chiefly at rising agricultural imports from Russia, did a great deal to create a favourable climate for agricultural protectionism in the public political sphere, Reichstag parties and government.

As willing as the state was to provide help for agriculture, the problem was that all the important agricultural tariffs – above all the cereal tariffs – were fixed by trade treaty until 1903/4 and were therefore unavailable as mechanisms of control over the short term. There was a certain room for manoeuvre, meanwhile, with respect to nontariff support measures for the agrarian sector that were unaffected by the trade treaties: the abolition of the certificate of identity (*Identitätsnachweis*), the extension of tax concessions, the granting of export premiums and the tightening of animal disease controls. In one way or another, the government made use of all these options over the course of the 1890s to appease the agrarian protesters.

It was the protectionist instrumentalization of animal disease controls that played the key role in Germany's trading relationship with Russia. The regulations that applied in the early 1890s already resembled a virtual caricature of a system combining veterinary and protectionist motives, a common phenomenon during this period in both the German Empire and many other countries.[15] Over the course of the 1880s, the German government – keeping pace with the raising of cereal tariffs – had increasingly closed its borders to imports of foreign livestock through import bans justified on the basis of disease control. In mid-1889 a decree was issued prohibiting the remaining imports of live pigs. These had amounted to the substantial figure of 700,000 animals a year one decade earlier, but now Russian imports faced a complete ban.[16] Two years later, however, an exception was granted that made a mockery of veterinary justifications: in order to meet the needs of the Upper Silesian industrial region, the import of a weekly contingent of 2,550 pigs from Russia was permitted.

On the basis of the imperial law on livestock diseases, amended in 1894, in the spring of 1896 the German government reduced this quota to just 1,300 pigs per week. At the same time, the import of small amounts of fresh pork, which the inhabitants of the border districts had been permitted, was prohibited, while the inspection of horses coming over the border was tightened up significantly.[17] In both the public sphere and in the debate between the various ministries and imperial offices, the Prussian Ministry of Agriculture put forward purely veterinary reasons for these measures and could point to numerous cases of foot-and-mouth disease and other animal diseases.[18] Even the representatives of the Foreign Ministry, however, cautiously pointed out that the 'motivation for reducing' the Upper Silesian pig contingent was 'not entirely logical, for if Russian pigs are necessary to the industrial area and a figure of 1,300 seems permissible from a veterinary perspective, it is unclear why a larger number of pigs cannot be allowed in'. In Russia, the measures imposed by Germany had 'raised fears that we wish to wage a systematic campaign against Russia's agricultural production'.[19] The vice president of the Prussian State Ministry, Heinrich von Boetticher, backed this view: 'We cannot blame the Russians for describing the measures as protectionist rather than veterinary in character.'[20] In the meeting of the State Ministry that dealt with this issue, the trade policy differences between the various Prussian and imperial ministries came to light yet again; more than this, though, it was evident that genuine arguments relating to the control of animal disease and agricultural protectionist motives had become almost indistinguishably fused. Tellingly, by opting to uphold the reduction of the pig contingent, most of the key actors in the State Ministry ultimately followed the ambivalent argument put forward by Miquel, namely, that a failure to do so would increase 'sanitary risks' and engender 'disgruntlement in agricultural circles'.[21]

The trade policy squabbles prompted by the German disease control initiative made it abundantly clear how quickly a relatively unimportant matter could develop into a major conflict in the tense field of international trade policy around 1900, characterized by the global rise of protectionism. The Russian government immediately lodged a complaint about the new import restrictions imposed by Germany. When it received no immediate reply from the Foreign Ministry, Witte, the Russian finance minister, decided to take action. Just fourteen days after the Foreign Ministry had received the complaint, he issued a decree subjecting a number of German export commodities to 'customs reprisals'.[22] Further, should the German disease control measures not be removed, the Russian government aired the possibility of further countermeasures – such as prohibiting Russian-Polish migrant workers from crossing the border into the eastern provinces of Prussia, an influx on which agriculture east of the Elbe, which suffered from a 'dearth of people', had become highly dependent.[23]

In November 1896, at the behest of Russia, a German-Russian conference was convened to resolve these contentious issues. It too initially achieved nothing.[24] As Paul Reichardt, director of the Trade Policy Department of the Foreign Ministry, warned, because the German delegates in particular were essentially unwilling to make concessions, towards the end of 1896 Germany and Russia stood on the brink of a 'latent customs war'.[25] In the meantime, the situation had become even more complicated as those affected negatively by the veterinary measures within the German Empire began to make their voices heard. In the submissions put forward by their organizations, the Upper Silesian Mining and Metallurgical Union (Oberschlesischer Berg- und Hüttenmännischer Verein) and the Eastern Group of the VDEStI, Upper Silesian heavy industrialists expressed strong support for allowing the full, original contingent of Russian pigs to enter the country.[26] First, they asserted that the livestock from Russia was needed to cover the meat requirements of Upper Silesian industrial workers – supply shortfalls and extreme price rises would otherwise be likely, and this would ultimately have an effect on wages. Second, and even more important for them, they were afraid of retaliatory measures against their own exports to Russia, which they claimed would hit the Upper Silesian iron and steel industry particularly hard because it had expanded massively in the preceding years in the expectation of a rapid expansion of German-Russian trade.

Finally, under pressure from the export interests at stake on both sides, the German-Russian conference came to a conclusion. The German government upheld the lowering of the pig contingent, but made a number of minor concessions in other fields. In return, Russia eliminated the obstacles to German imports it had imposed.[27] In the State Ministry, the Foreign Ministry trade experts managed to push through even the minimal German concessions – such as the unofficial assurance desired by the Russians that certain cereal entrepôts would remain open for the time being[28] – only in the face of substantial resistance and by pointing out that, should no agreement be reached, the Russian government was in a position to 'almost entirely cripple our industrial exports to Russia'.[29] The domestic political pressure built up by the agricultural interest organizations over the preceding years was obviously too great for the Prussian-German executive to have been willing to dismantle in any substantial way the agricultural protectionist measures now in force.

The trade policy interlude of 1896/97, however, was merely a foretaste of the conflict likely to occur upon expiry of the trade treaty between Germany and Russia in 1904. For the ten-year duration of the treaty both states had pledged not to raise a number of tariffs of particular importance to the other side, but now the entire protective tariff system could be redesigned at the discretion of the German and Russian authorities. In preparation for the trade treaty negotiations now imminent due to the impending expiry of the Caprivi treaties at the turn of the century, from 1897 on the German customs tariff had been completely reworked amid intense domestic political conflicts (see chapter 5). The new customs tariff adopted by the Reichstag in late 1902 did much to accommodate the protectionist demands of the agricultural interest organizations – though they vociferously disputed this. For the agrarians, what mattered now was to ensure that the agricultural tariff protection achieved in the Bülow tariff was retained to the greatest possible degree and not undercut in the trade treaty negotiations with Russia and the other treaty states. The introduction of legally enshrined minimum tariffs for the four main types of cereals, which went hand-in-hand with a drastic increase in the existing tariff level, was a significant advance achievement for the agricultural producers that naturally hit Russia particularly hard as the main supplier of cereals to Germany.

But in the run-up to the trade treaty negotiations the agrarian interest organizations also presented a comprehensive catalogue of demands beyond the level of pure tariff protection, and this too was aimed primarily at Russian agricultural exports. Once again disease control issues played a major role. From the BdL to the Christian peasants' associations, all the agricultural organizations were unanimous in their vehement protests against any trade treaty concessions on sanitary measures and disease control – the virtually total ban on Russian livestock must be retained in its present form at all costs.[30]

But agrarian protests also targeted the so-called Loco clause in the final protocol to Article 19 of the existing German-Russian trade treaty, according to which consignments of Russian cereals to the German Baltic ports of Danzig, Königsberg and Memel would be conveyed at the lower Russian rather than the higher Prussian freight rates on the Prussian stretches of the railway. While there was no reason to believe that this regulation, which aimed to maintain the competitiveness of the Prussian Baltic cities vis-à-vis the Russian ports, would have damaged agriculture east of the Elbe by flooding eastern Germany with Russian cereals – and an enquiry set up specifically to examine this claim came to the opposite conclusion in 1903 – from the mid-1890s the struggle against the Loco clause was as much a part of the standard repertoire of agrarian concerns as the demand for the abolition of the cereal entrepôts, which primarily targeted Russian cereal imports. In the Reichstag, conservative deputy Count Clemens von Klinckowstroem put forward a motion in 1901 calling on the government to seek changes to the contested provision in the final protocol at the impending trade treaty negotiations with Russia.[31] The resolution that bore his name demanded that the reduced freight rates should apply only to that portion of Russian cereals that would be shipped onwards from the German Baltic seaports to locations beyond the customs area (Trans-mare clause).

In the Prussian-German executive, the Ministry of Agriculture immediately declared itself entirely in agreement with the motion. At the same time, the ministry let it be known prophylactically that as far as it was concerned the result of the enquiry that had been initiated to examine the economic consequences of the Loco clause for agriculture east of the Elbe would 'carry no decisive weight, since the issue has essentially become a political one'.[32] For the other Prussian ministries and imperial offices, meanwhile, and above all the Foreign Ministry, which was dealing directly with the treaty negotiations, the situation was far more problematic. First, they were aware that the renewal of the Loco clause would inevitably face energetic resistance from the agrarian interest organizations and many conservative deputies in the Reichstag. Second, should Germany insist on amending the final protocol, they feared negative consequences for the Prussian Baltic ports and another serious impediment to the German-Russian trade treaty negotiations.

The protectionist package that the Russian government took to the talks on the extension of the trade agreement was every bit as weighty as its German counterpart. Of course, in the late nineteenth century, the average protection level of the Russian customs tariff was far higher than that of its German equivalent. The trade treaty concluded in 1894 had done nothing to change this. Since then, many of the Russian tariffs of importance to the German economy had been fixed by treaty. But in August 1900 the Russian government had raised more than 120 nonfixed tariff rates by between 10 and 50 per cent.[33] In preparation for the trade treaty negotiations, the Russian customs tariff was then subjected to comprehensive revision under Witte's leadership. The Russian tariff, adopted just one month after its German counterpart in January 1903, again significantly increased most of the already highly protectionist industrial tariffs. At the same time, it provided for a distinction between tariffs on imports to Russia by sea and land that privileged the former.[34]

Witte's new customs tariff was in part a response to the protectionist desires of Russian industry, which was unable to cope with world market competition and had been suffering a deep depression since 1900. But like the Bülow tariff, it was at least as much an element in the customs tariff arms race that had become an established feature of international relations since the 1880s (see chapter 3). It was not just Russia and Germany but also Austria-Hungary, Switzerland, Serbia and Romania that entered negotiations on the new trade treaties with new customs tariffs drawn up specifically for this purpose, all of which featured a substantially increased tariff level. Beyond those duties intended to protect parts of a given national economy against ever more intense global competition, all the tariffs contained a number of items or increases whose sole function was to serve as bargaining chips in the imminent trade treaty negotiations. The Russian customs tariff of 1903 must thus be understood in significant part as a response to the German tariff reform of 1902, whose massive increases in agricultural duties were generally well known in Russia from mid-1901 at the latest and had provoked the ire of agrarians dependent on exports to Germany.[35] To some extent at least, Witte aimed to persuade the German government to back down on agricultural tariffs in the impending trade treaty negotiations by threatening to hurt German exporters.

In line with this, the increased duties in the customs tariff drawn up under Witte's leadership primarily targeted German industrial products exported to Russia. Within the German Empire, this immediately prompted input from the associations of trade and industry, which were in turn besieged by their members with an interest in exports to Russia. From the Central Association of German Industrialists (Centralverband Deutscher Industrieller or CVDI), dominated by heavy industry, through the economically liberal Trade Treaty Association (Handelsvertragsverein), to the German-Russian Association (Deutsch-Russischer Verein), founded in 1899 to represent those circles with an interest in trade with Russia, all the relevant organizations were as one in protesting against the planned Russian tariff increases.[36] In its submission to the imperial chancellor on the Russian customs tariff, the Association of Export Commissioning Firms (Vereinigung der Export-Commissions-Firmen), whose executive director, Hjalmar Schacht, was just twenty-six years old at the time, came to the conclusion that 'if it proves impossible to get the rates set in this tariff at least down to around the level of the tariff rates that still apply at present', then it would be 'curtains' for German exports to Russia. The association made it clear to the government that it should not 'be deterred ... by the clamour of the agrarians ... from pushing for the conclusion of trade treaties that would at least not worsen the position of German industry and German trade any more than the present treaties do'.[37] In a resolution drawn up by its general assembly on 18 April 1903, the German-Russian Association called on the German government 'to ensure significant reductions in the proposed tariff rates through a treaty-based tariff to be established by a trade treaty covering several years, featuring as many fixed items as possible for goods exported from Germany'.[38] The CVDI too described the 'numerous increases in the rates of the new Russian customs tariff' as 'self-evidently detrimental to German exports' and called on the government 'to ensure the reduction of all items to the rates that apply at present'.[39]

The distinction between imports by land and sea provided for in the new Russian customs tariff was a particular thorn in the flesh of German exporters. This imposed a duty on goods imported to Russia across its western land border about 20 per cent higher than on imports by sea and, given the existing trade routes, was clearly a retaliatory measure aimed at German exports. The differential tariff, the German-Russian Association underlined, 'would put Germany at a huge disadvantage compared to its competitors on the Russian market'. The imposition of additional duties on goods entering Russia across Germany's eastern border would 'be so detrimental to exports from central and eastern Germany, particularly Silesia, while at the same time being so beneficial to our competitors from England, Belgium and the United States of America, that eliminating the distinction between sea and land duties set out in the new general tariff must be one of the first preconditions for a trade treaty'.[40] The CVDI also feared that the introduction of a differential tariff would shift competitive conditions to the advantage of international competitors in one of the most important German export markets. It too pressed the German government to 'enshrine ... in the new trade treaty ... the equality of tariffs for both borders stipulated in the final protocol to the current trade treaty'.[41]

Beyond the desire for Russian tariff reductions, the submissions, petitions and announcements of the organizations of trade and industry boiled down to two fundamental demands. First, and this was one of the key demands made during the protests against the differential tariff, German imports to Russia should enjoy comprehensive most-favoured-nation status, in other words, be treated no worse than the products of Germany's foreign industrial competitors. Second, the government should again conclude a trade treaty of at least ten years' duration that laid down as many Russian tariff rates as possible for the full duration of the treaty. Only a long-term trade treaty with comprehensive fixed tariffs would protect German exporters from unpredictable state interventions in foreign trade and thus provide it with the kind of predictability that would limit the transaction costs of exporting to Russia, which were fairly high in any case, or at least the most risky portion of such costs.[42] Particularly in view of the 'difficulties associated with doing business with Russia', the German-Russian Association underlined that it was 'absolutely necessary that the manufacturer and exporter can count on fixed factors that apply for a good number of years when making their calculations'.[43]

The circumstances that pertained on the eve of the trade treaty negotiations with Russia, as outlined above, perfectly capture the pincer movement to which German trade policy was exposed as a result of globalization, one that had increased in intensity since the 1890s. First, the emergence of a functioning world agricultural market had provoked a protectionist backlash among the German agrarians, as it had done in France and other continental European countries as well; this protest movement achieved its first major victory in the shape of the Bülow tariff and pushed relentlessly for the extension of the German system of agricultural protection. Second, the German economy's export dependency made it seem imperative to conclude a new long-term trade treaty that established conditions tolerable to German exporters. To defend at all costs the enhanced agricultural tariff protection set out in the customs tariff of 1902, while simultaneously responding to the Russian high protectionist retaliatory measures aimed at German exports – this was the virtually irresolvable dual task confronting German foreign trade policy in the impending trade treaty negotiations.

## *The German-Russian Trade Treaty of 1904 and Its Consequences*

On the German side, concrete preparations for the trade treaty negotiations with Russia began immediately after adoption of the Bülow tariff in late 1902. They kicked off with three important preliminary decisions.

First, the Foreign Ministry accepted the new Russian customs tariff as the basis for the treaty negotiations. This was by no means an uncontested decision. The German consul general in St. Petersburg, Erich Maron, argued that the German government must go out of its way to insist that the negotiations proceed not on the basis of the revised Russian tariff but of its predecessor, which was more favourable to Germany. He proposed instructing the 'better part of our press' to 'quickly [adopt] an uncompromising position on this matter', thus enabling the German negotiators 'to make compelling reference to German public opinion'[44] – a suggestion immediately taken up by Bülow, who set great store by a favourable press reaction.[45] By now, however, key figures in the Foreign Ministry had already decided that there was no point in continuing to refuse the Russian government's demand that Germany enter the negotiations with a new tariff and had officially conceded this point.[46] Paul Ernst von Körner, director of the Foreign Ministry's Trade Policy Department since 1899, responded to Maron's assessment that the Russian customs tariff, whose increased duties hit German exporters particularly hard, was 'not meant seriously'[47] by stating acerbically: 'It is no doubt meant as seriously as our tariff is.'[48] Remarkably sober-minded, Körner concluded that Germany could not avoid recognizing the new Russian customs tariff as the basis for negotiations since ultimately even the revised German tariff of 1902 had 'admittedly been drawn up, every bit as much as the new Russian [tariff], as a weapon in the treaty negotiations' and hit 'Russian exports (cereals, livestock, hops) with greatly increased duties'.[49]

Second, the German government decided not to involve the Economic Committee in the preparations for the trade treaty negotiations with Russia. This was surprising in the sense that it was only in 1897 that the Economic Committee, composed of representatives of economic interest groups, had been explicitly established to function as a semistate trade policy advisory body. In line with this, during the preliminary commissarial departmental consultations, the Imperial Treasury suggested convening the Economic Committee and giving it responsibility for hearing expert testimony.[50] The Foreign Ministry immediately raised an objection to this suggestion and gained the support of the other departments for its view that it was 'not feasible at present' to 'convene the Economic Committee and expect it to address this matter'.[51] Instead, it suggested other means of obtaining the economic information necessary for preparing for the trade treaty negotiations. The 'experts' – mostly the representatives of specific companies – should be given the opportunity to express their views on the Russian customs tariff through unofficial, individual surveys carried out by officials at the Imperial Ministry of the Interior and the Ministry of Trade.[52]

The aim of this procedure, which was ultimately approved on a consensual basis, was not to strictly exclude the representatives of economic interests. In cutting out the Economic Committee, the goal was in fact to maintain a distance from the interest associations represented in it. As sources of information, the ministerial bureaucracy was keen to hear from the representatives of economic interest groups and to take their views into consideration; but officials sought to evade the pressure exercised by organized economic interests as far as possible – apart from anything else, they had learned how important this was from the problems and conflicts that beset the period immediately before the customs tariff reform of 1902, in the initial stages of which the Economic Committee played an important role. The decision not to convene the Economic Committee was primarily a move against the agricultural interest organizations, first and foremost the BdL. In the election campaign that was taking place at the time, this organization was vociferous in expressing its dissatisfaction with the agricultural protection achieved in the Bülow tariff and launched a crusade against the conclusion of long-term trade treaties. The Economic Committee would have provided the agrarians, who made up such a major contingent of its members, with another platform to advocate their extreme protectionist demands; it was essential that the government fight these if the trade treaties were to have any chance. As the treaty negotiations continued, therefore, the government stuck with its decision not to involve the Economic Committee.[53] Within the framework of the expert hearings, the representatives of agricultural interests were also largely excluded; virtually the only voices that were heard were those of the export industry.

Third, the Foreign Ministry was also successful with its proposal not to conclude a completely new trade treaty but merely a supplementary agreement with Russia – as well as with Austria-Hungary, Italy, Switzerland, Belgium, Serbia and Romania[54] – which was intended to cover only changes to the existing treaty. The decisive factor in choosing this approach to designing the treaty was the fact that 'in this way certain more or less contested provisions in the current treaty, such as those concerning most-favoured-nation status and railway tariffs, [would be] removed if not from the debate then at least from the ambit of specific decisions in the Reichstag'.[55] Still smarting from the parliamentary battle over the Bülow tariff, the Foreign Ministry and the other ministries were keen to allow the absolute minimum of highly explosive trade policy material into the Reichstag. Above all, by presenting a supplementary convention that merely contained treaty changes, the aim was to do everything possible to deny the agrarian conservatives in the parliament any opportunity to question the present foundations of the treaty – and thus hack at the roots of the trade treaty system.

At the same time, with its proposal that Germany limit itself to a supplementary agreement, the Foreign Ministry aimed to block more extensive proposals for change on the level of the ministerial bureaucracy as well.[56] Despite the warning, repeated by representatives of the Foreign Ministry on a number of occasions, that it was vital 'to make as few changes as possible to the existing treaty text', however, the Foreign Ministry was far from entirely successful in this respect.[57] The Prussian Ministry of Agriculture in particular insisted that 'all important matters requiring changes' should in fact 'be subject to revision'.[58] Once again, the agriculture minister's concrete proposals for changing the existing treaty were very much in line with the demands that the agrarian interest organizations had been making for years. First, the agreement reached in Article 19 of the 1894 trade treaty and in the related clause in the final protocol on both sides' approach to calculating railway tariffs should be revised to reflect agrarian needs.[59] Second, the Ministry of Agriculture intended to break with the universal most-favoured-nation principle as the foundation stone of German trade policy by proposing that the trade treaties with Russia and the other states stipulate that the concessions listed should remain limited to the trade treaty states.[60]

While the representatives of the Foreign Ministry decided to play for time with respect to the railway tariffs and keep the issue open for the time being, they energetically opposed the attack on unlimited application of the most-favoured-nation principle. In a reply to a motion put forward by Prussian agriculture minister Podbielski, Richthofen, the undersecretary of state, explained that any attempt to restrict the most-favoured-nation principle would be neither technically enforceable nor economically advisable. If one were to break 'with the most-favoured-nation principle', the 'self-evident consequence [would be] that foreign countries' would 'reciprocate' with respect to the German Empire. This was bound to have disastrous consequences for the German export industry because across the world it was exposed 'almost everywhere to competition from highly developed industries' and could therefore be 'driven fairly easily from the relevant foreign markets by any differential tariff treatment'.[61]

While many of the conflicts within the Prussian-German executive rumbled on unresolved, the official trade treaty negotiations between Germany and Russia began in St. Petersburg on 5 August 1903. The nine-member German delegation included, in addition to the St. Petersburg consul general Maron, representatives of the Foreign Ministry, the Imperial Treasury, the Imperial Ministry of the Interior and – testimony to the extensive fusion of the Prussian and German governments – the Prussian Finance Ministry, Ministry of Trade and Ministry of Agriculture. They were led by Körner, head of the Trade Policy Department of the Foreign Ministry. The first round of negotiations, which lasted until 28 August, proved quite unproductive overall.[62] On three occasions, the talks were close to breaking down – twice because of the minimum tariff rates for cereals stipulated in the Bülow tariff and once because, in line with their instructions, the German negotiators showed no willingness to back down on disease control issues. When they had finished the first reading of the treaty text and both customs tariffs, they were not much closer to finding a compromise than they had been at the start of the negotiations. Both delegations made their demands and declared the other side's concessions inadequate.[63]

As expected, the German agricultural tariff increases were a particular bone of contention, above all the minimum cereal tariffs, which constituted a substantial extra burden compared to the current conventional tariff. When the talks began, at the first meeting the Russian negotiators went so far as to describe German willingness to go below the minimum rates, adopted just six months earlier in the Reichstag amid intense struggles, as a prerequisite for entering into more extensive negotiations. Körner soon informed the imperial chancellor of his view that 'it really will be necessary to grant compensation for the raising of our cereal and livestock tariffs in one area or another … we should perhaps already be seriously considering whether this can be done with respect to feed barley or meat imports'.[64] Even the conclusion of the second reading did nothing to change this assessment. With the exception of the representative of the Ministry of Agriculture, Wolfgang Kapp, the German trade treaty commission had 'become convinced that without a concession' on the disease control issue – the Russian government was calling for the abolition of the general ban on the import of Russian livestock and recognition of Russia's veterinary certificates in Germany – 'it will be impossible to conclude the treaty, particularly because the minimum rates are to be maintained'.[65]

The second round of negotiations, which took place in Berlin in November 1903, was even more disastrous than the first. In an informal discussion before the official start of the negotiations, Körner and Posadowsky, secretary of the interior, explained to Vasily Timiryazev, the Russian chief negotiator, the German government's proposals, which the various Prussian and imperial ministries had agreed to at a conference chaired by Bülow in early November. Any attempt to go below the minimal rates for cereals was categorically ruled out, as was the treaty-based restriction of German freedom of action with respect to disease control measures. The German government wished to accommodate Russian demands with respect to duties on feed barley, lubricating oils, horses, geese and eggs; the possibility of raising the Upper Silesian pig contingent was also aired.

In return, the Russian government should essentially maintain the existing conventional tariffs and forego the threatened tariff increases and the distinction between imports by land and sea. In view of the mood in Germany and particularly in the Reichstag, as Posadowsky explained the German government's inability to make far-reaching concessions in the agrarian field, 'a treaty that failed to include increased protection for agriculture compared to the current situation [would have] no prospect of being adopted and no government could present such a treaty to the Reichstag'.[66]

Unimpressed, Timiryazev made it abundantly clear that he regarded the German offer, which amounted to a massive increase in the burden on Russian exports to Germany, while Russian import tariffs would remain largely unchanged, as totally inadequate and unacceptable. Given the Germans' complete intransigence on the issue of minimum tariffs and with respect to all the other key Russian demands, the Russian delegate signalled that his government might have no interest in a tariff treaty, but only in a straightforward most-favoured-nation agreement. Körner responded that Germany was not prepared to conclude a pure most-favoured-nation treaty with Russia since Russia would benefit from the tariff reductions in the other German tariff treaties while the same would not apply to Germany. This was because the Russian government would not conclude any more tariff treaties if it did not manage to conclude one with Germany. Timiryazev explained that this meant that his instructions had become obsolete and he would have to confer with his government.[67]

The negotiations had in effect broken down before they had officially begun. With a great deal of effort, the negotiators maintained the fiction that the talks were continuing by agreeing to at least go through the text of the treaty and the final protocol over five sessions, while abandoning discussion of the customs tariffs. With virtually nothing to show for their efforts, the Russian delegation prepared to head back to St. Petersburg. Posadowsky had already given Timiryazev a document drawn up by the Foreign Ministry outlining the 'prerequisites for the continuation of the negotiations concerning renewal of the German-Russian trade treaty'.[68] In written and more detailed form, this document again specified the outer limits of the concessions, already set out verbally to the leader of the Russian delegation, that the German government was willing to countenance, along with the demands it insisted on. At the same time, Timiryazev was informed that 'the German delegates would be unable to come to St. Petersburg to continue the discussions before receiving a response to these proposals that holds out at least a reasonable prospect of concluding the treaty'.[69] The Russian government could scarcely have responded more brusquely. In January 1904 it informed the German ambassador in St. Petersburg, Friedrich Johann von Alvensleben, that it regarded the German offer as inadequate and was only willing to make further concessions if Germany offered adequate compensation for raising the cereal tariffs.[70]

In early 1904 German trade policy seemed to have hit a dead end. The trade treaty negotiations with Russia had reached a deadlock. The Russian government had proved intransigent and aimed to force Germany to make further concessions that, given the structure of Russian exports, could only lie in the sphere of agriculture. Yet it was precisely here that the German government's room for manoeuvre was all but exhausted – not least because it had tied its own hands through the legally enshrined minimum tariffs for the four main types of cereals. This messy situation appeared to suggest that the opponents of the customs tariff reform of 1902 had been right to complain that it would be impossible to conclude trade treaties on the basis of the Bülow tariff, or at least any acceptable to German exporters.

To make matters worse, the German government faced increasing time pressure. So far, it had refrained from abrogating the existing trade treaty with Russia and the other Caprivi treaties, as this would have deprived it of an important means of pressurising the Reichstag to accept new treaties.[71] The Russian chief negotiators had made full use of this fact and delayed the negotiations whenever possible; ultimately, as Alvensleben remarked, 'every day that goes by with the lower German cereal tariffs ... is a boon for Russia'.[72] At the same time, however, there had been a marked increase in the domestic political pressure within the German Empire to abrogate the old trade treaties and finally enforce the increased agrarian protection provided by the Bülow tariff. The situation was also complicated by the fact that Germany was negotiating not just with Russia but also with the other tariff treaty states on the conclusion of new trade treaties; for administrative reasons, all of these ought to come into force at the same time. This further restricted the time horizon for further negotiations with Russia and made it seem imperative to rescind the present treaty before the end of 1904.[73] But if negotiations failed to produce results within the year prior to abrogation, there was a risk that German-Russian trade would be unregulated by treaty, and this would have resulted in the termination of most-favoured-nation status and the imposition of the general tariffs on both sides. Under these circumstances the most likely outcome would have been a repeat of the customs war of 1893/94, with all its disastrous consequences for both imports and exports.

The fact that the German government ultimately managed to overcome the trade policy deadlock and conclude a trade treaty with Russia was due to an event external to trade policy, namely, the outbreak of the Russo-Japanese War. From the beginning of the military conflict in early 1904, the Japanese, hugely underestimated by the Russian leadership, imposed a series of heavy defeats on the Russian Empire.[74] The fact that the war was going so badly put Russia in a position of dual dependency on the German Empire. First, it was strategically dependent on the 'benevolent neutrality' of its western neighbour. Second, it needed access to the German finance market to meet Russian borrowing requirements, which had grown tremendously as a result of the military conflict.

As Russia's military and financial situation grew worse in the spring of 1904 and the German-Russian trade treaty negotiations remained stalled, with no prospect of resolution in sight, the German leadership sought to exploit the Russian government's predicament.[75] To circumvent Witte, the key figure in the Russian government insisting on reduced German minimum tariffs, Bülow asked the emperor to write to the czar personally, requesting that he send 'some prominent figure to Berlin to deal with Bülow directly' in order to speed up the trade treaty negotiations.[76] In parallel to this political initiative, pressure was imposed on the banking firms involved in the Russian consortium to avoid agreeing to loans with the Russian Empire. While the Foreign Ministry took up contact with the Deutsche Bank, the Prussian trade minister informed the other major banks in Berlin and Frankfurt that he expected 'the German banking firms [to be] so loyal and patriotic' as to desist from lending to Russia 'as long as a new trade treaty has not been concluded with [it]'.[77] At the same time, through the intermediary figure of Anton Lessing, the locomotive industrialist, the Foreign Ministry made it known to Vladimir Nikolaevich Kokovtsov, the new Russian finance minister, that the German capital market would be open to Russia only after the conclusion of a new trade treaty.[78]

The alarming scenario evoked by the German government had the desired effect. At the ministerial conference of 14 May, the Russian finance minister explained to his colleagues in stark terms that given the 'terrible strains on Russia's financial strength' as a result of the war with Japan, the 'use of foreign credit [is] a national imperative'. The French capital market, he pointed out, was already saturated with Russian borrowing. The 'other proven and solid market, namely, the German', would, however, 'remain closed as long as the issue of the Russian-German trade treaty [remains] unresolved'. The ministerial conference therefore decided to bring the negotiations on the trade agreement to a close as quickly as possible: 'no demands [should] be made of Germany' that 'the German government would be unable to accept'.[79] In early June, via Lessing, Kokovtsov was able to inform the Foreign Ministry confidentially that 'against the wishes of Witte he had obtained the czar's written authorization to conclude a treaty on the basis of our [the German] minimum tariffs'.[80] Just one month later, in July 1904, a small Russian delegation met at Norderney, Bülow's summer residence, to conclude the trade treaty negotiations. The task of negotiating the minutiae of the agreement fell to none other than Witte, who had been so intransigent with respect to the German minimum tariffs. But the wishes of the Russian ministerial committee and the czar's express instructions to bring the negotiations to a positive conclusion at any price left him with no choice but to broadly accept the German conditions.[81] Furthermore, Witte's influence within the Russian government had diminished markedly by 1903 and he had been compelled to move to the fairly insignificant post of chair of the ministerial committee. If he wished to prevent the further erosion of his authority, he could not afford for the negotiations he led to fail.[82]

The new German-Russian trade treaty, soon signed by Bülow and Witte on 28 July, went a long way to satisfying German aspirations. The minimal rates for rye, wheat, oats and malting barley were retained in full. In terms of disease controls, the imperial government successfully resisted all treaty-based restrictions on its autonomy of action. The German concessions went only slightly further than what had been offered the year before in the 'prerequisites' outlined by Posadowsky: the tariff for feed barley was reduced not just to 2 marks per quintal, but to 1.3 marks – but this significant reduction affected a vanishingly small portion of German cereal producers and benefited many livestock farmers. In increasing the Upper Silesian pig contingent the German side went some way to meeting Russian desires. Rather than just 1,900 animals, 2,500 – almost exactly as many as prior to 1896 – would be allowed across the Russian border into the Upper Silesian industrial region on a weekly basis. Russia's concessions were far more substantial. The distinction between land and sea duties contained in the Russian tariff of 1903, which targeted German exports, was eliminated. The German side also got what it wanted from the negotiations with respect to a number of nontariff issues such as the taxation of business travellers and the permissibility of supplementary tariffs on Russian sugar, in accordance with the Brussels International Sugar Convention of 1902. Of the increased duties on German export goods in the new Russian tariff, almost none entered fully into force. Many returned to the level in the previous treaty tariff, and some were set even lower. The chief German negotiators did, however, have to accept a number of sometimes substantial duty increases for the products of the chemicals, iron and machine industries – whether these had much potential to damage German exports was, however, unclear, since there was as yet no serious import competition in Russia. Otherwise, key parameters of the old treaty remained unchanged. This applied both to the regulation of the railway tariff, as set out in Article 19 and the associated final protocol clause, and to the most-favoured-nation clause. Finally, Russia agreed to the German demand to again conclude a long-term trade treaty that, like the other German tariff treaties, was to last for twelve years.[83]

In exemplary fashion, the genesis of the German-Russian trade treaty of 1904 demonstrates how dramatically the increasing global economic integration at the beginning of the twentieth century had curtailed the German government's trade policy room for manoeuvre. On the one hand, the government felt it must defend the protective barriers erected by the Bülow tariff at all costs against the overwhelming competition on the world agricultural market. On the other hand, it believed it impossible to accept any intensification of Russian high protectionism, as this would have put at risk one of Germany's most important export markets. Taken together, these two imperatives – whether they were real or merely perceived is of little significance here – made the prospects for concluding the German-Russian negotiations seem hopeless. The imperial leadership only managed to overcome them by exploiting a favourable foreign policy situation to prompt Russia to accept its demands. In his report to Hermann Friedrich von Lucanus, head of the Secret Civil Cabinet (Geheimes Zivilkabinett), Bülow was quite open about this. According to the imperial chancellor, it was only Russia's precarious situation in East Asia and the position of the German capital market as a source of loans to Russia that had made it possible to conclude the trade treaty.[84]

The imperial government thus endowed trade policy with an entirely new significance. Formerly, it had engaged in international trade policy conflicts and resolved them with the help of genuine trade policy instruments – this was certainly true of the German-Russian customs war of 1893/94. In contemporaries' traditional understanding of politics, the relationship between foreign trade policy and so-called grand politics had a clear hierarchical structure: trade policy was to serve as an instrument of foreign policy – and even in the case of Caprivi this had remained an important side effect. Now, however, the instrumentalization of 'grand politics' to enforce trade policy demands had turned this hierarchy on its head. The consequences of economic globalization had placed such limits on the German government's trade policy room for manoeuvre, while so greatly enhancing its significance, that at least in situational terms it had taken precedence over traditional foreign policy.

Along with the treaties with Austria-Hungary, Italy, Switzerland, Belgium, Serbia and Romania, the trade agreement with Russia was presented to the Reichstag on 1 February 1905. The trade treaties were linked in this way not just for practical reasons but also – like their design as supplementary conventions – to give the parliament as little opportunity as possible to debate highly conflictual trade policy issues. In any case, the

Reichstag deputies had little scope for action: they could merely accept each individual treaty as a whole or reject it, but could make no changes to it. In addition, in the Reichstag committee the government had threatened to abandon all seven treaties should one of them fail 'contrary to expectation … to be approved by the Reichstag'.[85] This fear was testimony to the trauma suffered by members of the executive in the struggle over the Bülow tariff, but was largely unjustified: though they were unenthusiastic, most important economic interest groups and most of the press signalled their support for the trade treaties.

On one side of the political spectrum, the agrarian right emphasized that the 'improvements' entailed in the new treaties 'are very far from approaching what German agriculture has always demanded and should in fact be able to expect'. But in spite of themselves, and in a frankly shameless manner given the massive agricultural tariff increases, the agrarian right conceded that 'in a number of areas the new treaty tariffs [were] slightly though not a great deal better' than the previous ones and made their peace with the government.[86] The associations of trade and industry and those close to them, meanwhile, were relieved that any long-term trade treaties had been concluded on the basis of the Bülow tariff, though the left-liberal press had labelled the new treaties the 'work of the agrarians' and complained that they were less favourable to industry than the preceding ones.[87] Overall, a broad social and political consensus seemed to take shape that there was ultimately no viable alternative to ratifying the trade treaties. The majority in favour of the treaties in the Reichstag was correspondingly large. In contrast to the customs tariff reform of 1902, this time the agrarian conservatives voted en bloc for the government bill. The only ones to vote against the trade treaties were the Social Democrats and a few scattered deputies from the left-liberal parties and the Bavarian Peasants' League (Bayerischer Bauernbund).[88] The political left, however, did not reject the trade treaties as such – in principle they firmly supported them – but rather the Bülow tariff on which they were based.

All seven agreements came into force on 1 March 1906. This meant that the German Empire retained its position as the undisputed centre of the European network of trade treaties; in other words, it continued to play the role it had taken over from France in the early 1890s. The German-Russian trade treaty set the parameters for a further period of dramatic growth in trade between the two countries. German imports from Russia, which were still worth 805 million marks in 1904, climbed to more than twice this amount within just seven years – by 1911 – to 1,634 million marks, before falling slightly to 1,425 million marks by 1913 (see table 1.7). Since the growth rate of Russian exports to Germany greatly exceeded that of Russian exports as a whole, the empire became ever more important as a purchaser of Russian goods. In 1910, just under half of Russian exports went to Germany; twenty years earlier it had been less than one-third.[89]

The products of agriculture and forestry continued to make up the lion's share of Russian exports to Germany – in 1913, for example, they accounted for a share of 91.6 per cent.[90] Cereals occupied a special position among agrarian products: between 1910 and 1913, wheat, rye, barley and oats alone made up no less than 38 per cent on average of Russian exports to Germany.[91] All in all, the new German cereal tariffs that applied to imports from 1906 on, had failed to curb or even significantly reduce the growth rate of cereal imports from Russia. If we compare, for example, the total quantity of rye, wheat, barley and oats (in tonnes) imported to Germany from the Russian Empire for the three years of 1900, 1905 and 1910, for the first five-year period – in other words, while the Caprivi tariffs applied – the growth rate was 57 per cent, while this had reached 70 per cent for the 1905–10 period.[92]

Of course, this does not mean that the German tariffs made no impact. Two of their effects are particularly evident. First, while they did not detach the cereal price trend in Germany from that of the world market, they did ensure that the gap between the German and the world market price grew larger. From 1906 on, German cereal prices, or to be more precise, those in areas of high cereal demand west of the Elbe, regularly lay above prices on the global market to the full amount of the increased tariffs. Second, under the influence of the new duties there was a fundamental shift in the structure of German cereal imports from Russia. The import of wheat and oats, to which the high minimum duties of 55 and 50 marks per tonne applied from 1906 on, showed only a moderate increase of 21 per cent and 36 per cent, respectively, between 1902/3 and 1912/13. But over the same period imports of feed barley, to which a duty of just 13 marks per tonne applied, shot up by 535 per cent. This corresponded to an increase in barley's share of total cereal imports from 22 to 60 per cent.[93] The import of Russian rye, once the Russian Empire's major export item to Germany, meanwhile, collapsed by more than half (57 per cent) between 1902/3 and 1912/13; on the eve of the First World War, it had become almost insignificant compared to imports of wheat and barley. This development becomes understandable only if we take into account the intertwining of the increased duty on rye with the bill of entry system that had existed since 1894 (see chapter 4). The increased duty triggered a concurrent rise in the level of export subsidies, which is what the bills of entry de facto functioned as. Because of this, German rye exports – and to a lesser extent exports of oats and wheat as well – grew remarkably from 1908 on; in turn, and indirectly, this provided a major stimulus to cereal production. Russian rye was increasingly driven from the German market, while the German Empire ceased to be a rye-importing state and became a rye-exporting one. Not only this, but Germany outstripped Russia, still the world's biggest producer of rye, as rye's greatest exporter, and made increasing advances in the Russian market itself.[94]

German export industry had in principle welcomed the conclusion of the trade treaty with Russia, but responded to increases in certain Russian import duties with prophecies of doom. The increased Russian duties were, it was claimed, 'likely to seriously impede and limit [German exports to Russia] and paralyze them completely in some sectors' – this was the general tenor of the response.[95] None of this turned out to be true. German exports to Russia surged in the years following the conclusion of the trade treaty. They grew much faster than German exports as a whole – which were already booming – and Russian imports, which also showed an upward trend. German exports to Russia had largely stagnated for five years from 1899 before advancing in leaps and bounds: from 300 million marks in 1904, through 445 million marks in 1909, to 880 million marks in 1913. This also meant that as an export market Russia's importance to the German economy grew in a way that applied to no other major German market. As late as 1904, just 5.7 per cent of German exports had gone to the Russian Empire, but by 1913 this had already increased to 8.7 per cent. Within just a few years, Russia had become Germany's third-largest export market (see table 1.5). Even those groups of commodities – such as machines and electrotechnical products – for which the new trade treaty had brought sometimes substantial increases in Russian duties generally enjoyed marked and often disproportionate growth in exports to Russia.

It would be rash to take this to mean that individual tariff rates and Russian high protectionism as a whole had no consequences for German foreign trade. It seems quite possible, probable even, that without Russian trade barriers German exports to Russia would have developed even more dynamically. But whether, and if so to what extent, this would have been the case could only be explored through a counterfactual simulation that presupposed free trade between Germany and Russia. This would inevitably be hypothetical and theoretically problematic in many ways. All we can say with confidence is that the rapid Russian economic growth in the boom years between 1909 and 1913, which was based on an industrial upsurge propelled by the state and reinforced by an influx of foreign capital, clearly generated so much Russian import demand that even tariff increases could not impede the accelerated growth in imports from Germany. The dynamism of economic development proved stronger than the trade barriers erected by the state. Those contemporaries who were involved directly in trade with Russia came to the same conclusion. 'The conditions for commerce with Russia were particularly favourable', as a report by the German-Russian Association with reference to 1911 summed things up, 'in the sense that over the last few years that country has undergone phenomenal economic development that has made demands on foreign trade that render the exact level of import duties quite insignificant'.[96]

Given the intensification of German-Russian economic relations on the eve of the First World War, we could be forgiven for assuming that the trading relationship between the two countries was unproblematic and that the trade treaty due to expire at the end of 1917 must have had good prospects of trouble-free extension without the need for major changes. In fact, the opposite was the case. First of all, the trade treaty, and above all the process of its emergence, provoked constant trade policy tensions. At every possible opportunity, the last being the German-Russian 'newspaper war' in the spring of 1914, the Russian press singled out the 1904 treaty for criticism.[97] 'Russian public opinion', as the German consul in Moscow described the dominant tendency within Russian political discourse until the First World War, 'continued to [regard] the fixing of the German minimum tariffs in the treaty as gravely detrimental to Russian agriculture and Russian exports, an impediment, moreover, that Germany has enforced by unscrupulously exploiting Russia's political and financial difficulties'.[98]

Second, after the turn of the century Russian economic interest groups increasingly made their presence felt, hampering the smooth extension of the trade treaty. It was 'characteristic of the profoundly different situation in Russia compared with the period before the trade treaties of 1894 and 1904', as a report by the German consulate summed things up, 'that while on that occasion the government made all the preparations in secret and in consultation with just a small number of interested parties, now every issue is discussed by the various interest organizations in the most public way'.[99] Several years in advance, the Russian agrarian and industrial interest organizations signalled their views on the renegotiation of the German-Russian agreement, due in 1917, through a major media campaign. The Russian government, mutatis mutandis, now found itself confronted with the same phenomenon with which the German government had been struggling since the 1890s as a result of the German economy's earlier and deeper integration into the global market. As a result of the increasing pressure from economic interests – on which economic globalization impacted ever more radically and in profoundly different ways – its room for manoeuvre on trade policy was increasingly constrained. German experts on Russian economic policy were therefore certain that 'there [would be] no new trade treaties with Russia without protracted and difficult negotiations'. 'Public opinion, or rather the powerful agitation of the major associations representing individual economic sectors, [is forcing] the government to do all it can to champion the interests of the country – that is, of the producers, not so much the consumers'.[100] The First World War rendered this highly realistic prognosis obsolete. When a new trade treaty was finally agreed between Germany and Russia in early 1918 in Brest-Litovsk, it was no more than a footnote to the far-reaching provisions in the peace treaty, and the German side was largely able to dictate terms.

## The United States

### *The Challenge of U.S. High Protectionism*

The United States was the homeland of modern protectionism. The first secretary of the treasury, Alexander Hamilton, produced his famous *Report on Manufactures* in 1791, which is considered the classical formulation of the 'infant industry' argument in favour of protectionist interventions.[101] Without protective tariffs and a state premiums policy, Hamilton believed, effective industrialization would be impossible in an industrial latecomer such as the U.S., because the nascent economic sectors were incapable of withstanding superior foreign competition. Over the following decades, this theoretical manifesto was turned into practical action: step-by-step, up until the 1820s, the American system of protective tariffs was developed into a massive bulwark. After a phase of generally moderate protectionism between 1846 and 1860, the U.S. returned to high protectionism through the Morrill tariff of 1861 – at a time when free trade was taking hold in Europe.

Finally, towards the end of the nineteenth century, American protectionism reached a new peak. The McKinley tariff of 1890, named after one of the chairs of the House Ways and Means Committee, raised the average tariff burden of dutiable imports to almost 49 per cent (1891–94; see figure 6.1).[102] The Wilson-Gorman tariff (1894), implemented by the Democrats with their majority in both houses of Congress, only slightly reduced this exorbitant tariff level despite the announcements made in the preceding election campaign, and was in any case merely a short-lived interlude. By 1897, the Republicans had taken advantage of the change in the composition of Congress and McKinley's presidency to introduce a new customs tariff, the legendary Dingley tariff. This represented the peak of American high protectionism before the First World War. While it is true that during its twelve-year period of validity the average tariff burden on dutiable imports lay slightly below that of the McKinley tariff at 47.3 per cent, this figure is already diluted by tariff-induced shifts in imports. More instructive is the level of protection immediately after the Dingley tariff came into force, which grew to an average annual level of 50 per cent for the years 1898–1902 and reached a peak of more than 52 per cent in 1899. Furthermore, the new customs tariff expanded the proportion of dutiable goods as a share of imports so that the tariff burden of total imports increased markedly.[103] The Payne-Aldrich tariff of 1909, which resulted in a mild reduction in tariffs overall, also did nothing to fundamentally change the ultraprotectionist character of U.S. trade policy. Only when the Democrats won the presidential election of 1912 for the first time since the early 1890s, while also gaining a majority in Congress, was there a temporary break with the preceding policies. The Underwood-Simmons tariff, adopted in October of the following year, expanded the list of duty-free import goods through the addition of numerous foodstuffs and raw materials and substantially reduced duties on a wide array of products. The First World War and its consequences, however, rendered this shift in tariff policy virtually irrelevant.[104]

The American protectionism of the McKinley and Dingley tariffs was flanked by a policy of reciprocity inaugurated in 1890 by secretary of state James G. Blaine. This strategy, which built on Blaine's pan-American vision, was intended to ensure that the U.S. export industry conquered the markets of South and Central America. First of all, this was intended to create a growth-stabilizing export outlet for North American industry and agriculture, which were in desperate need of markets. Second, the strengthening of the U.S. economic presence in Latin America and concomitant displacement of European influence was intended to provide

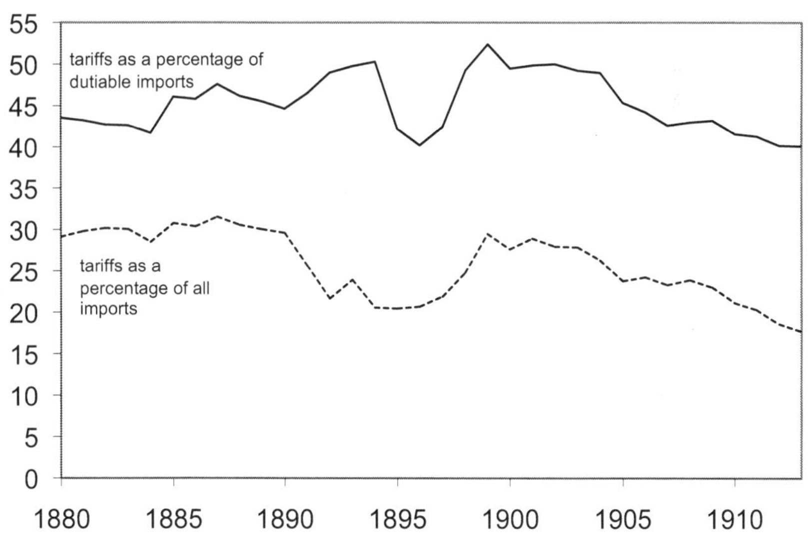


**Figure 6.1.** American protectionism, 1880–1913
*Source:* Bureau of the Census, *Historical Statistics of the United States,* vol. 2, 888.

economic backing for the Monroe Doctrine, and, over the long term, to integrate the states of South and Central America into a coherent, U.S.-dominated trade system. In order to achieve this goal, Blaine managed to ensure that Congress included a reciprocity clause in the McKinley tariff. This empowered the American president – Benjamin Harrison in 1890 – to conclude bilateral trade treaties granting U.S. treaty partners duty-free import of sugar, molasses, coffee, tea and skins if they in turn made tariff policy concessions with respect to certain North American export goods – exclusively to the benefit of the U.S. and not to be extended to other trading partners. Should trade treaty negotiations break down, the reciprocity clause also gave the president the power to impose punitive tariffs on the above-mentioned products, the vast majority of which entered the U.S. from Latin America.[105]

The Dingley tariff contained a similar provision. In addition to the option of lowering the duties on a narrowly circumscribed range of luxury goods within the context of trade treaty negotiations, which was only of much relevance to French exports, Section 3 gave the president the right to impose punitive tariffs on coffee, tea, tonka beans and vanilla beans from other countries if he felt they had failed to open themselves sufficiently to U.S. exports. In addition, in Section 4, the Dingley tariff empowered the president to conclude comprehensive reciprocal treaties in which U.S. tariffs could be reduced by up to 20 per cent in exchange for similar concessions on American exported goods. Such agreements, however, required the approval of both the Senate and the House of Representatives – a safeguard Congress was unwilling to give up.

Beyond their protectionist function, the insertion of the reciprocity clause made both the McKinley and Dingley tariffs instruments of economic expansion. Essentially, what all this amounted to was a policy of blackmail dressed up – with difficulty – as a matter of reciprocity. In formal terms this policy had no specific goal but de facto targeted the states of Latin America and, secondarily, the Pacific region. The aim was to exploit the high level of dependency on exports to the United States characteristic of many of the countries of South and Central America in order to provide U.S. exports with advantageous access to their markets. In this way, the U.S. aimed finally to snatch away major market shares from its European competitors, mainly the British but also the Germans, who had dominated the South American market hitherto. At the turn of the century it could not be clearly foreseen how limited the economic success of this strategy would prove to be. Initially, the numerous reciprocity treaties with Latin American states concluded after implementation of the McKinley and Dingley tariffs seemed to indicate that the U.S. had found an effective means of penetrating South America economically and driving out European exports.[106]

In contrast to Russia, much of whose foreign trade policy can be understood in light of its interactions with German policy, the United States, the other major high protectionist power towards the end of the nineteenth century, proved largely unaffected by the currents of international trade policy. The key to understanding the course of U.S. foreign trade policy, therefore, lies not in the external stimulus of other states' trade policies, but in the sectorally and regionally variable way in which globalization, and thus state intervention in trade, impacted on the various economic interest groups within the United States. It is only by looking at the conflicts of interest to which this gave rise that we can explain why, just as in Germany, U.S. tariff and trade policy around the turn of the century had become one of the most important and contested fields of domestic politics. The famous 'Cui bono?' question is fairly easy to answer with respect to American trade policy. The main beneficiary of both high protectionism and the reciprocity policy – as well as the other typical attributes of trade imperialism – was the industrial Northeast. The industries of the manufacturing belt, first and foremost the iron and steel and textile industries, benefited from protection from their European competitors – this at least was what contemporaries believed, as evident in the intensive lobbying efforts of industrial associations in favour of protectionist measures. Furthermore, it was primarily American industrial products for which the policy of reciprocity promised to open up new markets in less developed countries. Big industrialists such as Andrew Carnegie were thus among the most passionate supporters of reciprocity, viewing it as 'the best step' towards conquering new markets for American industrial exports.[107]

The industrially underdeveloped south of the U.S., meanwhile, lost out in two ways from a trade policy strategy that combined protectionism and reciprocity. First, the southern states had to bear part of the cost of protectionism in the form of increased goods prices. In contrast to businesses and industrial workers in the Northeast, however, they did not benefit from the protective effects of the tariffs. Second, U.S. tariff and trade policy was a threat to the export industry of the southern states. The South was by far the most export-dependent region of the U.S. In contrast to the exports of American industrial regions, more than 80 per cent of the South's exports were raw materials, above all cotton, that went almost exclusively to Europe.[108] This made the raw material producers of the American South particularly vulnerable to any retaliatory trade measures imposed by the European industrial nations, which were provoked unnecessarily, as they saw it, by an aggressive U.S. trade policy. Amid the tariff policy disputes around the turn of the century, therefore, the political and economic representatives of the southern states were virtually united in calling for a lowering of tariffs and attacking the policy of reciprocity.

But the profoundly protectionist attitudes of much of American industry and the preeminent economic and social importance of America's industrial core in the Northeast do not in themselves explain why high protectionism gained such a firm foothold from 1890 on. Ultimately, it was in the arena of national politics rather than economic interests that decisions on tariff policy were made. Since the presidential election of 1888 at the latest, in which Cleveland, the Democratic candidate, made lowering the tariffs a major campaign theme before losing the election, the two parties had been sharply divided. Since then, the Republicans had been even more clearly committed to tightening tariff protection, just as the Democrats were determined to reduce it.[109]

Under these conditions, the crucial factor in enforcing high protectionism and the policy of reciprocity that flanked it was the Republican Party's success in forging a political coalition in favour of high protectionism and trade imperialism that went far beyond the groups in the Northeast directly interested in them. In order to achieve this, party strategists greatly expanded the circle of potential beneficiaries of the planned trade policy, in two main ways. First, they extended the protectionist programme through the addition of protective tariffs for a number of agricultural goods. Wool tariffs in particular helped win over the sheep farmers of the American West. Second, the Republicans used most of the revenue from the new tariffs to finance a generous system of military pensions provided exclusively for veterans of the American Civil War who had fought for the northern states. Because the majority of those entitled to such a pension lived in rural areas of the northern U.S., by linking protectionism with a pension system the Republicans gained another important source of potential support beyond the manufacturing belt. Through these additional incentives, the Republican Party integrated new social groups into the phalanx of those with an interest in high protectionism. In the run-up to both the McKinley and Dingley tariffs, in elections and in Congress, the party thus managed to put together a political coalition that covered almost the entire highly populated North of the United States. This completely isolated the South and produced a broad majority in favour of the projected tariff increases.[110]

## *German Exports and the 'American Peril'*

As usual, it is very difficult to assess the extent to which American high protectionism had an adverse effect on German exports. Viewed in isolation, the increase in German exports to the U.S. – the overwhelming majority of which were finished industrial goods, first and foremost textiles, chemical and pharmaceutical products, and leather goods[111] – seemed highly impressive in the quarter century before the First World War. Between 1889–91 and 1911–13, on an average annual basis, the value of exports increased from 390 to 684 million marks – no less than 75 per cent (see table 1.5). If we relate these figures to other statistics, however, we must relativize our positive assessment of German export trends. First, they did not come close to keeping up with the increase in German imports from the U.S., which climbed from 372 to 1,547 million marks over the same period and thus increased by 316 per cent. As a consequence, the slight trade surplus with the U.S. that the German Empire had achieved by the early 1890s was transformed into a massive deficit by the time of the First World War. Second, the increase in German exports to North America lagged far behind the growth in other German exports. As a consequence, the proportion of total German exports that went to the U.S. steadily declined: in 1889–91, it still made up a good 12 per cent, but had fallen to just 7.6 per cent in 1911–13 (see table 1.5). This was a significant drop that accelerated immediately after the McKinley and Dingley tariffs came into force. Third, German exports to the U.S. expanded more slowly than aggregate American imports, which increased by 110 per cent between 1889–91 and 1911–13, a period during which non-European regions became increasingly important as suppliers of goods to the U.S.[112]

Against this background, if we compare the rather disappointing trends in German exports to the U.S. with exports to Russia, we find a remarkable discrepancy. While German exports to the U.S. increased by 75 per cent between 1889–91 and 1911–13, exports to Russia shot up over the same period by 334 per cent – despite the fact that the Russian tariff level was higher on average than its American equivalent during the quarter century before the First World War. The comparison suggests that we cannot explain the relatively slow growth of German exports to the U.S. solely with reference to American high protectionism. Only if we also take account of the burgeoning development of American industry, which proved increasingly capable of producing import-competitive products as well as goods for export, do we begin to grasp the problems facing German exports.

In the perception of the contemporaries affected by them, however, it was the consequences of American tariffs that stood out. In numerous submissions and petitions presented to the imperial government, in annual reports and at meetings, the associations of trade and industry, chambers of commerce and individual firms articulated their protest against U.S. protectionism. 'German industry' had been 'pushed step-by-step out of the market that the U.S. formerly represented as a result of the United States' repeated major tariff increases', the Cologne Industrialists' Union (Verein der Industriellen des Regierungsbezirks Köln) complained in early 1899 in a submission to the imperial chancellor.[113] In its annual report for 1899, the Gera Chamber of Commerce also came to the conclusion that 'as a result of its extremely high protectionism', the 'ruthless tariff policy being pursued by the United States of North America [*sic*] … [had] brought things to the point' where 'exports to that market have declined very significantly'.[114] Sentiments had changed little a decade later. At the U.S. conference organized in late 1909 by the Trade Treaty Association and the Industrialists' League, or BdI, after the Payne-Aldrich tariff had come into force, a delegate from Stuttgart stated that of 150 industrialists who had been surveyed, 'a full third' had declared that they were now unable to export the goods they produced as a result of new tariff increases.[115]

But the tariffs, which were often between 30 and 50 per cent, and sometimes even higher, were just one aspect of the import barriers hindering German exports to the U.S. American tariff administrative regulations and the way in which they were enforced also had a significant trade-hampering effect. In fact, they were often central to the complaints of German exporters – and this changed little between 1890 and the First World War. Beginning with de facto functionless hygiene provisions through excessive rules on declaration to the demand for fee-based authentication of all papers by a specially created American consulate in Germany, the American tariff administration law contained a large number of regulations that, particularly if interpreted narrowly, inevitably hindered trade. But by far the greatest number of criticisms voiced by the export industry and trade were related to the fact that, in the two decades before the First World War, the American customs tariff consisted chiefly of value-based tariffs. While the German tariff system had been built on the principle of the specific duty, in which the quantitative unit of a good (the number of units, weight, etc.) formed the basis for calculating the duty, the American tariff was a mixture of specific and value-based tariff rates. Over the course of time, the value-based tariff system had been developed ever further by the legislative branch, so that it ultimately came to dominate. The pivot of every functional value-based tariff system is the clear and understandable determination of the commodity price that is to form the basis for the assessment of duty.[116] Yet this is just what the American tariff lacked in practice. In fact, the tariffing procedure with which German goods found themselves confronted upon entering the U.S. entailed a number of imponderables and risks apt to drive up transaction costs.[117]

The main complaints of German trade and the export industry concerned the activities of American 'appraisers'. In assessing the market value of incoming goods, these officials often came to conclusions that differed significantly from the information provided by exporters, no doubt often pushing values arbitrarily upwards. A typical experience with

American tariffing procedures was described by Faber, the pencil manufacturer, in the context of a survey of chambers of trade and commerce in Middle Franconia. A batch of pencils bound for New York, which the southern German industrialist had declared at the same value 'for which this article had been invoiced for many years over there and [had been] sold in Germany', was suddenly estimated by the American tariff authority at a market value around 50 per cent higher – at the behest, Faber claimed, of his American competitors.[118] The increase in declared value at the hands of the appraiser not only resulted in a proportional increase in the duty on the imported goods, calculated ad valorem, but also incurred a severe customs penalty due to underdeclaration. In the case of Faber, the deviation was in fact so high that the American customs authority identified all the elements of attempted fraud and confiscated the goods without further ado.

Certainly, in such cases the exporter or importer could raise an objection to the appraiser's decision. But the appeal procedure placed the burden of proof clearly on the businessman and cost him even more money, and there was no certainty about the outcome. Faber, the pencil manufacturer, tried to demonstrate the correctness of the price it had declared – in line with American tariff law – by producing affidavits from various buyers in Germany and other countries to show that 'the relevant customers sell the same pencil' produced by the company 'at no higher a price' than it 'was invoiced at in the United States'. Though he had his New York lawyer present these certificates, authenticated by American consuls, to the customs authority, 'the results of his action ... [were] wholly negative', since 'despite the proof brought forward on a number of occasions' of the correctness of the declared value, the customs authority insisted on its original decision and finally confiscated the goods.[119] The experience of unpredictability inherent in this and many similar cases severely undermined German exporters' sense of trust[120] that the American customs administration would function reliably, the institutional trust so central to long-term international business relations because it lowers transaction costs. This factor was so important that, as the *Frankfurter Zeitung* summed up the mood among German exporters to the U.S. in 1907, for the 'interested parties ... an improvement in American customs procedures almost [seems] more important' than a 'revision of the tariff'.[121]

In addition to the problems caused by the American protective tariffs and tariffing procedures, which were perceived as harassment, German industry faced another threat from the late 1890s on. Both in its own domestic market and in the markets of third-party states within and beyond Europe, it increasingly found itself confronted by competition from rapidly growing U.S. industrial exports. Beginning in 1897/98, and thus almost concurrent with the coming into force of the Dingley tariff, for a limited period American industry engaged in what we might call a major export offensive, which made its presence felt in the German market. Between 1895 and 1900, for example, German imports of American machines and machine parts – the most important individual industrial imports from the U.S. – shot up by a factor of ten, from 3.3 to 31.8 million marks.[122] It was tremendous growth rates like these that caused contemporaries to fear the imminent 'flooding' of Europe by U.S. industrial products.

The fear of American competition received new impetus in spring 1900. The economic boom in the German Empire that had lasted since 1895 came to a sudden end; the economy was plunged into deep recession. Though most economists agreed that this was a crisis of overproduction, a result of the overcapacity that had built up over the preceding boom years, the depression was often blamed, particularly by the spokesmen of German industry, on the U.S.[123] This attempt to apportion blame was based on a collapse in the value of shares following news from the U.S. that a number of major ironworks intended to close their plants because of overproduction. This in turn led to a crisis in Germany in April 1900, as key actors feared the imminent flooding of the German market due to U.S. export dumping and the associated negative price effects. In fact, however, economic developments in the U.S. acted at most as a trigger here; at the same time, though, the stock exchange's sensitive reaction shows how deeply the fear of American industrial competition was anchored in German economic circles.

Ultimately, the breathtaking growth rate of U.S. industrial exports to Germany shortly before the turn of the century proved a short-lived phenomenon. This was due in substantial part to the cyclical mismatch between the U.S. and Europe. Because economic activity accelerated later and more slowly in the U.S. than in Europe, prices and domestic demand were still low in the U.S. in 1897/98, while the European economy was already enjoying booms accompanied by a marked acceleration in prices. The extraordinary export stimulus that this constellation entailed for American industry did not last long. When the economic situation improved dramatically in the U.S. from 1901 onwards, while the economic crisis in Europe persisted, the initial conditions were reversed and now began to exercise a favourable effect on German industrial exports to the U.S. Overall, U.S. industrial exports to Germany after the turn of the century grew at a more moderate rate than in the previous years. Further, this growth was limited to a relatively narrow segment of products. The structure of German imports from the U.S. did not, therefore, change in any fundamental way before the First World War. They still consisted of approximately 90 per cent raw materials and agricultural products, compared with which finished industrial goods, which made up about 10 per cent, played little more than a marginal role.[124]

Despite this, the fear of what seemed to be superior American industrial competition remained a fixed element in the perceptual frame of German industrialists even after the turn of the century. One of the key reasons for this was undoubtedly the fact that not just in Germany and the other European industrial states but also, and perhaps even more, in overseas markets, they suddenly faced new American competitors. These, moreover, were supported by a vigorous state export policy. With respect to Latin America, for example, *Export* magazine summed up the impression widespread in the German export economy when it stated that the U.S. was doing everything it could 'to wrest away from the European industrial states these splendid markets in which England and Germany in particular have their least disturbed and most rewarding outlets'.[125] On the basis of its activities in Brazil, the Association of Itinerant Merchants of Germany (Verband Reisender Kaufleute Deutschlands) also concluded that 'in the shape of America, we have our greatest trading adversary for the future', since 'it will become our greatest and most successful competitor in the world market'.[126] But despite all the American export successes, even with respect to overseas markets it would be quite wrong to suggest that German exports were driven out. This is evident in the disproportionate growth of German exports to these regions and the increasing role they played for German exports – and this applies in particular to South America. Here too, the experience of American competitive pressure, which was real enough, and its significant exaggeration in the perception and discourse of German exporters are seamlessly interwoven.[127]

American high protectionism and trade imperialism, the impressive growth of American industry and its export offensive from 1897/98 onwards – all of this coalesced to form the 'American peril' syndrome that afflicted industrialists and the public political sphere in every European industrial state around the turn of the century. Nowhere did it persist as long as in Germany. The 'American peril' scenario was rooted in a peculiar mix of admiration for the technological-organizational achievements and dramatic economic rise of the U.S. and the fear of being crushed by this emerging economic colossus, which seemed to have unlimited human and material resources at its disposal, in the social Darwinist struggle for survival. While the 'American peril' was used repeatedly and deliberately by interest organizations and political parties to push their economic policy demands and mobilize voters, it would be too simple to interpret it merely as an instrument of manipulation. The broader debate on the 'American peril', carried on primarily by economists and journalists,[128] in fact suggests that it was more than just a tactically motivated construct.

The perception of actually existing tendencies was fused together with distorted constructions of these tendencies. This sometimes took grotesque forms. A good deal of evidence suggests that both the caricature of the 'American peril' and the closely associated fear of the 'Americanization of Europe' were products of a shift in the perception of the U.S. among the European and especially German bourgeoisie. This occurred in the final quarter of the nineteenth century and as it played itself out the political dimension that originally stood centre stage and that underlined the U.S.'s character as a model democracy receded into the background. Increasingly, it gave way to a perception of the country as an economic and social challenge. The causes of this shift of perspective were the stunning industrial development of the U.S. following the American Civil War and the increasing sense that within an increasingly integrated global economy, this new industrial power was fast catching up. But also important was high industrialization in Germany itself, which often projected German fears and desires concerning modernization onto the U.S.[129] In Germany around the turn of the century, the notion of the 'American peril' was further reinforced by its close linkage with other key contemporary principles and debates. Most prominent here was the theory, shared by many leading economists, of the three world empires that would dominate the globe in the future. Here the U.S. played an established role as a highly expansionist world power intent on implementing an 'economic Monroe Doctrine',[130] its ultimate aspiration to dominate the entire Western Hemisphere through a vast empire that would be largely sealed off from the rest of the world.[131]

Though there was broad agreement about the existence of an 'American peril' among the economic and political elites of the German Empire, they had different views about its specific form and above all about the correct trade policy tools needed to combat it. The agrarian right, highly fixated on the 'American peril' that, because of the superior agricultural competition in the U.S., represented such a great threat to it, took a clearly confrontational approach. The campaign promoting agricultural protectionism launched by the agrarian interest organizations before the turn of the century targeted the crucial agricultural imports from the U.S. It was thus no coincidence that the system of agricultural protection that the agrarians managed to achieve also had a clearly anti-American edge. This applied less to the cereal tariff increases in the Bülow tariff, which affected all cereal importers in the same way, than to the veterinary controls and sanitary measures aimed primarily at livestock and meat imports from the U.S. These included a ban on the import of cattle and beef from the U.S. enacted in 1894, supposedly in response to the risk of Texas fever, or the meat inspection law of 1900 through which German meat producers achieved an almost total ban on imports from their overseas competitors under the guise of disease control.[132]

But even after the agricultural protectionist firewall had been erected, there was no fundamental change in the conflictual strategy favoured by the agrarian right with respect to the U.S. The aim now was to defend the agricultural protection that had been achieved at any cost. Countless submissions to the government and innumerable articles in the agrarian press constantly repeated the mantra that agriculture had 'every right' to 'insist' that 'with respect to [U.S.] products there will be *no attempt to lower the rates of the treaty tariff* and with respect to *livestock imports no concessions* [will be] made' within the context of any trade agreement with the U.S.[133] The demands for an aggressive trade policy towards the U.S., put forward repeatedly by the extreme agrarians of the BdL in particular, essentially amounted to the desire to drive the German Empire into a customs war. Chief editor of the *Deutsche Tageszeitung*, Georg Oertel, expressed this in no uncertain terms at the general assembly of the BdL in the Zirkus Busch in 1907 and received a rapturous response from the delegates: a 'brisk and breezy war' was 'much better ... than a foul and musty peace (applause), than a peace bought at the expense of German honour, at the price of German prosperity. There should therefore be no attempt to avoid a customs war at all costs!'[134]

The organizations of trade and industry did not join in with the BdL's clamour for a customs war. Yet many of them also took the view that defending Germany against the 'American peril' required the imperial government to take a firmer trade policy approach than hitherto. The interests that undergirded this shared view, however, were highly heterogeneous. While some branches of industry primarily wanted increased tariffs to protect the German domestic market from its North American competitors, others wanted the duties in the German general tariff to be deployed as bargaining chips in order to achieve lower American import duties within the framework of trade treaty negotiations. At times, however, the 'American peril' proved such a strong binding agent that the conflicts of interest within German industry and to some extent even within specific branches could be overcome. This was the case in the run-up to the Bülow tariff, when the hysteria over the 'American peril', which was reaching its peak, did much to bring about a cohesive alliance within the BdI with respect to tariff increases and to prompt the league to temporarily support the 'politics of rallying together' (see chapter 5). After the turn of the century, the shared fear of the 'American peril' was the key reason why all the important economic associations, together with many chambers of commerce and notable representatives from trade, industry and politics, joined the Central European Economic Association (Mitteleuropäischer

Wirtschaftsverein) founded in 1904 under the aegis of Breslau economist Julius Wolf.[135] The new association's objective, the creation of a preferential economic system in continental Europe, whose character was not set out in detail, had a clear anti-American thrust.

In view of the impending German-American treaty negotiations, in its practical activities too the Central European Economic Association immediately turned its attention to trade relations with the U.S. In a comprehensive memorandum it expressed the 'bitterness' that prevailed 'in the relevant circles' about the fact 'that the Americans can permit such a rigorous approach to the customs tariff and tariffing procedures without retaliatory measures of any kind being taken on the German side'.[136] With respect to the trade treaty negotiations, the association advised the imperial government 'not [to be] intimidated' and 'to remain firm'. Given the negligible concessions the U.S. was likely to be willing to make, the German Empire should no longer grant unlimited most-favoured-nation status and instead merely a small portion of the reduced duties in the German treaty tariff.[137]

A few months later, much the same line was taken in a submission by the new umbrella organization known as the Syndicate of German Industry (Interessengemeinschaft der deutschen Industrie), launched shortly before by the CVDI, BdI and Central Department for Trade Treaties. In no doubt that they were speaking for the vast majority of organized German industry, and against the background of the unresolved trade policy relationship with the U.S., 'once again, at the last moment' the associations lent weight to the demands 'of broad industrial circles'. 'German industry' was convinced of 'the importance of an enduring trade agreement' between Germany and the U.S., but took the view that 'the loyal recognition of German interests requires the United States of America to grant more substantial concessions than those contained in Section 3 of the Dingley tariff if it is to be granted most-favoured-nation status by Germany to the same or to a similar extent as hitherto'. It was, moreover, 'urgently necessary to gain assurances from America that for the duration of the treaty there will be neither any increase in the Dingley tariff nor any differentiation to the disadvantage of German exports'.[138]

Opinions differed, however, on how far a trade policy confrontation with the U.S. should be taken and what constituted acceptable risks in this context. 'There are different views within German industry on the best approach to take', as secretary of the interior Posadowsky summed things up at the Prussian State Ministry in early 1906, a few days before the declaration of intent by the CVDI, BdI and Central Department for Trade Treaties. While industrialists agreed, he stated, that 'the full treaty tariffs should be granted to the United States only in return for equal concessions', 'only a few voices' had called for 'this demand to be enforced at the risk of a customs war'. 'Only those industries that had already lost a large part of their sales to the United States' wanted the government to lay down the law on tariff policy; those industries that remained dependent on the North American market for a large portion of their exports, had, 'meanwhile, declared that they could not tolerate a customs war with the United States, even one of short duration'.[139]

Three years later, when German-American trade relations were on the agenda again after the Payne-Aldrich tariff had come into force, a very similar picture emerged at the U.S. conference organized by the BdI and the Trade Treaty Association. Participants again assailed 'American ruthlessness and capricious self-aggrandizement'[140] and underlined the need to 'resolutely confront [the U.S.]'.[141] Even now, though, only those industrialists who had 'lost their sales to the [U.S.]' or feared they would lose out due to the new American customs tariff advocated trade policy retaliation. The representatives of those sectors that continued to export, who made up the overwhelming majority of those attending the conference, meanwhile, pointed out that imposition of the American maximum tariff, likely in the event of a trade policy conflict, would reduce German exports to the U.S. 'to a tiny fragment'. 'Whole industrial areas plagued by unemployment', 'frequent slumps, and major losses for the German shipping companies' would be the unavoidable consequences. The 'relocation of industrial firms to the [U.S.] (migration of labour *and* capital!), already a common occurrence', would also 'inevitably increase'. A customs war with the U.S. must therefore be 'avoided at all costs'.[142]

## German Trade Policy: Stages and Underlying Motives

The history of trade policy relations between the United States and the German Empire, the outraged *Plutus,* a weekly economic newspaper, claimed in 1907, would be a prime candidate for 'adaptation as Busch verses for the nursery', and suggested the title: '"The Clever Dick and the Scaredy-Cat"'. Should a historian of a future millennium ever 'dig up a book that did no more than describe the trade policy relationship between the two countries', he would almost inevitably come to the conclusion that 'Germany had been a vassal state of the great America. For it would not seem immediately obvious to succeeding generations why an independent, sovereign state would submit to so many instances of high-handed treatment' as had Germany at the hands of the U.S. with respect to trade policy.[143] Indeed, the successes of the German government's trade policy towards the U.S. did little to satisfy the great, and at times highly contradictory, expectations of the various economic and political interest groups within the German Empire. But even from a present-day perspective, taken as a whole and particularly in comparison to the approach taken with Russia, German trade policy towards the U.S. before the First World War has a peculiarly reactive, almost helpless character that seems to demand explanation. First, however, it is important to outline the key stages in German-American trade policy relations. From a trade treaty perspective, we can distinguish three periods before 1914.

First, until the turn of the century, the basis of German-American trade relations was, to put it mildly, of dubious legality. The only treaty-based foundation that existed was a treaty agreed upon by Prussia and the U.S. in 1828, together with a small number of similarly old agreements between the U.S. and the German coastal states. All these trade agreements were essentially simple most-favoured-nation treaties. The German Empire was not the legal successor of the individual states and the existing trade treaties had thus lost their validity with the founding of the empire. Nonetheless, contrary to normal practice and in the absence of formal ratification, both the empire and the U.S. applied their provisions to their relationship – initially in an implicit way through mutual, de facto granting of most-favoured-nation status, and then explicitly in the mid-1880s when circumstances made this necessary.[144]

Despite the differing interpretations that had emerged in the preceding negotiations, the unlimited most-favoured-nation relationship between Germany and the U.S. was confirmed again by the Saratoga Convention of 1891. This agreement, no more than an exchange of notes in formal terms, was a result of the difficulties in which the German government found itself as a result of the reciprocity clause in the McKinley tariff, which had just come into force. Because this gave the American president the option of disadvantaging German sugar on the American market by imposing a punitive tariff, it provided the U.S. government with an effective means of pressuring Germany to eliminate the ban on American pork imports in place since 1883. Confronted with the danger that U.S. tariffing distinctions would decimate the far from insignificant German sugar exports to the U.S., the Foreign Ministry believed that it had no other choice than to agree to the approach outlined by U.S. secretary of state Blaine. On 3 September 1891, the imperial government rescinded the ban on American pork imports ostensibly imposed to counter the threat of trichina. This was supposedly done because the obligatory inspections for meat exports introduced by the U.S. shortly before had rendered it unnecessary. The imperial government also assured the U.S. that it would be granted the tariff reductions agreed to for Austria-Hungary and other states in the ongoing trade treaty negotiations. In return, the American president refrained from imposing duty on German sugar. On a declaratory level, the

Saratoga agreement thus reinforced the two countries' commitment to deal with each other on a most-favoured-nation basis.[145]

The implementation of the Wilson-Gorman tariff of 1894 caused the first rupture in the trade treaty foundation hitherto accepted by both sides. The new customs tariff imposed a value-based duty of 40 per cent on sugar entering the U.S. Germany thus lost the concession granted by the U.S. three years earlier in the Saratoga agreement. Far more problematic in legal terms, however, was the fact that the Wilson-Gorman tariff also imposed supplementary duty on sugar imports from Germany and all other countries that paid export premiums. The German government lodged a protest about this measure on the basis that the payment of export premiums was an internal matter and the use of a differential tariff represented a break with the most-favoured-nation principle. The American president's attempt to prompt Congress to rescind the supplementary duty failed in the Senate. It took the view that there was in fact no most-favoured-nation relationship between the U.S. and the German Empire, since the empire had not inherited the treaty of 1828 with Prussia. Initially, however, none of this had much practical significance because Cuba, the most important American sugar supplier, was temporarily unable to maintain its exports due to domestic political turmoil, causing German sugar imports to the U.S. to increase markedly in subsequent years despite the supplementary duty.[146]

The imperial government hoped that following their electoral victory of 1896 the Republicans would take the same position as in the early 1890s and eliminate the supplementary sugar duties in the Wilson-Gorman tariff, but it was to be disappointed. The opposite was the case. The Dingley tariff adopted by the Republican majority now went so far as to burden German sugar with a differential duty to the full amount of the German export premium; this helped ensure that the American market was lost entirely to German sugar producers over the next few years. Furthermore, the American government concluded a reciprocal treaty with France on 28 May 1898 in line with Section 3 of the Dingley tariff and a far more extensive agreement one year later in accordance with Section 4. Neither the tariff privileges in the first treaty nor the far more comprehensive ones in the second – though this was not subsequently ratified by Congress – were to apply to imports from Germany.[147] While there had been room for interpretation with respect to sugar, this really was an open break with the unconditional application of the most-favoured-nation principle, though the empire continued to apply it to the U.S. When the German government lodged a complaint to this effect in the U.S. with reference to the treaty of 1828, the McKinley administration informed it, in a clearly flawed interpretation, that while it did not doubt the validity of the agreement it believed it entailed a conditional rather than unconditional most-favoured-nation approach that made extension of the tariff privileges granted to France dependent on reciprocal measures by Germany. Since the import bans – justified as usual in terms of health policy – that Germany had now imposed on American cattle, beef and fruit had proved entirely useless as a means of achieving Germany's objectives and had merely contributed to poisoning the trade policy atmosphere, it is fair to say that the imperial government's policy, which sought to maintain Germany's claim to unconditional most-favoured-nation status, had failed abysmally. As the Foreign Ministry resignedly acknowledged, 'under these circumstances there is nothing else [that the government can do] than adopt the same interpretation of the treaty as the United States' and enter into new trade treaty negotiations with the U.S. on this basis.[148]

In 1900, the era of 'stopgap' trade policies began; this represents the second period of trade relations with the U.S. Following the German government's unsuccessful attempt to gain acceptance for its interpretation of the most-favoured-nation principle, ultimately drawn from the British free trade tradition, it was initially quite unclear on what basis German-American trade relations were to be reorganized. What was supposed to happen in the interim was also uncertain. One obvious solution was for the German government to take the same approach as it had to Canada and cease treating the U.S. as a most-favoured nation. This would have meant that goods imported from the U.S. would no longer have faced the moderate duties in the German treaty tariff but instead the much higher ones in the general tariff. Given that anti-American sentiment was reaching its peak in agricultural and industrial circles and the Reichstag majority had responded with outrage to American trade policy, the imperial leadership could have reasonably counted on broad approval for such an approach within the empire's public political sphere. In the Prussian-German executive, however, it was the more moderate forces that wished to avoid a trade policy confrontation with the U.S., which were concentrated in the Foreign Ministry and the Imperial Treasury, that got their way. As the representatives of the Foreign Ministry pointed out at a commissarial meeting of the various ministries, were Germany to deny the U.S. the conventional tariff it would 'undoubtedly lead to an immediate customs war'.[149] In parallel to developments in Germany, anti-German sentiment was reaching its climax in the U.S. This had arisen over the preceding years in significant part because of German import bans, and had been further inflamed by the confrontation between German and American warships in Manila's harbour. These tensions made it seem likely that the application of the German general tariff to imports from the U.S. would provoke American countermeasures. In the case of such trade policy conflict, however, as the Imperial Treasury pointed out, the German Empire would have 'no weapons' at its disposal.[150]

The German government thus refrained from any further provocation and pursued a negotiated solution. It now sought a comprehensive reciprocal agreement on the model of the as-yet-unratified French-American trade treaty. But when it began to look as though the U.S. government was unwilling to agree to this, since the treaty with France had already come up against insurmountable obstacles in Congress, it settled for a 'small' agreement on the basis of Section 3 of the Dingley tariff, which the American president could conclude without approval from the legislature.[151] The German Empire assured the U.S. that it would enjoy its full conventional tariff and eliminated the import restrictions on American fruit. In return, it received tariff privileges on cream of tartar, spirits, wine and objets d'art, which the U.S. had already granted to France, Italy and Portugal in similar treaties.[152] As far as the mutually assured tariff reductions were concerned, the imbalance in the agreement was quite apparent. If we base ourselves on the figures on German-American trade for 1901, the German concessions were worth around 25 million marks, the American just 900,000 marks.[153] The German government had also tacitly, and finally, accepted the additional duties on sugar. As the German government saw it, however, this was an appropriate price to pay for avoiding a customs war with the U.S. Nonetheless, it dared not present the agreement with the U.S. to the Reichstag, as it feared vigorous resistance to the executive's compromise approach. With a unanimity unusual with respect to trade policy, all the Prussian and imperial departments were thus at great pains to refer to the German-American agreement as a 'stopgap' and give it as 'simple [a] form as possible', which did not 'require winning over the Bundesrat and Reichstag'.[154]

Like all the other trade treaties based on the old treaty tariff, the imperial government terminated the existing German-American agreement on 1 March 1906; otherwise, the Bülow tariff and the tariff treaties concluded on its basis could not have come into force. In view of the strong domestic political opposition, President Roosevelt initially declared himself unable to conclude a new agreement, so once again there was a risk of a treaty-free vacuum. In order to prevent this, the two governments agreed to extend the existing arrangement for another year through bespoke legislation. The government's decision to provisionally grant the German conventional tariff in full despite getting virtually nothing in return from the U.S., Posadowsky conceded at the Prussian State Ministry, would 'certainly come under vigorous attack in the public sphere and in the Reichstag'. As the German ambassador and consul general in the U.S. both reported, however, it was vital to do so to prevent a customs war.[155]

Because both Roosevelt and U.S. secretary of state Root had signalled their fundamental willingness to hold talks, most members of the German government thought there was nothing else to do now but wait and hope that the ultraprotectionist storm raging in the U.S. would die down.

The trade treaty negotiations were in fact resumed later in 1906. As a gesture of goodwill, in November Roosevelt sent three tariff experts, the so-called North Commission, to Berlin. The commissioners had no authority to make binding declarations but were tasked with sounding out the preconditions for achieving a trade treaty.[156] Once again, the chief German negotiators aimed to conclude a long-term and comprehensive tariff treaty, which should entail a reduction in the Dingley tariff duties on German exports to the U.S. of up to 20 per cent and which the American president appeared willing to countenance.[157] Once again, it emerged that 'the time' for such an agreement had 'not yet come'.[158] The main obstacle here was not so much the Roosevelt administration, which was quite open to a moderate tariff reduction, as the U.S. Senate, which would have had to approve any comprehensive tariff treaty by a two-thirds majority and in which the Republican high protectionists had in fact grown in strength in the elections of 1906.[159] Against this background, in early 1907 the Foreign Ministry could only state with disappointment that 'with respect to the great agreement … there is nothing more [to be heard] from over there' and it seemed 'to have been postponed for an indefinite period of time'.[160]

Once again, in its place a 'small' agreement was made, which the imperial government again referred to as a 'stopgap' and which was intended to bridge over the period until the conclusion of the desired 'big' treaty.[161] Since it was likely that a trade treaty with Germany would fail in the Senate, just as every similar agreement with other countries had done in previous years, right from the start the only concessions considered by the Americans were ones that Roosevelt could grant without the agreement of Congress. This meant, first, the relatively meaningless duty reductions in Section 3 of the Dingley tariff, which already applied to Germany. Second, and this was the real progress made by the German negotiators, the American president gave assurances in the treaty that administrative means would be found to ease up tariffing procedures.

By now, however, the German government too had come under massive domestic political pressure that curbed its room for manoeuvre in negotiations. A 'large number of influential chambers of commerce and interest groups' along with the 'overwhelming majority of the press' had protested sharply against granting the U.S. the entire German conventional tariff once again without more extensive reciprocal measures. If, 'despite this, we accommodate the United States across the board', as the Foreign Ministry, Imperial Ministry of the Interior and Imperial Treasury feared in advance of the transitional solution of 1906, 'then it will inspire vigorous and sometimes powerful opposition, consisting of the representatives of trade and industry and public opinion, which [would] find a great deal of support in the Reichstag, not just among the agrarians but among many left-wingers as well'.[162] Because of this, the German negotiators agreed to a compromise with their American counterparts that was domestically useful but whose benefits were more apparent than real. While the empire formally excluded the U.S. from part of the treaty tariff, it was only a symbolic remnant of 3 per cent of American imports that missed out on its reduced tariff rates.[163] The imperial government needed these modest negotiating successes chiefly because this time it did not believe it could bypass either the Economic Committee or the Reichstag. Both bodies ultimately gave their approval to the trade agreement, though they were far from enthusiastic. Despite the widespread disappointment about the outcome of the negotiations, particularly in industry, as Posadowsky summed things up as he closed the Economic Committee meeting, the view that generally took hold was that 'while this provisional agreement … does not satisfy the demands we must make of America in the interests of German economic life and in the interests of obtaining equal rights for Germany, for now it is advisable to accept it in order to avoid a customs war'.[164]

Third and finally, in 1909 the U.S. ushered in the final phase in German-American trade relations before the First World War. The Payne-Aldrich tariff adopted that year entailed a mild reduction in the average level of protectionism compared with the Dingley tariff, but this was achieved in a one-sided way through lower duties on raw materials. For finished industrial goods, meanwhile, by far the largest component of German exports to the U.S., the average tariff burden increased. At the same time, the Payne-Aldrich tariff marked the United States' transition to what was now a formally 'autonomous' tariff policy, an approach upheld by American trade policy even after the Underwood-Simmons tariff came into force in October 1913. From this point forward, American tariff policy was to face absolutely no restrictions on its autonomy of action through international treaties.[165] The American government therefore immediately rescinded all existing trade treaty agreements, including the 'small' agreement of 1907 with the German Empire. The German government could now finally abandon the hope, which it had harboured for years, of achieving a long-term trade treaty with the U.S. entailing comprehensive tariff reductions.

Furthermore, the U.S. linked the annulment of the treaty with an undisguised ultimatum. From 1 April 1910, imports from every country that 'unfairly discriminated against' the U.S. would be subject not to the normal Payne-Aldrich tariff but to a maximum tariff that exceeded its duty rates by 25 per cent. What 'unfair discrimination' meant was left to the interpretation of the American president. It was down to him to decree whether imports from a given country would continue to enter the U.S. at the duty rates in the Payne-Aldrich tariff that had applied since August 1909, which was a minimum tariff in legal terms. Should he fail to do so, the maximum tariff would come into force automatically in 1910.[166]

Faced with this threat, the imperial government went out of its way to ensure that German exports would enjoy the benefits of the American 'minimum tariff'. Key actors in trade and the export industry hammered home how damaging the maximum tariff would be,[167] rapidly decimating most German exports to the U.S. This was not just because of the tariff rates, which had increased again dramatically, but above all because German exporters would then be at a competitive disadvantage vis-à-vis their competitors in countries to which only the American minimum tariff applied. In the negotiations with the U.S. government, which extended into 1910, it soon emerged that the claim of undue discrimination against U.S. exports contained in the Payne-Aldrich tariff bill left plenty of room for interpretation, inviting the American negotiators to make far-reaching demands with two key focuses. First, beyond the conventional rates granted to the U.S. in 1907, they demanded that the German Empire now apply the remaining elements in the German treaty tariff as well. Second, the American delegates called for the elimination or reduction of the veterinary and sanitary provisions and import bans; over the preceding two decades, these had helped close the German market off from foreign imports of livestock and meat.[168]

The German government felt unable to make concessions with respect to livestock and meat imports. This was not really because of disease control or sanitary imperatives, but because the majority of the Reichstag was still in favour of agricultural protectionism and the powerful agricultural interest associations had announced prophylactically that any easing of import restrictions on livestock and meat would provoke 'a storm of indignation in agricultural circles'.[169] Without mincing his words, Körner, director of the Trade Policy Department in the Foreign Ministry, explained the government's motivations to the German ambassador in Washington, D.C., Johann Heinrich von Bernstorff, who had been entrusted with the negotiations.

> The decisive factor in our attitude towards the control of animal diseases is the domestic political factor. The elimination or reduction of the existing import bans, in as much as they rest on legal provisions, would under no circumstances be enforced given the present constellation of parties in the Reichstag, and, to the extent that they are dealt with through administrative

> channels, would lead to serious conflicts with the majority parties and likely rule out the possibility of getting the Reichstag's agreement on applying the treaty tariff to the United States.[170]

To ward off the danger of the maximum tariff, therefore, the imperial government saw no other option than to accommodate the Americans with respect to tariffs and ultimately grant them the remaining conventional rates retained in 1907.[171] What this ultimately meant was an extension of the tariff concessions on the German side while the conditions for German exports grew worse – both because of the industrial tariff increases contained in the Payne-Aldrich tariff and because the main improvements in American tariffing procedures made in 1907 were reversed.

Why did the German government, almost without exception, allow the U.S. to dictate the conditions of their bilateral trade relationship over the entire quarter century before the First World War? Why, in the trade agreements of 1891, 1900, 1906, 1907 and 1910 was the German side so much worse at getting what it wanted than its American counterpart? Why is there such a peculiar contrast between the cautious German trade policy approach to the U.S., which was geared towards avoiding conflict, and its far more forceful and confrontational approach to Russia? Aspects of 'grand politics' played at most a situational role here. In fact, the answer – not just from a modern-day perspective, but also in contemporaries' perceptions – lay in the field of economics, or to be more precise, in the structure of international economic relations.

Within the executive, Count Posadowsky, secretary of the interior, had been one of the advocates of an agricultural protectionist approach in the dispute over the Bülow tariff and was not, therefore, suspected of being too close to trade or the export industry. Behind the closed doors of the Prussian State Ministry, no one contradicted him when he summed up the motives that shaped German trade policy towards the U.S. before the First World War with unsurpassed analytical clarity.[172] According to him, it was impossible 'to deny that we [the Germans] would be the weaker party in any customs tariff conflict with the United States'. The German Empire lacked 'the means to make any substantial impact on imports from the United States'. Most 'American imports consist of duty-free raw materials (cotton, copper)', on which 'duties [cannot be] imposed' because these goods could not be 'obtained from other countries'. The application of the German maximum tariff on American cereals and other foodstuffs was out of the question, 'because of national food requirements; even an increased petroleum tariff' would 'be borne … for the most part' by the German economy 'itself because it is impossible to obtain sufficient supplies from other sources'. Those American industrial products on which it would be 'quite safe to impose additional tariffs' made up 'just a small percentage of American imports'. In contrast, German exports 'to the United States [consist] overwhelmingly of industrial products that the United States could in many cases have obtained from other countries'. Even if this were not the case, there was still 'a risk that German manufacturers would feel compelled to establish subsidiaries in the United States that would remain there even after the end of the customs war and compete against our indigenous industry'. Finally, it should be remembered that 'a customs conflict with the United States' would inevitably 'severely damage' German 'shipping'. Recognition of German dependency on non-substitutable American industrial raw materials (together, cotton, copper and petroleum alone made up a good 48 per cent of German imports from the U.S. in 1905),[173] the fear of losing one of the most important German export markets, anxieties over capital exports and the catastrophic effects on German shipping, to which German-American trade was of key importance – this was the motivational complex that caused Posadowsky and the other members of the imperial government to conclude that the U.S. 'holds all the important cards', and that therefore 'a way [must] be found that will allow us to avoid conflict with the United States at all costs'.

Once again, then, it was the German economy's deep integration into the global market that restricted the government's room for manoeuvre on trade policy. In this case, however, it was not just because of the political pressure exercised by those social groups affected by globalization within the German nation-state that world market integration constrained the trade policy decision-making process. It did so primarily because of the trade policy power imbalance arising from the different positions of Germany and the U.S. within the world economy, which was perceived in much the same way on the other side of the Atlantic as it was in Germany.[174] Before the First World War, the German Empire, which was far more dependent on foreign trade, could no longer afford the kind of trade policy autonomy enjoyed by the U.S., with its reserves of raw materials and enormous internal market. The key political actors in the imperial leadership were fully aware of this. In contrast to the situation with respect to Russia, they lacked any economic or political means of putting pressure on the U.S. They therefore believed they had no other choice than to accept, nolens volens, the rising twentieth-century hegemon's trade policy demands. In so doing, they were de facto pursuing the trade policy course favoured, within the political spectrum of the German Empire, by trade, the export industry and the left-liberal parties. This in turn exposed them to criticism from the protectionist Reichstag majority and to some extent also from the industrial associations, who called for a 'firm approach' to counter American high protectionism. Above all, however, the government came under attack from the agrarians, who were compensated for the lack of a customs war with the U.S. by the import bans on livestock and meat. The German government had its back against the wall in domestic political terms, and no real trade policy alternatives. The dilemma it faced in its trade policy towards the United States is perhaps the most impressive testimony to the loss of national political autonomy engendered by globalization in the nineteenth century.

# Conclusion

In the mid-nineteenth century a process began that we might describe, from a modern-day perspective, as the first wave of economic globalization. Facilitated and propelled by the concurrent revolution in transport and communication systems, within just a few decades global economic integration reached a level approaching, and in some cases surpassing, that of the present day. As evident in the convergence of international commodity and factor prices, on the cusp of the twentieth century a functioning world market had come into being, and this was reflected in world trade, the expansion of international capital mobility and the rise of mass migration. There are undoubted differences between present-day globalization and that of one hundred years ago. But the significant parallels and the high degree of global economic integration already reached during the 'long' nineteenth century justify the notion that these two periods of globalization are phases of the same economic process. From an economic history perspective, this process is a coherent and ongoing 'age of globalization'. It has lasted for more than 150 years, and differs from all previous tendencies towards global economic integration. Even the globalization backlash after 1914 could only temporarily halt the increasing integration of the global economy.

The economy of the German Empire was highly integrated into the global economy during its belle époque before the First World War. This is particularly true of global trade. As the second-largest trading nation before 1914, Germany accounted for a steadily growing share of world trade and challenged the global leadership of the U.K., which was increasingly losing ground. Conversely, foreign trade was becoming ever more important to the German economy. Because both imports and exports were growing more quickly than gross national product, with an export rate of 15.8 per cent and an import rate of 19.2 per cent, in the five-year period before the First World War Germany's integration into the world market reached an unprecedented level. On the one hand, this meant that the German economy was more dependent than ever before on obtaining foodstuffs, raw materials, and semifinished and finished industrial products from abroad. On the other hand, exports constituted a demand factor of crucial importance to German industry.

Over the long term and as a whole the German national economy benefited massively from its integration into the world market, but over the short and medium term this integration had a highly variable impact on different groups within the German nation-state. Among the winners of globalization were those parts of German industry – above all machine building and the mechanical and electrical industries – that were dependent on imports of raw materials and intermediate goods and that sold many of their products abroad. Often, export demand formed the basis for an expansion of production volume, which resulted in substantial economies of scale and thus a major drop in unit costs; in many cases the world market became more important than the domestic market. That service sectors such as foreign trade and shipping had a direct interest in the expansion of international trade relations seems self-evident. But the same applies, as long as we adopt a wholly consumption-based standpoint, to consumers, for whom the reduced prices of foodstuffs and other consumer goods brought about by international competition meant a significant increase in real income.

Among the clear losers of globalization, meanwhile, was German agriculture. Though farmers benefited from the world market in cheap feedstuffs and fertilizer, this was outweighed by the negative consequences that flowed from the development of a global market in agricultural products. Despite major advances in productivity, at the end of the nineteenth century large parts of German agriculture could not keep pace with their international competitors and their cheaper goods under free market conditions. This applies especially to cereal producers, who faced a secular fall in the prices of their products from the mid-1870s, and with some qualification to livestock breeders as well. Virtually all German agricultural producers who produced more than their subsistence needs thus had a shared interest in a comprehensive and graduated system of agricultural protection. Those branches of industry in which there was strong import competition or, as applied particularly to the highly capitalized and vertically integrated heavy industry, which had developed organizational forms that facilitated effective price differentiation between the domestic and world market, were also bound to benefit from protectionist measures. Quite often, however, the different foreign trade policy interests within industry did not correspond to the boundaries between different branches, but instead divided them into diametrically opposing camps, as exemplified by the antagonism between spinning and weaving within the textile industry.

Because there was so much at stake for both the losers and winners of increasing world market integration, globalization became one of the key forces driving the development of economic interest organizations. As in many other countries, in Germany before the First World War the most important economic interest groups emerged within the context of foreign trade policy conflicts and reflected the antagonisms within them. The process of their formation not only demonstrates how economic interests shape the structure of politics. It also shows that producers keen on protectionist measures had a structural organizational advantage over those circles that would benefit from the free exchange of goods. The incentive to get organized in order to ensure the imposition of certain trade restrictions was greater than the impulse to get together to prevent them, because as a rule their protective effect brought palpable benefits to a definable group of producers and made an impact within a short period of time, while their negative consequences tended to be indirect and widespread.

The relatively uniform interests found within German agriculture provided the most favourable point of departure for the formation of an influential protectionist organization. It is no coincidence that the Agrarian League (Bund der Landwirte) became by far the most powerful and successful interest organization in the producers' camp. Its success was due in part to the fact that the BdL was more successful than any other economic interest organization in using selective incentives to manage the difficulties involved in collective action. In industry too protectionist interests initially enjoyed an organizational advantage. This is evident not just in the history of the foundation of the Central Association of German Industrialists (Centralverband Deutscher Industrieller) but also in the superior ability of the protectionist branches of industry to achieve their goals while the Bülow tariff was still in the early stages of preparation. Over the course of time, however, the divergent interests within industry became ever more palpable, hindering the formulation of a uniform and sharply defined trade policy position with strong organizational backing. Even those organizations dedicated to the pursuit of a liberal trade policy make little difference to this overall picture of organizational weakness, which included trade as well as industry. At odds internally and defensive in orientation, founded too late and without the broad appeal needed to achieve mass mobilization, they were never in a position to exercise a decisive influence on the foreign trade policy decision-making process.

Overall, the consequences of globalization did much to fragment the society and politics of the German Empire along the lines of socioeconomic conflict. From the beginning of the 1890s on, the content and style of political disputes underwent a fundamental change. Increasingly the government lost, to the propaganda machines of right and left, the capacity to determine the key themes of elections. On one side of the political spectrum the tone was set by the highly organized agricultural protest movement, which had taken off through a complex interplay of rural self-mobilization and the leadership of key organizations, and which demanded the fencing-off of agriculture from the world market. On the other side, the Social Democrats engaged in a campaign of mass mobilization against calls for protective agricultural tariffs; even before the turn of the century, the SPD increasingly took on the mantle of the consumers' party. Tariff and trade policy had now become one of the dominant fields of conflict within German domestic politics. At the same time, the latent conflict of interest between rural producers and urban consumers was endowed with a lasting political charge.

The second major socioeconomic gulf that opened up under the pressure of world market integration was that between the agricultural and industrial sectors. The trade policy alliance that had existed between heavy industry and agriculture since 1879 had survived the 1880s largely unscathed, but the Caprivi trade treaties in the early 1890s opened up a serious rift between their organizations. The 'politics of rallying together', that is, the joint efforts of agriculture and heavy industry, launched in the late 1890s under the aegis of Prussian finance minister Johannes von Miquel, managed to patch up this breach over the short term. But in the buildup to the passing of the Bülow tariff, it became clear that this alliance was profoundly unstable: in key areas, the coalition partners' foreign trade interests conflicted radically. Within industry itself, as disputes over the customs tariff of 1902 dragged on, differences on trade policy became increasingly apparent. This is evident not just in the views of the numerous sectoral associations, which sometimes diverged greatly, but also in the massive tensions and policy disputes that fuelled the tariff issue in all the umbrella organizations – in the German Trade Association (Deutscher Handelstag), CVDI and Industrialists' League (Bund der Industriellen).

Linked with these processes within the German nation-state through the hinge of foreign trade policy, a development in the sphere of international relations was gaining a certain momentum of its own. A development running counter to protectionism had already occurred after the signing of the Cobden Treaty between the U.K. and France in 1860. Within a few years, a self-perpetuating process of trade liberalization had gained traction across Europe as a number of countries concluded trade treaties featuring a most-favoured-nation clause. As globalization advanced, it triggered an opposing trend. Globalization threatened certain social groups with a serious loss of income, not just in Germany but in every country, and this prompted calls for state protection from foreign competition. From the late 1870s, an antiglobalist tendency was in evidence: tariff increases in one country frequently provoked corresponding measures among trading partners. Quite often, this culminated in an upward spiral of protectionist measures, an extreme example being the Russo-German tariff war of 1893, which saw the escalating use of retaliatory tariffs.

Overall, the dynamic inherent within the international trade system prior to the First World War looked much like a tariff arms race. This is very much in line with contemporaries' perceptions. That tariffs and other trade policy instruments mutated into 'weapons' and 'arms' to be used in the impending 'tariff battles across the world', to quote some of the bellicose language used,[1] was testimony to a widespread social Darwinist worldview and influenced political action. Often the mere anticipation of tariff increases in a given country was enough to set in motion similar revisions in another country's tariff policies for preventative reasons, further propelling this spiral of protectionism. Almost every customs tariff entailed numerous tariffs exclusively intended to serve as bargaining chips in trade treaty negotiations. This method had unintended protectionist effects. The introduction of a tariff on purely tactical grounds aroused protectionist desires among domestic producers that might benefit from it, despite them having no need of protection; such attitudes then acquired a momentum of their own, and these protective tariffs were suddenly subject to passionate defence. Ultimately, the 'customs tariff arms race', the 'tactic of upping tariffs for use as bargaining chips', as the Prussian Ministry of Agriculture put it with hindsight in 1912, 'undeniably led to an enduring increase in the general level of tariffs'.[2]

Globalization imposed increasing restrictions on German trade policy. This occurred directly through increasing dependency on foreign trade and indirectly via the conduit of domestic political conditions, which were changing under the influence of globalization and the dynamics unleashed by globalization within the system of international relations. In the half century before the First World War, the Prussian-German government's room for manoeuvre in the trade policy field narrowed dramatically. World market integration and the pressure of economic interests played no major role in the reorganization of German trade policy along free trade lines in the 1860s and early 1870s. Instead, the key factor here was the ideological triumph of the free trade idea, which was fostered but not caused by economic developments, and the instrumentalization of this idea by the Prussian power elite as it strove to attain hegemony within central Europe. The change in global economic parameters – the world economic crisis that began in 1873 and the flooding of Europe with overseas cereals that began a little later on but whose consequences could scarcely have been predicted – was a prerequisite for the protectionist turn of 1879. But the overall genesis of this turn points to the key role of Bismarck, which enabled him to bring about a shift in the direction of trade policy while pursuing autonomous fiscal and domestic policy objectives that went far beyond the narrow field of tariff policy.

Fifteen years later – as clearly evident in the conflict over the Caprivi trade treaties – this degree of political freedom was no longer possible due to the pressures of globalization. More and more, German foreign trade policy found itself between the Scylla of German exports and consumer interests and the Charybdis of the agricultural protectionist movement. Just how dangerous this situation could be is evident in Caprivi's inability, despite comprehensive compensatory measures in the agricultural field, to escape the maelstrom unleashed by advocates of agricultural interests, which led to his political demise. When concluding trade treaties, foreign policy considerations had still played at least a secondary role for the second German imperial chancellor, but from the turn of the century even this last remnant of freedom of movement, namely, the ability to instrumentalize tariff and trade policy to other ends, had disappeared. During the serious domestic political conflicts over the customs tariff reform of 1902, all the imperial leadership really wished to do was somehow rid themselves of this can of worms without themselves being crushed between the millstones of different interests. Every long-term political strategy – whether that of the 'politics of rallying together' or that of the 'middle way' – increasingly fell by the wayside in favour of a policy of muddling through. There was no longer any room to pursue political goals beyond the field of tariff policy: even obvious and pressing fiscal problems were subordinated entirely to international economic considerations.

In the trade treaty negotiations that followed the adoption of the Bülow tariff, it became apparent just how much world market integration had now curtailed the German government's foreign trade policy room for manoeuvre. In view of the massive pressure from agricultural protectionists within German domestic politics, the government felt it could neither accept reductions in its own system of agricultural protection nor risk German exports by triggering retaliation from an already highly protectionist Russia. Because of this the imperial leadership saw only one way of achieving the urgently needed treaty with Russia: by exploiting favourable international conditions, in other words, Russia's precarious predicament in the war with Japan, in order to persuade the Russian government to relent. It thus used 'grand politics' to serve the needs of trade policy, turning on its head the hierarchical relationship between these two political fields, a hierarchy entrenched in contemporaries' mentality. That trade policy was able to gain primacy over traditional foreign policy, at least for a time, points to the key importance of foreign economic policies as a result of the first wave of globalization. At around the same time, trade relations between Germany and the U.S. revealed just how much autonomy of action the nation-state had lost with respect to international economic policy before the First World War. For want of an effective foreign policy or economic lever it might have used to free itself from its plight, the German government essentially allowed the U.S. to dictate the conditions of their trade relations, while domestically it struggled to resist the sweeping demands of the various interest groups.

Far from being a homogenous entity, in the thrust of its tariff and trade policy the Prussian-German executive was in fact deeply divided. The chasm within German society between the losers of globalization, who were pressing for policies to hold back the forces of the world market, and those in favour of globalization, who advocated an export- and consumer-friendly trade policy, remained. The fronts within the ministerial bureaucracy crosscut the division between the Prussian and imperial level: the Prussian Ministry of Agriculture pursued a more protectionist course, seeing itself as the champion of agrarian interests, along with the Prussian Finance Ministry and the Imperial Ministry of the Interior. The Foreign Ministry, the Imperial Treasury and the Prussian Ministry of Trade and Commerce advocated a moderate system of protective tariffs. In view of the balance of domestic political forces, this rather than a truly liberal trade policy was the alternative at the turn of the century.

The officials of the Trade Policy Department of the Foreign Ministry, who were entrusted with all issues pertaining to foreign trade policy, were particularly keen on a moderate tariff and trade policy. This approach remained essentially alien to the policy of national prestige and threatening gestures being pursued concurrently by the Foreign Ministry's Political Department. We find no pressing social historical reasons for this if we examine the origin of the personnel. If we look at affiliation to the nobility as a criterion likely to imply distance from the economy and a traditional understanding of politics, we find that nobles made up 55 per cent of higher officials in the Foreign Ministry's Trade Policy Department, only insignificantly less than in the Political Department (61 per cent) and markedly above the aristocratic element in the other Prussian and imperial departments.[3] In light of this, it makes sense to look at the professional praxis of the Foreign Ministry trade experts to explain their comparatively cautious and export-friendly trade policy views. Because they had mostly served for many years in the consular service and played a leading role in all trade treaty negotiations,[4] they were politically sensitive to the problems of the German export economy and the dangers of the international spiral of protectionism; other departments, above all the Prussian Ministry of Agriculture and the Imperial Ministry of the Interior, found themselves confronted primarily with the protectionist demands emanating from the losers of globalization within the German Empire.

The result of the escalating conflicts within the Prussian-German ministerial bureaucracy, particularly in the run-up to the Bülow tariff, was a compromise in which the moderately protectionist departments were able to achieve certain key aims. The German government ultimately advocated a tariff and trade policy far less protectionist than the one favoured by most members of the Reichstag. But this protectionist gulf between legislative and executive was not a feature special to the late German Empire; it was a pattern seen again and again both internationally and intertemporally. It pertained concurrently in the U.S., where the American president was far more willing than Congress to accommodate Germany with respect to trade policy. Earlier, in 1860, Napoleon III had managed to lower French import tariffs substantially only by avoiding the French parliament. And thirty years after the beginning of the twentieth century, it was once again the U.S. Congress that turned what President Hoover called 'limited changes in the tariff'[5] into the high protectionist monstrosity that was the Smoot-Hawley tariff. The structural reason for the much greater protectionist tendencies of parliamentary institutions lies in the fact that deputies are far more directly and existentially exposed than the executive to interest groups aiming to force through trade-restricting measures. Conversely, it is no great surprise that it was the export-friendly wing of the ministerial bureaucracy that sought to shut the Reichstag out of the foreign trade policy decision-making process as much as possible and keep to a minimum the influence of economic interest groups as institutionalized within the Economic Committee. In reality, then, this wing of the executive was more successful in serving the interests of the export industry, trade and consumers than their own organizations and representatives in parliament. In particular, this entailed taking account of the export interests of the emerging multinational companies in the chemical and electrical industries. Though highly dependent on the world market, there was no increased need for them to vociferously resist trade-restricting measures. As a result of capital exports and the development of branch operations abroad they had a completely new kind of exit option, enabling them to make up for setbacks on one level of globalization through action on another level.[6]

As a whole, the response of German foreign trade policy to the challenges inherent in the high phase of economic globalization before the First World War presents an ambivalent picture. On the one hand, this policy went a long way to accommodating the protectionist demands of those social groups for whom world market integration meant a marked worsening in their income prospects and who were effective in pursuing their aims. From 1879 on, this meant a significant increase in the nominal tariff burden, particularly on agricultural products – initially over the course of the 1880s and then, when the Caprivi treaties (which resulted in a temporary reduction) had ceased to apply, once again through the Bülow tariff. At the same time, the agriculturalists achieved comprehensive packages of nontariff measures – ranging from prohibitive veterinary regulations to the bill of entry system, which either protected them from world market competition or compensated them for loss of income. Together, over the long term, these two measures fixed German prices for agricultural products significantly above world market prices.

Though attempts to quantify the various consequences of German agricultural protectionism are beset by methodological difficulties, from a national economic perspective there is no doubt that these were negative overall. All measures to support agricultural prices were pure maintenance subsidies that artificially kept alive those parts of German agriculture no longer competitive on the world market. This meant not only forgoing the advantages of the international division of labour, but also the costly slowing of an ultimately inexorable shift in the overall economic structure. Tariffs and other state interventions diverted copious economic resources into inefficient factor combinations. Contrary to the long-standing myth, it was not just Prussian landowners but also farmers in the rest of Germany, though to differing degrees, who benefited from large-scale social redistribution, pocketing an at times substantial producer's surplus. It was consumers who picked up the tab. In comparison to the U.K., with its commitment to free trade, agricultural protectionism raised living costs markedly.[7] Going by the generally cautious calculations made by Wilhelm Gerloff, which are confirmed by other contemporary economists, the cereal tariffs included in the Bülow tariff alone cost urban working-class families more than 2 and often more than 3 per cent of their household income.[8]

Social democratic and liberal critics before the First World War – and in their wake, recent historical research – have thus been sharply critical of German tariff and trade policies, viewing them mainly as the work of a Prussian-German ministerial bureaucracy that acted willingly on behalf of the brutally selfish estate-owning class east of the Elbe. As we have seen, there can be no doubt about the negative economic and social consequences of German agricultural protectionism – however unclear we may be about the details. It is also true that the ministerial bureaucracy was overwhelmingly well-disposed towards the demands for state protection emanating from German agriculture. Finally, it is probably also true that around the turn of the century agriculturalists managed to erect a protectionist wall that went beyond what was economically necessary to securing the survival of German agriculture in the face of foreign competition. A number of indicators, such as the increase in the profitability of agricultural firms, the degree of mortgage debt, the development of commodity prices and the decreasing number of forced sales, suggest that most farmers – especially large estate owners – were again doing very well in the final decade before the First World War.[9] This is no doubt due in significant part to state support measures, but had at least as much to do with the enduring increase in the price of agricultural products internationally from the end of the 1890s.

The economic appropriateness of a less comprehensive system of agricultural protection is one thing; its political feasibility is quite another. And here there are grounds for scepticism. The entire prehistory of the Bülow tariff suggests that even if it had seriously tried to do so the Prussian-German government would not have succeeded in enforcing a significant reduction in agricultural protections (some already in place, some projected) in the face of the public pressure exerted by agricultural interest groups and a staunchly protectionist Reichstag majority. Here we must remember that historical actors at the turn of the century could not have anticipated the lasting reversal in the downward trend in agricultural prices, which had persisted across the world from the 1870s on. They could only have become aware of this a few years later, when the increased tariffs had been in place for more than a decade as stipulated in the new trade treaties. It is also important to bear in mind that in Germany around the turn of the century 38 per cent of workers were still involved in agriculture. In contrast to the U.K., where this applied only to a minority of 9 per cent, in the German Empire the globalization of the agricultural market thus dealt a major blow to many people's income prospects.[10] At the time, systems of social security and other mechanisms of compensation for the losses suffered as a result of world market integration were still underdeveloped. So even without the pronounced political influence of the Prussian landed aristocracy, there would likely have been no realistic alternative to providing state protection for the losers of globalization and reducing the pressure of international competition through protectionist measures (this is evident if we look at French agricultural protectionism, which was very similar to its German counterpart).[11] Anything else would have placed a massive question mark over social peace and the stability of the political system.

In a sense, agricultural protectionism, with its socially pacifying function, was the price that German foreign trade policy had to pay for its concurrent ability – and this is the other side of the coin – to reflect Germany's status, on the threshold of the twentieth century, as one of the most developed export nations, one highly dependent on the world market. So far, historians have been happy to concede this point with respect to Caprivi and the trade treaties concluded under his aegis, but have firmly denied it for the subsequent period. The findings of the present study suggest that we must revise this picture and place greater emphasis on the continuities in German foreign trade policy from the early 1890s until the First World War, which suggest an enduring focus on export interests. Above all, the basic principles of Caprivi's trade policies remained in force even after the turn of the century.[12] This was evident, first, in the continuation of the policy of long-term trade treaties, which were concluded partly on the basis of the Bülow tariff and again entailed comprehensive tariff reductions. Through them the German Empire remained at the centre of the European network of trade treaties; up until the First World War, then, it played the role it had taken over from France in the early 1890s. Second, despite massive attacks by the agriculturalists, the German government held to the principle of unlimited most-favoured-nation clauses, which prevented the disadvantaging of German exports in other countries and generalized the tariff reductions in the German conventional tariff. Third, though the champions of agricultural interests managed to achieve binding minimum rates for the four main types of cereals, even in the case of the customs tariff reform of 1902 the government favoured a flat tariff whose rates could be lowered within the context of trade treaty negotiations without a fixed lower limit. Sticking to these fundamental elements of traditional trade policy met the demands made by all the organizations of trade and industry, from the CVDI to the Trade Treaty Association; in this respect they were explicit and unanimous, regardless of how else they differed. Often, the stability of basic conditions, guaranteed primarily by the conclusion of long-term trade treaties, seems to have been more important to their members than tariff levels.

Further evidence of the continuity of German foreign trade policy in the quarter century before the First World War can be seen in the development of the average tariff burden of German imports during this period. If we use this as the measure of protectionism,[13] we find that in the twenty-five years before 1914 the actual level of German protectionism hardly changed. To put it more precisely, there is a tripartite finding.[14] Because of the movement in world market prices, absolute tariff changes between 1889 and 1913 – there is no valid data available for the period before – were not reflected in any corresponding development in the relative tariff burden of dutiable imports. After 1890, in other words, as a result of the Caprivi treaties, there was neither any reduction in the level of protectionism nor any increase after the Bülow tariff came into force in 1906. If we compare, for example, the five-year period from 1895 to 1899 with that between 1909 and 1913, it emerges that in both cases the average tariff burden of dutiable imports lay at 19 per cent, so tariff increases merely compensated for the increase in world market prices. Second, this applies especially to the field of foodstuffs and luxury consumables, which saw the biggest increase as a result of the new German customs tariff, though this merely kept pace with similar price trends in the world market. So their tariff burden also remained virtually unchanged (1895–99: 23.6 per cent, 1909–13: 23 per cent). Third and finally, the average tariff burden of total imports actually decreased slightly (1895–99: 10 per cent, 1909–13: 8.6 per cent), since dutiable imports as a proportion of total imports went down from 53 to 45.8 per cent.

In international comparison, with this tariff level the German Empire was at best in the lower middle range prior to the First World War. If we again take as the measure of protectionism the average tariff burden of total imports, for which we have comparative figures, we find that at an average of 8.6 per cent for the years 1909–13, Germany had approximately the same level as Austria-Hungary (7.6 per cent), France (8.7 per cent) and Sweden (9.0 per cent).[15] The only countries that were less protectionist were Denmark, Switzerland, the Netherlands and the U.K., though the latter still raised tariffs to the amount of 5.6 per cent of the value of its imports. Most other states of continental Europe, meanwhile, featured a higher tariff level, in some cases much higher. Finally, at the top of the protectionist hierarchy were the U.S. (21.4 per cent) and Russia (29.5 per cent). The picture that emerges from this approach is essentially confirmed by a recent study in economic history. To make an international comparison of the level of protectionism before the First World War, this study refers not to the tariff burden of imports as the key criterion, but instead uses an indicator of the openness of specific national economies to the world market based on the Heckscher-Ohlin model.[16] The main advantage of this method is that it takes account not just of the protectionist effects of tariffs, but also of nontariff trade restrictions. This, however, changes little about the assessment of German protectionism. According to this method of measurement as well, within a sample that includes fourteen countries of the 'old world' and four of the 'new world' for the year 1913, with the first-ranked country being the most protectionist, the German Empire is in eleventh place. Against this background and in view of the average tariff burden of German imports, which was comparatively moderate up until the First World War, it seems problematic, to put it cautiously, to claim that after the turn of the century German foreign trade policy made a transition to 'high protectionism', as historical accounts still tend to do.[17]

But the present study differs from the hitherto dominant view not just in its assessment of German customs and trade policy before the First World War, but above all in how it explains this policy. This has a lot to do with fundamentally different perspectives. In seeking to explain decisions and trends in German foreign trade policy, historians have tended to focus entirely on the constellation of social and political forces within the German Empire. This dovetails with the national historical perspective, which, emanating from Europe in the nineteenth century, went on to triumph across the globe. It is not just traditional political history but also social historical and other alternative models that have displayed an attachment to this nation-focused perspective. The nation-state has been and often still is taken as the self-evident unit of analysis. Even the oft-invoked method of historical comparison has done nothing to change this notion; in fact, in a certain sense it has reinforced it, because it is mostly national societies, cultures and policies that have been compared. This corresponds to an endogenous developmental model that, in terms of intellectual history – as Friedrich Tenbruck has rightly pointed out – is rooted in the Enlightenment notion of progress, but that was retained when the notion of unilinear 'progress' gave way to that of multifaceted 'change'.[18] It was thought that we can ultimately arrive at a causal explanation of social and political realities and developments by examining the internal structures and conflicts within national societies. This applies to almost all historical writing on the German Empire prior to 1914 and especially to interpretations of German foreign trade policy, which saw it as the product of an alliance between 'rye and iron'.

As that which must be explained, as the *explanandum,* the nation-state and its policies are also central to the present work. But the explanatory model I present here ascribes crucial importance to the first wave of globalization; so the *explanans* is a process that transcends the boundaries of the nation-state. Like the recent general turn towards transnational and global history, this is no doubt partly the result of a shift in epistemological interests inspired by changes in historians' lifeworlds as a result of the contemporary advance of globalization. But the explanatory method adopted here is also an attempt to provide better explanations than the national historical-genetic approaches that have dominated hitherto. While this does not mean that history should be entirely rewritten from the perspective of globalization, I have sought to do more than just supplement the established national historical perspective with a few transnational insights. Instead, my goal has been to link the increasing integration of the world economy *causally* with economic, social and political processes within the German nation-state. In this way we can capture within a more complex explanatory model the national and transnational level, economy, society and politics. At the same time, we see that those things formerly interpreted mainly as the result of endogenous forces were merely part of a general transnational reaction, whose country-specific manifestations depended at least as much on the world market position of the national economy and international contexts of interaction as on national historical factors. The history of German tariff and trade policies highlights the tense relationship between nation-state and globalization, a relationship that has shaped the world perhaps more than any other since the mid-nineteenth century.

# Appendix

**Table 1.** German exports and world exports, 1872–1913

| | *German exports in current prices (millions of marks)* | *German export index in current prices (1872 = 100)* | *World export index in current prices (1872 = 100)* | *German exports as a percentage of world exports* |
|---|---|---|---|---|
| *1872* | 2353 | 100 | 100 | 9.5 |
| *1873* | 2313 | 98.3 | 102.7 | 9.1 |
| *1874* | 2279 | 97.0 | 101.1 | 9.2 |
| *1875* | 2321 | 98.6 | 98.8 | 9.5 |
| *1876* | 2272 | 96.5 | 97.5 | 9.4 |
| *1877* | 2359 | 100.2 | 97.7 | 9.8 |
| *1878* | 2361 | 100.3 | 97.8 | 9.8 |
| *1879* | 2301 | 97.7 | 99.2 | 9.4 |
| *1880* | 2630 | 111.7 | 108.3 | 9.8 |
| *1881* | 2726 | 115.7 | 110.7 | 10.0 |
| *1882* | 2901 | 123.3 | 114.3 | 10.3 |
| *1883* | 2920 | 124.1 | 114.5 | 10.3 |
| *1884* | 2871 | 122.0 | 110.0 | 10.6 |
| *1885* | 2569 | 109.1 | 102.5 | 10.1 |
| *1886* | 2676 | 113.6 | 102.4 | 10.6 |
| *1887* | 2823 | 119.9 | 106.3 | 10.8 |
| *1888* | 2985 | 126.9 | 111.2 | 10.9 |
| *1889* | 3165 | 134.4 | 120.6 | 10.6 |
| *1890* | 3327 | 141.3 | 125.9 | 10.7 |
| *1891* | 3176 | 135.0 | 127.1 | 10.1 |
| *1892* | 2954 | 125.5 | 119.5 | 10.0 |
| *1893* | 3092 | 131.3 | 118.6 | 10.6 |
| *1894* | 2961 | 125.9 | 115.9 | 10.4 |
| *1895* | 3318 | 140.9 | 120.8 | 11.1 |
| *1896* | 3525 | 149.8 | 128.6 | 11.1 |
| *1897* | 3635 | 154.4 | 131.7 | 11.2 |
| *1898* | 3757 | 159.6 | 137.0 | 11.1 |
| *1899* | 4207 | 178.7 | 150.0 | 11.4 |
| *1900* | 4611 | 195.8 | 158.6 | 11.8 |
| *1901* | 4431 | 188.3 | 159.4 | 11.3 |

| | *German exports in current prices (millions of marks)* | *German export index in current prices (1872 = 100)* | *World export index in current prices (1872 = 100)* | *German exports as a percentage of world exports* |
|---|---|---|---|---|
| *1902* | 4678 | 198.3 | 163.6 | 11.6 |
| *1903* | 5015 | 213.1 | 176.5 | 11.5 |
| *1904* | 5223 | 221.9 | 182.4 | 11.6 |
| *1905* | 5732 | 243.5 | 198.2 | 11.7 |
| *1906* | 6359 | 270.1 | 220.5 | 11.7 |
| *1907* | 6846 | 290.9 | 233.1 | 11.9 |
| *1908* | 6399 | 271.9 | 215.1 | 12.1 |
| *1909* | 6594 | 280.1 | 231.2 | 11.6 |
| *1910* | 7475 | 317.5 | 255.6 | 11.8 |
| *1911* | 8106 | 344.4 | 269.2 | 12.2 |
| *1912* | 8957 | 380.6 | 296.1 | 12.3 |
| *1913* | 10097 | 429.0 | 311.6 | 13.1 |

*Sources:* Calculations based on *StDR*; Lewis, 'Rate of Growth', 30, table 2 (German exports 1872–89), 38–59, table 3.

**Table 2.** German balance of payments and foreign investment, 1883–1913 (millions of marks, current prices)

| | *Current account* | | | | | | *Capital account* | | | | |
|---|---|---|---|---|---|---|---|---|---|---|---|
| | *Trade balance* | | | *Invisible trade balance* | | | *Reserve account* | *Capital account proper* | | | |
| | *Exports* | *Imports* | *Balance* | *Return on capital (balance)* | *Other services (balance)* | *Balance* | *Precious metal imports (balance)* | *Capital exports (balance)* | *Foreign investment (Portfolio invest.) (balance)* | *Foreign investment (Direct invest.) (balance)* | *Total foreign investment (balance)* |
| | *I* | *II* | *III* | *IV* | *V* | *VI* | *VII* | *VIII* | *IX* | *X* | *XI* |
| *1883* | 2,920 | 3,221 | –301 | 691 | 70 | 460 | –37 | 497 | 7,398 | 5,397 | 12,795 |
| *1884* | 2,871 | 3,236 | –365 | 730 | 321 | 686 | –41 | 727 | 7,928 | 5,593 | 13,521 |
| *1885* | 2,569 | 2,922 | –353 | 768 | 289 | 704 | –3 | 707 | 8,438 | 5,790 | 14,228 |
| *1886* | 2,676 | 2,873 | –197 | 805 | 75 | 683 | 1 | 682 | 8,923 | 5,987 | 14,910 |
| *1887* | 2,823 | 3,109 | –286 | 838 | 76 | 628 | 21 | 607 | 9,333 | 6,184 | 15,517 |
| *1888* | 2,985 | 3,264 | –279 | 885 | 274 | 880 | 16 | 864 | 10,000 | 6,381 | 16,381 |
| *1889* | 3,165 | 3,989 | –824 | 927 | 684 | 787 | 6 | 781 | 10,584 | 6,578 | 17,162 |
| *1890* | 3,327 | 4,146 | –819 | 958 | 488 | 627 | 44 | 583 | 10,970 | 6,774 | 17,744 |
| *1891* | 3,176 | 4,150 | –974 | 982 | 523 | 531 | 89 | 442 | 11,215 | 6,971 | 18,186 |
| *1892* | 2,954 | 4,018 | –1,064 | 1,002 | 444 | 382 | 13 | 369 | 11,387 | 7,168 | 18,555 |
| *1893* | 3,092 | 3,962 | –870 | 1,033 | 429 | 592 | 19 | 573 | 11,763 | 7,365 | 19,128 |
| *1894* | 2,961 | 3,939 | –978 | 1,064 | 752 | 838 | 257 | 581 | 12,147 | 7,562 | 19,709 |
| *1895* | 3,318 | 4,121 | –803 | 1,092 | 245 | 534 | 19 | 515 | 12,465 | 7,759 | 20,224 |
| *1896* | 3,525 | 4,307 | –782 | 1,133 | 435 | 787 | 22 | 765 | 13,033 | 7,955 | 20,988 |
| *1897* | 3,635 | 4,681 | –1,046 | 1,178 | 731 | 863 | 33 | 830 | 13,666 | 8,152 | 21,818 |

| | *Current account* | | | | | | *Capital account* | | | | |
|---|---|---|---|---|---|---|---|---|---|---|---|
| | *Trade balance* | | | *Invisible trade balance* | | | *Reserve account* | *Capital account proper* | | | |
| | *Exports* I | *Imports* II | *Balance* III | *Return on capital (balance)* IV | *Other services (balance)* V | *Balance* VI | *Precious metal imports (balance)* VII | *Capital exports (balance)* VIII | *Foreign investment (Portfolio invest.) (balance)* IX | *Foreign investment (Direct invest.) (balance)* X | *Total foreign investment (balance)* XI |
| *1898* | 3,757 | 5,081 | –1,324 | 1,227 | 1,114 | 1,018 | 105 | 913 | 14,382 | 8,349 | 22,731 |
| *1899* | 4,207 | 5,483 | –1,276 | 1,251 | 596 | 571 | 140 | 431 | 14,616 | 8,546 | 23,162 |
| *1900* | 4,611 | 5,766 | –1,155 | 1,276 | 487 | 608 | 136 | 472 | 14,891 | 8,743 | 23,634 |
| *1901* | 4,431 | 5,421 | –990 | 1,300 | 337 | 647 | 208 | 439 | 15,133 | 8,939 | 24,072 |
| *1902* | 4,678 | 5,631 | –953 | 1,335 | 309 | 691 | 40 | 651 | 15,587 | 9,136 | 24,723 |
| *1903* | 5,015 | 6,003 | –988 | 1,359 | 270 | 641 | 202 | 439 | 15,829 | 9,333 | 25,162 |
| *1904* | 5,223 | 6,355 | –1,132 | 1,382 | 586 | 836 | 407 | 429 | 16,061 | 9,530 | 25,591 |
| *1905* | 5,732 | 7,129 | –1,397 | 1,452 | 1,446 | 1,502 | 197 | 1,305 | 17,169 | 9,727 | 26,896 |
| *1906* | 6,359 | 8,022 | –1,663 | 1,475 | 903 | 715 | 297 | 418 | 17,390 | 9,924 | 27,314 |
| *1907* | 6,846 | 8,747 | –1,901 | 1,494 | 764 | 357 | 7 | 350 | 17,543 | 10,120 | 27,663 |
| *1908* | 6,399 | 7,664 | –1,265 | 1,517 | 503 | 755 | 330 | 425 | 17,771 | 10,317 | 28,088 |
| *1909* | 6,594 | 8,527 | –1,933 | 1,546 | 1,002 | 615 | 69 | 546 | 18,120 | 10,514 | 28,634 |
| *1910* | 7,475 | 8,934 | –1,459 | 1,586 | 821 | 949 | 206 | 743 | 18,666 | 10,711 | 29,377 |
| *1911* | 8,106 | 9,706 | –1,600 | 1,622 | 818 | 840 | 183 | 657 | 19,126 | 10,908 | 30,034 |
| *1912* | 8,957 | 10,692 | –1,735 | 1,647 | 738 | 650 | 183 | 467 | 19,396 | 11,105 | 30,501 |
| *1913* | 10,097 | 10,770 | –673 | 1,690 | 119 | 1,136 | 335 | 801 | 20,000 | 11,301 | 31,301 |

*Sources and calculations:*

I Exports (special trade excluding precious metals): Lewis, 'Rate of Growth', 30, table 2 (1883–89); *StHbDR*, section 2; *StJbDR* (1890–1913).

II Imports (special trade excluding precious metals): *StHbDR*, section 2; *StJbDR*.

III Trade balance: III = I – II.

IV Balance of capital returns: IV = XI × 5.4 ÷ 100. Calculated as the return on total German net foreign investment (XI). Rate of return: 5.4 per cent (average of returns on foreign investments in Schaefer, *Deutsche Portfolioinvestitionen*, 589, table A.10).

V Balance of other services: calculated as balance of capital account and other current accounts: V = VII + VIII – (III + IV).

VI Balance of current accounts: VI = III + IV + V.

VII Balance of precious metals imports: precious metals imports – precious metals exports: *StHbDR*, section 2; *StJbDR*.

VIII Balance of capital exports: annual issuance of foreign securities according to the *Der deutsche Ökonomist*, 1900, 381 (1883–92), 1893ff. (1893–13) as an estimate of net capital exports in the form of portfolio investments + estimated average net direct investments of 197 million marks a year (see text for explanation).

IX Balance of German foreign investment (portfolio investments): calculated on the basis of an estimated balance of German investment abroad of 20 billion marks for 1913; back-calculation on the basis of issuance data in the *Der deutsche Ökonomist* (see text).

X Balance of German foreign investment (direct investment): see text for calculation.

XI Balance of total German foreign investment: XI = IX + X.

**Table 3.** Regional structure of German exports (on an annual basis), 1889–1913 (as a percentage of total exports)

| | *Europe* | *The Americas* | *Asia* | *Africa* | *Australia and Oceania* |
|---|---|---|---|---|---|
| *1889* | 77.1 | 18.8 | 2.6 | 0.7 | 0.7 |
| *1890* | 78.1 | 17.8 | 2.8 | 0.6 | 0.7 |
| *1891* | 79.4 | 15.9 | 2.9 | 0.9 | 0.9 |
| *1892* | 78.1 | 17.2 | 3.0 | 0.9 | 0.7 |
| *1893* | 77.3 | 17.4 | 3.6 | 1.1 | 0.6 |
| *1894* | 80.1 | 14.7 | 3.3 | 1.3 | 0.7 |
| *1895* | 76.8 | 17.6 | 3.6 | 1.3 | 0.7 |
| *1896* | 77.5 | 16.2 | 4.0 | 1.5 | 0.8 |
| *1897* | 78.2 | 15.7 | 3.7 | 1.6 | 0.9 |
| *1898* | 80.0 | 13.3 | 4.2 | 1.6 | 0.9 |
| *1899* | 79.5 | 13.8 | 4.2 | 1.6 | 0.9 |
| *1900* | 77.8 | 14.7 | 4.9 | 1.5 | 1.1 |
| *1901* | 78.7 | 13.8 | 4.7 | 1.6 | 1.2 |
| *1902* | 78.3 | 14.6 | 4.2 | 1.9 | 1.0 |
| *1903* | 77.3 | 15.1 | 4.5 | 2.0 | 0.9 |
| *1904* | 76.2 | 15.8 | 4.9 | 2.0 | 0.9 |
| *1905* | 75.0 | 16.4 | 5.4 | 2.1 | 0.9 |
| *1906* | 73.7 | 17.9 | 5.1 | 2.1 | 1.0 |
| *1907* | 73.7 | 18.0 | 5.1 | 2.0 | 1.0 |
| *1908* | 77.2 | 14.8 | 4.9 | 2.0 | 1.0 |
| *1909* | 75.7 | 16.5 | 4.3 | 2.2 | 1.0 |
| *1910* | 75.2 | 16.8 | 4.4 | 2.4 | 1.0 |
| *1911* | 74.9 | 16.8 | 4.7 | 2.3 | 1.1 |
| *1912* | 75.3 | 16.7 | 4.7 | 2.1 | 1.1 |
| *1913* | 76.0 | 15.3 | 5.4 | 2.1 | 1.0 |

*Sources: StHbDR,* section 2, 510–13 (1889–1905); *StJbDR* (1906–13). Until 1905, values refer to exports including precious metals and from 1906 onwards to exports excluding precious metals.

**Table 4.** Regional structure of German imports (on an annual basis), 1889–1913 (as a percentage of total imports)

| | *Europe* | *The Americas* | *Asia* | *Africa* | *Australia and Oceania* |
|---|---|---|---|---|---|
| *1889* | 79.3 | 15.5 | 3.1 | 1.0 | 0.9 |
| *1890* | 75.7 | 18.0 | 3.9 | 1.2 | 1.2 |
| *1891* | 72.6 | 20.5 | 4.6 | 1.3 | 0.9 |
| *1892* | 67.7 | 24.0 | 4.7 | 1.5 | 2.1 |
| *1893* | 68.9 | 21.3 | 5.7 | 1.7 | 2.3 |
| *1894* | 67.9 | 22.2 | 5.9 | 1.7 | 2.3 |
| *1895* | 66.4 | 22.6 | 6.3 | 1.9 | 2.8 |
| *1896* | 66.9 | 22.2 | 6.7 | 1.9 | 2.3 |
| *1897* | 66.8 | 22.2 | 7.2 | 1.9 | 1.8 |
| *1898* | 65.8 | 24.4 | 6.2 | 1.9 | 1.6 |
| *1899* | 64.6 | 24.4 | 5.9 | 2.8 | 2.1 |
| *1900* | 62.8 | 26.5 | 6.1 | 2.4 | 2.1 |
| *1901* | 61.0 | 27.9 | 6.9 | 2.2 | 1.9 |
| *1902* | 62.3 | 25.5 | 7.2 | 2.8 | 2.1 |
| *1903* | 63.1 | 25.0 | 6.9 | 2.8 | 2.0 |
| *1904* | 62.5 | 24.9 | 7.3 | 3.1 | 2.2 |
| *1905* | 62.3 | 25.5 | 6.8 | 3.1 | 2.2 |
| *1906* | 60.5 | 26.6 | 7.5 | 3.1 | 2.3 |
| *1907* | 58.8 | 26.4 | 8.5 | 3.5 | 2.7 |
| *1908* | 56.4 | 29.2 | 8.3 | 3.4 | 2.5 |
| *1909* | 58.2 | 26.8 | 7.8 | 4.3 | 2.9 |
| *1910* | 58.2 | 24.5 | 9.3 | 4.7 | 3.3 |
| *1911* | 58.6 | 25.4 | 8.8 | 4.3 | 2.8 |
| *1912* | 56.2 | 27.0 | 9.4 | 4.5 | 2.8 |
| *1913* | 54.7 | 27.8 | 9.7 | 4.6 | 3.0 |

*Sources*: *StHbDR*, section 2, 506–9 (1889–1905); *StJbDR* (1906–13). Until 1905, values refer to imports including precious metals and from 1906 onwards to imports excluding precious metals.

**Table 5.** Wheat: German production and foreign trade integration, 1880–1913

| | *German crop yields in 1,000s of tonnes* | *Imports in 1,000s of tonnes* | *Exports in 1,000s of tonnes* | *Net imports in 1,000s of tonnes* | *Import quota as a %* | *Net imports as a percentage of domestic demand* |
|---|---|---|---|---|---|---|
| | *I* | *II* | *III* | *IV* | *V* | *VI* |
| *1880* | 2353 | 228 | 178 | 50 | 9.7 | 2.1 |
| *1881* | 2066 | 362 | 53 | 309 | 17.5 | 13.0 |
| *1882* | 2562 | 687 | 63 | 624 | 26.8 | 19.6 |
| *1883* | 2359 | 642 | 81 | 561 | 27.2 | 19.2 |
| *1884* | 2487 | 755 | 36 | 719 | 30.4 | 22.4 |
| *1885* | 2608 | 572 | 14 | 558 | 21.9 | 17.6 |
| *1886* | 2666 | 273 | 8 | 265 | 10.2 | 9.0 |
| *1887* | 2831 | 547 | 3 | 544 | 19.3 | 16.1 |
| *1888* | 2531 | 340 | 1 | 339 | 13.4 | 11.8 |
| *1889* | 2372 | 517 | 1 | 516 | 21.8 | 17.9 |
| *1890* | 2831 | 673 | 0 | 673 | 23.8 | 19.2 |
| *1891* | 2334 | 905 | 0 | 905 | 38.8 | 27.9 |
| *1892* | 3163 | 1296 | 0 | 1296 | 41.0 | 29.1 |
| *1893* | 2995 | 703 | 0 | 703 | 23.5 | 19.0 |
| *1894* | 3012 | 1154 | 79 | 1075 | 38.3 | 26.3 |
| *1895* | 2808 | 1338 | 70 | 1268 | 47.6 | 31.1 |
| *1896* | 3008 | 1653 | 75 | 1578 | 55.0 | 34.4 |
| *1897* | 2913 | 1180 | 171 | 1009 | 40.5 | 25.7 |
| *1898* | 3293 | 1477 | 135 | 1342 | 44.9 | 29.0 |
| *1899* | 3848 | 1371 | 197 | 1174 | 35.6 | 23.4 |
| *1900* | 3841 | 1294 | 295 | 999 | 33.7 | 20.6 |
| *1901* | 2499 | 2134 | 93 | 2041 | 85.4 | 45.0 |
| *1902* | 3900 | 2075 | 82 | 1993 | 53.2 | 33.8 |
| *1903* | 3555 | 1929 | 180 | 1749 | 54.3 | 33.0 |
| *1904* | 3805 | 2021 | 160 | 1861 | 53.1 | 32.8 |
| *1905* | 3700 | 2288 | 165 | 2123 | 61.8 | 36.5 |
| *1906* | 3940 | 2008 | 200 | 1808 | 51.0 | 31.5 |
| *1907* | 3479 | 2455 | 96 | 2359 | 70.6 | 40.4 |
| *1908* | 3768 | 2091 | 261 | 1830 | 55.5 | 32.7 |
| *1909* | 3758 | 2433 | 210 | 2223 | 64.7 | 37.2 |
| *1910* | 3861 | 2344 | 281 | 2063 | 60.7 | 34.8 |
| *1911* | 4066 | 2488 | 310 | 2178 | 61.2 | 34.9 |
| *1912* | 4361 | 2297 | 323 | 1974 | 52.7 | 31.2 |
| *1913* | 4656 | 2546 | 538 | 2008 | 54.7 | 30.1 |

*Sources and calculations:*

I–III *StHbDR*, section 2; *StJbDR*.
IV Imports – exports: IV = II – III.
V Quotient of wheat imports and German wheat production as a %: V = (II ÷ I) × 100.
VI Quotient of net imports and domestic demand as a %: VI = IV ÷ (I + II – III) × 100.

**Table 6.** Copper: German production and foreign trade integration, 1880–1912

| | *German production in 1,000s of tonnes* | *Imports in 1,000s of tonnes* | *Exports in 1,000s of tonnes* | *Net imports in 1,000s of tonnes* | *Import quota as a %* | *Net imports as a percentage of domestic demand* |
|---|---|---|---|---|---|---|
| | *I* | *II* | *III* | *IV* | *V* | *VI* |
| *1880* | 14 | 12 | 6 | 6 | 85.7 | 30 |
| *1881* | 15 | 11 | 7 | 4 | 73.3 | 21.1 |
| *1882* | 15 | 10 | 6 | 4 | 66.7 | 21.1 |
| *1883* | 16 | 12 | 6 | 6 | 75.0 | 27.3 |
| *1884* | 16 | 14 | 7 | 7 | 87.5 | 30.4 |
| *1885* | 17 | 13 | 6 | 7 | 76.5 | 29.2 |
| *1886* | 17 | 12 | 6 | 6 | 70.6 | 26.1 |
| *1887* | 18 | 12 | 5 | 7 | 66.7 | 28.0 |
| *1888* | 19 | 8 | 5 | 3 | 42.1 | 13.6 |
| *1889* | 22 | 30 | 7 | 23 | 136.4 | 51.1 |
| *1890* | 23 | 31 | 8 | 23 | 134.8 | 50.0 |
| *1891* | 22 | 34 | 6 | 28 | 154.5 | 56.0 |
| *1892* | 23 | 32 | 6 | 26 | 139.1 | 53.1 |
| *1893* | 22 | 38 | 7 | 31 | 172.7 | 58.5 |
| *1894* | 23 | 37 | 6 | 31 | 160.9 | 57.4 |
| *1895* | 23 | 44 | 6 | 38 | 191.3 | 62.3 |
| *1896* | 27 | 59 | 9 | 50 | 218.5 | 64.9 |
| *1897* | 27 | 72 | 9 | 63 | 266.7 | 70.0 |
| *1898* | 28 | 78 | 10 | 68 | 278.6 | 70.8 |
| *1899* | 32 | 75 | 12 | 63 | 234.4 | 66.3 |
| *1900* | 30 | 88 | 11 | 77 | 293.3 | 72.0 |
| *1901* | 30 | 63 | 10 | 53 | 210.0 | 63.9 |
| *1902* | 29 | 81 | 9 | 72 | 279.3 | 71.3 |
| *1903* | 30 | 89 | 10 | 79 | 296.7 | 72.5 |
| *1904* | 29 | 116 | 9 | 107 | 400.0 | 78.7 |
| *1905* | 30 | 109 | 12 | 97 | 363.3 | 76.4 |
| *1906* | 32 | 131 | 11 | 120 | 409.4 | 78.9 |
| *1907* | 32 | 128 | 8 | 120 | 400.0 | 79.5 |
| *1908* | 30 | 160 | 9 | 151 | 533.3 | 83.0 |
| *1909* | 31 | 158 | 8 | 150 | 509.7 | 82.9 |
| *1910* | 35 | 185 | 8 | 177 | 528.6 | 83.9 |
| *1911* | 37 | 195 | 9 | 186 | 527.0 | 83.0 |
| *1912* | 45 | 206 | 10 | 196 | 457.8 | 81.3 |

*Sources and calculations:*

I–III *StHbDR*, section 2; *StJbDR*.
IV Imports – exports: IV = II – III.
V Quotient of copper imports and German copper production as a %: V = (II ÷ I) × 100.
VI Quotient of net imports and domestic demands as a %: VI = IV ÷ (I + II – III) × 100.

**Table 7.** Level of protectionism in Germany, 1889–1913

| | *Duties in millions of marks* | *Dutiable imports as a percentage of total imports* | *Duties as a percentage of total imports* | *Duties as a percentage of dutiable imports* | *Foodstuffs and luxury consumables: duties as a percentage of dutiable imports* |
|---|---|---|---|---|---|
| *1889* | 360 | 52 | 9 | 17 | 21 |
| *1890* | 395 | 54 | 10 | 17 | 21 |
| *1891* | 394 | 55 | 9 | 17 | 20 |
| *1892* | 393 | 56 | 10 | 18 | 20 |
| *1893* | 356 | 53 | 9 | 17 | 19 |
| *1894* | 390 | 55 | 10 | 18 | 20 |
| *1895* | 409 | 53 | 10 | 19 | 23 |
| *1896* | 463 | 54 | 11 | 20 | 25 |
| *1897* | 475 | 52 | 10 | 19 | 24 |
| *1898* | 515 | 55 | 10 | 19 | 23 |
| *1899* | 506 | 51 | 9 | 18 | 23 |
| *1900* | 521 | 50 | 9 | 18 | 23 |
| *1901* | 534 | 51 | 10 | 19 | 23 |
| *1902* | 539 | 50 | 10 | 19 | 22 |
| *1903* | 558 | 48 | 9 | 19 | 23 |
| *1904* | 551 | 46 | 9 | 19 | 22 |
| *1905* | 613 | 47 | 9 | 18 | 21 |
| *1906* | 668 | 47 | 8 | 18 | 23 |
| *1907* | 741 | 47 | 8 | 18 | 24 |
| *1908* | 684 | 47 | 9 | 19 | 24 |
| *1909* | 761 | 47 | 9 | 19 | 23 |
| *1910* | 795 | 45 | 9 | 20 | 25 |
| *1911* | 874 | 47 | 9 | 19 | 23 |
| *1912* | 896 | 46 | 8 | 18 | 21 |
| *1913* | 885 | 44 | 8 | 19 | 23 |

*Sources: StHbDR,* section 2, 588; *StJbDR* 31, 1910, 314; *StJbDR* 35, 1914, 364.

# Endnotes

## Introduction

1. Held and McGrew, 'Great Globalization Debate', 1.
2. See, e.g., Frank and Gills, *World System*; Frank and Gills, 'Cumulation of Accumulation'; Bentley, 'Cross-Cultural Interaction'; McNeill and McNeill, *Human Web.*
3. See Braudel, *Civilization*, vol. 3; Braudel, *Dynamik*; Wallerstein, *Modern World-System*, vols 1–3; Wallerstein, *Historical Capitalism.*
4. See James, *End of Globalization.*
5. See Topik and Wells, 'Commodity Chains', 628ff.; Harley, 'Ocean Freight Rates'; Harley, 'Late Nineteenth Century'; Mohammed and Williamson, 'Freight Rates'; Fremdling, 'European Foreign Trade Policies'; Standage, *Victorian Internet*; Winseck and Pike, *Communications*; Borchardt, *Globalisierung*; Bordo and Rockoff, 'Gold Standard'; Bordo and Kydland, 'Gold Standard'; Hardach and Hartig, 'Goldstandard'; Foreman-Peck and Michie, 'Performance'; Bordo and Schwartz (eds), *Retrospective*; Eichengreen (ed.), *Gold Standard*; Estevadeordal, 'Rise'.
6. See O'Rourke and Williamson, *Globalization and History*, 29–55; O'Rourke and Williamson, 'Late 19th Century'; O'Rourke, 'European Grain Invasion'; O'Rourke et al., 'Factor Price Convergence'; Harley, 'Transportation'; Klovland, 'Commodity Market Integration'; Findlay and O'Rourke, *Power and Plenty*, 402–7; Torp, 'Weltwirtschaft', 565–74.
7. See, e.g., Zevin, 'Financial Markets'; Bordo et al., *Is Globalization Today*; Taylor, *International Capital Mobility*; Craig and Fisher, *Integration*, 208ff.; Baldwin and Martin, 'Two Waves of Globalization'; Bordo et al., *International Financial Integration*; Jones and Obstfeld, *Saving.*
8. For arguments of this kind, see Williamson, 'Evolution'; Williamson, 'Globalization, Labor Markets and Policy Backlash'; O'Rourke and Williamson, *Globalization and History*, 119–66.
9. See, e.g., Mergel, 'Kaiserreich'; Conrad, 'Wilhelmine Nationalism'; Gosewinkel, 'Nationalisierung'.
10. This receives particular emphasis in Lang, 'Globalization'.
11. See only Bürgin, *Soziogenese*; Bürgin and Maissen, 'Begriff'; Frey, *Moderne Politische Ökonomie*; Rothschild, 'Political Economy'; Stolberg, 'Geschichte';

Whynes (ed.), *Political Economy*; more recently, see also Daunton and Trentmann (eds), *Worlds of Political Economy.*

12. See, e.g., Gilpin, *Political Economy*; Gilpin, *Global Political Economy*; the essays in Krasner (ed.), *International Regimes*; Grossman and Helpman, 'Trade Wars'; Gould and Woodbridge, 'Political Economy'; Keohane, *After Hegemony*; Trentmann, 'Political Culture'; Goldstein, 'Political Economy'; Kahler and Lake (eds), *Governance in a Global Economy.*
13. Woodruff, *Impact*, 313.
14. Maddison, 'Growth', 695.
15. Ricardo, *Principles*, 89ff.
16. On new trade theory, see Krugman, 'Free Trade'; Krugman, *Rethinking International Trade*; Brander and Spencer, 'International R+D Rivalry'; Brander and Spencer, 'Export Subsidies'; the essays in Krugman (ed.), *Strategic Trade Policy.* For the critique, see Bhagwati, 'Free Trade'; Baldwin, 'Evaluating'; Baldwin, 'Economists' Traditional Trade Policy Views'; Irwin, *Against the Tide*, 207ff.
17. Czempiel, *Machtprobe*, 363–64.
18. The most influential work was O'Rourke and Williamson, *Globalization and History.*
19. See, e.g., Topik and Wells, 'Commodity Chains'; Macfarlane and Martin, *Glass*; Topik and Clarence-Smith (eds), *Global Coffee Economy*; Beckert, 'Emancipation'; Riello and Parthasarathi (eds), *Spinning World*; Derks, *History of the Opium Problem.* The pioneering study here is, of course, Mintz, *Sweetness.*
20. See Bayly, *Birth*; Osterhammel and Petersson, *Globalization*; Osterhammel, *Verwandlung*; Darwin, *After Tamerlane*; Darwin, *Rise and Fall.*
21. See only Hirst and Thompson, *Globalization*; Chase-Dunn et al., 'Trade Globalization'; Marichal, *Century of Debt Crises*; Lang, 'Globalization'; O'Rourke and Williamson, *Globalization and History*; Bordo et al. (eds), *Globalization in Historical Perspective.*
22. See, e.g., Karl, *Staging the World*; Conrad, *Globalisation*; Conrad, *Globalgeschichte.*
23. See only Marsh, *Bargaining on Europe*; Howe, *Free Trade*; Marrison, *British Business*; Biagini, *Liberty*; the essays in Marrison (ed.), *Free Trade*, vol. 1; Lebovics, *Alliance*; Bensel, *Sectionalism*; Bensel, *Political Economy*; Trubowitz, *Defining the National Interest*; Lake, *Power*; Eckes, *Opening America's Market*; Goldstein, *Ideas*; Verdier, *Democracy.*
24. See Kehr, *Battleship Building*; Kehr, *Primat*; Gerschenkron, *Bread*; Rosenberg, *Große Depression*; Wehler, *German Empire.*
25. Rosenberg, *Große Depression*, 182.
26. See Hardach, *Bedeutung.*
27. See Hunt, 'Peasants'.
28. See only Evans (ed.), *Society*; Eley, *Reshaping*; Blackbourn, *Class*; Blackbourn and Eley, *Peculiarities.*
29. See esp. Eley, 'Sammlungspolitik'.
30. Webb, 'Tariff Protection'; Webb, 'Tariffs, Cartels, Technology, and Growth'; Webb, 'Agricultural Protection'; Hentschel, *Wirtschaft und Wirtschaftspolitik.*

## Chapter 1

1. Arndt, *Deutschlands Stellung,* 12; original emphasis.
2. *Statistik des Deutschen Reichs* (hereafter *StDR*) 22, 1876, II.93.
3. *StDR* 49, 1881, 9. See also Soetbeer, 'Bemerkungen', 770.
4. *Statistisches Handbuch für das Deutsche Reich* (hereafter *StHbDR*), section 2, 5.
5. See *StDR* 251, 1912, 1.
6. *StDR* 15, 1885, 1.
7. See the comments in Meerwarth, 'Wege', 680ff.
8. See *StDR* 15, 1885, 3.
9. Ibid., 2.
10. For a general overview of these points, see *StHbDR,* section 2, 1–8; Meerwarth, 'Wege'; Statistisches Bundesamt (ed.), *Bevölkerung,* 24–25; Hoffmann, *Wachstum,* 517ff.; Zimmermann, 'Handelsstatistik', 301ff., 443ff.; Roeske, 'Die amtliche Statistik', 89ff.; Buchheim, *Deutsche Gewerbeexporte,* 19ff.; Jasper, 'Strukturwandlungen', 4ff.
11. See Zimmermann, 'Handelsstatistik', 319, 323, 450–51; Meerwarth, 'Wege', 689ff.; Statistisches Bundesamt (ed.), *Bevölkerung,* 25.
12. *StHbDR,* section 2, 8. See also, e.g., *Statistisches Jahrbuch für das Deutsche Reich* (hereafter *StJbDR*) 30, 1909, 151; *StDR* 270, 1913, 1.
13. See StJbDR 28ff, 1907ff.
14. On the – at times highly complex – assignment of the numbers found in the German Statistical Index that applied at a given time to the categories of the 'Brussels Index', see Jasper, 'Strukturwandlungen', 382–83. Unfortunately, there are a number of mistakes in Jasper's calculations, some of them significant and some downright incomprehensible. This emerges if we scrutinize his statistical series for the export of chemical and pharmaceutical products in light of the assignment method he himself selected. See ibid., 361–62.
15. The German economic area included the territory of the German Empire apart from Heligoland and a number of small customs enclaves in Baden, as well as the Grand Duchy of Luxembourg and the two Austrian communities of Jungholz and Mittelberg. The free ports (Hamburg, Cuxhaven, Bremerhaven, Geestemünde) were part of the German economic area but not the customs area. The 1906 adjustment of the statistics so that they applied to the economic area rather than the customs area thus affected only the figures for general commerce, but had virtually no impact on those for the special trade of interest to us here.
16. *StDR* 41, 1889, I.2.
17. All quotations are from *StDR* 47, 1890, 16.
18. My own calculation, based on *StHbDR,* section 2, 9.
19. See *Tabellarische Uebersichten des Hamburgischen Handels,* years 1880-1889.
20. See Soltau, 'Statistische Untersuchungen', 18–19, 43.
21. See Lewis, 'Rate of Growth', 27ff.
22. My own calculations, based on *StDR* 41, 1889, I.2; *StDR* 48, 1890, I.2, I.4.
23. Buchheim, *Deutsche Gewerbeexporte,* 131, appendix, table 2, despite the objections he himself mentions (25), attempts to correct the figures for German

exports to the U.K. on the basis of the statistics for Hamburg and Bremen. In this way he reaches a figure of 715 million marks for German exports for 1882. This seems far too high given that after the Hanseatic cities joined the Customs Union, in other words, seven years later, the empire's exports amounted to just 647 million marks and exports exceeded the value calculated by Buchheim for the first time in 1898. Jasper, 'Strukturwandlungen', 6, sweepingly assigns the customs area's trade with the Hanseatic cities to 'Europe' and thus distorts the figures completely.

24. See Meerwarth, 'Wege', 674–75; Lewis, 'Rate of Growth', 35; Arndt, *Die Handelsbeziehungen Deutschlands zu England,* 43; Buchheim, *Deutsche Gewerbeexporte,* 21.
25. All figures are based on table 1 in the appendix.
26. Lewis, 'Rate of Growth', 48.
27. Hardach, *Deutschland in der Weltwirtschaft,* 99.
28. NDP: Hoffmann, *Wachstum,* 454–55, table 103. As in figure 1.2, for the development of real-term exports for the period from 1890 to 1913 I draw on Hoffmann, *Wachstum,* 531, table 129, while for the period 1872–89 I base my calculations on the improved data provided by Lewis, 'Rate of Growth', 30, table 2.
29. On the cycles of the German economy and world economy before the First World War, see Borchardt, 'Wirtschaftliches Wachstum', 255–75; Wehler, *Gesellschaftsgeschichte,* vol. 3, 552–610; Rostow, *World Economy,* 314–30; Craig and Fisher, *Integration,* 222–71; Grabas, *Konjunktur;* Kenwood and Lougheed, *Growth,* 160–73.
30. My calculations are based on the data sets informing figure 1.2. For real NDP at factor costs I used the figures provided in Holtfrerich, 'Growth', 130, who slightly revises Hoffmann's growth rates upwards. For a critique of Hoffmann's methodological approach, see also Fremdling, 'German National Accounts: A Critical Assessment'; Fremdling, 'German National Accounts'; Fremdling, 'Productivity Comparison'; Lewis, *Growth and Fluctuations.* Unfortunately, the most recent estimate of the German national product (Ritschl and Spoerer, 'Bruttosozialprodukt') reaches back only to 1901, so I was unable to use it here.
31. See, e.g., Wehler, *Gesellschaftsgeschichte,* vol. 3, 562ff.
32. See Hoffmann, *Wachstum,* 530–31, table 129; Lewis, 'Rate of Growth', 30, table 2.
33. Hoffmann, *Wachstum,* 537–38, table 131. As in figure 1.3, I have not factored in the growth figures for 1879–80 (–26.09 per cent) and 1888–89 (+19.37 per cent) in calculating the annual averages; this is because they are 'blips' brought about by the gaps in the statistics described above, which would have profoundly distorted the entire data set.
34. It is generally assumed that imports $M$ consist of an autonomous portion $M^a$ and an induced, income-dependent portion $M^{ind}$, which is linearly dependent on national income $Y$: $M^{ind} = gY$ (where $g$ is the marginal import rate). This means that: $M(Y) = M^a + M^{ind} = M^a + gY$. See, e.g., Rose and Sauernheimer, *Theorie der Außenwirtschaft,* 117–18.

35. There are no reliable estimates for German GDP before 1914. I drew instead on the best available calculations of real GNP for the period from 1901 to 1913 by Albrecht Ritschl and Mark Spoerer, 'Bruttosozialprodukt'. For the years between 1874 and 1900, I have estimated the GNP by taking the GNP level of 1913 calculated by Ritschl and Spoerer as my basis and using real net national product (NNP) growth rates based on Hoffmann, *Wachstum*. This approach entails a range of methodological problems. These include the implicit assumption that NNP and GNP grow at the same rate, in other words, that capital consumption and indirect taxes increase in proportion to total product. But if we test the calculation method proposed here for the period 1901–13 and compare it with the figures provided by Ritschl and Spoerer, the degree of deviation is tolerable. The key advantage of the estimate provided by Ritschl and Spoerer – the lowering of the general level of GNP prior to the First World War – is retained when we apply it to the period before 1901.
36. All figures in current prices. Maddison, *Dynamic Forces*, 326, table F.7.
37. Much the same applies when domestic service providers (transport companies, insurers) are involved in transportation of imports. Again, despite being carried out by domestic firms, the c.i.f. method adds services to the invoice value of imports. At the same time, these services artificially inflate the services balance because they are recorded as service exports. See Rose and Sauernheimer, *Theorie der Außenwirtschaft*, 7.
38. Calculation based on appendix, table 2. The corresponding value for 1883–88 (9.6 per cent) is based on the fact that until 1888 the German statistics systematically underestimate imports and thus understate the trade deficit as well. This value cannot, therefore, be used for comparison. See above.
39. Hoffmann, *Wachstum*, 817, table 241.
40. See *Der deutsche Ökonomist*, 1900, 381, for the period between 1883 and 1892. For the years from 1893, see *Der deutsche Ökonomist*, 1893 and the following years. There are some minor deviations from Hoffmann's figures. See Hoffmann, *Wachstum*, 262, table 43.
41. Feis, *Europe*, 23 (6.4 million pounds). See Schaefer, *Deutsche Portfolioinvestitionen*, 101, table 3 (German ownership of foreign securities on 1 August 1914 according to the results of the registration ordinance of 1916), for German investments in the U.K.
42. See Sartorius von Waltershausen, *Deutsche Wirtschaftsgeschichte*, 621.
43. Sartorius von Waltershausen, *Kapitalanlage*, 102–3; see also Arndt, *Deutschlands Stellung*, 28–29.
44. A linear regression of the values of German foreign portfolio investments for the period from 1883 to 1913 (see table 2 in the appendix) produced a high determination coefficient of $R^2 = 0.9963$.
45. See appendix, table 2.
46. Arndt, *Deutschlands Stellung*, 29. See also Sartorius von Waltershausen, *Deutsche Wirtschaftsgeschichte*, 441.
47. See Hoffmann, *Wachstum*, 817, table 241.
48. See ibid., 510.

49. Schaefer, *Deutsche Portfolioinvestitionen,* 589. See also the assessment in Sartorius von Waltershausen, *Kapitalanlage,* 104; for securities he suggests an interest rate of 4 per cent, and for direct investments a yield of 6 per cent.
50. Compare table 2 in the appendix with Hoffmann, *Wachstum,* 817, table 241.
51. See the early contribution by Borchardt, 'Währung und Wirtschaft', 32–33; Tilly, 'Der deutsche Kapitalmarkt', 218–19; Sommariva and Tullio, *German Macroeconomic History.*
52. In figure 1.5, Hoffmann's t.o.t. value for 1912 has been corrected on the basis of the export and import price index.
53. See, e.g., Rose and Sauernheimer, *Theorie der Außenwirtschaft,* 87ff., 496–505, 578ff.; Ethier, *Moderne Außenwirtschaftstheorie,* 230ff.; Glastetter, *Außenwirtschaftspolitik,* 202; Kindleberger, *Terms of Trade.*
54. Charles Kindleberger has already pointed this out in his still relevant study *Terms of Trade,* 68 and passim.
55. See, e.g., Eichengreen, 'Gold Standard', 64; Irwin, 'Terms of Trade', 93ff.; Kindleberger, *Terms of Trade,* 26.
56. Though Jasper, 'Strukturwandlungen', 18–36, is aware of this, he draws on the data from 1880 to 1888, which is significantly distorted by the fact that Hamburg and Bremen had not yet joined the customs area; he thus implies – particularly in his diagrams – a development that had not in fact occurred. Methodologically problematic in a number of ways and overall of little help in analyzing the structure of German foreign trade before 1914 is Höpfner, *Außenhandel.*
57. Bairoch, 'Geographical Structure', 572–73. Only 35.2 per cent of British exports went to other European countries in 1909–11.
58. *Statistisches Jahrbuch der Bundesrepublik Deutschland 2001.*
59. *StHbDR,* section 2, 522–23; *StJbDR* 35, 1914, 254.
60. Appendix, table 3.
61. *StJbDR* 35, 1914, 253–54.
62. Birken, 'Verhältnis', 342, table 3. The same picture emerges in northern Europe: in 1913 Sweden obtained 34.2, Denmark 38.4, Norway 40.9 and Finland 43.9 per cent of imports from the German Empire. Schröter, *Außenpolitik,* 397.
63. On the mathematical foundation, see Birken, 'Verhältnis', 324.
64. Appendix, table 4.
65. Ibid.; Statistisches Bundesamt, *Statistisches Jahrbuch 2012,* 417.
66. As with exports, supplier countries were ranked according to the total value of the goods obtained from them between 1889 and 1913.
67. The eight most important importing countries of 1889 were the U.K. (665 million marks), Austria-Hungary (530 million marks), Russia (519 million marks), Belgium (336 million marks), the U.S. (317 million marks), the Netherlands (284 million marks), France (271 million marks) and Switzerland (180 million marks).
68. The eight largest supplier countries of 1913 are identical with the key trading partners listed in table 1.7.
69. The most important goods in the individual categories were as follows. Foodstuffs: cereals, meat, sugar, fruit, milk products, eggs; luxury consum-

ables: coffee, cocoa, tobacco, spirits; raw materials: coal, ores, textile fibres, wood, skins and pelts; semifinished products: metals, yarns, coke, mineral oils; finished products: machines, metalware, motor vehicles, fine mechanical and electrical products, pharmaceutical and chemical products, fabrics, clothing.

70. All figures are my own calculations, based on Hoffmann, *Wachstum*, 524, table 127 (imports in current prices). See also Hoffmann, 'Strukturwandlungen', 292ff.
71. *StJbDR* 36, 1915, 182.
72. See figure 1.5.
73. My own calculations, based on *StHbDR*, section 1, 148; section 2, 150, 153; *StJbDR* 36, 1915, 51, 183.
74. Here no account has been taken of seed reserves and the like; I have not converted flour quantities into cereals. The consumption figures in *StJbDR* that factor in these quantities (see, e.g., *StJbDR* 34, 1913, 289) cannot be used here for a number of reasons. Among other things, the data acquisition periods are incompatible with those for foreign trade, and wheat and spelt are lumped together.
75. Ten-year averages for 1880–89, 1890–99 and 1900–10 are based on table 5 in the appendix.
76. My own calculations, based on *StHbDR*, section 1, 148; section 2, 150, 153; *StJbDR* 36, 1915, 51, 183.
77. See Harms, *Deutschlands Anteil*, 92.
78. *StJbDR* 34, 1913, 293.
79. See *StJbDR* 36, 1915, 34*–35*.
80. My own calculations, based on *StJbDR* 36, 1915, 310. See *StHbDR*, section 2, 112–17.
81. *StJbDR* 32, 1911, 220.
82. My own calculations, based on Fischer (ed.), *Statistik der Bergbauproduktion*, 121, table 162 (mining of iron ores in the German customs area); *StJbDR*; *StHbDR*, section 2 (imports and exports). Around 80 per cent of German iron ore was mined in Alsace-Lorraine and Luxembourg, which joined the German customs area in 1842. See Vorstand des Deutschen Metallarbeiter-Verbandes (ed.), *Schwereisenindustrie im deutschen Zollgebiet*, 180; Harms, *Deutschlands Anteil*, 40.
83. For all figures, see table 6 in the appendix.
84. Calculations based on Hoffmann, *Wachstum*, 520, table 125 (exports in current prices). Luxury consumables made up such a small proportion of German exports, at 2.3 per cent in 1880, 1.5 per cent in 1890, 1.2 per cent in 1900 and 0.8 per cent in 1910, that I have included them in the figures for foodstuffs in the text.
85. See the international surveys in *StJbDR*; Teichmann, *Politik der Agrarpreisstützung*, 314–46; Paasche, *Zuckerindustrie*; Paasche, *Zuckerproduktion der Welt*; Ellerbrock, *Geschichte*, 387–400.
86. My own calculations, based on the figures in *StJbDR*.
87. Wulf, 'Außenhandel', 75; see also Hoffmann, 'Strukturwandlungen', 290–91.

88. All figures calculated on the basis of Hoffmann, *Wachstum,* 520, table 125, and 530, table 129. See also Hoffmann, 'Strukturwandlungen', 288ff.; Wulf, 'Außenhandel', 74ff.; Fischer, 'Deutschland 1850-1914', 410–11.
89. This is also highlighted by Christoph Buchheim. Buchheim, 'Deutschland auf dem Weltmarkt', 199. In contrast to Buchheim, who places the key rupture in the German export structure after 1900 (ibid.), here the 'turning point' is identified ten years earlier. From the early 1890s the textile industry's share of exports shows a fairly continuous decline, while that of the 'new' export sectors shows an upward tendency.
90. All German export figures are calculations based on *StDR; StJbDR; StHbDR,* section 2; for the U.K., see Lewis, *Growth and Fluctuations,* 128. See also Borchardt, 'Wirtschaftliches Wachstum', 233; Wulf, 'Außenhandel', 69ff., 87ff.; Milward and Saul, *Development,* 60ff.; Maizels, *Growth,* 162ff.
91. Very much in line with this, Weber illustrates the ideal-typical method with reference to 'ideal types of social action' in economic theory, whose task it is to ask 'what course of action would take place if it were purely rational and oriented to economic ends alone. This construction can be used to aid in the understanding of action not purely economically determined but which involves deviations arising from traditional restraints, affects, errors, and the intrusion of other than economic purposes or considerations. This can take place in two ways. First, in analysing the extent to which in the concrete case, or on the average for a class of cases, the action was in part economically determined along with the other factors. Secondly, by throwing the discrepancy between the actual course of events and the ideal type into relief, the analysis of the non-economic motives actually involved is facilitated.' Weber, *Economy and Society,* 21. See also Weber, *Gesammelte Aufsätze zur Wissenschaftslehre,* 190ff.
92. In 1878, 1,819,248 hectares of productive agricultural land were used to grow wheat in the German Empire (*StHbDR,* section 1, 136). The figures for the U.S. are based on Henning, *Deutsche Wirtschafts- und Sozialgeschichte,* vol. 2, 900.
93. My own calculations, based on *StHbDR,* section 1, 148; section 2, 158, 464.
94. Lewis, *Growth and Fluctuations,* 280–81. The basis here is the Sauerbeck-Statist Index for American wheat in London, which was published annually in the *Journal of the Royal Statistical Society.*
95. On this paragraph and the following paragraphs generally, see Wehler, *Gesellschaftsgeschichte,* vol. 3, 685ff.; O'Rourke, 'European Grain Invasion', 775ff.; Aldenhoff-Hübinger, *Agrarpolitik,* 29ff.; Bittermann, *Landwirtschaftliche Produktion*; Harley, 'Late Nineteenth Century'; Nipperdey, *Deutsche Geschichte 1866-1918,* vol. 1:, 203ff.; Rolfes, 'Landwirtschaft', 498ff.; Achilles, *Deutsche Agrargeschichte,* 214ff.; Pollard, *Peaceful Conquest,* 264ff.; Henning, *Deutsche Wirtschafts- und Sozialgeschichte,* vol. 2, 889ff.; Schiller, *Vom Rittergut zum Großgrundbesitz,* 148ff.; Ritter, *Agrarwirtschaft,* 422ff.; Warstat, 'Preisentwicklung'; Gläsel, *Entwicklung der Preise*; Haushofer, *Landwirtschaft,* 205ff.
96. See Zanden, 'First Green Revolution', 220, 229. See also Bairoch, 'Les trois révolutions agricoles'.
97. See Zanden, 'First Green Revolution', 230–35.

98. See Henning, 'Produktionskosten', 221ff.; Kempter, *Agrarprotektionismus,* 185ff.
99. Mommsen and Aldenhoff (ed.), *Max Weber Gesamtausgabe I/4,* 191, 338. On the historical context of this statement, see Torp, *Max Weber,* 16–26, 49–61, 67–74.
100. Sauerbeck-Statist Index quoted in Mitchell, *British Historical Statistics,* 474. See also ibid., 476; Harley, 'World Food Economy', 247.
101. Kaiserliches Statistisches Amt, *Deutsche Landwirtschaft,* 200–1. See also Moeller, *German Peasants,* 13ff.; Achilles, 'Betriebswirtschaftliche Leitbilder', 202.
102. On the preceding remarks, see Haushofer, *Landwirtschaft,* 203; Nipperdey, *Deutsche Geschichte 1866-1918,* vol. 1, 192ff.; Perren, *Meat Trade*; Wehler, *Gesellschaftsgeschichte,* vol. 3, 693ff.; Achilles, 'Betriebswirtschaftliche Leitbilder'; Achilles, *Deutsche Agrargeschichte,* 252ff.; Ritter, *Agrarwirtschaft,* 1474ff.; Webb, 'Agricultural Protection', 317ff.; Harley, 'World Food Economy'; Hunt, 'Peasants', 321ff.; Moeller, *German Peasants,* 9–21.
103. In 1913, German machine exports amounted to 680 million marks, while the British figure was 742 million and the American 529 million marks. *StJbDR* 36, 1915, 67*; Huber, *Deutschland als Industriestaat,* 336; Maizels, *Growth,* 193.
104. Huber, *Deutschland als Industriestaat,* 333.
105. My own calculations, based on Däbritz and Metzeltin, *Hundert Jahre Hanomag,* 80, 99. The export shares calculated by the authors themselves (96) do not reflect the listed annual data for locomotive production and exports and must therefore be regarded as erroneous. Flawed figures on exports as a share of production are also found in Barth, *Entwicklungslinien,* 44 and 183, and – entirely unsourced – in Milward and Saul, *Development,* 39.
106. *Fünfundsiebzig Jahre Bosch,* 34.
107. *StJbDR* 33, 1912, 120. On the machine-building industry in general, see Hentschel, *Maschinenfabrik Esslingen AG*; Milward and Saul, *Development,* 38ff.; Feldman, *Weltkrieg,* 161–81; Wehler, *Gesellschaftsgeschichte,* vol. 3, 613–14; Fischer, 'Bergbau', 550ff.; Barth, *Entwicklungslinien*; Huber, *Deutschland als Industriestaat,* 330–55.
108. For the statistical data, see Feldenkirchen, *Siemens,* 43–44, 456, 646 (table 1), 647 (table 2), 662 (table 21), 678 (table 40); Schulz-Hansen, *Stellung,* 30; Czada, *Berliner Elektroindustrie,* 48ff. See Peschke, *Elektroindustrie,* 185ff.; Milward and Saul, *Development,* 35ff.; Koch, *Konzentrationsbewegung*; Fischer, 'Bergbau', 549–50; Feldenkirchen, 'Foreign Investments'; Feldenkirchen, 'Die Firma Siemens im Russischen Reich'; Kocka, *Siemens*; Hertner, 'Financial Strategies'; Jacob-Wendler, *Deutsche Elektroindustrie*; Fischer and Czada, 'Wandlungen', 148–49; Wittke, *Massenproduktion,* 48ff.
109. Data based on Plumpe, *I.G. Farbenindustrie,* 50ff.; Haber, *The Chemical Industry During the Nineteenth Century,* 128; Teltschik, *Geschichte,* 12; Hippel, 'Auf dem Weg', 100. See also Wetzel, *Naturwissenschaften,* 84ff.; Beer, *Emergence*; Travis, *Rainbow Makers*; Henning, *Deutsche Wirtschafts- und Sozialgeschichte,* vol. 2, 857–60; Haber, *Chemical Industry, 1900–1930,* 108ff.; Schröter, 'Auslandsinvestitionen'; for contemporary studies, see Lepsius, *Deutschlands Chemische Industrie*; Harms, *Deutschlands Anteil,* 55ff.

110. Perkin, 'Position', 558.
111. See, e.g., Plumpe, *I.G. Farbenindustrie,* 56.
112. On this topic and the preceding remarks, see Schallermair, 'Sodaindustrie', 36ff., 52, 64, 67; Krause, *Chemie,* 68–70, 102ff., 172–75. See also Müller, *Chemische Industrie,* 191; Goldstein, *Deutschlands Sodaindustrie,* 76, 98; Landes, *Unbound Prometheus,* 270–73; Hohenberg, *Chemicals,* 52; Haber, *The Chemical Industry During the Nineteenth Century,* 121, 217ff.
113. Trade Treaty Association (Handelsvertragsverein) to Bülow on 14 April 1903, Bundesarchiv (Federal Archives; hereafter BA), R 43, 314, fol. 52.
114. In 1913 there were 55.97 million cotton spindles in the U.K., 11.40 million in Germany and 142.19 million worldwide. *StJbDR* 36, 1915, 30*, table 16c.
115. Maizels, *Growth,* 192.
116. See *StHbDR,* section 2, 458, 475; Oppel, *Textilindustrie,* 9.
117. For a general take on this subject, see Landes, *Unbound Prometheus,* 211–15; Kirchhain, *Wachstum;* Brown, 'Market Organization' (unfortunately, the tables showing the empirical data on which Brown bases his argument appear to have fallen victim to printing errors); Clark, 'Whole World', 141ff.; Fischer, 'Bergbau', 553–55; Milward and Saul, *Development,* 31–32; Webb, 'Tariff Protection', 343–47; Oppel, *Textilindustrie,* 45–56; Kertesz, *Textilindustrie;* Landauer, *Handel;* Harms, *Deutschlands Anteil,* 47–50; Huber, *Deutschland als Industriestaat,* 421–56.
118. See Association of Southern German Cotton Industrialists (Verein Süddeutscher Baumwollindustrieller) to Hohenlohe on 20 December 1897, BA, R43, 305a, fol. 11–14; *StHbDR,* section 2, 462–63, 142–47; Oppel, *Textilindustrie,* 45–48, 116–22; Milward and Saul, *Development,* 32.
119. In 1907 486,456 individuals were employed in weaving and 207,025 in spinning. The corresponding figures for 1882 were 491,796 for weaving and 162,716 for spinning. Oppel, *Textilindustrie,* 20.
120. My own calculations, based on *StHbDR,* section 2, 504.
121. Kleinwächter, *Kartelle,* 143.
122. Burn, *Economic History,* 101–15. See Tolliday, 'Competition', 22–23; Allen, 'International Competition and the Growth of the British Iron and Steel Industry', 393–94; Wengenroth, *Unternehmensstrategien und technischer Fortschritt,* 136ff.; Webb, 'Tariffs, Cartels, Technology, and Growth', 310ff.
123. On this paragraph, see Hentschel, *Wirtschaft und Wirtschaftspolitik,* 99ff.; Webb, 'Tariffs, Cartels, Technology, and Growth', 310ff.; Webb, 'Tariff Protection', 337ff.; Webb, 'Cartels'; Zöllner, *Eisenindustrie;* Rips, 'Stellung', 47, 58ff.; Spanier, 'Exportpolitik', 4; Wehler, *Gesellschaftsgeschichte,* vol. 3, 632ff.; Wehler, 'Aufstieg des Organisierten Kapitalismus', 40–41; Fremdling and Krengel, 'Kartelle'; Wengenroth, *Unternehmensstrategien und technischer Fortschritt,* 136ff.; Wengenroth, 'Kartellbewegung'; Maschke, *Grundzüge;* Fremdling, 'German Iron and Steel Industry', 130ff. From the perspective of economic theory, see Aberle, *Wettbewerbstheorie,* 55ff.
124. For a general examination of what follows, see Feldenkirchen, *Eisen- und Stahlindustrie,* 110–49; Rips, 'Stellung', 71–78; Hentschel, *Wirtschaft und Wirtschaftspolitik,* 103ff.; Wengenroth, 'Unternehmensstrategien in Deutschland', 307–8.

125. The conclusion reached in the contemporary literature was that the various cost savings made during production of rolled steel for a 'mixed works' came to fifteen marks per tonne of finished product. Zöllner, *Eisenindustrie,* 25; Heymann, *Die gemischten Werke,* 213. See also Rips, 'Stellung', 73; Krengel, *Roheisenindustrie,* 31.
126. Supply shortfalls were a common occurrence during economic booms as a result of the cartels' quantitative restrictions, as in 1899/1900 in the case of pig iron. See *Kontradiktorische Verhandlungen,* vol. 3, 194ff.
127. See Williamson, 'Vertical Integration', 112ff.; Richter and Furubotn, *Neue Institutionenökonomik,* 71–72. The classic work is, of course, Coase, 'Nature of the Firm'. See also the early comments in Wengenroth, 'Unternehmensstrategien in Deutschland', 318.
128. See Hentschel, *Wirtschaft und Wirtschaftspolitik,* 110ff.; Rips, 'Stellung', 76; Blaich, *Kartell- und Monopolpolitik,* 152ff.
129. Feldenkirchen, 'Rivalität', 95, 97, 99; Feldenkirchen, *Eisen- und Stahlindustrie,* 224; Landes, *Unbound Prometheus,* 269.
130. See Burn, *Economic History,* 213; Burnham and Hoskins, *Iron and Steel,* 38, 45, 187; Orsagh, 'Progress', 216ff.; Landes, *Unbound Prometheus,* 262ff. For a critique, see McCloskey, *Economic Maturity,* 127. For an analysis of this critique, see Wengenroth, *Unternehmensstrategien und technischer Fortschritt,* 276ff.; Tolliday, 'Competition', 36.
131. See Webb, 'Tariffs, Cartels, Technology, and Growth', 328.
132. See Allen, 'International Competition in Iron and Steel', 932; Allen, 'International Competition and the Growth of the British Iron and Steel Industry'; Webb, 'Tariffs, Cartels, Technology, and Growth', 322–23; McCloskey, *Economic Maturity,* chap. 7; Elbaum, *Industrial Relations,* 260ff.
133. In 1913, the share of total steel production in Germany produced by the Siemens-Martin process was 40.2 per cent, versus 79.2 per cent in the U.K. Landes, *Unbound Prometheus,* 262.
134. See Wengenroth, 'Unternehmensstrategien in Deutschland'; Wengenroth, *Unternehmensstrategien und technischer Fortschritt;* Wengenroth, 'Deutscher Stahl', 204–5; Tolliday, 'Competition', 28, 32–33, 47; Feldenkirchen, *Eisen- und Stahlindustrie,* 187–88, 219–20; Suzuki, 'Rise', 2ff.; Fremdling, 'German Iron and Steel Industry', 126ff., 133; Treue, 'Innovation', 109ff.
135. *Protokolle über die Vernehmungen der Sachverständigen durch die Eisen-Enquete-Kommission,* 746.
136. Krugman, 'Import Protection'. Reprinted in Krugman, *Rethinking International Trade,* 185–98. For a mathematical version of this theory, see Zhang and Zhang, 'Analysis'.
137. In mathematical terms, marginal costs are the first derivative of the cost function $C$. So $C'' < 0$ as marginal costs fall. But the model is also valid with respect to other economies of scale. See Krugman, *Rethinking International Trade,* 192–98.
138. See Wehler, *Gesellschaftsgeschichte,* vol. 3, 562ff.; Wengenroth, *Unternehmensstrategien und technischer Fortschritt,* 128–52; Hentschel, *Wirtschaft und Wirtschaftspolitik,* 116; Sonnemann, *Auswirkungen des Schutzzolls,* 76ff.; Wa-

genführ, *Bedeutung des Außenmarktes,* 36ff.; Tiedemann, *Sechs Jahre,* 68–69; *Kontradiktorische Verhandlungen,* vol. 3.

139. Total production costs or – synonymously – average costs are total unit costs, in other words, variable unit costs plus fixed costs per unit.
140. For the essentials, see Wengenroth, *Unternehmensstrategien und technischer Fortschritt,* 148–52. See also Webb, 'Cartels', 95–98.
141. Minutes of the meeting of the governing board on 20 July 1878, quoted in Wengenroth, *Unternehmensstrategien und technischer Fortschritt,* 147; original emphasis. See also *Protokolle über die Vernehmung der Sachverständigen durch die Eisen-Enquete-Kommission,* 410.
142. My own calculations, based on Feldenkirchen, *Eisen- und Stahlindustrie,* 232, table 73.

## Chapter 2

1. Of the flood of literature on the Cobden Treaty, see Howe, *Free Trade,* 92–105; Marsh, *Bargaining on Europe,* 8–27; Bairoch, 'European Trade Policy', 37–40; Wendt, 'Freihandel'; Metzler, *Großbritannien,* 139–45; Dunham, *Anglo-French Treaty;* Iliasu, 'Cobden-Chevalier Commercial Treaty'.
2. Quoted in Bourne, *Foreign Policy of Victorian England,* 85.
3. The text of the Cobden Treaty can be found in Levi, *British Commerce,* 428–33. See also Marsh, *Bargaining on Europe,* 16; Dunham, *Anglo-French Treaty.*
4. See Bairoch, 'European Trade Policy', 38–39.
5. L. Mallet, Commercial Treaty with Austria, memo. 1866, 9, PRO, CAB 1/1.
6. See Böhme, *Deutschlands Weg,* 100–66; Böhme, 'Verfassungskonflikt', 206ff.; Henderson, 'Cobden-Vertrag', 233–39; Hahn, *Geschichte des Deutschen Zollvereins,* 166–80; Hahn, *Wirtschaftliche Integration,* 277ff.; and the early contribution from Weber, *Zollverein,* 356–411; Lotz, *Ideen der deutschen Handelspolitik,* 27–63; Delbrück, *Lebenserinnerungen,* vol. 2, 199ff.
7. See Hahn, *Geschichte des Deutschen Zollvereins,* 20–27; Helfferich, *Handelspolitik,* 103–10; Ohnishi, *Zolltarifpolitik,* 28–59; Brinkmann, *Handelspolitik;* Weber, *Zollverein,* 92–119.
8. Schmoller, *Grundriß,* 1288.
9. See Kindleberger, 'Rise of Free Trade', 64–65, who also underlines the importance of free trade theory's international ideological triumph.
10. Delbrück, *Lebenserinnerungen,* vol. 2, 201.
11. On the various groupings within the German free trade movement, see Hentschel, *Freihändler,* 17–22.
12. See, e.g., Lotz, *Ideen der deutschen Handelspolitik,* 20–26; Hentschel, *Freihändler,* 12–26, 61–78; Stalmann, *Kongreß;* Offermann, *Arbeiterbewegung,* 169ff.; Langewiesche, *Liberalismus in Deutschland,* 113–14; Hahn, *Geschichte des Deutschen Zollvereins,* 162; Böhme, 'Verfassungskonflikt', 200.
13. In this sense conditions were completely different from those twenty years earlier in the U.K., where the Manchester-based cotton industrialists were the prime movers in the establishment of the Anti-Corn Law League and

its free trade campaign. See Kadish, 'Free Trade'; Howe, *Cotton Masters*; McCord, *Anti-Corn Law League*, 16ff.; Bairoch, 'European Trade Policy', 11; Lloyd-Jones, 'Merchant City', 86ff.

14. Delbrück, *Lebenserinnerungen*, vol. 2, 204.
15. Ibid., 201.
16. Lotz, *Ideen der deutschen Handelspolitik*, 38; Delbrück, *Lebenserinnerungen*, vol. 2, 212. According to Delbrück, there was little to be gained from a survey, 'because, as we were well aware, the representatives of protected industries were reluctant to acknowledge publicly the legitimacy of reducing such protection'; Delbrück, *Lebenserinnerungen*, vol. 2, 212.
17. Second memorandum by Bruck, 30 May 1850, quoted in Böhme, *Deutschlands Weg*, 28.
18. On the paragraph, see Hahn, *Geschichte des Deutschen Zollvereins*, 140–64; Böhme, *Deutschlands Weg*, 19–50; Wehler, *Gesellschaftsgeschichte*, vol. 3, 225ff.; Henderson, 'Cobden-Vertrag', 221–26; Lotz, *Ideen der deutschen Handelspolitik*, 7ff.; Festenberg-Packisch, *Geschichte des Zollvereins*, 291–327; Mamroth, *Entwicklung*.
19. Quoted in Böhme, *Deutschlands Weg*, 55. See also Delbrück, *Lebenserinnerungen*, vol. 2, 77.
20. See Rosenberg, *Weltwirtschaftskrise*, 194–210; Rosenberg, *Machteliten*, 156ff.; Beer, *Handelspolitik*, 190ff.; Wagner, 'Österreichs Finanzen'; Böhme, *Deutschlands Weg*, 81–82, 90.
21. Delbrück, *Lebenserinnerungen*, vol. 2, 216.
22. On the content of the Franco-Prussian trade treaty, see Lotz, *Ideen der deutschen Handelspolitik*, 39–50; Delbrück, *Lebenserinnerungen*, vol. 2, 223ff.; Aegidi and Klauhold, *Krisis*, 198–205.
23. Delbrück, *Lebenserinnerungen*, vol. 2, 236–37. Cf. the Austrian memorandum, 7 May 1862, in Aegidi and Klauhold, *Krisis*, 216–22.
24. For the Austrian proposals in detail, see Rechberg to Karolyi, 10 July 1862, in Aegidi and Klauhold, *Krisis*, 228–34.
25. Delbrück, *Lebenserinnerungen*, vol. 2, 238.
26. Ibid., 243.
27. Promemoria for Wilhelm I, 25 December 1862, in Bismarck, *Die gesammelten Werke* (hereafter *GW*), vol. 4, supplement to no. 18; original emphasis.
28. See Delbrück, *Lebenserinnerungen*, vol. 2, 279–83; Schneider, 'Bismarck', 1064–65.
29. Bismarck's letter to the *chargé d'affaires* in Paris, Heinrich VII, Prinz Reuß, 27 December 1862, in Bismarck, *GW*, vol. 4, no. 19.
30. See Zorn, 'Zwischenstaatliche wirtschaftliche Integration'; Zorn, 'Die wirtschaftliche Integration Kleindeutschlands'; Zorn, 'Wirtschafts- und sozialgeschichtliche Zusammenhänge'; Fischer, *Wirtschaft*, 110-28; Megerle, 'Ökonomische Integration', 104–12, 120.
31. Zschok to Bismarck, 13 June 1864, in Historische Reichskommission (ed.), *Auswärtige Politik Preußens*, vol. 5, no. 144.
32. See Delbrück, *Lebenserinnerungen*, vol. 2, 307.
33. Ludwig to Schrenck, 26 August 1864, in Böhme (ed.), *Vor 1866*, 127.

34. The treaty of 16 May 1865 in *Verträge und Verhandlungen*, vol. 5, 43–67. For a general overview of the preceding topics, see Böhme, *Deutschlands Weg*, 100–66; Böhme, 'Verfassungskonflikt'; Wehler, *Gesellschaftsgeschichte*, vol. 3, 286ff.; Hahn, *Geschichte des Deutschen Zollvereins*, 165–80; Hahn, *Wirtschaftliche Integration*, 277–306; Hahn, 'Hegemonie', 65–67; Henderson, *Zollverein*, 286–303; Henderson, 'Cobden-Vertrag', 233–46; Meyer, *Zollverein*, 103–75; Franz, *Entscheidungskampf*, 319–403; Helfferich, *Handelspolitik*, 119ff.; Lotz, *Ideen der deutschen Handelspolitik*, 64–71; Schneider, 'Bismarck', 1048–79; Weber, *Zollverein*, 356–411; Festenberg-Packisch, *Geschichte des Zollvereins*, 360ff.
35. *Gesetzsammlung für die Königlich Preußischen Staaten*, 1865, no. 25, art. 25. See also Bismarck to Werther, 9 November 1864, in Poschinger, *Aktenstücke zur Wirtschaftspolitik*, vol. 1, no. 28; Bismarck to Werther, 9 November 1864, in Historische Reichskommission (ed.), *Auswärtige Politik Preußens*, vol. 5, no. 330.
36. Bismarck, *GW*, vol. 15, 238.
37. Ibid., 239.
38. Delbrück's memorandum quoted in Delbrück, *Lebenserinnerungen*, vol. 2, 319–23. On the threat of demission, see ibid., 324; Bismarck, *GW*, vol. 15, 239 (Abeken to Bismarck, 12 October 1864). See Meyer, *Zollverein*, 147–75; Lotz, *Ideen der deutschen Handelspolitik*, 72–73; Henderson, 'Cobden-Vertrag', 245; Schneider, 'Bismarck', 1068–79; Böhme, *Deutschlands Weg*, 173–83.
39. See Davis, *Britain and the German Zollverein*, 159–68; Marsh, *Bargaining on Europe*, 40–45; Metzler, *Großbritannien*, 241–50; Sydow, *Handelsbeziehungen*, vol. 1, 182–200; Schneider, 'Bismarck', 168–74; Meyer, *Zollverein*, 176–90; Lotz, *Ideen der deutschen Handelspolitik*, 74ff.
40. Bamberger, *Vertrauliche Briefe aus dem Zollparlament*, 182; see also 98ff., 143, 180ff.
41. See Hohenlohe-Schillingsfürst, *Denkwürdigkeiten*, vol. 1, 244–47; Delbrück, *Lebenserinnerungen*, vol. 2, 394ff.; Hahn, *Geschichte des Deutschen Zollvereins*, 182–88; Henderson, 'Cobden-Vertrag', 246–51; Henderson, 'The German Zollverein and the European Economic Community', 498; Böhme, *Deutschlands Weg*, 249ff.; Wehler, *Gesellschaftsgeschichte*, vol. 3, 304ff.; Schneider, 'Bismarck', 174–92; Lotz, *Ideen der deutschen Handelspolitik*, 83ff.; Weber, *Zollverein*, 461–75.
42. See Delbrück, *Lebenserinnerungen*, vol. 2, 227–28; Poschinger, *Fürst Bismarck und der Bundesrat*, vol. 3, 212. See also Lambi, *Free Trade and Protection*, 35–36; Lotz, *Ideen der deutschen Handelspolitik*, 84–85; Böhme, *Deutschlands Weg*, 256ff.; Gall, *Bismarck*, 394–95.
43. Bismarck to Wilhelm I, 22 October 1869, in Bismarck, *GW*, vol. 6b, no. 1443; Bismarck to Wilhelm I, 29 October 1869, in Bismarck, *GW*, vol. 6b, no. 1445.
44. Mohl's speech, in *Stenographische Berichte über die Verhandlungen des Deutschen Zollparlaments* (hereafter *StenBerZollparl.*), 1868, 132 (9 May 1868).
45. *StenBerZollparl.*, 1868, 186ff.
46. Miquel's speech, in *StenBerZollparl.*, 1868, 299 (19 May 1868), and the overall debate, in *StenBerZollparl.*, 1868, 289–78; see also the compilation of contributions to the debate in Maron, *Materialien zum Zolltarif*, 275–98.

47. See *StenBerZollparl.*, 1869, 85–86 (15 June 1869); *Hamburgischer Correspondent*, 15 June 1869.
48. On this paragraph, see Matlekovits, *Zollpolitik*, 143–49; Weber, *Zollverein*, 475–503; Schippel, *Grundzüge*, 185ff.; Helfferich, *Handelspolitik*, 126–27; Gerloff, *Finanz- und Zollpolitik*, 23–31; Lambi, *Free Trade and Protection*, 35–54.
49. See, e.g., *Vierteljahrsschrift für Volkswirtschaft, Politik und Kulturgeschichte*, 9, 1871, vol. 34; *Hamburgische Börsen-Halle*, 14 December 1870, 15 August 1872, 28 August 1872, 21 June 1873; *Hamburger Nachrichten*, 23 February 1872; *Hamburgischer Correspondent*, 11 August 1872.
50. See *Bericht über die erste und constituierende Versammlung des Deutschen Landwirtschaftsrats 1872*, 84–88; *Bericht über die zweite Versammlung des Deutschen Landwirtschaftsrats 1873*, 215ff.
51. *Stenographische Berichte über die Verhandlungen des Deutschen Reichstags* (hereafter *StenBerRT*), 1873, Attachments, no. 88; on the negotiations on this motion in the Reichstag, see *StenBerRT*, 1873, 832–37, 844–47, 1052–63.
52. *StenBerRT*, 1873, 1396–97; emphasis in original.
53. For Delbrück's announcement in the Reichstag, see *StenBerRT*, 1873, 1054 (10 June 1873). On the prehistory of the government's bill, see Geheimes Staatsarchiv Preußischer Kulturbesitz (Prussian Privy State Archives; hereafter GStAPK), I. HA, Rep. 120 – Ministerium für Handel und Gewerbe, dept. C VII 1 no. 10 vol. 15.
54. *StenBerRT*, 1873, Attachments, no. 192.
55. *StenBerRT*, 1873, 1058 (10 June 1873).
56. See *StenBerRT*, 1873, 1059–60, 1271.
57. See *StenBerRT*, 1873, 1289, 1294ff., 1414–15; Matlekovits, *Zollpolitik*, 152; Gerloff, *Finanz- und Zollpolitik*, 119; Bein and Goldschmidt, *Friedrich Hammacher*, 69–70; Böhme, *Deutschlands Weg*, 311; Lambi, *Free Trade and Protection*, 69–72.
58. *StenBerRT*, 1873, 1052.
59. See *StenBerRT*, 1873, 1058–59.
60. *Verhandlungen, Mitteilungen und Berichte des Centralverbands Deutscher Industrieller*, no. 7 (*Bericht des 2. Kongresses*), 29; *Protokolle über die Vernehmung der Sachverständigen durch die Eisen-Enquete-Kommission*, 50. See also Rips, 'Stellung', 19–20.
61. Lotz, *Ideen der deutschen Handelspolitik*, 28. See Borchardt, 'Protektionismus', 29.

## Chapter 3

1. For a recent analysis, see, e.g., Schonhardt-Bailey, 'Parties and Interests'; Schonhardt-Bailey, 'Interests, Ideology and Politics'; Klug, 'Why Chamberlain Failed and Bismarck Succeeded'; Gourevitch, *Politics in Hard Times*, 83–103; Gourevitch, 'International Trade', 285ff.; Rogowski, *Commerce*, 39–40.
2. See, e.g., Rosenberg, *Große Depression*, 169–91; Rosenberg, *Machteliten*, 102–17; Böhme, *Deutschlands Weg*; Böhme, 'Bismarcks Schutzzollpolitik'; Wehler, *German Empire*; Wehler, *Gesellschaftsgeschichte*, vol. 3, 936ff.; Winkler, *Weg*, vol. 1, 243–44. For a critique, see Barkin, '1878–1879'.

3. Rosenberg, *Große Depression,* 182.
4. See Spree, *Wachstumszyklen;* Rosenberg, *Große Depression,* 22–57; Rosenberg, 'Wirtschaftskonjunktur'; Böhme, *Deutschlands Weg,* 341–416; Ullmann, *Kaiserreich,* 60–68; Wehler, *Bismarck,* 61–111; Wehler, *Gesellschaftsgeschichte,* vol. 3, 100–5; Nipperdey, *Deutsche Geschichte, 1866-1918,* vol. 1, 284–85.
5. See Protokoll der Vorstandssitzung des VDEStI, 17 January 1875, BA, R 13 I, 79, fols 19–23; Bueck, *Centralverband,* vol. 1, 129.
6. Löwe to Baare, 11 August 1875, BA, R 13/I, 274.
7. Servaes to Rentzsch, 6 November 1875, quoted in Böhme, *Deutschlands Weg,* 388.
8. Lotz, *Ideen der deutschen Handelspolitik,* 125.
9. Bueck, *Centralverband,* vol. 1, 139.
10. Ibid., 182–83.
11. *Der Deutsche Handelstag,* vol. 2, 435.
12. See ibid., vol. 1, 51; vol. 2, 432. For a general discussion of these issues, see Lotz, *Ideen der deutschen Handelspolitik,* 122–37; Böhme, *Deutschlands Weg,* 359–78, 387–404; Lambi, 'Schutzzoll-Interessen'; Lambi, *Free Trade and Protection,* 113–30; Ullmann, *Interessenverbände,* 78; Kaelble, *Industrielle Interessenpolitik,* 3ff.; Wehler, *Gesellschaftsgeschichte,* vol. 3, 640ff.
13. See *StHbDR,* section 2, 463–64.
14. Perlmann, *Bewegung der Weizenpreise,* 23. See Conrad, 'Tarifreform', 5; Ritter, *Agrarwirtschaft,* 394.
15. Wehler, *Gesellschaftsgeschichte,* vol. 3, 687. See Ritter, *Agrarwirtschaft,* 394; Hardach, *Bedeutung,* 84.
16. Brentano, *Getreidezölle,* 10.
17. Bebel, *Aus meinem Leben,* 566.
18. *Bericht über die Verhandlungen des VSW 1876,* 55 (§ 2,3). Cf. *Bericht über die Verhandlungen des VSW 1879,* 112.
19. See Gottwald, 'Vereinigung der Steuer- und Wirtschaftsreformer', 358–67; Böhme, *Deutschlands Weg,* 400–4; Hardach, *Bedeutung,* 159–64; Lambi, *Free Trade and Protection,* 131–49.
20. *Bericht über die Verhandlungen der siebten Versammlung des Deutschen Landwirtschaftsrats,* 1879, 299, 302. See esp. Hardach, *Bedeutung,* 125–31.
21. See *Bericht über die Verhandlungen der siebten Versammlung des Deutschen Landwirtschaftsrats,* 1879, 299–93.
22. See esp. Hardach, *Bedeutung,* 91–123. See also Pyta, *Landwirtschaftliche Interessenpolitik,* who also underlines that for the agrarian organizations it was not the tariff issue but fiscal policy (lowering of direct taxes on property) that was most important (12).
23. Wehrenpfennig, 'Politische Correspondenz', 97–98.
24. Schmoller, 'Korreferat über die Zolltarifvorlage', 19, 23.
25. Rosenberg, *Große Depression,* 66–67. See ibid., 62–78; Wehler, *Gesellschaftsgeschichte,* vol. 3, 871; Hardach, *Bedeutung,* 144–48; Lambi, *Free Trade and Protection,* 73–96; Langewiesche, *Liberalismus in Deutschland,* 170ff.
26. Wittschewsky, 'Zoll- und Handelspolitik Rußlands', 372.

27. Bairoch, *Economics,* 39.
28. *StenBerRT,* 1879, 1065 (8 May 1879).
29. Schmoller, 'Korreferat über die Zolltarifvorlage', 24. On this paragraph, see Matlekovits, *Zollpolitik,* 47–60; Peez, 'Österreichische Handelspolitik', 177ff.; Sombart, 'Handelspolitik Italiens', 92–97; Wittschewsky, 'Zoll- und Handelspolitik Rußlands', 371–72; Mayo-Smith and Seligman, 'Commercial Policy', 10–33; Lotz, *Ideen der deutschen Handelspolitik,* 146–49; Schmoller, *Grundriß,* 716–27; Ashley, *Modern Tariff History,* 176–91; Bairoch, *Economics,* 35–43; Bairoch, 'European Trade Policy', 51–69, 137–53.
30. Bismarck to Bundesrat (hereafter BR), 15 December 1878, in Poschinger, *Fürst Bismarck und der Bundesrat,* vol 4, 48.
31. *StenBerRT,* 1879, 927ff. (2 May 1879).
32. Gerloff, *Finanz- und Zollpolitik,* 522. From 1876, the beginning of the financial year was changed from 1 January to 1 April. See ibid., 69.
33. Ibid., 521.
34. Reichstag speech, 22 November 1875, in Poschinger, *Fürst Bismarck als Volkswirth,* vol. 1, 72. See Bismarck to Camphausen, 13 February 1877, in Poschinger, *Aktenstücke zur Wirtschaftspolitik,* vol. 1, 249–50.
35. Bismarck to BR, 15 December 1878, in Poschinger, *Fürst Bismarck und der Bundesrat,* vol. 4, 50. See Bismarck to Prussian envoy, 28 October 1878, in Poschinger, *Aktenstücke zur Wirtschaftspolitik,* vol. 1, 287–90.
36. *StenBerRT,* 1879, 927 (2 May 1879).
37. Ibid. See also Bismarck's speech in the Reichstag (hereafter RT), 22 February 1878, in Kohl (ed.), *Die politischen Reden,* vol. 7, 109ff.
38. See Bismarck to Hobrecht, 25 May 1878, in Bismarck, *GW,* vol. 6c, 110–12.
39. Ibid., 6c,112.
40. Bismarck to BR, 15 December 1878, in Poschinger, *Fürst Bismarck und der Bundesrat,* vol. 4, 49. See also *StenBerRT,* 1879, 928ff.
41. On these issues, see Gerloff, *Finanz- und Zollpolitik,* 51ff., 134ff., 148–67; Poschinger, *Fürst Bismarck als Volkswirth,* vol. 1, 100–7; Nitzsche, *Handelspolitische Reaktion,* 145–49; Hardach, *Bedeutung,* 182–85; Nipperdey, *Deutsche Geschichte, 1866-1918,* vol. 2, 385–86; Gall, *Bismarck,* 542ff.; Pflanze, *Bismarck,* vol. 2, 190–95; Hobson, *Wealth of States,* 31ff.
42. See Lucius, 31 October 1875, in Bismarck, *GW,* vol. 8, 157; Bismarck to Hobrecht, 25 May 1878, in Bismarck, *GW,* vol. 6c, 110–12; Bismarck, *GW,* vol. 15, 28. See Wehler, *Bismarck,* 182–86.
43. Tiedemann, *Sechs Jahre,* 106 (meeting of the Crown Council, 3 December 1876). Cf. BA, R 43, 1616, fols 213–43.
44. Quotation: Conversation with Kardorff, 31 March 1878, in Bismarck, *GW,* vol. 8, 254–55. But cf. Bismarck to Wilhelm I, 3 July 1879, in Bismarck, *GW,* vol. 6c, 156; Gall, *Bismarck,* 549.
45. Bismarck to Camphausen, 13 February 1877, in Poschinger, *Aktenstücke zur Wirtschaftspolitik,* vol. 1, 250–51.
46. Bismarck to Wilhelm I, 9 October 1876, in Poschinger, *Aktenstücke zur Wirtschaftspolitik,* vol. 1, 239. Cf. Poschinger, *Aktenstücke zur Wirtschaftspolitik,* vol.

1, 202, 251; Poschinger, *Fürst Bismarck als Volkswirth,* vol. 1, 110–12; Lambi, *Free Trade and Protection,* 163–64.

47. Bismarck to Széchényi, late January 1879, in Bismarck, *GW,* vol. 8, 294–95.
48. Bismarck to Prussian envoy, 28 October 1878, in Poschinger, *Aktenstücke zur Wirtschaftspolitik,* vol. 1, 288. On the preceding remarks, see also *StenBerRT,* 1878, 142–44 (22 February 1878); *StenBerRT,* 1878, 199, 205–6 (25 February 1878); Kardorff, *Wilhelm von Kardorff,* 135–44; Lambi, *Free Trade and Protection,* 163–90; Plachetka, 'Getreide-Autarkiepolitik', 77–81.
49. Weber, *Gesammelte Politische Schriften,* 315.
50. Bismarck to Hobrecht, 25 May 1878, in Bismarck, *GW,* vol. 6c, 111–12.
51. *StenBerRT,* 1879, 1060 (8 May 1879).
52. Lucius von Ballhausen, *Bismarck-Erinnerungen,* 131.
53. On the preceding paragraphs, see Oncken, *Rudolf von Bennigsen,* vol. 2, 318ff.; Rosenberg, *Große Depression,* 132–91; Böhme, *Deutschlands Weg,* 474–561; Lambi, *Free Trade and Protection,* 171ff.; Matthes, 'Spaltung', 49ff.; Gall, *Bismarck,* 535–74; Langewiesche, *Liberalismus in Deutschland,* 164–80; Langewiesche, 'Bismarck und die Nationalliberalen', 87ff.; Nipperdey, *Deutsche Geschichte, 1866-1918,* vol. 2, 382ff.; Ullmann, *Kaiserreich,* 68ff.; Wehler, *Gesellschaftsgeschichte,* vol. 3, 934–36; Reif, 'Bismarck und die Konservativen', 29ff.; Morsey, 'Bismarck und das Zentrum', 56ff.
54. See Minutes of Expert Testimony to the Committee of Enquiry on the Iron Industry, GStAPK, I. HA, Rep. 120 Ministerium für Handel und Gewerbe, Abt. C VII 1 no. 31; GStAPK, I. HA, Rep. 120 Ministerium für Handel und Gewerbe, Abt. C VII 2 no. 8 vol. 16; Schulthess, *Europäischer Geschichtskalender,* vol. 19 (1879), 39; Bueck, *Centralverband,* vol. 1, 185; Nitzsche, *Handelspolitische Reaktion,* 127ff.; Böhme, *Deutschlands Weg,* 459–63, 510–16; Wehler, *Gesellschaftsgeschichte,* vol. 3, 645.
55. Ritter, *Wahlgeschichtliches Arbeitsbuch,* 38–39. See Engelberg, *Bismarck,* 274–75; Pflanze, *Bismarck,* vol. 2, 130–35; Nipperdey, *Deutsche Geschichte, 1866-1918,* vol. 2, 396ff.
56. On the exact date of the resolution and number of signatures, see BA, R 43, 1620, fol. 18 (according to which there were 203 signatures); Hardach, *Bedeutung,* 155; Matlekovits, *Zollpolitik,* 163; Poschinger, *Fürst Bismarck als Volkswirth,* vol. 1, 147; Schulthess, *Europäischer Geschichtskalender,* vol. 19 (1879), 168.
57. Quoted in Ritter (ed.), *Kaiserreich,* 210.
58. See Hardach, *Bedeutung,* 155–56. By agrarian eastern Germany, I mean the provinces of East Prussia, West Prussia, Pomerania and Posen, along with the grand duchies of Mecklenburg-Schwerin and Mecklenburg-Strelitz.
59. See Poschinger, *Aktenstücke zur Wirthschaftspolitik,* vol. 1, 287–94; Poschinger, *Fürst Bismarck als Volkswirth,* vol. 1, 168–70, 170–77.
60. On this issue and the following remarks, see Poschinger, *Fürst Bismarck als Volkswirth,* vol. 1, 150–62; Tiedemann, *Sechs Jahre,* 361; Oncken, *Rudolf von Bennigsen,* vol. 2, 399ff.; Matlekovits, *Zollpolitik,* 164–219; Lotz, *Ideen der deutschen Handelspolitik,* 156–74; Gerloff, *Finanz- und Zollpolitik,* 148–67; Lambi,

*Free Trade and Protection,* 207–25; Böhme, *Deutschlands Weg,* 484–86, 530–64; Hardach, *Bedeutung,* 150–81; Gall, *Bismarck,* 574–91; Pflanze, *Bismarck,* vol. 2, 194–216; Engelberg, *Bismarck,* vol. 2, 309–20.

61. Quoted in Ritter (ed.), *Kaiserreich,* 210–11. See also *Bericht über die Verhandlungen des VSW 1878,* 38ff.
62. See Böhme, *Deutschlands Weg,* 531, 540–43, 559–60; Gerloff, *Finanz- und Zollpolitik,* 156; *StenBerRT,* 1879, 1419, 1429.
63. Tiedemann, *Sechs Jahre,* 361.
64. Bismarck to the city council in Barmen, 20 January 1879, in Poschinger, *Fürst Bismarck als Volkswirth,* vol. 1, 184. See BA, R 43, 2110–11; Poschinger, *Fürst Bismarck als Volkswirth,* vol. 1, 180–84; Bismarck, *GW,* vol. 6a, 129–30; Bismarck, *GW,* vol. 14, 899, 902.
65. Bismarck to the agricultural association in Schönhausen, 13 January 1879, in Poschinger, *Fürst Bismarck als Volkswirth,* vol. 1, 182.
66. *StenBerRT,* 1879, 1047 (8 May 1879).
67. Thüngen-Roßbach to Bismarck, 12 April 1879, in Poschinger, *Fürst Bismarck als Volkswirth,* vol. 1, 214.
68. Bismarck to Thüngen-Roßbach, 16 April 1879, in Poschinger, *Fürst Bismarck als Volkswirth,* vol 1, 215.
69. Weber, *Gesammelte Politische Schriften,* 317.
70. See *StenBerRT,* 1879, 1036 (6 May 1879), 1066–70 (8 May 1879); Note by Frankkenstein, 1879, in Pyta, *Landwirtschaftliche Interessenpolitik,* 125–43; Bismarck's speech of 9 July 1879, in Kohl (ed.), *Die politischen Reden,* vol. 8, 137–55; Lucius von Ballhausen, *Bismarck-Erinnerungen,* 162ff.; Hohenlohe-Schillingsfürst, *Denkwürdigkeiten,* vol. 2, 270; Oncken, *Rudolf von Bennigsen,* vol. 2, 407–13; Lotz, *Ideen der deutschen Handelspolitik,* 171–72; Gerloff, *Finanz- und Zollpolitik,* 160–65; Lambi, *Free Trade and Protection,* 221–25; Böhme, *Deutschlands Weg,* 560–61; Gall, *Bismarck,* 582–88; Anderson, *Windthorst,* 229–35; Kruedener, 'Franckenstein Paradox', 111–23; Ullmann, *Kaiserreich,* 74–75.
71. For the details, see *Reichsgesetzblatt,* no. 17 (1885); *Reichsgesetzblatt,* no. 48 (1887); Conrad, 'Erhöhung der Getreidezölle'; S., 'Beitrag zur Beurteilung', 422–26; Schmoller, 'Analekten'; Matlekovits, *Zollpolitik,* 234–51.
72. *StenBerRT,* 1879, 1047 (8 May 1879).
73. The fixing of the rye tariff through the trade treaty of 1883 with Spain, which was an obstacle to the tariff increase of 1885, was eliminated following lengthy negotiations in return for minor German concessions in other fields. On this issue and the preceding remarks as a whole, see Bismarck's speech in the RT, 11 May 1885, in Kohl (ed.), *Die politischen Reden,* vol. 11, 216–18; Matlekovits, *Zollpolitik,* 251–72; Gerloff, *Finanz- und Zollpolitik,* 204–26; Lotz, *Ideen der deutschen Handelspolitik,* 98–101.
74. *StenBerRT,* Attachments, no. 156. Quoted in Kohl (ed.), *Die politischen Reden,* vol. 10, 443ff. See also Schmoller, 'Analekten', 192ff.
75. See *Der Deutsche Handelstag,* vol. 2, 439; Matlekovits, *Zollpolitik,* 248–51.
76. Herbert von Bismarck to Auswärtiges Amt (Foreign Ministry, hereafter AA), 27 August 1883, in Poschinger, *Aktenstücke zur Wirtschaftspolitik,* vol. 2, 139.

77. See, e.g., *StenBerRT,* 1881, 566 (28 March 1881); Kohl (ed.), *Die politischen Reden,* vol. 10, 360–64, 370–76 (8 January 1885), 452–74 (10 February 1885), 474–504 (12 February 1885); Bismarck to Scholz, 17 December 1884, in Poschinger, *Aktenstücke zur Wirtschaftspolitik,* vol. 2, 165–66; statement, 6 January 1885, in Poschinger, *Fürst Bismarck als Volkswirth,* vol. 3, 1–2; RT speech, 11 May 1885, in Poschinger, *Fürst Bismarck als Volkswirth,* vol. 3, 125–33.
78. Kohl (ed.), *Die politischen Reden,* vol. 10, 473 (10 February 1885). See also ibid., 465 (10 February 1885), 485 (12 February 1885).
79. Ibid., 477 (12 February 1885), 470 (10 February 1885).
80. *StenBerRT,* 1882, 422 (14 June 1882). See also *StenBerRT,* 1879, Attachments, no. 132 (A); *StenBerRT,* 1885, Attachments, no. 156; *StenBerRT,* 1885, 481–82 (8 January 1885); *Hamburger Nachrichten,* 15 March 1893, morning edition; Plachetka, 'Getreide-Autarkiepolitik', 108ff.
81. Lucius von Ballhausen, *Bismarck-Erinnerungen,* 398. See ibid., 386–88; GStAPK, I. HA, Rep. 90a, B III 2 b no. 6 vol. 98, fols 111–12; GStAPK, I. HA, Rep. 90a, B III 2 b no. 6 vol. 99, fols 154–57.
82. *Kreuzzeitung,* 29 October 1887.
83. See *StenBerRT,* 1881, Attachments, no. 147, 790–91. For the RT debate, see *StenBerRT,* 1881, 1388–417 (30 May 1881); Matlekovits, *Zollpolitik,* 219–20; Gerloff, *Finanz- und Zollpolitik,* 198.
84. See Wittschewsky, 'Zoll- und Handelspolitik Rußlands', 404–15; Peez, 'Österreichische Handelspolitik', 174–85; Sombart, 'Handelspolitik Italiens', 100–23; Matlekovits, *Zollpolitik,* 82–101, 105–9; Gerloff, *Finanz- und Zollpolitik,* 212–24; Schmoller, *Grundriß,* 717–18, 725–26; Coppa, 'Italian Tariff'; Geyer, *Der russische Imperialismus,* 104–10; Bairoch, 'European Trade Policy', 62–66; Smith, 'Méline Tariff', 230–43; Smith, *Tariff Reform;* Aldenhoff-Hübinger, *Agrarpolitik,* 117–23.

## Chapter 4

1. A trade treaty was also concluded with Spain in 1893, but did not come into force because the Spanish parliament failed to ratify it. See Lotz, 'Handelspolitik', 108.
2. *StenBerRT,* 1890–92, 3303 (10 December 1891).
3. See table 1.2.
4. *StHbDR,* section 2, 521.
5. According to the government's memorandum on the German-Russian trade treaty of 1894, German exports to Russia, including Finland, declined from 215 million marks in 1880 to 124 million marks in 1887. *StenBerRT,* 1893–94, Attachments, no. 190, 1005. See also Vogel, *Rußlandpolitik,* 13ff.; Wehler, 'Bismarcks Imperialismus und späte Rußlandpolitik', 242–55; Geyer, *Der russische Imperialismus,* 116–30; Müller-Link, *Industrialisierung,* 283–85, 319–38; Weitowitz, *Deutsche Politik,* 228–42.
6. *StenBerRT,* 1893–94, 18 (23 November 1893).

7. See the list in the government's Memorandum on the Austro-Hungarian, Italian and Belgian trade treaties, *StenBerRT,* 1890–92, Attachments, no. 570, 3343.
8. Speech by Caprivi in the RT, *StenBerRT,* 1890–92, 3302 (10 December 1891).
9. My own calculations, based on *StJbDR* 15, 1894, 12. Wehler, *Gesellschaftsgeschichte,* vol. 3, 544; Bade, 'Massenwanderung und Arbeitsmarkt im deutschen Nordosten', 270–75; Bade, 'Die deutsche überseeische Massenauswanderung', 262–76.
10. *StenBerRT,* 1890–92, 3307 (10 December 1891).
11. Confidential discussion at the State Ministry on 30 September 1890, GStAPK, I. HA, Rep. 90a, B III 2 b no. 6 vol. 103.
12. *StenBerRT,* 1890–92, 3302 (10 December 1891).
13. See, e.g., Weitowitz, *Deutsche Politik,* 300ff.; Puhle, *Agrarische Interessenpolitik,* 31–32.
14. My own calculations, based on *StHbDR,* section 2, 9, 13.
15. *StenBerRT,* 1890–92, 3302 (10 December 1891).
16. Ibid.
17. See Brentano, 'Handelspolitik', 20–22; Peez, *Handelspolitik,* 7–36, 65–82, 83–246, 249–74; Schmoller, 'Neuere Literatur'; Zimmermann, *Handelspolitik,* 150–61; Meyer, *Mitteleuropa*; Henderson, 'Mitteleuropäische Zollvereinspläne'; Theiner, '"Mitteleuropa"-Pläne'; Abelshauser, '"Mitteleuropa"', 268ff.; Mommsen, 'Mitteleuropaidee'; Brandt, 'Von Bruck zu Naumann'; Neitzel, *Weltmacht,* 129–44.
18. In 1890 the director of the Trade Policy Department of the Foreign Ministry was neither Berchem (Neitzel, *Weltmacht,* 140) nor Rotenhan (Weitowitz, *Deutsche Politik,* 41), but Reichardt, who held this office from 1886 to 1899. In 1886 Berchem moved to the post of undersecretary of state, which was taken over by Rotenhan in 1890. See PA AA, Materialien zu einer Darstellung der Zusammensetzung und der Wirksamkeit der früheren 2. (handelspolitischen) Abteilung des Auswärtigen Amtes von ihrer Gründung am 1. April 1885 an bis zu ihrer im Frühjahr 1920 erfolgten Auflösung, Anlage 1: Personalverhältnisse der Beamten.
19. Memorandum by Berchem, 25 March 1890, BA, R 43, 412.
20. My own calculations, based on table 1 in the appendix.
21. Memorandum by Berchem, 25 March 1890, BA, R 43, 412.
22. Sheehan, *Brentano,* 110.
23. Brentano, 'Handelspolitik', 21.
24. See PA AA, 008900: Freiherr von Lindenfels personal files.
25. See the memorandum by Lindenfels, 21 June 1890, BA, R 43, 412, fols 32–40.
26. Memorandum by Schraut, July 1890, BA, R 43, 412, fols 43–53; original emphasis.
27. Caprivi to Boetticher, 14 July 1890, BA, R 43, 412, fols 121–23.
28. Memorandum by Huber, 8 July 1890, BA, R 43, 412, fols 54–64.
29. See ibid.; GStAPK, I. HA, Rep. 87 Ministerium für Landwirtschaft, Domänen und Forsten, Abt. B no. 7230, fols 117ff.

30. On Lucius von Ballhausen's opposition, see Lucius von Ballhausen to Marschall, 12 September 1890, BA, R 901, 10058, 79–80; Lucius von Ballhausen to Caprivi, 23 September 1890, GStAPK, I. HA, Rep. 87 Ministerium für Landwirtschaft, Domänen und Forsten, Abt. B no. 7230, fol. 130; confidential discussion at the State Ministry on 30 September 1890, GStAPK, I. HA, Rep. 90a, B III 2 b no. 6 vol. 103, fols 229–42. For a general discussion, see Leibenguth, 'Modernisierungskrisis', 214–18; Weitowitz, *Deutsche Politik*, 42–48, 59–61; Bonham, *Ideology*, 108–21.
31. Quoted in Leibenguth, 'Modernisierungskrisis', 215.
32. *StenBerRT*, 1890–92, 3307 (10 December 1891).
33. See Neitzel, *Weltmacht*; Neitzel, 'Außenpolitische Zukunftsvorstellungen'.
34. *StenBerRT*, 1890–92, 3308 (10 December 1891).
35. Confidential discussion at the State Ministry on 30 September 1890, GStAPK, I. HA, Rep. 90a, B III 2 b no. 6 vol. 103.
36. Caprivi to Marschall, 25 September 1890, R 901, 10058, fol. 89.
37. On these issues, see also Weitowitz, *Deutsche Politik*, 59–60; Leibenguth, 'Modernisierungskrisis', 214–18; Lahme, *Deutsche Außenpolitik*, 227–38; Canis, *Von Bismarck zur Weltpolitik*, 71–91.
38. See also Bonham, *Ideology*, 135–43.
39. See *Der Deutsche Handelstag*, vol. 2, 455–58; memorandum by Lindenfels, 21 June 1890, BA, R 43, 412, fols 32–40; memorandum by Huber, 8 July 1890, BA, R 43, 412, fols 54–64.
40. Wermuth, *Beamtenleben*, 194.
41. See the petitions in GStAPK, I. HA, Rep. 87 Ministerium für Landwirtschaft, Domänen und Forsten, Abt. B no. 7230; BA, R 43, 2120–23.
42. See Wippermann, *Deutscher Geschichtskalender*, vol. 1 (1891), 42ff.; Schulthess, *Europäischer Geschichtskalender*, vol. 32 (1891), 14.
43. Quoted in Bueck, *Centralverband*, vol. 1, 451; see also ibid., 253–54; Hellwig, *Stumm-Halberg*, 454–55.
44. See CVDI to Caprivi, 25 April 1891, GStAPK, I. HA, Rep. 120 Ministerium für Handel und Gewerbe, Abt. C XIII 2 no. 1b vol. 3, fols 39–40.
45. See Lotz, 'Handelspolitik', 96.
46. See Bueck, *Centralverband*, vol. 1, 254. The same line of argument can also be found in Hellwig, *Stumm-Halberg*, 454–55, and Weitowitz, *Deutsche Politik*, 23–24.
47. See Bueck, *Centralverband*, vol. 1, 255–56; Marschall to Reuss, 6 March 1891, BA, R 901, 10064, fol. 205.
48. Association for the Protection of the Interests of the German Chemical Industry to AA, 23 March 1891, GStAPK, I. HA, Rep. 120 Ministerium für Handel und Gewerbe, Abt. C XIII 2 no. 1 b vol. 2, fol. 161.
49. *Der Deutsche Handelstag*, vol. 2, 458–59.
50. See Lotz, 'Handelspolitik', 93.
51. *StJbDR* 17, 1896, 127.
52. Ibid.; Borchard, *Wirkungen der Getreidezölle*, appended tables.
53. See Lotz, 'Handelspolitik', 77; *Monatshefte zur Statistik des Deutschen Reichs*, 1891, XII, 10; Borchard, *Wirkungen der Getreidezölle*, appended tables.

54. See *Deutsches Handels-Archiv* 1891, 949, 1070, 1107.
55. See Weitowitz, *Deutsche Politik,* 20–21; Tirrell, *German Agrarian Politics,* 96, 100–4.
56. See meeting of the State Ministry on 2 January 1891, GStAPK, I. HA, Rep. 90a, B III 2 b no. 6 vol. 105, fols 25–26; confidential discussion at the State Ministry on 28 May 1891, GStAPK, I. HA, Rep. 90a, B III 2b no. 6 vol. 105, fols 290–304; meeting of the State Ministry on 31 May 1891, GStAPK, I. HA, Rep. 90a, B III 2b no. 6 vol. 105, fols 326–31; meeting of the State Ministry on 15 August 1891, GStAPK, I. HA, Rep. 90a, B III 2 b no. 6 vol. 106, fols 150–58.
57. Confidential discussion at the State Ministry on 28 May 1891, GStAPK, I. HA, Rep. 90a, B III 2 b no. 6 vol. 105.
58. Meeting of the State Ministry on 31 May 1891, GStAPK, I. HA, Rep. 90a, B III 2 b no. 6 vol. 105.
59. See *Stenographische Berichte über die Verhandlungen des Preußischen Hauses der Abgeordneten* (hereafter *StenBerAH*), 1890/91, 2447–50 (1 June 1891).
60. *StenBerRT,* 1890–92, 3304 (10 December 1891).
61. Ibid., 3310 (10 December 1891).
62. Ibid., 3454 (15 December 1891).
63. See Nichols, *Germany,* 146–49; Bonham, *Ideology,* 149; Tirrell, *German Agrarian Politics,* 133–43; Weitowitz, *Deutsche Politik,* 148–52.
64. See, e.g., Bönker, 'Dog', 191–95.
65. *Monatshefte zur Statistik des Deutschen Reichs* 1893, I, 37; *Vierteljahrshefte zur Statistik des Deutschen Reichs* 1894, I, 5; ibid., 1895 I, 42; *StHbDR,* section 1, 474.
66. See chapter 1; Schmoller, 'Die amerikanische Konkurrenz'; Conrad, 'Agrarkrisis'; Kempter, *Agrarprotektionismus,* 66–67; Aldenhoff-Hübinger, *Agrarpolitik,* 73–75.
67. See Blackbourn, 'Peasants and Politics', 51ff.
68. Quoted in Kiesenwetter, *Zehn Jahre wirtschafts-politischen Kampfes,* 14–15.
69. See esp. Tirrell, *German Agrarian Politics*; Puhle, *Agrarische Interessenpolitik*; for a recent regional study of Württemberg, see Biland, *Deutsch-Konservative Partei,* 105–200.
70. On this paragraph, see also Farr, 'Peasant Protest'; Moeller, 'Introduction'; Blackbourn, 'Peasants and Politics'; Blackbourn, *Class*; Eley, *Wilhelminismus,* 174–208; Ullmann, *Interessenverbände,* 88–94; Aldenhoff, 'Agrarbewegungen'.
71. Quoted in Puhle, *Agrarische Interessenpolitik,* 314.
72. See ibid., 35, 167–68.
73. See White, *Splintered Party,* 141ff.; Eley, *Wilhelminismus,* 200ff.
74. See Loth, *Katholiken,* 39–51; for a general discussion, see also Mees, *Schorlemer-Alst.*
75. *Germania,* 24 May 1893.
76. See the government memorandum on the German-Russian trade treaty, *StenBerRT,* 1893/94, Attachments, no. 190, 1005. Lotz, 'Handelspolitik', 119; Gerschenkron, *Bread,* 52n48; Weitowitz, *Deutsche Politik,* 274; Löbel, 'Zollkrieg', 147, goes so far as to assume, wrongly, that the *Kronslastengelder* increased by a factor of twenty. On this topic as a whole, see also Vogel, *Rußlandpolitik,* 17–18; Geyer, *Der russische Imperialismus,* 122ff.

77. See table 1.5 and table 1.7.
78. These figures refer to the quantity of German imports of wheat, rye, barley, maize and oats. My own calculations, based on the memorandum by the German government on the German-Russian trade treaty, *StenBerRT,* 1893/94, Attachments, no. 190, 1007.
79. Report by the 13th Commission, *StenBerRT,* 1893/94, Attachments, no. 234, 1210–11. All figures refer to import quantities in quintals or tonnes.
80. See *Der Deutsche Handelstag,* vol. 2, 471; *StenBerRT,* 1897/98, 967 (11 February 1898).
81. Government memorandum on the German-Russian trade treaty, *StenBerRT,* 1893/94, Attachments, no. 190, 1008.
82. Ibid.
83. See ibid., 1012; Lotz, 'Handelspolitik', 122; Börner, 'Klassencharakter', 192ff.; Weitowitz, *Deutsche Politik,* 292–93, with contradictory figures on the number of fixed tariff items.
84. See Vogel, *Rußlandpolitik,* 18; Ullmann, *Bund der Industriellen,* 24; Geyer, *Der russische Imperialismus,* 124.
85. See the memorandum by Lindenfels and Pritsch, 27 November 1890, BA, R 43, 413, fols 156ff. See also the memorandum by Goering, 12 March 1891, BA, R 43, 414, fols 134ff.; confidential discussion at the State Ministry on 28 May 1891, GStAPK, I. HA, Rep. 90a, B III 2 b no. 6 vol. 105, fols 290–304. See Weitowitz, *Deutsche Politik,* 247–53.
86. See Lipset and Rokkan, 'Cleavage Structures'; Rokkan, 'Nation Building'; Rohe, *Wahlen,* 19–29.
87. *StenBerRT,* 1893/94, 1425 (26 February 1894).
88. Ibid., 1513 (1 March 1894).
89. Ibid., 1904 (16 March 1894).
90. Bueck, *Centralverband,* vol. 1, 477–78.
91. *StenBerRT,* 1893/94, 56 (24 November 1893); see Bueck, *Centralverband,* vol. 1, 475ff.
92. Suchsland to Stumm, 7 June 1893, quoted in Hellwig, *Stumm-Halberg,* 472.
93. *StenBerRT,* 1893/94, 1903 (16 March 1894).
94. Ibid., 1419 (26 February 1894).
95. Ibid., 52 (24 November 1893).
96. See the Reichstag voting results in Bonham, *Ideology,* 149, 172, 178.
97. Lieber to unknown addressee, 2 June 1894, quoted in Loth, *Katholiken,* 55.
98. On this and the following, see Bonham, *Ideology,* 101–82.
99. Wilhelm II to Miquel, 12 February 1894, quoted in Herzfeld, *Miquel,* vol. 2, 328–29.
100. *StenBerRT,* 1893/94, 1517–18 (1 March 1894).
101. Bernstorff had already voted against the German-Romanian trade treaty, while Gamp abstained from the votes on the treaties with Austria-Hungary and Romania. See *StenBerRT,* 1893/94, 441ff., 1750ff. See also Bonham, *Ideology,* 172ff.
102. Meeting of the State Ministry on 18 December 1893, GStAPK, I. HA, Rep. 90a, B III 2 b no. 6 vol. 112, fols 95–104.

103. *StenBerRT,* 1893/94, 1430 (26 February 1894).
104. Ibid.
105. See Marschall in *StenBerRT,* 1893/94, 1431 (26 February 1894); see Kanitz in *StenBerRT,* 1893/94, 1512 (1 March 1894); Lotz, 'Handelspolitik', 129.
106. *StenBerRT,* 1893/94, 1432 (26 February 1894). See also Miquel in *StenBerRT,* 1893/94, 1516 (1 March 1894).
107. Meeting of the State Ministry on 12 February 1894, GStAPK, I. HA, Rep. 90a, B III 2 b no. 6 vol. 113, fols 151–59, 164–65; see also GStAPK, I. HA, Rep. 90a, K II 3 no. 5 vol. 1, fols 169–214 (Prussian-Bavarian talks on 25–27 January 1894, letter from Caprivi of 9 February 1894); meeting of the State Ministry on 17 February 1894, GStAPK, I. HA, Rep. 90a, B III 2 b no. 6 vol. 112, fols 172–82.
108. See Fridrichowicz, *Technik,* 187ff.; Lotz, 'Handelspolitik', 129–32; Simon, *Getreideeinfuhrscheine*; Beckmann, *Einfuhrscheinsysteme,* 35ff.; Lexis, 'Identitätsnachweis', 578–81; Weitowitz, *Deutsche Politik,* 294–95; Teichmann, *Politik der Agrarpreisstützung,* 197–207; Steinkühler, *Agrar- oder Industriestaat,* 164–75; Aldenhoff-Hübinger, *Agrarpolitik,* 153–54.
109. For Kanitz, see *StenBerRT,* 1893/94, 1513 (1 March 1894).

## Chapter 5

1. Hohenlohe-Schillingsfürst, *Denkwürdigkeiten der Reichskanzlerzeit,* 31.
2. The most important of the countless contributions to the debate are probably Oldenberg, 'Ueber Deutschland als Industriestaat', and Weber, 'Diskussionsbeiträge zum Vortrag von Karl Oldenberg' (both contributions to the Protestant Social Congress [Evangelisch-sozialer Kongreß] of 1897; see also the other contributions in *Verhandlungen des Achten Evangelisch-sozialen Kongresses*); Arndt, *Wirtschaftliche Folgen*; Brentano, *Schrecken*; Dietzel, *Kornzoll*; Dietzel, *Socialpolitik*; Dietzel, 'Agrarstaat und Industriestaat'; Helfferich, *Handelspolitik*; Pohle, *Deutschland am Scheidewege*; Wagner, *Agrar- und Industriestaat*; see also *Verhandlungen des Vereins für Socialpolitik (1901).*
3. See, e.g., Oldenberg, 'Ueber Deutschland als Industriestaat', 104; Sering, 'Handelspolitik', 33.
4. Oldenberg, 'Ueber Deutschland als Industriestaat', 90.
5. Wagner, *Agrar- und Industriestaat,* 36; original emphasis.
6. See Lebovics, '"Agrarians"'; Barkin, *Controversy*; Tracy, *Government,* 92–94; Steinkühler, *Agrar- oder Industriestaat,* 30–55; Harnisch, 'Agrarstaat'; Etges, *Wirtschaftsnationalismus,* 287–93; Ambrosius, 'Agrarstaat', 50–53; Spree, 'Globalisierungs-Diskurse', 42–47.
7. Harnisch, 'Agrarstaat', 48. See also Barkin, *Controversy,* 4ff., 173ff., 278.
8. Pohle, *Deutschland am Scheidewege,* vi.
9. Rogowski, *Commerce*. See Rogowski, 'Political Cleavages'; Midford, 'International Trade'. For analyses based on the same theoretical premises, see, e.g., Kaempfer and Marks, 'Expected Effects of Trade Liberalization'; Balistreri, 'Performance of the Heckscher-Ohlin-Vanek Model'.

10. For a theoretical explanation, see Stolper and Samuelson, 'Protection'. See also Rose and Sauernheimer, *Theorie der Außenwirtschaft,* 599–605; Ethier, *Moderne Außenwirtschaftstheorie,* 140ff.
11. Rogowski, *Commerce,* 30–47.
12. Irwin, 'Political Economy'. See also Irwin, 'Industry'.
13. See Irwin, 'Political Economy', 89. For the origins of this model, see Mussa, 'Imperfect Factor Mobility'; Baldwin, 'Rent Seeking'.
14. See Irwin, 'Political Economy', esp. 95–105.
15. See Trentmann, 'Political Culture', 223.
16. See Frey, *Internationale Politische Ökonomie,* 22ff.; Weck-Hannemann, *Politische Ökonomie,* 58ff.; Ursprung, 'Modellierung'.
17. See Olson, *Logik*; Olson, *Rise,* 17–35. For a general discussion, see also Hardin, *Collective Action*; Sandler, *Collective Action*; Marwell and Oliver, *Critical Mass*; Arnold, *Theorie der Kollektivgüter*; Vanberg, 'Kollektive Güter'; Pies and Leschke, *Mancur Olsons Logik des kollektiven Handelns.* Here, as in the work of Olson and the theory of groups in general, 'group' means 'a number of individuals with a common interest' – regardless of the basis of this interest and whether and if so how it is expressed. See Olson, *Logik,* 7.
18. See Olson, *Logik,* 21–34, 48–49; Olson, *Rise,* 29ff.
19. See North, *Theorie des institutionellen Wandels,* 54–55, 59–60.
20. See Kehr, *Battleship Building,* esp. 282ff.; Gerschenkron, *Bread and Democracy*; Rosenberg, *Große Depression,* 187; Rosenberg, *Probleme,* 59, 68; Puhle, *Agrarische Interessenpolitik*; Barkin, *Controversy,* 30–31, 47–48, 105ff.; Flemming, *Landwirtschaftliche Interessen,* 27–28 (with reservations).
21. See Hunt, 'Peasants', 313, 322ff. Hunt bases himself here on a number of contemporary empirical studies such as Stumpfe, *Grundbesitz*; Koenig, *Statistische Mitteilungen*; Grebe, *Lage*; Keup and Mührer, *Bedeutung.*
22. See Hunt, 'Peasants', esp. 313ff. But see also the early contribution by Teichmann, *Politik der Agrarpreisstützung,* 596ff.
23. The same point is made by Nonn, *Verbraucherprotest,* 107ff.
24. For a general overview, see Kaiserliches Statistisches Amt (ed.), *Deutsche Landwirtschaft*; Sering, *Landwirtschaft*; Sering, 'Ländlicher Grundbesitz'.
25. See the compilation of submissions and petitions in BA, R 1501, 118948–51; *Württembergische Jahrbücher für Statistik und Landeskunde,* 1895, II, 25–26; Müller, 'Landwirtschaftliche Interessenvertretung'; Moeller, *German Peasants,* 13–16; Moeller, 'Introduction'; Farr, 'Peasant Protest'; Biland, *Deutsch-Konservative Partei,* 120–24.
26. Kaiserliches Statistisches Amt (ed.), *Deutsche Landwirtschaft,* 121.
27. The acreage devoted to the growing of breadstuffs for farms of varying sizes was as follows: 0.5–2 hectares: 31.2 per cent; 2–5 hectares: 34.9 per cent; 5–20 hectares: 35.3 per cent; 20–100 hectares: 32.9 per cent; over 100 hectares: 29.8 per cent. All figures for 1907. Kaiserliches Statistisches Amt (ed.), *Deutsche Landwirtschaft,* 120.
28. For the province of Hanover, see Flathmann (ed.), *Landbevölkerung,* 46–101.
29. *Deutsche Tageszeitung,* 23 September 1900; original emphasis.
30. *Deutsche Tageszeitung,* 25 December 1900; original emphasis.

31. VSW resolution regarding 'the creation of an autonomous customs tariff as a basis for concluding the new trade treaties', 5 March 1900, BA, R 1501, 118891, fol. 51; original emphasis.
32. See Puhle, *Agrarische Interessenpolitik,* 39, 72ff.
33. See esp. Blackbourn, *Class;* Blackbourn, 'Peasants and Politics'; Blackbourn, 'Politics of Demagogy'; Mock, '"Manipulation von oben"'; Moeller, 'The Kaiserreich Recast'.
34. See the summary of agrarian demands in the stenographic report on the 28th plenary assembly of the DHT in Berlin on 30 September 1901, BA, R 1501, 118908, fol. 179.
35. See BdL programme of 1893, point 4, quoted in Puhle, *Agrarische Interessenpolitik,* 314. See also ibid., 74; Fricke and Hartwig, 'Bund der Landwirte', 244.
36. *Kreuzzeitung,* 17 August 1901; *Deutsche Tageszeitung,* 13 August 1901. See also BA, R 1501, 118908, fol. 179.
37. See *Kreuzzeitung,* 17 August 1901.
38. See *Der Bund der Landwirte,* 19 September 1901, 243; *Deutsche Tageszeitung,* 25 December 1900.
39. See *Augsburger Abend-Zeitung,* 24 February 1901; *Korrespondenz des BdL,* 26 February 1901.
40. See, e.g., VSW resolution regarding 'the creation of an autonomous customs tariff as a basis for concluding the new trade treaties', R 1501, 118891, fol. 51; BdL to Bülow, 8 October 1900, R 1501, 118902, fol. 38; DLR to Bülow, 30 November 1900, BA, R 1501, 118903, fol. 64; *Deutsche Tageszeitung,* 23 September 1900; *Korrespondenz des BdL,* 23 October 1900; *Freisinnige Zeitung,* 10 November 1900.
41. Resolution by the standing committee of the DLR, *Kreuzzeitung,* 17 August 1901.
42. The double tariff system, which was ultimately implemented in the Bülow tariff only for the main cereal types, was based on the legally enshrined declaration of intention not to lower the tariff rates below the stipulated minimum tariffs in the context of trade treaty agreements. In legal terms, it is true, this did not definitively rule out the possibility of concluding and ratifying trade treaties featuring tariffs below the minimum rates. But it represented a serious political obstacle that was de facto never overcome, since the Reichstag would have been highly unlikely to approve such treaties.
43. VSW resolution regarding 'the creation of an autonomous customs tariff as a basis for concluding the new trade treaties', BA, R 1501, 118891, fol. 51; original emphasis.
44. See BdL to Bülow, 8 October 1900, BA, R 1501, 118902, fols 39–41; DLR to Bülow, 30 November 1900, BA, R 1501, 118903, fol. 66; *Kreuzzeitung,* 17 August 1901.
45. On the BdL and the other agrarian interest associations, see Puhle, *Agrarische Interessenpolitik;* Puhle, *Politische Agrarbewegungen,* 55–77; Ullmann, *Interessenverbände,* 85–94; Hunt, '"Egalitarianism"'; Biland, *Deutsch-Konservative Partei,* esp. 105–200; Flemming, *Landwirtschaftliche Interessen,* 29–53; Fricke and Hartwig, 'Bund der Landwirte'; Fritsch and Gottwald, 'Bayerischer Bau-

ernbund'; Gottwald, 'Vereinigung der Steuer- und Wirtschaftsreformer'; Farr, 'Populism'.

46. See Puhle, *Agrarische Interessenpolitik,* 50–55.
47. Ibid., 39n5. But see Fricke and Hartwig, 'Bund der Landwirte', 242, which gives different figures.
48. The DLR nominated Dr. von Frege (MdR [DKP], VSW, executive board of the BdL), Count von Kanitz (MdR [DKP], VSW), Rettich (MdR [DKP], Domains Council), Baron von Soden-Frauenhofen (vice chairman of the DLR) and Winkelmann (Regional Economic Council [Landesökonomierat], vice chairman of the Westphalian Peasants' Union [Westfälischer Bauernverein]). For agriculture, the government appointed von Arnim (president of the Brandenburg Agricultural Council [Brandenburgischer Landwirtschaftsrat]), Klein (president of the Baden Agricultural Council [Badischer Landwirtschaftsrat]), Count von Schwerin-Löwitz (president of the DLR), Count von Loë-Wissen (chairman of the Rhineland Peasants' Association [Rheinischer Bauernverein]) and von Ploetz (MdR [DKP], chairman of the BdL). For the membership list of the Economic Committee, or Wirtschaftlicher Ausschuß (hereafter WA), see BA, R 901, 3430, fols 17–18. The data in Stegmann, *Erben Bismarcks,* 71–72, quoted in Tischert, *Unterwegs,* 3–4, does not reflect the original composition of the WA, but rather the state of affairs in 1900. See also Ullmann, *Bund der Industriellen,* 365–66.
49. Apart from the ten agrarian delegates mentioned here, the only other members of the committee were Koenig (chairman of the German Sugar Industry Association [Verein Deutscher Zuckerindustrie], member of the CVDI executive board), Frentzel (chairman of the DHT) and Collenbusch (Dresden Chamber of Commerce [Handelskammer, hereafter HK], German Tobacco Association [Deutscher Tabakverein]). BA, R 901, 3430, fol. 19. For the proceedings of the committee, see BA, R 1501, 118940–42.
50. Puhle, *Politische Agrarbewegungen,* 73.
51. On the following, see Puhle, *Agrarische Interessenpolitik,* 165–212; Puhle, 'Radikalisierung'; Nipperdey, 'Organization', 101ff.; Ritter, *Parteien,* 23–27; Ullmann, *Interessenverbände,* 92–93; Eley, *Reshaping,* 19ff.; Eley, *Wilhelminismus,* 203ff.; Retallack, *Notables,* 100–12, 131–47; Wehler, *Gesellschaftsgeschichte,* vol. 3, 1038ff., 1060ff.; Sperber, *Kaiser's Voters,* 223–30; Fairbairn, 'Interpreting Wilhelmine Elections', 30–41; Fairbairn, *Democracy,* 51ff.
52. *Kölnische Zeitung,* 27 July 1901.
53. Kaelble, *Industrielle Interessenpolitik,* 9. For a general discussion, see ibid., 3–9, 51ff.; Blaich, *Staat,* 35–41; Schulze, 'Zentralverband Deutscher Industrieller'; Ullmann, *Interessenverbände,* 77ff.
54. *Verhandlungen, Mitteilungen und Berichte des Centralverbands Deutscher Industrieller,* vol. 77 (1897), 43. See Bueck's memorandum concerning the 'establishment of a body tasked with preparing the ground for the conclusion of trade treaties with foreign countries', 13 June 1897, BA, R 901, 3430.
55. On the founding of the WA, see *Berliner Politische Nachrichten,* 10 October 1900; Bueck, *Centralverband,* vol. 1, 519ff., 527ff., 549–50; Hacker, *Beiräte,* 34ff.; Tischert, *Unterwegs,* 2ff.; Kaulisch, 'Bildung', 135ff.; Stegmann, *Erben Bis-*

*marcks,* 70ff.; Stegmann, 'Wirtschaft', 182–83; Ullmann, *Bund der Industriellen,* 170–71; Blaich, *Staat,* 38.
56. *Jahrbuch des Handelsvertragsvereins,* 1901, 24.
57. See BA, R 901, 3430, fols 17–18; Kaelble, *Industrielle Interessenpolitik,* 62–63.
58. The individuals in question were Ballestrem (member of the Prussian House of Representatives [Centre Party], Silesian magnate), Moeller (CVDI), Rieppel (CVDI), Vogel (chairman of the Association of Textile Industrialists [Verband der Textilindustriellen], CVDI) and Wachler (CVDI). BA, R 901, 3430, fols 17–18; Stegmann, *Erben Bismarcks,* 71–72; Wermuth, *Beamtenleben,* 219.
59. The WA had a total of thirty members, half of whom were drawn equally from the DLR, CVDI and DHT, while the other half were nominated by the Imperial Ministry of the Interior. The DHT sent: Frentzel (chairman of the DHT, member of the Prussian House of Lords), Herz (oldest member of the Berlin Merchants' Association [Ältester der Kaufmannschaft von Berlin]), Laeisz (head of the Hamburg HK, Association for the Promotion of Trade Freedom [Verein zur Förderung der Handelsfreiheit]), Michel (chairman of the Mainz HK, executive board of the DHT), Weidert (chairman of the Munich HK, executive board of the DHT). The Imperial Ministry of the Interior also appointed von Dreyse (BdI, CVH), Collenbusch (CVH), Martius (Association for the Protection of the Interests of the German Chemical Industry [Verein zur Wahrung der Interessen der Chemischen Industrie Deutschlands], chairman of the CVH), Teschendorff and Widenmann (chairman of the Stuttgart HK). BA, R 901, 3430, fols 17–18. For the agrarian members of the WA, see above, note 48.
60. *Freisinnige Zeitung,* 16 November 1897.
61. See Bueck, *Centralverband,* vol. 1, 553–54.
62. See Bueck to the Imperial Ministry of the Interior (Reichsamt des Innern, hereafter RI), 28 September 1900, BA, R 1501, 118894, fol. 146.
63. Bueck, *Centralverband,* vol. 1, 565–66.
64. Ibid., 563.
65. See Bueck to RI, 28 September 1900, BA, R 1501, 118894, fols 147–48.
66. See CVDI, proposals on changing the tariff schedule and determining tariff rates, BA, R 1501, 118893, fols 3–105. See also Bueck, *Centralverband,* vol. 1, 563.
67. This and the preceding quotations in 'Rundschreiben des Direktoriums des CVDI an die Mitglieder', 6 October 1900, published in *Berliner Politische Nachrichten,* 10 October 1900. See also Bueck to RI, 28 October 1900, BA, R 1501, 118894, fols 149–50.
68. Ungewitter, *Ausgewählte Kapitel,* 379.
69. See Kaelble, *Industrielle Interessenpolitik,* 54.
70. See ibid.
71. See Kehr, *Battleship Building,* esp. 212ff.; Stegmann, *Erben Bismarcks,* 63ff.; Stegmann, 'Wirtschaft'; Berghahn, *Tirpitz-Plan*; Wehler, *German Empire,* 94ff.; Eley, 'Sammlungspolitik'; Eley, '"Kehrites"'; Eley, *Wilhelminismus,* 20ff.; Witt, 'Innenpolitik', 19ff.; Puhle, 'Legende', 111ff.; Hentschel, *Wirtschaft und Wirtschaftspolitik,* 184ff.

72. Bueck, *Centralverband,* vol. 1, 576.
73. Kehr, *Battleship Building,* 217.
74. See Eley, 'Sammlungspolitik', esp. 33–48.
75. See, e.g., 'Die konservative Partei und die Handelsverträge', *Hannoversche Tages-Nachrichten,* 19 December 1900.
76. Resolution of the CVDI executive board on 9 September 1901, quoted in *Berliner Tageblatt,* 12 August 1901.
77. See the report on the meeting of CVDI delegates on 1 October 1901, in *Deutsche Industrie-Zeitung,* 4 October 1901; Bueck, *Centralverband,* vol. 1, 586–606; 'Großindustrie und Landwirtschaft', *Kölnische Volkszeitung,* 3 March 1901.
78. The term 'agrarian industrialists' comes from Kaelble, *Industrielle Interessenpolitik,* 62ff., who describes the formation of three groups within the CVDI.
79. See *Verhandlungen, Mitteilungen und Berichte des Centralverbands Deutscher Industrieller,* vol. 91 (1901), 33ff. (Bueck), 48ff. (Koenig).
80. See also CVDI to Bülow, 18 September 1902, BA, R 1501, 118918, fol. 16, in the same vein.
81. Resolution by the general assembly of the VDEStI on 4 October 1901, in *Die Post,* 4 October 1901. The fact that from 1893 Bueck held the post of executive director of both organizations is likely to have been another significant reason for the close temporal relationship between the resolutions of the CVDI and VDEStI.
82. 'Vom Zolltarife', *Deutsche Tageszeitung,* 12 August 1901; original emphasis.
83. *Kreuzzeitung,* 3 October 1901, quoted in 'Großindustrie und Landwirtschaft', *Kölnische Volkszeitung,* 3 October 1901.
84. 'Gegen die Hanseaten!', *Hamburgischer Correspondent,* 27 August 1901.
85. *Berliner Tageblatt,* 12 August 1901.
86. 'Erhöhte Schutzzölle für die Industrie', *Freisinnige Zeitung,* 22 September 1901.
87. For a general discussion of this point and the following remarks, see Ullmann, *Bund der Industriellen*; Ullmann, *Interessenverbände,* 79ff.; Hohberg, 'Bund der Industriellen'.
88. See Ullmann, *Bund der Industriellen,* 166ff.
89. *Jahresbericht des Bundes der Industriellen,* 1897/98, 65.
90. Resolution of the BdI board of directors of May 1902, *Jahresbericht des Bundes der Industriellen,* 1901/2, 5.
91. See, e.g., BdI to Posadowsky, 18 October 1899, BA, R 1501, 118888, fols 2–3. The timing was also bad. The draft tariff composed by the Federal Bureau for the Preparation of Trade Treaties (Bundesstelle zur Vorbereitung von Handelsverträgen) reached the RI far too late to have any impact on its decision. See BdI to Posadowsky-Wehner, 15 May 1900, BA, 1501, 118891, fols 157ff. See also Ullmann, *Bund der Industriellen,* 179–80.
92. See ibid., 34–44, 79–109.
93. See *Jahrbuch des Handelsvertragsvereins,* 1901, 18ff.; Ungewitter, *Ausgewählte Kapitel,* 382ff.; Kaelble, *Industrielle Interessenpolitik,* 174; Stegmann, *Bismarcks Erben,* 75–76.

94. Quoted in Gottwald, 'Schutzverband', 128. The Protection Association against Agrarian Encroachments was absorbed into the Trade Treaty Association in 1901.
95. See Borgius, *Handelsvertragsverein*; Nussbaum, *Unternehmer,* 151ff.; Böhm, *Überseehandel,* 252–53; Stegmann, *Erben Bismarcks,* 77ff.; Mielke, *Hansa-Bund,* 24–25; Elm, 'Handelsvertragsverein', 85–86.
96. *Der Handelsvertragsverein, sein Wesen und seine Ziele,* 8.
97. See, e.g., 'Was bedeutet der Doppeltarif?', *Handelsvertragsverein,* 14 March 1901; 'Zum Zolltarifentwurf', *Mitteilungen des Handelsvertragsvereins,* 3 August 1901.
98. Central Department for Trade Treaties, memorandum regarding uniform and dual tariff presented to the imperial chancellor on 20 December 1900, BA, R 1501, 118902, fol. 299.
99. See Nussbaum, *Unternehmer,* 153–54; Stegmann, *Erben Bismarcks,* 88; Mielke, *Hansa-Bund,* 25; Blaich, *Staat,* 40–41.
100. See Tschirschky to Bülow, 30 October 1902, BA, R 1501, 118919, fols 91–92. Unfortunately, the biographies by Cecil and Straub cast very little light on Ballin's role in the Trade Treaty Association or his economic policy activities in general. See Cecil, *Ballin*; Straub, *Ballin.*
101. See Pogge von Strandmann, 'Widersprüche', 230; Peschke, *Elektroindustrie,* 238ff.; Plumpe, *I.G. Farbenindustrie,* 50ff.; Hippel, 'Auf dem Weg', 90ff.
102. See *Der Deutsche Handelstag,* vol. 1, 126–27; Krueger, 'Untersuchung', 654; Fischer, *Unternehmerschaft,* 108ff.
103. See John et al., 'Deutscher Industrie- und Handelstag', 136ff.; Kaelble, *Industrielle Interessenpolitik,* 177–81; Lichter, *Handelskammern,* 14ff.
104. *Der Deutsche Handelstag,* vol. 2, 516. See also the report on the 28th plenary assembly of the DHT in Berlin on 30 September 1901, 35, BA, R 1501, 118908, fol. 177.
105. DHT, *Mitteilungen an die Mitglieder,* vol. 41, no. 12, 13 September 1901: report on the meeting of the committee of 2 September 1901, 11–12, BA, R 1501, 118907, fol. 93; emphasis added.
106. Report on the plenary assembly of the DHT on 30 September 1901, 36, BA, R 1501, 118908, fol. 177.
107. Report on the plenary assembly of the DHT on 30 September 1901, 46, BA, R 1501, 118908, fol. 182. Beumer was executive director of both the Langnamverein and the Northwestern Group of the VDEStI, as well as being a member of the CVDI board and Reichstag deputy for the National Liberal Party from 1901 to 1907. See Kaelble, *Industrielle Interessenpolitik,* 250; Schulze, 'Verein zur Wahrung der gemeinsamen wirtschaftlichen Interessen', 379.
108. Report on the plenary assembly of the DHT on 30 September 1901, 58, BA, R 1501, 118908, fol. 188.
109. *Der Deutsche Handelstag,* vol. 2, 435.
110. Report on the plenary assembly of the DHT on 30 September 1901, 66–67, BA, R 1501, 118908, fols 192–93; original emphasis. The motion by the chambers of commerce of Bochum and associates was defeated by 244 votes to 65,

while the board's motion was carried by 228 to 34 protest abstentions. See BA, R 1501, 118908, p. 63, fol. 191.

111. See, e.g., the memorandum by the oldest member of the Berlin Merchants' Association regarding the new approach in German trade policy, 25 March 1901, BA, R 43, 316, fols 172–93; Breslau HK and others to Hohenlohe-Schillingsfürst, 10 July 1900, BA, R 1501, 118892, fols 39–42; Frankfurt am Main HK to BR, 5 October 1901, BA, R 1501, 118913, fols 114–70; compilation of submissions by members of the DHT in DHT, *Mitteilungen an die Mitglieder,* 28 September 1901, BA, R 1501, 118910, fols 289ff.; DHT, *Mitteilungen an die Mitglieder,* 24 October 1901, BA, R 1501, 118909, fols 288ff.; DHT (ed.), *Anträge zum Zolltarif aus dem Kreise der Mitglieder des DHT,* Berlin, December 1901, BA, R 1501, 118915.

112. The 'tendency towards the increasing depoliticization' of the DHT identified by Harm-Hinrich Brandt was thus interrupted, at least in the run-up to the Bülow tariff. See Brandt, 'Diskussionsbeitrag', 76–77. Nor is it correct to state, as Jörg Lichter does, that the DHT was 'paralyzed' for 'twenty years … with respect to tariff and trade policy issues' (Lichter, *Handelskammern,* 17). One resolution came out unambiguously against the agricultural tariff increases of 1887, for example, though this was far from uncontested. See *Der Deutsche Handelstag,* vol. 2, 445–46; Pohl, 'Stellungnahmen', 61ff.

113. Report by General Secretary Soetbeer at the DHT plenary assembly of 14 March 1898, in *Der Deutsche Handelstag,* vol. 2, 498; original emphasis.

114. See resolution of the DHT plenary assembly of 14 March 1898, in *Der Deutsche Handelstag,* vol. 2, 500.

115. Only the chambers of commerce of Metz and Saarbrücken voted against the resolution opposing minimum tariff rates. See compilation of DHT resolutions of 30 September 1901 regarding customs tariff law, BA, R 1501, 118908, fol. 192. See also, e.g., chair of Plauen HK to RI, 25 June 1900, BA, R 1501, 118892, fols 32–33; Breslau HK and others to Hohenlohe, 10 July 1900, BA, R 1501, 118892, fols 39–42; Solingen HK to Bülow, 3 November 1900, BA, R 1501, 118902, fol. 20; Oberbayern HK to RI, 10 November 1900, BA, R 1501, 118902, fols 31–33; memorandum by the oldest member of the Berlin Merchants' Association regarding the new approach in German trade policy, 25 March 1901, BA, R 43, 316, fols 172–93.

116. See, e.g., Weck-Hannemann, *Politische Ökonomie,* 58–59; Olson, *Logik,* 130.

117. Nonn, *Verbraucherprotest,* 23–83, 240–80, 313–14; see also Nonn, 'Arbeiter'; Nonn, 'Fleischteuerungsprotest'; Nonn, 'Parteien'; Nonn, 'Konsumentenprotest'.

118. Quoted in *Protokoll über die Verhandlungen des Parteitags der Sozialdemokratischen Partei Deutschlands,* 1898, 179. See also Kautsky, *Handelspolitik,* 26.

119. Quotations from *Protokoll über die Verhandlungen des Parteitags der Sozialdemokratischen Partei Deutschlands,* 1898, 183, 172, 179. See also Schippel, *Grundzüge,* esp. 321–52.

120. *Protokoll über die Verhandlungen des Parteitags der Sozialdemokratischen Partei Deutschlands,* 1898, 193.

121. Ibid., 205.

122. *Protokoll über die Verhandlungen des Parteitags der Sozialdemokratischen Partei Deutschlands,* 1900, 246.
123. Nonn's assertion that the Bülow tariff 'laid down only low rates' for meat (*Verbraucherprotest,* 59) is incorrect. The tariff burden for beef and pork, which had been reduced to 15 and 17 marks, respectively, per quintal in the Caprivi treaties, was raised to 45 marks in the general tariff, and no less than 35 marks in the later conventional tariff. In percentage terms, then, the tariff increase for meat exceeded that for wheat and rye. See Teichmann, *Politik der Agrarpreisstützung,* 598.
124. *Protokoll über die Verhandlungen des Parteitags der Sozialdemokratischen Partei Deutschlands,* 1902, 12. See Bebel's speech opposing the customs tariff bill, in *Protokoll über die Verhandlungen des Parteitags der Sozialdemokratischen Partei Deutschlands,* 1901, 284–91; Report on the party conference, in *Vorwärts,* 29 September 1901.
125. *Protokoll über die Verhandlungen des Parteitags der Sozialdemokratischen Partei Deutschlands,* 1902, 12.
126. Ibid., 13; original emphasis.
127. For a general discussion of this paragraph, see Sperber, *Kaiser's Voters,* esp. 212–40; Fairbairn, *Democracy,* 45–68, 209–40; Fairbairn, 'Interpreting Wilhelmine Elections'; Fairbairn, 'Limits'. Instructive regional studies include Moring, *Sozialdemokratische Partei*; Paetau, *Konfrontation*; Saldern, *Wege*; Nolan, *Social Democracy.*
128. See Sperber, *Kaiser's Voters,* 237. On a broad statistical foundation, Sperber revises the previously dominant view within the research that SPD voters in the German Empire were almost exclusively working-class Protestants and that the growth in its support was due chiefly to the mobilization of former nonvoters. See, e.g., Conze, 'Politische Willensbildung', 342–43; Ritter, 'Sozialdemokratie', 351; Saldern, 'Wer ging in die SPD?', 164; Rohe, *Wahlen,* 102; Schmädeke, *Wählerbewegung,* vol. 1, 537.
129. See Lehmann, *Agrarfrage,* 145–223.
130. See, e.g., Vosberg-Rekow, *Zolltarifvorlage,* 2–4.
131. See Thielmann to Brefeld, 1 October 1898, GStAPK, I. HA, Rep. 120, C VII 1 no. 41 vol. 1, fols 5–6. On this section generally, see also Herzfeld, *Miquel,* vol. 2, 587ff.; Witt, *Finanzpolitik,* 63ff.; Ullmann, *Bund der Industriellen,* 176ff.; Bonham, *Ideology,* 230ff.
132. Posadowsky to Thielmann, 26 January 1899, GStAPK, I. HA, Rep. 120, C VII 1 no. 41 vol. 1, fols 16, 20.
133. Draft customs tariff scheme for 'agriculture, along with the food and luxury consumables industry', GStAPK, I. HA, Rep. 120, C VII 1 no. 41 vol. 1, fols 22–52.
134. Hammerstein to Posadowsky, 29 March 1899, GStAPK, I. HA, Rep. 120, C VII 1 no. 41 vol. 1, fol. 139. See also Hammerstein to Posadowsky-Wehner, 8 December 1899, GStAPK, I. HA, Rep. 120, C VII 1 no. 41 vol. 2, fol. 70.
135. Hammerstein to Posadowsky, 29 March 1899, GStAPK, I. HA, Rep. 120, C VII 1 no. 41 vol. 1, fol. 139.
136. See ibid., fols 139–40.

137. Thielmann to Brefeld, 1 October 1898, GStAPK, I. HA, Rep. 120, C VII 1 no. 41 vol. 1, fol. 6.
138. Meeting of the State Ministry on 22 November 1897, BA, R 43, 2028, 30.
139. *Berliner Tageblatt,* 19 January 1898, morning edition.
140. Questionnaire for the coal and steel industry, metallurgical industry and metalworking, GStAPK, I. HA, Rep. 120, C VII 1 no. 41 vol. 1, fol. 95.
141. Posadowsky to Thielmann, 28 March 1899, GStAPK, I. HA, Rep. 120, C VII 1 no. 41 vol. 1, fol. 142; see also Posadowsky to Thielmann, 12 March 1899, GStAPK, I. HA, Rep. 120, C VII 1 no. 41 vol. 1, fols 73–76.
142. Ullmann, *Bund der Industriellen,* 179.
143. See Miquel to Thielmann, 6 November 1899, GStAPK, I. HA, Rep. 120, C VII 1 no. 41 vol. 2, fols 2–6; Posadowsky to Thielmann, 24 November 1899, GStAPK, I. HA, Rep. 120, C VII 1 no. 41 vol. 2, fols 20–25; statement by Miquel, 4 December 1899, GStAPK, I. HA, Rep. 120, C VII 1 no. 41 vol. 2, fols 66–68; Thielmann to Posadowsky, 18 December 1899, GStAPK, I. HA, Rep. 120, C VII 1 no. 41 vol. 2, fols 73–75; statement by Posadowsky, 24 December 1899, GStAPK, I. HA, Rep. 120, C VII 1 no. 41 vol. 2, fol. 106; Miquel to Thielmann, 23 December 1899, GStAPK, I. HA, Rep. 120, C VII 1 no. 41 vol. 2, fol. 107.
144. See Thielmann to Posadowsky, 4 May 1899, BA 1501, 118884, fols 275–76; Thielmann to Posadowsky, 13 November 1899, GStAPK, I. HA, Rep. 120, C VII 1 no. 41 vol. 2, fol. 18.
145. See Thielmann to the federal governments with their own customs administration and the governor of Alsace-Lorraine, 21 December 1899, GStAPK, I. HA, Rep. 120, C VII 1 no. 41 vol. 2, fol. 104. Comparison of the two Imperial Treasury (Reichsschatzamt, hereafter RSA) drafts of 1899 and 1900 shows the difference: plan for a new German customs tariff system, drawn up in the RSA, 1899, BA 1501, 118887, fols 17–214; plan for a new German customs tariff system, drawn up in the RSA, 1900, BA, R 1501, 118889.
146. Posadowsky to Bülow and Thielmann, 21 October 1899, R 1501, 118886, fols 272, 255.
147. Ibid., fols 272–73.
148. Ibid., fol. 256.
149. See also memorandum by the RI, 17 September 1900, R 1501, 118893, fols 139–57.
150. Posadowsky to Bülow and Thielmann, 21 October 1899, R 1501, 118886, fol. 292. See Posadowsky to Thielmann, 24 April 1900, BA, R 1501, 118891, fols 110–11.
151. Miquel to Posadowsky, 20 September 1900, BA, R 1501, 118894, fol. 35.
152. Statement by Hammerstein, 17 September 1900, BA, R 43, 316, fol. 3; original emphasis.
153. Ibid., fol. 4.
154. See Posadowsky to Bülow and Thielmann, 21 October 1899, BA, R 1501, 118886, fols 268ff.; memorandum by the RI, 17 September 1900, BA, R 1501, 118893, fols 145ff.
155. Memorandum by the RSA, 2 February 1900, BA, R 1501, 118891, fol. 83.
156. Ibid., fol. 85. See Ullmann, *Bund der Industriellen,* 182–83.

157. Memorandum by the RSA, 2 February 1900, BA, R 1501, 118891, fol. 86. See Herzfeld, *Miquel,* vol. 2, 593–94.
158. Bülow to Posadowsky, late May 1900, BA, R 1501, 118891, fol. 74. This was also the view taken by the Ministry of Trade and Commerce (Ministerium für Handel und Gewerbe, hereafter MHG); see Brefeld to Thielmann, 31 August 1900, BA, R 2, 24458, fols 175–82.
159. Bülow to Posadowsky, late May 1900, BA, R 1501, 118891, fol. 76.
160. Ibid., fol. 77. See also Bonham, *Ideology,* 236–37.
161. Bülow to Posadowsky, late May 1900, BA, R 1501, 118891, fol. 80.
162. See Thielmann to Posadowsky, 8 September 1900, BA, R 1501, 118894, fol. 31; *Frankfurter Zeitung,* 13 October 1900.
163. See Hammerstein to Bülow, 9 November 1900, BA, R 43, 316, fol. 42; Bleyberg, 'Government', 78–79.
164. The idea generally espoused in the research literature that the decision to introduce a dual tariff solely for agrarian but not for industrial goods had already been made at the sitting on 27 October 1900 is wrong. In fact, it was explicitly resolved that it was 'not advisable' to make 'a fundamental distinction between agricultural and industrial products, because in those … industrial circles requiring protection' this might lead to the assumption 'that in future they are to be the first to be sacrificed to the requirements of the trade treaties'. Record of the meeting on 27 October 1900, BA, R 901, 13316, fols 6–7; see also statement by the Foreign Ministry, 30 November 1900, BA, R 1501, 118902. But see Witt, *Finanzpolitik,* 67; Ullmann, *Bund der Industriellen,* 184–85; Lerman, *Chancellor,* 52.
165. See Wermuth, *Beamtenleben,* 223.
166. See *StenBerAH,* 1901, cols 2–6 (9 January 1901); draft of the opening speech with Posadowsky's corrections, BA, R 1501, 115532, fols 12–17. See also Kardorff, *Wilhelm von Kardorff,* 344–45; Horn, *Kampf,* 97ff.; Witt, *Finanzpolitik,* 68; Winzen, *Bülow,* 118.
167. See VSW resolution regarding 'the creation of an autonomous customs tariff as a basis for concluding the new trade treaties', BA, R 1501, 118891, fol. 51; BdL to Bülow, 8 October 1900, BA, R 1501, 118902, fol. 38; DLR to Bülow, 30 November 1900, BA, R 1501, 118903, fol. 64; *Deutsche Tageszeitung,* 23 September 1900; *Korrespondenz des BdL,* 23 October 1900; 'Rundschreiben des Direktoriums des CVDI an die Mitglieder', 6 October 1900, published in *Berliner Politische Nachrichten,* 10 October 1900; Bueck to RI, 28 October 1900, BA, R 1501, 118894, fols 149–50; *Freisinnige Zeitung,* 10 November 1900.
168. RSA to Bülow, 4 April 1901, BA, R 1501, 118904, fol. 171. For the same document, see also BA, R 43, 316, fols 92–113.
169. RSA to Bülow, 4 April 1901, BA, R 1501, 118904, fol. 174.
170. Ibid., fols 176–77.
171. See ibid., fols 177ff.; commissarial consultations among the relevant imperial and Prussian departments on the draft customs tariff law, minutes of the first meeting, 11 March 1901, BA, R 1501, 118904, fols 65–66.
172. RSA to Bülow, 4 April 1901, BA, R 1501, 118904, fol. 179. See statement by Hammerstein, 17 September 1900, BA, R 43, 316, fol. 9. See also Ullmann, *Bund der Industriellen,* 185; Bleyberg, 'Government', 106ff.

173. RSA to Bülow, 4 April 1901, BA, R 1501, 118904, fol. 179.
174. The following took part in the conference beginning on 11 March 1901 as representatives of their departments: AA: Koerner, Johannes, Goebel von Harrant; RI: Wermuth, Wolffram, van der Borght, Müller, Völcker, Martin, Boenisch; Finance Ministry (Ministerium der Finanzen, hereafter MF): Köhn, Rodatz; MHG: Lusensky, Jaeger; Ministry of Agriculture, Estates and Forestry (Ministerium für Landwirtschaft, Domänen und Forsten, hereafter ML): Donner, Kapp, Wesener; RSA: Fischer, Henle, Meuschel, Blau, Pinckernelle. See minutes of the first meeting, 11 March 1901, BA, R 1501, 118904, fols 65–66. On the background to the conference, see Thielmann to Brefeld, 25 February 1901, GStAPK, I. HA, Rep. 120, C VII 1 no. 41 vol. 3, fol. 3; Miquel to Bülow, 28 February 1901, GStAPK, I. HA, Rep. 120, C VII 1 no. 41 vol. 3, fols 5–6; Bleyberg, 'Government', 93–94.
175. See findings of the commissarial consultation among the relevant imperial and royal Prussian departments on the draft customs tariff law, 29 March 1901, BA, R 1501, 118904, fols 11–30.
176. Thielmann to Bülow, 25 May 1902, BA, R 43, 316, fols 320–21. See commissarial consultations on the draft customs tariff law, minutes of the sixth meeting, 16 March 1901, BA, R 43, 316, fol. 146.
177. See Thielmann to Bülow, 25 May 1902, BA, R 43, 316, fol. 292.
178. See commissarial consultations on the draft customs tariff law, minutes of the fifth meeting, 15 March 1901, BA, R 43, 316, fols 138–39; Thielmann to Bülow, 25 May 1902, BA, R 43, 316, fols 293–94.
179. BA, R 43, 316, fol. 294.
180. See Bülow, *Denkwürdigkeiten,* vol. 1, 522ff.; Kardorff, *Wilhelm von Kardorff,* 345–46; Herzfeld, *Miquel,* vol. 2, 637ff.; Witt, *Finanzpolitik,* 68; Horn, *Kampf,* 88ff.; Bleyberg, 'Government', 113ff.; Lerman, *Chancellor,* 67ff.
181. Jagemann to Brauer, 8 May 1901, quoted in Fuchs (ed.), *Großherzog Friedrich,* vol. 4, 318. See also telegram from Bülow to Wilhelm II, 4 December 1901, BA, R 43, 317, fol. 26.
182. Minutes of the meeting on 27 October 1900, BA, R 901, 13316, fol. 7.
183. See the list of attendees, appendix 1 to the first meeting, BA, R 1501, 118905, fol. 120. Alexander, *Freikonservative Partei,* 273, mixes up the tariff policy conference on 4–5 June 1901 with what Wermuth called the 'battle of the nations' interdepartmental conference of 27 October 1900 and wrongly identifies the results of the latter as those of the former.
184. Bülow, *Denkwürdigkeiten,* vol. 1, 531.
185. See ibid.; Neumann, 'Innenpolitik', 53; Bleyberg, 'Government', 121–22.
186. Tariff policy conference, first meeting, 4 June 1901, BA, R 1501, 118905, fol. 104.
187. See ibid., fol. 107.
188. See ibid., fol. 114.
189. See above; *Der Deutsche Handelstag,* vol. 2, 516; Gensel, *Der Deutsche Handelstag,* 170.
190. Regrettably, the recent Bülow biographies pay little attention to the customs tariff reform; see Fesser, *Bülow,* 69ff.; Winzen, *Bülow,* 118ff. More revealing is Lerman, *Chancellor,* 51ff., 71ff., 76.

191. See Witt, *Finanzpolitik*, 70.
192. See Bülow, *Denkwürdigkeiten*, vol. 1, 532–33. Bülow himself claims in his *Denkwürdigkeiten* that by publishing the tariff bill he intended to drive the extreme agrarians onto the defensive. Whether this is correct or whether he had other motives is unclear. See also Alexander, *Freikonservative Partei*, 273–74.
193. 'Zum Zolltarif', *Berliner Börsen-Zeitung*, 28 July 1901.
194. 'Der neue Zolltarif', *Vorwärts*, 21 July 1901.
195. *Frankfurter Zeitung*, 31 July 1901.
196. 'An die Gewehre!', *Freisinnige Zeitung*, 30 July 1901; original emphasis.
197. See, e.g., *Berliner Börsen-Courier*, 27 July 1901; *National-Zeitung*, 27 July 1901; *Hamburger Nachrichten*, 27 July 1901; *Berliner Börsen-Zeitung*, 28 July 1901; *Münchener Neueste Nachrichten*, 1 August 1901; *Hamburgischer Correspondent*, 2 August 1901; *Mitteilungen des Handelsvertragsvereins*, 3 August 1901.
198. Telegram from Bülow to Posadowsky, 23 July 1901, BA, R 1501, 118905, fols 344–45.
199. See *Post*, 25 July 1901; *Kreuzzeitung*, 29 July 1901, 30 July 1901.
200. *Deutsche Tageszeitung*, 27 July 1901, quoted in *Berliner Börsen-Zeitung*, 28 July 1901.
201. See the overviews of the international press reaction in *National-Zeitung*, 29 July 1901; *Vorwärts*, 30 July 1901; *Breslauer Zeitung*, 31 July 1901. The reports produced by the German embassies and consulates point in the same direction. See Romberg to Bülow, 1 August 1901, BA, R 1501, 118906, fol. 194; Maron to Bülow, 18 August 1901, BA, R 901, 11014, fols 93–94.
202. Wermuth, *Beamtenleben*, 225.
203. See *StenBerRT*, 1900–3, Attachments, no. 373.
204. See *StenBerRT*, 1900–3, 2883–84. (2 December 1901).
205. Ibid., 2909 (3 December 1901). The following quotation is from the same source.
206. Ibid., 2908 (3 December 1901).
207. On the following, apart from *StenBerRT*, 1900–3, 2883–3195 (2 December 1901 to 12 December 1901), and minutes of the meetings of the Customs Tariff Committee, BA, R 43, 318 and 319, see also Beidler, 'Kampf', 5ff., 21ff.; Bachem, *Vorgeschichte*, vol. 6, 129ff.; Schöne, 'Verflechtung'; Bleyberg, 'Government', 161–255; Alexander, *Freikonservative Partei*, 275ff.
208. See also the vote of the Eisenach conference of delegates on 12 October 1902 in *National-Zeitung*, 13 October 1902.
209. This relationship was embodied above all in the person of Wilhelm Beumer, executive director of the Langnamverein and of the Northwestern Group of the VDEStI, who entered the Reichstag in 1901 in place of Theodor Möller. See Schwarz, *MdR*, 269; Kaelble, *Industrielle Interessenpolitik*, 198.
210. See *Kreuzzeitung*, 29 August 1901; Bachem, *Vorgeschichte*, vol. 6, 153; Puhle, *Agrarische Interessenpolitik*, 193ff.; Bleyberg, 'Government', 181ff.
211. See Puhle, *Agrarische Interessenpolitik*, 215.
212. *Deutsche Tageszeitung*, 4 September 1901.
213. *StenBerRT*, 1900–3, 3052 (7 December 1901); 26th meeting of the Customs Tariff Committee, 21 February 1902, BA, R 43, 318, fol. 122.

214. 'Die Aussichten der Zolltarifvorlage', *Germania,* 24 December 1901. On this article, see also 'Zentrum und Zolltarif', *Berliner Neueste Nachrichten,* 24 December 1901; *Kölnische Zeitung,* 24 December 1901; 'Das Zentrum und der Zolltarif', *Vossische Zeitung,* 24 December 1901.
215. Report by the *Hamburger Echo* on a public gathering in Hamburg on 2 November 1901, quoted in Beidler, 'Kampf', 11; original emphasis.
216. Speech by Richter, *StenBerRT,* 1900–3, 2920 (3 December 1901); original emphasis.
217. Speech by Richter, *StenBerRT,* 1900–3, 6740ff. (1 December 1902).
218. See the speech by Bebel, *StenBerRT,* 1900–3, 6745ff. (1 December 1902). See also Beidler, 'Kampf', 7–8; Bleyberg, 'Government', 200.
219. See the statement by Thielmann, 5 March 1902, BA, R 43, 318, fol. 150; meeting of the State Ministry on 6 March 1902, BA, R 43, 318, fols 179–80; 34th meeting of the Customs Tariff Committee, 7 March 1902, BA, R 43, 318, fol. 181; *StenBerRT,* 1900–3, 5116–41 (28 April 1902); *StenBerRT,* 1900–3, 5231–66 (2 May 1902); 'Wie steht's mit dem Zolltarif', *Kölnische Volkszeitung,* 21 March 1902. See also Alexander, *Freikonservative Partei,* 280–81; Butzer, *Diäten,* 222ff.
220. *Zukunft,* 25 January 1902.
221. See Kardorff, *Wilhelm von Kardorff,* 347; Bleyberg, 'Government', 218ff.; Alexander, *Freikonservative Partei,* 278.
222. 22nd meeting of the Customs Tariff Committee, 14 February 1902, BA, R 43, 318, fol. 105.
223. Kardorff to his wife, 21 February 1902, quoted in Kardorff, *Wilhelm von Kardorff,* 348.
224. 'Die Herabsetzung der Industriezölle', *Deutsche Tageszeitung,* 19 April 1902; original emphasis. See also *Deutsche Tageszeitung,* 23 April 1902, 3 May 1902. See also: 'Der Bund der Freihändler mit den Agrariern', *Berliner Neueste Nachrichten,* 18 February 1902.
225. 65th meeting of the Customs Tariff Committee, 18 June 1902, BA, R 43, 319.
226. See esp. the 65th to the 70th meetings of the Customs Tariff Committee, 18 June 1902 to 25 June 1902, BA, R 43, 319. See also Bleyberg, 'Government', 241–45.
227. Jagemann to Brauer, 21 February 1902, quoted in Fuchs (ed.), *Großherzog Friedrich,* vol. 4, 384.
228. See Lerman, *Chancellor,* 76–77.
229. See *StenBerRT,* 1900–3, Attachments, no. 704, 4374–75.
230. The so-called Schwerin-Herold-Kardorff compromise motion, which proposed increasing the minimum tariff, was signed by fifteen members of the committee. Of these, seven (Herold, Gröber, Klose, Pingen, Spahn, Speck, Trimborn) were deputies for the Centre Party and five (Schwerin, Kardorff, Gamp, Kanitz, Rettich) for the Conservatives or the Imperial Party. Of the National Liberals, only Sieg, a manorial lord, signed. See 24th meeting of the Customs Tariff Committee, 19 February 1902, BA, R 43, 318, fol. 110.
231. 26th meeting of the Customs Tariff Committee, 21 February 1902, BA, R 43, 318, fol. 121.

232. Posadowsky's statement to the Customs Tariff Committee, 25th meeting of the Customs Tariff Committee, 20 February 1902, BA, R 43, 318, fol. 115. See also Bülow's speech at an Agricultural Council banquet, *Kreuzzeitung,* 16 February 1902; Thielmann's statement, 27th meeting of the Customs Tariff Committee, 24 February 1902, BA, R 43, 318.
233. See *StenBerRT,* 1900–3, Attachments, no. 704, 4374–75; *StenBerRT,* 1900–3, Attachments, no. 704 b, 4586ff.
234. 42nd meeting of the Customs Tariff Committee, 15 April 1902, BA, R 43, 318, fol. 252. See 41st meeting of the Customs Tariff Committee, 11 April 1902, BA, R 43, 318, fols 240–48.
235. 41st meeting of the Customs Tariff Committee, 11 April 1902, BA, R 43, 318, fol. 247.
236. 42nd meeting of the Customs Tariff Committee, 15 April 1902, BA, R 43, 318, fol. 253.
237. *StenBerRT,* 1900–3, Attachments, no. 704, 4393ff.
238. Quotations can be found in the confidential discussion at the State Ministry on 10 February 1902, BA, R 43, 2031, fols 196, 199. See also BA, R 43, 2031, fols 201–2.
239. *StenBerRT,* 1900–3, 5687 (16 October 1902).
240. Ibid.
241. See Bülow, *Deutsche Politik,* 311–15; Bülow, *Denkwürdigkeiten,* vol. 1, 591–92.
242. See, e.g., Bleyberg, 'Government', passim; Alexander, *Freikonservative Partei,* 288–89.
243. Cf. the states' declarations of agreement with Bülow's intransigent attitude in the Reichstag: BA, R 1501, 118919.
244. Confidential note by Bülow on his discussion with the emperor, meeting of the State Ministry on 11 November 1901, GStAPK, I. HA, Rep. 90a, B III 2 b no. 6 vol. 143, fols 77 a–c.
245. *StenBerRT,* 1900–3, 5690 (16 October 1902).
246. On this complex, see Rauh, *Parlamentarisierung;* Langewiesche, 'Das Deutsche Kaiserreich'; Zwehl, 'Verhältnis von Regierung und Reichstag'; Boldt, 'Von der konstitutionellen Monarchie zur parlamentarischen Demokratie'; Kühne, 'Parlamentarismusgeschichte'; Schönberger, 'Parlamentarisierung'; Anderson, *Practicing Democracy.*
247. *StenBerRT,* 1900–3, 5706 (16 October 1902).
248. Ibid.
249. *Nation,* 18 October 1902.
250. See, e.g., *Kreuzzeitung,* 17 October 1902; *Post,* 17 October 1902; *Germania,* 17 October 1902; *Kölnische Volkszeitung,* 17 October 1902.
251. See *StenBerRT,* 1900–3, 5690–704 (16 October 1902).
252. See ibid., 5820–41 (17 October 1902).
253. See Beidler, 'Kampf', 11–12.
254. *StenBerRT,* 1900–3, 5834 (21 October 1902).
255. Ibid., 5854 (22 October 1902).
256. On this point, and the following remarks in general, see Kardorff, *Wilhelm von Kardorff,* 351–52; Beidler, 'Kampf', 29ff.; Bachem, *Vorgeschichte,* vol. 6,

155ff.; Witt, *Finanzpolitik,* 71–72; Bleyberg, 'Government', 266ff.; Alexander, *Freikonservative Partei,* 283ff.

257. Witt's notion (*Finanzpolitik,* 72n92) that a minimum tariff of 1.3 marks per quintal was set for feed barley is incorrect. In fact it was the tariff, included in the general tariff, of 7 marks per quintal that applied to feed barley. Only through the later trade treaties was it reduced to 1.3 marks per quintal.
258. The import of barley as animal feed greatly exceeded that of oats. See Dade, 'Agrarzölle', 95. The proposal to divide the barley tariff in two already appears here.
259. Bachem, *Vorgeschichte,* vol. 6, 155.
260. Kardorff's motion also included the agreed-to reduction in tariffs on agricultural machinery. See *StenBerRT,* 1900–3, Attachments, no. 775.
261. Motion by Herold, *StenBerRT,* 1900–3, Attachments, no. 790.
262. *StenBerRT,* 1900–3, 6651 (27 November 1902).
263. See ibid.; Beidler, 'Kampf', 32; Bachem, *Vorgeschichte,* vol. 6, 157; Alexander, *Freikonservative Partei,* 287n73.
264. *StenBerRT,* 1900–3, 6655 (27 November 1902).
265. See ibid., 6654 (27 November 1902), and the account in *Berliner Tageblatt,* 28 November 1902.
266. *StenBerRT,* 1900–3, 6743 (1 December 1902).
267. See the voting record in *StenBerRT,* 1900–3, 7240–47. The Centre Party voted unanimously for the customs tariff, while Büsing from the National Liberals and Gersdorff from the Free Conservatives voted against. Alexander's (*Freikonservative Partei,* 288) claim that the Imperial Party voted as one for the tariff is thus incorrect.
268. See Bhagwati, *Protectionism,* 22–23, 41–42; Eichengreen, 'Political Economy'; Irwin, 'From Smoot-Hawley'; Irwin and Kroszner, 'Log-Rolling'; the classical analysis is Schattschneider, *Politics.*
269. Meeting of the State Ministry on 22 November 1897, BA, R 43, 2028, fol. 30.
270. See *Korrespondenz des BdL,* 13 December 1902, BA, R 1501, 118928, fols 48–55. Kardorff himself resigned from the BdL in late December 1902 after it had attacked him and his party on a number of occasions, declaring: 'In view of the fact that the president of the Agrarian League has seen fit to declare war on the German Imperial Party, my party colleagues self-evidently *cannot* be members of the Agrarian League.' 'Reichspartei und Bund der Landwirte', *Die Post,* 27 December 1902. See also Kardorff, *Wilhelm von Kardorff,* 354ff.
271. See, e.g., Puhle, *Agrarische Interessenpolitik,* 241–42; Stegmann, *Erben Bismarcks,* 14, 111; Vogel, *Rußlandpolitik,* 28; Wehler, *German Empire,* 97. The locus classicus is Kehr, *Battleship Building,* 212ff.
272. Bleyberg, 'Government', 308, ultimately comes to the same conclusion. Eley's critique, meanwhile, is based on an empirical analysis restricted to the events of 1897/98. See Eley, 'Sammlungspolitik'.
273. The most prominent example here is the assurance given by Thielmann on 1 May 1900 in the Reichstag budgetary committee that the 'allied governments ... are determined to do their utmost to uphold the interests of German agriculture with respect to the protection of its products in designing the

customs tariff now underway and in concluding new trade treaties', a statement on which Kehr also based his arguments. See Kehr, *Battleship Building*, 215–16.

274. For an argument very much in this vein, see Bönker, *Militarism*, 229–32.
275. The contemporary historical actors could not know that the survivors' fund established through the Trimborn Act would not benefit financially over the long term through the bill of entry system. See Gerloff, *Finanz- und Zollpolitik*, 388–89; Witt, *Finanzpolitik*, 72ff.
276. Borchardt, 'Protektionismus', 26, 42ff.; Marsh, *Joseph Chamberlain*, 564ff.; Verdier, *Democracy*, 142–43.

## Chapter 6

1. See above, chapter 4.
2. If we retain the calculation basis that applied up to and including 1896 and thus treat Finland as part of Russia, we come up with a figure for German imports for 1903 of no less than 838 million marks. For the figures, see table 1.7.
3. German exports to Russia, including Finland, were worth 366 million marks in 1899. For the figures, see table 1.5.
4. See *StDR* 165 A. 1905, V. 5; head of the statistical office to RI, 2 May 1902, BA, R 901, 10567; Arndt, 'Zum Abschluß eines neuen deutsch-russischen Handelsvertrages', 12–20; Ballod, 'Die deutsch-russischen Handelsbeziehungen', 279ff.; Vogel, *Rußlandpolitik*, 66ff.
5. See Maron to Bülow, 8 May 1903, BA, R 901, 10569; Biermann to Bülow, 28 May 1906, in Lemke (ed.), *Deutsch-russische Wirtschaftsbeziehungen*, 60; Arndt, 'Zum Abschluß eines neuen deutsch-russischen Handelsvertrages', 12–20; Human, *Der deutsch-russische Handels- und Schiffahrtsvertrag*, 55ff.; Ballod, 'Die deutsch-russischen Handelsbeziehungen', 279ff.; Vogel, *Rußlandpolitik*, 66ff.
6. See, e.g., the AA note on the Russian proposals on the new German-Russian trade treaty, 24 June 1903, BA, R 901, 11027, fol. 28; German response to the Russian proposals, forwarded to Alvensleben on 16 July 1903, BA, R 901, 11027, fols 94ff.
7. My own calculations, based on *StHbDR*, section 2, 528, and table 1.7 in this text.
8. My own calculations, based on *StDR* 165 A. 1905, V. 3. See *StHbDR*, section 2, 148ff.; Beckmann, 'Entwicklung des deutsch-russischen Getreideverkehrs'.
9. See Geyer, *Der russische Imperialismus*, 110, table 8; Wixforth, 'Wirtschaft', 231ff. See also Nötzold, *Wirtschaftspolitische Alternativen*, 121ff.; Hildermeier, *Russische Revolution*, 26.
10. My own calculations based on *StHbDR*, section 2, 94–102.
11. *StDR* 165 A. 1905, V. 5.
12. See Geyer, *Der russische Imperialismus*, 34; Metzer, 'Railroads'; Wixforth, 'Wirtschaft', 231–32.
13. *StHbDR*, section 2, 299, 305, 307.

14. See Plumpe, *I.G. Farbenindustrie*, 57ff.; Pohl, *Geschäft*, 40ff.
15. See Esslen, *Fleischversorgung*, 113ff.; Teichmann, *Politik der Agrarpreisstützung*, 596ff.; Hunt, 'Peasants', 314–15; Wottawa, *Protektionismus*, 52ff.; Aldenhoff-Hübinger, *Agrarpolitik*, 155ff.
16. See *StHbDR*, section 2, 421; meeting of the State Ministry on 3 November 1896, BA, R 43, 419, fol. 48 (the minutes, fols 44–53, can also be found in BA, R 901, 10669, fols 39–48).
17. Meeting of the State Ministry on 3 November 1896, BA, R 43, 419, fol. 44.
18. See the meeting of the various imperial and Prussian ministries on the trade in agricultural products with Russia and the U.S., 3 October 1896, BA, R 1501, 104866, fol. 31; memorandum, late 1896, BA, R 901, 10669, fols 222–30.
19. Meeting of the various imperial and Prussian ministries on the trade in agricultural products with Russia and the U.S., 3 October 1896, BA, R 1501, 104866, fol. 33.
20. Meeting of the State Ministry on 3 November 1896, BA, R 43, 419, fol. 50.
21. Ibid., fol. 51. See also Hammerstein's statement that it would 'cause uproar among agrarian circles' were 'the measure to be withdrawn'. Ibid., fol. 48.
22. Ibid., fol. 45.
23. See the meeting of the various imperial and Prussian ministries on the trade in agricultural products with Russia and the U.S., 3 October 1896, BA, R 1501, 104866, fol. 34; meeting of the State Ministry on 31 December 1896, BA, R 901, 10669, fol. 252.
24. Minutes of the conference sessions, BA, R 901, 10669, fols 117–88.
25. Meeting of the State Ministry on 9 December 1896, BA, R 43, 419, fol. 86.
26. See Upper Silesian Mining and Metallurgical Union to Marschall, 19 November 1896, BA, R 1501, 104866, fols 88ff.; executive board of the Eastern Group of the VDEStI to Marschall, 20 November 1896, BA, R 1501, 104866, fols 92–93.
27. See the final protocol to the German-Russian conference, Berlin 1896/97, BA, R 43, 419, fols 104–11; Hohenlohe-Schillingsfürst to Wilhelm II, 12 January 1897, BA, R 901, 10669, fols 335–37.
28. See the meetings of the State Ministry on 31 December 1896, 6 January 1897 and 28 January 1897, BA, R 901, 10669, fols 248ff., 302ff., 386ff.
29. Reichardt at the meeting of the State Ministry on 6 January 1897, BA, R 901, 10669, fol. 305.
30. See only the petition of the executive boards of the Christian peasants' associations concerning the conclusion of a trade treaty, BA, R 43, 314, fols 85–89; 'Deutscher Eigensinn?', *Deutsche Tageszeitung*, 2 September 1903; 'Ueber die Handelsvertragsverhandlungen mit Rußland', *Deutsche Tageszeitung*, 24 March 1904.
31. Klinckowstroem had already broached the subject of the railway tariff on several occasions in the Prussian House of Lords. See the meeting of the State Ministry on 29 November 1897, BA, R 43, 2028, fol. 49. On the Klinckowstroem resolution, see also the statement by Thielen, 24 January 1901, BA, R 43, 305 b, fols 1–6; Imperial Railway Office (Reichseisenbahnamt), outline of a statement to be submitted to the RT budgetary committee, BA, R 43, 305 b,

fols 7–9; statement by Thielen, 8 May 1901, BA, R 43, 305 b, fols 14–15; office of the president of the Königsberg Merchants' Association (Kaufmannschaft zu Königsberg) to RT, 20 January 1901, BA, R 901, 11019, fol. 66 (41 pages); 'Zum deutsch-russischen Handelsvertrage', *Deutsche Tageszeitung,* 24 March 1901. For a general discussion, see also Vogel, *Rußlandpolitik,* 69–72.

32. Meeting concerning the extension of the German-Russian trade treaty, 23 February 1903, BA, R 1501, 104887, fol. 19. See also the statement by Podbielski, 5 March 1903, GStAPK, I. HA, Rep. 120, C XIII 6 a no. 35 vol. 8.
33. See the report on the fourth annual general meeting of the German-Russian Association, held on 23 May 1902, 16, BA, R 901, 11017.
34. See Vogel, *Rußlandpolitik,* 125–26; Geyer, *Der russische Imperialismus,* 129; Kestler, *Betrachtungen,* 274.
35. See Maron to Bülow, 18 August 1901, BA, R 901, 11014, fols 93–94; *National-Zeitung,* 29 July 1901; *Breslauer Zeitung,* 31 July 1901; *Hamburgischer Correspondent,* 7 August 1901.
36. For details of the demands made by the associations of trade and industry, see CVDI to Bülow, 12 February 1903, BA, R 901, 11020, fols 169ff.; preferences of the Black Forest HK in Villingen with respect to the trade treaty with Russia, BA, R 901, 11020, fols 207–16; HVV memorandum setting out its preferences with respect to the new trade treaties, sent on 2 March 1903, BA, R 901, 11021, fols 24ff.; Association of German Dyestuff and Tanning Agent Extract Manufacturers (Verein Deutscher Farbstoff- und Gerbstoff-Extract Fabrikanten) to Bülow, February 1903, BA, R 901, 11021, fols 75–76; Upper Silesian Coke Works and Chemicals Plants (Oberschlesische Kokswerke und Chemische Fabriken AG) to Bülow, 11 March 1903, BA, R 901, 11021, fols 77ff.; submission by the German-Russian Association, 30 March 1903, BA, R 901, 11022, fols 59–60 (3 issues); CVDI to Bülow, 25 April 1903, BA, R 901, 11024, fols 42–46.
37. Association of Export Commissioning Firms, Berlin, to Bülow, 23 February 1903, BA, R 901, 10087.
38. Report on the fifth annual general meeting of the German-Russian Association, held on 18 April 1903, 60, BA, R 901, 11030. See also German-Russian Association to Bülow, 30 March 1903, dispatch of materials and proposals regarding a new trade treaty between Germany and Russia, BA, R 901, 11022, fols 64–65.
39. CVDI to Bülow, 12 February 1903, BA, R 901, 11020, fol. 169.
40. German-Russian Association to Bülow, 30 March 1903, dispatch of materials and proposals regarding a new trade treaty between Germany and Russia, BA, R 901, 11022, fols 68, 71.
41. See CVDI to Bülow, 12 February 1903, BA, R 901, 11020, fol. 169. See also CVDI to Richthofen, 25 April 1903, BA, R 901, 11024, fols 42ff.; Association of Export Commissioning Firms, Berlin, to Bülow, 23 February 1903, BA, R 901, 10087.
42. On the concept of transaction costs, see only Williamson, *Economic Institutions;* Picot and Dietl, 'Transaktionskostentheorie'; North, 'Institutions'; Richter and Furubotn, *Neue Institutionenökonomik,* 45ff.

43. German-Russian Association to Bülow, 30 March 1903, dispatch of materials and proposals regarding a new trade treaty between Germany and Russia, BA, R 901, 11022, fol. 64. See the report on the fifth annual general meeting of the German-Russian Association, held on 18 April 1903, 25, BA, R 901, 11030.
44. Maron to Bülow, 30 January 1903, BA, R 901, 11020, fols 142, 145. On the following, see also Vogel, *Rußlandpolitik,* 127–28.
45. See Bülow to Richthofen, 3 February 1903, BA, R 901, 11020, fol. 146.
46. See Richthofen to Osten-Sacken, 30 January 1903, BA, R 901, 11019.
47. See PA AA, 007781, Körner personal files.
48. Maron to Bülow, 30 January 1903, BA, R 901, 11020, fol. 145 (marginal note added by Körner).
49. Note by Körner on Maron's reports of 30 January and 9 February 1903, undated, BA, R 901, 11020, fol. 152.
50. See Thielmann to Richthofen, 19 March 1903, BA, R 901, 11021, fol. 126.
51. Note by Johannes, 11 March 1903, BA, R 901, 11021, fol. 61.
52. See minutes of the commissarial meetings on 25 February and 6 March 1903, BA, R 1501, 104887, fols 45–51, 80–84; note by Johannes, 11 March 1903, BA, R 901, 11021, fol. 61; Thielmann to Richthofen, 19 March 1903, BA, R 901, 11021, fol. 126.
53. See note by Körner, 24 June 1903, BA, R 901, 11027, fol. 30: 'At this point in the proceedings, as Count Posadowsky agrees, it is probably best to refrain from consulting the Economic Committee.'
54. See *StenBerRT,* 1903–5, attachments, no. 543, memorandum, 2.
55. Goebel's note to Bülow, 24 April 1903, BA, R 901, 11024, fol. 145.
56. See Vogel, *Rußlandpolitik,* 130ff.
57. Goebel's note, 10 April 1903, BA, R 901, 11023, fol. 73.
58. Kapp's statement at the commissarial meeting on 21 February 1903, BA, R 1501, 104887, fol. 2.
59. See minutes of the commissarial meeting on 23 February 1903, BA, R 1501, 104887, fols 19ff.
60. See Podbielski to Bülow, 11 March 1903, BA, R 43, 314, fols 40–43; Goebel's note to Bülow, 24 April 1903, BA, R 901, 11024, fol. 145.
61. Statement by Richthofen, 30 April 1903, BA, R 43, 314, fol. 75. See also Möller's statement in favour (MHG), 11 May 1903, BA, R 43, 314, fol. 83.
62. See the detailed account in Vogel, *Rußlandpolitik,* 140–47.
63. See Körner to Bülow, 28 August 1903, BA, R 901, 11029, fols 168–77; Körner to Bülow, 2 September 1903, BA, R 901, 11029, fols 194–99; note by Körner, 21 June 1904, BA, R 901, 11035, fol. 151.
64. Körner to Bülow, 16 August 1903, BA, R 901, 11029, fol. 139.
65. Körner to Bülow, 2 September 1903, BA, R 901, 11029, fol. 195.
66. Note by Körner, 18 November 1903, BA, R 901, 11032, fol. 126. On the meeting of the departmental heads on 6 November 1903, see note by Körner, 6 November 1903, BA, R 901, 11032, fol. 22–24; preparatory survey, BA, R 901, 11032, fol. 30; Posadowsky to Bülow, 29 October 1903, BA, R 43, 305 b, fols 24–28.
67. Note by Körner, 18 November 1903, BA, R 901, 11032, fols 131–32.

68. See prerequisites for the continuation of the negotiations concerning renewal of the German-Russian trade treaty, BA, R 901, 11033, fols 22–25; note by Körner, 21 June 1904, BA, R 901, 11035, fol. 152.
69. AA note, 21 February 1903, BA, R 901, 11034, fol. 78.
70. See Vogel, *Rußlandpolitik,* 152; AA note, 21 February 1904, BA, R 901, 11034, fol. 78.
71. See note by Körner, 15 October 1903, BA, R 43, 305 b, fols 18–23; Posadowsky to Bülow, 29 October 1903, BA, R 43, 305 b, fols 24–28. The Caprivi treaties were due to lapse at the end of 1903, but had to be rescinded a year earlier. They would otherwise have automatically continued to apply until twelve months after their abrogation. As long as they existed the Bülow tariff could not come into force.
72. Alvensleben to Bülow, 8 March 1904, BA, R 901, 11034, fol. 118.
73. See, e.g., ibid., fol. 119.
74. For a general account of the origins and course of the war, see Nish, *Origins of the Russo-Japanese War*; Westwood, *Russia against Japan*; Connaughton, *War of the Rising Sun.*
75. For a general account of what follows, see also Vogel, *Rußlandpolitik,* 174ff.; Wulff, 'Handelsvertrag'; Spaulding, *Osthandel,* 81ff.; Kusber, *Krieg,* 200–1.
76. Wilhelm II to Nikolai II, 29 March 1904, in Goetz, *Briefe Wilhelms II.,* no. 33.
77. Moeller to state commissioner at the stock exchange in Frankfurt am Main, 28 April 1904, quoted in Vogel, *Rußlandpolitik,* 177.
78. See note by Lehmann, 17 April 1904, BA, R 901, 11034, fols 168–69; Maron to Bülow, 22 April 1904, BA, R 901, 11034, fols 173ff.
79. Minutes of the meeting of the Russian ministerial conference of 14 May 1904, quoted in Wulff, 'Handelsvertrag', 134–35.
80. Romberg to AA, 5 June 1904, BA, R 901, 11035, fol. 93. See also Romberg to Bülow, 10 June 1904, BA, R 901, 11035, fols 120–22.
81. See Witte, *Memoirs,* 413–14.
82. See Grimm, 'Graf Witte', 41ff.; Vogel, *Rußlandpolitik,* 179.
83. On the preceding remarks, see prerequisites for the continuation of the negotiations concerning renewal of the German-Russian trade treaty, BA, R 901, 11033, fols 22–25; note by Körner, 21 June 1904, BA, R 901, 11035, fols 151–58; Bülow to Lucanus, 28 July 1904, BA, R 43, 305 b, fols 63–74a; *StenBerRT,* 1903–5, attachments, no. 543; *StenBerRT,* 1903–5, memorandum, 9–17; 'Die Handelsverträge', *Berliner Tageblatt,* 30 January 1905; 'Die gegenseitigen Zugeständnisse im deutsch-russischen Handelsvertrag', *Münchener Allgemeine Zeitung,* 31 January 1905; 'Die neuen Handelsverträge', *Dresdner Journal,* 30 January 1905; Reichsamt des Innern, *Die Handelsverträge des Deutschen Reichs,* 836–911; Vogel, *Rußlandpolitik,* 181, 291–92; Spaulding, *Osthandel,* 83.
84. Bismarck to Lucanus, 28 July 1904, BA, R 43, 305 b, fols 70, 74. See also Bülow's message to Rheinbaben and Stengel of 29 July 1904 – the day after the signing of the treaty – explaining that Witte had been given an assurance that the German market would now be open to Russian bonds; BA, R 43, 305 b, fols 75–77.
85. Richthofen on the RT committee, quoted in Schulthess, *Europäischer Geschichtskalender,* vol. 21 (1905), 42–43.

86. 'Der letzte Akt', *Deutsche Tageszeitung,* 8 February 1905. Cf. 'An der Schwelle der neuen Entwickelung', *Leipziger Neueste Nachrichten,* 9 February 1905.
87. 'Die neuen Handelsverträge', *Frankfurter Zeitung,* 8 February 1905. See also 'Die Handelsverträge', *Berliner Tageblatt,* 30 January 1905; 'Eine Erschwerung der deutschen Ausfuhr', *Berliner Tageblatt,* 31 January 1905.
88. See *StenBerRT,* 1903–5, 4715–17 (22 February 1905). The trade treaty with Russia was adopted by 228 votes to 81 with 3 abstentions; *StenBerRT,* 1903–5, 4713. See also Vogel, *Rußlandpolitik,* 186; Altrichter, *Konstitutionalismus,* 176ff.
89. *Export,* 29 June 1911. The percentages provided by Ehrl, *Entwicklung der Wirtschaftsbeziehungen,* 31, and Spaulding, *Osthandel,* 87, meanwhile, are based on the erroneous Russian statistics. Even informed contemporaries knew better.
90. *StDR* 271, 1914, V. 1.
91. My own calculations, based on *StJbDR* 35, 1914, 281.
92. My own calculations, based on the figures in *Export,* 29 June 1911.
93. These and the following figures are my own calculations, based on *StHbDR,* section 2, 154–55; *StJbDR* 35, 1914, 182–83.
94. See *Export,* 29 June 1911; Brentano, *Getreidezölle,* 25ff.; Teichmann, *Politik der Agrarpreisstützung,* 193ff.; Hentschel, *Wirtschaft und Wirtschaftspolitik,* 198ff.
95. Report on the extraordinary general meeting of the German-Russian Association on 3 June 1905, BA, R 901, 11040–1, fol. 46. See also BA, R 901, 11040–1, fol. 18; Löhr, *'Zukunft Rußlands',* 60–64.
96. 1911 report by the German-Russian Association, p. 22, BA, R 901, 6270, fol. 118. See BA, R 901, 6270, p. 24, fol. 119. On the preceding remarks, see also Zuckermann, *Warenaustausch,* iv–xii; Lehrfreund, *Entwicklung der deutsch-russischen Handelsbeziehungen*; Geyer, *Der russische Imperialismus,* 198ff.; Löhr, *'Zukunft Rußlands',* 143–70; Spaulding, *Osthandel,* 84ff.
97. See *National-Zeitung,* 26 June 1912; *Berliner Börsen-Courier,* 14 October 1913; *Kölnische Zeitung,* 2 March 1914; *Rheinisch-Westfälische Zeitung,* 22 March 1914; Wernecke, *Wille zur Weltgeltung,* 249ff.; Altrichter, *Konstitutionalismus,* 178ff.; Spaulding, *Osthandel,* 88ff.
98. Kohlhaas to German embassy in St. Petersburg, 16 September 1907, quoted in Lemke, *Deutsch-russische Wirtschaftsbeziehungen,* 114.
99. Report by Consul Kohlhaas to Bethmann, 19 June 1911, BA, R 901, 6270, fols 24–25. See *Berliner Börsen-Courier,* 14 October 1913; German-Russian Association to AA, 31 January 1914, BA, R 901, 6273, fols 203–4.
100. Report by consul general Biermann to Bethmann, 8 July 1913, BA, R 901, 6273, fols 8–9.
101. On this and the following remarks, see Hamilton, 'Report', 296ff.; Bairoch, *Economics,* 32ff.; Gilpin, *Political Economy,* 180–81; Irwin, *Against the Tide,* 121–22; Eckes, *Opening America's Market,* 15ff.
102. The ratio of duties to imports is often cited in the research as an indicator of the level of protectionism, but this entails a dual methodological problem. First, it takes no account of the impact of nontariff trade restrictions. Second, it is blind to duties so high that they have a prohibitive effect and are therefore de facto not collected.
103. See figure 6.1. All figures based on Bureau of the Census, *Historical Statistics of the United States,* vol. 2, 888.

104. On the preceding remarks, see Taussig, *Tariff History*, 155–446; Fisk, 'Handelspolitik', 4ff.; Terrill, *Tariff*, 159ff.; Becker, *Dynamics*, 69ff.; Bairoch, *Economics*, 36ff.; Trubowitz, *Defining the National Interest*, 80ff.
105. See Fisk, 'Handelspolitik', 23ff.; Stanwood, *American Tariff Controversies*, vol. 2, 243ff.; Taussig, *Tariff History*, 275ff.; Terrill, *Tariff*, 159–83; Crapol, *America*, 166ff.; Crapol and Schonberger, 'Shift', 172ff.; Fiebig-von Hase, *Lateinamerika*, 591–92.
106. For a general take on the last two paragraphs, see Wehler, *Aufstieg des amerikanischen Imperialismus*, 74–91; Pletcher, 'Reciprocity'; Pletcher, *Diplomacy*, 256ff.; Terril, *Tarriff*, 159–83, 53ff.; Fiebig-von Hase, *Lateinamerika*, 589ff., 665ff.; Trubowitz, *Defining the National Interest*, 75ff.; Eckes, *Opening America's Market*, 70–77.
107. Quoted in Trubowitz, *Defining the National Interest*, 84.
108. On the export dependency and foreign markets of the different U.S. regions, see Hutchinson, 'Regional Exports to Foreign Countries'; Hutchinson, 'Regional Exports of the United States'; Novack and Simon, 'Some Dimensions'.
109. See Bensel, *Political Economy*, 469–70, 475ff. On the 'Great Debate' of 1888, see Reitano, *Tariff Question*.
110. For a superb analysis, see Bensel, *Sectionalism*, 62–73; Bensel, *Political Economy*, 457–509; Trubowitz, *Defining the National Interest*, 75–95. See also Dearing, *Veterans*, 287–88, 364ff.; Verdier, *Democracy*, 115ff.; Lake, *Power*, 19–65.
111. See Jasper, 'Strukturwandlungen', 270–71; Fiebig-von Hase, 'Wirtschaftsbeziehungen', 332.
112. See Bureau of the Census, *Historical Statistics of the United States*, vol. 2, 906–7.
113. Quoted in memorandum for the International Trade Conference in Philadelphia, presented by J. van der Zypen, 20 September 1899, BA, R 901, 12218. For a general account, see the flood of submissions and petitions in the files of the Trade Policy Department of the AA, BA, R 901, 12216–57, and BA, R 901, 4576–82.
114. Quoted in memorandum for the International Trade Conference in Philadelphia, presented by J. van der Zypen, 20 September 1899, BA, R 901, 12218.
115. Minutes of the confidential conference organized by the HVV and BdI on the commercial and trade policy relations between the German Empire and the U.S. on 29 November 1909, BA, R 901, 4615, fol. 147.
116. See, e.g., Glastetter, *Außenwirtschaftspolitik*, 185–86.
117. On this and the following, see note on the current state of sanitary measures and Germany's trade relations with the U.S. in general, sent to the AA from the RI on 18 October 1899, BA, 1501, 103090, fols 26–27; compilation of proposals by interested German parties (United States of America. Printed matter no. 3. Confidential) as at the end of August 1905, BA, R 901, 12260, fols 178–213; CVDI, CVH and BdI to Bülow, 7 February 1906, BA, R 43, 308, fols 45–46; memorandum for the WA, April 1907, BA, R 901, 4585, fols 55–61; excerpt from the statements of trade representatives on the decrees by the MHG of 7 April 1906, concerning the tariffing regulations of the U.S., BA, R 901, 4576, fols 8–22; Harburg HK to Bülow, 8 December 1906, BA, R 901, 4576, fols 134–38; *Berliner Lokalanzeiger*, 21 November 1906; *Deutsche Tageszeitung*, 27 January 1907; *Vossische Zeitung*, 8 March 1907; *Der Tag*, 14 April 1907;

*Frankfurter Zeitung,* 27 April 1907; *Der Deutsche Handelstag,* vol. 2, 583–85; Fisk, 'Handelspolitik', 9–23.

118. The Faber company to the chambers of trade and commerce for Middle Franconia, Nuremberg, 24 September 1906, BA, R 901, 4576, fol. 36.
119. Ibid.
120. See only Ripperger, *Ökonomik des Vertrauens;* Siegenthaler, *Regelvertrauen;* Fiedler, 'Vertrauen'; Zucker, 'Production of Trust'.
121. *Frankfurter Zeitung,* 27 April 1907. See *Berliner Lokalanzeiger,* 21 November 1906; Richthofen to Sternburg, etc., 16 March 1905, BA, R 901, 12260, 10–11.
122. *StHbDR,* section 2, 550–51. See Ballod, 'Die deutsch-amerikanischen Handelsbeziehungen', 181.
123. See Steinberg, *Wirtschaftskrise;* Eulenburg, 'Wirtschaftskrise'; Lotz, 'Wirtschaftliche Krisis'; Vagts, *Deutschland,* 349ff.; Fiebig-von Hase, *Lateinamerika,* 325ff.
124. See *StDR* 165, B. 1904, XIX, 24ff.; *StDR* 271, 1914, XIX, 26–27; Prager, *Handelsbeziehungen,* 17–18.
125. *Export,* 13 June 1901.
126. Memorandum of the Association of Itinerant Merchants of Germany (Verband Reisender Kaufleute Deutschlands), 9 October 1901, quoted in Fiebig-von Hase, *Lateinamerika,* 347.
127. For an analysis in this vein, see also Fiebig-von Hase, *Lateinamerika,* 351ff. But cf. Vagts, *Deutschland,* 390ff.
128. See, e.g., Prager, *Die amerikanische Gefahr;* Sartorius von Waltershausen, *Handelsbilanz;* Wolf, 'Volkswirtschaft'; Lenschau, *Die amerikanische Gefahr;* Wiese, 'Die nordamerikanische Konkurrenz'; Knebel-Doberitz, *Besteht für Deutschland eine amerikanische Gefahr?;* Dietzel, *Der deutsch-amerikanische Handelsvertrag.*
129. See Schmidt-Gernig, 'Zukunftsmodell Amerika?', 88ff., and, more generally, Schmidt-Gernig, *Reisen in die Moderne.*
130. Schmoller, 'Wandlungen', 380.
131. On this paragraph, see Vagts, *Deutschland,* 345–425; Stegmann, *Erben Bismarcks,* 82ff.; Ullmann, *Bund der Industriellen,* 168–69, 204ff.; Fiebig-von Hase, *Lateinamerika,* 320–60; Fiebig-von Hase, 'USA und Europa', 20ff.; Fiebig-von Hase, 'United States', 42–43; Etges, *Wirtschaftsnationalismus,* 295–300.
132. On the meat inspection law, see Nonn, *Verbraucherprotest,* 116–21. This law was not, however, 'largely overlooked' by historians to the extent claimed by Nonn (116). See Böhm, *Überseehandel,* 224–35, and Teichmann, *Politik der Agrarpreisstützung,* 599ff., neither of whom Nonn mentions.
133. *Deutsche Tageszeitung,* 24 February 1907; original emphasis. See *Deutsche Tageszeitung,* 16 January 1907, 16 February 1907, 26 February 1907, 6 April 1907, 20 April 1907; Rhineland Peasants' Association (Rheinischer Bauern-Verein) to Bülow, 27 March 1907, BA, R 901, 4576, fol. 180; eighteenth report of the RT committee on petitions, BA, R 901, 4586, fols 6–7.
134. 'Bericht über die 14. Generalversammlung des BdL', *Deutsche Tageszeitung,* 12 February 1907.
135. See Kaelble, *Industrielle Interessenpolitik,* 155ff.; Ullmann, *Bund der Industriellen,* 204ff.; Theiner, '"Mitteleuropa"-Pläne', 134; Gottwald, 'Mitteleuropa-

organisationen', 365–66; Fiebig-von Hase, 'Wirtschaftsbeziehungen', 353ff.; Wolf, *Materialien*, 17ff., 36ff.

136. Central European Economic Association in Germany, memorandum concerning the reorganization of Germany's trade relations with the U.S., Berlin 1905, 36, BA, R 1501, 103086.
137. See ibid., 28ff., 88–89.
138. CVDI, CVH and BdI to Bülow, 7 February 1906, BA, R 43, 308, fol. 45.
139. Meeting of the Prussian State Ministry on 12 February 1906, BA, R 43, 308, fol. 78.
140. Summary of the results of the confidential discussion on German-American trade relations held on 29 November 1909 at the invitation of the BdI and HVV, BdI to Kempff, 14 October 1910, BA, R 901, 4615, fol. 151.
141. Minutes of the confidential conference organized by the HVV and BdI on the commercial and trade policy relations between the German Empire and the U.S. on 29 November 1909, BA, R 901, 4615, fol. 137.
142. Summary of the results of the confidential discussion on German-American trade relations held on 29 November 1909 at the invitation of the BdI and HVV, BdI to Kempff, 14 October 1910, BA, R 901, 4615, fols 151ff.; original emphasis. See the minutes of the conference, BA, R 901, 4615, fols 136–48.
143. *Plutus*, 11 May 1907.
144. See Fisk, *Beziehungen*, 176; Kaufmann, *Welt-Zuckerindustrie*, 380ff.; Prager, *Handelsbeziehungen*, 21ff.; Vagts, *Deutschland*, 10–11.
145. See Marschall's speech, *StenBerRT*, 1895–97, 5707 (3 May 1897). Similar arguments are made by Prager, *Handelsbeziehungen*, 29–30, and Vagts, *Deutschland*, 59. But cf. Sartorius von Waltershausen, *Deutschland*, 51; Borgius, *Deutschland*, 48.
146. See Prager, *Handelsbeziehungen*, 32ff.; Vagts, *Deutschland*, 82–120; Stone, 'Most-Favored Nation Relations', 433–34; Pommerin, *Kaiser*, 43–44.
147. See note on the current state of sanitary measures and Germany's trade relations with the U.S. in general, RI to AA, 18 October 1899, BA, R 1501, 103090, fols 25–26; *New Yorker Handelszeitung*, 23 December 1899.
148. AA memorandum, Bülow to Posadowsky-Wehner, 23 August 1899, BA, R 1501, 103085, fol. 5. See also note by Richthofen, 13 December 1899, BA, R 1501, 103090, fols 117–20; memorandum for the WA, April 1907, BA, R 901, 4585, fol. 55.
149. Commissarial meeting on the stance to be adopted in the negotiations with the U.S., 16 December 1899, BA, R 1501, 103090, fol. 257 (Schuckmann). See BA, R 1501, 103090, fol. 259 (Körner).
150. BA, R 1501, 103090, fol. 258 (Henle). See also Thielmann to Bülow, 3 December 1899, BA, R 1501, 103085, fols 12–13.
151. See Bülow to Posadowsky, 28 April 1900, BA, R 1501, 103091, fols 33–37. On the German preparations for the negotiations, see also note by Richthofen, 13 December 1899, BA, R 1501, 103090, fols 117–20; list of German preferences regarding the American customs tariff, undated, BA, R 1501, 103090, fols 212–17; explanation of German demands concerning the treaty negotiations with the U.S., undated, BA, R 1501, 103090, fols 218–48; German preferences

with respect to the procedures for dealing with the American consuls and the tariffing procedures in the U.S., undated, BA, R 1501, 103090, fols 24951; Posadowsky to AA, 22 December 1899, BA, R 1501, 103090, fols 253–54.

152. Körner to Posadowsky, 12 July 1900, BA, R 1501, 103091, fol. 66; American proclamation of the agreement, BA, R 1501, 103091, fol. 70.
153. See Goldberger, *Land,* 270.
154. Summary minutes of the commissarial meeting of 2 May 1900, BA, R 1501, 103091, fol. 55. See Prager, *Handelsbeziehungen,* 42–43.
155. Meeting of the State Ministry on 12 February 1906, BA, R 43, 308, fol. 79. See BA, R 43, 308, fols 77–84; Mühlberg, Posadowsky and Stengel to Bülow, 4 February 1906, BA, R 901, 4671; Bülow to Wilhelm II, 9 February 1906, BA, R 43, 308, fols 60–61; Sternburg to AA, 29 January 1906, BA, R 43, 308, fols 62–63; Sternburg to AA, 1 February 1906, BA, R 43, 308, fols 64–65; Sternburg to AA, 6 February 1906, BA, R 43, 308, fols 66–67; Sternburg to Bülow, 25 January 1906, BA, R 43, 308, fols 69–75.
156. See the reports on the North Commission in the German press: *Kölnische Zeitung,* 1 November 1906; *Hamburger Nachrichten,* 1 November 1906; *Deutsch-Amerikanische Korrespondenz,* 5 November 1906; *Vossische Zeitung,* 6 November 1906; *Berliner Tageblatt,* 17 November 1906; *Frankfurter Zeitung,* 17 November 1906; *Export,* 6 December 1906; *New Yorker Handelszeitung,* 5 January 1907; *New Yorker Handelszeitung,* 12 January 1907.
157. See Sternburg to AA, 10 January 1907, BA, R 901, 4583, fols 43–44; AA to Sternburg, 28 January 1907, BA, R 901, 4583, fols 126–48; the German commissioners' response to the American declarations of 3 and 5 December 1906, 10 December 1906, BA, R 901, 4589, fols 7–8; minutes of the negotiations with the North Committee, confidential discussions on the organization of German-American trade relations, BA, R 1501, 103098.
158. Memorandum for the WA, April 1907, p. 7, BA, R 901, 4585, fol. 58.
159. See *Deutsche Export-Revue,* 1 July 1906; *Hamburgischer Korrespondent,* 10 November 1906; *Der Tag,* 19 January 1907.
160. Körner to Sternburg, 19 March 1907, BA, R 901, 4584, fols 147–48.
161. See Posadowsky's speech, *StenBerRT,* 1907, 1469 (7 May 1907); stenographic record of the WA's negotiations on the trade agreement with the U.S. held in the RI on 22 April 1907, BA, R 1501, 103097; note by AA, undated (January 1907), BA, R 901, 4583, fol. 59; AA to Sternburg, 28 January 1907, BA, R 901, 4583, fol. 132; Bülow to Wilhelm II, 21 April 1907, BA, R 901, 4585, fols 152–54.
162. Mühlberg, Posadowsky and Stengel to Bülow, 4 February 1906, BA, R 43, 308, fols 57–58.
163. See note by AA, undated (January 1901), BA, R 901, 4583, fol. 61; AA to Sternburg, 28 January 1907, BA, R 901, 4583, fol. 143; Bülow to Wilhelm II, 21 April 1907, BA, R 901, 4585, fol. 153; memorandum for the WA, April 1907, p. 12–13, BA, R 901, 4585, fol. 61.
164. Stenographic record of the WA's negotiations on the trade agreement with the U.S. held in the RI on 22 April 1907, BA, R 1501, 103097, fol. 288. Cf. *Der Tag,* 25 April 1907.

165. The Underwood-Simmons tariff meant that trade treaties could again be concluded with the approval of Congress. But while the tariff negotiations were still going on the Democrats declared that they had no intention of using this law, so it was of no practical significance. See Prager, *Handelsbeziehungen,* 54.
166. See meeting on the reorganization of German-American trade relations, 14 September 1909, BA, R 1501, 103099, fols 72–73; memorandum for the WA, January 1909, p. 1ff., BA, R 901, 4615, fol. 83; Prager, *Handelsbeziehungen,* 47ff.
167. See submission from the Hamburg HK, 18 September 1909, BA, R 901, 4613, fols 174–75; minutes of the confidential conference organized by the HVV and BdI on the commercial and trade policy relations between the German Empire and the U.S. on 29 November 1909, BA, R 901, 4615, fols 128–48.
168. See memorandum for the WA, January 1909, BA, R 901, 4615, fol. 83; note by AA, undated, BA, R 901, 4613, fols 171–72; Bernstorff to Bethmann, 3 December 1909, BA, R 901, 4614, fols 27ff.; Bernstorff to AA, 28 December 1909, BA, R 901, 4614, fol. 105.
169. *Deutsche Tageszeitung,* 28 October 1909.
170. Körner to Bernstorff, 17 October 1909, BA, R 1501, 103099, fol. 69.
171. See Bernstorff to AA, 23 December 1909, BA, R 901, 4614, fols 59–60; Bernstorff to AA, 23 January 1910, BA, R 901, 4615, fols 112–13; Bernstorff to AA, 26 January 1910, BA, R 901, 4615, fol. 185; Bernstorff to AA, 31 January 1910, BA, R 901, 4615, fol. 215.
172. The following quotations: meeting of the State Ministry on 12 February 1906, BA, R 43, 308, fol. 78. For very similar sentiments, see also commissarial meeting on the stance to be adopted in the negotiations with the U.S., 16 December 1899, BA, R 1501, 103090, fols 256–64; Mühlberg, Posadowsky and Stengel to Bülow, 4 February 1906, BA, R 901, 4671.
173. My own calculations, based on *StHbDR,* section 2, 550.
174. We need only compare Posadowsky's analysis with the *Post*'s assessment of America's prospects should a customs war break out with Germany: 'What we sell to her [Germany] we can find a market for elsewhere. What she buys from us – 60 per cent of it – she can get nowhere else, and she is bound to have it or shut up shop. Thus we can contemplate the threatened war with considerable complacency. Germany must have our cotton or stop her looms; she must have our copper or close her shops; she must have our provisions or go supperless to bed. We can get sugar without going to Germany for it. We can get practically everything Germany has to sell without buying it off Germany'; the *Post,* 30 January 1907.

## Conclusion

1. For just one example, see the Reichstag debate on Germany's trade relations with the U.K. in June 1899: *StenBerRT,* 1898/99, 2602, 2609, 2611–12 (17 June 1899).
2. Memorandum by ML, 'Zur Revision des Zolltarifs', sent on 16 January 1912, BA, R 43, 324, fol. 131.

3. But there were differences between the Trade Policy Department and the Political Department in terms of officials' affiliation to the various groups within the nobility. The higher nobility were disproportionately represented in the Political Department. Junkers from east of the Elbe, meanwhile, made up almost as large a share of the Trade Policy Department as of the Political Department. See Cecil, *German Diplomatic Service,* 10, 58ff.; Cecil, 'Der diplomatische Dienst'; PA AA, Materialien zu einer Darstellung der Zusammensetzung und der Wirksamkeit der früheren 2. (handelspolitischen) Abteilung des Auswärtigen Amtes von ihrer Gründung am 1. April 1885 an bis zu ihrer im Frühjahr 1920 erfolgten Auflösung, 91–92.
4. See the biographical information on Franz von Aichberger and Adolf Boyé in Auswärtiges Amt (ed.), *Biographisches Handbuch,* vol. 1; and PA AA, personal files 004517–18 Goebel von Harrant; 004633–42 Goetsch; 004947–50 Grunenwald; 006814–16 Johannes; 007777–83 Körner; 008420–27 Ladenberg; 008661 Lehmann; 008747–51 Lentze; 008999–9000 Lindenfels; 009118–21 Loehr; 009831–36 Mertens; 010477–79 Nadolny; 011471–78 Pritsch; 011697–703 Raffauf; 013140–48 Schelling; 014143–48 Schwartzkoppen; 014298–301 Seeliger; 014965–67 Stockhammern.
5. Hoover on 4 March 1929, quoted in Irwin and Kroszner, 'Log-Rolling', 4.
6. The term 'exit' (along with 'voice') goes back to A. O. Hirschman. See Hirschman, *Exit.*
7. See the early contribution by Tyszka, *Löhne und Lebenskosten,* 259–90.
8. My own calculations, based on Gerloff, 'Verbrauch', 35. According to Gerloff, at 10 marks duty for every tonne of breadstuff, the income burden amounted to 0.65 per cent of household income below 800 marks, 0.61 per cent of income between 800 and 1,200 marks and 0.46 per cent of income between 1,200 and 2,000 marks, if we assume that the full force of duties was felt in prices. See Gerloff, 'Beiträge zur Reichsfinanzreform', 454; Hentschel, *Wirtschaft und Wirtschaftspolitik,* 200ff.
9. See, e.g., Heß, *Junker,* 306 and passim; Schiller, *Vom Rittergut zum Großgrundbesitz,* 160ff.; Hentschel, *Wirtschaft und Wirtschaftspolitik,* 199–200; Wehler, *Gesellschaftsgeschichte,* vol. 3, 696.
10. Percentages based on Haupt, *Konsum,* 116.
11. See, e.g., Aldenhoff-Hübinger, *Agrarpolitik,* 168.
12. In light of this, it seems problematic to describe Caprivi's trade treaty policies as 'in any event a failure'. See Petersson, 'Kaiserreich', 64.
13. On the methodological difficulties resulting from this approach, see chapter 6, note 102.
14. On the following, see table 7 in the appendix.
15. Figures in Bairoch, 'European Trade Policy', 76, 139. Bairoch wrongly puts the German level at just 7.9 per cent.
16. See Estevadeordal, 'Measuring Protection'.
17. For a recent example, see Schmidt, 'Nationalstaat', 197.
18. See Tenbruck, 'Gesellschaftsgeschichte', 420–21. Tenbruck's general critique applies less to historiography than to his own discipline of sociology.

# Sources and Bibliography

## Unpublished Sources

### *Bundesarchiv (BA) Berlin-Lichterfelde (Federal Archives)*

R 2 – Reichsschatzamt (Imperial Treasury)
24458
R 13 I – Verein Deutscher Eisen- und Stahlindustrieller (Association of German Iron and Steel Industrialists)
79, 274
R 43 – Reichskanzlei (Imperial Chancellery)
305a, 305b, 308, 314, 316–19, 324, 412–13, 419, 1616, 1620, 2028, 2031, 2110–11, 2120–23
R 901 – Auswärtiges Amt, Handelspolitische Abteilung (Foreign Ministry, Trade Policy Department)
3430, 4576–86, 4589, 4613–15, 4654–57, 4671, 6270, 6273, 10058, 10064, 10087, 10567, 10569, 10669, 11014, 11017, 11019–24, 11027, 11029–35, 11040–41, 11041–45, 12216–57, 12260, 13316
R 1501 – Reichsamt des Innern (Imperial Ministry of the Interior)
103085–86, 103090–91, 103097–100, 104866, 104887, 115532, 118884, 118886–89, 118891–94, 118902–10, 118913, 118915, 118918–19, 118923–28, 118940–42, 118948–51

### *Geheimes Staatsarchiv Preußischer Kulturbesitz (GStAPK) Berlin (Prussian Privy State Archives)*

I. HA, Rep. 87 – Ministerium für Landwirtschaft, Domänen und Forsten (Ministry of Agriculture, Estates and Forestry)
Abt. B Nr. 7230
I. HA, Rep. 90a – Preußisches Staatsministerium (Prussian State Ministry)
Abt. B III 2 b Nr. 6 Bd. 98–99, 103, 105–6, 112–13, 143
Abt. K II 3 Nr. 5 Bd. 1
I. HA, Rep. 120 – Ministerium für Handel und Gewerbe (Ministry of Trade and Commerce)
Abt. C VII 1 Nr. 10 Bd. 15
Abt. C VII 1 Nr. 31
Abt. C VII 1 Nr. 41 Bd. 1–3

Abt. C VII 2 Nr. 8 Bd. 16
Abt. C XIII 2 Nr. 1 b Bd. 2–3
Abt. C XIII 6 a Nr. 35 Bd. 8

### *Politisches Archiv des Auswärtigen Amtes (PA AA) Berlin (Foreign Ministry Political Archive)*

004517–18 Personalakte Goebel v. Harrant
004633–42 Personalakte Goetsch
004947–50 Personalakte Grunenwald
006814–16 Personalakte Johannes
007777–83 Personalakte v. Körner
008420–27 Personalakte v. Ladenberg
008661 Personalakte Lehmann
008747–51 Personalakte Lentze
008999–9000 Personalakte v. Lindenfels
009118–21 Personalakte v. Loehr
009831–36 Personalakte Mertens
010477–79 Personalakte Nadolny
011471–78 Personalakte Pritsch
011697–703 Personalakte Raffauf
013140–48 Personalakte v. Schelling
014143–48 Personalakte v. Schwartzkoppen
014298–301 Personalakte Seeliger
014965–67 Personalakte v. Stockhammern
Materialien zu einer Darstellung der Zusammensetzung und der Wirksamkeit der früheren 2. (handelspolitischen) Abteilung des Auswärtigen Amtes von ihrer Gründung am 1. April 1885 an bis zu ihrer im Frühjahr 1920 erfolgten Auflösung. Gesammelt im Auftrage des Auswärtigen Amtes (Materials relating to the composition and effectiveness of the former Second [Trade Policy] Department of the Foreign Ministry from its foundation on 1 April 1885 until its dissolution in the spring of 1920. Compiled by order of the Foreign Ministry).

## Newspapers and Journals

Augsburger Abend-Zeitung
Berliner Börsen-Courier
Berliner Börsen-Zeitung
Berliner Lokalanzeiger
Berliner Neueste Nachrichten
Berliner Politische Nachrichten
Berliner Tageblatt
Breslauer Zeitung
Der Bund der Landwirte

Deutsch-Amerikanische Korrespondenz
Deutsche Export-Revue
Deutsche Industrie-Zeitung
Der deutsche Ökonomist
Deutsches Handels-Archiv
Deutsche Tageszeitung
Dresdner Journal
Export
Frankfurter Zeitung
Freisinnige Zeitung
Germania
Hamburger Nachrichten
Hamburgische Börsen-Halle
Hamburgischer Correspondent
Handelsvertragsverein
Hannoversche Tages-Nachrichten
Jahrbuch des Handelsvertragsvereins
Kölnische Volkszeitung
Kölnische Zeitung
Korrespondenz des BdL
Kreuzzeitung
Leipziger Neueste Nachrichten
Mitteilungen des Handelsvertragsvereins
Münchener Allgemeine Zeitung
Münchener Neueste Nachrichten
Nation
National-Zeitung
New Yorker Handelszeitung
Plutus
Die Post
The Post
Rheinisch-Westfälische Zeitung
Der Tag
Vierteljahrsschrift für Volkswirtschaft, Politik und Kulturgeschichte
Vorwärts
Vossische Zeitung
Württembergische Jahrbücher für Statistik und Landeskunde
Zukunft

## Published Sources, Statistics and Contemporary Literature

Aegidi, L. and A. Klauhold. 1862. *Die Krisis des Zollvereins: Urkundlich dargestellt.* Hamburg: Meissner.

Arndt, P. 1899. *Wirtschaftliche Folgen der Entwicklung Deutschlands zum Industriestaat.* Berlin: Simion.

———. 1900. *Die Handelsbeziehungen Deutschlands zu England und den englischen Kolonien*. Berlin: Simion.

———. 1901. 'Zum Abschluß eines neuen deutsch-russischen Handelsvertrages'. In *Beiträge zur neuesten Handelspolitik Deutschlands*, vol. 3. Leipzig: Duncker und Humblot, 1–46.

———. 1913. *Deutschlands Stellung in der Weltwirtschaft*. 2nd ed. Leipzig: Teubner.

Ballod, C. 1900. 'Die deutsch-russischen Handelsbeziehungen'. In *Beiträge zur neuesten Handelspolitik Deutschlands*, vol. 1. Leipzig: Dunker und Humblot, 273–336.

———. 1901. 'Die deutsch-amerikanischen Handelsbeziehungen'. In *Beiträge zur neuesten Handelspolitik Deutschlands*, vol. 2. Leipzig: Duncker und Humblot, 173–222.

Bamberger, L. 1870. *Vertrauliche Briefe aus dem Zollparlament*. Breslau: Günther.

Bebel, A. (1911) 1997. *Aus meinem Leben*. Bonn: Dietz.

Beckmann, F. 1911. *Einfuhrscheinsysteme: Kritische Betrachtung mit besonderer Berücksichtigung der Getreideeinfuhrscheine* Karlsruhe: Braun.

———. 1913. 'Die Entwicklung des deutsch-russischen Getreideverkehrs unter den Handelsverträgen von 1894 und 1904'. *Jahrbücher für Nationalökonomie und Statistik* 101, 145–71.

Beer, A. 1891. *Die österreichische Handelspolitik im neunzehnten Jahrhundert*. Vienna: Manz.

*Berichte über die Verhandlungen der ersten, zweiten und siebten Versammlung des Deutschen Landwirtschaftsrats*. 1872/1873/1879. Berlin.

*Bericht über die Verhandlungen der Vereinigung der Steuer- und Wirthschaftsreformer zu Berlin am 22., 23. und 24. Februar 1876*. 1876. Berlin: Niendorf.

*Bericht über die Verhandlungen der Generalversammlung der Vereinigung der Steuer- und Wirthschaftsreformer zu Berlin am 14. und 15. Februar 1878*. Berlin: Niendorf.

*Bericht über die Verhandlungen der IV. Generalversammlung der Vereinigung der Steuer- und Wirthschaftsreformer zu Berlin am 26. und 27. Februar 1879*. 1879. Berlin: Niendorf.

Bismarck, O. von. 1924–35. *Die gesammelten Werke*. 15 vols. Berlin: Stolberg.

Böhme, H. (ed.). 1966. *Vor 1866: Aktenstücke zur Wirtschaftspolitik der deutschen Mittelstaaten*. Frankfurt: Europäische Verlagsanstalt.

Borchard, C. 1913. *Die Wirkungen der Getreidezölle auf die Getreidepreise*. Berlin: Trenkel.

Borgius, W. 1899. *Deutschland und die Vereinigten Staaten*. Berlin: Guttentag.

———. 1903. *Der Handelsvertragsverein: Ein Rückblick auf die ersten drei Jahre seiner Tätigkeit*. Berlin: F. Siemenroth.

Brentano, L. 1885. 'Ueber eine zukünftige Handelspolitik des Deutschen Reichs'. *Schmollers Jahrbuch* 9, 1–29.

———. 1901. *Die Schrecken des überwiegenden Industriestaates*. Berlin: Simion.

———. 1911. *Die deutschen Getreidezölle*. 2nd ed. Stuttgart: Cotta.

Bueck, H. A. 1902–5. *Der Centralverband Deutscher Industrieller, 1876–1901*. 3 vols. Berlin: Deutscher Verlag.

Bülow, B. von. (1912) 1992. *Deutsche Politik*. Edited by P. Winzen. Bonn: Bouvier.

———. 1930/31. *Denkwürdigkeiten*. 4 vols. Berlin: Ullstein.

Bureau of the Census. 1975. *Historical Statistics of the United States: Colonial Times to 1970.* 2 vols. Washington, D.C.: Bureau of the Census.

Conrad, J. 1879. 'Die Tarifreform im Deutschen Reiche nach dem Gesetze vom 15. Juli 1879'. *Jahrbücher für Nationalökonomie und Statistik* 34, 1–42.

———. 1885. 'Die Erhöhung der Getreidezölle im Deutschen Reiche im Jahre 1885'. *Jahrbücher für Nationalökonomie und Statistik* 44, 237–62.

———. 1909. 'Agrarkrisis'. *Handbuch der Staatswissenschaften* 1, 206–11.

Dade, H. 1901. 'Die Agrarzölle'. In *Beiträge zur neuesten Handelspolitik Deutschlands,* vol. 2. Leipzig: Duncker und Humblot, 1–102.

Delbrück, R. von. 1905. *Lebenserinnerungen 1817–1867: Mit einem Nachtrag aus dem Jahre 1870.* 2 vols. Leipzig: Duncker und Humblot.

*Der Deutsche Handelstag.* 1911–13. 2 vols. Berlin: Heymann.

*Der Handelsvertragsverein, sein Wesen und seine Ziele.* 1900. Berlin: J. Springer.

Dietzel, H. 1901. *Kornzoll und Sozialreform.* Berlin: Simion.

———. 1902. *Socialpolitik und Handelspolitik.* Berlin: Simion.

———. 1905. *Der deutsch-amerikanische Handelsvertrag und das Phantom der amerikanischen Industriekonkurrenz.* Berlin: Simion.

———. 1909. 'Agrarstaat und Industriestaat'. *Handbuch für Staatswissenschaften* 1, 226–37.

Esslen, J. B. 1912. *Die Fleischversorgung des Deutschen Reiches: Eine Untersuchung der Ursachen und Wirkungen der Fleischteuerung und der Mittel zur Abhilfe.* Stuttgart: Enke.

Eulenburg, F. 1902. 'Die gegenwärtige Wirtschaftskrise: Symptome und Ursachen'. *Jahrbücher für Nationalökonomie und Statistik* 24, 305–88.

Festenberg-Packisch, H. von. 1869. *Geschichte des Zollvereins mit besonderer Berücksichtigung der staatlichen Entwickelung Deutschlands.* Leipzig: Brockhaus.

Fischer, W. (ed.). 1989. *Statistik der Bergbauproduktion Deutschlands, 1850–1914.* St. Katharinen: Scripta Mercaturae.

Fisk, G. M. 1897. *Die handelspolitischen und sonstigen völkerrechtlichen Beziehungen zwischen Deutschland und den Vereinigten Staaten von Amerika.* Stuttgart: Cotta.

———. 1900. 'Die Handelspolitik der Vereinigten Staaten 1890–1900'. In *Beiträge zur neuesten Handelspolitik Deutschlands,* vol. 1. Leipzig: Duncker und Humblot, 1–101.

Flathmann, J. 1902. *Die Landbevölkerung der Provinz Hannover und die Agrarzölle.* Berlin: Baensch.

Fridrichowicz, E. von. 1908. *Die Technik des internationalen Getreidehandels.* Berlin: P. Parey.

Fuchs, W. P. (ed.). 1968–80. *Großherzog Friedrich I. von Baden und die Reichspolitik, 1871–1907.* 4 vols. Stuttgart: Kohlhammer.

Gensel, J. 1902. *Der Deutsche Handelstag in seiner Entwicklung und Thätigkeit, 1861–1901.* Berlin: Heymann.

Gerloff, W. 1908. 'Verbrauch und Verbrauchsbelastung kleiner und mittlerer Einkommen in Deutschland um die Wende des 19. Jahrhunderts: Eine konsum- und finanzstatistische Studie'. *Jahrbücher für Nationalökonomie und Statistik* 35, 1–44, 145–72.

———. 1909. 'Beiträge zur Reichsfinanzreform'. *Jahrbücher für Nationalökonomie und Statistik* 37, 433–68.

———. 1913. *Die Finanz- und Zollpolitik des Deutschen Reiches nebst ihren Beziehungen zu Landes- und Gemeindefinanzen von der Gründung des Norddeutschen Bundes bis zur Gegenwart.* Jena: Fischer.

*Gesetzsammlung für die Königlich Preußischen Staaten.* 1810–1906. Berlin: Decker.

Gläsel, E. J. 1917. *Die Entwicklung der Preise landwirtschaftlicher Produkte und Produktionsmittel während der letzten 50 Jahre.* Berlin: Parey.

Goetz, W. (ed.). 1920. *Briefe Wilhelms II. an den Zaren, 1894–1914.* Berlin: Ullstein.

Goldberger, L. M. 1911. *Das Land der unbegrenzten Möglichkeiten: Beobachtungen über das Wirtschaftsleben der Vereinigten Staaten von Amerika.* 8th ed. Berlin: Fontane.

Goldstein, J. 1896. *Deutschlands Sodaindustrie in Vergangenheit und Gegenwart.* Stuttgart: Cotta.

Grebe, E. 1904. *Die Lage der bäuerlichen Landwirtschaft auf dem Schiefergebirge im Eisenberger Kreise des Fürstentums Waldeck nebst Untersuchungen aus 96 bäuerlichen Betrieben über Erzeugung, Verbrauch, Zukauf und Verkauf von Getreide.* Berlin: Ebering.

Hacker, P. 1903. *Die Beiräte für besondere Gebiete der Staatstätigkeit im Deutschen Reiche und in seinen bedeutenden Gliedstaaten.* Tübingen: Laupp.

Hamilton, A. (1791) 1966. 'Report on the Subject of Manufactures'. In H. C. Syrett (ed.), *The Papers of Alexander Hamilton,* vol. 10. New York: Columbia University Press, 230–340.

Harms, B. 1916. *Deutschlands Anteil an Welthandel und Weltschiffahrt.* Stuttgart: Union.

Helfferich, K. 1901. *Handelspolitik.* Leipzig: Duncker und Humblot.

Heymann, H. G. 1904. *Die gemischten Werke im Deutschen Großeisengewerbe.* Stuttgart: Cotta.

Historische Reichskommission (ed.). 1932–45. *Die auswärtige Politik Preußens 1858–1871: Diplomatische Aktenstücke.* 10 vols. Oldenburg: Stalling.

Hohenlohe-Schillingsfürst, C. von. 1907. *Denkwürdigkeiten.* Edited by F. Curtius. 2 vols. Stuttgart: Deutsche Verlags-Anstalt.

———. 1931. *Denkwürdigkeiten der Reichskanzlerzeit.* Edited by K. A. von Müller. Stuttgart: Deutsche Verlags-Anstalt.

Huber, F. C. 1901. *Deutschland als Industriestaat.* Stuttgart: J. G. Cotta.

Human, A. 1900. *Der deutsch-russische Handels- und Schiffahrtsvertrag vom 20. März 1894.* Leipzig: Duncker und Humblot.

*Jahresberichte des Bundes der Industriellen.*

Kaiserliches Statistisches Amt (ed.). 1913. *Die Deutsche Landwirtschaft: Hauptergebnisse der Reichsstatistik.* Berlin: Puttkammer and Mühlbrecht.

Kaufmann, W. 1904. *Welt-Zuckerindustrie und internationales und koloniales Recht.* Berlin: F. Siemenroth.

Kautsky, K. 1911. *Handelspolitik und Sozialdemokratie.* 2nd ed. Berlin: Vorwärts.

Kertesz, A. 1915. *Die Textilindustrie Deutschlands im Welthandel: Bearbeitet nach den statistischen Unterlagen der verschiedenen Staaten für die Industrien der Baumwolle, Wolle, Seide, Jute und des Leinens.* Braunschweig: Vieweg.

Keup, E. and R. Mührer. 1913. *Die volkswirtschaftliche Bedeutung von Groß- und*

*Kleinbetrieb in der Landwirtschaft: Untersuchungen über den Wert der inneren Kolonisation im Osten der preußischen Monarchie.* Berlin: Parey.

Kiesenwetter, O. von. 1903. *Zehn Jahre wirtschafts-politischen Kampfes: Historische Darstellung der Gründung, des Werdeganges und des bisherigen Wirkens des Bundes der Landwirte.* Berlin: Bund der Landwirte.

Kleinwächter, F. 1883. *Die Kartelle.* Innsbruck: Wagner.

Knebel-Doberitz, H. von. 1904. *Besteht für Deutschland eine amerikanische Gefahr?* Berlin: E. S. Mittler und Sohn.

Koch, W. 1907. *Die Konzentrationsbewegung in der deutschen Elektroindustrie.* Munich: Oldenbourg.

Koenig, R. 1901. *Statistische Mitteilungen aus 62 kleinbäuerlichen Betrieben über Erzeugung, Verbrauch, Verkauf und Zukauf von Getreide.* Jena: Fischer.

Kohl, H. (ed.). 1892–1905. *Die politischen Reden des Fürsten Bismarck, 1847–1897.* 14 vols. Stuttgart: J. G. Cotta.

*Kontradiktorische Verhandlungen über deutsche Kartelle: Die vom Reichsamt des Innern angestellten Erhebungen über das inländische Kartellwesen in Protokollen und stenographischen Berichten.* 1903–6. 6 vols. Berlin: Siemenroth.

Krueger, H. E. 1909. 'Historische und kritische Untersuchung über die freien Interessenvertretungen von Industrie, Handel und Gewerbe in Deutschland: Teil II'. *Jahrbuch für Gesetzgebung, Verwaltung und Volkswirtschaft* 33, 617–68.

Landauer, E. 1912. *Handel und Produktion in der Baumwollindustrie.* Tübingen: Mohr.

Lemke, H. (ed.). 1991. *Deutsch-russische Wirtschaftsbeziehungen 1906–1914: Dokumente.* Berlin: Akademie-Verlag.

Lenschau, T. 1902. *Die amerikanische Gefahr.* Berlin: Siemenroth.

Lepsius, B. 1914. *Deutschlands Chemische Industrie: 1888–1913.* Berlin: Stilke.

Levi, L. 1880. *The History of British Commerce.* 2nd ed. London: Murray.

Lexis, W. 1910. 'Identitätsnachweis'. In *Handwörterbuch der Staatswissenschaften*, vol. 5. Jena: Fischer, 576–82.

Lotz, W. 1892. *Die Ideen der deutschen Handelspolitik von 1860 bis 1891.* Leipzig: Duncker und Humblot.

———. 1900. 'Die Handelspolitik des Deutschen Reiches unter Graf Caprivi und Fürst Hohenlohe, (1890–1900)'. In *Beiträge zur neuesten Handelspolitik Deutschlands*, vol. 3. Leipzig: Duncker und Humblot, 47–218.

———. 1902. 'Die wirtschaftliche Krisis des Jahres 1901'. In *Verhandlungen des ersten Allgemeinen Deutschen Bankiertages zu Frankfurt a. M.*. Berlin: Verlag des Centralverbandes des Deutschen Bank- und Bankiergewerbes, 32ff.

Lucius von Ballhausen, R. 1921. *Bismarck-Erinnerungen.* Stuttgart: J. G. Cotta.

Mamroth, K. 1887. *Die Entwicklung der Österreichisch-Deutschen Handelsbeziehungen: Vom Entstehen der Zolleinigungsbestrebungen bis zum Ende der ausschließlichen Zollbegünstigungen (1849–1865).* Berlin: Carl Heymanns Verlag.

Maron, H. (ed.). 1868. *Materialien zum Zolltarif: Zusammenstellung der auf den Zolltarif bezüglichen Anträge und Petitionen sowie der Verhandlungen des ersten Deutschen Zoll-Parlaments.* Berlin: Stilke und van Munden.

Matlekovits, A. von. 1891. *Die Zollpolitik der Österreichisch-Ungarischen Monarchie und des Deutschen Reiches seit 1868 und deren nächste Zukunft.* Leipzig: Duncker und Humblot.

Mayo-Smith, R. and E. R. A. Seligman. 1892. 'The Commercial Policy of the United States of America, 1860–1890'. In *Die Handelspolitik der wichtigeren Kulturstaaten in den letzten Jahrzehnten*, vol. 1. Leipzig: Duncker und Humblot, 1–74.

Meerwarth, R. 1915. 'Wege und Ziele der modernen Außenhandelsstatistik'. *Allgemeines Statistisches Archiv* 9, 657–702.

*Monatshefte zur Statistik des Deutschen Reichs.* Berlin: Verlag für Sozialpolitik, Wirtschaft und Statistik.

Müller, G. 1909. *Die chemische Industrie.* Leipzig: Teubner.

Nitzsche, M. 1905. *Die handelspolitische Reaktion in Deutschland: Eine historisch-politische Studie.* Stuttgart: Cotta.

Oldenberg, K. 1897. 'Ueber Deutschland als Industriestaat'. In *Die Verhandlungen des Evangelisch-Sozialen Kongresses zu Leipzig.* Göttingen: Vandenhoeck und Ruprecht, 64–104.

Oncken, H. 1910. *Rudolf von Bennigsen: Ein deutscher liberaler Politiker: Nach seinen Briefen und hinterlassenen Papieren.* 2 vols. Stuttgart: Deutsche Verlags-Anstalt.

Oppel, A. 1912. *Die deutsche Textilindustrie: Entwicklung. Gegenwärtiger Zustand. Beziehungen zum Ausland und zur deutschen Kolonialwirtschaft.* Leipzig: Duncker und Humblot.

Paasche, H. 1891. *Zuckerindustrie und Zuckerhandel der Welt.* Jena: Fischer.

———. 1905. *Die Zuckerproduktion der Welt.* Berlin: Teubner.

Peez, A. 1892. 'Die österreichische Handelspolitik der letzten fünfundzwanzig Jahre'. In: *Die Handelspolitik der wichtigeren Kulturstaaten in den letzten Jahrzehnten*, vol. 1. Leipzig: Duncker und Humblot, 167–93.

———. 1895. *Zur neuesten Handelspolitik.* Vienna: Szelinski im Komm.

Perkin, W. H. 1915. 'The Position of the Organic Chemical Industry'. *Journal of the Chemical Society: Transactions* 107, 557–78.

Perlmann, L. 1914. *Die Bewegung der Weizenpreise und ihre Ursachen.* Munich: Hartung.

Pohle, L. 1902. *Deutschland am Scheidewege: Betrachtungen über die gegenwärtige volkswirtschaftliche Verfassung und die zukünftige Handelspolitik Deutschlands.* Leipzig: Teubner.

Poschinger, H. von. 1889–91. *Fürst Bismarck als Volkswirth.* 3 vols. Berlin: Henning.

———. 1890. *Aktenstücke zur Wirthschaftspolitik des Fürsten Bismarck.* 2 vols. Berlin: Henning.

———. 1898. *Fürst Bismarck und der Bundesrat.* 5 vols. Stuttgart: Deutsche Verlagsanstalt.

Prager, L. 1926. *Die Handelsbeziehungen des Deutschen Reiches mit den Vereinigten Staaten von Amerika bis zum Ausbruch des Weltkrieges im Jahre 1914.* Weimar: Böhlau.

Prager, M. 1902. *Die amerikanische Gefahr.* Berlin: Simion.

*Protokolle über die Verhandlungen des Parteitags der Sozialdemokratischen Partei Deutschlands.* 1890–1913.

*Protokolle über die Vernehmungen der Sachverständigen durch die Eisen-Enquete-Kommission.* 1878. Berlin: Sittenfeld.

Reichsamt des Innern (ed.). 1906. *Die Handelsverträge des Deutschen Reichs: Eine Zusammenstellung der geltenden Handels- Zoll- Schiffahrts- und Konsularverträge des Reichs und einzelner Bundesstaaten mit dem Auslande.* Berlin: Mittler.

Ritter, G. A. 1980. *Wahlgeschichtliches Arbeitsbuch: Materialien zur Statistik des Kaiserreichs, 1871–1918*. Munich: Beck.

——— (ed.). 1992. *Das Deutsche Kaiserreich, 1871–1914: Ein historisches Lesebuch*. 5th ed. Göttingen: Vandenhoeck und Ruprecht.

S. 1887. 'Beitrag zur Beurteilung der Wirkungen der neuen Getreidezölle'. *Jahrbücher für Nationalökonomie und Statistik* 49, 422–26.

Sartorius von Waltershausen, A. 1898. *Deutschland und die Handelspolitik der Vereinigten Staaten von Amerika*. Berlin: Siemenroth und Troschel.

———. 1901. *Die Handelsbilanz der Vereinigten Staaten von Amerika*. Berlin: J. Guttentag.

———. 1907. *Das volkswirtschaftliche System der Kapitalanlage im Auslande*. Berlin: G. Reimer.

———. 1923. *Deutsche Wirtschaftsgeschichte 1815–1914*. 2nd ed. Jena: Fischer.

Schippel, M. 1902. *Grundzüge der Handelspolitik: Zur Orientierung in den wirtschaftlichen Kämpfen*. Berlin: Akademischer Verlag für sociale Wissenschaft.

Schmoller, G. 1979. 'Korreferat über die Zolltarifvorlage'. In *Verhandlungen der sechsten Generalversammlung des Vereins für Socialpolitik über die Zolltarifvorlagen am 21. und 22. April 1879 in Frankfurt a. M.* Leipzig: Duncker & Humblot.

———. 1882. 'Die amerikanische Konkurrenz und die Lage der mitteleuropäischen, besonders der deutschen Landwirthschaft'. *Schmollers Jahrbuch* 6, 247–84.

———. 1885. 'Analekten und Randglossen zur Debatte über Erhöhung der Getreidezölle'. *Schmollers Jahrbuch* 9, 559–82.

———. 1891. 'Neuere Literatur über unsere handelspolitische Zukunft'. *Schmollers Jahrbuch* 15, 275–82.

———. 1900. 'Die Wandlungen in der europäischen Handelspolitik des 19. Jahrhunderts'. *Schmollers Jahrbuch* 24, 373–82.

———. 1919. *Grundriß der Allgemeinen Volkswirtschaftslehre*. Munich: Duncker und Humblot.

Schneider, O. 1910. 'Bismarck und die preußisch-deutsche Freihandelspolitik (1862–1876)'. *Schmollers Jahrbuch* 34, 1047–108.

Schulthess, H. (ed.). 1860–1940. *Europäischer Geschichtskalender*. 81 vols. Munich: Beck.

Sering, M. 1900. 'Die Handelspolitik der Grossstaaten und die Kriegsflotte'. In G. Schmoller et al. (eds), *Handels- und Machtpolitik: Reden und Aufsätze im Auftrage der 'Freien Vereinigung für Flottenvorträge'*, 2nd ed., vol. 2. Stuttgart: Cotta, 1–44.

———. 1911. 'Ländlicher Grundbesitz'. In *Wörterbuch der Volkswirtschaft*, vol. 2. Jena: Fischer, 221–35.

———. 1932. *Die deutsche Landwirtschaft*. Berlin: Parey.

Simon, F. 1909. *Die Getreideeinfuhrscheine*. Königsberg: Gräfe und Unzer.

Soetbeer, A. 1875. 'Bemerkungen über die Handelsbilanz Deutschlands'. *Annalen des Deutschen Reichs für Gesetzgebung, Verwaltung und Statistik*, 731ff.

Sombart, W. 1892. 'Die Handelspolitik Italiens seit der Einigung des Königreichs'. In *Die Handelspolitik der wichtigeren Kulturstaaten in den letzten Jahrzehnten*, vol. 1. Leipzig: Duncker und Humblot, 75–166.

Stanwood, E. (1903) 1967. *American Tariff Controversies in the Nineteenth Century*. 2 vols. New York: Russell and Russell.

*Statistik des Deutschen Reichs*. Edited by Kaiserliches Statistisches Amt.

*Statistisches Handbuch für das Deutsche Reich.* 1907. Edited by Kaiserliches Statistisches Amt. 2 parts. Berlin: Carl Heymanns Verlag.

*Statistisches Jahrbuch für das Deutsche Reich.* 1885–1914. Edited by Kaiserliches Statistisches Amt. Vol. 1–35. Berlin: Schmidt.

Steinberg, J. 1902. *Die Wirtschaftskrise 1901, ihre Ursachen, Lehren und Folgen.* Bonn.

*Stenographische Berichte über die Verhandlungen des Deutschen Reichstags.*

*Stenographische Berichte über die Verhandlungen des Deutschen Zollparlaments.*

*Stenographische Berichte über die Verhandlungen des Preußischen Hauses der Abgeordneten.*

Stone, N. I. 1906. 'Most-Favored Nation Relations between Germany and the United States'. *North American Review* 182, 433–45.

Stumpfe, E. 1897. *Der kleine Grundbesitz und die Getreidepreise.* Leipzig: Duncker und Humblot.

*Tabellarische Uebersichten des Hamburgischen Handels, zusammengestellt vom handelsstatistischen Büreau.* 1880–89. Hamburg: Herold.

Tiedemann, C. von. 1910. *Sechs Jahre Chef der Reichskanzlei unter dem Fürsten Bismarck.* 2nd ed. Leipzig: Hirzel.

Tischert, G. 1901. *Unterwegs zu den neuen Handelsverträgen: Eine kritische Darstellung der Vorbereitung der neuen Handelsverträge, 1897–1900.* Berlin: Siemenroth und Troscher.

Tyszka, C. von. 1914. *Löhne und Lebenskosten in Westeuropa im 19. Jahrhundert.* Munich: Duncker und Humblot.

Ungewitter, C. 1927. *Ausgewählte Kapitel aus der Chemisch-industriellen Wirtschaftspolitik, 1877–1927.* Berlin: Chemie.

*Verhandlungen des Achten Evangelisch-sozialen Kongresses, abgehalten zu Leipzig am 10. u. 11. Juni 1897: Nach den stenographischen Protokollen.* 1897. Göttingen: Vandenhoeck und Ruprecht.

*Verhandlungen des Vereins für Socialpolitik über die Wohnungsfrage und die Handelspolitik (1901).* 1902. Leipzig: Duncker und Humblot.

*Verhandlungen, Mitteilungen und Berichte des Centralverbands Deutscher Industrieller.* Berlin: Elsner.

*Verträge und Verhandlungen aus dem Zeitraume von 1833 bis einschließlich 1870 über die Bildung und Ausführung des deutschen Zoll- und Handels-Vereins.* 1871. 5 vols. Reprint, Frankfurt: Keip, 1986.

*Vierteljahrshefte zur Statistik des Deutschen Reichs.* Berlin: Verlag für Socialpolitik, Wirtschaft und Statistik.

Vorstand des Deutschen Metallarbeiter-Verbandes (ed.). 1912. *Die Schwereisenindustrie im deutschen Zollgebiet, ihre Entwicklung und ihre Arbeiter: Nach vorgenommenen Erhebungen im Jahre 1910.* Stuttgart: Schlicke.

Vosberg-Rekow, M. 1902. *Die Zolltarifvorlage und ihre Begründung.* Berlin: J. Guttentag.

Wagner, A. 1863. 'Österreichs Finanzen seit dem Frieden von Villafranca'. *Unsere Zeit: Jahrbuch zum Conversationslexikon* 7, 1–38.

———. 1902. *Agrar- und Industriestaat: Die Kehrseite des Industriestaats und die Rechtfertigung agrarischen Zollschutzes mit besonderer Rücksicht auf die Bevölkerungsfrage.* 2nd ed. Jena: Fischer.

Weber, M. (1897) 1993. 'Diskussionsbeiträge zum Vortrag von Karl Oldenberg'. In W. J. Mommsen and R. Aldenhoff (eds), *Max Weber Gesamtausgabe I/4*. Tübingen: Mohr, 626–40.

Weber, W. (1871) 1972. *Der deutsche Zollverein: Geschichte seiner Entstehung und Entwickelung*. Glashütten: Auvermann.

Wehrenpfennig, W. 1876. 'Politische Correspondenz'. *Preußische Jahrbücher* 37, 97–108.

Wermuth, A. 1922. *Ein Beamtenleben*. Berlin: Scherl.

Wiese, L. von 1905. 'Die nordamerikanische Konkurrenz: Die Industrie'. In E. von Halle (ed.), *Amerika*. Hamburg: Hamburger Börsenhalle, 194–242.

Wippermann, K. (ed.). 1887–1919. *Deutscher Geschichtskalender*. 33 vols. Leipzig: Meiner.

Witte, S. J. 1921. *Memoirs of Count Witte*. Garden City, N.Y.: Doubleday.

Wittschewsky, V. 1892. 'Die Zoll- und Handelspolitik Rußlands während der letzten Jahrzehnte'. In *Die Handelspolitik der wichtigeren Kulturstaaten in den letzten Jahrzehnten*, vol. 1. Leipzig: Duncker und Humblot, 361–449.

Wolf, J. 1901. 'Volkswirtschaft und Weltwirtschaft'. In J. Wolf (ed.), *Das Deutsche Reich und der Weltmarkt*. Jena: Fischer, 1–50.

———. 1904. *Materialien betreffend den Mitteleuropäischen Wirtschaftsverein*. Berlin: Reimer.

Zimmermann, A. 1899. *Handelspolitik des Deutschen Reiches vom Frankfurter Frieden bis zur Gegenwart*. Berlin: E. S. Mittler und Sohn.

Zimmermann, F. W. R. 1908. 'Die deutsche Handelsstatistik in ihrer geschichtlichen Entwicklung und ihrem derzeitigen Stand'. *Jahrbücher für Nationalökonomie und Statistik* 35, 289–324, 433–73.

Zöllner, A. 1907. *Eisenindustrie und Stahlwerksverband*. Leipzig: Deichert.

Zuckermann, S. 1906. *Der Warenaustausch zwischen Russland und Deutschland wie er tatsächlich vor dem Kriege war und wie er in Zukunft zu sein verspricht*. 2nd ed. Berlin: Verlag Russischer Kurier.

## Bibliography

Abelshauser, W. 1994. '"Mitteleuropa" und die deutsche Außenwirtschaftspolitik'. In C. Buchheim et al. (eds), *Zerrissene Zwischenkriegszeit: Wirtschaftshistorische Beiträge:. Knut Borchardt zum Geburtstag*. Baden-Baden: Nomos, 263–86.

Aberle, G. 1992. *Wettbewerbstheorie und Wettbewerbspolitik*. 2nd ed. Stuttgart: Kohlhammer.

Achilles, W. 1993. *Deutsche Agrargeschichte im Zeitalter der Reformen und der Industrialisierung*. Stuttgart: Ulmer.

———. 1994. 'Betriebswirtschaftliche Leitbilder in der ostdeutschen Gutswirtschaft seit dem Ende des 19. Jahrhunderts'. In H. Reif (ed.), *Ostelbische Agrargesellschaft im Kaiserreich und in der Weimarer Republik*. Berlin: Akademie-Verlag, 191–212.

Aldenhoff, R. 1995. 'Agrarbewegungen und Agrarpolitik in Preußen/Deutschland 1890–1894'. *Zeitschrift für Geschichtswissenschaft* 43, 795–808.

Aldenhoff-Hübinger, R. 2002. *Agrarpolitik und Protektionismus: Deutschland und Frankreich im Vergleich, 1879–1914*. Göttingen: Vandenhoeck und Ruprecht.

Alexander, M. 2000. *Die Freikonservative Partei, 1890–1918: Gemäßigter Konservatismus in der konstitutionellen Monarchie*. Düsseldorf: Droste.

Allen, R. C. 1975. 'International Competition and the Growth of the British Iron and Steel Industry, 1830–1913'. Ph.D. diss., Harvard University.

———. 1979. 'International Competition in Iron and Steel, 1850–1913'. *Journal of Economic History* 39, 911–37.

Altrichter, H. 1977. *Konstitutionalismus und Imperialismus: Der Reichstag und die deutsch-russischen Beziehungen, 1890–1914*. Frankfurt: Lang.

Ambrosius, G. 2001. 'Agrarstaat oder Industriestaat – Industriegesellschaft oder Dienstleistungsgesellschaft? Zum sektoralen Strukturwandel im 20. Jahrhundert'. In R. Spree (ed.), *Geschichte der deutschen Wirtschaft im 20. Jahrhundert*. Munich: Beck, 50–69.

Anderson, M. L. 1981. *Windthorst: A Political Biography*. Oxford: Clarendon.

———. 2000. *Practicing Democracy: Elections and Political Culture in Imperial Germany*. Princeton, N.J.: Princeton University Press.

Arnold, V. 1992. *Theorie der Kollektivgüter*. Munich: Vahlen.

Ashley, P. 1920. *Modern Tariff History: Germany – United States – France*. London: Murray.

Auswärtiges Amt (ed.). 2000. *Biographisches Handbuch des deutschen Auswärtigen Dienstes, 1871–1945*. Vol. 1. Paderborn: Schöningh.

Bachem, K. (1932) 1967. *Vorgeschichte, Geschichte und Politik der deutschen Zentrumspartei, zugleich ein Beitrag zur Geschichte der katholischen Bewegung, sowie zur allgemeinen Geschichte des neueren und neuesten Deutschland, 1815–1914*. 9 vols. Aalen: Scientia.

Bade, K. J. 1980. 'Massenwanderung und Arbeitsmarkt im deutschen Nordosten von 1880 bis zum Ersten Weltkrieg: Überseeische Auswanderung, interne Abwanderung und kontinentale Zuwanderung'. *Archiv für Sozialgeschichte* 20, 265–323.

———. 1985. 'Die deutsche überseeische Massenauswanderung im 19. und frühen 20. Jahrhundert'. In K. J. Bade (ed.), *Auswanderer – Wanderarbeiter – Gastarbeiter: Bevölkerung, Arbeitsmarkt und Wanderung in Deutschland seit der Mitte des 19. Jahrhunderts*. 2nd ed., vol. 1. Ostfildern: Scripta Mercaturae, 259–99.

Bairoch, P. 1974. 'Geographical Structure and Trade Balance of European Foreign Trade from 1800 to 1970'. *Journal of European Economic History* 3, 557–608.

———. 1989. 'European Trade Policy, 1815–1914'. In P. Mathias and S. Pollard (eds), *The Cambridge Economic History of Europe*, vol. 8, *The Industrial Economies: The Development of Economic and Social Policies*. Cambridge: Cambridge University Press, 1–160.

———. 1989. 'Les trois révolutions agricoles du monde dévéloppé: Rendements et productivité de 1800 à 1985', *Annales ESC* 44, 317–53.

———. 1993. *Economics and World History: Myths and Paradoxes*. Chicago: University of Chicago Press.

Baldwin, R. 1984. 'Rent Seeking and Trade Policy: An Industry Approach'. *Weltwirtschaftliches Archiv* 120, 662–77.

———. 1988. 'Evaluating Strategic Trade Policies'. *Aussenwirtschaft* 43, 207–33.

———. 1992. 'Are Economists' Traditional Trade Policy Views Still Valid?' *Journal of Economic Literature* 30, 804–29.

Baldwin, R. and P. Martin. 1999. 'Two Waves of Globalization: Superficial Similarities, Fundamental Differences'. In H. Siebert (ed.), *Globalization and Labor.* Tübingen: Mohr, 3–58.

Balistreri, E. J. 1997. 'The Performance of the Heckscher-Ohlin-Vanek Model in Predicting Endogenous Policy Forces at the Individual Level'. *Canadian Journal of Economics* 30, 1–17.

Barkin, K. D. 1970. *The Controversy over German Industrialization, 1890–1902.* Chicago: University of Chicago Press.

———. 1987. '1878–1879: The Second Founding of the Reich: A Perspective'. *German Studies Review* 10, 219–35.

Barth, E. 1973. *Entwicklungslinien der deutschen Maschinenbauindustrie von 1870 bis 1914.* Berlin: Akademie.

Bayly, C. A. 2004. *The Birth of the Modern World, 1780–1914: Global Connections and Comparisons.* Malden, M.A.: Blackwell.

Becker, W. H. 1982. *The Dynamics of Business-Government Relations: Industry and Exports, 1893–1921.* Chicago: University of Chicago Press.

Beckert, S. 2004. 'Emancipation and Empire: Reconstructing the Worldwide Web of Cotton Production in the Age of the American Civil War'. *Amercan Historical Review* 109, 1405–38.

Beer, J. J. 1959. *The Emergence of the German Dye Industry.* Urbana: University of Illinois Press.

Beidler, F. W. 1929. 'Der Kampf um den Zolltarif im Reichstag 1902: Ein Beitrag zur Geschichte des deutschen Parlamentarismus'. Ph.D. diss., Berlin.

Bein, A. and H. Goldschmidt. 1932. *Friedrich Hammacher: Lebensbild eines Parlamentariers und Wirtschaftsführers, 1824–1904.* Berlin: Mittler.

Bensel, R. F. 1987. *Sectionalism and American Political Development, 1880–1980.* Madison: University of Wisconsin Press.

———. 2000. *The Political Economy of American Industrialization, 1877–1900.* Cambridge: Cambridge University Press.

Bentley, J. 1996. 'Cross-Cultural Interaction and Periodization in World History'. *American Historical Review* 101, 749–70.

Berghahn, V. R. 1971. *Der Tirpitz-Plan.* Düsseldorf: Droste.

Bhagwati, J. 1989. 'Is Free Trade Passé After All?' *Weltwirtschaftliches Archiv* 125, 17–44.

———. 1995. *Protectionism.* 7th ed. Cambridge, M.A.: MIT Press.

Biagini, E. F. 1992. *Liberty, Retrenchment and Reform: Popular Liberalism in the Age of Gladstone, 1860–1880.* Cambridge: Cambridge University Press.

Biland, S. 2002. *Die Deutsch-Konservative Partei und der Bund der Landwirte in Württemberg vor 1914: Ein Beitrag zur Geschichte der politischen Parteien im Königreich Württemberg.* Stuttgart: Jan Thorbecke.

Birken, A. 1979. 'Das Verhältnis von Außenhandel und Außenpolitik und die Quantifizierung von Außenbeziehungen: Beobachtungen zum "Zeitalter des Imperialismus", 1880–1913'. *Vierteljahrschrift für Sozial- und Wirtschaftsgeschichte* 66, 317–61.

Bittermann, E. 1956. *Die landwirtschaftliche Produktion in Deutschland 1800 bis 1950: Ein methodischer Beitrag zur Ermittlung der Veränderungen des Umfanges der landwirtschaftlichen Produktion und der Ertragssteigerung in den letzten 150 Jahren*. Halle: Niemeyer.

Blackbourn, D. 1980. *Class, Religion, and Local Politics in Wilhelmine Germany: The Center Party in Württemberg before 1914*. Wiesbaden: Steiner.

———. 1984. 'Peasants and Politics in Germany, 1871–1914'. *European History Quarterly* 14, 47–75.

———. 1986. 'The Politics of Demagogy in Imperial Germany'. *Past and Present* 113, 152–84.

Blackbourn, D. and G. Eley. 1984. *The Peculiarities of German History: Bourgeois Society and Politics in Nineteenth-Century Germany*. Oxford: Oxford University Press.

Blaich, F. 1973. *Kartell- und Monopolpolitik im kaiserlichen Deutschland: Das Problem der Marktmacht im deutschen Reichstag zwischen 1879 und 1914*. Düsseldorf: Droste.

———. 1979. *Staat und Verbände in Deutschland zwischen 1871 und 1945*. Wiesbaden: Steiner.

Bleyberg, D. M. 1979. 'Government and Legislative Process in Wilhelmine Germany: The Reorganization of the Tariff Laws under Reich Chancellor von Bülow, 1897–1902'. Ph.D. diss., University of East Anglia.

Böhm, E. 1972. *Überseehandel und Flottenbau: Hanseatische Kaufmannschaft und deutsche Seerüstung, 1879–1902*. Düsseldorf: Bertelsmann.

Böhme, H. 1966. *Deutschlands Weg zur Großmacht: Studien zum Verhältnis von Wirtschaft und Staat während der Reichsgründungszeit, 1848–1881*. Cologne: Kiepenheuer und Witsch.

———. 1968. 'Bismarcks Schutzzollpolitik und die Festigung des konservativen Staates'. In H. Böhme (ed.), *Probleme der Reichsgründungszeit, 1848–1879*. Cologne: Kiepenheuer und Witsch, 328–52.

———. 1968. 'Verfassungskonflikt und Handelspolitik: Die Frage der Kontinuität im Jahre 1862'. In H. Böhme (ed.), *Probleme der Reichsgründungszeit 1848–1879*. Cologne: Kiepenheuer und Witsch.

Boldt, H. 1993. 'Von der konstitutionellen Monarchie zur parlamentarischen Demokratie'. In *Wendemarken der deutschen Verfassungsgeschichte*. Berlin: Duncker und Humblot, 151–72.

Bonham, G. 1991. *Ideology and Interests in the German State*. New York: Garland.

Bönker, D. 2012. *Militarism in a Global Age: Naval Ambitions in Germany and the United States before World War I*. Ithaca, N.Y.: Cornell University Press.

Bönker, F. 1995. 'The Dog That Did Not Bark? Politische Restriktionen und ökonomische Reformen in den Visegrád-Ländern'. In H. Wollmann et al. (eds), *Transformation sozialistischer Gesellschaften: Am Ende des Anfangs*. Opladen: Westdeutscher Verlag, 180–206.

Borchardt, K. 1976. 'Währung und Wirtschaft'. In *Deutsche Bundesbank, Währung und Wirtschaft in Deutschland, 1876–1975*. Frankfurt: Fritz Knapp, 32–33.

———. 1976. 'Wirtschaftliches Wachstum und Wechsellagen 1800–1914'. In H. Aubin and W. Zorn (eds), *Handbuch der deutschen Wirtschafts- und Sozialgeschichte*, vol. 2. Stuttgart: Klett, 198–275.

———. 1984. 'Protektionismus im historischen Rückblick'. In A. Gutowski (ed.), *Der neue Protektionismus*. Hamburg: Weltarchiv, 17–47.

———. 2001. *Globalisierung in historischer Perspektive*. Munich: Beck.

Bordo, M. and F. E. Kydland. 1995. 'The Gold Standard as a Rule: An Essay in Exploration'. *Explorations in Economic History* 32, 423–64.

Bordo, M. and H. Rockoff. 1996. 'The Gold Standard as a "Good Housekeeping Seal of Approval"'. *Journal of Economic History* 56, 389–428.

Bordo, M. and A. J. Schwartz (eds). 1984. *A Retrospective of the Classical Gold Standard, 1821–1931*. Chicago: University of Chicago Press.

Bordo, M. et al. 1998. *Was There Really an Earlier Period of International Financial Integration Comparable to Today?* NBER Working Paper 6738. Cambridge, M.A.: National Bureau of Economic Research.

Bordo, M. et al. 1999. *Is Globalization Today Really Different than Globalization a Hundred Years Ago?* NBER Working Paper 7195. Cambridge, M.A.: National Bureau of Economic Research.

Bordo, M. et al. (eds). 2003. *Globalization in Historical Perspective*. Chicago: University of Chicago Press.

Börner, A. 1961. 'Der Klassencharakter der Caprivischen Handelspolitik, vornehmlich dargestellt am Beispiel des Kampfes um den Abschluß des deutsch-russischen Handelsvertrages von 1894'. Ph.D. diss., Leipzig.

Bourne, K. 1970. *The Foreign Policy of Victorian England, 1830–1902*. Oxford: Oxford University Press.

Brander, J. A. and B. J. Spencer. 1983. 'International R+D Rivalry and Industrial Strategy'. *Review of Economic Studies* 50, 707–22.

———. 1985. 'Export Subsidies and International Market Share Rivalry'. *Journal of International Economics* 18, 83–100.

Brandt, H.-H. 1987. 'Diskussionsbeitrag'. In H. Pohl (ed.), *Zur Politik und Wirksamkeit des Deutschen Industrie- und Handelstages und der Industrie- und Handelskammern 1861 bis 1949*. Stuttgart: Steiner, 76–77.

———. 1996. 'Von Bruck zu Naumann: "Mitteleuropa" in der Zeit der Paulskirche und des Ersten Weltkriegs'. In M. Gehler et al. (eds), *Ungleiche Partner? Österreich und Deutschland in ihrer gegenseitigen Wahrnehmung: Historische Analysen und Vergleiche aus dem 19. und 20. Jahrhundert*. Stuttgart: Steiner, 315–52.

Braudel, F. 1984. *Civilization and Capitalism, 15th–18th Century*. Vol. 3. New York: Harper and Row.

———. 1991. *Die Dynamik des Kapitalismus*. 2nd ed. Stuttgart: Klett-Cotta.

Brinkmann, C. 1922. *Die preußische Handelspolitik vor dem Zollverein und der Wiederaufbau vor hundert Jahren*. Berlin: de Gruyter.

Brown, J. C. 1997. 'Market Organization, Protection, and Vertical Integration: German Cotton Textiles before 1914'. In J. Komlos and S. Eddie (eds), *Selected Cliometric Studies on German Economic History*. Stuttgart: Steiner, 101–9.

Buchheim, C. 1983. *Deutsche Gewerbeexporte nach England in der zweiten Hälfte des 19. Jahrhunderts*. Ostfildern: Scripta Mercaturae.

———. 1984. 'Deutschland auf dem Weltmarkt am Ende des 19. Jahrhunderts'. *Vierteljahrschrift für Sozial- und Wirtschaftsgeschichte* 71, 199–216.

Bürgin, A. 1993. *Zur Soziogenese der Politischen Ökonomie: Wirtschaftsgeschichtliche und dogmenhistorische Betrachtungen.* Marburg: Metropolis.

Bürgin, A. and T. Maissen. 1999. 'Zum Begriff der politischen Ökonomie heute', *Geschichte und Gesellschaft* 25, 177–200.

Burn, D. C. 1961. *The Economic History of Steelmaking, 1867–1939.* 2nd ed. Cambridge: Cambridge University Press.

Burnham, T. H. and G. O. Hoskins. 1943. *Iron and Steel in Britain, 1870–1930.* London: Allen and Unwin.

Butzer, H. 1999. *Diäten und Freifahrt im Deutschen Reichstag: Der Weg zum Entschädigungsgesetz von 1906 und die Nachwirkung dieser Regelung bis in die Zeit des Grundgesetzes.* Düsseldorf: Droste.

Canis, K. 1999. *Von Bismarck zur Weltpolitik: Deutsche Außenpolitik 1890 bis 1902.* 2nd ed. Berlin: Oldenbourg.

Cecil, L. 1969. *Albert Ballin: Wirtschaft und Politik im deutschen Kaiserreich, 1888–1918.* Hamburg: Hoffmann und Campe.

———. 1976. *The German Diplomatic Service, 1871–1914.* Princeton, N.J.: Princeton University Press.

———. 1985. 'Der diplomatische Dienst im kaiserlichen Deutschland'. In K. Schwabe (ed.), *Das Diplomatische Korps 1871–1945.* Boppard: Boldt, 15–39.

Chase-Dunn, C. et al. 2000. 'Trade Globalization since 1795: Waves of Integration in the World-System'. *Amercian Sociological Review* 65, 77–95.

Clark, G. 1987. 'Why Isn't the Whole World Developed?' *Journal of Economic History* 47, 141–73.

Coase, R. H. 1937. 'The Nature of the Firm'. *Economica* 4, 386–405.

Connaughton, R. M. 1988. *The War of the Rising Sun and Tumbling Bear: A Military History of the Russo-Japanese War, 1904/05.* London: Routledge.

Conrad, S. 2010. *Globalisation and the Nation in Imperial Germany.* Cambridge: Cambridge University Press.

———. 2011. 'Wilhelmine Nationalism in Global Contexts: Mobility, Race, and Global Consciousness'. In S. O. Müller and C. Torp (eds), *Imperial Germany Revisited: Continuing Debates and New Perspectives.* New York: Berghahn Books, 281–96.

———. 2013. *Globalgeschichte: Eine Einführung.* Munich: Beck.

Conze, W. 1978. 'Politische Willensbildung im deutschen Kaiserreich als Forschungsaufgabe historischer Wahlsoziologie'. In H. Berding (ed.), *Vom Staat des Ancien Regime zum modernen Parteienstaat: Festschrift für Theodor Schieder.* Munich: Oldenbourg, 331–47.

Coppa, F. 1970. 'The Italian Tariff and the Conflict between Agriculture and Industry: The Commercial Policy of Liberal Italy, 1860–1922'. *Journal of Economic History* 30, 742–69.

Craig, L. A. and D. Fisher, 1997. *The Integration of the European Economy, 1850–1913.* New York: St. Martin's Press.

Crapol, E. P. 1972. *America for Americans: Economic Nationalism and Anglophobia in the Late Ninteenth Century.* Westport, C.T.: Greenwood Press.

Crapol, E. P. and H. B. Schonberger. 1972. 'The Shift to Global Expansion, 1865–1900'. In W. A. Williams (ed.), *From Colony to Empire.* New York: Wiley, 136–202.

Czada, P. 1969. *Die Berliner Elektroindustrie in der Weimarer Zeit: Eine regionalstatistisch- wirtschaftshistorische Untersuchung*. Berlin: Colloquium.

Czempiel, E.-O. 1989. *Machtprobe: Die USA und die Sowjetunion in den achtziger Jahren*. Munich: Beck.

Däbritz, W. and E. Metzeltin. 1935. *Hundert Jahre Hanomag*. Düsseldorf: Stahleisen.

Darwin, J. 2008. *After Tamerlane: The Rise and Fall of Global Empires, 1400–2000*. London: Penguin Books.

———. 2011. *The Rise and Fall of the British World-System, 1830–1970*. Cambridge: Cambridge University Press.

Daunton, M. and F. Trentmann (eds). 2004. *Worlds of Political Economy: Knowledge and Power in the Nineteenth and Twentieth Centuries*. Basingstoke, U.K.: Macmillan.

Davis, J. R. 1997. *Britain and the German Zollverein, 1848–66*. Basingstoke, U.K.: Macmillan.

Dearing, M. R. 1952. *Veterans in Politics: The Story of the G. A. R.* Baton Rouge: Louisiana State University Press.

Derks, H. 2012. *History of the Opium Problem: The Assault on the East, ca. 1600–1950*. Leiden: Brill.

Dunham, A. L. 1930. *The Anglo-French Treaty of Commerce of 1860 and the Progress of the Industrial Revolution in France*. Ann Arbor: University of Michigan Press.

Eckes, A. E. 1995. *Opening America's Market: U.S. Foreign Trade Policy since 1776*. Chapel Hill: University of North Carolina Press.

Ehrl, R. 1993. *Die Entwicklung der Wirtschaftsbeziehungen zwischen Rußland bzw. der Sowjetunion und Deutschland von der Jahrhundertwende bis 1941*. Weiden: Eurotrans.

Eichengreen, B. 1989. 'The Political Economy of the Smoot-Hawley Tariff'. *Research in Economic History* 12, 1–35.

———. 1992. 'The Gold Standard since Alec Ford'. In S. N. Broadberry and N. F. R. Crafts (eds), *Britain in the International Economy*. Cambridge: Cambridge University Press, 49–79.

——— (ed.). 1985. *The Gold Standard in Theory and History*. New York: Methuen.

Elbaum, B. 1982. 'Industrial Relations and Uneven Development: Wage Structure and Industrial Organization in the British and U.S. Iron and Steel Industries, 1870–1970'. Ph.D. diss., Harvard University.

Eley, G. 1974. 'Sammlungspolitik, Social Imperialism and the Navy Law of 1898'. *Militärgeschichtliche Mitteilungen* 15, 29–63.

———. 1978. 'Die "Kehrites" und das Kaiserreich: Bemerkungen zu einer aktuellen Kontroverse'. *Geschichte und Gesellschaft* 4, 91–107.

———. (1980) 1991. *Reshaping the German Right: Radical Nationalism and Political Change after Bismarck*. 2nd ed. Ann Arbor: University of Michigan Press.

———. 1991. *Wilhelminismus, Nationalismus, Faschismus: Zur historischen Kontinuität in Deutschland*. Münster: Westfälisches Dampfboot.

Ellerbrock, K.-P. 1993. *Geschichte der deutschen Nahrungs- und Genußmittelindustrie, 1750–1914*. Stuttgart: Steiner.

Elm, L. 1985. 'Handelsvertragsverein'. In D. Fricke (ed.), *Lexikon zur Parteiengeschichte*, vol. 3. Leipzig: VEB Bibliographisches Institut, 84–90.

Engelberg, E. 1990. *Bismarck: Das Reich in der Mitte Europas*. Berlin: Dietz.

Estevadeordal, A. 1997. 'Measuring Protection in the Early Twentieth Century'. *European Review of Economic History* 1, 89–125.

———. 2003. 'The Rise and Fall of World Trade, 1870–1939'. *Quarterly Journal of Economics* 118, 359–407.

Etges, A. 1998. *Wirtschaftsnationalismus: USA und Deutschland im Vergleich (1815–1914).* Frankfurt: Campus.

Ethier, W. J. 1997. *Moderne Außenwirtschaftstheorie.* 4th ed. Munich: Oldenbourg.

Evans, R. J. (ed.). 1978. *Society and Politics in Wilhelmine Germany.* London: Croom Helm.

Fairbairn, B. 1990. 'The Limits of Nationalist Politics: Electoral Culture and Mobilization in Germany, 1898–1903'. *Historical Journal* 33, 811–38.

———. 1992. 'Interpreting Wilhelmine Elections: National Issues, Fairness Issues, and Electoral Mobilization'. In L. E. Jones and J. Retallack (eds), *Elections, Mass Politics, and Social Change in Modern Germany.* Cambridge: Cambridge University Press, 17–48.

———. 1997. *Democracy in the Undemocratic State: The German Reichstag Elections of 1898 and 1903.* Toronto: University of Toronto Press.

Farr, I. 1978. 'Populism in the Countryside: The Peasant Leagues in Bavaria in the 1890s'. In R. J. Evans (ed.), *Society and Politics in Wilhelmine Germany.* London: Croom Helm, 136–59.

———. 1986. 'Peasant Protest in the Empire: The Bavarian Example'. In R. G. Moeller (ed.), *Peasants and Lords in Modern Germany.* Boston: Allen and Unwin, 110–39.

Feis, H. (1930) 1964. *Europe: The World's Banker 1870–1914: An Account of European Foreign Investment and the Connection of World Finance with Diplomacy before the War.* New York: A. M. Kelley.

Feldenkirchen, W. 1980. 'Die wirtschaftliche Rivalität zwischen Deutschland und England im 19. Jahrhundert'. *Zeitschrift für Unternehmensgeschichte* 25, 77–107.

———. 1982. *Die Eisen- und Stahlindustrie des Ruhrgebiets, 1879–1914: Wachstum, Finanzierung und Struktur ihrer Großunternehmen.* Wiesbaden: Steiner.

———. 1994. 'Foreign Investments in the German Electrical Industry'. In H. Pohl (ed.), *Transnational Investment from the 19th Century to the Present.* Stuttgart: Steiner, 117–51.

———. 1995. *Siemens, 1918–1945.* Munich: Piper.

———. 1998. 'Die Firma Siemens im Russischen Reich vor 1914'. In D. Dahlmann and C. Scheide (eds), *'. . . das einzige Land in Europa, das eine große Zukunft vor sich hat': Deutsche Unternehmen und Unternehmer im Russischen Reich im 19. und frühen 20. Jahrhundert.* Göttingen: Hubert, 167–88.

Feldman, G. D. 1984. *Vom Weltkrieg zur Weltwirtschaftskrise: Studien zur deutschen Wirtschafts- und Sozialgeschichte, 1914–1932.* Göttingen: Vandenhoeck und Ruprecht, 161–81.

Fesser, G. 1991. *Reichskanzler Bernhard Fürst von Bülow: Eine Biographie.* Berlin: Deutscher Verlag der Wissenschaften.

Fiebig-von Hase, R. 1986. *Lateinamerika als Konfliktherd der deutsch-amerikanischen Beziehungen, 1890–1903.* 2 vols. Göttingen: Vandenhoeck und Ruprecht.

———. 1988. 'Die deutsch-amerikanischen Wirtschaftsbeziehungen, 1890–1914, im Zeichen von Protektionismus und internationaler Integration'. *Amerikastudien* 33, 329–57.

———. 1993. 'The United States and Germany in the World Arena, 1900–1917'. In H.-J. Schröder (ed.), *Confrontation and Cooperation: Germany and the United States in the Era of World War I, 1900–1924*. Providence, R.I.: Berg, 33–68.

———. 1994. 'Die USA und Europa vor dem Ersten Weltkrieg'. *Amerikastudien* 39, 7–41.

Fiedler, M. 2001. 'Vertrauen ist gut, Kontrolle ist teuer: Vertrauen als Schlüsselkategorie wirtschaftlichen Handelns'. *Geschichte und Gesellschaft* 27, 576–92.

Findlay, R. and K. H. O'Rourke. 2007. *Power and Plenty: Trade, War, and the World Economy in the Second Millennium*. Princeton, N.J.: Princeton University Press.

Fischer, W. 1964. *Unternehmerschaft, Selbstverwaltung und Staat: Die Handelskammern in der deutschen Wirtschafts- und Staatsverfassung des 19. Jahrhunderts*. Berlin: Duncker und Humblot.

———. 1972. *Wirtschaft und Gesellschaft im Zeitalter der Industrialisierung*. Göttingen: Vandenhoeck und Ruprecht.

———. 1976. 'Bergbau, Industrie und Handwerk'. In H. Aubin and W. Zorn (eds), *Handbuch der deutschen Wirtschafts- und Sozialgeschichte*, vol. 2. Stuttgart: Klett, 527–62.

——— (ed.). 1985. 'Deutschland 1850-1914'. In *Handbuch der Europäischen Wirtschafts- und Sozialgeschichte*, vol. 5. Stuttgart: Klett, 357-437.

Fischer, W. and P. Czada. 1970. 'Wandlungen in der deutschen Industriestruktur im 20. Jahrhundert'. In G. A. Ritter (ed.), *Entstehung und Wandel der modernen Gesellschaft: Festschrift für Hans Rosenberg*. Berlin: de Gruyter, 116–65.

Flemming, J. 1978. *Landwirtschaftliche Interessen und Demokratie: Ländliche Gesellschaft, Agrarverbände und Staat 1890–1925*. Bonn: Verlag Neue Gesellschaft.

Foreman-Peck, J. and R. Michie. 1986. 'The Performance of the Nineteenth Century International Gold Standard'. In W. Fischer et al. (eds), *The Emergence of a World Economy, 1500–1914*, vol. 2. Wiesbaden: Steiner, 383–411.

Frank, A. G. and B. Gills. 1990. 'The Cumulation of Accumulation: Theses and Research Agenda for 5000 Years of World System Theory'. *Dialectical Anthropology* 15, 19–42.

——— (eds). 1993. *The World System: Five Hundred Years or Five Thousand?* London: Routledge.

Franz, E. (1933) 1973. *Der Entscheidungskampf um die wirtschaftspolitische Führung Deutschlands (1856–1867)*. Munich: Scientia.

Fremdling, R. 1988. 'German National Accounts for the 19th and Early 20th Century: A Critical Assessment'. *Vierteljahrschrift für Sozial- und Wirtschaftsgeschichte* 75, 33–57.

———. 1991. 'The German Iron and Steel Industry in the 19th Century'. In E. Abe and Y. Suzuki (eds), *Changing Patterns of International Rivalry: Some Lessons from the Steel Industry*. Tokyo: University of Tokyo Press, 113–36.

———. 1991. 'Productivity Comparison between Great Britain and Germany, 1855–1913'. *Scandinavian Economic History Review* 39, 28–42.

———. 1995. 'German National Accounts for the 19th and Early 20th Century'. *Scandinavian Economic History Review* 43, 77–100.

———. 2003. 'European Foreign Trade Policies, Freight Rates and the World Markets of Grain and Coal during the 19th Century'. *Jahrbuch für Wirtschaftsgeschichte* 2003(2), 83–98.

Fremdling, R. and J. Krengel. 1985. 'Kartelle und ihre volks- bzw. einzelwirtschaftliche Bedeutung bis 1914'. In H. Pohl (ed.), *Kartelle und Kartellgesetzgebung in Praxis und Rechtsprechung vom 19. Jahrhundert bis zur Gegenwart.* Stuttgart: Steiner, 28–37.

Frey, B. S. 1977. *Moderne Politische Ökonomie.* Munich: Piper.

———. 1985. *Internationale Politische Ökonomie.* Munich: Vahlen.

Fricke, D. and E. Hartwig. 1983. 'Bund der Landwirte'. In D. Fricke (ed.), *Lexikon zur Parteiengeschichte,* vol. 1. Leipzig: VEB Bibliographisches Institut, 241–70.

Fritsch, W. and H. Gottwald. 1983. 'Bayerischer Bauernbund'. In D. Fricke (ed.), *Lexikon zur Parteiengeschichte,* vol. 1. Leipzig: VEB Bibliographisches Institut, 135–51.

*Fünfundsiebzig Jahre Bosch.* 1961. Stuttgart: Bosch.

Gall, L. 1980. *Bismarck: Der weiße Revolutionär.* Frankfurt: Propyläen.

Gerschenkron, A. (1943) 1989. *Bread and Democracy in Germany.* Ithaca, N.Y.: Cornell University Press.

Geyer, D. 1977. *Der russische Imperialismus: Studien über den Zusammenhang von innerer und auswärtiger Politik, 1860–1914.* Göttingen: Vandenhoeck und Ruprecht.

Gilpin, R. 1987. *The Political Economy of International Relations.* Princeton, N.J.: Princeton University Press.

———. 2001. *Global Political Economy: Understanding the International Economic Order.* Princeton, N.J.: Princeton University Press.

Glastetter, W. 1998. *Außenwirtschaftspolitik.* 3rd ed. Munich: Oldenbourg.

Goldstein, J. 1986. 'The Political Economy of Trade: Institutions of Protection'. *American Political Science Review* 80, 161–84.

———. 1993. *Ideas, Interests, and American Trade Policy.* Ithaca, N.Y.: Cornell University Press.

Gosewinkel, D. 2009. 'Die Nationalisierung der Staatsangehörigkeit im Deutschen Kaiserreich'. In S. O. Müller and C. Torp (eds), *Das Deutsche Kaiserreich in der Kontroverse.* Göttingen: Vandenhoeck and Ruprecht, 392–405.

Gottwald, H. 1985. 'Mitteleuropaorganisationen', in D. Fricke (ed.), *Lexikon zur Parteiengeschichte,* vol. 3, Leipzig: VEB Bibliographisches Institut, 365–375.

———. 1986. 'Schutzverband gegen agrarische Übergriffe', in D. Fricke (ed.), *Lexikon zur Parteiengeschichte,* vol. 4, Leipzig: VEB Bibliographisches Institut, 128–130.

———. 1986. 'Vereinigung der Steuer- und Wirtschaftsreformer'. In D. Fricke (ed.), *Lexikon zur Parteiengeschichte,* vol. 4. Leipzig: VEB Bibliographisches Institut, 358–67.

Gould, D. M. and G. L. Woodbridge, 1998. 'The Political Economy of Retaliation, Liberalization and Trade Wars'. *European Journal of Political Economy* 14, 115–37.

Gourevitch, P. 1977. 'International Trade, Domestic Coalitions and Liberty: Comparative Responses to the Crisis of 1873–1896'. *Journal of Interdisciplinary History* 8, 281–313.

———. 1986. *Politics in Hard Times: Comparative Responses to International Economic Crises.* Ithaca, N.Y.: Cornell University Press.

Grabas, M. 1992. *Konjunktur und Wachstum in Deutschland von 1895 bis 1914.* Berlin: Duncker und Humblot.

Grimm, A. 1930. 'Graf Witte und die Deutsche Politik'. Ph.D. diss., Freiburg.

Grossman, G. M. and E. Helpman. 1995. 'Trade Wars and Trade Talks'. *Journal of Political Economy* 103, 675–708.

Haber, L. F. 1958. *The Chemical Industry During the Nineteenth Century.* Oxford: Clarendon.

———. 1971. *The Chemical Industry, 1900–1930: International Growth and Technological Change.* Oxford: Clarendon.

Hahn, H.-W. 1982. *Wirtschaftliche Integration im 19. Jahrhundert: Die hessischen Staaten und der Deutsche Zollverein.* Göttingen: Vandenhoeck und Ruprecht.

———. 1984. *Geschichte des Deutschen Zollvereins.* Göttingen: Vandenhoeck und Ruprecht.

———. 1984. 'Hegemonie und Integration: Voraussetzungen und Folgen der preußischen Führungsrolle im Deutschen Zollverein'. In H. Berding (ed.), *Wirtschaftliche und politische Integration in Europa im 19. und 20. Jahrhundert.* Göttingen: Vandenhoeck und Ruprecht, 45–70.

Hardach, G. 1977. *Deutschland in der Weltwirtschaft, 1870–1970.* Frankfurt: Campus.

Hardach, G. and S. Hartig. 1998. 'Der Goldstandard als Argument in der internationalen Währungsdiskussion'. *Jahrbuch für Wirtschaftsgeschichte* 1998(1), 125–41.

Hardach, K. W. 1967. *Die Bedeutung wirtschaftlicher Faktoren bei der Wiedereinführung der Eisen- und Getreidezölle in Deutschland 1879.* Berlin: Duncker und Humblot.

Hardin, R. 1982. *Collective Action.* Baltimore: Johns Hopkins University Press.

Harley, K. C. 1980. 'Transportation, the World Wheat Trade, and the Kuznets Cycle, 1850–1913'. *Explorations in Economic History* 17, 218–50.

———. 1986. 'Late Nineteenth Century Transportation, Trade and Settlement'. In W. Fischer et al. (eds), *The Emergence of a World Economy 1500–1914,* vol. 2. Wiesbaden: Steiner, 593–617.

———. 1988. 'Ocean Freight Rates and Productivity, 1740–1913: The Primacy of Mechanical Invention Reaffirmed'. *Journal of Economic History* 48, 851–76.

———. 1992. 'The World Food Economy and Pre-World War I Argentina'. In S. N. Broadberry and N. F. R. Crafts, *Britain in the International Economy.* Cambridge: Cambridge University Press, 244–68.

Harnisch, H. 1994. 'Agrarstaat oder Industriestaat: Die Debatte um die Bedeutung der Landwirtschaft in Wirtschaft und Gesellschaft Deutschlands an der Wende vom 19. zum 20. Jahrhundert'. In H. Reif (ed.), *Ostelbische Agrargesellschaft im Kaiserreich und in der Weimarer Republik.* Berlin: Akademie, 33–50.

Haupt, H.-G. 2003. *Konsum und Handel: Europa im 19. und 20. Jahrhundert.* Göttingen: Vandenhoeck und Ruprecht.

Haushofer, H. 1963. *Die deutsche Landwirtschaft im technischen Zeitalter.* Stuttgart: Ulmer.

Held, D. and A. McGrew. 2000. 'The Great Globalization Debate: An Introduction'. In D. Held and A. McGrew (eds), *The Global Transformations Reader: An Introduction to the Globalization Debate.* Cambridge: Polity, 1–45.

Hellwig, F. 1936. *Carl Ferdinand Freiherr von Stumm-Hallberg, 1836–1901*. Heidelberg: Westmark.

Henderson, W. O. 1966. 'Mitteleuropäische Zollvereinspläne'. *Zeitschrift für die gesamte Staatswissenschaft* 122, 130–62.

———. 1968. *The Zollverein*. 2nd ed. London: Cass.

———. 1981. 'The German Zollverein and the European Economic Community'. *Zeitschrift für die gesamte Staatswissenschaft* 137, 491–507.

———. 1987. 'Cobden-Vertrag und handelspolitischer Liberalismus'. In H. Pohl (ed.), *Die Auswirkungen von Zöllen und anderen Handelshemmnissen auf Wirtschaft und Gesellschaft vom Mittelalter bis zur Gegenwart*). Stuttgart: Steiner, 221–51.

Henning, F.-W. 1977. 'Produktionskosten und Preisbildung für Getreide in den letzten Jahrzehnten des 19. Jahrhunderts'. *Zeitschrift für Agrargeschichte und Agrarsoziologie* 25, 214–36.

———. 1996. *Deutsche Wirtschafts- und Sozialgeschichte im 19. Jahrhundert*. Vol. 2. Paderborn: Schöningh.

Hentschel, V. 1975. *Die deutschen Freihändler und der volkswirtschaftliche Kongreß 1858 bis 1885*. Stuttgart: Klett.

———. 1977. *Wirtschaftsgeschichte der Maschinenfabrik Esslingen AG*. Stuttgart: Klett.

———. 1978. *Wirtschaft und Wirtschaftspolitik im wilhelminischen Deutschland: Organisierter Kapitalismus und Interventionsstaat?* Stuttgart: Klett-Cotta.

Hertner, P. 1986. 'Financial Strategies and Adaptation to Foreign Markets: The German Electro-Technical Industry and Its Multinational Initiatives, 1890s to 1939'. In A. Teichova (ed.), *Multinational Enterprise in Historical Perspective*. Cambridge: Cambridge University Press, 145–59.

Herzfeld, H. Johannes. 1938. *Von Miquel: Sein Anteil am Ausbau des Deutschen Reiches bis zur Jahrhundertwende*. 2 vols. Detmold: Staercke.

Heß, K. 1990. *Junker und bürgerliche Großgrundbesitzer im Kaiserreich: Landwirtschaftlicher Großbetrieb, Großgrundbesitz und Familienfideikommiß in Preußen (1867/71–1914)*. Stuttgart: Steiner.

Hildermeier, M. 1989. *Die Russische Revolution, 1905–1921*. Frankfurt: Suhrkamp.

Hippel, W. von. 2002. 'Auf dem Weg zum Weltunternehmen (1865–1900)' In W. Abelshauser (ed.), *Die BASF: Eine Unternehmensgeschichte*. Munich: Beck, 17–116.

Hirschman, A. O. 1970. *Exit, Voice, and Loyalty: Responses to Declines in Firms, Organizations, and States*. Cambridge, M.A.: Harvard University Press.

Hirst, P. and G. Thompson. 1999. *Globalization in Question: The International Economy and the Possibilities of Governance*. 2nd ed. Cambridge: Polity.

Hobson, J. M. 1997. *The Wealth of States: A Comparative Sociology of International Economic and Political Change*. Cambridge: Cambridge University Press.

Hoffmann, W. G. 1965. *Das Wachstum der deutschen Wirtschaft seit der Mitte des 19. Jahrhunderts*. Berlin: Springer.

———. 1967. 'Strukturwandlungen im Außenhandel der deutschen Volkswirtschaft seit der Mitte des 19. Jahrhunderts'. *Kyklos* 20, 287–306.

Hohberg, C. 1983. 'Bund der Industriellen'. In D. Fricke (ed.), *Lexikon zur Parteiengeschichte*, vol. 1. Leipzig: VEB Bibliographisches Institut, 217–34.

Hohenberg, P. M. 1967. *Chemicals in Western Europe*. Amsterdam: North Holland.

Holtfrerich, C.-L. 1983. 'The Growth of Net Domestic Product in Germany, 1850–1913'. In R. Fremdling and P. K. O'Brien (eds), *Productivity in the Economies of Europe*. Stuttgart: Klett-Cotta, 124–32.

Höpfner, B. 1993. *Der deutsche Außenhandel, 1900–1945: Änderungen in der Waren- und Regionalstruktur*. Frankfurt: Lang.

Horn, H. 1964. *Der Kampf um den Bau des Mittellandkanals: Eine politologische Untersuchung über die Rolle eines Wirtschaftlichen Interessenverbandes im Preußen Wilhelms II*. Cologne: Westdeutscher Verlag.

Howe, A. 1984. *The Cotton Masters, 1830–1860*. Oxford: Oxford University Press.

———. 1997. *Free Trade and Liberal England, 1846–1946*. Oxford: Oxford University Press.

Hunt, J. C. 1974. 'Peasants, Grain Tariffs, and Meat Quotas: Imperial German Protectionism Reexamined'. *Central European History* 7, 311–31.

———. 1975. 'The "Egalitarianism" of the Right: The Agrarian League in Southwest Germany, 1893–1914'. *Journal of Contemporary History* 3, 513–30.

Hutchinson, W. K. 1982. 'Regional Exports to Foreign Countries: United States, 1870–1914'. *Research in Economic History* 7, 133–237.

———. 1986. 'Regional Exports of the United States to Foreign Countries: A Structural Analysis, 1870–1910'. *Research in Economic History* 10, 131–54.

Iliasu, A. A. 1971. 'The Cobden-Chevalier Commercial Treaty of 1860'. *Historical Journal* 14, 67–98.

Irwin, D. A. 1991. 'Terms of Trade and Economic Growth in Nineteenth Century Britain'. *Bulletin of Economic Research* 43, 93–101.

———. 1994. 'The Political Economy of Free Trade: Voting in the British General Election of 1906'. *Journal of Law and Economics* 37, 75–108.

———. 1996. *Against the Tide: An Intellectual History of Free Trade*. Princeton, N.J.: Princeton University Press.

———. 1996. 'Industry or Class Cleavages over Trade Policy? Evidence from the British General Election of 1923'. In R. C. Feenstra et al. (eds), *The Political Economy of Trade Policy: Papers in Honor of Jagdish Bhagwati*. Cambridge, M.A.: MIT Press, 53–75.

———. 1998. 'From Smoot-Hawley to Reciprocal Trade Agreements: Changing the Course of U.S. Trade Policy in the 1930s'. In M. D. Bordo et al. (eds), *The Defining Moment: The Great Depression and the American Economy in the Twentieth Century*. Chicago: University of Chicago Press, 325–52.

Irwin, D. A. and R. S. Kroszner. 1996. 'Log-Rolling and Economic Interests in the Passage of the Smoot-Hawley Tariff'. *Carnegie-Rochester Conference Series on Public Policy* 45, 173–200.

Jacob-Wendler, G. 1982. *Deutsche Elektroindustrie in Lateinamerika: Siemens und AEG (1890–1914)*. Stuttgart: Klett-Cotta.

James, H. 2001. *The End of Globalization: Lessons from the Great Depression*. Cambridge, M.A.: Harvard University Press.

Jasper, K. 1996. 'Die regionalen Strukturwandlungen des deutschen Außenhandels von 1880 bis 1938'. Ph.D. diss., Berlin.

John, J. et al. 1983. 'Deutscher Industrie- und Handelstag'. In D. Fricke (ed.), *Lexikon zur Parteiengeschichte*, vol. 1. Leipzig: VEB Bibliographisches Institut, 136–56.

Jones, M. T. and M. Obstfeld. 1997. *Saving, Investment, and Gold: A Reassessment of Historical Current Account Data.* NBER Working Paper 6103. Cambridge, M.A.: National Bureau of Economic Research.

Kadish, A. 1998. 'Free Trade and High Wages: The Economics of the Anti-Corn Law League'. In A. Marrison (ed.), *Free Trade and Its Reception 1815–1960*, vol. 1. London: Routledge, 14–27.

Kaelble, H. 1967. *Industrielle Interessenpolitik in der Wilhelminischen Gesellschaft: Centralverband Deutscher Industrieller, 1895–1914.* Berlin: de Gruyter.

Kaempfer, W. H. and S. V. Marks. 1993. 'The Expected Effects of Trade Liberalization: Evidence from U.S. Congressional Action on Fast-Track Authority'. *The World Economy* 16, 725–40.

Kahler, M. and D. A. Lake (eds). 2003. *Governance in a Global Economy: Political Authority in Transition.* Princeton, N.J.: Princeton University Press.

Kardorff, S. von. 1936. *Wilhelm von Kardorff: Ein nationaler Parlamentarier im Zeitalter Bismarcks und Wilhelms II., 1828–1907.* Berlin: Mittler.

Karl, R. E. 2002. *Staging the World: Chinese Nationalism at the Turn of the Twentieth Century.* Durham, N.C.: Duke University Press.

Kaulisch, B. 1973. 'Die Bildung des "Wirtschaftlichen Ausschusses zur Vorbereitung und Begutachtung handelspolitischer Maßnahmen" im Jahre 1897: Ein Beitrag zum Problem der "Sammlungspolitik" beim Übergang zum Imperialismus'. *Jahrbuch für Wirtschaftsgeschichte* 1973(3), 115–42.

Kehr, E. 1965. *Der Primat der Innenpolitik.* Edited by H.-U. Wehler. Berlin: de Gruyter.

———. 1973. *Battleship Building and Party Politics in Germany, 1894–1901.* Chicago: University of Chicago Press.

Kempter, G. 1985. *Agrarprotektionismus: Landwirtschaftliche Schutzzollpolitik im Deutschen Reich von 1879 bis 1914.* Frankfurt: Lang.

Kenwood, A. G. and A. L. Lougheed. 1983. *The Growth of the International Economy, 1820–1980.* London: Unwin.

Keohane, R. O. 1984. *After Hegemony: Cooperation and Discord in the World Political Economy.* Princeton, N.J.: Princeton University Press.

Kestler, S. 2002. *Betrachtungen zur kaiserlich deutschen Rußlandpolitik: Ihre Bedeutung für die Herausbildung des deutsch-russischen Antagonismus zwischen Reichsgründung und Ausbruch des Ersten Weltkriegs (1871–1914).* Hamburg: Kovac.

Kindleberger, C. P. 1956. *The Terms of Trade: A European Case Study.* London: Chapman and Hall.

———. 1978. 'The Rise of Free Trade in Western Europe, 1820 to 1875'. In C. P. Kindleberger, *Economic Response: Comparative Studies in Trade, Finance, and Growth.* Cambridge, M.A.: Harvard University Press, 39–65.

Kirchhain, G. 1977. *Das Wachstum der deutschen Baumwollindustrie im 19. Jahrhundert.* New York: Arno.

Klovland, J. T. 2000. 'Commodity Market Integration 1850–1913: Evidence from Britain and Germany'. *European Review of Economic History* 9, 163–97.

Klug, A. 2001. 'Why Chamberlain Failed and Bismarck Succeeded: The Political Economy of Tariffs in British and German Elections'. *European Review of Economic History* 5, 219–50.

Kocka, J. 1969. *Unternehmensverwaltung und Angestelltenschaft am Beispiel Siemens 1847–1914: Zum Verhältnis von Kapitalismus und Bürokratie in der deutschen Industrialisierung.* Stuttgart: Klett.

Krasner, S. D. (ed.). 1983. *International Regimes.* Ithaca, N.Y.: Cornell University Press.

Krause, W. 1997. *Chemie, Strategie und Zölle: Zollpolitik und die Sodaindustrie im Kaiserreich.* St. Katharinen: Script Mercaturae.

Krengel, J. 1983. *Die deutsche Roheisenindustrie, 1871–1913: Eine quantitativ-historische Untersuchung.* Berlin: Duncker und Humblot.

Kruedener, J. von. 1987. 'The Franckenstein Paradox in the Intergovernmental Fiscal Relations of Imperial Germany'. In P.-C. Witt (ed.), *Wealth and Taxation in Central Europe.* Leamington Spa, U.K.: Berg, 111–23.

Krugman, P. 1984. 'Import Protection as Export Promotion: International Competition in the Presence of Oligopoly and Economics of Scale'. In H. Kierzkowski, *Monopolistic Competition and International Trade.* Oxford: Clarendon, 180–93.

———. 1987. 'Is Free Trade Passé?' *Journal of Economic Perspectives* 1, 131–44.

———. 1996. *Rethinking International Trade.* 5th ed. Cambridge, M.A.: MIT Press.

——— (ed.). 1995. *Strategic Trade Policy and the New International System.* 7th ed. Cambridge, M.A.: MIT Press.

Kühne, T. 1998. 'Parlamentarismusgeschichte in Deutschland: Probleme, Erträge und Perspektiven einer Gesamtdarstellung'. *Geschichte und Gesellschaft* 24, 323–38.

Kusber, J. 1997. *Krieg und Revolution in Rußland, 1904–1906: Das Militiär im Verhältnis zu Wirtschaft, Autokratie und Gesellschaft.* Stuttgart: Steiner.

Lahme, R. 1990. *Deutsche Außenpolitik, 1890–1894: Von der Gleichgewichtspolitik Bismarcks zur Allianzstrategie Caprivis.* Göttingen: Vandenhoeck und Ruprecht.

Lake, D. A. 1988. *Power, Protection, and Free Trade: International Sources of U.S. Commercial Strategy, 1887–1939.* Ithaca, N.Y.: Cornell University Press.

Lambi, I. N. 1963. *Free Trade and Protection in Germany, 1868–79.* Wiesbaden: Steiner.

———. 1968. 'Die Schutzzoll-Interessen der deutschen Eisen- und Stahlindustrie, 1873–1879'. In H. Böhme (ed.), *Probleme der Reichsgründungszeit, 1848–1879.* Cologne: Kiepenheuer und Witsch, 317–27.

Landes, D. S. 2003. *The Unbound Prometheus: Technological Change and Industrial Development in Western Europe from 1750 to the Present.* 2nd ed. Cambridge: Cambridge University Press.

Lang, Michael. 2006. 'Globalization and Its History'. *Journal of Modern History* 78, 899–931.

Langewiesche, D. 1979. 'Das Deutsche Kaiserreich: Bemerkungen zur Diskussion über Parlamentarisierung und Demokratisierung Deutschlands'. *Archiv für Sozialgeschichte* 19, 628–42.

———. 1988. *Liberalismus in Deutschland.* Frankfurt: Suhrkamp.

———. 2001. 'Bismarck und die Nationalliberalen'. In L. Gall (ed.), *Otto von Bismarck und die Parteien.* Paderborn: Schöningh, 73–89.

Lebovics, H. 1967. '"Agrarians" versus "Industrializers": Social Conservative Resistance to Industrialism and Capitalism in Late Nineteenth Century Germany'. *International Review of Social History* 12, 31–65.

———. 1988. *The Alliance of Iron and Wheat in the Third French Republic, 1860–1914: Origins of the New Conservatism.* Baton Rouge: Louisiana State University Press.

Lehmann, H. G. 1970. *Die Agrarfrage in der Theorie und Praxis der deutschen und internationalen Sozialdemokratie.* Tübingen: Mohr.

Lehrfreund, L. 1921. *Die Entwicklung der deutsch-russischen Handelsbeziehungen.* Leipzig: Carnegie.

Leibenguth, P. 1975. 'Modernisierungskrisis des Kaiserreichs an der Schwelle zum wilhelminischen Imperialismus: Politische Probleme der Ära Caprivi (1890–1894)'. Ph.D. diss., Cologne.

Lerman, K. A. 1990. *The Chancellor as Courtier: Bernhard von Bülow and the Governance of Germany, 1900–1909.* Cambridge: Cambridge University Press.

Lewis, W. A. 1978. *Growth and Fluctuations 1870–1913.* London: Allen and Unwin.

———. 1981. 'The Rate of Growth of World Trade, 1830–1973'. In S. Grassman and E. Lundberg (eds), *The World Economic Order: Past and Prospects.* London: Macmillan, 11–81.

Lichter, J. 1996. *Die Handelskammern und der Deutsche Handelstag im Interessengruppensystem des Deutschen Kaiserreichs.* Cologne: Selbstverlag.

Lipset, S. M. and S. Rokkan. 1967. 'Cleavage Structures, Party Systems and Voter Alignments'. In S. M. Lipset and S. Rokkan (eds), *Party Systems and Voter Alignments: Cross-National Perspectives.* New York: Free Press, 1–64.

Lloyd-Jones, R. 1998. 'Merchant City: The Manchester Business Community, the Trade Cycle and Commercial Policy, c. 1820–1846'. In A. Marrison (ed.), *Free Trade and Its Reception, 1815–1960,* vol. 1. London: Routledge, 86–104.

Löbel, U. 1988. 'Der deutsch-russische Zollkrieg 1893/94: Zu seinen innen- und außenpolitischen Hintergründen'. *Jahrbuch für Geschichte der sozialistischen Länder Europas* 32, 147–71.

Löhr, B. 1985. *Die 'Zukunft Rußlands': Perspektiven russischer Wirtschaftsentwicklung und deutsch-russische Wirtschaftsbeziehungen vor dem Ersten Weltkrieg.* Wiesbaden: Steiner.

Loth, W. 1984. *Katholiken im Kaiserreich: Der politische Katholizismus in der Krise des wilhelminischen Deutschlands.* Düsseldorf: Droste.

Macfarlane, A. and G. Martin. 2002. *Glass: A World History.* Chicago: Chicago University Press.

Maddison, A. 1987. 'Growth and Slowdown in Advanced Capitalist Economies: Techniques of Quantitative Assessment'. *Journal of Economic Literature* 25, 649–98.

———. 1991. *Dynamic Forces in Capitalist Development: A Long-Run Comparative View.* Oxford: Oxford University Press.

Maizels, A. 1970. *Growth and Trade.* Cambridge: Cambridge University Press.

Marichal, C. 1989. *A Century of Debt Crises in Latin America: From Independence to the Great Depression, 1820–1930.* Princeton, N.J.: Princeton University Press.

Marrison, A. 1996. *British Business and Protection 1903–1932.* Oxford: Clarendon.

——— (ed.). 1998. *Free Trade and Its Reception 1815–1960.* Vol. 1. London: Routledge.

Marsh, P. T. 1994. *Joseph Chamberlain: Entrepreneur in Politics.* New Haven, C.T.: Yale University Press.

———. 1999. *Bargaining on Europe: Britain and the First Common Market, 1860–1892.* New Haven, C.T.: Yale University Press.

Marwell, G. and P. Oliver. 1993. *The Critical Mass in Collective Action*. New York: Cambridge University Press.

Maschke, E. 1964. *Grundzüge der deutschen Kartellgeschichte bis 1914*. Dortmund: Ardey.

Matthes, H.-E. 1953. 'Die Spaltung der Nationalliberalen Partei und die Entwicklung des Linksliberalismus bis zur Auflösung der Deutsch-Freisinnigen Partei, 1878–1893'. Ph.D. diss., Kiel.

McCloskey, D. N. 1973. *Economic Maturity and Entrepreneurial Decline: British Iron and Steel, 1870–1913*. Cambridge, M.A.: Harvard University Press.

McCord, N. 1958. *The Anti-Corn Law League, 1838–1846*. London: Allen and Unwin.

McNeill, W. and J. R. McNeill 2003. *The Human Web: A Bird's Eye View of World History*. New York: Norton.

Mees, G. 1956. *Schorlemer-Alst und der Westfälische Bauernverein in der deutschen Innenpolitik, vornehmlich der Jahre 1890–1894*. Ph.D. diss., Münster.

Megerle, K. 1984. 'Ökonomische Integration und politische Orientierung deutscher Mittel- und Kleinstaaten im Vorfeld der Reichsgründung'. In H. Berding (ed.), *Wirtschaftliche und politische Integration in Europa im 19. und 20. Jahrhundert*. Göttingen: Vandenhoeck und Ruprecht, 102–27.

Mergel, T. 2011. 'The Kaiserreich as a Society of Migration'. In S.O. Müller and C. Torp (eds), *Imperial Germany Revisited: Continuing Debates and New Perspectives*. New York: Berghahn Books, 267–80.

Metzer, J. 1976. 'Railroads in Tsarist Russia: Direct Gains and Implications'. *Explorations in Economic History* 13, 85–111.

Metzler, G. 1997. *Großbritannien – Weltmacht in Europa: Handelspolitik im Wandel des europäischen Staatensystems 1856 bis 1871*. Berlin: Akademie.

Meyer, A. 1986. *Der Zollverein und die deutsche Politik Bismarcks: Eine Studie über das Verhältnis von Wirtschaft und Politik im Zeitalter der Reichsgründung*. Frankfurt: Lang.

Meyer, H. C. 1955. *Mitteleuropa in German Thought and Action, 1815–1945*. The Hague: Martinus Nijhoff.

Midford, P. 1993. 'International Trade and Domestic Politics: Improving on Rogowski's Model of Political Alignments'. *International Organization* 47, 535–64.

Mielke, S. 1976. *Der Hansa-Bund für Gewerbe, Handel und Industrie 1909–1914: Der gescheiterte Versuch einer antifeudalen Sammlungspolitik*. Göttingen: Vandenhoeck und Ruprecht.

Milward, A. S. and S. B. Saul. 1977. *The Development of the Economies of Continental Europe, 1850–1914*. London: Allen and Unwin.

Mintz, S. W. 1985. *Sweetness and Power: The Place of Sugar in Modern History*. New York: Viking Press.

Mitchell, B. R. 1971. *Abstract of British Historical Statistics*. Cambridge: Cambridge University Press.

Mock, W. 1981. '"Manipulation von oben" oder Selbstorganisation an der Basis? Einige neuere Ansätze in der englischen Historiographie zur Geschichte des Deutschen Kaiserreichs'. *Historische Zeitschrift* 232, 358–75.

Moeller, R. G. 1984. 'The Kaiserreich Recast? Continuity and Change in Modern German History'. *Journal of Social History* 17, 655–83.

———. 1986. *German Peasants and Agrarian Politics, 1914–1924: The Rhineland and Westphalia.* Chapel Hill: University of North Carolina Press.

———. 1986. 'Introduction: Locating Peasants and Lords in Modern German Historiography'. In R. G. Moeller (ed.), *Peasants and Lords in Modern Germany.* Boston: Allen and Unwin, 1–23.

Mohammed, S. I. S. and J. G. Williamson 2004. 'Freight Rates and Productivity Gains in British Tramp Shipping, 1869–1950'. *Explorations in Economic History* 41, 172–203.

Mommsen, W. J. 1995. 'Die Mitteleuropaidee und die Mitteleuropaplanungen im Deutschen Reich vor und während des Ersten Weltkriegs'. In R. G. Plaschka et al. (eds), *Mitteleuropa-Konzeptionen in der ersten Hälfte des 20. Jahrhunderts.* Vienna: Verlag der Österreichischen Akademie der Wissenschaften, 3–24.

Mommsen, W. J. and R. Aldenhoff (ed.). 1993. *Max Weber Gesamtausgabe I/4: Landarbeiterfrage, Nationalstaat und Volkswirtschaftspolitik: Schriften und Reden, 1892–1899.* Tübingen: Mohr.

Moring, K.-E. 1968. *Die Sozialdemokratische Partei in Bremen, 1890–1914.* Hannover: Verlag für Literatur und Zeitgeschehen.

Morsey, R. 2001. 'Bismarck und das Zentrum'. In L. Gall (ed.), *Otto von Bismarck und die Parteien.* Paderborn: Schöningh, 43–72.

Müller, H. P. 1994. 'Landwirtschaftliche Interessenvertretung und völkisch-antisemitische Ideologie: Der Bund der Landwirte/Bauernbund in Württemberg 1893–1918'. *Zeitschrift für Württembergische Landesgeschichte* 53, 263–300.

Müller-Link, H. 1977. *Industrialisierung und Außenpolitik: Preußen-Deutschland und das Zarenreich von 1860 bis 1890.* Göttingen: Vandenhoeck und Ruprecht.

Mussa, M. 1982. 'Imperfect Factor Mobility and the Distribution of Income'. *Journal of International Economics* 12, 125–41.

Neitzel, S. 2000. *Weltmacht oder Untergang: Die Weltreichslehre im Zeitalter des Imperialismus.* Paderborn: Schoeningh.

———. 2002. 'Außenpolitische Zukunftsvorstellungen in Deutschland um 1900'. In S. Neitzel (ed.), *Zukunftsvisionen der Großmächte.* Paderborn: Schoeningh, 55–79.

Neumann, W. 1949. 'Die Innenpolitik des Fürsten Bülow von 1900 bis 1906'. Ph.D. diss., Kiel.

Nichols, J. A. 1958. *Germany after Bismarck: The Caprivi Era 1890–1894.* Cambridge, M.A.: Harvard University Press.

Nipperdey, T. 1973. 'Die Organisation der bürgerlichen Parteien in Deutschland'. In G. A. Ritter (ed.), *Deutsche Parteien vor 1918.* Cologne: Kiepenheuer and Witsch, 100–19.

———. 1990–92. *Deutsche Geschichte, 1866–1918.* 2 vols. Munich: Beck.

Nish, I. H. 1985. *The Origins of the Russo-Japanese War.* London: Longman.

Nolan, M. 1981. *Social Democracy and Society: Working-Class Radicalism in Düsseldorf, 1890–1920.* Cambridge: Cambridge University Press.

Nonn, C. 1993. 'Arbeiter, Bürger und "Agrarier": Stadt-Land-Gegensatz und Klassenkonflikt im wilhelminischen Deutschland am Beispiel des Königreiches Sachsen'. In H. Grebing et al. (eds), *Demokratie und Emanzipation zwischen Elbe und Saale: Beiträge zur Geschichte der sozialdemokratischen Arbeiterbewegung vor 1933.* Essen: Klartext, 101–13.

———. 1994. 'Fleischteuerungsprotest und Parteipolitik im Rheinland und im Reich 1905–1914'. In M. Gailus and H. Volkmann (eds), *Der Kampf um das tägliche Brot: Nahrungsmangel, Versorgungspolitik und Protest, 1750–1990.* Opladen: Westdeutscher Verlag, 305–15.

———. 1996. 'Parteien und Wahlen im wilhelminischen Deutschland (1890–1914)'. *Neue Politische Literatur* 41, 30–42.

———. 1996. *Verbraucherprotest und Parteiensystem im wilhelminischen Deutschland.* Düsseldorf: Droste.

———. 1999. 'Vom Konsumentenprotest zum Konsens: Lebensmittelverbraucher und Agrarpolitik in Deutschland 1900–1955'. In H. Berghoff (ed.), *Konsumpolitik: Die Regulierung des privaten Verbrauchs im 20. Jahrhundert.* Göttingen: Vandenhoeck und Ruprecht, 23–46.

North, D. C. 1988. *Theorie des institutionellen Wandels: Eine neue Sicht der Wirtschaftsgeschichte.* Tübingen: Mohr.

———. 1991. 'Institutions'. *Journal of Economic Perspectives* 5, 97–112.

Nötzold, J. 1966. *Wirtschaftspolitische Alternativen der Entwicklung Rußlands in der Ära Witte und Stolypin.* Berlin: Duncker und Humblot.

Novack, D. E. and M. Simon. 1964. 'Some Dimensions of the American Commercial Invasion of Europe, 1871–1914: An Introductory Essay'. *Journal of Economic History* 24, 591–605.

Nussbaum, H. 1966. *Unternehmer gegen Monopole: Über Struktur und Aktionen antimonopolistischer bürgerlicher Gruppen zu Beginn des 20. Jahrhunderts.* Berlin: Akademie.

Offermann, T. 1979. *Arbeiterbewegung und liberales Bürgertum in Deutschland, 1850–1863.* Bonn: Verlag Neue Gesellschaft.

Ohnishi, T. 1973. *Zolltarifpolitik Preußens bis zur Gründung des Deutschen Zollvereins: Ein Beitrag zur Finanz- und Außenhandelspolitik Preußens.* Göttingen: Schwartz.

Olson, M. 1982. *The Rise and Decline of Nations: Economic Growth, Stagflation and Social Rigidities.* New Haven, C.T.: Yale University Press.

———. 1998. *Die Logik des kollektiven Handelns: Kollektivgüter und die Theorie der Gruppen.* 4th ed. Tübingen: Mohr.

O'Rourke, K. H. 1997. 'The European Grain Invasion, 1870–1913'. *Journal of Economic History* 57, 775–801.

O'Rourke, K. H. and J. G. Williamson. 1994. 'Late 19th Century Anglo-American Factor Price Convergence: Were Heckscher and Ohlin Right?' *Journal of Economic History* 54, 892–916.

———. 1999. *Globalization and History: The Evolution of a Nineteenth-Century Atlantic Economy.* Cambridge, M.A.: MIT Press .

O'Rourke, K. H. et al. 1996. 'Factor Price Convergence in the Late Nineteenth Century'. *International Economic Review* 37, 499–530.

Orsagh, T. J. 1960/61. 'Progress in Iron and Steel: 1870–1913'. *Comparative Studies in Society and History* 3, 216–30.

Osterhammel, J. 2009. *Die Verwandlung der Welt: Eine Geschichte des 19. Jahrhunderts.* Munich: Beck.

Osterhammel, J. and N. P. Petersson. 2005. *Globalization: A Short History.* Princeton, N.J.: Princeton University Press.

Paetau, R. 1988. *Konfrontation oder Kooperation: Arbeiterbewegung und bürgerliche Gesellschaft im ländlichen Schleswig-Holstein und der Industriestadt Kiel zwischen 1900 und 1925.* Neumünster: Wachholtz.

Perren, R. 1978. *The Meat Trade of Britain, 1840–1914.* London: Routledge.

Peschke, H.-P. von. 1981. *Elektroindustrie und Staatsverwaltung am Beispiel Siemens, 1847–1914.* Frankfurt: Lang.

Petersson, N. P. 2004. 'Das Kaiserreich in Prozessen ökonomischer Globalisierung'. In S. Conrad and J. Osterhammel, *Das Kaiserreich transnational: Deutschland in der Welt, 1871–1914.* Göttingen: Vandenhoek und Ruprecht, 49–67.

Pflanze, O. 1998. *Bismarck.* 2 vols. Munich: Beck.

Picot, A. and H. Dietl. 1990. 'Transaktionskostentheorie'. *Wirtschaftswissenschaftliches Studium* 19, 178–84.

Pies, I. and M. Leschke (eds). 1997. *Mancur Olsons Logik kollektiven Handelns.* Tübingen: Mohr.

Plachetka, M. G. 1969. 'Die Getreide-Autarkiepolitik Bismarcks und seiner Nachfolger im Reichskanzleramt'. Ph.D. diss., Bonn.

Pletcher, D. M. 1978. 'Reciprocity and Latin America in the Early 1890s: A Foretaste of Dollar Diplomacy'. *Pacific Historical Review* 47, 53–89.

———. 1998. *The Diplomacy of Trade and Investment: American Economic Expansion in the Hemisphere, 1865–1900.* Columbia: University of Missouri Press.

Plumpe, G. 1990. *Die I.G. Farbenindustrie AG: Wirtschaft, Technik und Politik, 1904–1945.* Berlin: Duncker und Humblot.

Pogge von Strandmann, H. 1978. 'Widersprüche im Modernisierungsprozeß Deutschlands: Der Kampf der verarbeitenden Industrie gegen die Schwerindustrie'. In D. Stegmann et al. (eds), *Industrielle Gesellschaft und politisches System: Beiträge zur politischen Sozialgeschichte: Festschrift für Fritz Fischer.* Bonn: Neue Gesellschaft, 225–40.

Pohl, H. 1987. 'Stellungnahmen des Deutschen Handelstags zur Verkehrs- und Außenwirtschaftspolitik 1861 bis 1914'. In H. Pohl (ed.), *Zur Politik und Wirksamkeit des Deutschen Industrie- und Handelstages und der Industrie- und Handelskammern 1861 bis 1949.* Stuttgart: Steiner, 50–65.

Pohl, M. 1988. *Geschäft und Politik: Deutsch-russisch/sowjetische Wirtschaftsbeziehungen, 1850–1988.* Mainz: von Hase und Koehler.

Pollard, S. 1981. *Peaceful Conquest: The Industrialization of Europe, 1760–1970.* Oxford: Oxford University Press.

Pommerin, R. 1986. *Der Kaiser und Amerika: Die USA in der Politik der Reichsleitung, 1890–1917.* Cologne: Böhlau.

Puhle, H.-J. 1973. 'Radikalisierung und Wandel des deutschen Konservatismus vor dem ersten Weltkrieg'. In G. A. Ritter (ed.), *Deutsche Parteien vor 1918.* Cologne: Kiepenheuer und Witsch, 165–86.

———. 1975. *Agrarische Interessenpolitik und preußischer Konservatismus im wilhelminischen Reich (1893–1914).* 2nd ed. Bonn-Bad Godesberg: Neue Gesellschaft.

———. 1975. *Politische Agrarbewegungen in kapitalistischen Industriegesellschaften: Deutschland, USA und Frankreich im 20. Jahrhundert.* Göttingen: Vandenhoeck und Ruprecht.

———. 1978. 'Zur Legende von der "Kehrschen Schule"'. *Geschichte und Gesellschaft* 4, 108–19.

Pyta, W. 1991. *Landwirtschaftliche Interessenpolitik im Deutschen Kaiserreich: Der Einfluß agrarischer Interessen auf die Neuordnung der Finanz- und Wirtschaftspolitik am Ende der 1870er Jahre am Beispiel von Rheinland und Westfalen.* Stuttgart: Steiner.

Rauh, M. 1977. *Die Parlamentarisierung des Deutschen Reiches.* Düsseldorf: Droste.

Reif, H. 2001. 'Bismarck und die Konservativen'. In L. Gall (ed.), *Otto von Bismarck und die Parteien.* Paderborn: Schöningh, 17–42.

Reitano, J. 1994. *The Tariff Question in the Gilded Age: The Great Debate of 1888.* University Park: Pennsylvania State University Press.

Retallack, J. N. 1988. *Notables of the Right: The Conservative Party and Political Mobilization in Germany, 1876–1918.* Boston: Unwin Hyman.

Ricardo, D. (1817) 1996. *Principles of Political Economy and Taxation.* New York: Prometheus.

Richter, R. and E. G. Furubotn. 1999. *Neue Institutionenökonomik: Eine Einführung und kritische Würdigung.* 2nd ed. Tübingen: Mohr.

Riello, G. and P. Parthasarathi (eds). 2009. *The Spinning World: A Global History of Cotton Textiles, 1200–1850.* Oxford: Oxford University Press.

Ripperger, T. 2003. *Ökonomik des Vertrauens: Analyse eines Organisationsprinzips.* 2nd ed. Tübingen: Mohr.

Rips, F. 1941. 'Die Stellung der deutschen Eisenindustrie in der Außenhandelspolitik 1870 bis 1914'. Ph.D. diss., Jena.

Ritschl, A. and M. Spoerer. 1997. 'Das Bruttosozialprodukt in Deutschland nach den amtlichen Volkseinkommens- und Sozialproduktstatistiken, 1901–1995'. *Jahrbuch für Wirtschaftsgeschichte* 1997(2), 27–54.

Ritter, G. A. 1985. *Die deutschen Parteien 1830–1914: Parteien und Gesellschaft im konstitutionellen Regierungssystem.* Göttingen: Vandenhoeck und Ruprecht.

———. 1989. 'Die Sozialdemokratie im Deutschen Kaiserreich in sozialgeschichtlicher Perspektive'. *Historische Zeitschrift* 249, 295–362.

Ritter, K. 1956. *Agrarwirtschaft und Agrarpolitik im Kapitalismus.* 2nd ed. Berlin: Deutscher Bauernverlag.

Roeske, U. 1978. 'Die amtliche Statistik des Deutschen Reichs 1872 bis 1939: Historische Entwicklung, Organisationsstruktur, Veröffentlichungen'. *Jahrbuch für Wirtschaftsgeschichte* 1978(4), 85–107.

Rogowski, R. 1987. 'Political Cleavages and Changing Exposure to Trade'. *American Political Science Review* 81, 1121–37.

———. 1989. *Commerce and Coalitions: How Trade Affects Domestic Political Alignments.* Princeton, N.J.: Princeton University Press.

Rohe, K. 1992. *Wahlen und Wählertraditionen in Deutschland: Kulturelle Grundlagen deutscher Parteien und Parteiensysteme im 19. und 20. Jahrhundert.* Frankfurt: Suhrkamp.

Rokkan, S. 1970. 'Nation Building, Cleavage Formation and the Structuring of Mass Politics'. In S. Rokkan, *Citizens, Elections, Parties: Approaches to the Comparative Study of the Processes of Development.* Oslo: Universitetsforlaget, 73–144.

Rolfes, M. 1976. 'Landwirtschaft 1850–1914'. In H. Aubin and W. Zorn (eds), *Handbuch der deutschen Wirtschafts- und Sozialgeschichte*, vol. 2. Stuttgart: Klett, 495–526.

Rose, K. and K. Sauernheimer. 1995. *Theorie der Außenwirtschaft*. 12th ed. Munich: Vahlen.

Rosenberg, H. (1934) 1974. *Die Weltwirtschaftskrise, 1857–1859*. 2nd ed. Göttingen: Vandenhoeck und Ruprecht.

———. (1967) 1976. *Große Depression und Bismarckzeit: Wirtschaftsablauf, Gesellschaft und Politik in Mitteleuropa*. Frankfurt: Ullstein.

———. 1968. 'Wirtschaftskonjunktur, Gesellschaft und Politik in Mitteleuropa, 1873 bis 1896'. In H.-U. Wehler (ed.), *Moderne deutsche Sozialgeschichte*. Cologne: Kiepenheuer und Witsch, 225–53.

———. 1969. *Probleme der deutschen Sozialgeschichte*. Frankfurt: Suhrkamp.

———. 1978. *Machteliten und Wirtschaftskonjunkturen: Studien zur neueren deutschen Sozial- und Wirtschaftsgeschichte*. Göttingen: Vandenhoeck und Ruprecht.

Rostow, W. W. 1978. *The World Economy*. London: Macmillan.

Rothschild, K. W. 1989. 'Political Economy or Economics? Some Terminological and Normative Considerations'. *European Journal of Political Economy* 5, 1–12.

Saldern, A. von. 1984. *Auf dem Wege zum Arbeiter-Reformismus: Parteialltag in sozialdemokratischer Provinz. Göttingen 1870–1920*. Frankfurt: Materialis.

———. 1990. 'Wer ging in die SPD? Zur Analyse der Parteimitgliedschaft in wilhelminischer Zeit'. In G. A. Ritter (ed.), *Der Aufstieg der deutschen Arbeiterbewegung*. Munich: Oldenbourg, 161–83.

Sandler, T. 1992. *Collective Action*. Ann Arbor: University of Michigan Press.

Schaefer, K. C. 1995. *Deutsche Portfolioinvestitionen im Ausland 1870–1914: Banken, Kapitalmärkte und Wertpapierhandel im Zeitalter des Imperialismus*. Münster: LIT.

Schallermair, C. 1997. 'Die deutsche Sodaindustrie und die Entwicklung des deutschen Sodaaußenhandels, 1872–1913'. *Vierteljahrschrift für Sozial- und Wirtschaftsgeschichte* 84, 33–67.

Schattschneider, E. E. 1935. *Politics, Pressures and the Tariff: A Study of Free Private Enterprise in Pressure Politics as Shown in the 1929–1930 Revision of the Tariff*. New York: Prentice-Hall.

Schiller, R. 2003. *Vom Rittergut zum Großgrundbesitz: Ökonomische und soziale Transformationsprozesse der ländlichen Eliten in Brandenburg im 19. Jahrhundert*. Berlin: Akademie-Verlag.

Schmädeke, J. 1995. *Wählerbewegung im Wilhelminischen Deutschland*. 2 vols. Berlin: Akademie.

Schmidt, G. 2000. 'Nationalstaat, Weltmarkt und imperiale Expansion: Zum Verhältnis von Politik und Ökonomie im 19. Jahrhundert'. In J. Siegelberg and K. Schlichte (eds), *Strukturwandel internationaler Beziehungen: Zum Verhältnis von Staat und internationalem System seit dem Westfälischen Frieden*. Wiesbaden: Westdeutscher Verlag, 194–216.

Schmidt-Gernig, A. 1997. *Reisen in die Moderne: Der Amerika-Diskurs des deutschen Bürgertums vor dem Ersten Weltkrieg im europäischen Vergleich*. Berlin: Akademie.

———. 2000. 'Zukunftsmodell Amerika? Das europäische Bürgertum und die amerikanische Herausforderung um 1900'. In U. Frevert (ed.), *Das Neue*

*Jahrhundert: Europäische Zeitdiagnosen und Zukunftsentwürfe um 1900.* Göttingen: Vandenhoeck und Ruprecht, 79–112.

Schönberger, C. 2001. 'Die überholte Parlamentarisierung: Einflußgewinn und fehlende Herrschaftsfähigkeit des Reichstags im sich demokratisierenden Kaiserreich'. *Historische Zeitschrift* 272, 623–66.

Schöne, G. (1901/2) 1934. 'Die Verflechtung wirtschaftlicher und politischer Motive in der Haltung der Parteien zum Bülowschen Zolltarif'. Ph.D. diss., Halle.

Schonhardt-Bailey, C. 1998. 'Interests, Ideology and Politics: Agricultural Trade Policy in Nineteenth-Century Britain and Germany'. In A. Marrison (ed.), *Free Trade and Its Reception, 1815–1960,* vol. 1. London: Routledge, 63–81.

———. 1998. 'Parties and Interests in the "Marriage of Iron and Rye"'. *British Journal of Political Science* 28, 291–330.

Schröter, H. G. 1983. *Außenpolitik und Wirtschaftsinteresse: Skandinavien im außenwirtschaftlichen Kalkül Deutschlands und Großbritanniens, 1918–1949.* Frankfurt: Lang.

———. 1990. 'Die Auslandsinvestitionen der deutschen chemischen Industrie 1870 bis 1930'. *Zeitschrift für Geschichtswissenschaft* 35, 1–22.

Schulze, G. 1986. 'Verein zur Wahrung der gemeinsamen wirtschaftlichen Interessen in Rheinland und Westfalen (Langnamverein)'. In D. Fricke (ed.), *Lexikon zur Parteiengeschichte,* vol. 4. Leipzig: VEB Bibliographisches Institut, 379–402.

———. 1986. 'Zentralverband Deutscher Industrieller'. In D. Fricke (ed.), *Lexikon zur Parteiengeschichte,* vol. 4. Leipzig: VEB Bibliographisches Institut, 509–43.

Schulz-Hansen, K. 1970. 'Die Stellung der Elektroindustrie im Industrialisierungsprozeß'. Ph.D. diss., Berlin.

Schwarz, M. 1965. *MdR: Biographisches Handbuch der Reichstage.* Hannover: Verlag für Literatur und Zeitgeschehen.

Sheehan, J. J. 1966. *The Career of Lujo Brentano: A Study of Liberalism and Social Reform in Imperial Germany.* Chicago: University of Chicago Press.

Siegenthaler, H. 1993. *Regelvertrauen, Prosperität und Krisen: Die Unregelmäßigkeit wirtschaftlicher und sozialer Entwicklung als Ergebnis individuellen Handelns und sozialen Lernens.* Tübingen: Mohr.

Smith, M. S. 1980. *Tariff Reform in France, 1860–1900: The Politics of Economic Interest.* London: Cornell University Press.

———. 1992. 'The Méline Tariff as Social Protection: Rhetoric or Reality?' *International Review of Social History* 37, 230–43.

Soltau, F. 1926. 'Statistische Untersuchungen über die Entwicklung und die Konjunkturschwankungen des Außenhandels'. *Vierteljahrshefte zur Konjunkturforschung* 1, suppl. 2, 15–48.

Sommariva, A. and G. Tullio. 1987. *German Macroeconomic History, 1880–1979.* London: St. Martin's Press.

Sonnemann, R. 1960. *Die Auswirkungen des Schutzzolls auf die Monopolisierung der deutschen Eisen- und Stahlindustrie, 1879–1892.* Berlin: Akademie.

Spanier, A. 1926. 'Die Exportpolitik der Eisenkartelle'. Ph.D. diss., Cologne.

Spaulding, R. M. 1997. *Osthandel and Ostpolitik: German Foreign Trade Policies in Eastern Europe from Bismarck to Adenauer.* Providence, R.I.: Berghahn Books.

Sperber, J. 1997. *The Kaiser's Voters: Electors and Elections in Imperial Germany.* Cambridge: Cambridge University Press.

Spree, R. 1977. *Die Wachstumszyklen der deutschen Wirtschaft von 1840 bis 1880.* Berlin: Duncker and Humblot.

———. 2003. 'Globalisierungs-Diskurse: Gestern und heute'. *Jahrbuch für Wirtschaftsgeschichte* 2003(2), 35–56.

Stalmann, G. 1926. *Der Kongreß deutscher Volkswirte.* Düsseldorf: Voß.

Standage, T. 1998. *The Victorian Internet: The Remarkable Story of the Telegraph and the Nineteenth Century's On-line Pioneers.* New York: Walker Publishing.

Statistisches Bundesamt (ed.). 1972. *Bevölkerung und Wirtschaft, 1872–1972.* Stuttgart: Kohlhammer.

Stegmann, D. 1970. *Die Erben Bismarcks: Parteien und Verbände in der Spätphase des Wilhelminischen Deutschlands.* Cologne: Kiepenheuer und Witsch.

———. 1974. 'Wirtschaft und Politik nach Bismarcks Sturz: Zur Genesis der Miquelschen Sammlungspolitik, 1890–1897'. In I. Geiss and B. J. Wendt (eds), *Deutschland in der Weltpolitik des 19. und 20. Jahrhunderts,* 2nd ed. Düsseldorf: Bertelsmann, 161–84.

Steinkühler, M. 1992. *Agrar- oder Industriestaat: Die Auseinandersetzungen um die Getreidehandels- und Zollpolitik des Deutschen Reiches, 1879–1914.* Frankfurt: Lang.

Stolberg, G. 1977/78. 'Zur Geschichte des Begriffs "Politische Ökonomie"'. *Jahrbücher für Nationalökonomie und Statistik* 192, 1–35.

Stolper, W. F. and P. A. Samuelson. 1941/42. 'Protection and Real Wages'. *Review of Economic Studies* 9, 58–73.

Straub, E. 2001. *Albert Ballin: Der Reeder des Kaisers.* Berlin: Siedler.

Suzuki, Y. 1991. 'The Rise and Decline of Steel Industries: A Business Historical Introduction'. In E. Abe and Y. Suzuki (eds), *Changing Patterns of International Rivalry: Some Lessons from the Steel Industry.* Tokyo: University of Tokyo Press, 1–17.

Sydow, H. 1979. *Die Handelsbeziehungen zwischen Belgien und dem Zollverein, 1830–1885: Vertragspolitik und Warenaustausch.* 2 vols. Cologne: Böhlau.

Taussig, F. W. 1964. *The Tariff History of the United States.* 8th ed. New York: Putnam.

Taylor, A. M. 1996. *International Capital Mobility in History: The Saving-Investment Relationship.* NBER Working Paper 5743. Cambridge, M.A.: National Bureau of Economic Research.

Teichmann, U. 1955. *Die Politik der Agrarpreisstützung.* Cologne: Bund.

Teltschik, W. 1992. *Geschichte der deutschen Großchemie: Entwicklung und Einfluß in Staat und Gesellschaft.* Weinheim: VCH.

Tenbruck, F. 1989. 'Gesellschaftsgeschichte oder Weltgeschichte?' *Kölner Zeitschrift für Soziologie und Sozialpsychologie* 41, 417–39.

Terrill, T. E. 1973. *The Tariff, Politics, and American Foreign Policy, 1874–1901.* Westport, C.T.: Greenwood.

Theiner, P. 1984. '"Mitteleuropa"-Pläne im Wilhelminischen Deutschland'. In H. Berding (ed.), *Wirtschaftliche und politische Integration in Europa im 19. und 20. Jahrhundert.* Göttingen: Vandenhoeck und Ruprecht, 128–48.

Tilly, R. 1992. 'Der deutsche Kapitalmarkt und die Auslandsinvestitionen von 1870 bis 1913'. *ifo Studien* 38, 199–225.

Tirrell, S. R. 1951. *German Agrarian Politics after Bismarck's Fall: The Formation of the Farmers' League.* New York: Colombia University Press.

Tolliday, S. 1991. 'Competition and Maturity in the British Steel Industry, 1870–1914'. In E. Abe and Y. Suzuki (eds), *Changing Patterns of International Rivalry: Some Lessons from the Steel Industry*. Tokyo: University of Tokyo Press, 20–72.

Topik, S. and W. G. Clarence-Smith (eds). 2003. *The Global Coffee Economy in Africa, Asia, and Latin America, 1500–1989*. Cambridge: Cambridge University Press.

Topik, S. C. and A. Wells. 2012. 'Commodity Chains in a Global Economy'. In E. S. Rosenberg (ed.), *A World Connecting*. Cambridge, M.A.: Harvard University Press, 591–812.

Torp, C. 1998. *Max Weber und die preußischen Junker*. Tübingen: Mohr.

———. 2004. 'Weltwirtschaft vor dem Weltkrieg: Die erste Welle ökonomischer Globalisierung vor 1914'. *Historische Zeitschrift* 279, 561–609.

Tracy, M. 1989. *Government and Agriculture in Western Europe, 1880–1988*. 3rd ed. New York: Harvester Wheatsheaf.

Travis, A. S. 1993. *The Rainbow Makers: The Origins of the Synthetic Dyestuffs Industry in Western Europe*. Bethlehem, P.A.: Lehigh University Press.

Trentmann, F. 1998. 'Political Culture and Political Economy: Interest, Ideology and Free Trade'. *Review of International Political Economy* 5, 217–51.

Treue, W. 1982. 'Innovation, Know-How, Rationalization and Investment in the German Shipbuilding Industry, 1860–1930'. In H. Pohl (ed.), *Innovation, Know-How, Rationalization and Investment in the German and Japanese Economies, 1868/71–1930/80*. Wiesbaden: Steiner, 103–23.

Trubowitz, P. 1998. *Defining the National Interest: Conflict and Change in American Foreign Policy*. Chicago: University of Chicago Press.

Ullmann, H.-P. 1976. *Der Bund der Industriellen: Organisation, Einfluß und Politik klein- und mittelbetrieblicher Industrieller im Deutschen Kaiserreich 1895–1914*. Göttingen: Vandenhoeck und Ruprecht.

———. 1988. *Interessenverbände in Deutschland*. Frankfurt: Suhrkamp.

———. 1995. *Das Deutsche Kaiserreich, 1871–1918*. Frankfurt: Suhrkamp.

Ursprung, H. 2000. 'Die Modellierung endogener Handelspolitik: "The Rake's Progress"'. *Aussenwirtschaft* 55, 85–119.

Vagts, A. 1935. *Deutschland und die Vereinigten Staaten in der Weltpolitik*. 2 vols. New York: Macmillan.

Vanberg, V. 1978. 'Kollektive Güter und kollektives Handeln'. *Kölner Zeitschrift für Soziologie und Sozialpsychologie* 30, 652–79.

Verdier, D. 1994. *Democracy and International Trade: Britain, France, and the United States, 1860–1990*. Princeton, N.J.: Princeton University Press.

Vogel, B. 1973. *Deutsche Rußlandpolitik: Das Scheitern der deutschen Weltpolitik unter Bülow, 1900–1906*. Düsseldorf: Bertelsmann Universitätsverlag.

Wagenführ, R. 1936. *Die Bedeutung des Außenmarktes für die deutsche Industriewirtschaft: Die Exportquote der deutschen Industrie von 1870 bis 1936*. Berlin: Hanseatische Verlagsanstalt Hamburg.

Wallerstein, I. 1974/1980/1989. *The Modern World-System*. 3 vols. New York: Academic Press.

———. 1983. *Historical Capitalism*. London: Verso.

Warstat, H.-G. 1933. 'Die Preisentwicklung landwirtschaftlicher Produkte und Produktionsmittel vor dem Kriege und nach der Inflation und ihr Einfluß auf die Betriebsweise der deutschen Landwirtschaft'. Ph.D. diss., Bonn.

Webb, S. B. 1977. 'Tariff Protection for the Iron Industry, Cotton Textiles and Agriculture in Germany, 1879–1914'. *Jahrbücher für Nationalökonomie und Statistik* 192, 336–57.

———. 1980. 'Tariffs, Cartels, Technology, and Growth in the German Steel Industry, 1879 to 1914'. *Journal of Economic History* 40, 309–29.

———. 1982. 'Agricultural Protection in Wilhelminian Germany: Forging an Empire with Pork and Rye'. *Journal of Economic History* 42, 309–26.

———. 1997. 'Cartels and Business Cycles in Germany, 1880 to 1914'. In J. Komlos and S. Eddie (eds), *Selected Cliometric Studies on German Economic History*. Stuttgart: Steiner, 83–100.

Weber, M. 1979. *Economy and Society: An Outline of Interpretive Sociology*. Berkeley: University of California Press.

———. 1988. *Gesammelte Aufsätze zur Wissenschaftslehre*. Edited by J. Winckelmann. 7th ed. Tübingen: Mohr.

———. 1988. *Gesammelte Politische Schriften*. Edited by J. Winckelmann. 5th ed. Tübingen: Mohr.

Weck-Hannemann, H. 1992. *Politische Ökonomie des Protektionismus: Eine institutionelle und empirische Analyse*. Frankfurt: Campus.

Wehler, H.-U. (1969) 1985. *Bismarck und der Imperialismus*. 2nd ed. Frankfurt: Suhrkamp.

———. 1970. 'Bismarcks Imperialismus und späte Rußlandpolitik unter dem Primat der Innenpolitik'. In M. Stürmer (ed.), *Das kaiserliche Deutschland: Politik und Gesellschaft, 1870–1918*. Düsseldorf: Droste, 235–64.

———. 1974. 'Der Aufstieg des Organisierten Kapitalismus und Interventionsstaates'. In H. A. Winkler (ed.), *Organisierter Kapitalismus*. Göttingen: Vandenhoeck und Ruprecht, 36–57.

———. 1985. *The German Empire, 1871–1918*. Leamington Spa, U.K.: Berg.

———. 1987. *Der Aufstieg des amerikanischen Imperialismus: Studien zur Entwicklung des Imperium Americanum, 1865–1900*. 2nd ed. Göttingen: Vandenhoeck und Ruprecht.

———. 1995. *Deutsche Gesellschaftsgeschichte*. Vol. 3, Munich: Beck.

Weitowitz, R. 1978. *Deutsche Politik und Handelspolitik unter Reichskanzler Leo von Caprivi, 1890–1894*. Düsseldorf: Droste.

Wendt, B.-J. 1974. 'Freihandel und Friedenssicherung: Zur Bedeutung des Cobden-Vertrages von 1860 zwischen England und Frankreich'. *Vierteljahrschrift für Sozial- und Wirtschaftsgeschichte* 61, 29–64.

Wengenroth, U. 1985. 'Die Entwicklung der Kartellbewegung bis 1914'. In H. Pohl (ed.), *Kartelle und Kartellgesetzgebung in Praxis und Rechtsprechung vom 19. Jahrhundert bis zur Gegenwart*. Stuttgart: Steiner, 15–24.

———. 1986. *Unternehmensstrategien und technischer Fortschritt: Die deutsche und die britische Stahlindustrie, 1865–1895*. Göttingen: Vandenhoeck und Ruprecht.

———. 1987. 'Deutscher Stahl – Bad and Cheap: Glanz und Elend des Thomasstahls vor dem Ersten Weltkrieg'. *Technikgeschichte* 54, 197–208.

———. 1992. 'Unternehmensstrategien in Deutschland, England und Frankreich vor dem Ersten Weltkrieg'. In O. Dascher and C. Kleinschmidt (eds), *Die Eisen- und Stahlindustrie im Dortmunder Raum.* Dortmund: Gesellschaft für Westfälische Wirtschaftsgeschichte, 305–20.

Wernecke, K. 1970. *Der Wille zur Weltgeltung: Außenpolitik und Öffentlichkeit im Kaiserreich am Vorabend des Ersten Weltkrieges.* Düsseldorf: Droste.

Westwood, J. N. 1986. *Russia against Japan: A New Look at the Russo-Japanese War.* London: Macmillan.

Wetzel, W. 1991. *Naturwissenschaften und chemische Industrie in Deutschland: Voraussetzungen und Mechanismen ihres Aufstiegs im 19. Jahrhundert.* Stuttgart: Steiner.

White, D. S. 1976. *The Splintered Party: National Liberalism in Hessen and the Reich, 1867–1918.* Cambridge, M.A.: Harvard University Press.

Whynes, D. (ed.). 1984. *What Is Political Economy? Eight Perspectives.* Oxford: Blackwell.

Williamson, J. G. 1995. 'The Evolution of Global Labor Markets since 1830: Background Evidence and Hypotheses'. *Explorations in Economic History* 32, 141–96.

———. 1998. 'Globalization, Labor Markets and Policy Backlash in the Past'. *Journal of Economic Perspectives* 12(4), 51–72.

Williamson, O. E. 1971. 'The Vertical Integration of Production: Market Failure Considerations'. *American Economic Review* 61, 112–23.

———. 1985. *The Economic Institutions of Capitalism: Firms, Markets, Relational Contracting.* New York: Free Press.

Winkler, H. A. 2000. *Der lange Weg nach* Westen. Vol. 1. Munich: Beck.

Winseck, D. R. and R. M. Pike 2007. *Communications and Empire: Media, Markets, and Globalization, 1860–1930.* Durham, N.C.: Duke University Press.

Winzen, P. 2003. *Reichskanzler Bernhard Fürst von Bülow: Weltmachtstratege ohne Fortune – Wegbereiter der großen Katastrophe.* Göttingen: Muster-Schmidt.

Witt, P.-C. 1970. *Die Finanzpolitik des Deutschen Reiches von 1903 bis 1913: Eine Studie zur Innenpolitik des Wilhelminischen Deutschland.* Lübeck: Matthiesen.

———. 1975. 'Innenpolitik und Imperialismus in der Vorgeschichte des 1. Weltkrieges'. In K. Holl and G. List (eds), *Liberalismus und imperialistischer Staat: Der Imperialismus als Problem liberaler Parteien in Deutschland, 1890–1914.* Göttingen: Vandenhoeck und Ruprecht, 7–34.

Wittke, V. 1996. *Wie entstand industrielle Massenproduktion? Die diskontinuierliche Entwicklung der deutschen Elektroindustrie von den Anfängen der 'großen Industrie' bis zur Entfaltung des Fordismus (1880–1975).* Berlin: Sigma.

Wixforth, H. 1992. 'Wirtschaft und Staat in Russland und der Sowjetunion 1890–1941'. In S. Pollard and D. Ziegler (eds), *Markt, Staat, Planung: Historische Erfahrungen mit Regulierungs- und Deregulierungsversuchen der Wirtschaft.* St. Katharinen: Scripta Mercaturae, 228–66.

Woodruff, W. 1966. *Impact of Western Man: A Study of Europe's Role in the World Economy, 1750–1960.* London: Macmillan.

Wottawa, D. 1985. *Protektionismus im Außenhandel Deutschlands mit Vieh und Fleisch zwischen Reichsgründung und Beginn des Zweiten Weltkrieg.* Frankfurt: Lang.

Wulf, J. 1965. 'Der Deutsche Außenhandel seit 1850: Entwicklung, Strukturwandlungen und Beziehungen zum Wirtschaftswachstum'. Ph.D. diss., Basel.

Wulff, D. 1988. 'Der russisch-deutsche Handelsvertrag von 1904: Hintergründe und Motive seines Abschlusses'. *Jahrbuch für Geschichte der sozialistischen Länder Europas* 32, 129–45.

Zanden, J. L. van. 1991. 'The First Green Revolution: The Growth of Production and Productivity in European Agriculture, 1870–1914'. *Economic History Review* 44, 215–39.

Zevin, R. 1992. 'Are Financial Markets More Open? If So, Why and With What Effects?' In T. Banuri and J. B. Schor (eds), *Financial Openness and National Autonomy: Opportunities and Constraints.* Oxford: Clarendon, 43–83.

Zhang, A. and Y. Zhang. 1998. 'An Analysis of Import Protection as Export Promotion under Economies of Scale'. *Japan and the World Economy* 10, 199–219.

Zorn, W. 1968. 'Wirtschafts- und sozialgeschichtliche Zusammenhänge der deutschen Reichsgründungszeit (1850–1879)'. In H.-U. Wehler (ed.), *Moderne deutsche Sozialgeschichte.* Cologne: Kiepenheuer und Witsch, 296–316.

———. 1973. 'Die wirtschaftliche Integration Kleindeutschlands in den 1860er Jahren und die Reichsgründung'. *Historische Zeitschrift* 216, 304–34.

———. 1978. 'Zwischenstaatliche wirtschaftliche Integration im Deutschen Zollverein, 1867–1870'. *Vierteljahrschrift für Sozial- und Wirtschaftsgeschichte* 65, 38–76.

Zucker, L. G. 1986. 'Production of Trust: Institutional Sources of Economic Structure, 1840–1920'. In B. Staw and L. Cummings (eds), *Research in Organizational Behaviour,* vol. 8. Greenwich, C.T.: JAI, 53–112.

Zwehl, K. von. 1983. 'Zum Verhältnis von Regierung und Reichstag im Kaiserreich (1871–1918)'. In G. A. Ritter (ed.), *Regierung, Bürokratie und Parlament in Preußen und Deutschland von 1848 bis zur Gegenwart.* Düsseldorf: Droste, 90–116.

# Subject Index

# Name Index